Wiltrud Mihatsch, Inga Hennecke, Anna Kisiel,
Alena Kolyaseva, Kristin Davidse and Lieselotte Brems (Eds.)
Type Noun Constructions in Slavic, Germanic and Romance Languages

Trends in Linguistics
Studies and Monographs

Editors
Chiara Gianollo
Daniël Van Olmen

Editorial Board
Walter Bisang
Tine Breban
Volker Gast
Hans Henrich Hock
Karen Lahousse
Natalia Levshina
Caterina Mauri
Heiko Narrog
Salvador Pons
Niina Ning Zhang
Amir Zeldes

Editor responsible for this volume
Daniël Van Olmen

Volume 352

Type Noun Constructions in Slavic, Germanic and Romance Languages

—

Semantics and Pragmatics on the Move

Edited by
Wiltrud Mihatsch, Inga Hennecke, Anna Kisiel,
Alena Kolyaseva, Kristin Davidse and Lieselotte Brems

DE GRUYTER
MOUTON

ISBN 978-3-11-162735-9
e-ISBN (PDF) 978-3-11-070110-4
e-ISBN (EPUB) 978-3-11-070116-6
ISSN 1861-4302

Library of Congress Control Number: 2022948125

Bibliographic information published by the Deutsche Nationalbibliothek
The Deutsche Nationalbibliothek lists this publication in the Deutsche Nationalbibliografie;
detailed bibliographic data are available on the internet at http://dnb.dnb.de.

© 2024 Walter de Gruyter GmbH, Berlin/Boston
This volume is text- and page-identical with the hardback published in 2023.
Typesetting: Integra Software Services Pvt. Ltd.

www.degruyter.com

Preface

Type nouns or taxonomic nouns, i.e. nouns with meanings such as 'class of people or things that share specific features' or 'model', cross-linguistically show a strong tendency to develop a great variety of new pragmatic as well as grammatical uses. New pragmatic meanings include approximative categorization, hedging, focus marking, quotative marking and filler uses. New grammatical functions, in which the type nouns typically lose their head noun status, include the expression of (i) nominal categories such as quantity, phoricity, and adjective or noun modification, (ii) adverbial-like modification of predicates and whole clauses, (iii) inter- and intraclausal relations such as prepositional and conjunctive relations and quotatives. Quite strikingly, across the language branches the lexical item 'type' seems to be particularly prone to take on new pragmatic functions in all the language branches studied, which is why we decided to employ the term 'type noun' alongside the more general term 'taxonomic noun'.

Arguably, these derived uses arise in particular discourse strategies which exploit the original categorizing function of type nouns. The origins of the new uses tend to be tied to specific historical stages and to dialectal, sociolectal and diatypic varieties. The type nouns that extend to new constructions are often cognates from Latin and Greek – obviously so in the Romance languages, but also in the Germanic languages (e.g. English *sort*, *type*, Dutch *soort*, *type*, German *Typ*) and Slavic languages (e.g. Russian *tip*, Polish *typ*, Czech *typ*). At the same time, in the latter two language groups, nouns of indigenous stock manifest the same – often very early – paths of change such as English *kind*, *manner*, Dutch and Norwegian *slag*, German *Art*, Russian *rod*, and Czech *druh*.

Many of the new uses seem to emerge in informal, spoken language use, even though some diachronic developments can also be situated in specific formal, written genres. Likewise, some type noun-constructions show different distributions across dialectal, sociolectal and diatypic varieties. For instance, grammaticalized *kind of* is more common in British English and *sort of* in American English, and quotative uses are more frequent in the language of younger speakers and on fora such as the Internet.

All these dimensions demand research in multiple domains of linguistics: synchronic morphology and syntax, semantics and pragmatics, historical study, theory of change, contrastive linguistics, sociolinguistic description. The challenges type noun-constructions constitute to all these domains have so far only partially been met and for some languages these remain largely uncharted territories.

The importance of this volume resides in the gaps it seeks to fill by bringing together contributions about type noun constructions in Slavic, Germanic and

Romance languages. The majority of contributions were presented at the workshop "Pragmatic functions of type nouns: a crosslinguistic perspective", convened by Wiltrud Mihatsch and Inga Hennecke at Eberhard Karls Universität Tübingen (18.6–20.6.2018) funded by the DFG (Deutsche Forschungsgemeinschaft/German Research Foundation). This workshop consisted of invited talks, whose speakers had been selected to achieve maximal coverage of research on type noun-constructions in terms of a number of factors. First and foremost, the workshop extended the languages in which type nouns are being studied from core Germanic and Romance languages to hitherto neglected languages of these groups and, most importantly, to Slavic languages (Russian, Polish and Czech). Secondly, participants in the workshop were encouraged to address neglected phenomena such as the omnipresence of cognates of 'type' in all languages studied (albeit with different degrees of grammaticalization) and the different uses of the surface string 'X of the type Y' (which has barely been studied in Germanic languages). Thirdly, contributions from the various relevant domains of linguistics were invited, thus addressing synchronic, diachronic, contrastive and sociolinguistic aspects. Fourthly and finally, invitations were sent to both authors with a publication history about type noun constructions and – relative – newcomers to the field, whose promising contributions had been noticed.

This volume stands out for its thematic coherence due to the clear conceptual focus on taxonomic nouns and the emergence of new grammatical and pragmatic functions as well as a common theoretical and methodological framework. The contributions are based on broadly compatible versions of construction grammar and usage-based theories in combination with sound data-based descriptions, in most cases corpus data. The individual chapters investigate the parallels and differences between the new functions of different taxonomic nouns of one language and in the case of the comparative chapters in the last section of two or more languages, with a special focus on the following aspects:
- the range and interchangeability of type noun-constructions in various languages
- discourse contexts and discourse functions of type noun-constructions
- sociolinguistic and variational factors in the choice of particular type noun-constructions
- functional and morphosyntactic characteristics of type-noun-based pragmatic markers in individual languages
- mechanisms and motivations of change, language-specific constraints and preconditions, intra- and extralinguistic factors; the role of language contact
- one remarkable, but hitherto neglected phenomenon is the striking omnipresence of the lexical item 'type' in all the language branches studied and the different uses of the surface string 'X of the type Y'.

In addition to the papers dealing with particular languages, the volume includes survey chapters about type noun constructions in Germanic, Romance and Slavic languages, focusing on formal recognition criteria and semantic-pragmatic features of the constructions from a contrastive and comparative point of view. The surveys offer coherent syntheses, with the aim of providing a sound framework for future work in these and other language branches.

This volume could not have been accomplished without the people and institutions involved. We would like to thank the DFG (Deutsche Forschungsgemeinschaft/German Research Foundation) for funding the workshop that brought us together, all the participants of the workshop for contributing debate and new insights, and the editorial team of TiLSM, in particular series editor Daniel Van Olmen and managing editor Barbara Karlson, for supervising the editing process with great care and patience. We also thank Joanne Kehr, Kathrin Fotler, Ina Berner and Nina Schieting for their practical help in the editing process. A very special thank you goes to Emma Walters, whose stylistic suggestions as well as linguistic comments helped to make this volume coherent. Within the editorial time, Inga, Anna, Alena, Kristin and Lieselotte feel they owe a great debt of gratitude to Wiltrud, who was the prime mover behind both the workshop and the volume. She convened the workshop and secured funding for its organization. She also coordinated the editing of the volume, supervising the whole process from the conception of its structure, over the gathering and reviewing of the contributions, to the correct application of the style sheet. For all this, and for her courtesy and enthusiasm, we say a very big thank you.

Wiltrud Mihatsch, Lieselotte Brems, Kristin Davidse,
Inga Hennecke, Alena Kolyaseva, Anna Kisiel

Contents

Preface —— V

Wiltrud Mihatsch
1   General introduction: Taxonomic nouns and their derived functions in Germanic, Romance and Slavic languages —— 1

Part 1: Type noun constructions in Germanic languages

Kristin Davidse, Lieselotte Brems & An Van linden
2   Type noun-constructions in English and Dutch —— 55

Kristin Davidse & Lieselotte Brems
3   English type noun-constructions with lexical functions: A new functional-structural typology —— 95

Karin Aijmer
4   Type nouns in some varieties of English —— 141

Evelien Keizer
5   The function and use of NP-external *sort/kind of*: The case of *sort/kind of DEF NP* —— 181

Carla Umbach
6   Ways of classification: German *Art* and *Typ* —— 211

Part 2: Type noun constructions in Romance languages

Wiltrud Mihatsch
7   A panoramic overview of the extended uses of taxonomic nouns in Romance languages —— 245

Pierre Chauveau-Thoumelin
8   Classification, qualification, typification: Categorizing with *genre de* and *espèce de* 'kind of' in French —— 311

Miriam Voghera
9 The network of *specie, genere, sorta, tipo* constructions: From lexical features to discursive functions —— 351

Maria Aldina Marques
10 Pragmatic functions and contexts of use of TIPO in European Portuguese —— 393

Laura Malena Kornfeld
11 Taxonomic nouns and markers of mitigation in Río de la Plata Spanish —— 415

Part 3: Type noun constructions in Slavic languages

Alena Kolyaseva & Anna Kisiel
12 Taxonomic nouns in Slavic: An overview —— 457

Anna Kisiel & Alena Kolyaseva
13 Towards a comprehensive typology of type noun constructions in Slavic languages, with a special focus on Polish and Russian —— 501

Anna Kisiel
14 Polish *w stylu* and the rise of hedges —— 545

Markéta Janebová, Michaela Martinková & Volker Gast
15 Czech type nouns: Evidence from corpora —— 571

Part 4: Comparative analyses

Valentina Benigni
16 The complementizer function of *type*-nouns in ad hoc concept construction: Evidence from Italian and Russian —— 621

Hélène Vassiliadou, Elena Vladimirska, Marie Lammert, Céline Benninger, Francine Gerhard-Krait, Jelena Gridina & Daina Turla
17 Clear vs. approximate categorization in French and Latvian —— 655

Kate Beeching
18 Sociopragmatic variation, *sort of* and *genre* in English and French —— 695

Language index —— 723

Subject index —— 725

Wiltrud Mihatsch
1 General introduction: Taxonomic nouns and their derived functions in Germanic, Romance and Slavic languages

Abstract: This survey chapter gives a comparative overview of the most important derived uses of taxonomic nouns in the three Indo-European language branches treated in this volume, i.e. Germanic, Romance and Slavic languages. The observations of this chapter are mainly taken from the contributions to this volume as well as previous analyses. After a sketch of the communicative and cognitive functions of taxonomic nouns the most important etymological sources of taxonomic nouns are presented, followed by a description of the main functions derived from subtype binominals (such as *a type of NP*), i.e. attributive modifier and semi-suffix uses which support nominal modification, emerging postdeterminers, i.e. constructions combining taxonomic nouns with determiners or quantifiers, and nominal qualifier or approximator uses. A second group of derived, mostly pragmaticalized functions goes back to taxonomic nouns linking two NPs, this construction is a source of mitigators, quotative markers, focus markers and other pragmatic functions. The grammatical functions linked to the noun phrase based on subtype binominals can be observed to a greater or lesser degree in all the languages presented and start to arise very early on. However, not all languages show pragmaticalized functions. These seem to arise as late as the second half of the twentieth century in several, but not in all the languages discussed in this volume. In many cases formal, mostly morphosyntactic changes, accompany these processes and reflect the loss of the nominal properties of the taxonomic nouns undergoing these changes. All in all, the survey shows striking parallels, but also language-particular developments of taxonomic nouns crosslinguistically, which are thus a highly productive source of new grammatical and pragmatic functions. These new functions are an outcome of functional changes which are more or less advanced in different languages and in the case of individual taxonomic nouns. Interestingly, the observed parallels and differences are not correlated with particular language branches.

Wiltrud Mihatsch, Romanisches Seminar, University of Tübingen, Wilhelmstr. 50, D-72074 Tübingen, e-mail: w.mihatsch@uni-tuebingen.de

1 Introduction

The aim of this volume is to investigate non-nominal uses of type nouns or taxonomic nouns (TN), i.e. nouns designating categories, such as *sort*, *kind* and *type*, from a cross-linguistic perspective. The contributions analyse their very striking common functional and morphosyntactic features, but also highlight language-particular tendencies. This volume includes analyses of TNs in languages such as English and German, French, Italian, Portuguese and Spanish, Czech, Polish and Russian, as well as Latvian, and thus covers languages from the major branches of Indo-European languages. The papers elaborate talks presented at a DFG-sponsored workshop on type nouns in Tübingen in 2018 organised by Inga Hennecke and Wiltrud Mihatsch. The papers focus on the synchrony and diachrony of TNs in particular languages, but also offer comparative analyses of the pragmatic functions of etymological equivalents of *type* and other categorizing nouns, complemented by overviews of each of the Indo-European branches studied, i.e. Germanic, Romance and (Balto-)Slavic languages.

Particular attention will be paid to the following aspects:
- Functional, morphosyntactic, sociolinguistic and variational characteristics of TN-derived functions, both grammaticalized and pragmaticalized expressions in individual languages
- Insights from a diachronic perspective on type nouns such as the loss of the head status of TNs, processes of fossilization, and the emergence of new functions
- Cross-linguistic analyses of common as well as diverging semantic, pragmatic and morphosyntactic properties.

TNs, that is, nouns referring to categories, such as English *type*, *kind* and *sort*, French *genre*, *espèce* and *sorte*, Italian *specie*, *sorta* and *tipo* and Russian *tip* and *rod* show a strong cross-linguistic tendency to relinquish their nominal status. Many TNs develop a wide range of grammatical functions within the domain of the functional complex of the noun phrase. These include phoric uses and modifying uses in the context of nominal determination and a large array of more pragmatic functions such as markers of approximation, mitigation and other related functions. Most previous research on this topic is based on English (e.g. Aijmer 2002; Brems 2011; Brems and Davidse 2010; Denison 2002; Keizer 2007; and many more), although in the last few years in particular TNs have also been studied in other languages, as the references in the introductory chapters on Germanic, Slavic and Romance languages show.

While uses in determiner-like functions started emerging over 500 years ago, most of the pragmatic functions evolving from TNs are based on the more recent TNs which are etymological equivalents (either cognates or loanwords, in some cases calques) of *type* in several Germanic, Slavic and Romance languages. These functions are in many cases equivalent to those of colloquial English *like* (Andersen 2001; D'Arcy 2017). In the past few years, a growing number of studies investigated these uses, for instance, Rosenkvist and Skärlund (2013) on Swedish, Odden (2019) on Norwegian, Daiber (2010), Sakhno (2010), Kolyaseva and Davidse (2018), as well as Kolyaseva (2018) and (2021a) on Russian, Voghera (2013, 2017) on Italian, Lima Hernandes (2005) and Marques (2015) on Portuguese, Kornfeld (2013), Fernández (2017) and Mihatsch (2018) on Spanish, and from a comparative cross-linguistic perspective Mihatsch (2010, 2016) on Romance languages. Other TNs or related nouns that show similar patterns are French *genre* (Yaguello 1998 and Fleischman 1998 for early studies, Mihatsch, Ch.7, this volume, and Chauveau-Thoumelin, Ch.8, this volume, for recent references) and Romanian *gen* (Zafiu 2012; Terian 2018; Popescu and Ionescu 2019) as well as etymological equivalents of *style* in some languages (see Kisiel, Ch.14, this volume, on Polish). It is also striking that the absolute and relative chronology of development in the above-mentioned languages is very similar. Remarkably, the pragmatic functions of the etymological equivalents of *type* and analogous TNs French *genre* and Romanian *gen* do not exist in English and German and are not equally well established in all the languages and varieties which have them.

The contributions to this volume set out to analyse and explain the grammatical and pragmatic functions derived from TNs and offer an overview of cross-linguistically common tendencies as well as particularities in Slavic, Germanic and Romance languages.

This chapter offers a synthesis of the most important common tendencies in the evolution of TN constructions found in the three language sub-families, starting out with their lexical origins, then addressing the formal and functional changes as they develop modifier, complex determiner and approximator uses as well as the less widely observable TN-based prepositions and pragmatic markers.

2 Cognitive and communicative functions of TNs

Categorization and the manipulation of categories, i.e. sets of individuals grouped together on the basis of common properties (Smith 1995), seem to be cognitively hard-wired or acquired at a very early age (Gelman and Brandone 2010). However, we do not require TNs to refer to categories and subcategorization. Categories may be expressed by generic NPs (*the dog* 'the subspecies dog') and taxonomic or kind readings of quantified NPs (*a cheese* 'a kind of cheese', *many cheeses* 'many kinds of cheese', *three cheeses* 'three kinds of cheese') in many languages, not only in Western literate societies (see Corbett 2000: 84–87).

In all these contexts TNs such as English *sort, kind, class, category* and *type*, which refer to the abstract notion of category, may be used in order to render the reference to a category more explicit. Although categorization as such is a general human cognitive ability, TNs seem to originate in scholarly contexts, as the introductory chapters to the language families in this volume show. Many central TNs can be traced back to Latin and Greek sources and ultimately seem to be rooted in Greek philosophy, where metareflection on categories developed in Europe, beginning with Plato, who elaborated a definition technique based on inclusion relationships and in particular the relation between a generic and a more specific term (see Klix 1993: 345). This principle is also at the heart of the Aristotelian definition technique based on a combination of *genus proximum* and *differentiae specificae* (Klix 1993: 347–348). The foundational text which triggered European reflection on categories is Aristotle's work on general categories (Studtmann 2007) and the development of logic reasoning in the context of syllogisms and definition techniques linked to taxonomies (see also Gingras, Keating, and Limoges 2000: 43–44, 80). These ideas and notably the taxonomic definition technique entered medieval European school logic via Boethius (Gingras, Keating, and Limoges 2000: 96). The principle of taxonomic organization remains ubiquitous in scientific and general academic categorization today and not only contributes to knowledge organization and storage, but may also lead to the discovery of underlying general principles. TNs provide linguistic labels which allow explicit communication about categorization principles. In learned contexts TNs allow us to speak of categories as abstract mental constructs. They also help in structuring particular domains of knowledge and are then used as relational nouns.

In all the languages discussed in this volume, TNs became part of the general lexicon early on, beginning with the most ancient texts in European vernaculars. Today, many of the originally learned TNs have long been integrated into everyday language, even into colloquial registers, while others retain their learned connotation, as is the case with English *species* and *genus*, and to some extent *category*. As the contributions to this volume show, the relational power of TNs is exploited in discourse and leads to a series of grammaticalization and pragmaticalization processes. A look at the early attestations of TNs in the OED and the contexts found in diachronic corpora (see the introductory chapters to the language families covered in this volume) shows that relational uses in complex noun phrases seem to prevail in everyday language early on, notably in the binominal construction DET TN PREP N such as *that kind of person*, but also in a binominal construction with the TN in the second position (*a person of that kind*, DET N PREP DET TN). As Davidse and Brems (Ch. 3, this volume) point out, this source construction has been neglected in the literature so far, since here the TN does not have head status from the outset, so that there is no categorical change involved and the change is very subtle. In languages with an inflectional genitive such as Old English, but also the contemporary Slavic languages (e.g. Kolyaseva and Davidse 2018, Kolyaseva 2022, Kolyaseva and Kisiel, Ch. 12, this volume, Kisiel and Kolyaseva, Ch. 13, this volume; Davidse and Brems, Ch. 3, this volume), we observe constructions with either a genitival TN or a genitival non-taxonomic noun (reflecting the two variants with prepositions), with the genitive preceding or following the head. Odden (2019) shows that NPs with close apposition in Scandinavian languages go back to an earlier prenominal genitive. Davidse and Brems (Ch. 3, this volume) also argue that constructions with a preceding genitival TN (with a later insertion of the preposition *of*) are the source of the complex determiner, quantifier, identifier, modifier and qualifier or hedging uses in English.

While the discussion of taxonomic hierarchies as such may not be central for speakers, explicit categorization is useful when talking about unknown or unnamed referents, when referring metalinguistically to categorization and formulation processes, when stressing the existence of category-internal variation and when grouping together instances or categories on the basis of shared properties.

3 Etymological origins of TNs

TNs originate in Classical Greek and Latin and are attested from the earliest documents onward in the Germanic, Romance and Slavic vernaculars, in several cases as calques. In all three language families TNs show a strong link to the Greco-Latin tradition. Ancient Greek γένος (*genos*) 'genus' and εἶδος (*eîdos*) 'species'; 'appearance, look' plausibly underly the Latin cognate *genus* 'birth, race, stock, kind, genus' and the calque *speciēs* 'appearance, aspect, kind, species' from *specĕre* 'to look, behold' (OED, s.v. *species*; Ernout and Meillet 1994). Learned taxonomic structures might at first sight seem rather marginal in everyday speech; however, the early integration and appearance of TNs in European vernaculars certainly indicate that they are useful to speakers. Attestations are found in the earliest texts: both English *kind* (and the Old English *gecynd*, OED, s.v. *kind*) and Slavic *rod* and *vid* are attested in the eleventh century with a taxonomic meaning (see the overview of Slavic TNs by Kolyaseva and Kisiel, Ch. 12, this volume).

When studying the origins of TNs in European vernacular languages, two general correlated tendencies stand out.

First of all, TNs tend to originate from learned vocabulary. The learned provenance is obvious in the case of the Greco-Latin loanwords such as English *genus* and *species* as well as *category* and *type*. However, in many cases we find less obvious calques from Classical Greek or Latin as is the case with Slavic *rod* (Kolyaseva and Kisiel, Ch. 12, this volume) and, probably, English *kind* (see OED, s.v. *kind*), for which the entry in the OED includes a reference to Latin *genus*. French *genre* is also a very early TN borrowed directly from Latin *genus* (FEW, TLFi, s.v. *genre*).

Furthermore, TNs which cannot be directly traced back to Latin or Classical Greek are often borrowed from other languages, plausibly also via scholarly contact. For instance, English *sort* was borrowed from Old French (OED, s.v. *sort*), German *Sorte* is a loanword from French or Italian (GDWB, s.v. *Sorte*), Russian *tip* is a French loanword, Czech *typ* seems to be a nineteenth-century borrowing from German, Polish *kstalt* stems from Middle High German *gestalt* and Polish *gatunek* is a German loanword from German *Gattung* (see the introductory chapters to Slavic, Romance and Germanic TNs). Norwegian *slag* seems to be a loanword from Middle Low German and Norwegian *sort* was arguably borrowed from Middle Low German and French (Odden 2019: 207). As a matter of fact, many languages have borrowed *type* and *sort* from Western European languages such as French, German or Italian, though the loanwords are now used with varying language-particular frequencies. In some cases, further studies are needed to investigate the existence of calques; the striking parallels between the different, often very specific, subsenses may be an important argument in favour of semantic borrowing. For instance, in all the languages analysed, etymological equivalents of *type* also show the meaning 'guy' or 'person', a sense derived from 'prototype, model' from the nineteenth century onward (see the introductory chapters to Slavic, Romance and Germanic TNs). Furthermore, in many languages etymological equivalents of *genus* also display a subsense 'category of goods'[1] as in the case of Spanish *género* and Italian *genere*, possibly also inherited from the subsenses 'crop' and 'produce' of Classical Greek γένος 'genus' (LSJ). A systematic classification and comparison of all the subsenses of the etymological equivalents in each language may indeed shed light on the exact processes and chronology of borrowing.

The etymological sources may also help us to understand how speakers conceptualize categories.

We find three main etymological sources, but have to take into account that in many cases, we probably do not observe independent paths of semantic change leading to a taxonomic meaning, but calques, i.e. polysemy copying.

---

[1] Anna Kisiel (personal communication) observes a similar polysemy in the case of Polish *gatunek* (<Ger. *Gattung* 'genus').

a) *Semantic source 'family', 'social class'*
TNs such as English *kind* are etymologically derived from a relationship (of similarity) between the members of a category via family ties, and etymologically derive from meanings such as 'tribe', 'family' or 'clan', as in Classical Greek γένος (*genos*) and its Latin cognate *genus* 'birth, descent' which has been borrowed into many European languages and in particular Romance languages. Another case is German *Gattung* 'genus', still today used in the biological sense as well as for literary genres (GDWB).

There are a great number of TNs with a comparable background, some of which have become obsolete; see, for instance, West Old Norse *kyn* 'kind, ancestry', *ætt* 'ancestry' and *kind* 'ancestry, class, kind' (Odden 2019: 211), or Old High German *kunni* (Köbler 2014, s.v. *kunni*). The metaphor based on the idea of a social group is also the conceptual source of the TNs *sort* (from 'lot, fate' via 'rank, social group, category'). The origin of German *Art* is unclear; the GDWB relates *Art* to a Germanic root meaning 'to give birth' and from there to 'family'.

The Western and Western South Slavic languages show a parallel semantic development for *vrsta* from 'age, time of life, generation, person of the same age, turn' in the Western South Slavic languages and *druh*, derived from 'companion, follower, friend, comrade' in the Czech-Slovak branch (Kolyaseva and Kisiel, Ch. 12, this volume). The taxonomic meaning of the etymological equivalents of *class* is also derived from a meaning in the domain of social groups from the Latin meaning 'draft, levy, fleet, class of citizens' (Ernout and Meillet 1994) via 'rank, class'.[2]

The idea of grouping together similar individuals into a collective may also explain why *genus* and many of its etymological equivalents, as well as other TNs of this group, specialize in higher-level taxons and tend to denote superordinates, the *genus proximum*. Interestingly, Traugott (2008: 28) shows a diachronic transition of English *kind* from the meaning 'superordinate class' in Old English *gecynd* to a member of a set and internal differentiation closer to *species* in the early sixteenth century. Today, English *kind* is not designated for a particular hierarchical level.

b) *Semantic source 'outer appearance'*
A second path of semantic change derives TNs from concepts referring to 'shape' or 'outer appearance' as in the case of Greek εἶδος (*eîdos*) 'species', 'appearance, look' and the Latin calque *species* and its equivalents, particularly in the Romance languages, a source also underlying the Slavic calque *vid/vyd* (Kolyas-

---

[2] For both of Latin *classis* and *sors* the taxonomic reading develops rather late; for *sors* the meaning of 'rank, class, order' appears in Late Latin, and for *classis* in post-Augustan texts (Lewis and Short 1879, s.v. *classis*).

eva and Kisiel, Ch. 12, this volume). The same conceptual basis explains the taxonomic reading of Old Polish *kstalt* from Middle High German *gestalt* (Kolyaseva and Kisiel, Ch. 12, this volume). This is also the conceptual basis of the TN *form* and its etymological equivalents, with the idea that defining visual properties can distinguish different subcategories. While the path in a), related to the concept of family, clan or social class, reflects the cognitive process of assembling several category members within one superordinate category and therefore tends to create higher-level taxons, the path related to visual characteristics which distinguish category members unsurprisingly leads to TNs establishing subkinds via *differentiae specificae*.

The Norwegian and Swedish TNs *slag* 'kind' from Middle Low German 'battle, punch, stroke' via the minting of coins also follows this path, just like Old High German *slahta* (Köbler 2014, s.v. *slahta*). The taxonomic meaning is still preserved in German *Schlag*, but is now restricted to categories of people characterized by a particular mentality as in *Menschenschlag* ('type of person'), both in compounds and on its own. At first sight the etymology of *type* and its equivalents seems to belong to this group. These ultimately stem from Classical Greek τύπος (*typos*) 'impression, imprint, matrix, engraving, cast or replica made in a mould, sketch, model, outline' from the root of τύπτειν (*typtein*) 'to beat, strike' (LSJ), resembling the etymology of North Scandinavian *slag* and German *Schlag*. However, the taxonomic meaning of *type* arises centuries later than that of *slag*; in the case of English *type*, not until the nineteenth century (OED, s.v. *type*). Here the immediate source of the taxonomic reading is that of a prototypical representative category member, a principle also adopted in botanical and zoological taxonomies in the eighteenth and nineteenth centuries, where exemplars or specimens were used to stabilize taxons (Daston 2004).

c) *Semantic source 'manner', 'way of doing sth'*
The third source for TNs is less prominent, since many of these nouns have not retained their former taxonomic reading. One such case is English *manner*, a loan from Anglo-Norman (OED, s.v. *manner*) and its etymological equivalents in Romance, Germanic and Slavic languages. Again, we find an intricate network of inter-European loanwords, mostly via Romance languages. French *manière* and equivalents in other Romance languages are derived from Classical Latin MANUĀRIUS 'operated by hand', 'tractable', 'skilful'. Etymological equivalents of *manner* are now predominantly used in the sense of 'way of being or doing something'. Early on they all developed categorizing senses corresponding to 'type, sort, kind', which have disappeared, except in fixed postdeterminer expressions such as *what manner of* and *all manner of* (OED, s.v. *manner*). Denison (2002) suggests that the loss of the taxonomic reading of *manner* was related to its disyllabic

structure which set it apart from other TNs in English. However, that explanation does not hold for Romance languages, for instance, some of whose well-established TNs do contain more than one syllable. English *fashion* has a similar origin related to 'manner of making something' and a tendency to relinquish an earlier taxonomic sense, now obsolete, or French *façon* which means 'way of doing or making something', but also has a now rather rare sense of 'sort' or 'kind', from Latin FACTIONEM 'power, way of doing something' (TLFi, OED). Similar cases are Polish *fason* 'way of doing something', 'style (referring to human behaviour' and Russian *fason* 'cut, model on which something is sewn (clothes or shoes)', 'style', and, rather restricted to older texts, 'way of doing things' (Anna Kisiel and Alena Kolyaseva, p.c.). Similarly, in West Old Norse *háttr* 'manner, kind' or *konr* 'man, kind, manner' and *lund* 'way, manner, condition', *lei/led* 'way, direction' combined the senses 'manner' and 'kind' (Odden 2019: 211). These are currently preserved in fixed expressions, often with a determiner and a genitival TN which can be traced back to an early Germanic pattern of type noun constructions (Odden 2019: 213). These old taxonomic meanings also survive in German, mostly as grammaticalized univerbated postdeterminers containing an adjectival component with a fossilized genitive, as in *vielerlei* 'all kinds of', *allerhand* 'a variety of', and *keinerlei* 'no kind of' (GDBW). Dutch also has *allerhande* 'all kinds of', *velerlei* 'many kinds of' (Lot Brems, p.c.). Similarly, English *way* shows an obsolete taxonomic reading 'specified type or class of things; kind, sort' (OED, s.v. *way*).

Rather restricted to 'way of doing something' or 'manner' in the modern sense is German *Weise* (formerly also English *wise*, mainly preserved as an adverb-forming suffix and other fixed expressions) and the now archaic Germanic loans Spanish *guisa* and French *guise* (and others in other Romance languages). These have a root meaning reminiscent of the etymology of *species*: intially meaning 'to see' via 'appearance', then 'way of doing sth', and 'character' and, marginally, 'kind' (see Mihatsch 2019: 446–447).

Perhaps this path might even point to an alternative etymology of German *Art*, since Walde (2008 [1910]) highlights a link between Latin *ars* 'craftmanship, skill, art, science', and Middle High German *art* 'manner, way of doing sth'. Also belonging to the periphery of TNs closer to 'way of being made' are *style* and its etymological equivalents, Spanish *corte* 'cut' and the etymological equivalents of English *mode* from Classical Latin *modus* 'measure, size, limit of quantity, manner, method, musical mode' (OED, s.v. *mode*).

This path is revealing in two ways. Firstly, it points to the conceptual differentiation between 'manner of doing or being' and 'kind of thing'. Secondly, it shows the diachronic transitions and conceptual permeability between the reference to subcategories of nominal concepts and verbal concepts. It would certainly be worthwhile to study in greater detail the hitherto understudied nouns designating 'manner' and their dynamics (see Moline 2011 on French constructions with *manière*) in the vein of Moline and Stosic (2016), who offer the first comprehensive onomasiological overview of linguistic expressions of manner.

Table 1 gives an overview of these three principal paths of semantic change leading to taxonomic meanings, including now obsolete TNs (of course, there are also diverging etymologies for some TNs; see the introductory chapters to the language families):

Table 1: Overview of the main etymological sources of TNs.

Path a) 'family, rank, social group'	Path b) 'outer appearance, shape'	Path c) 'manner, way of doing sth'
Classical Greek γένος (*genos*)	Greek εἶδος (*eîdos*)	Etymological equivalents of English *manner*
Latin GENUS and etymological equivalents (cognates directly going back to Latin, loans and calques) in modern languages	Latin SPECIES and etymological equivalents	Etymological equivalents of English *fashion*
	Etymological equivalents of English *form*	West Old Norse *háttr* 'manner, kind', *konr* 'man; kind, manner', and *lund* 'way, manner condition'; *lei led* 'way, direction'
English *kind*	Norwegian and Swedish *slag* and Germanic etymological equivalents	
West Old Norse *kyn* 'kind, ancestry', *ætt* 'ancestry' and *kind* 'ancestry, class, kind'		
	Slavic *vid/vyd*	Etymological equivalents of German *Weise*
German *Gattung*	Old Polish *kstałt* and etymological equivalents	
German *Art* (source unclear)		German *Art*
West Slavic/Western South Slavic *vrsta*	Special case based on 'model, prototype':	Meanings close to taxonomic readings: etymological equivalents of *style*
Czech-Slovak *druh*	Classical Greek τύπος (*typos*) and etymological equivalents	
Slavic *rod*		
Etymological equivalents of English *class*		
Etymological equivalents of English *sort*		
Also the taxonomic terms *family* and *kingdom* in biological taxonomies		

(for sources, see the introductory chapters for each language family treated in this volume)

Two central and predominantly learned terms do not fit into this grid. English *category* and its etymological equivalents, from Greek κατηγορία (*katīgoría*) 'accusation, assertion, predication' via Latin *catēgoria* (OED, s.v. *categoria*) originated from Aristotle's ten most general categories or predicaments and now refers to a class or division in general. Although these nouns are still not part of colloquial vocabulary; they are also at the root of current debates about high-level ontologies (OED s.v. *category*). English *taxonomy* and its etymological equivalents are ultimately derived from ancient Greek τάξις (*táxis*) 'arrangement, order' (OED, s.v. *taxonomy*).

This overview shows that the three largest language families in Europe are linked by an intricate network of borrowings and calques, often via learned contexts and from languages with a certain prestige in science and education, adopted by languages (or rather their speakers) perhaps aspiring to gain prestige. In many cases indirect loans seem plausible. A systematic comparison and analysis of lexicographic data cross-linguistically might shed light on the complex network of (learned) linguistic and cultural contacts in the domain of TNs.

Generally, their learned origins and borrowability might also explain their great diachronic fluctuations: new TNs seem to arise time and again, often via learned borrowing. In some cases they show a specialization for higher- or lower-level taxons and, particularly when still belonging to the scientific domains, preferences for specific domains of use (see Umbach, Ch. 6, this volume, for German *Art* and *Typ*). TNs further display different degrees of integration into everyday language; compare English *species* or *genus* to *kind* and *sort*.

4 Derived functions of TNs

The relational nature of TNs which manifests itself in an overwhelmingly binominal use, in addition to the subtle interplay between TNs and other nominal constituents, certainly facilitates the functional reinterpretation of TNs and their loss of head status. In this section, I will sketch the most important types of grammaticalized and pragmaticalized uses cross-linguistically and describe possible triggers for the emergence of these new functions.

We assume two main groups of functions based on two general underlying constructions, subtype binominals (DET TN PREP N as in *this kind of thing* and DET N PREP TN as in *a thing of this kind*) and "trinominal" uses corresponding to (NP PREP (DET) TN PREP NP as in *a car of the category of a luxury V-class*) where a prepositional phrase or genitival construction containing a TN relates two NPs. This latter construction sounds awkward in English, but is common in many of the languages covered in this volume.

4.1 Subtype binominals

Binominals which show the pattern DET TN PREP N basically establish subcategories of a noun, for example, of chocolate, in *this type of chocolate*.³ The subtype (or subkind) relation of both DET TN PREP N and DET N PREP DET TN may be exploited strategically in discourse in order to achieve particular communicative effects. If these strategies are used frequently enough, the structures employed may become entrenched and reanalysed. The DET TN PREP N-construction then seems to lose the original taxonomic reading and refers to instances designated by N2, suggesting the loss of head, and then noun status of the TN. Davidse and Brems (Ch. 3, this volume) argue that the Old English preposed genitival taxonomic noun plausibly represented the first step in this development; at least for English this would mean that the taxonomic noun was never a head in this position, just as Odden (2019: 135–137) shows for Scandinavian, where the fossilized genitive and the juxtaposition of the two nouns still reflect the older construction. Possibly, the German construction *eine Art* N, literally 'a kind N' without an inflectionally marked relation between *Art* 'kind' and N also goes back to a genitival taxonomic noun preceding N. The Romance languages focussed on this volume never had an inflectional genitive; here we must assume a binominal source with a preposition. It would be certainly worth looking at taxonomic noun uses in Latin, which has an inflectional genitive, and which heavily influenced the Romance languages, especially in the Renaissance.

The changes of the DET N PREP DET TN construction (as in *chocolate of this kind*) are altogether less conspicuous than that of DET TN PREP N, which may explain why this construction has been much overlooked.

Early analyses of subkind constructions with TNs overtaking new functions in English are summarized in Davidse, Brems, and De Smedt (2008). Denison (2002, 2005) first established a fine-grained classification of partly grammaticalized uses of TNs within the noun phrase. This classification has been further developed by Keizer (2007) as well as Brems and Davidse (2010).

In this section, I will largely follow Brems and Davidse (2010) and discuss the principal tendencies of non-nominal uses of TNs derived from binominal TN constructions whose subtype reading can be exploited by speakers in various ways and can then trigger subsequent reinterpretations.

---

3 This construction has to be distinguished from a superficially identical appositional construction not addressed here as in (*a car of*) *the type of a SUV*, more common in Romance languages than in English, which prefers close apposition ((*a car of*) *the type SUV*).

Before we discuss the different emerging functions of TN binominals we need to consider two positional variants related to the general duality of lexically specified noun phrases which combine the semantic categorization provided by the lexical item and a referential relation indicated by the determiner. This hybrid function of noun phrases remains implicit in most cases but surfaces when taxonomic readings are combined with referential uses, i.e., when type and instance readings conflate, as in *I bought three cheeses*. Alternatively, we may also use explicit TNs in referring expressions as in *I bought three kinds of cheese* (see Mihatsch 2021 on this type of conflation). Here, the argument of *buy* is not *kind*, but *cheese*. This explains why *This kind of tree* appears to be synonymous with *A tree of this kind* (cf. OED, s.v. *kind*) and thus shows a very inconspicuous, but probably very frequent, case of "dual reference" following Ward and Birner (1995: 732), who use the term "dual reference" to mean reference to a new (indefinite) instance of a known (or definite) type or category, such as *the usual crowd* in *There was the usual crowd at the beach today* (Ward and Birner 1995: 732).

In binominals in which the TN follows another noun, as in *A tree of this kind*, the dual reference is evident in the two determiners (*a* and *this*), while the indefinite article is implicit in referential uses with a preposed TN such as *this kind of tree*, as in the following example:

(1) English
    (...) *loblolly pine tree (parents planted **this kind of tree** in front of the house they lived in when I was born).* (https://www.sandiegoreader.com/photos/galleries/tattoo-you/26772/#, accessed 12 June 2018)[4]

Cases of near equivalence between positional variants in binominals are also analysed (in terms of functional layers and raising) by Zamparelli (2000). Such referential equivalents are not only found with TNs:

(2) English
    a dress that size / that size (of) dress is hard to find (Zamparelli 2000: 79)

(3) English
    all kinds of cars / cars of all kinds (Zamparelli 2000: 91)

---

4 Here and in the following examples the bold typeface is mine.
  Morpheme-by-morpheme glosses are only given if relevant for the analysis.

Both positional variants allow reference to individual instances (see also Zamparelli 2000: 87). However, the two variants are not entirely symmetrical, since the pure kind reading is not possible with the kind-final construction, i.e. *a dog of this kind* refers to an individual dog of a certain kind, not to the kind itself (Zamparelli 2000: 87). This also shows in agreement variants where the TN introduces an NP and can here lose its head status (4), while the postposed variant, as in (5), requires agreement with the head noun:

(4) Italian
    Questo tipo di persone {è / sono}
    'This kind of people {is / are}' (Zamparelli 2000: 103)

(5) Italian
    Le persone di questo tipo {*è / sono}
    'The people of this kind {*is / are}' (ibid.)

The ease of transition from taxonomic or kind readings to reference to individual instances is plausibly the underlying mechanism that leads to a readily available reinterpretation of TNs and the loss of their noun status (see also Mihatsch 2016, 2021).

Binominal constructions with TNs are not isolated phenomena. They share features such as a complex interplay between the two nouns and a referential function with other binominals such as partitive and pseudopartitive constructions, as well as the tendency of the first noun to lose its head properties and often also its nominal properties, as in the formerly nominal expressions *a lot of* or *a bunch of* (Brems 2011). Thus, functional and categorial changes of TNs are facilitated by the general competition of the two nominal elements in their contribution to the reference of the whole NP, and in many cases a conflation of the semantics of the two nominal elements.

Davidse, Brems, and De Smedt (2008) offer a systematic classification of derived uses in terms of functional layers of the noun phrase, which we will follow here, starting with the innermost layer closest to the lexical noun. To the immediate left of the noun in English we find the attribute and classifier layer producing modifier uses (discussed in 4.1.1), followed by the determiner complex comprising identifying and quantifying expressions (see section 4.1.2). Davidse, Brems, and De Smedt (2008) point out different grammaticalization processes involving subjectification (most clearly in the domain of the determiners), in some cases leading to a coalescence of the TN with determiners, quantifiers and modifiers respectively.

4.1.1 Modification

An emphasis on a careful, detailed description is at the root of uses linking TNs and noun modifiers, typically adjectives, but also other parts of speech modifying a noun (Denison 2005, and Brems and Davidse 2010 for English; Mihatsch 2016: 148–151 for Romance languages). Reanalysed modifier uses are plausible when the taxonomic reading is backgrounded and when the whole NP refers to an individual instance. Denison (2002, 2005) and subsequent analyses assume two subtypes: the attributive modifier and the semi-suffix.[5]

The first construction type is the attributive modifier use incorporating rather unexpected or unusual characterizing adjectives, as in *a very dramatic sort of person*. Apart from highlighting deliberate categorization with a strong subjective evaluation the TN construction may secondarily help to overcome selection restrictions of adjectives in the case of unusual adjective-noun combinations (Mihatsch 2016).

The second construction type, the classifying semi-suffix use, exemplified in *Quick reaction type missions* or *a keeping-up-with-the Joneses sort of person*, facilitates modification with possibly unusual or ad hoc classifying adjectives but also other parts of speech, also often with subjective connotations.

Davidse, Brems, and De Smedt (2008) argue in favour of a cline from the less entrenched attributive modifier use to the more strongly grammaticalized, and therefore cross-linguistically probably less widespread, semi-suffix use which facilitates a greater flexibility of modifier expressions.[6] With growing entrenchment, the TN merges with the preceding modifier and thus becomes a semi-suffix, whose status becomes evident in hyphenated uses, but fulfils this function whether hyphenated or not. Such uses frequently adopt overtones of approximation, possibly influenced by independently arising approximative uses (as discussed in 4.1.4).

However, a secondary emerging function is the transformation of very diverse and often creative lexical material into eligible modifiers, thus enabling unusual adjective-noun combinations.

---

[5] So far, the focus in the literature has been on prenominal uses based on a subkind construction with a taxonomic head. As mentioned above, at least for English, Davidse and Brems (this volume) argue that the modifying uses were derived from quantifying and phoric uses with a prenominal genitival taxonomic noun in Old English, which then lost the genitive element and was then reanalysed, with the preposition inserted later. Thus, according to this analysis, the evolution of the prenominal modifier use in English does not involve a modifier-head shift.

[6] According to Emma Walters (p.c.) in English the more grammaticalized semi-suffix construction seems to be more widespread than the attributive modifier construction, following Davidse, Brems, and De Smedt (2008: 148–149), who state that "[a]ll in all, the attributive modifier construction has a rather limited application in Present-day English".

The general impression is that these uses exist to some extent in all the languages studied in this volume, although they seem most established in English, possibly because present-day English generally favours extended premodification (Davidse, personal communication, see also Chauveau-Thoumelin (2020) on French, Odden (2019) on Norwegian, Mihatsch (2016) on Romance languages and Kolyaseva and Kisiel (Ch. 12, this volume) for general observations of these uses in Slavic languages, where according to Alena Kolyaseva (p.c.) they do not seem to be established).

In the Romance languages and in Polish the very frequent postposition of classifying adjectives might explain why modifier uses are less entrenched, since in postposition as in (6) there is no scope ambiguity of the adjective either modifying the TN or the whole NP, which in turn may facilitate reinterpretation. Nevertheless, there are occurrences such as (6) where the taxonomic reading fades out and just seems to support modification:

(6) French
l-a   charade   incit-e   à   un
DET.DEF-F.SG charade.F.SG elicit-PRS.3SG to DET.INDF.M.SG
genre   très   subtil   de   commutation
sort.M.SG very subtle.M.SG of commutation.F.SG
'the charade elicits a very subtle sort of commutation' (FT, Willemse, Brems, and Davidse 2008)

For the Romance languages Mihatsch (2016) shows a complex picture where pre- and postmodification lead to a variety of positions and scope relations so that even an adjective to the right of N2, impossible for most adjectives in English, can be reanalysed as modifying the preceding material with a TN as a head, although there are cases where the adjective agrees with the N2 despite clearly modifying the whole binominal:

(7) Spanish
Pero hay   un   tipo   de persona
But   have.PRS.3SG DET.INDF.M.SG type.M.SG of person.F.SG
muy   específic-a   que   no   solo   recuerd-a
very specific-F.SG   who   not   only   remember-PRS.3SG
l-a   fecha (...)
DET.DEF-F.SG date.F.SG
'But there is a very specific type of person who doesn't only remember the date (...)' (http://ciegaacitas.tv/, accessed 24 April 2012)

According to Anna Kisiel (p.c.), the analogous position of an adjective to the right of an NP following the TN in a modifying function is possible in Polish, although restricted to stylistically marked uses with a very specific prosody.

However, in Romance languages as well as Slavic languages[7] (in Polish and Russian, see Kolyaseva and Davidse 2018, there are postnominal adpositional phrases (in Russian principally with *rod*) and in the Slavic languages we also find the corresponding genitival NPs (preferably *typ* in Polish, and *rod* and *tip* in Russian).[8] Russian shows a strong association of *tip* with classifying adjectives (Alena Kolyaseva, p.c.). These constructions with TNs modified by adjectives or other elements such as NPs are a clearer and more current equivalent of the modifier uses in English (Willemse, Brems, and Davidse 2008):

(8) Italian
abbiamo anche / messo in evidenza / come / &he / i problemi / di tipo linguistico / fossero di / importanza preminente
'we have- also shown how the problems of a linguistic nature were of utmost importance' (C-ORAL-ROM inatte02)

(9) Polish
instalacja   gazowa   starego   typu
installation   gas   old   type
'an old type of gas installation'(lit. 'installations of the old type')

(10) Russian
originalnost'   samogo   nizmennogo   roda
original   same   old   type
'the cheapest kind of originality' (lit. originality of the cheapest kind) (Kisiel and Kolyaseva, Ch. 13, this volume)

Postnominal modifier uses, hitherto neglected in the literature, also occur in English and should be subsumed under the function of an extended modifier complex together with the better studied premodifers. It is possible that the variety of positional variants and the postposition of the majority of lexical adjectives in Romance languages and Polish block further entrenchment and favour the postnominal prepositional phrase. A further reason might be that the patterns

---

[7] Janebová and Martinková (2017) also argue that there is no Czech equivalent of the English attributive modifier construction.
[8] In Russian, the genitival modifier can also, less frequently, precede the head noun (Kolyaseva and Davidse 2018).

with adjectives following the TNs or the whole binominal construction diverge too strongly from the emerging complex determiner uses with clearly preposed identifying adjectives and quantifiers in all the languages discussed.

4.1.2 Emerging postdeterminer or complex determiner uses

As with modifier uses, emerging prenominal complex determiners[9] containing TNs show a loss of taxonomic interpretation and a tendency to refer to individual instances,[10] although many cases are ambiguous, i.e. bridging contexts in the sense of Heine (2002). Aijmer (2020) very aptly shows that English TN-based constructions with quantifying, modifying and identifying functions are often translated into Swedish by quantifiers, lexical NPs directly modified by adjectives, or determiners or determiner-like adjectives without the TN element. This clearly points to a loss of head status of the former TN and a reinterpretation as part of the determiner and modifier complex. Further analyses of translation equivalents might reveal interesting crosslinguistic differences regarding the degree of entrenchment of the TN constructions and the degree of reinterpretation.

In most cases, postnominal TN uses (as in Det NP *of this type/of all sorts*) may have an equivalent function to the preposed variant with an original type noun head and should be analysed together with the prenominal uses.

Two different emerging categories within the determiner layer which originate from different communicative strategies can be distinguished: identifiers and quantifiers.

a) Identifier uses
Type noun binominals frequently combine with determiner-like adjectives (see Davidse, Brems, and De Smedt 2008), and also interrogative determiners, for

---

9 According to Davidse and Brems (this volume) English complex determiner uses emerged in Middle English and involved extension from quantifying to phoric premodifiers, they argue that the taxonomic noun in these uses derives from a prenominal genitive, a change which does not require a loss of head status.

10 Denison (2002, 2005) and Keizer (2007) adopt a narrower definition and restrict postdeterminer uses to cases where the determiner agrees with N2 and where the TN is fossilized in the singular, as in *these sort of skills*, which is certainly a clear indicator for reinterpretation. However, crosslinguistically, other patterns may point to grammaticalization, such as a fossilization of the singular for both the TN and the preceding determiner or the agreement between the determiner, the TN and the N2, two tendencies observed in Romance languages (Mihatsch 2016).

instance, *which type, the same kind of, such a kind of, another kind of, different kinds of, that kind of*. Excepting the interrogative use these tend to establish links of similarity or differentiation to antecedents (and in some cases cataphorically to following NPs or contextually given entities). With identifying expressions TNs add an explicit reference to categories, thus overtly signalling a taxonomic structure, often in contexts of ad hoc classification. This explicit reference to categorization may be used strategically, not only in colloquial registers. TNs may underline the rational foundations of lexical choices and suggest careful formulations, which may at the same time conceal problems with lexical access or naming unknown concepts. If speakers exploit this strategy, arguably not in overly colloquial registers but in semi-formal contexts, the pretended thoughtful classification and care of formulation may be backgrounded over time and the uses may acquire emphatic functions in the nominal complex. The loss of head status of the TN becomes evident in cases in which uses without TNs are referentially equivalent to the postdeterminer uses with TNs (compare *a different view* and *a different kind of view*). Apart from underlining identification relations, identifying uses may create implicit superordinate categories assembling different entities or subordinate categories within a (usually implicit) superordinate. This also explains why the pre- and postposed variants of type noun binominals are not always equivalent. The TN in *a kind of X* establishes a subcategory of X, while in *an X of this kind*, X is assigned to a superordinate category. Contemporary French, which distinguishes between *genre* 'genus' for more general inclusive categories and *espèce* 'species' for specifying subcategories, therefore shows a differentiation between the pre- and the postposed variant:[11]

(11) French
      cette espèce de dossier / ? Un dossier de cette espèce.[12]
      'this kind of file / ? A file of this kind'

Languages distinguishing between TNs for higher- and lower-level taxons therefore generally prefer higher-level taxons such as French *genre* and not *espèce* in constructions establishing (implicit) superordinates (for Romance languages, see Mihatsch 2016).

---

[11] This is unlike colloquial English, where *kind* and *sort* do not specialize in higher- or lower-level taxons.
[12] This example has been adapted from Rosier (2002: 82), who gives an example with *genre* 'kind, genus' allowing both constructions.

Phoric uses such as *that kind of thing* also belong to the group of identifying postdeterminers. These are the source for general extender constructions, i.e. *and/or that sort of thing*.

Apart from the identifying function, phoric uses may also acquire a quantifying force referring to degrees, as in *that kind of energy* (Davidse, Brems, and De Smedt 2008: 153).

b) Quantifier uses

Davidse, Brems, and De Smedt (2008) assume a separate quantifying type noun complex. The communicative strategy behind quantifying uses is indeed different from the identifying uses (Mihatsch 2016: 142–144). Uses of TNs with the universal, negative and free-choice quantifiers arguably allow expressive readings heightening quantificational force. The quantification of subkinds leads to an expressive quantification of individual entities via implicature. As with identifying uses, there is an easy transition from kind to instance readings, facilitated by referential equivalence in many contexts, at least in the Romance languages, where the quantifier uses arise in a binominal construction with a taxonomic noun as a head followed by a preposition phrase: for instance, French *toutes sortes de NP*, thus implies that all instances of NP are referred to. *All kinds of NP* is more expressive than *all NP*, since the presence of the TN highlights the fact that all of the different subcategories, even marginal ones, are included.

As in the case of the other derived prenominal uses, for English, Davidse and Brems (Ch. 3, this volume) assume that historically, there was no head-modifier shift, but a shift from a genitival premodifier like *ælces*$_{GEN.SG}$ *cynnes*$_{GEN.SG}$ *déor* 'each kind of wild animal' to a premodifier as in *alle kind of fishis* 'all kinds of fish'. From the OED-entries of *kin*, n. 6b, *kind*, n. 4a, and *manner* n. 1, they gather that the genitive, which was typically placed before the head noun, came to be treated as an attributive or adjective-like phrase once the inflection had been lost. The preceding adjective also dropped its genitive *-s*, sometimes transferring it to the TN, as in *Alle skynnes*$_{GEN.SG}$ *condiciouns* (1384). As illustrated by the insert in *four kin maner* [a1425 *fowrkins maners*] *of glotony* (1400), early scribes must have been aware of this genitive singular origin. As Odden (2019: 135–137) shows for Norwegian, the genitival source of taxonomic nouns in NPs with close apposition is obvious in the fossilized genitive of the taxonomic nouns *slags* and *sorts* and the lack of a preposition.

Furthermore a as in the case of the modifier, complex determiner and identifier uses, in the future, greater attention will also have to be paid to the corresponding postnominal uses as in the case of *services of all kinds*.

4.1.3 Crosslinguistic tendencies in the evolution of non-nominal uses of TNs within the NP

Quantifying and identifying uses seem to be very widespread crosslinguistically, involving both old and recent TNs in all the languages analysed in this volume. They are not restricted to colloquial language. De Smedt, Brems and Davidse (2007: 249–252) show for English that even today postdeterminer uses are more frequent in press texts than in colloquial (youth) language; a comparable tendency can be observed for French (Chauveau-Thoumelin 2020).

Complex determiner uses arise very early in all the language families treated in this volume and arguably all the languages within these families: for English see Denison (2002, 2005), Keizer (2007), Davidse, Brems, and De Smedt (2008); for North Scandinavian languages notably Odden (2019) on Norwegian and Swedish; for French see Chauveau-Thoumelin (2020) and Mihatsch (2021); for Italian see Voghera (2013, 2017); for a Romance overview see Mihatsch (2016) and for a comprehensive overview of Slavic languages see Kolyaseva and Kisiel (Ch. 12, this volume), For Czech see Janebová and Martinková (2017) and Janebová, Martinková and Gast, Ch. 15, this volume.

As new TNs are continually integrated into the lexicon they also start developing complex determiner uses some time after they are first attested. For English *kind*, these uses are attested from the earliest texts in the fourteenth century onwards, for the somewhat later loanword *sort*, they appear in postdeterminer uses in the sixteenth century and for *type*, in the nineteenth century, almost simultaneously with its first occurrences as a TN (see notably Denison 2005 and Brems and Davidse 2010; Odden 2019 for Norwegian; Mihatsch 2010, 2016 for Romance languages). Kolyaseva and Kisiel (Ch. 12, this volume) also point out medieval quantifying uses of Russian *vid* in translations from Greek. We certainly cannot exclude calques from Latin and Greek; see the Latin collocation *omnis generis* 'of all kinds' (for example, in Lewis and Short 1879, s.v. *gĕnus*).

Although these uses seem to emerge very easily, there are language-particular preferences as to the degree of entrenchment of particular TNs in these functions (Davidse, Brems, and De Smedt 2008; Mihatsch 2016; Kolyaseva and Kisiel (Ch. 12, this volume)). There might also be different degrees of entrenchment of the constructions in different languages. According to Willemse, Brems, and Davidse (2008), the complex determiner uses are generally less developed for French, at least in literary texts, than for English, while determiner uses of *genre* seem to be more common in internet data. Here, further comparative studies are needed for a full crosslinguistic picture.

Interestingly, all the languages discussed in this volume have numerous fossilized coalesced expressions with TNs, in some cases even preserving obsolete TNs, as in *what manner* and *all manner of* (OED, s.v. *manner*). Odden (2019: 213–214) gives a detailed overview of such fixed expressions in Norwegian, for example, *soleis, således* 'so, in such a way', *allehånde*, 'all kinds', *hvadhaande* 'whatever kind' and *ingahanda* 'no kind', 'nothing'. In some cases, the loss of transparency even leads to etymologically redundant expressions combining the now archaic TN *handa* in genitive form and the TN *slags* with a fossilized genitive as in *alla-handa slags gräs* 'all kinds of kinds of grass' ('all.GEN.PL-kind.GEN.PL sort-GEN.SG grass').

For English, many such fossilized merged uses are mentioned in the OED, such as Middle English *alkin, nakin, whatkin* (OED, s.v. *kind*). Other collocations are less conspicuous; in such cases frequencies have to be taken into account, such as with *no sort of* which is listed as a negative reinforcer in the entry for *sort* in the OED.

The Romance languages do not seem to show coalesced forms, but, nevertheless, dictionaries indicate fixed constructions with quantifiers, for instance, with the universal quantifier ('all kinds'), as in French *de toute espèce* (PR, s.v. *espèce*), *toutes sortes de* (PR, s.v. *sorte*), Italian *ogni sorta di*, NP *di ogni sorta* (ZVI, s.v. *sorta*), and Portuguese *todo gênero de* (ADLP, s.v. *gênero*). Remarkably, the equivalent Latin phrase *omne genus* was frequently used (Bambeck 1959: 25). There are also negative reinforcers ('no kind of') such as *aucune espèce de* (PR, s.v. *espèce*) and Italian *di sorta* 'not at all, in no way' (ZVI, s.v. *sorta*). Old French and Catalan have grammaticalized negative expressions *giens* and *gens* (LDAF; FEW, s.v. *genus*; DCLIC, s.v. *gens*), although without a determiner or quantifier, thus preserving in these expressions the bare noun uses of earlier periods.

Such lexicalized constructions are also well attested in Slavic languages (Kolyaseva and Kisiel, Ch. 12, this volume) as in the case of Polish *wszelkiego rodzaju/typu* 'of all possible kinds', *różnego rodzaju/typu* 'of different kinds', Russian *всех родов* (*vsex rodov*) 'of all kinds', *разного рода* (*raznogo roda*) of different kinds', *разного типа* (*raznogo tipa*) 'of different types', *всяческого рода* (*vsjačeskogo roda)* 'of all possible kinds' and many others (see the impressive list in the Slavic overview by Kolyaseva and Kisiel, Ch. 12, this volume).

4.1.4 Nominal qualifier or approximator uses

In all the languages investigated in this volume, a subset of TNs, usually the ones best integrated into the common lexicon, are reinterpreted as imprecision or approximation markers, often with subjective or metalinguistic overtones (or both) introducing unusual terms, signalling distance or insecurity or marking metaphors, such as in the following example:

(12) French
Ça moutonnait le long des boutiques. Le tramway, **un genre de girafe obèse,** *il dépassait les bicoques, il laminait la cohue, il godaillait dans les vitres* ...
'People strolled along the shops. The tram, **a kind of obese giraffe**, passed the shacks, it toppled the crowd, it dug into the shop windows' (FRANTEXT, Céline, Louis-Ferdinand (1936): *Mort à crédit*)

In emerging identifier and quantifier complexes the original complement N2 tends to acquire the function of a head and determine the referent, while the TN no longer contributes to the propositional content, at least in the Romance languages, while again, for English, Davidse and Brems (Ch. 3, this volume) suggest a genitival source. In approximator uses, the former TN does change the truth-conditions of the proposition by flexibilizing the category boundaries of the N2. Approximation therefore seems neither to belong to the inventory of grammatical categories, nor is the new function purely pragmatic, so it is not clear whether this is a case of grammaticalization (see also Denison 2005). As for the communicative trigger, neither careful categorization (even if used as a subterfuge) nor expressive quantification lead to approximation. Rather, we have a case of wear and tear of a category frequently employed for peripheral or doubtful category members, just as the frequent wearing of clothes that are actually too tight renders them baggy in the long run (also see Mihatsch 2010: 144–146). Such uses can be due to laziness, but also due to a lack of adequate expressions for speaking about abstract concepts such as spiritual experiences and the need to deal with unknown, unfamiliar or hard-to-classify referents, for instance, while expressing the new reality of the New World, as in the following example where the writer only manages to give a (rough) assignment of an object to a superordinate:

(13) French
Je crois que c'étoit **une espèce de baleine** *dont les naturalistes ne font point de mention*
'I think that was **a kind of whale** that the natural historians do not mention at all.' (FRANTEXT, Foigny (1676): *La Terre australe connue*)

Such uses easily lead to a reinterpretation of the subordination relation as a relation of cohyponymy with a wider implicit superordinate and subsequently even signalling a loose similarity relation if the target concept and the noun following the TN do not belong to one common superordinate, thus becoming an approximation marker.

The difference between postdeterminer uses and qualifying or approximative uses is evident in the different timeline of the emergence of approximators, which evolve substantially later than the postdeterminer uses. Approximators seem to require a more complex reinterpretation, which is also seen in the smaller selection of TNs for this function.

In English we find *sort of* (*sorta*) and *kind of* (*kinda*); in the Romance languages the most entrenched approximators are derived from the etymological equivalents of *species* (Mihatsch 2010, 2016), although most languages have several qualifying uses derived from different TNs (see Mihatsch, Ch. 7, this volume). The binominal source construction expressing a subkind relation explains the preference for TN associated with lower levels of generalization and the idea of a subdivision (*differentiae specificae*), which is why etymological equivalents of *species* are more established than those of *genus*.

Qualifying or approximating uses are attested from the sixteenth century at the latest for English *kind of* (OED, s.v. *kind*), Swedish *slags* (Odden 2019), French *espèce de* (Mihatsch 2016) and Polish *rodzaj*, but also for other (sometimes also more recent) TNs such as *tip* in Serbian, *vid* in Bulgarian, Czech *druh* and others (Kolyaseva and Kisiel, Ch. 12, this volume Kisiel and Kolyaseva, Ch. 13, this volume; Janebová, Martinková and Gast, Ch. 15, this volume).

In colloquial language approximating constructions may be exploited for further purposes such as the cover-up of lexical retrieval problems, the pragmatic mitigation of (possibly offensive) nouns and for signalling innovative uses such as the unexpected use of metaphors (as in example 13 above), often with subtle differences between the different approximators (see Chauveau-Thoumelin 2020; Kisiel and Kolyaseva, Ch. 13, this volume; Willemse, Brems, and Davidse 2008). Sometimes we observe dialectal and sociolinguistic differences, as in the case of the rather British *sort of* and the rather American *kind of* (Aijmer 2002).

Despite the differences between postdeterminers and qualifying or approximative uses, they have in common the tendency of the TN to lose semantic, and in some cases morphosyntactic,[13] nominal properties. However, with the exception of English *sort of/sorta* and *kind of/kinda*, in the languages analysed in this volume the new functions arising from binominals do in fact maintain their original position within the NP, even as they acquire additional pragmatic functions such as mitigation or metalinguistic comment (for a synthesis see Mihatsch 2007, 2010: 155–160, 174–178).

---

[13] For instance, in the Romance languages this is evident in some (still stigmatized) uses where the TN adopts the gender of the following NP. However, morphosyntactic indicators of a loss of nominal status have not become generalized (yet). For the qualifying uses of Russian *rod*, Kolyaseva (2021) shows that the new function has not lead to a loss of nominal inflection such as case marking (as in the case of the prepositional and particle uses of *rod*); according to Anna Kisiel (p.c.) this is also true for qualifying uses of Polish TNs.

In English, *kind of* and *sort of* are syntactically and functionally more versatile than their equivalents in the other languages analysed, since they can modify constituents other than N, including NPs (as in *a sort of a gangway*) VPs and APs, and even appear with sentential scope (Bolinger 1972: 113; De Smedt, Brems and Davidse 2007: 246; Aijmer 2002: 175–209; Beeching 2016: 156–182); they may then also function as pragmatic markers without the truth-conditional effects of approximators:

(14) English
   ((^it was . a !little)) **sort of** *'rather un:pl\easant in the /end# (. . .)* (Aijmer 2002: 200)

(15) English
   ^can't we **sort of** *'leave 'Belgium and :L\uxembourg# and the ^south of 'France to an:\/other *'year#* (Aijmer 2002: 205)

English *kinda/kind of* and *sorta/sort of* may also, although marginally, express numerical imprecision (16) and introduce direct speech (17):

(16) English
   And they were ^all **sort of** */eighty#* (Aijmer 2002: 185)

(17) English
   ..and **sort of** *going oh no, gotta cover up..* (Aijmer 2002: 183)

According to Tabor (1993: 458), adverbial uses arise in structures with adjectives, such as *a sort/kind of* + Adj. + N (see also Aijmer 2002: 180 and Keizer 2007: 168), and the subsequent reanalysis of the TN (plus preposition) as an adverbial modifier with scope over the adjective. This might then lead to the particular NP-external uses attested for English (see Keizer, Ch. 5, this volume).

4.1.5 Overview of the diachronic links and crosslinguistic tendencies of subtype binominals

The relative chronology of appearance of the new functions sketched so far, starting with lexical taxonomic uses, leading to postdeterminer and then approximator uses (see Denison 2005), seems to suggest a linear development linking all these functions. However, Brems and Davidse (2010) suggest a more complex diachronic network with quantifier and descriptive modifiers facilitating the evolution of identifying, postdeterminer and approximator functions, Davidse and Brems (Ch. 3, this volume) further suggest, at least for English, a preposed genitival taxonomic noun as source.

In the sections above I have sketched three particular and distinctive communicative strategies leading to new uses: expressive quantification via kinds, ostensibly careful classification for the descriptive modifier and the identifying uses, and wear and tear of loose uses of subcategorization leading to approximators. This is certainly an argument for three distinct paths of change which arise easier and therefore earlier if used more frequently, allowing very productive kinds of reinterpretation, and arise later if more complex processes of reinterpretation are involved, as in the case of the approximators. However, even if one assumes different independent paths for these uses, mutual influences between the different paths are plausible.

Approximator uses derived from TNs also develop in languages outside Europe, for instance, for Persian (Parvaresh and Sheikhan 2019; see also Parvaresh and Zhang 2019), but also in Hindi (Walters, in preparation), the Austronesian language Acehnese and in Thai, as Odden (2019: 233) argues on the basis of data collected within the framework of Natural Semantic Metalanguage in Goddard and Wierzbicka (1994).

Further crosslinguistic comparisons are needed to discover in how far the phenomena of postdeterminer uses and approximation are due to universal cognitive and communicative properties of TNs, and how far particular cultural and communicative conditions and discourse traditions contribute to these developments which seem so amazingly uniform in European languages.

4.1.6 Formal changes related to the non-nominal uses of TNs

As the TNs lose their head status, they tend to lose their nominal properties too. This may be revealed in an inability for the TN to inflect and in some cases a fossilization of an inflected form, but also the inability to be modified and the loss of governance, for instance, when the verb agrees not with the TN but with the second head of a binominal NP in subject position. These effects might be seen in differing frequencies for particular expressions. Head reversal effects, or at least ambiguities, and a tendency to be backgrounded may affect even binominals with a taxonomic reading; however, overall the effects seem to be stronger for the new grammatical and approximative uses.

In what follows, I will give a rough outline of the principal formal changes which can be observed in Germanic, Romance and Slavic languages as TNs relinquish their nominal status.

a) Determiners and definiteness
The new functions in the domain of quantification and identification arise from the univerbation of a TN with a determiner, determiner-like adjective or quantifier. This is less clear for the qualifier or approximator uses. However, here indefinite determiners are more frequent due to the mostly rhematic positions of hedged NPs, usually 'first-mention' cases (Mihatsch 2010: 171). Except for NP-external uses in English (Keizer, Ch. 5, this volume), where the taxonomic noun precedes a noun phrase with its own determiner, the second noun does not usually appear with a determiner. In Norwegian and Swedish Odden (2019: 118) observes frequent omissions of the definiteness suffix on type binominals and differing variability of determiners with different TNs: stronger restrictions for the older *slags* and *sorts*, and greater variation of determiners but also a frequent lack of determiners in binominals with the more recent *typ(e)*. Odden (2019: 175–179) also observes varying agreement of the determiner either with the TN or the following noun; again, the deviation is more frequent with the more entrenched *slags* than the less entrenched *sorts* or the more recent *typ(e)*. She also notes different patterns for singular and plural nouns following Norwegian *slags*: with a singular N2 the indefinite article agrees with N2; with a plural N2 the masculine/common gender *en* is used indiscriminately Odden (2019: 307).

The lack of grammaticalized determiners in Slavic languages makes it harder to distinguish the binominal derived uses from the "trinominal" derived uses discussed in section 4.2 below. The following example is a qualifying use derived from a binominal:

(18) Polish
 (…) *sam* *uważam* *WOŚP* *za* **rodzaj**
 myself consider-PRS.1SG WOŚP for kind(M)-NOM.M.SG
 wielkiej *mistyfikacji*
 huge-GEN.SG.F hoax-GEN.SG.F
 'I personally see WOŚP as **a kind of big hoax**.'
 (https://encyklopedia.biolog.pl/index.php?haslo=Wikipedysta:Stotr/Archiwum2, accessed 8 of February 2022, from Kolyaseva and Kisiel, Ch. 12, this volume)

In postnominal uses, both the first noun and the taxonomic noun have their own determiner as in *a problem of this kind*.

b) Number inflection
Similarly, a loss of number inflection may indicate head reversal. The loss of number inflection may surface in different realizations depending on the lan-

guage. Denison (2002, 2005) and Keizer (2007) highlight the fossilized singular form of grammaticalized postdeterminer TNs and plural agreement between the determiner and the N2, as in *these sort of problems*, and between the N2 and the verb in the case of subject uses. This phenomenon does not seem to be established in the languages investigated in this volume apart from English. An initial study shows that Romance languages have different patterns for the non-nominal uses of TNs. In Spanish and, to some extent, in Portuguese, plural reference tends to be expressed by singular TNs with a singular determiner followed by a plural noun in expressive quantification, interrogation, phoric uses, and identifying uses. French shows a certain tendency for plural agreement between the determiner, the TN and N2 for both expressive quantification and approximation (Mihatsch 2016). Examples (19) and (20) show qualifying uses: example (19) illustrates a use with the singular TN with a singular determiner in Spanish; example (20) from French is a typical case of pluralization of the determiner and both nouns in an approximative function:

(19) Spanish
 L-a especie de interludio-s
 DET.DEF-F.SG kind.F.SG of interlude.M-PL
 'the sort of interlude' (CREA, El Periódico de Aragón, 14.05.2004 : ESTRENO)

(20) French
 des espèce-s de satellite-s
 DET.INDEF-PL kind.F-PL of satellite.M-PL
 'kinds of satellites' (FRANTEXT, Char (1980): *Sous ma casquette amarante*)

Number agreement in Norwegian and Swedish is not always visible (Odden 2019); however, Odden (2019: 176) notes "a clear tendency to drop the plural suffix -r from the TN, as in *sånn-e type avgift-er* (such-PL type.SG fee-PL; 'those kind of fees') and she observes that quantifiers and determiners tend to agree with the N2.

For Russian, Kolyaseva (2021a: 23–24) observes number incongruences in specifying clauses following the TN construction. In the Slavic languages there is a tendency for the reinterpreted TN to occur in the singular in genitival uses. Anna Kisiel (p.c.) points to a slight preference for plural N2 in Polish postdeterminer constructions where the TN is pluralized but also points out that in Slavic in general pronominal adjectives agree with TN, never with N2.

c) Gender agreement

Parallel phenomena surface with gender agreement. While English nouns do not have gender, Romance and Slavic languages as well as German, Swedish and Norwegian do. Head reversal becomes evident when the first determiner of a Det TN (PREP) N2 construction agrees with the gender of the N2; this has been shown for French *espèce de*, notably in qualifying, i.e. approximating, uses, and also, although less frequently, with *genre* (Davidse, Brems, Willemse, Doyen, Kiermeer & Thoelen 2013, and Chauveau-Thoumelin 2020; Mihatsch 2010). Aijmer (p.c.) confirms the same phenomenon for Swedish, where the indefinite article tends to agree with the N2 (the common gender as in *en slags stol* 'a kind of chair' vs. the neuter gender as in *ett slags bord* 'a kind of table').[14] This is also true for Norwegian to some extent; Odden (2019: 119–126) shows a complex interplay between the respective TN, determiner type, number and register, which determine the agreement patters and in particular gender agreement between the determiner preceding the TN and N2 in Norwegian and Swedish.

Agreement between the determiner and the N2 can also be observed for the German approximator *Art*, as in the following example referring to a chess term, although I do not consider this stigmatized use to be very common even in colloquial German:

(21) German
So   ein   Art   Wartezug
Such DET.INDEF.M.SG kind.F.SG   waiting.move.M.SG
'such a kind of waiting move' (Kolde 2004: 138)

d) Links between the TN and the lexical NP

The languages analysed in this volume use three different methods for linking the taxonomic noun and the lexical NP (N2 if following the TN) in binominal constructions: genitive marking, a preposition expressing a genitival relation and close apposition.

English and Romance subkind binominals are exclusively based on a semantically very general preposition which assumes functions of the genitive. TNs introduced by adpositions are also attested in the other Germanic and Slavic languages (Kisiel and Kolyaseva, Ch. 13, this volume). Languages with an inflectional case system such as the Slavic languages and German also have TN binominals with a genitival NP in addition to other prepositional constructions. Typically, the lexical NP (usually N2) is in the genitive case functioning as a complement (see also Keizer (2007: 241, 257). West Old Norse, Old English and Old High German (Odden 2019: 211–212, Schrodt [2011] 2004: 23) predominantly used preposed genitive NPs in binominal constructions, which explains a fossilized subtype of gen-

---

14 See also https://www.iklartext.se/en-slags-mobel-eller-ett-slags-mobel/, accessed 6 August 2021.

itival use comprising a TN in the genitive preceded by a qualifying adjective or a quantifier to the left of the N2 (Toft 2009: 268–269 in Odden 2019: 211–212):

(22) West Old Norse
Alls   háttar   íþrótt
all.GEN.SG kind.GEN.SG   sport/ART.SG
'All kinds of sports/art' (Nygaard 1905: 135, in Odden 2019: 211)

This once productive pattern is preserved in fossilized genitive forms of TNs such as Norwegian (and Swedish) *slags* as in *en slags äppelkaka* 'a kind of apple cake' (Odden 2019: 133) and *sorts* (and some more recent analogous forms of *typs*) as well as fixed expressions in Norwegian (Odden 2019). This is also evident in some fixed expressions in German, such as *allerhand, allerlei* 'all kinds of' and *keinerlei* 'no kind of', showing traces of the genitive on quantifier in the NP containing the TN (GDWB, s.v. *allerhand, allerlei, keinerlei*). Since the genitival form is not the head of the binominal NP, there is no head reversal.

As mentioned before, Davidse and Brems (Ch. 3, this volume) assume that this construction is the source of the English prenominal determiner, modifier, quantifier, identifying and hedging uses.

In Slavic languages (where word order is quite free) we find a similar construction with a preposed or postposed TN in the genitive case (Kolyaseva and Davidse 2018):

(23) Russian
*On   bal'zakskogo   **tipa**   mužčina*
He.NOM.SG.M   Balzacian.GEN.SG.M   **type.gen.sg.m** man.NOM.SG.M
'He's a Balzacian **sort of** man.' (RNC Š. Martynova and E. Lixačeva. Interv'ju v peredače 'Oni sdelali 'eto'. Finam_FM. 2009 in Kolyaseva and Davidse 2018: 194)

The genitival TN seems to correspond to binominals in modern Germanic languages and Romance languages, where the TN modifies a (preceding) head noun (as in *trees of all kinds*). German, Swedish, Norwegian and Flemish/Dutch also use juxtaposition (or close apposition) to link the TN to the lexical NP (mostly N2). Apposition is also possible in Russian for the lexical uses of *tip* and *rod* in the biological sense of 'genus' (Kolyaseva 2021a: 8–9).

Preferences for a particular type of linking strategy are language-particular. German TN binominals show all three possibilities, although the genitive N2 is rather rare and formal. Old Norse and Old English showed a genitive N2, which is still possible in modern Norwegian; however, Swedish now seems to prefer the prepositional link, and Norwegian apposition (Odden 2019: 92–93). Romance languages only display TN binominals with prepositions expressing genitive functions. Russian and Polish have genitival constructions as well as apposition (Kolyaseva 2021a: 9).

In the case of juxtaposition (or close apposition) the N2 adopts the case assigned to the whole NP and thus shows the same case as the TN. (24) is an example of dative case marking assigned to *Art* 'kind' as well as the second noun:

(24) German
Der   Weg   war   mit   ein-er
DET.M.NOM way.M.SG   be.PST.3.SG with   DET.INDEF-F.DAT.SG
Art   grob-em   Schotter   befestigt.
kind.F.SG coarse-M.DAT.SG   gravel.M.SG pave.PST.PRT.
'The path was paved with a kind of coarse gravel' (DDUW, in Kolde 2004: 141)

Diachronically, Germanic close apposition arguably goes back to a binominal NP with a prenominal genitival element. Odden (2019: 135–137) provides arguments for Scandinavian languages, one clear piece of evidence is the fossilized genitive in Norwegian *slags* 'kind', Davidse and Brems (Ch. 3, this volume) now also assume a prenominal genitive as a source for English conventionalized type noun binominals where the type noun precedes NP2 and the close apposition in German might also go back to an earlier prenominal genitive.

4.2 Pragmatic markers based on a trinominal construction

Remarkably, in some, but not all, languages analyzed in this volume (for example, not in English and German), recent type nouns which are etymological equivalents of *type* (and in a few cases other TNs such as French *genre*) give rise to highly multifunctional and syntactically flexible markers in colloquial language, especially in youth language. The markers are stunningly similar to English *like* (see Andersen 2001; D'Arcy 2017). Arguably, these functions are based on a particular source construction, namely the "trinominal" one where the TN links two other NPs: "NP1 (is) of the (same) type as NP2" or rather where a binominal with a TN modifies a preceding NP. These type-noun derived pragmatic markers are attested to varying degrees in many languages: Italian *tipo* (Voghera 2013, Ch. 9, this volume), Brazilian and European Portuguese *tipo* (Lima Hernandes 2005; Marques 2015, Ch. 10, this volume), Spanish *tipo* (Kornfeld 2013, this volume; Fernández 2017; Mihatsch 2018), French *genre* (Fleischman and Yaguello 2004), Swedish and Norwegian *typ* (Rosenkvist and Skärlund 2013; Odden 2019) and cognates of *type* in Slavic languages, in particular Russian (Kolyaseva 2018; Kolyaseva and Kisiel, Ch. 12, this volume, Kisiel and Kolyaseva, Ch. 13, this volume).

The following example is a typical mitigating use found in languages which display pragmaticalized uses derived from trinominal constructions (Kolyaseva and Kisiel, Ch. 12, this volume):

(25) Russian
Èto   čto/   ja   dolžna   delat'? - Nu / net /
this-ACC.N.SG what   I.NOM   must-F.SG do-INF   well   no
nu ... nu   ja   dumal /   **tipa /** pomožeš'.
well   well I.NOM   think-PST.PRT.M.SG **type.** help-FUT.2.SG
'What / is it me who has to do that?
- well / no / well ... well I thought / **like** / you would help.' (RNC)

In 4.2.1 I will sketch the form and function of the source construction which results in a similative preposition, in 4.2.2 I will discuss the plausible paths leading from the prepositional use to adverbial functions developing into pragmatic markers. The most important tendencies in the languages presented in this volume will be summarized in 4.2.3. In 4.3. I will briefly reflect on phonetic and prosodic characteristics of markers based on TNs and will close with an overview of the timeline of this development in the languages covered in this volume.

4.2.1 Source construction

Several studies (for instance, Voghera 2013; Mihatsch 2018) point to a source construction "NP1 (is) of the (same) type as NP2", which can be paraphrased as 'X belongs to same superordinate category as Y', which seems to get more strongly established from the nineteenth century onward. In the "trinominal" source construction the TN is not the head. This structure rather resembles the postposed constructions discussed above (*trees of all kinds*), with the particularity that the TN is followed by another prepositional phrase. In Russian, the genitival TN followed by a genitive lexical noun is the source construction of the highly entrenched and polyfunctional marker *tipa*; this is also true for Polish *tipu*. Latvian seems to have the Russian loans *tipa* and *kipa* (Vassiliadou et al., Ch. 17, this volume). The even more frequent Russian *vrode* (from *v rode* 'in the kind of', a calque from French *dans le genre de*, see Kolyaseva 2021b) shows a similar array of pragmatic functions. Anna Kisiel (p.c.) also highlights the productivity of preposition-based TN constructions in Polish, which are more productive than their genitival equivalents. Here, the taxonomic relation expressed by the TN is one of superordination, not subcategorization, so, unsurprisingly, we do not find cognates of *species* but *genus* in such trinominal constructions (see the overview of Romance languages in Mihatsch, Ch. 7, this volume) as well as the most common choice, *type*, which is arguably also closer to superordination, since the TNs based on etymological equivalents of *type* construe a more general category on the basis of a prototype.

As with phoric uses (*that kind of thing*), the construction "NP1 (is) of the (same) type as NP2" creates an implicit (ad hoc) superordinate (see Mauri 2017 on the linguistic means of creating ad hoc categories). The reinterpretation of the TN (with or without preposition) as a similative preposition simplifies the semantics of the construction and a complex construal via an implicit superordinate is thus avoided, so we have a kind of semantic shortcut.

For Romance and North Scandinavian languages, the first step toward more pragmaticalized uses of the trinominal construction is the evolution of a similative preposition formally accompanied by reduction of the semantically general prepositions preceding and following the TN. For Russian *tipa* the first step is a fossilization of the genitive, whereas for Russian *vrode* it is the coalescence of the preposition and the TN.

(26) Russian
 zvezda **tipa** *Solnca* *našego*
 star.NOM.SG.F **type** sun.GEN.SG.M our.GEN.SG.M
 'a star **like** the Sun of ours' (Kolyaseva and Davidse 2018: 206)

(27) Polish
 Relacja *typu* „*twarzą* w *twarz*
 Relation type face-INSTR.SG in face-ACC.SG
 'face-to-face-like relation' (Kolyaseva and Kisiel, Ch. 12, this volume)

These prepositions typically link two NPs, but there are also uses introducing a prepositional phrase which modifies VPs:

(28) Italian
 La *tratta-va* **tipo** *me*
 her treat-PST.3.SG **type** me
 'He/She treated her **like** me.' (Voghera 2013: 298)

While the prepositional use of Russian *tipa* is predominantly adnominal linking two NPs, Russian *vrode* is also common in predicative complements (Kolyaseva and Davidse 2018: 205). Uses of TN-based prepositions beyond adnominal uses linking to NPs are also attested in the other Romance languages (see Mihatsch 2021, in press, and Ch. 7, this volume). Since the development of the prepositional use is very inconspicuous when compared to the subsequent evolution of pragmatic markers, there seem to be less studies on the particularities of this stage than on the pragmatic functions (see Mihatsch in press on the case of French *genre*).

The trinominal construction can also be used in copular sentences, linking the subject NP of the sentence with a prepositional phrase containing a TN. This may be the bridging context and the locus of reinterpretation of the preposition as an adverb, since copula complements may be realized by a variety of syntactic constituents, such as NPs, adjectival phrases or prepositional phrases:
– Subject copula [$_{PP}$ *tipo*$_P$ [NP]]
– Subject copula [$_{NP}$ *tipo*$_{ADV}$ [NP]]

Clear adverbial uses are found in direct object position, such as in the following example:

(29) Spanish
[...] *Quer-ía-n*   *hac-er*   **tipo**   *charla-s*
[...] Want-IMPRF-3.PL   make-INF   **type**   talk-PL
'[...] they wanted to have **like** (*tipo*) talks' (COLA Buenos Aires)

4.2.2 From adverb to pragmatic marker

Adverbs may further develop particle uses, for instance, in sentence-initial and (although more restricted and not found in all languages) in sentence-final position, or in independent constituents in short answers:

(30) Italian
Partiamo domani // **tipo** *//*
'We'll leave tomorrow, **like**' (Voghera 2013)

(31) Norwegian
dataskärmen lyser lika starkt i mina ögon som solen gör i Thailand, **typ** *:)*
'the pc-screen shines as strongly in my eyes as the sun does in Thailand, **kinda** (typ) :)' (Odden 2019: 195)

(32) Polish
A: *Interesujesz się takimi facetami?*
B: ***Typu?*** (Kolyaseva and Kisiel, Ch. 12, this volume)

'A: You fancy such men?
B: **Like what?** (*Typu?*)'

As with English *like*, the transitions from comparative preposition to approximating preposition and then approximating adverb and from comparison to exemplification are rather smooth. These functions of (former) TN exist in all the languages discussed in this volume except for English and German, and these steps are also attested for more established similative prepositions such as French *comme*, Spanish and Portuguese *como* and Italian *come*, as well as lexemes in other Romance languages, also rather marginally with German *wie*.

Starting out from approximation, new functions as pragmatic markers such as mitigation (often with epistemic or evidential values), focus markers and imprecise quantification arise, while exemplification (including explanation and illustration markers) seems to lead to quotation markers and general discourse structuring devices (see Mihatsch 2018 on the implicatures facilitating these hypothesized paths and Mihatsch 2020b for arguments in favour of these paths):

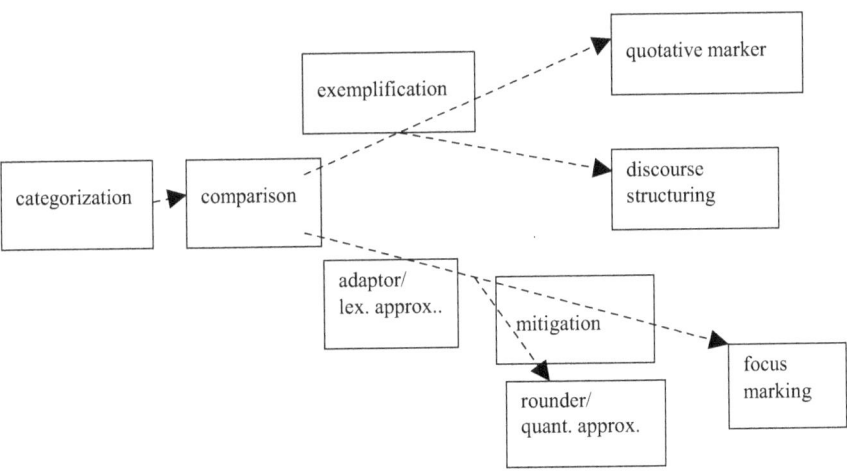

Figure 1: A semantic map for TN-based pragmatic markers (Mihatsch 2020b).

4.2.3 A brief crosslinguistic overview of pragmatic markers derived from trinominal constructions

The evolution of adverbial and pragmatic marker uses in the three language families will be treated in greater detail in the introductions to the language families and in many of the contributions to this volume. In what follows, I will present an overview of the general tendencies observed in the three language families.

In the Slavic languages analogous functions, although with differing degrees of entrenchment, are expressed both by the rather recent TN *tip/typ > tipa*, mostly fossilizing a genitive, and also by fossilized prepositional constructions such as Russian *vrode* (<*v rode* lit. 'in the kind of') and *po tipu* (lit. 'by the type'), and Polish *w rodzaju* (lit. 'in the kind of'), *z rodzaju* (lit. 'from the kind of'), and *w typie* (lit. 'in the type'). For Russian *tipa* and *vrode* the whole array of functions can be observed, although with interesting semantic and pragmatic differences (see Sakhno (2010), Kolyaseva (2021a), Kisiel and Kolyaseva, Ch. 13, this volume, and Daiber (2010) on the quotative function), while other Slavic languages often show the weakly pragmaticalized approximator and exemplifier functions, but not rounder uses, quotative uses (although frequent in Polish, Anna Kisiel, p.c.), focus markers or discourse structuring functions (see Kisiel and Kolyaseva, Ch. 13, this volume), since these seem to require further pragmaticalization processes (Mihatsch 2018, 2020b). This confirms the semantic map sketched above, which was originally based solely on Romance data. Similar paths in Slavic languages are derived from other TNs and often with coalesced adpositions. In Slavic languages, parallel (incipient) developments affect prepositional phrases with nouns semantically close to TNs translating 'style', 'taste' and 'shape'. These and others may develop analogous uses as pragmatic markers (see Polish *w stylu, w guście* (<*gust* 'taste'), *na kształt* (<*kształt* 'a shape'), *na wzór* (<*wzór* 'pattern'), *spod znaku* (<*znak* 'a sign'), *z nurtu* (<*nurt* 'a stream') and *z serii* (*seria* 'series'), Kisiel, Ch. 14, this volume). Janebová, Martinková and Gast (Ch. 15, this volume) detect incipient changes of Czech *tip* leading to uses in similative comparison, exemplification and quotation, thus the functions which do not correspond to an advanced stage of pragmaticalization.

In the North Scandinavian Germanic languages Swedish and Norwegian, *typ* is derived from a reduced prepositional construction *av typen av* (Odden 2019); the pragmatic marker *typ* seems more established in Swedish than in Norwegian.

German does not have such type noun derived markers, but now has an equivalent derived from the similative deictic *so* 'so, such' which covers the same array of functions, although with some of the rather more strongly pragmaticalized functions still restricted to colloquial teenage language or at least that of younger adults (Umbach and Ebert 2009; Wiese 2011). Ekberg, Opsahl, and Wiese (2015) show comparable uses for Swedish and Norwegian *sån/sånn*, which are also evolving in contemporary urban vernaculars. Remarkably, Rumantsch seems to have a corresponding calque from German *so* (see Mihatsch, Ch. 7, this volume).

The standardized national Romance languages Portuguese, Spanish, Catalan (to some extent), French, Italian and Romanian have established type-noun-based pragmatic markers derived from a trinominal structure. These are mostly based on *type* cognates, with the exception of French and Romanian *genus*-based markers (and some incipient uses of Portuguese *género*). A first pilot study, in which native speakers with a professional linguistic background (linguists, language teachers and members of institutions promoting minority languages) were consulted, confirms that such uses have not developed in Catalan, Galician, Romansh, Ladin, and Sardinian, which do, nevertheless, show loans (or calques) of pragmaticalized TNs from contact languages. This is a very intriguing discovery which points to the importance of either standard language or possibly rather a flourishing urban youth culture in each respective language for the evolution of the markers in the standardized national languages (see Mihatsch, Ch. 7, this volume). In addition to competing lexemes French *comme*, Spanish and Portuguese *como* and Italian *come*, some Romance languages show analogous paths through nouns semantically close to TNs like the etymological equivalents of *style* (Mihatsch 2010; Masini and Mauri 2020), and dialectally and sociolinguistically, more restricted Spanish *en plan*[15] (< 'with the intention'), *onda* (< 'vibes', 'atmosphere') (Mihatsch 2020a; Mondaca 2020) and *corte* (*que*) (< 'cut') (Rojas 2012).

4.3 Phonetic and prosodic changes accompanying the loss of noun status

There are hardly any systematic phonetic and prosodic studies of TNs, with the exception of Dehé and Stathi (2016) on English *sort/kind/type of* constructions, and Hennecke and Mihatsch (in press) on French *genre*. These studies as well as many relevant observations in analyses with a semantic, pragmatic and morphosyntactic focus, such as Davidse, Brems, and De Smedt (2008), point to a loss of prosodic prominence as TNs lose their head status and their nominal properties.

Hennecke and Mihatsch (in press) compare lexical uses of French *genre* within, as well as, outside binominals and show rather clear rising intonation contours in combination with a relatively high intensity and a slightly shorter duration within binominals than lexical uses external to binominals. The reduced length may be partly due to the position of the TN, since in French the stress is at

---

[15] On the pragmaticalization paths of *en plan* see Borreguero Zuloaga (2020) and Rodríguez Abruñeiras (2020).

the end of an intonation unit, whereas here, depending on the speech rate, stress should rather fall on the N2 or subsequent elements. However, this might also point to a close interaction between the two nouns and the backgrounding of the syntactic head in a binominal construction. Regardless, the length of the nominal uses was found to be shorter than the length of the pragmaticalized functions discussed in 4.2.

The approximative uses in our subcorpus are all sentence-internal with narrow scope, and truth-functional with additional pragmatic effects such as hesitation. This might explain their greater length in comparison with the other functions, but they also show generally flat intonational contours with low intensity and no prosodic prominence and an overall loss of stress compared to the nominal functions of *genre*, as well as no rise in their prosodic autonomy. In our opinion this reflects the combination of truth-functional and sentence-internal use and a certain degree of proceduralization alongside the adoption of additional pragmatic effects, paralleling the observations by Siegel (2002) on the functional properties of English *like*. In its discourse marker function with sentence scope, *genre* has a flat intonational contour with low intensity, a loss of stress, and no prosodic prominence. However, we observe a higher degree of prosodic autonomy (framed by pauses) and greater length than the lexical uses. This also corresponds to what previous studies have found, to a greater or lesser extent, for the prosodic detachment of English *like* (Miller and Weinert 1995: 373; Andersen 2001) and *sort of* and *kind of* (Aijmer 2002: 188).

Beside the prosodic effects, there are also more conspicuous segmental changes. As pointed out above, there is a tendency for the TNs to agglutinate with either determiners or quantifiers, as can be seen in fossilized expressions such as Middle English *alkin* (OED, s.v. *alkin*), in addition to the German and Norwegian expressions mentioned in section 4.1.3. In some cases phonetic reduction is quite developed, as in the reduction of *hva slags* to *kass, kassas* and *kala* in some Norwegian dialects (Odden 2019: 240). An example of fusion with the preceding preposition is Russian *vrode*, which is formed from a prepositional phrase *v* + *rod-(e)* 'in the kind of' (Kisiel and Kolyaseva, Ch. 13, this volume). English shows a fusion of the TN with the following preposition followed by segmental reduction as *sort of* is reduced to *sorta* and *kind of* to *kinda* (Aijmer 2002: 187), and Norwegian *slags* and Russian *tipa* (discussed below) fossilize a genitive form. Interestingly, Russian *tipa* shows an alternative spelling *tipo* in informal texts such as internet forums; for a discussion of plausible explanations see Kisiel and Kolyaseva (Ch. 13, this volume). Similarly, Swedish and Norwegian *slags* /ʃlaks/ has a short vowel, unlike the lexical *slag* with a long /a:/ pronounced as /ʃlaːg/ (Odden 2019: 12).

4.4 Comparing the timelines of the evolving pragmatic markers

Unlike derived modifier, quantifier and identifier uses, the pragmatic functions seem to evolve later and with a stronger restriction to particular TNs. In the case of the nominal qualifier use based on a binominal akin to 'a kind of NP' there is a strong European tendency for first approximative uses to arise in the sixteenth century (see section 4.1.3), possibly because the affected TNs need to be well integrated into their respective vernacular lexicon. Perhaps there are other external reasons, such as the discovery of the New World and the necessity to deal with hitherto unknown realities or intensive translation activities and related lexical problems in the Renaissance. In any case, in the following century new TNs also began to adopt qualifying (i.e. approximating) functions, so that the process kept repeating itself over several hundred years.

The timeline of the type noun based pragmatic markers is much more focused and very similar in all the languages analysed, with first possible source constructions getting established in the nineteenth century, then developing prepositional uses and from the last third of the twentieth century leading in most cases to pragmatic marker uses in colloquial language, in particular among young speakers.

The development of the more intensively studied English *like* seems to show a strong link to contemporary urban colloquial teenage language in the States. However, a closer look shows that many of the pragmatic functions such as mitigation are much older, some of them originating in the eighteenth century (OED, s.v. *like*), and they are found in rural communities in Great Britain (Miller and Weinert 1995). Further pragmatic uses seem to become a characteristic feature of the beat and jazz movements in the middle of the twentieth century. The massive increase in pragmatic uses, in particular the quotative use, seems to have occurred in the 1980s and is often associated with middle-class female teenagers on the West Coast of the United States.[16]

The chronology of first appearances of the type noun derived markers differs from that of English *like*. Since the etymological equivalents of *type* start appearing with their taxonomic reading in the eighteenth and nineteenth centuries, first prepositional uses of these TNs are attested some time later toward the end of the nineteenth and the beginning of the twentieth centuries. These uses are often found in technical and generally specialized, sometimes scientific, contexts (Rosenkvist and Skärlund 2013; Mihatsch 2020a, 2020b).

---

16 For the myth of the Valley girls and a very detailed critical evaluation of sociolinguistic beliefs concerning the evolution of *like*, see D'Arcy (2017).

Remarkably, the timeline of the evolution of the more pragmaticalized uses is comparable to that of English *like*, although the lack of colloquial data in the first two thirds of the twentieth century makes an exact diachronic study rather difficult. First pragmaticalized uses of Spanish *tipo*, Portuguese *tipo*, French *genre*, and Russian *tipa*, and also some related (quasi-)TNs, seem to appear from the seventies onward (for an overview see Lapteva 1983; Lima Hernandes 2005; Isambert 2016; Mihatsch 2020a; Mihatsch, Ch. 7, this volume) and further functions such as quotative uses begin in the eighties and nineties (also see Kolyaseva and Kisiel, Ch. 12, this volume). The more pragmaticalized uses are colloquial and often associated with teenage language, and in some cases related to particular social classes, while the less pragmaticalized prepositional uses and the qualifying function based on binominals tend to be adopted by adult speakers of all ages (see Beeching 2016).

The very similar timeline observed in all the languages with such pragmatic markers is rather puzzling. One might think of language contact and particularly the influence of English *like*. However, in some cases pragmaticalized uses appear very early as Kisiel (Ch. 14, this volume) shows for Polish *w stylu*, appearing well before the new English quotatives and also slightly earlier than Russian *tipa*. As discussed in Kolyaseva (2018: 85–86) and Kisiel and Kolyaseva (Ch. 13, this volume), the countries of the Soviet bloc had very restricted contact with the Western world, so borrowing via informal discourse seems implausible.

For Swedish, Rosenkvist and Skärlund (2013) suggest that the adverbial and particle uses appear towards the end of the twentieth century, after typical uses in the domain of military aircraft in the twenties and thirties became generalized.

Some studies propose contact between neighbouring languages or immigration as decisive factors. Odden (2019: 64) mentions a hypothesis by Olofsson (2016), who suggests that pragmaticalized uses may have been reinforced by Italian immigration before and after World War II and by Chilean immigration in the seventies; however, these theories are hard to prove since clear attestations of pragmatic marker uses in Spanish and Italian pointing to a solid degree of entrenchment appear rather later. Odden (2019: 300) points to a later development in Norwegian with a sharp increase in the twenty-first century, possibly influenced by Swedish *typ*. In Belarusian and Ukrainian there also seems to be a very recent parallel development for *kštaltu*, possibly influenced by Polish and Russian (Kolyaseva and Kisiel, Ch. 12, this volume). As Kolyaseva and Kisiel (Ch. 12, this volume) show, a dialect of Croatian from the region of Rijeka, as well as Istria contains a highly colloquial borrowing from Italian (*tip*).

Language contact might be one factor, at least in some well-documented cases; however, general tendencies towards the increased use of direct speech and the evolution of quotatives might be related to general international communicative tendencies (see also Foolen 2008). A rather external factor triggering the earlier mitigating uses might be the communicative tendencies of mid-century counter cultures, in particular the transitions of type noun constructions from formal academic texts to colloquial speech.

There are still many unsolved questions, many of which are related to the international character of the described tendencies, the role of general or perhaps even universal paths of grammaticalization and pragmaticalization, the role of discourse traditions and communicative patterns, language contact and external sociocultural factors, and also morphosyntactic differences between the languages.

5 The contributions to this volume

This volume is organized in language-specific sections with extensive overviews provided for each language family.

Part 1: Type noun constructions in Germanic languages

The first section of the volume focuses on Germanic languages and starts with an overview of TN-derived uses in Germanic languages by Lot Brems (University of Liège/Leuven). Kristin Davidse (University of Leuven) and An Van Linden (University of Liège) entitled **Towards a comprehensive typology of type noun constructions in Germanic languages with special focus on English and Dutch.**

In their contribution on **Taxonomizing and characterizing TN constructions in English: a new functional-structural typology** Kristin Davidse (University of Leuven) and Lot Brems (University of Liège/Leuven) address a number of research gaps by investigating in greater detail the lexical uses of TNs expressing sub- and superordination as well as characterization and the different construction types associated with these functions. Based on Langacker's cognitive functional-structural analysis of constructions with a focus on the mechanisms of modification and complementation of heads they establish a refined typology of the constructions containing lexical TNs which do not show any signs of decategorialization, but which are nevertheless, highly differentiated in their functions.

Karin Aijmer (University of Göteborg) contributes an analysis on **Type nouns in some varieties of English.** In this article, Karin Aijmer argues for a more global view on TNs by comparing American English to other varieties of English, both inner-circle ones like New Zealand English, and outer-circle ones like Hong Kong English. Based on extensive corpus research, the study aims to ascertain whether the uses of TNs described in earlier works are also attested in these other varieties and with what frequency. Based on semantic, formal and collocational analyses the division of labour between the various TNs is revealed. The corpus study also yields innovative and non-standard patterns, such as *kinda of*, as well as a TN expression that seems to be making a comeback in certain patterns, namely *all manner of*. Incorporating other varieties also lends further support to the view that elements typically shift from propositional uses to non-propositional ones.

Evelien Keizer (University of Vienna) analyses **The function and use of NP-external *sort/kind-of*: the case of *sort/kind of* DEF.DET.** Her contribution is dedicated to a hitherto understudied subtype of English *sort/kind of* binominals in which the taxonomic noun precedes a definite NP. Based on corpus data she argues that the NP external uses share functions with both the adverbial qualifier or discourse marker uses of *sort/kind of*, as well as with the NP-internal qualifying use. Related to the scope over the NP, the NP-external *sort/kind of* rather aims at the categorization of the referent than the (mitigated) appropriateness of the linguistic description. She further points out diverging properties of *sort of* and *kind of* in these constructions, with a greater proportion of pragmatic functions of *kind of* when compared with *sort of*, which in some positions seems to specialize in exemplification and specification.

Carla Umbach (University of Berlin/Cologne) focuses on **Ways of categorization: German *Art* and *Typ*.** Umbach's paper compares the meaning and usage of two German TNs, i.e. *Art* and *Typ*. Dictionaries, corpus research and an experimental study confirm that they construe two distinct ways of classification. *Art* makes use of essential properties shared by the instances of a kind while classification by *Typ* makes use of prototypes. Furthermore, while classification by *Art* makes use of linguistic knowledge in a broad sense, classification by *Typ* tends to use expert-knowledge. The corpus study, moreover, showed that there are two basic forms of *Art-* and *Typ*-phrases in which the specified noun is either juxtaposed or embedded in a genitive or prepositional *von*-phrase. Finally, the findings on *Art* and *Typ* are considered more generally against the background of the notions of 'kind' and 'type' and their role in semantics theory.

Part 2. Type noun constructions in Romance languages

The section on Romance languages starts with a general overview by Wiltrud Mihatsch (University of Tübingen) with the title **A panoramic overview of the extended uses of taxonomic nouns in Romance languages** sketching the parallels and differences between the major and some minor Romance languages.

In his paper on **Classification, qualification, typification: categorizing with *genre de* and *espèce de* 'kind of' in French**, Pierre Chauveau-Thoumelin (University of Lille) investigates three different functions of constructions formed with the TNs *genre* 'genus; kind' and *espèce* 'species; kind'. In his paper, he offers a fine-grained analysis of the classifying construction, the qualifying construction and the typifying construction. The particular focus is on the third kind, the typifying construction, whose status is not as well established. This construction helps create a category on the basis of individuals usually previously mentioned in the discourse, often creating an ad hoc category (see Barsalou 1983). Analysis is based on corpus data of recent formal and informal written language and special attention is given to the type of determiner, agreement patterns, type of noun in the N-slot, and constraints with regard to modifiers in each construction.

Miriam Voghera (University of Salerno) studies **The network of *specie, genere, sorta, tipo* constructions: from lexical features to discursive functions.** Her paper offers an analysis of the network of the non-nominal head constructions (TNCxs$_{[-N]}$) derived from the Italian TNs (TNs) *specie, genere, sorta* and *tipo* (SGST). The focus is on the relationship between the semantic development of these TNs and their diffusion in various types of texts on the basis of diachronic and synchronic Italian corpora. Miriam Voghera considers, in particular, the interaction between, firstly, an increase in frequency and determinologization of the TNs, and secondly, the evolution of different functions such as categorization, comparison, approximation, exemplification and focusing, and the concomitant syntactic flexibilization required. This allows us to determine the different degrees of flexibility and versatility of the analysed TN constructions.

Maria Aldina Marques (Braga) offers a study of the ***Pragmatic functions and contexts of use of* tipo *in European Portuguese.*** In her analysis, Maria Aldina Marques focuses on the discourse marker *tipo* 'type' in European Portuguese. After a review of the semantic and pragmatic characteristics of the uses of *tipo* in spontaneous speech, she analyses the characteristics of each context in which the discourse marker *tipo* occurs, including the syntactic structures and, in particular, the clusters of discourse markers occuring with *tipo* and the semantic-pragmatic values that they convey. The analysis is based on oral data from two corpora, the CRPC-Oral and the corpus *Perfil Sociolinguístico da Fala Bracarense* (Sociolinguistic profile of Braga speech), both corpora of colloquial spontaneous speech.

In her contribution on **Taxonomic nouns and markers of mitigation in Río de la Plata Spanish** Laura Malena Kornfeld (Buenos Aires) presents an analysis of three items, the TN *tipo* ('type'), and the semi-taxonomic nouns *onda* ('wave, vibes', 'style') and *corte* (lit. 'cut', 'type, style'), which have analogous functions as prepositions, adverbial items, and pragmatic markers in some colloquial varieties of Río de la Plata Spanish, particularly among young people. Functions with sentential scope, notably mitigation, are at the heart of her analysis; one central aim of this paper is to systematize their basic grammatical properties such as distribution, and compatibility with various modalities, moods and polarities. The paper closes with an overview of the processes involved in the grammaticalization of nouns with (semi-)taxonomic meanings into markers of mitigation, contrasting them with other mitigating expressions in colloquial Río de la Plata Spanish (*como que*, 'like that', *medio*, 'half' or *un poco*, 'a bit') and the case of English *kind (of)/kinda*.

Part 3. Type noun constructions in Slavic languages

The third part of the volume brings together studies of TN constructions in Slavic languages and starts with a detailed comparative chapter **Taxonomic nouns in Slavic: an overview** sketching the diachronic and synchronic tendencies of extended TN uses in the Slavic language family by Anna Kisiel and Alena Kolyaseva (University of Leuven).

In the opening chapter with the title **Towards a comprehensive typology of type noun constructions in Slavic languages, with a special focus on Polish and Russian,** Anna Kisiel and Alena Kolyaseva present a comprehensive typology of TN constructions in Slavic languages, with a special focus on Polish and Russian. The typology builds on a reanalysed classification of lexical and grammaticalized uses of TNs in Russian proposed by Alena Kolyaseva and Kristin Davidse (2018). Their paper aims to demonstrate the range of possibilities for TN development attested in Slavic to date. The typology is based on similarities and differences identified between the meanings and usages of Polish *typ* and *rodzaj* and Russian *tip* and *rod*, both within and across languages. By analysing collocational patterns of *typ/tip* and *rodzaj/rod*, and their constructions, the authors aim to identify grammaticalization processes in Slavic. The authors show that two languages from one language group can be alike in their nominal uses and differ greatly in their non-representational meanings. The analysis is based on examples extracted from the Polish and Russian national corpora, compared with analogous contexts in Ukrainian and Bulgarian.

Anna Kisiel (Leuven) contributes a case study with the title **Polish *w stylu* and the rise of hedges.** In this study, Anna Kisiel investigates whether the development paths followed by TN constructions are replicated by grammaticalized constructions formed with non-taxonomic nouns and as such serve as more general developmental patterns. As a test case, she has chosen Polish prepositional phrase *w stylu* (lit. 'in the style of'), based on the noun *styl*, which acquires functions identical to those of TN constructions. The analysis of diachronic data from the National Corpus of Polish suggests that *w stylu* progresses through the stages of development in a similar manner to TN-based *w typie*, but that the time lapse between obtaining similarity and exemplification functions is shorter than that of grammaticalized TN constructions. At the same time the author observes *w stylu*'s further development into an explanation marker. In Polish the evolution of *w stylu* may be more striking than that of TN constructions, the patterns are identical.

The Slavic section closes with a contribution by Markéta Janebová, Michaela Martinkova (both University of Olomouc) and Volker Gast (University of Jena) on **Czech type nouns: evidence from Spoken Czech**. The authors present the development of two major TNs in another Slavic language, Czech. By analysing distributional patterns in informal spoken Czech as represented by the ORAL v.1 corpus (Kopřivová et al. 2017) and in original Czech fiction translated into English, they investigate the discourse functions of *druh* 'kind/sort' (whose taxonomic meaning developed from the animate reading 'a member of a group, companion'), and *typ* 'type' (a nineteenth-century borrowing, arguably via German). The statistical analyses suggest that the development of *druh* is less advanced than that of *typ*. *Druh* mostly retains its taxonomic function, even though there is evidence of its gaining quantifying and hedging functions. The functions acquired by *typ* include exemplifying, similative, and quotative functions.

Part 4. Comparative analyses across Indo-European language branches

The fourth and final section closes the volume with three analyses comparing languages from different language branches.

Valentina Benigni contributes an analysis with the title **The complementizer function of *TYPE*-nouns in ad hoc concept construction: evidence from Italian and Russian**. This paper sheds light on the role of TNs in the construction of ad hoc concepts from a Relevance-theoretic perspective. It provides a comparative account of the non-nominal Italian *tipo* and Russian *tipa* as part of the abstract syntactic pattern [X (of) type (of) Y] with a focus on pre-TN and post-TN discourse segments. In doing so, it complements the typology of TNs and their grammaticalized derivatives in Slavic languages presented in Kisiel and Kolyaseva (this volume) by offering an alternative, unifying account of *type*-words (cognates of *type*) as general complementizers that can take chunks of discourse with varying degrees of syntactic complexity, from word forms to sentences, as their argument. The empirical data are extracted from multiple web corpora containing collections of spoken discourse and computer-mediated communication (Araneum Russicum Maius, the Russian National Corpus, Araneum Italicum Maius, Perugia and InterCorp), and a usage-based constructional approach of functional-cognitive orientation within the framework of Construction Grammar is adopted for the analysis of the semantic and pragmatic aspects of the complementizer function.

The chapter with the title **Clear vs approximate categorization in French and Latvian** by Hélène Vassiliadou, Marie Lammert, Céline Benninger, Francine Gerhard-Krait (University of Strasbourg), Jelena Gridina, Daina Turla and Elena Vladimirska (University of Latvia) investigates TNs employed for hierarchical categorization and approximation. The paper begins with a scrutiny of the distinction between categorization and approximation, two frequently opposed yet essentially indissociable operations, and the interrelated phenomena *approximation, imprecision, vagueness* and *categorization*. The refined notions are then applied first to French taxonomic expressions and derived functions, then to Latvian TNs and their uses. The aim of this comparative analysis is to verify in particular whether the expressions exhibit the same kind of semantic multifunctionality in the studied languages or, on the contrary, if there are any specific semantic and morphosyntactic constraints in each language. One indicator of possible differences is the selection of the nouns preceding and following the TNs in the binominal structures. Another indicator is morphosyntax, which, according to the authors, explains why Latvian with its rich morphology leads to more clear-cut distinctions between the functions in comparison with French.

The section as well as the volume, closes with the chapter **Sociopragmatic variation, *sort of* and *genre* in English and French** by Kate Beeching (University of Bristol). She compares the English TN *sort of* with French *genre* in order to present similarities and differences in their pragmatic uses and related syntactic positions, in particular the syntactic flexibilization required for quotative uses.

With a focus on Quebec French, she further investigates the uses of *genre* and its equivalent *comme* 'sort of/like' in a corpus of oral speech data of Quebec French in order to examine current processes of language change and the sociolinguistic tendencies that characterize the recently emerging pragmatic uses.

6 Outlook

The aim of this overview has been to give a rough outline of the general tendencies of TN-derived functions in the language branches treated in this volume. Further systematic studies will be required to address the tendencies in these languages as well as other languages of the Germanic, Slavic and Romance branches, as well as other, also non-Indo-European languages: We hope this volume may serve as a starting point for future analyses beyond the phenomena and languages addressed in the contributions.

References

ADLP = Ferreira, Aurélio Buarque de Holanda. 1999 [1988]. *Novo Aurélio Século XXI: o dicionário da língua portuguesa* [The new 21st century Aurélio: the dictionary of the Portuguese language]. 3rd edn. Rio de Janeiro: Nova Fronteira.

Aijmer, Karin. 2002. *English discourse particles: Evidence from a corpus*. Amsterdam: John Benjamins.
Aijmer, Karin. 2020. *Sort of* and *kind of* from an English-Swedish perspective. In Ewa Jonsson & Tove Larsson (eds.), *Voices Past and Present – Studies of Involved, Speech-related and Spoken Texts: In honor of Merja Kytö*. 248–263 (Studies in Corpus Linguistics 97). Amsterdam: John Benjamins. https://doi.org/10.1075/scl.97.15aij (accessed 6 August 2021).
Andersen, Gisle. 2001. *Pragmatic markers and sociolinguistic variation. A relevance-theoretic approach to the language of adolescents*. Amsterdam: John Benjamins.
Bambeck, Manfred. 1959. *Lateinisch-romanische Wortstudien*. Wiesbaden: Steiner.
Barsalou, Lawrence W. 1983. Ad hoc categories. *Memory and Cognition* 11 (3). 211–227.
Beeching, Kate. 2016. *Pragmatic markers in British English: Meaning in social interaction*. Cambridge: Cambridge University Press.
Bolinger, Dwight. 1972. *Degree words*. The Hague: De Gruyter Mouton.
Borreguero Zuloaga, Margarita. 2020. Los marcadores de aproximación (en el lenguaje juvenil): it. *tipo* vs. esp. *en plan*. In Miguel Ángel Cuevas Gómez, Fernando Molina Castillo & Paolo Silvestri (eds.), *España e Italia: Un viaje de ida y vuelta. Studia in honorem Manuel Carrera Díaz*, 53–78. Sevilla: Editorial Universidad de Sevilla.
Brems, Lieselotte. 2011. *Layering of size and type noun constructions in English*. Berlin: De Gruyter Mouton.
Brems, Lieselotte & Kristin Davidse. 2010. The grammaticalization of nominal type noun constructions with *kind/sort of*: Chronology and paths of change. *English Studies* 91 (2). 180–202.
Chauveau-Thoumelin, Pierre. 2020. *Une approche constructionnelle des enclosures* genre et espèce. Lille: Université Lille 3 doctoral thesis.
COLA = *Corpus Oral de Lenguaje Adolescente*. http://www.colam.org/ (accessed 7 April 2021).
C-ORAL-ROM = Cresti, Emanuela & Massimo Moneglia: *C-ORAL-ROM: Integrated reference corpora for spoken Romance languages*. CD-ROM. Amsterdam & Philadelphia: Benjamins.
Corbett, Greville G. 2000. *Number*. Cambridge: Cambridge University Press.
CREA = Real Academia Española: *Corpus de Referencia del Español Actual*. http://corpus.rae.es/creanet.html (accessed 25 April 2021).
D'Arcy, Alexandra. 2017. *Discourse-pragmatic variation in context: Eight hundred years of* LIKE. Amsterdam: John Benjamins.
Daiber, Thomas. 2010. Quotativmarker im Russischen (типо/типа). *Zeitschrift für Slawistik* 55 (1). 69–89.
Daston, Lorraine. 2004. Type specimens and scientific memory. *Critical Inquiry* 31 (1). 153–182.
Davidse, Kristin, Lieselotte Brems & Liesbeth De Smedt. 2008. Type noun uses in the English NP: A case of right to left layering. *International Journal of Corpus Linguistics* 13 (2). 139–168.
Davidse, Kristin, Lieselotte Brems, Peter Willemse, Emeline Doyen, Jessica Kiermeer & Elfi Thoelen. 2013. A comparative study of the grammaticalized uses of English *sort (of)* and French *genre (de)* in teenage forum data. In Miola E. (ed.), *Standard and non-standard languages on the Internet. Languages Go Web. Studi e Ricerche*, 41–66. Alessandria: Edizioni dell' Orso.
DCLIC = Coromines, Joan. 1991 [1980]. *Diccionari etimológic i complementari de la llengua catalane* [Etymological and complementary dictionary of Catalan]. 9th edn. Barcelona: Curial.

De Smedt, Liesbeth, Lieselotte Brems & Kristin Davidse. 2007. NP-internal functions and extended uses of the ‚type' nouns *kind, sort*, and *type*: towards a comprehensive, corpus-based description. In Roberta Facchinetti (ed.), *Corpus Linguistics 25 Years on*, 225–255. Amsterdam & New York: Rodopi.

Dehé, Nicole & Katerina Stathi. 2016. Grammaticalization and prosody: The case of English *sort/kind/type of* constructions. *Language* 92 (4). 911–946.

Denison, David. 2002. History of the *sort of* construction family. Paper presented at the Second International Conference on Construction Grammar, University of Helsinki, 7 September.

Denison, David. 2005. The grammaticalization of *sort of, kind of* and *type of* in English. Paper presented at New Reflections on Grammaticalization 3, University of Santiago de Compostela, 17–20 July.

Ekberg, Lena, Toril Opsahl & Heike Wiese. 2015. Functional gains: A cross-linguistic case study of three particles in Swedish, Norwegian and German. In Jacomine Nortier & Bente A. Svendsen (eds.), *Language, youth and identity in the 21st century. Linguistic practices across urban spaces*, 93–115. Cambridge: Cambridge University Press.

Ernout, Alfred & Antoine Meillet (eds.). 1994. *Dictionnaire étymologique de la langue latine: Histoire des mots*. Paris: Klincksieck.

Fernández, Julieta. 2017. The language functions of *tipo* in Argentine vernacular. *Journal of Pragmatics* 114. 87–103.

FEW = von Wartburg, Walther. 1922. *Französisches etymologisches Wörterbuch: eine Darstellung des galloromanischen Sprachschatzes*. Bonn & Leipzig: Kurt Schroeder.

Fleischman, Suzanne & Marina Yaguello. 2004. Discourse markers across languages? Evidence from English and French. In Carol Lynn Moder & Aida Martinovic-Zic (eds.), *Discourse across languages and cultures*, 129–147. Amsterdam: John Benjamins.

Fleischman, Suzanne. 1998. Des jumeaux du discours: *Genre* et *like*. *La linguistique* 34 (2). 31–47.

Foolen, Ad. 2008. New quotative markers in spoken discourse. In Bernt Ahrenholz, Ursula Bredel, Wolfgang Klein, Martina Rost-Roth & Romuald Skiba (eds.), *Empirische Forschung und Theoriebildung: Beiträge aus Soziolinguistik, Gesprochene-Sprache- und Zweitspracherwerbsforschung. Festschrift für Norbert Dittmar zum 65. Geburtstag*, 117–128. Frankfurt am Main: Lang.

FRANTEXT = Base textuelle *FRANTEXT*. 2021. https://www.frantext.fr/ (accessed 7 April 2021).

GDWB = Grimm, Jacob & Wilhelm Grimm. 1854–1893. *Deutsches Wörterbuch*. Leipzig: Hirzel. http://dwb.uni-trier.de/de/ (accessed 06 August 2021). GDWB = Grimm, Jacob & Wilhelm Grimm. 1854–1893. *Deutsches Wörterbuch*. Leipzig: Hirzel. http://dwb.uni-trier.de/de/ (accessed 06 August 2021).

Gelman, Susan A. & Amanda C. Brandone. 2010. Fast-mapping placeholders: Using words to talk about kinds. *Language Learning and Development* 6 (3). 223–240.

Gingras, Yves, Peter Keating & Camille Limoges. 2000. *Du scribe au savant: les porteurs du savoir de l'Antiquité à la révolution industrielle*. Paris: Presses Universitaires de France.

Goddard, Cliff & Anna Wierzbicka (eds.). 1994. *Semantic and lexical universals: Theory and empirical findings*. Amsterdam: John Benjamins.

Heine, Bernd. 2002. On the role of context in grammaticalization. In Ilse Wischer & Gabriele Diewald (eds.), *New reflections on grammaticalization*, 83–101. (Typological studies in language 49). Amsterdam/Philadelphia: John Benjamins.

Hennecke, Inga & Wiltrud Mihatsch. In press. From taxonomic to pragmatic uses of French *genre*: Degrees of prosodic prominence as an indicator of pragmaticalization. In

Hélène Vassiliadou & Marie Lammert (eds.), *Clear versus approximate categorization: A crosslinguistic perspective*. Cambridge: Cambridge Scholars.

Isambert, Paul. 2016. *Genre*: une mode récente mais qui vient de loin. *Journal of French language studies* 26 (1). 85–96.

Janebová, Markéta, Martinková, Michaela. 2017. NP-Internal *Kind of* and *Sort of*: Evidence from a Parallel Translation Corpus. In Markéta Janebová, Ekaterina Lapshinova-Koltunski & Micaela Martinková (eds.), *Contrasting English and Other Languages through Corpora*. 164–217. Newcastle upon Tyne: Cambridge ScholarsPublishing.

Keizer, Evelien. 2007. *The English noun phrase: The nature of linguistic categorization*. Cambridge: Cambridge University Press.

Klix, Friedhart. 1993. *Erwachendes Denken: Geistige Leistungen aus evolutionspsychologischer Sicht*. Heidelberg: Spektrum.

Köbler, Gerhard. 2014. *Althochdeutsches Wörterbuch*. 6th edn. http://www.koeblergerhard.de/ahdwbhin.html (accessed 6 August 2021).

Kolde, Gottfried. 2004. Gehört der Heckenausdruck *(so)(ei)n(e) Art (von) X* ins Valenzwörterbuch? In Speranta Stanescu (ed.), *Die Valenztheorie. Bestandsaufnahme und Perspektiven*, 133–146. Frankfurt am Main: Peter Lang.

Kolyaseva, Alena. 2018. The 'new' Russian quotative *tipa*: Pragmatic scope and functions. *Journal of Pragmatics* 128. 82–97.

Kolyaseva, Alena. 2021a. The nominal uses of the Russian *rod* ('genus', 'genre', 'kind') and *tip* ('type'): the starting point of desemanticization. *Slovo a Slovesnost* 82. 3–44.

Kolyaseva, Alena. 2021b. The divergent paths of pragmaticalization: The case of the Russian particles *tipa* and *vrode*. *Journal of Pragmatics*. https://doi.org/10.1016/j.pragma.2021.08.003. (accessed 18 January 2022)

Kolyaseva, Alena & Kristin Davidse. 2018. A typology of lexical and grammaticalized uses of Russian *tip, tipa, po tipu*. *Russian linguistics* 42 (2). 191–220.

Kornfeld, Laura. 2013. Atenuadores en la lengua coloquial argentina. *Lingüística* 29. 17–49.

Lapteva, Olga Alekseevna. 1983. *Tipa* ili *vrode* [*Tipa* or *vrode*]. *Voprosy jazykoznanija* [Topics in linguistics] 1. 39–51.

LDAF = Greimas, Algirdas J. 1992 [1968]. *Dictionnaire de l'ancien français. Le Moyen Âge*. 2nd edn. Paris: Larousse.

Lewis, Charlton T. and Short, Charles. 1879. *A Latin Dictionary*. Founded on Andrews' edition of Freund's Latin dictionary. revised, enlarged, and in great part rewritten by. Charlton T. Lewis, Ph.D. and. Charles Short, LL.D. Oxford: Clarendon Press. https://www.perseus.tufts.edu/hopper/text?doc=Perseus%3Atext%3A1999.04.0059%3 (accessed 13 December 2021).

Lima Hernandes, Maria Célia. 2005. *A interface sociolingüística / gramaticalização: estratificação de usos de tipo, feito, igual e como – sincronia e diacronia* [The interface sociolinguistics /grammaticalization: stratification of the uses of *tipo, feito, igual* and *como* – synchrony and diachrony]. Campinas: Unicamp doctoral dissertation.

LSJ = Roelli, Philippe (ed.). 1940. *Liddell-Scott-Jones Greek-English Lexicon*. https://outils.biblissima.fr/fr/eulexis-web/ (accessed 24 April 2021).

Marques, Maria Aldina. 2015. 'Tipo'. Référenciation et modalisation dans des interactions verbales orales. In Maria Helena Araújo Carreira (ed.), *Faits de langue et de discours pour l'expression des modalités dans les langues romanes. Travaux et documents* 60. 249–260. Paris: Université Paris 8-Vincennes-Saint-Denis.

Masini, Francesca & Caterina Mauri. 2020. Questione di stile. L'espressione analitica della maniera indessicale. *Testi e linguaggi* 14. 259–271.

Mauri, Caterina. 2017. Building and interpreting ad hoc categories: a linguistic analysis. In Joanna Blochowiak, Cristina Grisot, Stephanie Durrlemann-Tame, & Christopher Laenzlinger (eds.), *Formal models in the study of language. Applications in Interdisciplinary Contexts*, 297–326. Berlin: Springer.

Mihatsch, Wiltrud. 2007. The Construction of vagueness: 'Sort of' expressions in Romance languages. In Günter Radden, Klaus-Michael Koepcke, Thomas Berg & Peter Siemund (eds.), *Aspects of meaning construction*, 225–245. Amsterdam & Philadelphia: John Benjamins.

Mihatsch, Wiltrud. 2010. „Wird man von Hustensaft wie so ne art bekifft?" *Approximationsmarker in romanischen Sprachen*. Frankfurt am Main: Klostermann.

Mihatsch, Wiltrud. 2016. Type-noun binominals in four Romance languages. In Lieselotte Brems, Bernard De Clerck & Katrien Verveckken (eds.), *Binominal syntagms as a neglected locus of synchronic variation and diachronic change: Towards a unified approach*. Special issue in Language Sciences, 136–159.

Mihatsch, Wiltrud. 2018. From ad hoc category to ad hoc categorization: The proceduralization of Argentinian Spanish *tipo*. *Folia Linguistica* 52. 147–176.

Mihatsch Wiltrud. 2019. *De manera, de forma, de modo*: construcciones adverbiales de manera en tres variedades del español. In Franz Lebsanft & Sebastian Greußlich (eds.), *El español, lengua pluricéntrica. Discurso, gramática, léxico y medios de comunicación masiva*, 431–459. (Sprache in kulturellen Kontexten 4). Göttingen: V&R unipress.

Mihatsch, Wiltrud. 2020a. Los orígenes discursivos de los atenuadores procedimentalizados 'tipo', 'onda', 'corte' y 'rollo': Una exploración microdiacrónica. *Revista Signos* 53 (104). 686–717.

Mihatsch, Wiltrud. 2020b. A semantic-map approach to pragmatic markers: the complex approximation/mitigation/quotation/focus marking. [Peninsular Spanish (*tipo, así, como*) and European Portuguese (*tipo, assim, como*) based on a corpus analysis of C-ORAL-ROM]. In Isabel Margarida Duarte & Rogelio Ponce de Léon (eds.), *Marcadores discursivos. O português como referência contrastiva*, 137–162. Bern: Peter Lang.

Mihatsch, Wiltrud. 2021. French type-noun constructions based on *genre*: From the creation of ad hoc categories to ad hoc categorization. In Caterina Mauri, Ilaria Fiorentini & Eugenio Goria (eds.), *Building categories in interaction: Linguistic resources at work*, 373–414. New York & Amsterdam: John Benjamins.

Miller, Jim & Regina Weinert. 1995. The function of *like* in dialogue. *Journal of Pragmatics* 23 (4). 365–393.

Moline, Estelle & Dejan Stosic. 2016. *L'expression de la manière en français*. Paris: Ophrys.

Moline, Estelle. 2011. Une manière d'article en manière d'hommage. Sur les tournures en *une manière de N*. In Dany Amiot, Walter de Mulder, Estelle Moline & Dejan Stosic (eds.), *Ars Grammatica. Hommages à Nelly Flaux*, 389–402. Bern: Peter Lang.

Mondaca Becerra, Lissette. 2020. Aproximación al estudio de las funciones pragmáticas y a la atenuación en la partícula 'onda' en el español de Chile. *Revista Signos* 53 (104). 718–743.

Odden, Oda Røste. 2019. *North Scandinavian type noun constructions: Patterns with slags, SORTs and TYP(E)*. Oslo: University of Oslo doctoral dissertation.

OED = Oxford English Dictionary. *OED Online*. Oxford University Press. http://dictionary.oed.com (accessed 6 August 2021).

Olofsson, Arne. 2016. Svensk typ är inte unik [Swedish typ is not unique]. *Språktidningen* 2016 (1). 58–62.

Parvaresh, Vahid & Sheikhan, Amir. 2019. Pragmatic functions of 'sort of' in Persian: A vague language perspective. *Journal of Asian Pacific Communication* 29. 86–110.

Parvaresh, Vahid & Zhang, Grace Qiao. 2019. Sort of across languages of the Asia and Oceania region. *Journal of Asian Pacific Communication* 29. 2–8.

Popescu, Cecilia-Mihaela & Alice Ionescu. 2019. Étude comparative des marqueurs métadiscursifs *gen* du roumain et *genre* du français. Distribution et valeurs pragmatiques. *Studii de lingvistică* 9 (2). 93–112.

PR = Rey-Debove, Josette & Alain Rey (eds.). 2017. *Le Petit Robert de la langue française*, Nouvelle édition millésime 2017. Paris: Dictionnaires Le Robert.

Rodríguez-Abruñeiras, Paula. 2020. Outlining a grammaticalization path for the Spanish formula *en plan (de)*: A contribution to crosslinguistic pragmatics. *Linguistics* 55 (6). https://doi.org/10.1515/ling-2020-0229 (accessed 17 January 2022)

Rojas, Edgardo Gustavo. 2012. *Caracterización pragmático discursiva de la partícula conversacional "corte/corte que" en la variedad juvenil del español metropolitano*. Paper presented at I Congreso de la Delegación Argentina de la Asociación de Lingüística y Filología de América Latina (ALFAL) y V Jornadas Internacionales de Filología Hispánica, La Plata, Argentina. http://sedici.unlp.edu.ar/bitstream/handle/10915/42397/Documento_completo__.pdf?sequence=1&isAllowed=y (accessed 14 of December 2021).

Rosenkvist, Henrik & Sanna Skärlund. 2013. Grammaticalization in the present. The changes of modern Swedish *typ*. In Anna Giacalone Ramat, Caterina Mauri & Piera Molinelli (eds.), *Synchrony and Diachrony: A dynamic interface*, 313–338. Amsterdam: John Benjamins.

Rosier, Laurence. 2002. Genre: le nuancier de sa grammaticalisation. *Travaux de Linguistique* 44 (1). 79–88.

Sakhno, Serguei. (2010). Les avatars du sens et de la fonction dans le phénomène de la grammaticalisation: Description systématique du lexème russe vrode 'dans le genre de' comparé à d'autres lexèmes russes grammaticalisés à fonctionnement proche. Université Paris Ouest, unpublished habilitation thesis.

Schrodt, Richard. 2004 [2011]. *Althochdeutsche Grammatik II: Syntax*. Berlin: De Gruyter.

Siegel, Muffy E. A. 2002. *Like*: The Discourse Particle and Semantics. *Journal of Semantics* 19 (1). 35–71.

Smith, Edward E. 1995. Concepts and categorization. In Edward E. Smith & Daniel N. Osherson (eds.), *Thinking. An invitation to cognitive science*, vol. 3, 3–33. Cambridge, MA: MIT Press.

Studtmann, Paul. 2007. Aristotle's Categories. *Stanford Encyclopedia of Philosophy*. https://plato.stanford.edu/entries/aristotle-categories/ (accessed 25 February 2021).

Tabor, Whitney. 1993. The gradual development of degree modifier *sort of* and *kind of*: A corpus proximity model. In Katherine Beals, Gina Cooke, David Kathman, Sotaro Kita, Karl-Erik McCullough & David Testen (eds.), *Papers from the 29th Regional Meeting of the Chicago Linguistic Society*, 451–465. Chicago: Linguistic Society.

Terian, Simina-Maria. 2018. (Inter)subiectificare și gramaticalizare: *gen* în limba română contemporană [(Inter)subjectification and grammaticalization: *gen* in contemporary Romanian]. *Transilvania review* 11–12. 129–134.

TLFi = Trésor de la Langue Française informatisé (http://atilf.atilf.fr/) (accessed 25 April 2021).

Toft, Ellen H. 2009. Adnominal and adverbal genitive constructions in Old Norse: a cognitive construction grammar account. Oslo: University of Oslo doctoral dissertation.

Traugott, Elizabeth Closs. 2008. The grammaticalization of *NP of NP* patterns. In Alexander Bergs & Gabriele Diewald (eds.), *Constructions and language change*, 23–45. Berlin: De Gruyter Mouton.

Umbach, Carla & Cornelia Ebert. 2009. German demonstrative *so*. Intensifying and hedging effects. *Sprache & Datenverarbeitung: International Journal for Language Data Processing* 33 (1–2). 153–168.

Voghera, Miriam. 2013. A case study on the relationship between grammatical change and synchronic variation: The emergence of *tipo*[-N] in Italian. In Anna Giacalone Ramat, Caterina Mauri & Piera Molinelli (eds.), *Synchrony and diachrony: A dynamic interface*, 283–312. Amsterdam: John Benjamins.

Voghera, Miriam. 2017. La nascita delle costruzioni non nominali di *specie, genere, sorta* e *tipo*: Uno studio basato su corpora. In Paolo D'Achille & Maria Grossmann (eds.), *Per la storia della formazione delle parole in italiano: Un nuovo corpus in rete (MIDIA) e nuove prospettive di studio*, 277–307. Florenz: Franco Cesati.

Walde, Alois. 2008. [1910]. *Lateinisches etymologisches Wörterbuch*, 6th edn. Heidelberg: Winter.

Walters, Emma (manuscript): Semantic innovation and grammaticalization of the English loanword *type* in colloquial *Hindi*. PhD-thesis. London: Birkbeck College, University of London.

Ward, Gregory & Betty Birner. 1995. Definiteness and the English existential. *Language* 71 (4). 722–742.

Wiese, Heike. 2011. *So* as a focus marker in German. *Linguistics* 49 (5). 991–1039.

Willemse, Peter, Lieselotte Brems & Kristin Davidse. 2008. Synchronic layering of type nouns in English and French. Paper presented at the 41st SLE Meeting (Languages in Contrast: Grammar, Translation, Corpora), University of Bologna at Forli, 17–20 September.

Yaguello, Marina. 1998. *Genre,* une particule d'un genre nouveau. *Petits Faits de Langue*, 18–24.

Zafiu, Rodica. 2012. Gen. Sau ceva de genul. . ..[gen. Or something like that] *Dilema veche* 460. https://dilemaveche.ro/tag/cuvinte-nepotrivite?page=33 (accessed 25 April 2021).

Zamparelli, Roberto. 2000. *Layers in the determiner phrase*. New York: Garland.

ZVI = Zingarelli, Niccolò Antonio (ed.). 1999. *Lo Zingarelli. Vocabolario della lingua italiana*. 11th edn. Bologna: Zanichelli.

Part 1: **Type noun constructions in Germanic languages**

Kristin Davidse, Lieselotte Brems & An Van linden
2 Type noun-constructions in English and Dutch

Abstract: The articles of this section focus on specific issues in the synchronic description of the functions of constructions with type nouns (TNs) in English and German. This introduction addresses a number of problems in the received view of the diachrony of TN-constructions in English, viz. the absence of essential data such as TN-constructions in Old English and what we argue are errors and gaps in earlier analyses of English TN-constructions. It is important to provide a more adequate and comprehensive diachronic reconstruction, as these earlier studies have had a major impact on accounts of Germanic languages, amongst which those of English predominated. We start by establishing that there were two – not one – lexical source constructions in Old English, in which the TN is either head or modifier, and in which the dependent element is coded by a genitive. We show that the TN/head and TN/modifier constructions formed the source of two – rather than one – diachronic paths, along which constructions with grammaticalized functions developed in different ways than posited hitherto. We describe the transition from the synthetic coding of Old English to analytic coding in Middle English, noting that this was accompanied by a general tendency to develop variants with both pre- and postdependents. In this period, the defining steps were taken in the development of the TN/modifier constructions, whose historical trajectory we outline. We then focus on the trajectory of the TN/head constructions, whose constitutive developments took place in Modern English. For Present-day English we present a comprehensive typology, recognizing more TN-constructions and structural variants than distinguished in the literature on English so far. We research the counterparts of these in Present-day Dutch, by way of a first test of the newly proposed model.

1 Introduction

Some of the earliest accounts of type noun (TN) constructions from the perspective of language change have focused on English (e.g. Tabor 1993; Denison 2002).

Kristin Davidse, KU Leuven (University of Leuven), e-mail: kristin.davidse@kuleuven
Lieselotte Brems, Université de Liège, e-mail: lbrems@uliege.be
An Van linden, Université de Liège, e-mail: an.vanlinden@uliege.be

Central to their approach were two claims. Firstly, one source construction was posited for all the derived uses, viz. the construction in which a TN, used with the meaning of 'subtype', is the head followed by *of* + a superordinate noun (N2), as in (1).

(1) Crabbe is **an manere of fissce.** (1225, OED)[1]
    'Crab is **a type of fish.**'

Secondly, this source construction was claimed to have undergone a structural shift from head–postmodifier to premodifier–head, which was the mechanism ultimately responsible for all derived constructions. The locus of grammaticalization processes was restricted to syntagms with the order TN + N2. Denison (2002) identified the complex determiner construction with quantifying meaning, as in (2), as the earliest attested premodifier–head construction on the path of change. The illogical singular form of the TN was viewed as a sign of the decategorialization accompanying the alleged shift from head to premodifier.

(2) Spices & **all manere of marchandises** (?a1425 (c1400), *Mandeville's Trav.*, OED)
    'spices and **all manner of merchandise**'

On this path of change, further constructions were said to develop such as (3), which was analysed by Tabor (1993) as a degree modifying use and by Denison (2002) as a qualifying use.

(3) But I suppose it's as a that's as a **sort of holiday**, kind of doing you know nothing but sitting around (ICE-GB, quoted in Denison 2002: 2).

The locus of grammaticalization processes was thus restricted to syntagms with the order TN + N2.

This diachronic account has influenced not only the – relatively sparse – studies of Germanic languages like Dutch and German, but also certain aspects of studies of Romance languages. By contrast, Odden (2019) does consider binominal genitive constructions in Old Norse, while the Romance tradition has tended to cover, in its

---

[1] Following each attested example its source is indicated between brackets by the Internet url or the abbreviation of the corpus, WordbanksOnline (WB), The York–Toronto–Helsinki Parsed Corpus of Old English Prose (YCOE), Corpus of Late Modern English – extended version (CLMETEV), Oxford English Dictionary (OED), The Santa Barbara Corpus of Spoken American English (SBCAE), Russian National Corpus (RNC).

diachronic and synchronic studies, TN-constructions with both the order TN + N2, e.g. *ce genre d'évènement* 'this type of event' and N2 + TN, e.g. *un concert de ce genre* 'a concert of this kind' (see Mihatsch's General Introduction to this volume).

In this introduction, we will show that there are major problems with the received take on the history of English TN-constructions, which pertain both to the historical data considered and the functional-structural shift said to link examples like (1) and (2). As we will explain presently, these problems were revealed to us by Kolyaseva's analysis of TN-constructions in Russian (e.g. Kolyaseva 2021).

Historical studies of TN-constructions like Tabor (1993), Denison (2002) and Brems and Davidse (2010) basically considered data starting in Middle English only. Yet, TN-constructions are attested from Old English on. Importantly, the Old English constructions feature genitive dependents, not the analytically coded dependents of Middle English illustrated in the TN + *of* + N2 syntagms in (1) and (2). If the data with genitives from Old English are taken into account, then it becomes clear, we will argue, that not one but two source constructions existed in Old English, one in which the N2/genitive is a complement of the TN/head, and one in which the TN/genitive is a modifier of the N2/head. In fact, the Middle English examples of TN/head (1) and TN/modifier (2) quoted above will be suggested to have developed from these two source constructions rather than ones like (2) having derived from ones like (1). We will further propose that the TN/head and TN/modifier constructions of Old English formed the start of two distinct diachronic paths, yielding a different and more complex picture than that posited so far in grammaticalization studies of TN-constructions, including our own earlier work (Brems and Davidse 2010). Thus, whereas qualifying TN-constructions as in (3) very likely did develop from the TN/head construction via a change of headedness, we argue that TN/modifier constructions with quantifying meaning like (2) derived from the TN/modifier construction in Old English, without any shift of headedness having taken place. The new view on the history of TN-constructions that we propose dovetails fully with the revised synchronic typology of lexically used TN-constructions (Davidse and Brems this volume), which is based on synchronic functional-structural analysis. Both the new diachronic and synchronic account have been crucially inspired by the analysis of TN-constructions in Russian (Kolyaseva p.c.; Kolyaseva and Davidse 2018; Kolyaseva 2021; Kisiel and Kolyaseva this volume).

In these studies it has been shown that Russian has two nominal source constructions with a TN and a second N (N2). Because of the Russian systems of case, number and gender marking on the one hand and of agreement on the other, the different head–dependent relations in these two constructions can be identified very clearly. The semantics coded by the different dependency structures were elucidated with concepts from Langacker's Cognitive Grammar.

In the first source construction, illustrated in (4), the TN, e.g. *tip* ('type'), is the head, which can take any of the six Russian cases, symbolized as 1–6, and is elaborated by a noun in the genitive, which can be either singular or plural. This is the TN/head construction, whose morphosyntax can be represented as $tip_{1-6,SG-PL}$ + $N2_{GEN, SG-PL}$. This is the counterpart of the English TN/head construction illustrated in (1), in which N2 has generally been analysed as a postmodifier (e.g. Denison 2002; Brems, Davidse and De Smedt 2007).

(4) *Dannyj   avtomobil'   proizvoditsja   i   postavljaetsja*
    This.NOM.M.SG car.NOM.M.SG   produce.3SG.PASS and   supply.3SG.PASS
    *na   naš   rynok   v   **trex   tipax***
    onto   our.ACC.M.SG   market.ACC.M.SG in   tree.PRP   type-PRP.PL
    kuzovov.
    body.GEN.PL
    'This car is manufactured and supplied to our market in **three types of bodies**.' (http://auto.obozrevatel.com/news/2006/04/18/450.htm) (Kolyaseva and Davidse 2018: 198)

However, Kolyaseva (p.c.) and Kolyaseva and Davidse (2018) analyse the second noun (N_{GEN}) in (4) as a complement. For this, they invoke Langacker's (1987: 277f) conceptually motivated definition of complementation. The head of a complementation relation is conceptually incomplete: it needs to be semantically completed by a complement. In the construction illustrated in (4), the relational 'subtype' meaning of the TN head can indeed only be conceptualized in terms of the supertype it is a subtype of, 'three types of bodies'.

In the second source construction, illustrated in (5), the N is the head that can occur in all six cases and the TN is part of the dependent in the genitive case, which modifies the head. Of this modifier, the TN is the head, which is typically, but not obligatorily, singular. This is the TN/modifier construction, whose morphosyntax can be represented as $N2_{1-6}$ + $Adj_{GEN.M.SG.}$ + $tip\text{-}(a)_{GEN}$. Its English counterpart is illustrated in (2) above.

(5) *Delaetsja   popytka   ocenit'   perspektivy*
    Do.3SG.PASS   attempt.NOM.F.SG   evaluate.INF   prospect.ACC.PL
    *razvitija   **sistem**   **različnogo**   **tipa.***
    development.GEN.N.SG system.GEN.F.PL   various.GEN.M.SG   type.GEN.M.SG
    'An attempt is being made to assess the prospects of development of **systems of various sort**. (2004, *Voprosy statistiki*, RNC) (Kolyaseva and Davidse 2018: 201)

The modifier analysis of the genitive constituent is motivated by Langacker's (1987: 235–236, 309–310) definition of modification as a relation in which the modifier is the relational element that cannot stand on its own but needs a conceptually autonomous head. For instance, in (5), the head *sistem* 'systems' is an ordinary noun designating entities, which can be conceptualized as such. In this construction, the 'subtype' meaning of the TN, e.g. *tipa* 'of type' in (5) dovetails with the relational meaning of a modifier.

This introductory section to TN-constructions in Germanic languages will be devoted mainly to correcting the received view on the history of English TN-constructions. The new account of the diachronic development of English TN-constructions has to be developed largely from scratch. In the first place, it requires analysing data that earlier studies failed to consider, viz. Old English data in which binominal constructions involved genitives as well as attestations of NPs with N2 *of* TN-order. These data have been retrieved mainly from the Oxford English Dictionary (OED) corpus, making use of the search function, which ranges all examples of individual TNs on a time line. In the second place, new descriptions have to be thrashed out for TN-constructions not studied so far while for some constructions that have been recognized alternative analyses have to be developed. We then widen this focus by providing a survey of Present-day Dutch TN-constructions, which is novel in comparison with existing accounts. By trying out the newly proposed typology on Dutch synchronic data, we put it to a first test for its soundness and explanatory power.

This introduction differs in terms of its focus and scope from the introductions to TNs in Romance and Slavic languages. Because of its aim to correct the earlier influential studies on English TN-constructions, this introduction is strongly grammar-oriented and focused on one language. By contrast, the other introductions approach the field with a stronger emphasis on the lexicosemantic development of TNs, providing comprehensive lexical inventories and cover more languages within their respective language family. However, we think that there is room for this diversity of contributions to the large field of TN-research, in which errors and gaps of different types remain to be addressed.

The structure of this chapter is as follows. In Section 2, we start by establishing the two source constructions in Old English. In Section 3, we describe the transition from synthetic to analytic coding in Middle English. In this period, the defining steps are taken in the development of the TN/modifier constructions, whose historical trajectory we outline. In Section 4, we focus on the trajectory of the TN/head constructions, whose constitutive developments took place in Modern English. In Section 5, we turn to Present-day English and present a comprehensive survey, recognizing more TN-constructions and structural variation than distinguished in the literature on English so far. In Section 6, we address the question whether or not there are counterparts in Present-day Dutch of all the TN-constructions in Present-day English.

2 Two nominal source constructions in Old English

In this section, we reconstruct the emergence of the source constructions with TNs in Old English (OE), 650 to 1150. Old English is typologically more similar to Russian than Present-day English in having case, number and gender marking as well as agreement. Old English attests constructions in which a relation between TN and N2 is expressed by the genitive. It is these data that were not taken into account in the historical trajectories proposed in Denison (2002) and Brems and Davidse (2010). The earliest TN-noun to be used in constructions with genitive dependents was the neuter noun *cynn/kin*. It is with *cynn* that the two different TN-constructions illustrated for Russian in (4) and (5) above, viz. the TN/head and the TN/modifier construction, are attested in Old English.

The TN/head + complement construction is the source construction that the literature on English TNs has exclusively focused on so far. As noted in Section 1, Denison (2002), De Smedt et al (2007) and Brems and Davidse (2010) analysed it as a head–postmodifier construction, wrongly so, we now argue. Cogent arguments for a head–complement analysis were given by Keizer (2007) from a functional discourse grammar perspective, which largely square with the cognitive grammar analysis we present below. The Old English coding of this construction with genitival complement is illustrated in (6).

(6) **Feower** synt **muneca** **cyn.** Đæt
 four are monk.GEN.PL kind.NOM.PL that.NOM/ACC.N.SG.
 forme is **mynster-monna** [...]. *Oþer*
 first.NOM/ACC.N.SG is monastery-man.GEN.PL other.NOM/ACC.N.SG
 cyn is **ancrena.**
 kind.NOM.SG is anchorite.GEN.PL
 'There are **four kinds of monks**. **The first** [kind] is **of the monastery men**. **The second kind** is **of the anchorites**.' (*c*960, *Rule St. Benet*, OED)

The first sentence features the complex NP *feower muneca cyn*, in which the genitive plural *muneca*, i.e. 'of monks', precedes the TN/head *cyn*. As *cyn* is a conceptually incomplete head, its dependent *muneca* is a pre-complement. The semantic relation between *muneca* and *cyn* is one of *superordination*: 'four kinds of monks'. In the last two sentences in (6), the subjects are *Ðæt forme (cyn)* and *Oþer cyn*, which are complemented by the predicative genitives *mynster-monna* and *ancrena*. The genitive-marked nouns specify the members that fall within the 'type' referred to by the subject NP. In this inclusion sense, there is an *appositional* relation between the subject and the predicative complement NP. Semantically, the context in (6) construes a 'type' interpretation of religious orders: there are four subtypes of religious men, of which two subtypes are specified, viz. monks living in a monastery and anchorites.² Example (7) contains a TN/head construction with a genitival postcomplement expressing a superordination relation: 'two types of martyrdom'. Example (8) contains two coordinated TN/head constructions with genitival pre-complements expressing an appositional relation: 'the entire kind of angels and the kind of men'.

(7) Gregorius andswarode him, **twa cyn** beoþ, Petrus,
    Gregory answered him two kin.NOM.PL be.PRS.3PL Peter
    þæs martyrhades
    that.GEN.M.SG martyrdom.GEN.SG
    'Gregory answered him: "**Two kinds** there are, Peter, **of that martyrdom**"'
    (c1055–1090, YCOE)

(8) Him biþ beforan andweard **eal engla cynn &**
    Him.DAT is before present all angel.GEN.PL kind.NOM.SG &
    manna cynn
    man.GEN.PL kind.NOM.SG
    'Before Him **the whole kind of angels and kind of men** is present.' (971, Blickl. Hom. OED)

We conclude that in Old English we find TN/head constructions with genitive complements either preceding or following the head and semantically expressing either superordination or apposition. The referents of TN/head constructions are located in the 'type universe' of interpretation.

In Old English, an appositional relation between TN *kin* and N2 naming the specific type could also be expressed by compounds like *déorcynn* ('animalkind'), *fisccynn* ('fishkind'), *fugolcynn* ('fowlkind'), *wifcynn* ('womankind'), etc. (*kin*, n, †5. OED). These compounds are right-headed (Ackema and Neeleman 2004): the

---

2 In the following sentence (not excerpted here) two more subtypes are listed, the sarabaites and the gyrovagues (itinerant monks) (see: https://christdesert.org/rule-of-st-benedict/chapter-1-the-kinds-of-monks/).

category referred to is determined by *kin* or *kind*, meaning 'a large natural group or division, a race', whose composition is expressed by the pre-head complement, as in *mankind*, 'the kind of man', e.g. (9).

(9) *Godspell   is   [þa]   word   þe   he   spræc   on   þissere*
    gospel   is   the   word.NOM.PL REL   he   spoke   on   this.DAT.SG
    *worulde,   **mancynne**   to   lare*
    world.DAT.SG mankind.DAT.SG   to   lore.DAT.SG
    'The Gospel is . . . the words that he spoke on this world, (to serve) as knowledge for **mankind**.' (OE, ÆLFRIC *Homily*, OED)

The second source construction has remained under the radar in the literature on English TNs so far. This is the TN/modifier construction. Its coding in Old English with genitival modifier is illustrated by (10) and (11): a premodifier consisting of a quantifying adjective + *kin* is dependent on the following head noun. These NPs express a superordination relation: the genitive TN designates subtypes, e.g. *monigra cyna* 'of many kinds' in (11), and N2 designates the supertype, *wil deor* 'wild animals' in (11). The modifiers with adjective + TN can be genitive singular, e.g. *ælces cynnes déor* 'animals of each kind', *nanes cynnes anlicnyssa* 'images of no kind' (c.11th c. OED), or genitive plural, e.g. *monigra cyna* 'of many kinds'. The first attestations of the TN/modifier construction in the OED-data predate those of the TN/head constructions.

(10) ***ælces   cynnes   déor***
     each.GEN.SG   kind.GEN.SG   animal.NOM.PL
     '**animals of each kind**' (?c825, *kin*, n. †6 †b, OED)

(11) ***monigra   cyna   wil   deor***
     many.GEN.PL   kind.GEN.PL   wild   animal.NOM.PL
     '**animals of many kinds**' (a899, *Old Eng. Martyrol.* OED)

Strikingly, the TN/modifiers emerged in Old English with quantifying adjectives. They 'literally' quantify subtypes of the head noun. The TN is not semantically bleached. At the same time, we can note that these TN/modifier constructions contain the same semantic elements as quantifying complex determiner constructions like (2) *all manner of merchandise*, viz. quantifier + TN followed by N2/head. Indeed, as we will argue below, it is the TN/genitive modifier-construction in OE, not the TN/head–complement construction, that is the source construction of the later *all kind/manner/sort of* N-pattern. A number of changes were involved in this but not modifier–head reversal. Hence, the explanations given for the emergence of quantifying complex determiners in the literature on English TNs so far have to be revised. But first we wrap up this discussion of TN-constructions in OE with Table 1, which visualizes the three types attested: TN/head + superordinate or appositional genitive complement, appositional compound, and N2/head + genitive modifier with TN.

Table 1: TN-constructions in Old English.

	predependent + head	head + postdependent
NP with TN/head + superordinate genitive complement	*feower muneca*$_{GEN.PL}$ *cynn*$_{NOM.PL}$ (c960) 'four kinds of monks'	*twa cynn*$_{NOM.PL}$ *þæs*$_{GEN.SG}$ *martyrhades*$_{GEN.SG}$ (c 1050–1099, YCOE) 'two kinds of that martyrdom'
NP with TN/head + appositional genitive complement	*eal engla*$_{GEN.PL}$ *cynn*$_{NOM.SG}$ & *manna*$_{GEN.PL}$ *cynn*$_{NOM.SG}$ (c971) 'the whole kind of angels and the kind of humans'	*wið þa missenlican* $_{ACC.PL}$ *cynd*$_{ACC.PL}$ *nædrena*$_{GEN.PL}$ (c1000) 'against the various kinds of adders'
appositional compound with TN/head	*fugolcynn, manncynn* (c971) 'fowlkind', 'mankind'	—
NP with genitive TN/modifier + superordinate N2/head	*ælces*$_{GEN.SG}$ *cynnes*$_{GEN.SG}$ *déor*$_{NOM.PL}$ (?c825) 'animals of each sort' *monigra*$_{GEN.PL}$ *cyna*$_{GEN.PL}$ *wil deor*$_{NOM.PL}$ (899) 'wild animals of many kinds'	—

3 From synthetic to analytic coding in Middle English and the development of the TN/modifier constructions

Middle English (ME), 1150–1500, is a transitional period for TN-constructions in many ways. On the lexical level, we see an expansion of the set of TNs occurring in them, with *kin, kind, sort* and *manner* being the most frequent. Structurally, the expression of the relations between head and dependent gradually shifts from genitive marking to analytic coding, typically involving the linking of head to dependent by *of*. Table 2 gives an overview of the TN-constructions in Middle English.

Table 2: TN-constructions in Middle English.

	predependent + head	head + postdependent
complex NP with TN/head + appositional genitive complement	*deres-kin* (1324) *mans kind* [*manes-kind*] (1400->a1325) *aungels kynde* (1425)	---
appositional compound with TN/head	*angel kind* (1400->a1325)	---
complex NP with TN/head + appositional *of*-complement	---	*tweie kyndes, of þe Godhede and manhede* (1387) *þe kind of man* (1425->1400)
complex NP with TN/head + superordinate genitive complement	*that sterys kind* (a1500)	---
complex NP with TN/head + superordinate *of*-complement	---	*feole cunne of weldede* (c1175) *an manere of fissce* (1225) *any kinnes of corne* (1500)
NP with genitive TN/modifier + superordinate N2/head	*alles*_{GEN.SG} *cunnes*_{GEN.SG} *wilde deor* (c1384) *alle skynnes*_{GEN.SG} *condiciouns* (1384)	*Þe Gast is unʒesæʒenlices*_{GEN.SG} *cyndes*_{GEN.SG} (1175)[3]
NP with TN/(*of*-)modifier + superordinate N2/head	*alle kind* [L. *genere*] *of fishis* (1384) *alle kinde Of women* (1393) *the worste kynde of Infortune* (1413–1385) *foure-kin maner* [a1325 *fowrkins maners*] *of glotony* (1400) *what kynne tidynges* (1440)	*al þe folk of þis soort* (1380) *a kirnelle of conforte kynde* (1430–1378) *othere eglis of a lowere kynde* (1430–1380) *many Fysches of kynes sere* (c1450)

---

3 This is an early Middle English example in which a TN/genitive used as the predicative complement of a copular clause contains a descriptive adjective:

Þe	Gast	is	unʒesæʒenlices	cyndes
The	Ghost	is	unspeakable.GEN.SG	kind.GEN.SG

'The Ghost is of an unspeakable kind.' (c1175 (►OE) *Homily* in A. O. Belfour *12th Cent. Homilies in MS Bodl*).

This section will show that, for the TN/head–complement constructions, the shift from synthetic to analytic coding was not accompanied by an extension of their general semantic functions in Middle English. By contrast, for the TN/modifier constructions, this shift involved an expansion of functions. In Old English, TN/modifiers contained only quantifying adjectives, but in Middle English, they came to also feature interrogative and phoric adjectives as well as descriptive lexical modifiers. We will describe this development up till the state it reached, via Early Modern English, in Present-day English. On the basis of the chronology of emergence of the 'grammatical' and 'lexical' functions of TN/modifier constructions we have to reject the hypotheses that were formulated in earlier work.

We start with the TN/head–complement constructions. In Middle English we see, besides the older constructions with typical pre-head genitive + TN/head, the emergence of the analytic TN/head + *of*-complement construction. This shift from synthetic to analytic coding is accompanied by a reversal of N2 – TN order to TN – N2 order, but the analytic structures code the same appositional and superordinate semantics, as visualized in Figure 1.

source construction 1:
**N2/genitive complement
+TN/head**   OE
muneca$_{GEN.PL}$ ^{cyn}$_{NOM.SG.}$ (c960)

	N2$_{GEN}$–TN	TN *of* N2	
appositional	*angel kind* (1400->a1325)	*feole cunne of weldede*	
	aungels kynde (1425)	(c1175)	
		þe kind of man (1425->1400)	ME
superordinate	*that sterys kind* (a1500)	*any kinnes of corne* (1500)	

Figure 1: Main Middle English paths that developed from the Old English source N2/genitive complement +TN/head.

For the *appositional* relation, we see its two synthetic codings from Old English moving into Middle English, i.e. NPs with genitive N2 + TN/head and compounds. However, the distinction between them becomes fuzzy, as illustrated by variants such as *deres-kin* (1324, OED), *mans kind* (1400 -> a1325, OED), *aungels kynde* (1425, OED), and *angel kind* (1400 -> a1325, OED). It was the forms in which N2 does not have genitive marking that continued into Modern and Present-day English, either as clear compounds like *mankind* or as NPs with pre-complement like *sed-*

iment rock types (WB). In the same period, the appositional relation comes to be expressed analytically in constructions headed by the TN and complemented by *of* + NP with N2, as in *Tweie kyndes, of þe Godhede and manhede* ('two kinds, of the godhood and manhood') (1387, OED), and *þe kind of man* (1425–1400, OED). This construction moved into Modern and Present-day English.

The expression of a *superordination* relation between TN and N2 gradually shifted from NPs with genitive precomplement, e.g. *that sterys kind* ('that kind of star') (a1500, OED), to analytic coding. In the latter, the supertype is expressed by an *of*-complement with N2, as in the existential clause in (12), whose subject is expressed by a discontinuous NP with fronted TN/head, *feole cunne,* and postverbal *of*-phrase, *of weldede*.

(12) **Feole   cunne   beoð   of   weldede**
       many.NOM.PL kind.NOM.PL   be.PRS.3PL of   good-deeds
      '**many kinds** (there) are **of good deeds**' (c1175, *Lamb. Hom.* OED)

Other examples are *an manere of fissce* (1225, OED), and *any kinnes of corne* (1500, OED).[4] This is the construction that has hitherto – erroneously – been viewed as the single one source construction of English TN-constructions.

Turning to the TN/modifier constructions, we find co-occurrence of three main structural variants in Middle English. Besides the older TN/genitive–N2/head construction, there emerged not only the expected analytic counterpart of N2/head + TN/*of*-postmodifier, but also a TN/premodifier (+ *of*) + N2 structure, whose origin we will discuss further down. The premodifiers of the TN expanded from quantifying adjectives over interrogative and phoric ones to lexical premodifiers. These diachronic developments are visualized in Figure 2.

Structurally, the shift from genitival premodifier to *of*-postmodifier is entirely predictable. Just as in Middle English *of*-postcomplements like *þe kind of man* (1425->1400, OED) emerged besides the older genitive pre-complements *aungels kynde* (1425, OED), *of*-postmodifiers as in *any Fysches of kynes sere* (c1450, OED) ('any fish of diverse kind') emerged besides the older genitive premodifiers as in *ælces*$_{GEN.SG}$ *cynnes*$_{GEN.SG}$ *déor* (c1384, OED) ('animals of each kind').

A much less predictable development of the genitival TN/premodifier was the analytic TN/premodifier that emerged in Middle English, as in *foure-kin*$_{SG}$ *maner*$_{SG}$ [a1425 *fowrkins maners*] *of glotony* (1400, OED), *what kynne*$_{SG}$ *tidynges* (1440,

---

4 As noted in Davidse and Brems (this volume), whereas appositional *of*–complements contain a full NP, *of*–complements coding a superordinate type may either contain the noun as such, e.g. *many breeds of dogs* or a full NP, as in *many breeds of the same species*.

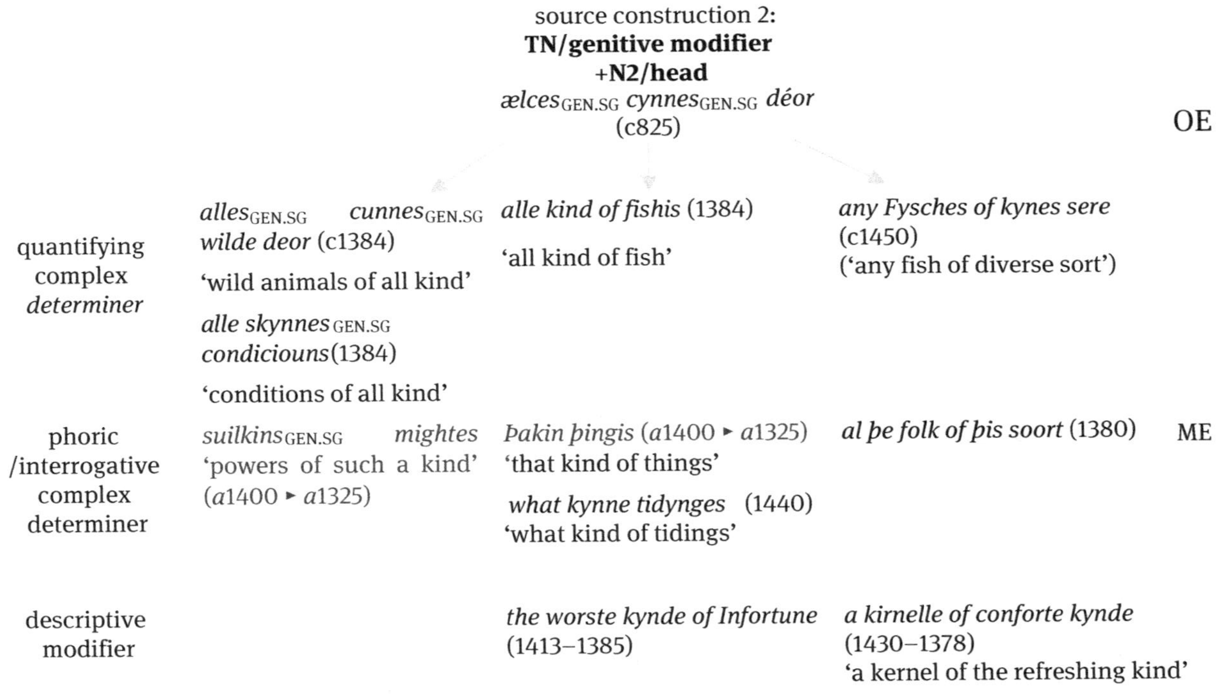

2 Type noun-constructions in English and Dutch — 67

	source construction 2: **TN/genitive modifier +N2/head** ælces_GEN.SG cynnes_GEN.SG déor (c825)		
			OE
quantifying complex determiner	alles_GEN.SG cunnes_GEN.SG wilde deor (c1384) 'wild animals of all kind' alle skynnes_GEN.SG condiciouns (1384) 'conditions of all kind'	alle kind of fishis (1384) 'all kind of fish'	any Fysches of kynes sere (c1450) ('any fish of diverse sort')
phoric /interrogative complex determiner	suilkins_GEN.SG mightes 'powers of such a kind' (a1400 ▸ a1325)	þakin þingis (a1400 ▸ a1325) 'that kind of things' what kynne tidynges (1440) 'what kind of tidings'	al þe folk of þis soort (1380) ME
descriptive modifier		the worste kynde of Infortune (1413–1385)	a kirnelle of conforte kynde (1430–1378) 'a kernel of the refreshing kind'

Figure 2: Main Middle English paths that developed from the Old English source TN/genitive modifier + N2/head.

OED), *all sortes*$_{PL}$ *of people* (1520, OED), *these kinde*$_{SG}$ *of vestures* (1566, OED). As shown in these examples, in Middle English the TN/premodifiers are often, albeit not always, linked to the head with *of*. With Langacker (1991: 87–9) and Sinclair (1991: 87–90), we do not view *of* as a typical preposition but as a particle with highly schematic meaning, able to link heads to postdependents as well as predependents to heads (Kruisinga 1932: 391). A striking feature is that some (but not all) examples with a notionally or formally plural premodifier combine with a singular TN, as in *these kinde*$_{SG}$ *of vestures*. It was in fact this number incongruence that was treated by Denison (2002) as an important formal feature of the 'complex determiner' construction. While it is not an absolute recognition criterion (see below), it is, as a typical feature, associated with the complex determiner construction with its quantifying, interrogative and phoric functions.

How, then, can the shift be explained from the genitival premodifier as in *monigra*$_{GEN.PL}$ *cyna*$_{GEN.PL}$ *wil deor*$_{NOM.PL}$ to complex determiners as in *all sortes*$_{PL}$ *of people* (1520, OED) and *these kinde*$_{SG}$ *of vestures* (1566, OED)? From the OED-entries of *kin*, n. 6b, *kind*, n. 4a, and *manner* n. 1, we can gather the following explanatory factors. The genitive, which was typically placed before the head noun, gradually lost its inflection and came to be treated as an attributive or adjective-like phrase. Transitional forms like *Alle skynnes*$_{GEN.SG}$ *condiciouns* 'Conditions of all kind' (1384, OED) illustrate loss of insight in the genitive marking. Inserts like *[fowrkins maners, a*1425*, Galba]* in (13) show that some early scribes were aware of the genitive singular origin, when they used the inflectionless form.

(13) it   es   funden   **bodily foure-kin   maner**
     there   be.PRS.3SG   found   bodily   four-kind   manner
     [fowrkins   maners]   **of   glotony**
     fourkin.GEN.SG manner.GEN.SG of   gluttony
     'there is found **bodily gluttony of four kinds**' (*a*1400 (▸*a*1325), *Cursor Mundi*, OED)

As noted in the OED entry for *kind* n., 8b "analogy with use of the genitive [...] would explain the use in the singular within an otherwise plural syntax". The use of a singular TN with plural quantifiers like *four* in (13), extended to cases with plural *these*, as in (14).

(14) It is not lawfull to vse **these kinde of vestures** (1566, *Briefe Exam*, OED)

While common, number incongruence is not a defining formal feature of the complex determiner construction, as it is also attested with plural TNs, as in (15). *All sortes of people* is clearly a TN/premodifier construction with *people* as head because it refers to the individuals making up the army. This excludes it being a TN/head–N2/complement construction, which designates types of a subtype (for further discussion, see below).

(15) A Iugurth ... anone prepared the greattest army that he coude of **all sortes of people** (?1520, *Cron. Warre agaynst Iugurth*, OED)

Of-insertion may have been supported by the equivalent use of *manere* borrowed from Old French, in which at an early stage *of* was inserted, as in *al maner o suet spices* 'all manner of sweet spices' (1400 (*a1325*), *Cursor Mundi*, OED). The particle *of* generalized to the structures with *kin*, *kind* and *sort*. The OED entry for *kin*, n. †6 †b, notes that in Middle English *kin* and its premodifiers often combined, yielding such forms as *alkin(s)* 'all kind(s)', *anykin(s)* 'any kind(s)', *fele-kin(s)* 'many kind(s)', *manykin(s)* 'many kind(s)', *nokin(s)* or *nakin(s)* 'no kind(s)', *otherkin(s)* 'other kind(s)', *sere-kin(s)* 'distinct kind(s)', *swilkin(s)* 'such kind(s)', *same-kin(s)* 'same kind(s)', *thiskin(s)* 'this kind(s)', *whilk-kin(s)* (*hwil-kyn*) 'which kind(s)', *whatkin(s)* 'what kind(s)'. Few came down to 1500, except *whatkin*, which is attested in the 16th century and which survives in Scottish and north English as *what'n*. These univerbated forms appear as prototypical "compound determiners" (Huddleston and Pullum 2002: 391), in which the TN is semantically bleached and decategorialized.[5]

In sum, from the Old English genitival TN/premodifier construction, the complex determiner construction developed in Middle English and early Modern English as the result of the loss of genitive marking combined with three tendencies: generalization of the singular form of the TN, compounding of premodifier and TN, and *of*-insertion. We have to reject the earlier hypotheses which assumed that examples like *alle kind of fishis* (1384, OED), with grammatical, quantifying meaning developed from lexical TN-structures like *feole cunne of weldede* (c1175). This was thought to be the result of re-analysis of the erstwhile lexical TN/head into a decategorialized premodifying noun. The quantifying complex determiners were viewed as the first grammaticalized construction type. In fact, as the Old English and Middle English data show, there was a straight line from TN/genitival premodifiers with quantifying adjective, e.g. *ælces*$_{GEN.SG}$ *cynnes*$_{GEN.SG}$ *déor* (c825) to quantifier + TN/premodifier + *of*, e.g. *alle kind of fishis* (1384, OED), as visualized in Figure 2. The development did not involve any head–modifier reversal. Since Old English, the TN had been part of the premodifier and the N2 had been the head. What was re-interpreted is the genitive singular TN into an uninflected TN, which

---

5 This is confirmed by the fact that such compound determiners co-occur in a number of examples with a less bleached TN as in *foure-kin maner* in (13).

yielded the apparent number incongruence. There was also a meaning shift from quantifying subtypes, *ælces*$_{GEN.SG}$ *cynnes*$_{GEN.SG}$ *déor* 'animals of each kind', to the quantifying meaning, as in *alle kind of fishis* (1384), which refers to 'manifold, very many fish' in the Gospel story of the miraculous catch of fish. In view of the formal and semantic changes involved, the emergence of the complex determiner construction can certainly be viewed as constituting a process of grammaticalization.

While our earlier hypotheses about its genesis stand corrected, the complex determiner construction can still meaningfully be distinguished and we can largely keep its definition of form and meaning as in De Smedt et al. (2007) and Brems and Davidse (2010). We have to distinguish complex determiner constructions very clearly from TN/head–complement constructions because, in their analytic coding, they may manifest as the same surface string (Janebová and Martinková 2017), in contrast with Old English, where the genitive clearly marked the dependent, as either the complement or the modifier. Table 3 summarizes the grammatical and semantic distinctions between the two which were invoked in the above discussion, and which we further elaborate with examples (16)–(22).

Table 3: Grammatical and semantic differences between TN/head and complex determiner constructions.

	TN/head construction	Complex determiner construction
Grammar	det. [TN$_{head}$ + N2$_{complement}$]	[det. + TN]$_{premodifier}$ N2$_{head}$
Designatum	subtype of supertype	Instances
Examples	*alle kyndes of bestis* (1348) 'all kinds of animals'	*alle kind of fishis* (1384) 'manifold fish'
	These two sortes of the chyldren of Israel (1562)	*these kind of reasonings* (1744) 'such reasonings'
	What Sorts of Manure (1754)	*what kynne tidynges* (1440) 'what tidings'
		generic class: *those sort of Ulcers the Farriers call cankers* (c1720) 'canker-type ulcers'
	subtype (of) 'x' *the kinde of man* (1583)	

(16) In **alle kyndes of bestis** þe femel is more febil þan þe male.
    'In **all kinds of animals**, the female is more feeble than the male'. (1398, *De Proprietatibus Rerum*, OED)

(17) **These two sortes of the chyldren of Israel** (1562, *Pilgr. Perf.*, OED)

(18) **What Sorts of Manure or Amendment** do they chiefly use for their Land...?
(1754, *Queries proposed Gentlemen*, OED)

(19) A nette sent in to the see, and of **alle kind** [L. *genere*] **of fishis** gedrynge.
'A net sent in to the see, and saturated with **all kinds of fish**' (c1348, *Bible*, OED)

(20) "Our very pride, methinks, should be a sufficient guard, and turn whatever favourable thoughts we might have of such a one, unknowing his design, into aversion, when once convinced, he presumed upon our weakness." In **these kind of reasonings** did she continue some time. (1744, CLEMETEV)

(21) He shall telle yow **what kynne tidyinges** that he hathe browte.
'He shall tell you **what kind of tidings** he has brought.' (c1440, *Gesta Romanorum*, OED)

(22) A mishapen or rusty Bit... will create **those sort of Ulcers the Farriers call cankers**. (c1720, *Farriers New Guide*, OED)

With TN/head–N2/complement constructions, the determiner + TN/head intrinsically designate a (sub)*type* (of a supertype). Hence, their referents are situated in what Langacker (1991: 71) calls the "type" universe of interpretation.[6] Most commonly, they refer to subtypes of a supertype within established taxonomies, as in examples (16)–(18), which illustrate how the subtypes may be quantified (16), pointed to (17), or inquired into (18). The determiner scopes over the TN_{head} + $N2_{complement}$ unit.

Complex determiner constructions clearly contrast semantically and structurally with the TN/head construction. The complex determiner, made up of simple determiner and TN, scopes over N2 only, which is the head of the NP. The referents of the NP are typically concrete instances of N2,[7] as in (19)–(21), but can also be generic subtypes, as in (22). *Alle kind of fishis* (1384) in (19) refers to the 'very many and manifold' fish caught miraculously in the Gospel story. In (20), the

---

6 In Davidse and Brems (this volume), we explain that this 'subtype' reference may figure in NPs with generic reference, like (16)–(18), as well as NPs with dual reference, i.e. overtly to a subtype but with pragmatically implied reference to concrete spatiotemporal referents, and non-referential predicate nominatives.

7 In the OED entry of *kind*, n. 8b, it is noted that "In the [...] attributive or adjective-like use of *kind of*... [i]n early modern English the reference *to individual members* [italics ours] of a class becomes clear".

complex determiner *these kind of* gives the reader instructions to infer properties that characterize the *reasonings* referred to anaphorically from the preceding representation of specific reasonings. In (21) the interrogative complex determiner *what kynne* enquires into a property of the *tidings* in question, e.g. whether bad or good. Complex determiner constructions may also realize generic reference. An example is given in (22), in which *those sort of* instructs the reader to cataphorically retrieve the subclass of the head noun *ulcers* referred to, viz. 'canker-type (of) ulcers'. All these complex determiners with TNs have simple determiner counterparts: *multiple fishes* (19), *such reasonings* (20), *what tidings* (21), *such ulcers as the farriers call cankers* (22).

We can now situate the complex determiner construction within the wider set of the main subtypes of the schematic TN/modifier construction, i.e. its pre- and postmodifier variants, and the various modifiers the TNs can take. These include not only quantifying, phoric and interrogative modifiers but also lexical modifiers of the TN, as visualized in Table 4.

Table 4: TN/modifier constructions.

Semantics	Construction in De Smedt et al (2007)	TN/premodifier + N2/head	Modifier of TN	N2/head + TN/postmodifier
Quantification	Complex determiner	*alle kind of fishis* (1384)	Quantifying	*ij. quartelettes, of dyvers sortes* (1459)
Class or quality specification		*these kind of reasonings* (1744) *those sort of Ulcers the Farriers call cankers.* (c1720)	Phoric	*al þe folk of þis soort* (1385) *lovers of such a sort, That feignen hem an humble port* (1390)
		what kynne tidyinges (1440)	Interrogative	*of which sorte bee these sayings* (1547)[8]
	Descriptive modifier	*the worste kynde of Infortune* (1413–1385) *a counterfeit kind of curtesie* (a1522)	Lexical	*fysche of the smalliste sorte.* (1545) *a kirnelle of conforte kynde* (1430–1378)

In Table 4, the fourth column indicates the four main subtypes of modifier of the TN: quantifying (in a broad sense), phoric, i.e. ana- and cataphoric, interrogative and lexical. The complex determiner construction subsumes the subtypes with TN/*premodifiers* containing quantifying, phoric and interrogative modifiers, which are put in grey shading in Table 4. As we saw, these subtypes

---

8 In this example the 'postmodifier' *of which sorte* of *these sayings* is actually fronted.

resulted from a number of formal and semantic changes which together constitute a grammaticalization process. The TN/*postmodifiers* containing quantifying, phoric and interrogative modifiers did not grammaticalize or idiomatize to the same extent. In Middle English, the postmodifier variants with quantifier occurred in both the singular, e.g. (23), and plural, e.g. (24), and tended to keep the sense of 'different' subtypes, as reflected by the use of adjectives like *sondry* (23) and *diverse* (24).

(23) What pepyll they were that came to that dysport I shall yow declare **of many a sondry sort.**
'What people they were that came to that entertainment I shall explain to you (to be) **of many a different sort**' (*c*1420, *Assembly of Gods*, OED)

(24) ij. quartelettes, **of dyvers sortes**
'II quarters [vesssels] **of various sorts**' (1459, *Paston Lett.*, OED)

In Present-day English, TN/postmodifiers with quantifiers still seem to have largely compositional semantics, with numbers like *one* and *two*, and quantifiers like *many* and *various* quantifying subtypes, e.g. *digestive disturbances of many sorts* (WB), *lilies of many kinds* (WB). However, there are two patterns with quantifiers that are processed non-compositionally and can convey quantifying meaning. The first is formed by the idiomatized expressions *of all sorts/kinds*. The universal relative quantifier *all* generally means 'very many', and while the notion of 'many subtypes' remains present, they also tend to invite the inference of 'a great number', as in (25). The second pattern features negation + postmodifier of *any kind/sort* and conveys emphatic negative quantification, as in (26).

(25) The children crept closer and there were gasps of pleasure and excitement. There were **trinkets of all kinds.** (WB)

(26) there must be **no publicity of any kind.** (WB)

Because of their 'closed class', quantifying meaning, these two patterns can functionally be grouped together with quantifying complex determiners.

If we look at the TN/modifier constructions from a broad semantic point of view, then the main opposition is between those with quantifying modifier and those with phoric, interrogative and lexical modifier, as indicated in the second column of Table 4. Ultimately, phoric, interrogative and lexical modifiers serve the same semantic goal, viz. *characterization* of the referents of the NP, which can be instances of the type designated by the head noun or, less commonly, generic subtypes. TN/modifier constructions with these three modifier types are all about adding semantic specifications to the subtype or instance referred to. TN/premodifiers with phoric and interrogative modifiers emerged in Middle English. Examples of TN/premodifiers with lexical modifiers appear with some frequency from Early Modern English on, as in (27).

(27) Giuing her the *vale* with **a counterfeit kind of curtesie**.
'bidding her goodbye with **a false kind of curtsy**' (*a*1522, tr. *Æneid*, OED)

This is, of course, an example of the attributive, or descriptive, modifier construction associated with instantial reference in Kruisinga (1932: 391) and De Smedt et al. (2007). Brems and Davidse (2010) stated that this construction, like the complex determiner construction, resulted from re-analysis of the erstwhile head of the TN/head construction into a modifier. They situated its emergence at the start of Early Modern English. Again, this has to be corrected. The analytic TN/premodifier constructions attributing semantic specifications to instances or generic subclasses descended from the TN/genitival premodifiers of Old English. No shift of headedness was involved. A process of change that can be argued for is semantic bleaching of the TN. Already in Middle English, some examples with a lexical modifier are attested, as in (28), in which reference is to a generic subclass, viz. 'the worst misfortune'.

(28) **The worste kynde of Infortune** is þis A man to haue be in prosperite And it remembren whan it passed is.
'**The worst kind of misfortune** is this: a man to have been in prosperity and remembering it when it is over.' (*a*1413 (*c*1385), *Troilus & Criseyde*, OED)

The category of the descriptive (pre-)modifier construction as such can be kept if one recognizes its ability for both instantial and generic reference. But, it is important to see the larger pattern it is part of, as visualized in Table 4. When it comes to describing class or quality properties of the referents, not only the TN/premodifier variants but also the TN/postmodifier variants, as illustrated in (29) and (30), have to be considered.

(29) **Al þe folk of þis soort** is a world þat shal be dampned.
'**All the people of this sort** is a world that shall be damned.' (*c*1380, *Eng. Wycliffite Serm*, OED)

(30) There myghte men the ryal egle fynde..And **othere eglis of a lowere kynde**.
'There might men find the royal eagle, and **other eagles of a lower kind**' (1430->1380, *Parl. Fowls*, OED)

In (29), *of þis sort* instructs the hearer to retrieve properties of *the folk*, e.g. 'sinful', from the preceding text. In (30), the adjective *lower* directly characterizes the subtype of eagles.

In this section, we have sketched the development from the Old English source construction of the genitival TN/modifier construction to analytic TN/modifier constructions, for which Middle English was a crucial period. Much more detailed data-study will be required to verify and flesh out this outline in terms of finer processes of change and the semantic-pragmatic effects accompanying them.

4 Modern English: The trajectory of development of the TN/head constructions

In this section, we focus on the trajectory starting from the Old English N2/genitival complement + TN/head construction (Section 2), which may convey a superordination relation, as in *feower muneca*$_{COMPL}$ *cyn*$_{HEAD}$ 'four kinds of monks' (6) or an appositional relation, as in *manna*$_{COMPL.}$ *cynn*$_{HEAD}$ 'the kind of man' (8). As we saw in Section 3, this construction was gradually replaced by analytic construals of the TN/head–complement relation, as in *feole cunne*$_{HEAD}$ *of weldede*$_{COMPL}$ 'many kinds of good deeds' (12) and *þe kind*$_{HEAD}$ *of man*$_{COMPL}$ 'the kind of man' (1425->1400, OED). It is these constructions that, in Modern English, led to the nominal qualifier construction, e.g. *he is a sort of genius*, via a shift of head-status from the TN to N2. The nominal qualifier construction then broke free from the limits of the NP (Denison 2002: 12): *sort of* and *kind of* came to function as adverbials modifying grammatical classes like the whole NP, the verb, the VP, and the whole proposition. Apart from our analysis of the source construction as containing a complement rather than a postmodifier, we follow Denison's (2002) hypotheses about this trajectory.

Mihatsch (this volume: 23) points out that nominal qualifier constructions may evolve by wear-and-tear of the TN/head–N2/complement construction into "a (rough) assignment of an object to a superordinate" category with unfamiliar, hard-to-classify entities. In (31) from Captain Cook's *The First Voyage* we find an example of such a precursor of the qualifier TN-construction.

(31) The Trees we saw were **a small kind of Cabbage Palms**. (CLMETEV, 1768–71)

Grammatically, this example still has many features of the TN/head–N2/complement construction.[9] *A small kind* is not a premodifier as suggested by the non-equivalence to (30) of an alternate in which the TN-constituent is construed as postmodifier: *The Trees we saw were Cabbage Palms of a small kind*. At the same time, N2 *Cabbage Palms* is the most important constituent for the representational meaning of the predicative NP categorizing the subject *the trees*. In other words, examples like (31) seem to prepare the shift of head status from TN to N2 without actually manifesting it in any full sense.

In examples like (32), N2 *spiritualitie* has acquired full head status, with *some kind of* functioning as its premodifier.

(32)   There must be..in the passions..**some kind of spiritualitue** (1683, *Theologia Mystica*, OED)

There is no notion of superordination here. *Spirituality* is the only category that is being considered. The 'subtype' meaning of the TN has bleached into that of 'peripheral variant', conveying absence of some of its canonical semantic features. The hedging of N2 by the premodifier TN-constituent may also convey interpersonal effects such as degree modification of gradable features in the head noun, as in (33), attenuation of pejorative features and metalinguistic framing of a stylistically marked noun (Aijmer 2002).

(33)   I haue the wit to thinke my Master is **a kinde of a knaue**. (1616, *Two Gentlemen of Verona*, OED)

At a later stage, the qualifying constituent also developed postmodifier variants such as *of sorts*, in (34).

(34)   In the old days Spain provided **an outlet of sorts**. (1902, *Daily Chron*, OED)

In Modern English, the qualifying constituent and the element in its scope occur not only as the modifier and lexical head of a NP but develop the new structure of a qualifying adverbial able to scope over other elements of the NP or the whole NP as well as (elements of) the VP. In (35), which represents colloquial speech, we see adverbial *kind of* qualifying the whole following predication.

---

9 Kolyaseva (2021: 11) notes that in Russian, TN/head–complement/N2 constructions, which can be clearly identified by their case marking, may be used with qualifying meaning.

(35) Captain Davis had a gun, He **kind of** clapt his head on 't. (1775, *Amer. Broadside Verse*, OED)

As noted in the OED entry of *sort* n., 5c, the full form *sort of* can also follow the statement it qualifies, as in (36).

(36) Except I feel like, well, what you're doing anyway is just sitting here and saying all these things just to tease me and to taunt me, **sort of.** (1959, *Psychiatry*, OED)

The adverbial qualifier developed further into "a parenthetic qualifier expressing hesitation, diffidence, or the like, on the speaker's part" (*sort* n., 5c. *(a) sort of, o', a, sorter*, OED). Denison (2002: 4, 14) categorizes these uses as discourse particles because they do not apply to any clear scopal domains. In this respect, they are not part of a structure.[10] They apply more diffusely to the discourse, through which they are scattered, as in (37), a diffident student's reaction to an explanation by a professor.

(37) S: Yes, I think I'm er beginning to understand it better now and I must say, I'm **sort of** impressed . . .I quite like the idea of, er, **sort of,** er, **sort of** flexibility I think is the key word, isn't it? . . . in the **sort of** Prospectus. (Martin 1980)

From the adverbial qualifier also developed quotative markers like *be/go sorta/ kinda* or simply *sorta/kinda*, as in (38) (Aijmer 2002).

(38) "I just got a visual, Sharon standing in front of the class going, (SCREAM), while these little kids **kinda** 'Señorita Flynn? Hee hee hee hee hee." (SBCAE)

This extension was probably motivated by the similative meaning component of *sorta/kinda*, which is cross-linguistically a source of quotatives introducing 'replicas' of utterances (Güldemann 2002). In English, this last development has not been very productive yet.

In conclusion to this section we can note that the path starting from the lexical TN/head construction yielding the qualifying and related constructions

---

10 Keizer (this volume) focuses in depth on English expressions like *sort of the enemy of Trump, kind of the pageant world*, investigating, amongst others, whether we are dealing here with adverbial qualifier or discourse marker uses, and in what way these differ semantically and pragmatically from qualifying complex NPs like *a sort of enemy of Trump*.

is a straightforward grammaticalization path to which the loss of head status of TN and the reanalysis of (determiner +) TN + *of* into a qualifying constituent was central. We can now turn to a survey of TN-constructions in Present-day English.

5 Survey of TN-constructions in Present-day English

In this section we survey the sets of TN-constructions used in Present-day English: (1) nominal TN-constructions with lexical functions, (2)) nominal TN-constructions with grammatical functions, and (3) non-nominal TN-constructions serving grammatical and discursive functions. In comparison with earlier typologies, this survey adds the constructions whose structural assemblies are realized with N2 – TN order.

We begin by surveying the nominal TN-constructions with lexical functions visualized in Table 5. This set subsumes the analytic counterparts that emerged in Middle English from the two source constructions with genitivally coded dependents in Old English. Central to it is the functional-structural opposition between head–complement and head–modifier and the different semantics these code.

Table 5: English NP-constructions with TN with lexical functions.

meaning	lexicogrammar	predependent + head	head + postdependent
reference to subtype(s) of supertype	NP with TN/head + superordinate complement	*a rare marble*$_{PRECOMPLEMENT}$ *type*$_{HEAD}$	*a rare type*$_{HEAD}$ *of marble*$_{POSTCOMPLEMENT}$
reference to subtype (of) 'x'	NP with TN/head + appositional complement	*the horror film*$_{PRECOMPLEMENT}$ *genre*$_{HEAD}$	*the genre*$_{HEAD}$ *of the horror film*$_{POSTCOMPLEMENT}$
attributing semantic specifications to instances or generic subclasses	NP with TN/modifier + superordinate N2/head	*pop and lock kind*$_{PREMODIFIER}$ *(of) dance moves*$_{HEAD}$	*dance moves*$_{HEAD}$ *of the pop–and–lock kind*$_{POSTMODIFIER}$.
	(be) of + NP with TN	---	*be of the skinny sort*

The TN/head–N2/*of*-complement construction referring to subtypes of a supertype has been called the binominal construction (Denison 2002) and the referential construction (Keizer 2007) in the literature. However, this conception of the binominal construction was incomplete in two ways. Firstly, it did not include TN/head constructions with precomplements. Secondly, it tended to overlook the point that TN/head constructions, with either pre- or postcomplements, can have appositional semantics. The more comprehensive typology in Table 5 includes this structural variation and the options of superordination and apposition.[11]

The TN/premodifier + N2/head construction was referred to as the descriptive modifier construction in our earlier work (Brems and Davidse 2010). We now argue that these semantics can also be expressed by N2/head + TN/*of*-postmodifier (Davidse and Brems this volume). Finally, we also point out the use of predicative *of* + NP with TN to ascribe semantic properties to the subject, as in (39), a construction that has been around from ME on (see footnote 3).

(39) ... the skeletons at Skhul and at Qafzeh are **of the AMHS type**. (WB)

Table 6 gives an overview of NP-constructions in which the TN-constituent serves grammatical functions. None of them have a complementation structure, which is associated with designating superordination, as in *a rare type*$_{HEAD}$ *of marble*$_{POSTCOMPLEMENT}$ or apposition, as in *the genre*$_{HEAD}$ *of the horror film*$_{POSTCOMPLEMENT}$. All TN-constructions with grammatical functions have a head–modifier structure. They also all have a pre- and a postmodifier variant. The third column of Table 6 lists the determiners that are typically used in the TN-modifier.

Table 6: English NP-constructions with TN with grammatical functions.

meaning	TN/premodifier + N2/head	determiner of TN	N2/head +TN/ *of*-postmodifier
qualifying of category designated by N2	*some sort of*$_{PREMODIFIER}$ *plans* *a kind of*$_{PREMODIFIER}$ *groupie*	*some, a*	*comfort of a sort*$_{POSTMODIFIER}$ *a suit of some sort*$_{POSTMODIFIER}$
modifying degree	*that kind of* $_{PREMODIFIER}$ *pressure* *what sort of*$_{PREMODIFIER}$ *monster*	*that, what, some*	*pressure of that kind*$_{POSTMODIFIER}$
quantifying of instances designated by NP	*all sorts of*$_{PREMODIFIER}$ *problems*	*all, no*	*trinkets of all kinds*$_{POSTMODIFIER}$. *no regard of any sort*$_{POSTMODIFIER}$

---

[11] Umbach (this volume) studies the semantic distinction between 'identity' and 'subsumption' for binominal NPs with *Art* and *Typ* in German.

Table 6 (continued)

meaning	TN/premodifier + N2/head	determiner of TN	N2/head +TN/ of-postmodifier
instructing retrieval of semantic specifications ascribed to referent of NP	*those kind of* $_{\text{PREMODIFIER}}$ *scare tactics*	*that, this, those, these, the*	*suicide bombings or attacks of that kind* $_{\text{POSTMODIFIER}}$
inquiring into semantic specifications of NP	*what sort of* $_{\text{PREMODIFIER}}$ *clients*	*what*	*Union of what sort* $_{\text{POSTMODIFIER}}$

In the top half of Table 6, we have put the qualifying and degree modifying constructions, which are related to each other in terms of their diachronic development and their semantics. The qualifying constructions in a strict sense are those that modify the category designated by N2: they allow for absence of canonical category features, e.g. *comfort of a sort*, or attenuate some of its attitudinal overtones, e.g. *a kind of groupie*. In the degree modifying use, gradable features of N2 are modified, either upgraded, as in *what sort of monster*, or downgraded, as in (40), which besides the qualifying meaning has a downtoning inference.

(40) are you in **trouble of some sort** (WB)

Quantifying TN/modifiers quantify the instances referred to by the NP in a hyperbolic way, either as a very large quantity (*all sorts of problems*) or as no quantity at all (*no publicity of any kind*). TN/modifiers with interrogative and phoric determiners ultimately serve the same semantic goal as descriptive modifiers, viz. ascription of semantic specifications to the referents of the NP, which in Present-day English are typically instances of the type designated by the head noun but can also be generic subtypes. We subsume TN/modifiers with interrogative and phoric determiners under TN-constructions with grammatical functions because determiner and TN together form a unit with determining, procedural meaning (Traugott and Dasher 2002), which instructs the addressee to retrieve semantic specifications. They do not name semantic specifications the way descriptive TN/modifiers do. TN/modifiers with interrogative determiners inquire into semantic specifications still to be identified, as illustrated for premodifiers in (41) and postmodifiers in (42).

(41) Prostitution has existed as long as history has been recorded . . . Many people have no concept of **what sort of clients** use sex services and seem to think it is the dregs of society. (WB)

(42) Nevertheless most responsible opinion saw no alternative to a Union of the two countries, but **Union of what sort** was less an object of agreement. (WB)

Those with phoric determiners instruct the addressee to retrieve semantic specifications either from the preceding text (43) or from information following in the NP itself (44). This retrieval often involves inferencing, rather than literal retrieval, and this further entails that generalization beyond the actual textual 'antecedent' may be involved. For instance, in (43) *these sort of scare tactics* refers back to 'linking plastic milk bottles and cancer', requiring the addressee to infer a generalization like 'unproven or exaggerated risk claims', under which many other *'such'* claims fall. Indeed, as noted by Mackenzie (1997: 89) phoric complex determiners can often be replaced by *such (a)*. In TN/phoric postmodifiers as in (44) *of the kind* can signal a relation of exemplification, which also requires the addressee to infer a generalization.

(43) We were only able to respond that we were unaware of any evidence linking plastic milk bottles and cancer, but your investigative report puts the whole issue into perspective. Unfortunately **these sort of scare tactics** do a lot of harm (WB)

(44) He led me down a hallway that was lined with **nineteenth-century American country antiques of the sort one finds all over Port Frederick.** (WB)

Finally, we survey the TN-constructions that have broken free from the boundaries of NP structure, which were discussed in Section 2.4. They are listed in Table 7. The most productive are the qualifying adverbial, illustrated in (35)–(36) above, and the discourse particle, e.g. (37).[12] Whereas the qualifying adverbial is an element of structure relating to the constituent it scopes over, the discourse particle is not an element of a clear structure. Two more constructions can be identified, which are infrequent in English. One is the quotative marker, illustrated in (38) above, which Aijmer (2002) has drawn attention to. The other is the emergent complex preposition in examples like (45), where *of the type* means 'like'. This is probably a further development of cataphoric postmodifiers as in (44). Whereas complex prepositions with TN have received attention in studies

---

[12] Aijmer (this volume) presents a further semantic subclassification of qualifying adverbials in terms of the various following grammatical categories and of the various discourse marker types.

on Romance languages (e.g. Voghera 2013; Rosier 2002) and Slavic language (e.g. Kolyaseva 2021; Kisiel and Kolyaseva this volume), they have been largely overlooked in work on English hitherto.

(45) words **of the type** *elentri* 'star-queen' seldom occur in Quenya. (WB)

Table 7: English extra-NP-constructions with TN with grammatical and discursive functions.

meaning	structure	
qualifying (hedging, approximating, attenuating, degree modifying, metalinguistic framing)	adverbial – scopal domain	*There are kinda three ways to do this;* (Google) *Gomez was kind of a smart ass.* (2005, OED) *He was sort of proud of them.* (1858, OED) *He kind of clapt his head on 't.* (1775, OED)
quotative	marker – report	*these little kids kinda 'Señorita Flynn* (SBCSE)
exemplifying, similative ('like, such as')	preposition – complement	*words of the type elentri 'star-queen'* (WB)
tentativeness, diffidence, filler	discourse particle	*I quite like the idea of, er, sort of, er, sort of flexibility I think is the key word, isn't it? . . . in the sort of Prospectus*

It is with these inventories of TN-constructions in Present-day English that, in the next section, we turn to Present-day Dutch, one of the closest living languages to English, to take stock of its TN-constructions.

6 Survey of TN-constructions in Present-day Dutch

Very little research has hitherto been done on TN-constructions in Dutch with some important exceptions like Schermer-Vermeer (2008) and De Troij and Van de Velde (2020). This section presents a first exploration focusing on the TNs *soort* 'sort' and its cognates, *type* 'type', and *aard* 'type, nature', using attested examples found with Google searches. As in the preceding sections, our main question is which TN-constructions, in the sense of Langacker's (2021) functional-structural assemblies, are available in Dutch.

We start with nominal TN-constructions with lexical functions, visualized in Table 8.

Table 8: Dutch NP-constructions with TN with lexical functions.

meaning	lexicogrammar	predependent + head	head + postdependent
reference to subtype(s) of supertype	NP with TN/head + superordinate complement	*een roze marmer*$_{\text{PRECOMPLEMENT}}$ *soort*$_{\text{HEAD}}$ 'a pink marble type'	*een echt roze soort*$_{\text{HEAD}}$ *marmer*$_{\text{POSTCOMPLEMENT}}$ 'a really pink type of marble' *het type*$_{\text{HEAD}}$ *van de verpakking*$_{\text{POSTCOMPLEMENT}}$ 'the type of packaging'
reference to subtype 'x'	NP with TN/head + appositional complement	*het griezelfilm*$_{\text{PRECOMPLEMENT}}$ *genre*$_{\text{HEAD}}$ 'the horror film genre'	*de soort*$_{\text{HEAD}}$ *hout*$_{\text{POSTCOMPLEMENT}}$ 'the sort wood' *het genre*$_{\text{HEAD}}$ *van de musical*$_{\text{POSTCOMPLEMENT}}$ 'the genre of the musical'
	NP with TN/modifier + superordinate N2/head	*een no-nonsense soort (van)*$_{\text{PREMODIFIER}}$ *kerel*$_{\text{HEAD}}$ 'a no-nonsense sort (of) bloke'	*een man*$_{\text{HEAD}}$ *van het type 'niet lullen, maar poetsen'*$_{\text{POSTMODIFIER}}$ 'a man of the type 'don't waffle but clean''
	zijn van 'be of' + NP with TN	---	*is van het rancuneuze soort* 'is of the rancorous sort'

Table 8 shows that Dutch has exactly the same lexical TN-constructions as English (Table 5). As in English, the main structural and semantic opposition is between TN/head–N2/complement constructions and TN/modifier–N2/head constructions. The TN/head–N2/complement constructions can designate either superordination or apposition, and have pre- and postcomplements. The one morphosyntactic difference with English is that reference to subtypes of a supertype can be grammatically realized with a postcomplement not linked to the head by particle *van* 'of', as in (46).[13]

(46) als je **een echt roze soort**$_{\text{HEAD}}$ **marmer**$_{\text{POSTCOMPL}}$ zoekt
 if you a really pink sort$_{\text{HEAD}}$ marble$_{\text{POSTCOMPL}}$ search
 'if you are looking for **a really pink type of marble'**, (salontafelmarmer.nl)

The Dutch TN/modifier + N2/head constructions, e.g. (47), are fully parallel with English, offering the same semantic and morphosyntactic options. The descriptive TN/postmodifier construction is illustrated in (47).

---

[13] Like De Troij and Van de Velde (2020), we provide for the sentences containing the TN-construction a word-by-word English transliteration followed by a more idiomatic translation.

(47) Timmerman Nico was **een man**$_{HEAD}$ **van het type 'niet lullen,**
Carpenter Nico was a man$_{HEAD}$ of the type not waffle
maar poetsen'$_{POSTMOD.}$
but clean$_{POSTMOD.}$
'Carpenter Nico was **a man of the type "don't waffle but clean"**'
(https://www.ad.nl/gouda/timmerman-nico-was-een-man-van-het-type-niet-lullen-maar-poetsen~a8295889/)

Table 9 lists nominal TN-constructions with grammatical functions in Dutch. As in English (Table 6), they are all TN/modifier–N2/head constructions, but unlike English, they do not all have postmodifiers. It is the qualifying and degree modifying constructions that have a premodifier realization only.

This split coincides with the different source constructions that we identified in English for the qualifying and degree modifying constructions versus the quantifying, phoric and interrogative modifiers. Qualifying and degree modifying constructions emerged as TN/premodifier–N2/head constructions through a shift of headedness from the lexical TN/head–superordinate N2/complement construction, and developed postmodifier variants at a later stage. In Dutch, no such postmodifier variants are available, as far as we can see. We can notice that, just as in their source construction illustrated in (46) above, the Dutch qualifying (48) and degree modifying (49) constructions do not feature the particle *van* 'of'. In the nominal qualifying construction, the TN *soort* 'sort' can also occur as its cognate *soortement*, which is restricted to this construction. The suffix *-ement* added to *soort* seems to be used here in the pseudo-learned but colloquial and somewhat pejorative sense in which it is also added to *kaak* 'jaw', yielding *kakement* 'face, mug', or to *ziel* 'soul', yielding *zielement* '(pitiable) body' (*zielement* n., De Coster 2002). The pejorative element in *soortement* conveys that N2 applies only to a certain extent to the phenomenon referred to and imposes a pejorative slant on it.

(48) Onze Braziliaanse chauffeur heeft er lol in dat hij Maarten Goffin naar zijn biologische moeder voert,. . .. Voor Maarten is het bittere ernst.
'Alsof ik in **een soortement**$_{HEAD}$ **Blind date-show**$_{POSTMOD.}$ ben
as if I in a sort$_{HEAD}$ Blind date-show$_{POSTMOD.}$ have
beland'.
ended up
'Our Brazilian driver is amused that he is driving Maarten Goffin to his biological mother. For Maarten it is dead serious. "As if I have ended up in **a (bad) sort of Blind date-show.**"' (https://www.standaard.be/plus/20170909/bijlage/dsw/optimized)

Table 9: Dutch NP-constructions with TN with grammatical functions.

meaning	TN/premodifier + N2/head	determiner of TN	N2/head + TN/postmodifier
qualifying of category designated by N2	een soort_PREMODIFIER "uniform" 'a sort of "uniform"'	een	---
modifying degree	dat soort_PREMODIFIER geweld 'that sort of violence' wat voor een (soort)_PREMODIFIER monster 'what sort of monster'	dat, wat voor een	---
quantifying of instances designated by NP	allerlei/allerhande (soort)_PREMODIFIER problemen 'all sorts of problems'	allerhande, veler-/allerlei	problemen allerhande_POSTMODIFIER. 'problems of all sorts'
instructing retrieval of semantic specifications ascribed to referent of NP	dat soort (van)_PREMODIFIER uitwassen	dat, het	herinneringen van dien aard 'memories of that sort' elke vergunning van die aard_POSTMODIFIER 'each permit of that sort'
inquiring into semantic specifications of NP	wat voor soort_PREMODIFIER mens 'what sort of person' welke 'soort' (van)_PREMODIFIER mensen 'what sort of people'	wat voor een, welke	een boef, maar van welke soort_POSTMODIFIER 'a criminal, but of which sort'

Degree modifying constituents typically have a demonstrative determiner. As shown by the use of neutral singular *dat* 'that.N' in *dat soort geweld* 'that sort of violence' in (49), *soort* used in degree modifiers has neutral gender,[14] whereas in its original lexical 'subtype' sense, as in *de soort hout* 'the sort wood', it has feminine gender and takes *de* 'the.F' rather than *het* 'the.N' as article.

---

[14] Presumably, this shift from feminine to neutral gender is motivated by semantic shift and bleaching.

(49) Tiener krijgt levenslang voor moord op meisje van 10:
"Nooit **dat soort**~HEAD~ **geweld**~POSTMOD.~ gezien bij 15-jarige."
never that sort~HEAD~ violence~POSTMOD~ seen with 15-year old
'Teenager gets life sentence for murder of 10 year old girl. "Never seen **that sort of violence** in a 15 year old." ' (Tiener krijgt levenslang voor moord op meisje van 10: "Nooit dat soort geweld gezien bij 15-jarige" | Buitenland | hln.be)

Let us now turn to the quantifying, phoric and interrogative modifiers, which in Present-day Dutch do have pre- and postmodifier variants. In Old English, the TN/modifier construction started off with a quantifying genitive premodifier. In Middle English, the premodifier lost its genitive inflexion and came to be viewed as a premodifying noun which could be linked by *of* to the head. TN/*of*-postmodifier variants gradually developed. In Middle and Modern English, the TN/modifier construction developed a wider range of quantifying, phoric and interrogative pre- and postmodifiers (Table 4). In Dutch, the premodifier variants, which typically lack particle *van* 'of', seem to us to be more common and TN/postmodifier constructions seem subject to more restrictions. This might be the result of a diachronic development similar to English. Beginning with the quantifying type, we find compound modifiers like *allerhande/allerlei*, and *velerlei*. The origin of *allerhande* 'of all sorts' is the Middle Dutch genitive plural *aller* of *al* 'all' plus *hand* 'hand' in its derived meaning 'sort' (Philippa et al. 2003–2009). *Allerlei* and *velerlei* likewise derive from the genitive plural *aller* of *al* 'all' and *veler* of *veel* 'many' plus *lei* 'law, principle, manner', yielding the meanings 'of all/many sorts'. As compound predeterminers they can be followed by another TN, as in (50). They can also be used as postmodifier, as in *problemen allerhande* 'problems of all sorts'.

(50) Ik heb dagelijks mensen over de vloer met **allerhande**
I have daily people over the floor with of all hands
soort~PREMOD~ **problemen**~HEAD~.
sort~PREMOD~ problems~HEAD~
'Every day I have people in my shop with **all sorts of problems**.' (https://www.wintersport.be/forum/topic/90239)

This historical trajectory has many parallels with the development from Old English genitival (pre)modifiers of Middle English compound determiners like *alkin(s)* 'all kind(s)' and *fele-kin(s)* 'many kind(s)' discussed in Section 3.

TN/premodifiers with interrogative determiners, then, serve the grammatical function of complex determiner, as shown by the fact that they can be replaced by other (simple and complex) determiners. But, like descriptive TN/modifiers, they are concerned with the ascription of semantic properties to the referents of the NP, as shown in the example with interrogative complex determiner in (51). The *wh*-interrogative with *wat voor soort mens* (lit. 'what for sort person') is followed by more specific polar interrogatives in which the alternative properties of 'super normal' versus 'very abnormal' are substituted for interrogative 'what sort of'.

(51) **Wat   voor   soort**$_{PREMOD}$ **mens**$_{HEAD}$ ben   jij?
      what   for   sort$_{PREMOD}$ person$_{HEAD}$ are   you
      Ben jij super normaal? Of een heel abnormaal mens???
      '**What sort of person** are you? Are you super normal? Or a very abnormal person???'
      (https://www.quizlet.nl/quiz/74978/wat-voor-soort-mens-ben-jij)

Besides the form *wat voor soort* in (51), interrogative complex determiners in Dutch can take variant forms like *welk soort* 'which sort' and *wat voor een*, which can perhaps be compared to North English *what'n* (Section 3). Example (52) illustrates the postmodifier variant *van welk soort* 'of which sort'.

(52) Hij   is   een   **boef**$_{HEAD}$, **maar   van   welk   soort**$_{POSTMOD}$?
      He   is   a   crook$_{HEAD}$ but   of   which   sort$_{POSTMOD}$
      Hij oogstte ongeloof. Net als de stelling van de Neus dat hij niet „is geïnteresseerd in geld".
      'He is **a crook, but of which sort**? He met with disbelief. Just like the claim by the Nose that he is not "interested in money".' (Holleeder zegt dat hij snakte naar een burgermansbestaan – NRC)

Phoric TN/modifiers give the addressee instructions to retrieve semantic specifications either from the preceding text (53) or from information following in the NP itself (54).

(53) Wat beleefd van u dat u de moeite neemt om nog te reageren op Petra en Frank. Beiden leven in een fantasiewereld dat wij in Nederland een soort DDR2.0 hebben.
      Dat   soort$_{PREMOD}$ **uitwassen**$_{HEAD}$ zit   vooral
      that   sort$_{PREMOD}$ excesses$_{HEAD}$ sits   mainly

aan het uiterst rechtse politieke spectrum van de FvD.
'How polite of you that you go to the trouble of reacting to Petra and Frank. Both are living in a fantasy world that in Netherlands we have a sort of DDR2.0. **That sort of excesses** is located mainly at the extreme right political spectrum of the FvD.[15]
(comment to Inboedel na ontruiming zaak van gemeente (binnenlandsbestuur.nl))

(54) Het is niet goed dat de mensch alleen zij. Deze woorden, of woorden van gelijke strekking, zijn gezegd of geschreven door de heer Saulus te D. **Vage herinneringen**$_{HEAD}$ **van dien aard**$_{POSTMOD}$
vague memories$_{HEAD}$ of that sort$_{POSTMOD}$
jagen althans, als mistflarden in december, door mijn brein.
'It is not good for man to be alone. These words, or words to the same effect, were said or written by mister Saul at D. At least, **vague memories of that sort** fleet, like trails of mist in December, through my brain.(from: Andreas Burnier, 1983. *De litteraire salon*, Querido)

In (53) the complex determiner *dat soort* ('such') contains the neutral noun *soort*, just like the degree modifier in *dat soort geweld* in (49), which confirms the association of the neutral noun with grammaticalized constructions, as opposed to feminine *die soort* found in lexical taxonomizing constructions. The reader is instructed to infer the properties of the 'excesses' from the preceding discourse, which refers to commentators calling Nederland ('Netherlands') NeDDRland. In (53), instructions for anaphoric retrieval are expressed by the postmodifier *van dien aard* ('of that nature').

The third and final set to consider is the extra-NP-constructions with grammatical and discursive functions, set out in Table 10, which can be compared with Table 7 for English.

---

15 FvD stands for Forum for Democracy, which is viewed as an extreme right wing party.

Table 10: English extra-NP-constructions with TN with grammatical and discursive functions.

meaning	structure	
qualifying (hedging, approximating, attenuating, degree modifying, metalinguistic framing)	adverbial – scopal domain	*Het is soort van mooi.* 'It's kind of pretty' *Ik zeg soort van uitdagend:* 'I say sort of defiantly' *Hij is soort begraven bij de raffinaderij* 'he is sort of buried at the refinery' *Dit is soort van wat wij doen.* 'This is sort of what we do'
quotative	marker – report	--
exemplifying, similative ('like, such as')	preposition – complement	*Imperatieven van het type 'niet te lang pruylen*[16]*'* 'imperatives of the type "not pout too long" '
tentativeness, diffidence, filler	discourse particle	*Het regent eigenlijk een soort van.* 'It's raining actually sort of'

Present-day Dutch has adverbial qualifiers like *soort* and *soort van* 'sort of' (De Troij and Van de Velde 2020). In informal registers they can be used in a variety of grammatical contexts, scoping over, amongst others, adjectives, adverbials (55), verbs and predicative complements, as illustrated in Table 10.

(55) Ik   probeer cool te   blijven en   zeg **soort van** **uitdagend**: 'jij
      I   try   cool to   remain   and say sorta   defiantly   you
      niet zeker'
      not surely
      'I try to remain cool and say **sort of defiantly**: 'don't you?'' (M'n vrienden willen wel een MILF-je... | Wine-up!)

Dutch *soort* and *(een) soort van* 'sort of' are also developing discourse particle uses, as in (56), heard on television and explained as an interpersonal marker of tentativeness and politeness on the website quoting it. In contrast with adverbial qualifiers, discourse particles do not have a clear scopal domain.

(56) Het regent eigenlijk **een** **soort** **van**'.
      it   rains   actually   a   sort   of
      It is actually **sort of** raining. (Is 'soort van' eigenlijk wel vaagheid? Of is het een vorm van beleefdheid soort van? (trouw.nl)

---

[16] The cited form *pruylen*, Present-day Dutch *pruilen*, is from an older stage of Dutch.

Finally, emergent complex preposition with TNs are attested, as in (57), in which *van het type* means 'like, such as'.

(57) Imperatieven **van het type** *niet te lang pruylen*
 imperatives of the type *niet te lang pruylen*
 'imperatives **like** "don't pout too long" ' (De Nieuwe Taalgids. Jaargang 33. dbnl)

Dutch does not have quotative markers with TNs. However, it has developed an innovative quotative marker with a similative meaning, *ik heb zoiets van*, as in (58), generally accepted to be the equivalent of *I'm like*.

(58) En ik heb zoiets van wees niet zo hard voor jezelf
 And I have something like be not so hard for yourself
 'And I'm like, don't be so hard on yourself'

In this section it has become clear that there is extensive parallelism between Present-day English and Dutch in terms of their great variety of TN-construction-types. In English, we have shown, this great variety is due to the different changes affecting the developmental paths from the two source constructions with genitival dependents in Old English. There have not been any diachronic studies of Dutch TN-constructions from the perspective we have outlined. However, in historical relics in some Dutch TN-constructions, parallels could be observed with the English diachrony such as the development of compound determiners like *allerhande* (all sorts of) and *velerlei* ('many sorts of') from older genitival TN-modifiers. However, systematic quantitative corpus-based studies are needed to verify the inventory of constructions offered here and to assess the relative productivity of the TN-constructions in our typology. This might reveal that Dutch is lagging somewhat behind English in speed of grammaticalization (see Vandevelde and Lamiroy 2017).

7 Conclusion

The field of TNs in any language covers an exceptionally extended area of the lexicogrammar, which moreover has undergone substantial diachronic change and extension. This field can be approached mainly from the lexical or the grammatical end. To the grammatical analyst, the field presents a great number of constructions, which further multiply if one increases the degree of granularity with which they are described. The processes of change that led to these multiple constructions are varied and complex. TN-constructions thus constitute a vast field to be charted grammatically, semantically and pragmatically and to be studied in terms of language variation and change.

In this chapter we have addressed gaps and errors of analysis in the existing interpretations of the grammaticalization of TN-constructions in English. Firstly, we have remedied the gap in the data studied hitherto by including Old English data, in which binominal NPs involved a genitive dependent. We have argued that the analysis developed by Kolyaseva (2021) and Kisiel and Kolyaseva (this volume) for binominal NPs with genitives in Russian largely applies to Old English, which was typologically similar. Contra received thinking on English, not one but two source constructions have to be recognized. The earliest and hitherto overlooked source construction was that with TN/genitive, *ælces cynnes*$_{GEN.SG}$ *déor*$_{NOM.PL}$ 'animals of each kind', which we analysed as a TN/modifier–N2/head construction. The second source construction with N2/genitive, *muneca*$_{GEN.PL}$ *cyn*$_{NOM;PL}$ 'kinds of monks', was analysed as a N2/complement–TN/head construction.

Secondly, we showed that not one, but two distinct diachronic paths developed from these two source constructions when their dependents came to be coded analytically, correcting analyses in our earlier work that were shown to be untenable. The construction with TN/genitival (pre-)modifier led to the complex determiner and the descriptive modifier constructions. When the genitive inflexion was lost, the TN was re-interpreted as a nominal premodifier that didn't need to but could be linked to the head noun by *of*. Postmodifiers coded analytically as *of* + TN also developed. Contra claims in the literature, as in Brems and Davidse (2010), no modifier– head reversal took place on this path. The second source construction, N2/genitival complement–N/head, we proposed, came to be realized analytically as N/head + of + N2/complement. For this lexical source construction, we do see the earlier posited shift of headedness as the most likely mechanism to have led to the nominal qualifying construction, in which the TN is part of a premodifier. The nominal qualifying construction also developed postmodifier variants. From the nominal qualifier construction developed adverbial qualifiers with their variety of scopal domains, which eventually led to discourse particles used in speech, and more marginally, quotative markers and complex prepositions.

For Present-day English we presented a comprehensive typology, recognizing more TN-constructions and structural variants than distinguished in the literature on English so far. By way of a first test of the newly proposed model, we researched the counterparts in Present-day Dutch of the TN-constructions in Present-day English. We found that, with the exception of some minor variants, the synchronic typology of Dutch is in its basic outlines very similar to that of

English. Moreover, Present-day Dutch TN-constructions feature relics from earlier stages such as TN/genitive-derived quantifiers like *allerhande* (lit. 'of all hands/sorts'), which also appear to support the proposed model.

These findings call for future grammar-oriented research. First of all, more qualitative and quantitative corpus study is needed to verify and flesh out the diachronic model proposed for English. Secondly, the proposed lines of development have to be investigated for other Germanic languages. It should be studied whether their diachronic development of TN-constructions involved not only analytic complex NPs but also ones with genitives. Diachronic studies of Scandinavian languages (e.g. Toft 2009, Odden 2019) have recognized the role played by these two types of constructions, i.e. analytically coded NPs like *Swedish flygplan av typen Boeing 777* 'plane of the type Boeing 777' (Odden 2018), and binominal genitive constructions. The latter type, Odden (2018) observes, developed mainly into idiosyncratic and semi-fixed constructions, particularly with quantifiers and demonstratives", as in Norwegian *allskens* (all.GEN.SG-kind.GEN.SG), 'of all kind'. The more specific hypotheses to be investigated in the history of other Germanic languages pertain to the two main source constructions posited by us for English, i.e. TN/head–N2/complement and N2/head–TN/modifier. Is there evidence in other languages for the central contrast we posit between complementation and modification constructions – both within their genitival and analytic realizations? Is there support for the two distinct developmental trajectories we have hypothesized for the complementation and modification source constructions? In sum, the more comprehensive diachronic model of English TN-constructions developed in this introduction calls for new grammar-oriented studies addressing these questions in other Germanic languages. Such studies will, in turn, allow to better flesh out the synchronic inventories of TN-constructions and elucidate their rich semantics-pragmatics.

References

Ackema, Peter & Ad Neeleman. 2004. *Beyond morphology: Interface conditions on word formation*. Oxford: Oxford University Press.

Aijmer, Karin. 2002. *English discourse particles: Evidence from a corpus*. Amsterdam: Benjamins.

Brems, Lieselotte & Kristin Davidse. 2010. The grammaticalization of nominal type noun constructions with *kind/sort of*: chronology and paths of change. *English Studies* 91. 180–202.

De Coster, Marc. 2002. *Woordenboek van populaire uitdrukkingen, clichés, kreten en slogans*. Den Haag: Sdu.

Denison, David. 2002. History of the *sort of* construction family. Paper presented at the Second International conference on Construction Grammar, Helsinki, September 6–28, 2002.

De Smedt, Liesbet, Lieselotte Brems & Kristin Davidse. 2007. NP-internal functions and extended uses of the 'type' nouns *kind, sort,* and *type*: Towards a comprehensive, corpus-based description. In Roberta Facchinetti et al. (eds.), *Corpus Linguistics 25 years on*, 225–255. Amsterdam: Rodopi.

De Troij, Robbert & Van de Velde, Freek. 2020. Beyond mere text frequency: assessing subtle grammaticalization by different quantitative measures. A case study on the Dutch *soort* construction. *Langages* 5. 55.

Güldemann, Tom. 2002. When 'say' is not *say*: The functional versatility of the Bantu quotative marker *ti* with special reference to Shona. In Tom Güldemann & Manfred von Roncador (eds.), *Reported discourse: A meeting ground for different linguistic domains*, 253–287. Amsterdam: John Benjamins.

Huddleston, Rodney & Geoffrey Pullum. 2002. *The Cambridge grammar of the English language*. Cambridge: Cambridge University Press.

Keizer, Evelien. 2007. *The English noun phrase. The nature of linguistic categorization*. Cambridge: Cambridge University Press.

Kolyaseva, Alena. 2021. The nominal uses of the Russian *rod* ('genus', 'genre', 'kind') and *tip* ('type'): the starting point of desemanticization, *Slovo a Slovesnost* 82. 3–44.

Kolyaseva, Alena & Kristin Davidse. 2018. A typology of lexical and grammaticalized uses of Russian *tip*. *Russian Linguistics* 42. 191–220.

Kruisinga, Etsko 1932. *A handbook of Present-day English*. 5th edition. Groningen: Noordhoff.

Langacker, Ronald. 1987. *Foundations of Cognitive Grammar. Vol. 1: Theoretical preliminaries*. Stanford: Stanford University Press.

Langacker, Ronald. 1991. *Foundations of Cognitive Grammar. Vol. 2: Descriptive application*. Stanford: Stanford University Press.

Langacker, Ronald. 2021. Functions and assemblies. In Kazuhiro Kodama & Tetsuharu Koyama, (eds.), *The forefront of Cognitive Linguistics*, 1–54. Tokyo: Hituzi Syobo.

Janebová, Markéta &, Michaela Martinková. 2017. NP-internal *kind of* and *sort of*: evidence from an English-Czech parallel translation corpus In Markéta Janebová, Ekaterina Lapshinova-Koltunski & Michaela Martinková (eds.), *Contrasting English and other languages through corpora*, 164–217. Newcastle: Cambridge Scholars Publishing.

Mackenzie, J. Lachlan. 1997. Grammar, discourse and knowledge: the use of *such*. In Jan Aarts, Inge de Mönnink, Herman Wekker (eds.) *Studies in English language and teaching. In honour of Flor Aarts*. Amsterdam: Rodopi, 85–105.

Martin, James 1980. *Text grammar*. Course notes. Linguistics Department. University of Sydney.

Odden, Oda Røste. 2018. Dynamics of the Scandinavian type nouns as renewal, reinforcement and analogy in determiner/proform-like systems. Paper presented at Workshop Pragmatic functions of type nouns: a crosslinguistic perspective. University of Tübingen, 18.6.2018 – 20.6.2018.

Odden, Oda Røste. 2019. *North Scandinavian type noun constructions: Patterns with slags, SORTs and TYP(E)*. Oslo: University of Oslo doctoral dissertation.

Oxford English Dictionary. 1933. Oxford: Oxford University Press. (www.oed.com)

Prince, Ellen. 1981. Towards a taxonomy of given–new information. In Peter Cole (ed.), *Radical Pragmatics*, 223–255. New York: Academic Press.

Philippa, Marlies, Frans Debrabandere, Arend Quak, Tanneke Schoonheim, & Nicoline van der Sijs. 2003–2009. *Etymologisch woordenboek van het Nederlands*. Amsterdam: Amsterdam University Press.

Rosier, Laurence. 2002. *Genre*: le nuancier de sa grammaticalisation. *Travaux de Linguistique* 44. 79–88.

Schermer-Vermeer, Ina. 2008. De *soort*-constructie: Een nieuw patroon in het Nederlands. *Nederlandse Taalkunde* 13. 2–33.

Sinclair, John. 1991. *Corpus, concordance, collocation*. New York: Oxford University Press.

Tabor, Whitey. 1993. The gradual development of degree modifier *sort of* and *kind of*: a corpus proximity model. In Katherine Beals, Gina Cooke, David Kathman, Karl-Erik McCullough, Sotar Kita & David Testen (eds.), *Papers from the 29th Regional Meeting of the Chicago Linguistics Society*, 451–465. Chicago: Chicago Linguistics Society.

Toft, Ellen H. 2009. *Adnominal and adverbal genitive constructions in Old Norse: a cognitive construction grammar account*. Oslo: University of Oslo doctoral dissertation.

Traugott, Elizabeth Closs & Richard Dasher. 2002. *Regularity in semantic change*. Cambridge: Cambridge University Press.

Van de Velde, Freek & Beatrice Lamiroy. 2017. External possessors in West Germanic and Romance: differential speed in the drift towards NP configurationality. In Hubert Cuyckens, Lobke Ghesquière & Daniel Van Olmen (eds.), *Aspects of grammaticalization: (Inter)subjectification, analogy and unidirectionality*, 353–399. Berlin: Mouton de Gruyter.

Voghera, Miriam. 2013. A case study on the relationship between grammatical change and synchronic variation: the emergence of *tipo*[–N] in Italian. In Anna Giacalone Ramat, Catarina Mauri Piera Molinelli (eds.), *Synchrony and diachrony. A dynamic interface*, 283–312. Amsterdam: Benjamins.

Kristin Davidse & Lieselotte Brems

3 English type noun-constructions with lexical functions: A new functional-structural typology

Abstract: This chapter addresses a number of gaps in the description of English binominal NPs with a type noun (TN) and a second noun (N2) with lexical functions. So far the literature has concentrated mainly on NPs with the surface order 'TN + N2', neglecting NPs which manifest as a surface string with reversed N2 – TN order. We thrash out a functional-structural account of all the nominal constructions with lexical functions featuring these two surface sequences. We do this within the framework of Langacker's cognitive construction grammar, which derives the meanings of constructions from the modification and complementation of heads at different levels of structural assembly. Semantically, the constructions are concerned with either *taxonomies* in the 'type' universe of interpretation or with the *characterization* of entities in terms of (sub)types. Grammatically, we argue, the fundamental contrast is between constructions to which either a *complementation* or a *modification* structure is central. The result is an extended and refined typology of English NP-constructions with lexical functions.

1 Introduction

The literature on English type noun (TN) constructions has so far concentrated on the different constructions thought to derive from one source structure, variously referred to as the binominal construction (Denison 2002), the referential con-

---

Acknowledgements: The research reported on in this article was made possible by the following research grants: (1) "Competition in emergent grammatical paradigms" (FSR-S-SH-CDR-19/09), awarded to Lieselotte Brems by the research council of the University of Liège, and (2) "The grammaticalization of constructions with taxonomic nouns in Polish and Russian" (C1-3H190236) granted by the research council of KU Leuven: primary investigator: Anna Kisiel, subsidiary investigator: Kristin Davidse, funded investigator: Alena Kolyaseva. We sincerely thank the two anonymous referees for their generous and insightful comments to the first draft. We are also endebted to Yuchan Li and An Van linden for their helpful feedback on central issues of this study.

Kristin Davidse, KU Leuven (University of Leuven), e-mail: kristin.davidse@kuleuven.be
Lieselotte Brems, Université de Liège, e-mail: lbrems@uliege.be

https://doi.org/10.1515/9783110701104-003

struction (Keizer 2007) or the TN/head construction (Davidse, Brems, and De Smedt 2008; Brems 2011), in which both the TN and the second noun (N2) are used in a full lexical sense. In (1) *pietra paesina* is categorized as *a rare type of marble*, i.e. as a specific subtype with its own character of a superordinate type. This is the 'taxonomic' lexical sense of TNs that is generally assumed to form the source of derived uses in constructions with grammatical functions.

(1) The late-17th century console has an elaborate top inlaid with agate and pietra paesina, **a rare type of marble**. (WB)[1]

(2) determiner (adjective/noun) TN + *of* + (adjective/noun) N

Initially approached from the perspective of processes of change such as grammaticalization, lexicalization or pragmaticalization (e.g. Aijmer 2002, Denison 2002), attention first went to TN-constructions involving decategorialization and functional shift of the TN. For nominal TN-constructions, this led Denison (2002)[2] to identify the qualifying construction (3) and complex determiner construction (4), assumed to have derived from the binominal construction illustrated in (1) via a shift in head status from TN to N2. In *some sort of plans* in (3), *some sort of* qualifies, or hedges, the category *plans*, which is the head noun of the NP. In *these sort of skills like [. . .] driving* in (4), *these sort of* functions as the complex determiner of the head noun *skills* and as a whole points forward into the discourse to a specific instance, viz. *driving*. The meaning of *these sort of* is akin to *such*. The number agreement between *these* and *skills*, rather than *sort*, is taken as a reflex of the latter's decategorialization.

(3) Lieutenant Colonel Gary Lydiate said: "We found arms, explosives and documents which appear to be **some sort of plans**." (WB)

(4) I don't associate you with [..] one of **these sort of skills** like [. . .] driving. (ICE-GB, quoted in Denison 2002: 3)

---

[1] Following each attested example its source is indicated between brackets by the Internet url or the abbreviation of the corpus, WordbanksOnline (WB), ICE-Great-Britain (ICE-GB), Oxford English Dictionary (OED), York-Toronto-Helsinki Parsed Corpus of Old English Prose (YCOE), Corpus of Late Modern English Texts (CLMETEV) and the Russian National Corpus (RNC).
[2] Denison (2002) acknowledged Keizer (p.c.) for the syntactic part of this analysis.

Denison (2002) also singled out the "semi-suffix" construction, in which TN-expressions like *type of* and *type* in (5), follow a premodifier of N2 as an affix-type marker.

(5) what you're saying is we need multiple **type of** I mean ideally we need a multiple **type** building [. . .] sorry a building with multiple **type** rooms. (ICE-GB, quoted in Denison 2002: 4)

In this chapter we address a number of gaps and remaining issues in the literature on nominal TN-constructions in English. The most glaring gap is that little or no attention has gone so far to constructions such as (6) and (7) which manifest as the surface string in (8) with reversed N2 – TN order in comparison with the TN – N2 string in (2).

(6) But the presence of lymphatic tissue may give rise to lymphoproliferative processes, namely **lymphoma of the non-Hodgkin type**. (The primary gastric lymphoma: definition (surgical-oncology.net))

(7) Damask was **a model of the plumper kind**. (WB)

(8) (determiner) (adjective/noun) N + *of* (determiner) (adjective/noun) TN

Work on TN-constructions in Romance languages (e.g. Mihatsch 2016; Voghera 2013) and Slavic languages (e.g. Kisiel and Kolyaseva this volume; Kolyaseva 2021) has been more comprehensive in this respect.

We will focus on 'lexical' constructions with TN – N2 and N2 – TN order, that is, constructions in which the TN contributes to conveying lexical functions. These functions are of two main types: *taxonomizing*, i.e. expressing relations between (sub- and super-)types, as in (1) and (6), and *characterization* of entities (Kolyaseva 2021: 7), as in (7). Of course, the description of TN-constructions with grammatical functions will also have to be extended to include not only the qualifying and complex determiner constructions with TN – N2 order in (3) and (4), but also those with N2 – TN order as in (9) and (10). These nominal, as well as extra-nominal, constructions with grammatical functions are considered in Davidse, Brems, and Van linden (this volume).

(9) There was **comfort of a sort**, perhaps, in that harsh image for the mustering forces of law and order . . . (WB)

(10) At the end of the day the Afrika Korps had lost a third of its tank strength and achieved **no tactical success of any kind**. (WB)

We will approach the lexical TN-constructions in terms of Langacker's (1987, 1991, 2021) cognitive construction grammar, which analyses constructions as the hierarchical integration of various component structures deriving their meanings from the modification and complementation of heads at different levels. Assuming such an approach to Russian TN-constructions, Kolyaseva and Davidse (2018) and Kolyaseva (2021) showed that the contrast between *complementation* and *modification* structures is central to their typology. We will argue that the contrast between complementation and modification is likewise central to English lexical TN-constructions.

The new typology we propose distinguishes complementation from modification constructions, and, within each, post- from precomplements and post- from premodifiers. In a *complementation* structure, the head is conceptually incomplete and needs to be completed by complements. *A rare type of marble* in (1) we analyse, like Keizer (2007) and contra Denison (2002) and Davidse et al (2008), as a *complementation* construction. Its relational head noun *type* needs to be complemented by a second noun specifying the superordinate it is a subtype of, viz. *marble*. The TN/head may also take a precomplement, like *sediment rock* in (11), which specifies the superordinate of the coordinated heads *types and sizes* (the latter being a relational noun similar to *type*s).

(11) Moraines, which include a broad mixture of **sediment rock types and sizes**, can also change the character of the exposed parts of the coastal region. (WB)

In a *modification* structure, the modifier is the relational element which inherently makes schematic reference to a head. In (6), the superordinate type denoted by N2, *lymphoma*, is construed as the head, which is narrowed down to a specific subtype by the postmodifier with TN *of the non-Hodgkin type*. The N2/head may also take a premodifier with TN, like *non-Hodgkin type* in (12).

(12) AIDS-related lymphoma is typically **a non-Hodgkin type lymphoma**. (AIDS-Related Lymphoma Treatment, Symptoms & Survival Rate (emedicinehealth.com)

The genre of the love story in (13), finally, is an appositional construction, which has been largely overlooked in the literature on English TNs so far, together with its alternate with reversed word order in (14), *the horror film genre*.

(13) Chaucer keeps forcing us to deal with different values and perspectives. **The genre of the love story**, for instance, is never certain. Are we to read it as though it were courtly romance, history, tragedy or moral allegory? (WB)

(14) How dare you be so disrespectful to the man who basically invented **the horror film genre**? (WB)

We analyse these two constructions as TN/head + complement constructions, with (13) featuring a postcomplement and (14) a precomplement. Structurally, they are very similar to the TN/head–N2/complement-constructions construing a superordinate relation, illustrated in (1) *a rare type of rock* and (11) *sediment rock types*. However, as we will see, the appositional semantics impose more restrictions on the fillers of the elements of structure than the superordinate semantics.

Our focus will be on grammatical-semantic analysis per se. Assuming the theoretical position that grammatical structure codes semantic structure in a natural, language-specific way (e.g. Bolinger 1968, 1977; Halliday 1967a, 1994; Langacker 1987, 1991, 2021) (Section 2), we offer a close analysis of the distinct semantics coded by the different structural assemblies. In this way, we lay out the grammatical and semantic recognition criteria – the two always go together – that can be used to distinguish construction types. We discuss the construction types in the following order:
- TN/head constructions with postcomplements (Section 3),
- TN/head constructions with precomplements (Section 4),
- TN/postmodifying constructions (Section 5)
- TN/premodifying constructions (Section 6)
- TN/appositional constructions (Section 7).

In Section 8, we consider the relevance of the new typology for lexical TN-constructions to synchronic variation and diachronic trajectories in English and comparison across language families such as the Germanic, Romance and Slavic languages.

2 Theoretical premises and analytical constructs

Theoretically, we situate ourselves in the cognitive-functional tradition with a shared commitment to the tenet that grammatical structure codes semantic structure in a natural, language-specific way (e.g. Hjelmslev [1943]1961; Bolinger 1968, 1977; Halliday 1967a, 1994, and Matthiessen 2004; Langacker 1987, 1991, 2015, 2021;

McGregor 1997). Langacker's cognitive construction grammar is of particular relevance to this study both with regard to theory and constructs for analysis of the NP.

Langacker (1987: 1) rejects the conception of "syntax as an autonomous formal system" and the pursuit of meaning with "apparatus derived from formal logic". Rather, he (Langacker 1987: 3) argues, grammar is symbolic in nature and exists to symbolize semantic structure. Under grammar, he understands the continuum of symbolic structures formed by the lexicon, morphology and syntax, for which Halliday (1985: xiv) coined the term "lexicogrammar". The lexicogrammar can be approached from its two sides: "structures . . . and functions . . . are not distinct but represent alternate perspectives on the same assemblies". One can seek to identify which functions are symbolized by a grammatical structure like the NP (Langacker 1991: 148). At the same time, "[a] full structural description – characterizing the elements and connections at multiple levels – is also a functional description" (Langacker 2021: 9).

For functional-structural analysis, we adhere to Langacker's (1987, 1991, 2021) theory of how elements are combined into structures. Clauses and phrases, and their combinations, involve composite structures, some of whose components are transparently assembled, whilst others are "only partially discernible (or even indiscernible) within the composite whole" (Langacker 1999: 152). This latter caveat allows for certain functions to be *not* separately symbolized, such as the definiteness of NPs coded by proper names (Langacker 1991: 148), but canonical structural assemblies are assumed to code semantic structure compositionally. Structural analysis is concerned with "the order in which component structures are successively combined to form progressively more elaborate composite structures" (Langacker 1987: 310). The order of assembly that analysts have to identify is the one that accounts best for the semantics of the structure, as conceptual dependencies between elements are "largely responsible, in the final analysis, for their combinatory behaviour" (Langacker 1987: 306). The notion of the 'behaviour' of component structures refers in the first place to the specific way in which they are integrated into the overall structure. Secondly, we use the notion of 'grammatical behaviour' (Levin 1993: 1–3) to refer to the possible and impossible alternations of constructions, which are revealing of their structural integration and of the semantics they code (Gleason 1966; Halliday 1968; Davidse 1998).[3]

---

[3] If we use the term "construction" in this study, we do so with reference to the long cognitive-functional tradition (see e.g. Halliday 1968: 195, 210; Langacker 2009, 2021), not with reference to the Goldberg tradition. We do not subscribe to the idea that we can only speak of a construction if its meaning is more than the sum of its parts (Goldberg 1995), since retracted in Goldberg (2006), but still commonly invoked. This idea overlooks the crucial point that grammatical meaning resides in the different *relations* between its 'parts', which are not simple rela-

3 English type noun-constructions with lexical functions — 101

Structural assembly in NP and clause hinges on two types of dependency structures: head-modifier and head-complement (Langacker 1987: 277f). While with both, the head determines the semantic profile of the whole structure, the head of a modification structure is conceptually autonomous, whereas the head of a complementation structure is conceptually incomplete.

In the NP, combinations such as *electric trains* and *old trains* are widely accepted to be examples of modifier-head structures, which provide semantic specifications for the representation of the entity-type denoted by the head noun. A noun like *train* is conceptually autonomous as it suffices to conceive of the entity-type in question (Langacker 1987: 235–236). Adjectives like *electric* and *old* are semantically dependent. They cannot be conceptualized as such, but only as features of entities, such as 'trains powered by electricity' or 'trains built a long time ago'. This relationship of semantic composition, in which relational features are added to the entity, motivates the modifier-head dependency structure. Following the convention used by Hudson (1984) and McGregor (1997), modifier head relations can be represented by an arrow arc pointing from modifier (M) to head H), as illustrated for *old trains* in Figure 1.

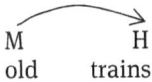

M   H
old   trains

Figure 1: Modifier-head structure of *old trains*.

In the clause, the verb-argument structure is interpreted as a complementation structure by Langacker (1987: 277f). The clausal head is the verb, e.g. *hit* in (15), which determines the semantic profile of a clause as the representation of a process.

(15) The vicar hit the burglar in the hallway.

---

tions of juxtaposition or addition, but involve the hierarchical integration of various component structures deriving their meanings from the modification and complementation of heads at different levels. Neither do we subscribe to the idea that semantic generalizations should be based on surface features of syntagms and that no relevant information can be got from alternations (Goldberg 2002). This idea was critiqued in Davidse (2011) and Perek (2012), and retracted in Perek and Goldberg (2017). We hold that an in-depth characterization of different constructions has to consider their possible and impossible alternates, which may reveal differences in their structural assembly and make aspects of their different semantics explicit.

A verb is conceptually incomplete, as one cannot conceive of the meaning of *hit* without mentally picturing someone hitting and someone or something being hit. Verbs are traditionally viewed as having 'valence', in the sense of determining all their possible case frames. According to Langacker (1987: 304), valence relations are motivated by semantic correspondences between schematic aspects of meaning present in the valence head and the more specific semantic profile of the elements that enter into a valence relation with it. It is in this sense that *hit* in (15) is the complement-taking head which contains schematic semantic substructures which are elaborated by the nominal complements designating the agent and patient in the process. Prepositions, which designate atemporal relations, are likewise conceptually dependent heads, which require NP complements (Langacker 1987: 300ff). The internal structure of a prepositional phrase such as in (15) is motivated by the valence relation between relational *in* and *the hallway*, with the whole structure designating a stative relation (Langacker 1987: 300f). Externally, the preposition phrase functions as a circumstantial modifier (M) of the whole clause nucleus, which is its head (H), as visualized in the top row of Figure 2. In the middle row, the dependency relations within these two units are visualized, which are, head (H) – complement (C) relations. The arrows go from dependent to head.

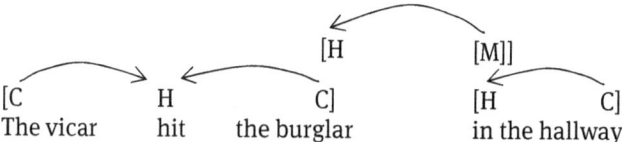

```
                           [H           [M]]
[C         H         C]    [H           C]
The vicar  hit   the burglar  in the hallway
```

Figure 2: Head–complement structures in *The vicar hit the burglar in the hallway*.

Head nouns designating entity-types are typical examples of conceptually autonomous heads and verbal clausal heads of conceptually dependent heads. However, some types of nouns are conceptually dependent, with deverbal nouns as the most obvious example. For instance, *belief* in (16) has valence and makes schematic reference to something believed in, which is provided by the proposition *that there was a God who had made all things to a certain design*. Complex NPs of this type feature a complementation relation between the head *belief* and its propositional complement (Davidse 2018).

(16) the belief that there was a God who had made all things to a certain design (WB)

Lexically used TNs like *sort, kind, type, genre,* etc. are not conceptually autonomous either. They are inherently relational, as they designate, in terms of Sinclair et al's (1987: 1391) gloss of *sort*, a "class of things that have particular features in common and that belong to a larger group of related things". This makes TNs fit to function as the conceptually dependent element in both complementation and modification, i.e. as the head of a complementation structure and as the modifier of a modification structure. In (1) *a rare type of marble*, we find the relational 'subtype' meaning of *type* construed as the head. This meaning cannot be conceived of on its own but needs to be completed by the supertype it is a subtype *of* (p.c. Alena Kolyaseva). This is the conceptual substrate of a complementation relation. In (6) *lymphoma of the non-Hodgkin type*, *type* with its relational 'subtype' meaning is part of the postmodifier subcategorizing the supertype head. In examples like (13) *the genre of the love story*, the meaning 'type characterized by distinctive features' of the TN *genre* is foregrounded. This is also a relational meaning, which is elaborated by the complement *of the love story*.

We will show that a fine-grained typology of taxonomizing and characterizing TN-constructions in English can be arrived at by a precise analysis of
(i) their structural assembly, i.e. their *internal* grammar;
(ii) the clause functions they can occur in, i.e. their *external* grammar;
(iii) their meanings and referential types.

It is in terms of these three dimensions that we propose an argued account, whose grammatical and semantic components have been developed on the basis of extensive qualitative corpus consultation. This broad data consultation is reflected in the extension of the typically considered set of *sort, kind, type* to other TNs like *genre, species, variety,* etc. The functional-structural types that we distinguish are argued for and characterized in the following sections: TN/head constructions with postcomplements (Section 3), TN/head constructions with precomplements (Section 4), TN/postmodifying constructions (Section 5), TN/premodifying constructions (Section 6), TN/appositional constructions (Section 7).

3 The TN/head + postcomplement construction

We start drawing up our typology with the construction-type that is generally viewed as the most prototypical *taxonomizing* construction. This construction denotes *(a) subtype(s)*, designated by the TN/head, *of a superordinate type*, described by the postcomplement containing N2.

(17) The Royal Fruit Company produces **two types of fruit drinks. The first type** is 25% pure fruit juice, and **the second type** is 75% pure fruit juice. (Placeholder | Royal Fruit Company)

(18) Pop is **the favourite type of recorded music** followed by rock. (WB)

(19) Our sun is **a type of star called a yellow dwarf.** (https://www.universetoday.com/16350/what-kind-of-star-is-the-sun/)

(20) Rocks are broadly classified into **three groups – igneous, sedimentary and metamorphic types of rock** (Rock (geology) – Wikipedia)

(21) **Anthropological types of Corded Ware and Yamna cultures.** [. . .] The corded Ware culture includes about **twenty variants.** (Dienekes' Anthropology Blog: Anthropological types of Corded Ware and Yamna cultures)

(22) The Latin name of the oil concerned should be noted, together with **the variety or chemotype which contains the constituent chemical(s) responsible for any hazard,** as **some varieties or chemotypes of the same species,** or from a different part of the plant, may be innocent. (WB)

3.1 Functional-structural assembly

3.1.1 The complementation relation between TN/head and postcomplement

We approach the TN/head + postcomplement construction with the aim of analysing the progressive assembly of its component structures in a way that accounts for how they are semantically computed. As with all NPs with common noun heads, the last layer of structural integration is formed by the determiner scoping over the rest of the assembled structure (Langacker 2002: 9–13). By his/her choice of determiner, the speaker assigns the 'cognitive status' to the referent that will allow the hearer to track that referent in the discourse (Gundel et al. 1993). In TN/head constructions, the determiner agrees with the singular or plural TN/head. All determiner types associated with count nouns can occur, a sample of which is illustrated in (17)–(22). To the representation built up by the rest of the NP, the complementation relation between the TN/head and the *of*-modifier is central. The postcomplement often contains just a noun, like *of rock* in (20), but it can also be a full NP with its own determiner, as in *some varieties or chemotypes of the same species* in (22). The basic structure of the TN/head construction can thus be represented as in (23).[4]

(23) [determiner [TN$_{head}$ [*of* + N/NP]$_{complement}$]]

The superordinate type may be designated by an overt postcomplement, but may also be retrievable, because presupposed, from the preceding discourse (Halliday 1967a: 206). By the very relational nature of their meaning, *the first type* and *second type* in (17) give instructions to retrieve the superordinate from the preceding text, i.e. 'the first/second type <u>of fruit drinks</u>'. Likewise, *three groups* in (20) refers to 'three groups <u>of rock</u>', and *the variety or chemotype which contains the constituent chemicals responsible for any hazard* in (22) refers to 'the variety or chemotype <u>of the oil concerned</u> which contains the constituent chemicals responsible for any hazard'.

The head is selected from the lexical set of nouns which have 'subtype' among their senses such as *kind, type* (17), *sort, species, group* (20), *variety* (22), *chemotype* (22), etc. The postcomplement contains either a noun or a NP, which have different referents (Langacker 1991). Whereas a common noun merely designates an entity-*type*, an *instance* of such a type can only be depicted by a full NP with a determiner that situates the designated instance vis-à-vis the speech event. Langacker (1991: 77–81) further clarifies the conceptual distinctions between uncount and count nouns, and within the latter, singular and plural (Langacker 1991: 77–81). A singular count noun such as *pebble* designates a type of 'discrete entity'. By contrast, the designatum of plural count nouns and uncount nouns can be generalized over as a 'mass'. The mass depicted by a plural count noun like *pebbles* conceptually involves replication of instances of a discrete entity-type, and is therefore a heterogeneous mass. The mass designated by a mass noun, e.g. *gravel*, is represented as homogeneous, i.e. a mass whose internal uniformity is highlighted. Common nouns are mostly used as heads of NPs, which refer to instances, as in *their dog, the late queen of England*. Their pure type meaning, Langacker (1991: 69–75) notes, is found in only some specific grammatical environments, such as compounds like *dog lover*, where *dog* designates the type, not a specific dog, and in a small subclass of predicate nominatives in English such as *Elizabeth Windsor became queen of England in 1952*, where *queen of England* likewise designates the pure type, not an individual. We point out that the postcomplements of TN/head-constructions are also a natural grammatical environment

---

4 This is a correction of the structure we posited in Davidse, Brems and De Smedt (2008: 144), [determiner [TN$_{head}$ [*of* + N]$_{postmodifier}$]].

for the pure type meaning: the TN/head's meaning of 'subtype' inherently needs to be elaborated by a supertype, for which a noun naming the pure entity-type is the unmarked option. If N2 is a count noun, it often allows the choice between singular or plural, as illustrated in (24) and (25). In (24), the supertype is evoked by the singular noun *comedian* in terms of one discrete entity type, in (25) the supertype is construed by *comedians* as a mass of replicated discrete entity-types.

(24) There's **two sorts of comedian** – ones who are alcoholics, and ones who used to be alcoholics. (Lunch with Ross Noble (smh.com.au)

(25) There are **many different kinds of comedians** . . . the observational humorist, the impressionist, the character creator, the physical comedian, the self-deprecator, the dirty-joke teller. (http://www.quotehd.com/quotes/damon-wayans)

In *types of rock* in (20) the supertype is construed as a homogeneous mass.

How is the supertype construed by a full NP? This NP always contains a definite determiner followed by a count noun. Typically, the hearer is instructed to retrieve the supertype from the preceding discourse, as in (22), where *of the same species* refers back anaphorically to *the oil concerned*. In (26) *of the same enzyme* refers to one and the same supertype of many subtypes operating at different temperatures.

(26) The difference from head to tail was an astonishing 60 degrees C. . . . Enzymes and proteins are generally adapted to operate at a set temperature. But this animal is essentially operating over a broad range. Either it has **many types of the same enzyme which can operate at different temperatures**, or it has enzymes that work over a broad range of temperatures. (WB)

3.1.2 Modifiers in the TN/head + postcomplement construction

Functional-structural analysis of TN/head-constructions often requires us to account for modification structures at various levels of the whole construction. By way of premodifiers in ordinary NPs, two different types are traditionally distinguished: classifiers and epithets (Halliday 1994). Classifying modifiers express semantic components that contribute to the conception of the entity-*type*. They typically "restrict the denotative scope" of the head noun (Adamson 2000: 57), as in *electric trains* versus *steam trains*, where the classifiers carve out different subtypes. However, classifiers may also be non-restrictive as in *demographic types of families* versus *psychological types of families*, where the classifiers indicate different principles for comprehensive classification of all families (p.c. Kolyaseva). Epithet modifiers ascribe a property to the *instance* referred to by the whole NP. These properties are inherently located on scales, either closed or open (Kennedy and McNally 2005), and can be graded accordingly, as in *a very fast train*. They too are typically restrictive but may also be non-restrictive. For instance, if a speaker talks about *old trains* versus *new trains* different sets of instances are involved. But epithets may also apply non-restrictively, for instance in specific types of definite NPs like *the modern genre of metal* core, where there is no contrast with 'an older genre of metalcore'. Regarding the order of assembly, classifying modifiers integrate first with the head, while epithet modifiers integrate with the whole type designation-part, as reflected in the word order, e.g. *a very fast*$_{epithet}$ *[electric*$_{classifier}$ *train*$_{head}$*]*.

In the TN/head constructions considered in this section, N2 may be premodified, typically by a classifier, like *recorded* in (18), which narrows down the superordinate type 'music' into *recorded music*. Adjectives preceding the TN can be classifiers or epithets, and often modify the whole head + postcomplement unit, like the epithet *favourite* does with *type of recorded music* in (18). Semantically, the adjective delineates the 'favourite' subtype of *recorded music*, in implied opposition to 'less favourite' subtypes. The resulting representation *favourite type of recorded music* is scoped over by determiner *the*. The structural analysis of the whole construction is visualized with square brackets and subscripts indicating the functions in (27).

(27) [the$_{determiner}$ [favourite$_{premodifier}$ [type$_{head}$ [of [recorded$_{premodifier}$ music$_{head}$]$_{prepositional\ complement}$]]$_{postcomplement}$]]

In (20), *igneous, sedimentary and metamorphic types of rock*, the three classifying adjectives together offer an exhaustive subclassification of the type *rock*. Classifying adjectives preceding the TN may also modify the TN only, when they name the principle of classification (p.c. Alena Kolyaseva), as *anthropological* does in (21). Semantically, the relation between *anthropological* and *types* is not one of subclassification but of appositional categorization. In such cases, the *of*-complement has the unit of classifier + TN, *anthropological types*, as its head, as visualized by the structural assembly in (28).

(28) [Ø$_{determiner}$ [[anthropological$_{premodifier}$ types$_{head}$]$_{head}$ [of [[Corded Ware and Yanna]$_{premodifier}$ cultures$_{head}$]$_{prepositional\ complement}$]$_{postcomplement}$]

This close integration of classifier and TN may be signalled by a hyphen, as in *chemical-type* in (29), or it may be realized morphologically by compounding, as in *chemotypes* in (22).

(29) Study on morphological classification and **chemical-type of Perilla frutescens cultivated germplasm**. ([Study on morphological classification and chemical-type of Perilla frutescens cultivated germplasm] – PubMed (nih.gov)

The final issue we consider is the different ways in which NP-internal relative clauses (RCs) and other NP-internal postmodifiers may be integrated into the TN/head + *of*-complement construction. NP-internal relative clauses modify the nominal head, and this composite structure is then scoped over by the determiner (Langacker 1991: 430–432). Semantically, such relative clauses characterize the entity by its role in a clausal process (Langacker 1991: 430–435). In TN/head + *of*-complement constructions, relative clauses may be appositional to or narrow down the whole unit comprising the TN + *of*-complement unit. The first possibility is illustrated by *a type of star called a yellow dwarf* in (19). The participial postmodifier *called a yellow dwarf* is appositional to type of *star*. The appositional complementation relation is discussed in more detail in Section 7. The structural analysis of the whole NP is given in (30).

(30) [a $_{determiner}$ [[type $_{head}$ [of star]$_{complement}$]$_{antecedent}$ [called a yellow dwarf]$_{RC-postmod}$]]

The case of a restrictive relative clause narrowing down head/TN + *of*-complement is illustrated in (22), *the variety or chemotype which contains the constituent chemical(s) responsible for any hazard*. In this example, N2 of the complement is not expressed overtly. As argued in Section 3.1.1, the conceptually incomplete TN/head *variety or chemotype* gives instructions to retrieve the complement, the supertype, from the preceding discourse. The context in (22) is concerned with a step-by-step classification of oils, in which *the Latin name of the oil concerned should be noted*, together with noxious and innocent subtypes of each oil. The antecedent of the RRC is thus formed by the unit *variety or chemotype (of the oil concerned)*, to which the complementation relation is internal. This unit as a whole is subcategorized by *which contains the constituent chemicals responsible for any hazard*. The structural analysis of this TN/head + *of*-complement-construction is given in (31).

(31) [the_determiner [[variety or chemotype_head (of the oil concerned)_complement]_antecedent [which contains the constituent chemical(s) responsible for any hazard]_RRC postmod]]

3.2 Referential types

The reference of TN/head-postcomplement constructions is constructed by the combination of the determiner and the type noun that forms the head. This entails that the referents are intrinsically situated in what Langacker (1991: 71) calls the "type" universe of interpretation. The reference is not to concrete instances in the spatio-temporal universe of interpretation. The type universe is structured by multiple 'superordination' taxonomies of supertypes and subtypes involving different principles of classification. Rocks, for instance, can be classified in terms of their composition as igneous, sedimentary and metamorphic, as in (20) above, or in terms of mode of occurrence, which distinguishes for instance venous from eruptive rock. The relation from supertype to subtype is characterized by progressive semantic specification (Langacker 1991: 61). The subtypes have all the features of the supertype, to which finer specifications are added. The referents of TN/head-postcomplement constructions thus involve clusters of subcategorizing features, represented as entities in type space. The examples in (17)-(22) illustrate some of the fields that can be interpreted as type universes: commerce with its product-types in (17), and various scientific fields of interpretation in (18)–(22). More subjective ad hoc subclassifications, as of the types of comedians in (24) and (25), can just as well be construed by TN/head-postcomplement constructions.

There seem to be few restrictions on the external grammar of these constructions. They may occur in any of the nominal clause functions such as:
- subject, e.g. *the first type* and *the second type* in (17),
- direct object complement, e.g. *The Royal Fruit Company produces two types of fruit drinks* in (17),
- predicative complement, in either predicative copulars, e.g. *Our sun is a type of star called a yellow dwarf* in (19), or in specificational copulars, e.g. *Pop is the favourite type of recorded music followed by rock* in (18).

Interacting with these different external functions and specific types of discourse, TN/head-postcomplement-NPs can realize three different types of reference, which all involve their 'type'-reference: generic reference, dual reference and non-referential predicate nominatives. The latter are found in contexts of primary and secondary predication.[5] We discuss each type below.

Firstly, TN/head-postcomplement-NPs can be used to refer to 'subtypes-of-a-supertype' *as such* in taxonomizing contexts, as in (20) *Rocks are broadly classified into three groups – igneous, sedimentary and metamorphic types of rock*. We can view this as a case of generic reference. If established taxonomies are involved such as product-types and scientific taxonomies, then alternates with simple NPs without TN/head are possible, as in (17)' and (20)'. In these alternates, the 'subkind' meaning (Carlson 1978: 204–216; Carlson and Pelletier 1995: 74–77) of singular and plural count nouns is activated, which, in (20)', involves the mass noun *rock* being converted into a count noun to designate the subkind meaning (Lumsden 1988: Ch. 4; Langacker 1991: 30–31).

(17)' The Royal Fruit Company produces **two fruit drinks**.

(20)' Rocks are broadly classified into three groups – **igneous, sedimentary and metamorphic rocks**.

With ad hoc taxonomies, the subkind meaning of the count noun is less easily activated, as illustrated by the non-equivalence between (24) *There's two sorts of comedian* and *There's two comedians*.

Secondly, TN/head-postcomplement constructions can – fairly marginally – be used with what Ward and Birner (1995: 732) have called *dual reference*, i.e. overt reference to a generalization coupled to pragmatically implied reference to instances of that generalization. In (32), the advice is to investigate specific spatio-temporal instances of *types of work not considered before*, i.e. specific jobs. The uncount noun *work* does not allow conversion into a count noun to express a 'subkind' meaning without explicit TN, **works which he may not have fully considered before*.

(32) If he is seeking work or wants to change his present job, he would do well to investigate **types of work which he may not have fully considered before**. (WB)

---

[5] This is a correction of our earlier claim in Davidse, Brems and De Smedt (2008) that TN/head-constructions always have generic reference.

Thirdly and finally, NPs with TN/head and *of*-complement can be used as *non-referential* predicative complements. Predicative complements are generally accepted to be 'non-referential' (e.g. Kuno 1970; Declerck 1988), i.e. they do not pick out a specific individual or thing the speaker is talking about. It is also generally accepted that they have a categorizing meaning, categorizing the subject entity as a member of a class. Langacker (1991: 68) glosses the meaning of the copular with simple predicative NP in (33) as 'Alice is "an arbitrary member of the *thief* category" (*Ibid.*)', i.e. Alice can be categorized as 'an' instance of the type *thief*. He (Langacker 1991: 67) points out that the instance meaning of the full NP *a thief* is "conjured up [...] solely for purposes of making a type attribution, and has no status outside the confines of this predicate nominative construction" (Langacker 1991: 67).

(33) Alice is a thief. (Langacker 1991: 67)

This analysis can be straightforwardly extended to examples with a TN/head construction like (19) *Our sun is a type of star called a yellow dwarf*, in which a subject with specific reference, *our sun*, is categorized *as an instance of the category* 'star called a yellow dwarf'. Unlike with simple predicative copulars like (33), the 'category' meaning is explicitly expressed by the TN in (19). Examples like (19) systematically alternate with a copular clause with simple predicate nominative (19)' *Our sun is a star called a yellow dwarf*. NPs with TN/head and *of*-complement can also be predicated of subjects with generic reference, like *juice-only diets* in (34).

(34) Juice-only diets are **a type of detox programme suitable for one or two days only**. (WB)

Juice-only diets is what Carlson (1978) has called a "bare" generic plural NP, i.e. a NP without any determiner. There is 'nothing' in either form or meaning in the determiner slot. This analysis goes against the oft-made claim that generic reference is equivalent to universal quantification. Carlson (1978: 28–29) showed this claim to be untenable in view of generic examples like *Koalas/*All koalas are widespread in Australia*. He (Carlson 1978: 33, 196, 2005) argued that generic NPs are truly 'bare' and have no determiner, which he correlated with them not designating a finite set of individuals. Put in terms of Langacker's approach to the NP, Davidse (1999a, 2004) has argued that generic NPs lack the instantiation function associated with determiners. Their type specifications give mental access to the generic class *as such*.

We conclude that the reference to type meaning of TN/head + *of*-complement NPs is central to the three types of reference they can convey: generic reference, dual reference and non-referential predicate nominatives.

4 The TN/head + precomplement construction

In the previous section we looked at the construction in which the 'subtype' meaning of the TN/head is completed by the supertype in the following *of*-complement, e.g. *a species of mineral* in (35). The conceptually incomplete TN/head may also be *preceded* by a 'precomplement' supplying the supertype, as in *a rock type* in (35). Because of their shared head-complement relation, the two constructions share many structural and semantic features. Hence, this section on TN/head-precomplement constructions, illustrated in (35)–(39), can presuppose many aspects of the description from the previous section and focus on the features specific to this construction.

(35) The definition of **a rock type** is generally looser than that of **a species of mineral**. (WB)

(36) Moraines, which include a broad mixture of **sediment rock types and sizes,** can also change the character of the exposed parts of the coastal region

(37) this winter will see a higher than average frequency of **northerly weather types** (WB)

(38) His bone marrow turned out to be a 100 per cent match for **Nick's rare tissue type.** (WB)

(39) Prune in late spring. . . . **Late-flowering or good evergreen foliage types** are mentioned here. (WB)

4.1 Functional-structural assembly

The main difference with the construction with *of*-complements, is that the precomplement can only contain a noun, not a NP. The supertype can thus not be anaphorically linked to earlier mentions. The basic structure of a TN/head + precomplement construction, e.g. *a rock type*, can be represented as in (40).

(40) [determiner [N2$_{precomplement}$TN$_{head}$]]

The modification patterns at lower and higher levels than the central complementation relation are partly parallel to those found in the *of*-complement constructions. The N2 expressing the supertype in the precomplement may take classifying modifiers, like *sediment rock* in (36) and *northerly weather* in (37). In (36) the precomplement *sediment rock* specifies the superordinate of the coordinated heads *types and sizes* (the latter being a relational noun similar to *types*). The structural analysis of this construction is given in (41).

(41) [Ø$_{determiner}$[[sediment$_{premod}$ rock$_{head}$]$_{precomplement}$ types and sizes$_{head}$]]

The whole unit of precomplement + TN/head may also take premodifiers, either epithets, like *rare* in (38) and *good* in (39), or classifiers like *late-flowering* and *ever-green* in (39). Restrictive relative clauses and other NP-internal postmodifiers may modify the whole precomplement + TN/head unit, as illustrated in (42), whose structural analysis is given in (43).

(42) The main volcanoes, then, are separately connected to the deep underworld. Yet to the casual eye **the rock-type making up the lavas** looks extremely similar. (WB).

(43) [the$_{determiner}$ [[rock$_{premodifier}$ types$_{head}$]$_{head}$ [making up the lavas]$_{postmodifier}$]]

Alternates without TN seem less often possible with precomplement constructions than with postcomplement constructions, as shown in (37)', (39)' and (42)'. This grammatical environment seems less conducive to triggering the 'subkind' meaning of count nouns.

(37)' ? this winter will see a higher than average frequency of northerly weathers.

(39)' ? Prune in late spring. Late-flowering or good evergreen foliages are mentioned here

(42)' ?To the casual eye the rocks making up the lavas look extremely similar.

4.2 Referential types

Like the constructions with postcomplement, those with precomplement can occur in any of the nominal clause functions like subject, e.g. (39) and (42), and predicative complement, e.g. (44).

(44) The Bndnerschiefer are known to be the time equivalents of the massive limestone cliffs of Malm that we passed in the cable car above Flims. They are **an utterly different rock type**. (WB)

Due to their compressed form, they occur frequently as part of NPs whose heads are nominalizations of lexical predicators, as in *a broad mixture of sediment rock types and sizes* (36), *a higher than average frequency of northerly weather types* (37).

They can convey the same three referential statuses as the constructions with *of*-complement: generic, dual reference to type and implied instances, and the non-referential status associated with predicative complements. Generic reference is often conveyed by the bare generic plural of the TN/head, as in (39), *Prune in late spring. Late-flowering or good evergreen foliage types are mentioned here*. The subject refers here to the classes as such: it is these types, not some instances of them, that should be pruned in late spring. Dual reference is illustrated in (37) *this winter will see a higher than average frequency of northerly weather types*, in which reference is made to future but individual temporally-located instances of *northerly weather types*. Non-referential predicative reference is illustrated in (44).

5 TN/postmodifier construction

Section 5 deals with constructions in which N2 designating the superordinate is the head, which is elaborated by a postmodifier comprising *of* + NP, which itself contains a premodified TN, as illustrated in (45)–(51).

(45) But the presence of lymphatic tissue may give rise to lymphoproliferative processes, namely **lymphoma of the non-Hodgkin type**. (The primary gastric lymphoma: definition (surgical-oncology.net)

(46) Muscles involved: Mid and lower back Erector spinae (including Longissimus dorsi). These are **deep spinal supporting muscles of the postural type**. (WB)

(47) Alexander Pope wrote, when his friend Johnson had been rejected as a schoolmaster, "He has **an infirmity of the convulsive kind** . . . so as to make him a sad spectacle. (WB)

(48) Timberlake showed off **some intricate dance moves of the pop-and-lock kind that suited his musical style.** (WB)

(49) Take a brilliant half-price Sun breakaway at a Butlins Family Entertainment Resort and you're sure to see **stars of the showbiz kind.** (WB)

(50) Olivia's concern was to present the Fellowship in a way that would be agreeable to a person that could read and write properly. And not come out with **pseudo-science of a dippy sort**, taking any psychic messages as being true – you know, everything I say is true, which is nonsense. (WB)

(51) Damask was **a model of the plumper kind,** though thin enough by ordinary standards. (WB)

5.1 Functional-structural assembly

5.1.1 The modification relation

In the construction with postmodifier, e.g. *an infirmity of the convulsive kind* in (46), the lexical head noun, *infirmity*, takes an *of*-postmodifier with a NP whose head is a TN, which itself is modified by *convulsive*. The postmodifier always contains a full NP with a determiner; it cannot be a mere noun with its pure type meaning, as shown by the impossibility of **an infirmity of convulsive kind*. The construction is hence a complex NP, involving a combination of NPs. This structure can be represented as in (52).

(52) [determiner [N2$_{head}$ [*of* + [determiner [adjective/noun$_{premodifier}$ TN$_{head}$]] NP]$_{postmodifier}$]]

The modification relation between the supertype/head and the postmodifier with subtype TN is central to this construction. Semantically, this sequence involves moving down the superordination cline, from super- to subtype, as in (45) *lymphoma of the non-Hodgkin type*. In this respect, it contrasts with the TN/head–*of*-complement construction, e.g. (1) *a rare type of marble*, in which the head designates the subtype and the postcomplement the supertype, i.e. a sequence moving up the superordination cline, from subordinate to superordinate. Distinguishing the two sequences of taxonomizing requires close analysis in context. For instance, an example like *some varieties or chemotypes of the same species* in (22) is tricky because it features two TNs, which is not surprising as the two nouns describe types. The sequence in (22) is from subtype (head) to supertype (complement).

5.1.2 Modifiers at other levels

We now turn to the various other modification relations found in the postmodifier/TN-construction. The postmodifying NP has to add information to the TN to designate the subtype. This information may be provided by a lexical modifier of the TN, as in *of the non-Hodgkin type* (45), but it may also have to be retrieved discursively, as in (53), in which the complex determiner *another* gives instructions to think of a subtype different from the earlier mentioned *solar radiation*.

(53) It became clear that most of the energy that manifests itself on the Earth is ultimately derived from solar radiation [. . .]. But what is the origin of that solar energy? It could in principle be transformed from **energy of another type**. (WB)

The lexical modifiers of the TN are typically premodifiers, which in a number of cases can be analysed as either classifiers, e.g. *of the non-Hodgkin type* (45), or epithets, e.g. *of the plumper kind* (51). However, this distinction may collapse if the premodifier is a nonce expression, like *trial-of-strength*, in (54), which evokes specific subtypes of games as well as gradable qualities like 'competitive'.

(54) the outdoor games were mostly **macho affairs of the trial-of-strength kind** (WB)

The relation between the premodifier and the TN may be either non-restrictive or restrictive, or vague between the two. In *of the non-Hodgkin type* in (45), the classifier *non-Hodgkin* names *the type*, and is in this sense appositional (Kolyaseva 2021: 7) or non-restrictive. Of course, the whole postmodifier *of the non-Hodgkin type* is restrictive and carves out a subtype of the head *lymphoma*. In *of the trial-of-strength kind* in (54), the expression *trial-of-strength* also seems appositional to *kind*, setting up a unique type specific to the context (Li 2022). On the other hand, within the NP in *of a dippy sort* in (50), *dippy* is a restrictive qualitative modifier of *sort*.

The TN in the postcomplement may also take postdependents, as illustrated in (55) and (56), which may be restrictive or appositional. In (55), *of the kind that humans called Hish* designates a subtype narrowing down the Free Magic Elements referred to (see Section 3.1.2). The relation between *the genus* and *Homo sapiens* in (56) is appositional.[6]

(55) **Free Magic Elements of the kind that humans called Hish** (WB).

(56) They both belonged to **the female sex of the genus Homo sapiens**. (WB)

The lexicogrammatical template of the *of*-postmodifier with TN offers ample scope for pragmatic effects like hedging, humor, irony, etc. In (49), *stars of the showbiz kind*, showbiz is a member of the paradigm of fields like sports, politics, etc., but the very use of the TN *kind* in the informal style of this example triggers hedging of the class. In (51) *Damask was a model of the plumper kind, though thin enough by ordinary standards*, the use of the TN in *of the plumper kind* suggests that the speaker is creating or invoking taxonomies within the *model* category, where above par weight stands out. It is important to note the hedging and other pragmatic effects that may be associated with these *of*-modifier uses. The literature on English TN-constructions has rightly pointed out such effects for premodifier uses as in (57) (see e.g. Aijmer 2002), but we also have to be aware of the comparable pragmatic potential of the postmodifier uses.

(57) Brandon Moss seems to be **a pop and lock kind of guy** (Unearthed Solutions For the Royals Offense – Bleeding Royal Blue)

The N2/head may also take modifiers, as in *deep spinal supporting muscles of the postural type* (46). Correct semantic computing of such examples requires analysis of the progressive narrowing down of the subtype as coded by the structural assembly. The context of (46) contains the Latin counterpart in which the type 'muscle', *(musculus) erector spinae*, is narrowed down by *rightward* progressive recursion of subclassifying adjectives, visualized in (58). In the English example,

---

[6] In Section 7 we give arguments for analysing *Homo sapiens* as an appositional complement of *genus*.

the same meaning is arrived at by *leftward* progressive recursion, as visualized in (59).

(58)
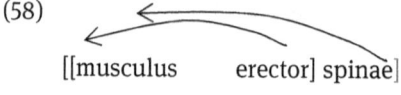
[[musculus   erector] spinae]

(59)

[spinal [supporting   muscles]]

The parsing of the complete example is given in (60). As the whole complex NP in (60) is a bare generic, it has no determiner.

(60) [deep$_{premod}$[spinal$_{premod}$[supporting$_{premod}$muscles$_{head}$]]]$_{head}$
[of [the [postural$_{premod}$ type$_{head}$]] NP/$_{prepositional\ complement}$]$_{postmodifier}$]

5.2 Referential types

We approach the referential types of TN/postmodifying constructions by comparing them with those that TN/head constructions can convey. Because the determiner + TN/head of the latter construction intrinsically designate a (sub)*type* (of a supertype), their referents are situated in what Langacker (1991: 71) calls the "type" universe of interpretation. TN/head-NPs can convey three types of reference, which each involve their subtype denotatum: (i) dual reference (overtly to a subtype but with implied reference to concrete spatiotemporal instances), (ii) generic reference, and (iii) non-referential predicate nominatives. In this section, we show that postmodifier/TN constructions can convey: (i) straight reference to spatiotemporal instances, (ii) generic reference and (iii) non-referential predicate nominatives.

In TN/postmodifying constructions, the determiner combines with the lexical head/N2. Because of this, they refer to *instances* of N2 *in the spatio-temporal world*, as in (48) *Timberlake showed off some intricate dance moves of the pop-and-lock kind* and (49) *you're sure to see [Ø] stars of the showbiz kind*. In (48), reference to spatiotemporal instances is realized by the indefinite determiner *some*, which presupposes instantiation of the type 'dance moves'. The paradigm of indefinite determiners also includes the zero-article, as in (49). Plural count nouns like *stars* in (49) have a determiner function with zero-realization (Langacker 1991: 103ff; Davidse 1999). This is what McGregor (2003) refers to as a 'semiotically significant' zero-element. To posit a zero-element that is 'there' in the grammar, McGregor argues, it has to be shown to be a member of a paradigm of elements realizing the same general function in a particular grammatical environment, whereby zero occupies a distinct and constant semantic value. This is the case with the zero-article in (49) *you're sure to see [ø] stars of the showbiz kind* because it is a member of the determiner paradigm used with plural count and uncount nouns, which also subsumes *some*, as in (49)', and *any* as in (49)". The zero-article contrasts with assertive *some* and non-assertive *any* by having a more general meaning that can be used in both assertive and non-assertive contexts.

(49)' you're sure to see some stars of the showbiz kind

(49)" are you sure to see any stars of the showbiz kind

Whereas the combination of determiner plus head/TN in TN/head constructions intrinsically realizes reference to entities in the type universe of interpretation, postmodifier/TN constructions with N2/head have to use exactly the same mechanisms as other English NPs with lexical head nouns to convey generic reference, i.e. bare uncount or plural NPs, singular NPs with article *a* and singular NPs with article *the*, as illustrated in (61) for the class 'koalas'. Recall that bare generic NPs like *koalas* in (61) truly have no determiner slot at all (Carlson 1978), in contrast with the zero-article in (49), *you're sure to see [ø] stars of the showbiz kind*, which has a value realized by zero. For postmodifier/TN constructions, the three realizations of generic reference are illustrated below: bare (62), singular NP with *a* (63), and singular NP with *the* (64).

(61) Koalas/a koala/the koala normally does not drink water.

(62) **Narcissists of every type** undermine our self-confidence. (The most dangerous types of narcissist (and how to avoid them) | by E.B. Johnson | Practical Growth | Medium)

(63) Real intimacy and real meaningfulness with another person cannot come from a covert narcissist or **a narcissist of any type**. (7 Common Traits of a Covert Narcissist (iheartintelligence.com)

(64) What follows is a description of some characteristics of **the narcissist of this particular type**. (lifeissues.net/writers/mcm/mcm_219narcissisminpriesthood.html)

When postmodifier/TN constructions are used as *predicate nominatives*, as in (46) and (51), they behave just like any NP with lexical head noun. The complex NP is used non-referentially. Although a full NP, it is used "solely for purposes of making a type attribution" (Langacker 1991: 67). In example (46), which is a definition (Declerck 1988: 113–4), the type-attribution is made of a subject denoting a class, *These (i.e. Mid and lower back Erector spinae) are deep spinal supporting muscles of the postural type*, while in (51), *Damask was a model of the plumper kind*, it is made of subjects referring to instances.

In the context of discussing the predicative use of TN/postmodifier constructions, it has to be pointed out that particle *of* + premodifier + TN can also be used as such as predicative complement, as illustrated in (65)–(67). These uses make the categorizing meaning of predicative complements explicit by putting the subject referent in the category expressed by the TN and its modifiers. The semantics may be taxonomizing (65) or characterizing (66)–(67).

(65) Most meteorites observed to fall are **of the stony kind**. (WB)

(66) Dan's thinness, even after three months of good food, was **of the skinny sort**. (WB)

(67) Mr Salmond duly won his standing ovation, but it was **of the perfunctory kind**. (WB)

6 TN/premodifying constructions

This section deals with constructions in which the superordinate N2/head is subcategorized by a TN/*pre*modifier. De Smedt et al. (2007) drew attention to Kruisinga's (1932) early semantic-structural account, which clearly distinguished it from the TN/head-postcomplement construction, even though the two constructions may manifest as the same surface string of determiner + TN + *of* + N2. Kruisinga (1932: 391) makes the crucial point that *of* "can sometimes make a preceding noun (instead of the following noun) into an adjunct" (1932: 391), "entirely subordinated in meaning" (1932: 395) to the head. Such adjunct N + *of* + head N-structures are found, Kruisinga notes, with measure nouns, like *a lot of* in (68),[7] and species

---

[7] As argued by Brems (2003, 2011, 2012), quantifiers like *a lot of, a bit of, heaps of,* etc. derived from NPs like *a five acres lot of land* by a shift in head status from the size noun to the second noun. In (68) *lot* has lost most of its nominal features and has become part of a new linguistic

nouns, like *what sort of* in (69)–(70). TN-constructions with *what sort of*, Kruisinga (1932: 178) notes, inquire about the quality of persons or things. In other words, these NPs ask the hearer to attribute a quality to the instance of the type N2 in that NP. In (71), the TN/premodifier construction answers such an implied question by ascribing the qualities *drizzly, misty, half-and-half* to *(English) weather*.

(68) there're **a lot of trees** ... separating the two places (WB)

(69) **What sort of weather** are we going to have? (*Spoken English*, by Collinson, Kruisinga 1932: 178)

(70) **What sort of a man** is he to see? (*The Strange case of Dr Jekyll and Mr Hyde*, by Robert L. Stevenson 1886, quoted in Kruisinga 1932: 178)

(71) When I lived in Canada I longed for English weather – for **drizzly, misty, half-and-half sort of weather.** (WB)

We extend Kruisinga's definition of the TN/premodifier-construction by claiming (i) that it can be realized by three structural variants (Section 6.1) and (ii) that it can be used not only to attribute a quality to the entity designated by the NP, but also to add further type specifications to the type named by the head noun (Section 6.2).

6.1 Internal grammar: Functional-structural assembly

If we consider examples (72)-(77), then the very way in which the TN/premodifier constructions are embedded in the discourse makes clear that they refer to entities of the N2-type. The TN is typically, but not obligatorily, singular, as illustrated by the plural in (77) by *these awful kinds of things*.

---

sign whose expression is *alotta* and whose denotatum is a relational notion of size (not an entity). *Trees* is the head designating the type of things referred to (Brems 2003, 2011, 2012). All TN-constructions in which the TN is not the head, e.g. *all kind of problems, these sort of problems*, etc. were hypothesized to derive via a similar head shift from the TN/head construction, e.g. *a rare type of marble*. However, Davidse, Brems, and Van linden (this volume) partly reject this hypothesis by showing that from the start in Old English, there were two lexical TN-constructions, the TN/head–complement and the TN/modifier construction, each of which formed the source of differentiated derivation paths (see also concluding section 8).

(72) It's thought that this would be the appropriate date, as it were, to complete the constitutional transition from communist dictatorship to **a West European-type democracy.** (WB)

(73) "I shut down and started to look for a job." "In diamonds?" "No, I wasn't trained in diamonds." "I'm **a specialized type of engineer.** I'm with the Cape offshore oil-from-gas platform at Mossel Bay. I was trained in oil rig engineering in Italy." (WB)

(74) News of the alleged attack has stunned families in the quiet town of Alford, Lincs. . . . One shopkeeper said: "Things like this aren't supposed to happen here. People know us as **an old-fashioned sort of place** – a market, a windmill, a grammar school." (WB)

(75) They could perhaps focus on helping their clients with their M&A-plans. That's more of **a corporate kind of a role.** (WB)

(76) It struck him as an uneasy type of thing to say, coming from her; later he decided it had marked the beginning of the end of their marriage, the first sign she was becoming a different person from **the straightforward sort of a female he'd got wed to.** (WB)

(77) Later on, after I had some time to think about it, I guessed that when **these awful kinds of things** happen to you, it helps to find a lot of things to feel good about. They don't have to be big deal things, but more like the hand business or combing Mom's hair, those kind of things. (WB)

For instance, the dialogue in (73) is concerned with characterizing the speaker's profession of *engineer*, subclassified as *a specialized type of engineer*, with this subclassification identified further down as *oil rig engineering*. The reference is to entities of the type of the N2/head. Premodifying/TN-constructions can in fact often alternate with a NP in which *type of* is left out, e.g. *a specialized engineer*, whose semantics and pragmatics are of course not fully equivalent. This contrasts with the way in which TN/head + complement constructions are embedded in the discourse, as in (17) above, reproduced as (78). The concern here is with product-*types*, designated by the determiner + TN/head, *two types of fruit drinks*, further developed by *the first type* and *the second type* in the following discourse. In sum, even though the surface manifestation of *a specialized type of engineer* and *two types of fruit drinks* involves the same grammatical classes, they differ in the ways they are semantically computed, and it is precisely these semantic computations that are coded by the different structural assemblies we propose for them.

(78) The Royal Fruit Company produces **two types of fruit drinks. The first type** is 25% pure fruit juice, and **the second type** is 75% pure fruit juice. (WB)

Observations such as these led Denison (2002: 4) to view the TN in (72)–(76), whether or not followed by *a*, as a semi-suffix. He argued that in examples like *a Western European-type democracy* (72), *an old-fashioned sort of place* (74), *type* and *sort of* sub-modify, as a sort of affix, the adjectives *Western European* and *old-fashioned*, which themselves modify N2. Diachronically, this semi-suffix was hypothesized to derive by re-analysis from the binominal construction (our TN/head–*of*-complement construction), by shift to head status of N2 and downranking of the TN to a sort of affix. The fact that the premodifiers of N2 may be nonce expressions, sometimes surrounded by quotation marks, as in (79), or hyphenated, as in (80), was felt to offer support for this analysis.

(79) Puts you down all the time. This is **the "I told you so" kind of partner.** (https://www.lovepanky.com/love-couch/broken-heart/types-of-toxic-relationships)

(80) Martin has written at length in The New Yorker about Andrew Motion's biography of Philip Larkin: **'A policeman-in-the-head kind of book'**. (WB)

On our analysis, the TN/premodifying construction is related to the TN/postmodifying construction. Circumstantial evidence for this claim is the fact that TN/postmodifying constructions also prominently feature nonce-expressions, hyphens, etc. as in (48) *moves of the pop-and-lock kind*, (54) *macho affairs of the trial-of-strength kind*. In other words, the premodifier slot of the TN in both the TN/postmodifying and TN/premodifying constructions attracts nonce expressions and ad hoc 'categorizations'. By contrast, such features are less prominent in the *of*-complement of TN/head constructions like *a rare type of marble*. We follow Nunberg, Sag and Wasow (1999) and Langacker (1999: 344) on the point that routinized and idiomatized expressions may keep their analysability. This, in our view, is also the case with the different construals of the strongly routinized expression *kind(s) of things* in (77) above. This binominal string is first used as the TN/postmodifier construction *awful kinds of things*, whose N2/head *things* refers to 'experiences'. *Things* then occurs as head in two simple NPs, *things to feel good about*, and *(no) big deal things*, in the latter of which the fixed expression *no big deal* directly pre-modifies the head *things*. Last comes *those kind of things*, in which the complex determiner *those kind of* ('such') generalizes from previous examples of concrete experiences. The fact that TN/premodifier constructions such as (79), *This is the "I told you so" kind of partner*, alternate with TN/postmodifier constructions, e.g. *This is a partner of the "I told you so" kind*, supports the analyzability of both. These alternations are motivated, we argue, by shared functional-structural features, viz. the central N2/head–TN/modifier relation, and within the modifier, the premodifier + TN/head relation.

The premodifying noun or adjective of the TN can be integrated in three ways into the whole NP. In the first variant, as in (72) *a West European-type* clearly functions as a premodifier of N2, akin to how a simple premodifier like *West European* relates to its head, but this premodifier is internally complex as it consists of the head *type* which is itself premodified by *West European*. The resulting unit, *West European-type democracy*, is scoped over by the determiner, as represented in (81).

(81) [a$_{determiner}$[[West European-$_{premodifier}$ type$_{head}$]$_{premodifier}$ democracy$_{head}$]]

If we then consider the second variant, as in (73) *a specialized type of engineer*, we see that it is structurally parallel to the first, except for the fact that the premodifier with TN is linked to N2 by the particle *of*. This yields a similar resulting unit of semantic specifications, *specialized type of engineer*, over which the determiner scopes.

(82) [a$_{determiner}$[[[specialized$_{premodifier}$ type$_{head}$] of]$_{premodifier}$ engineer$_{head}$]]

We can now turn to the third variant, as in (75) *a corporate kind of a role* and (76) *the straightforward sort of a female he'd got wed to*, in which *of* is followed by an indefinite article. We argue that this variant is also structurally parallel to the other two, its structural assembly being represented in (83).

(83) [a$_{determiner}$[[[corporate$_{premodifier}$ kind$_{head}$] of a]$_{premodifier}$ role$_{head}$]]

The semantic specifications in (75) are *corporate kind of a role* and those in (76) are *straightforward sort of a female he'd got wed to*. They are scoped over by an indefinite article in (75) and a definite article in (76), with the latter motivated by the following defining relative clause. In other words, the function of determining the entity designated by the whole NP is performed by the NP-initial determiner. The designated entity is an instance of the type named by N2, which is the head of the construction. The predicatively used TN-construction in (75) designates an instance of 'corporate *role*' and that in (76) refers to 'the straightforward *female* he'd got wed to'. This entails that in (75) and (76), the TN/premodifier is formed by the units *corporate kind of a* and *straightforward sort of a*. This in turn raises the question of the function of the article closing off this unit. This article is always indefinite, in contrast with the NP-initial determiner which offers the choice indefinite – definite to mark the referential status of the whole NP. We propose that *a* has the semantic effect of indicating that the semantic specifications expressed by the premodifier apply to an *instance* of an entity. TN/premodifier constructions of this last type cannot be used to refer to a type in type universe, as shown by the impossibility of *The mission is named after a massive type of *a snake that crushes its prey to death* as alternate of (84).

(84) The mission is named Operation Anaconda, after **a massive type of snake that crushes its prey to death**. (WB)

Just like the TN in *of*-modifiers, the premodifiers with TN require themselves modifiers, which are typically premodifiers, but can be postmodifiers, as in *type A blood*, which alternates with *blood of type A*. They do not take determiners because they are not full NPs. To the premodifiers of the TN, the difference between classifiers and epithets applies to a certain extent. For instance, *corporate* in (75), is classifying and *very frustrating* in (85) is obviously an epithet.

(85) I think the longer term test is will we share what the President says is his own patience with fighting **a very frustrating kind of a war** against an enemy scattered in as many as sixty countries. (WB)

At the same time, as in the TN/postmodifying construction, the very presence of the TN in the modifier confounds the difference between epithet and classifier. For instance, while *aggressive* would probably *prima facie* be thought of as a gradable property ascribed to individuals, the TN/premodifier *aggressive type of* in (86) may well be taken to refer to an established classification of soccer players.

(86) Everyone knows I am **an aggressive type of player**. (WB)

Moreover, the TN may be used either in its straight subtype-meaning or with a hedging meaning (Aijmer 2002), as in (72) where the TN in *Western European-type* indicates that the adjective is *not* to be taken as referring strictly to geographical location but to *qualities* metonymically associated with some democracies in Western Europe (Kolyaseva 2021). Nonce-expressions such as *the "I told you so" kind of partner* are often vague as to the distinction between subclass and quality.[8]

6.2 Referential types

TN/premodifier constructions are also fully parallel with TN/postmodifier constructions in their ability to convey the same three types of reference:
(i) straight reference to spatiotemporal instances, as in (76), **the straightforward sort of a female he'd got wed to**,
(ii) generic reference, as in (84) **a massive type of snake that crushes its prey to death**,
(iii) non-referential predicate nominatives, as in (86) *I am* **an aggressive type of player**.

This is because in the two constructions, the determiner combines with N2 as lexical head to construe the designatum (see Section 5.2).

7 TN appositional constructions

This section addresses the last type of construction in which TNs are used with full lexical meaning, viz. appositional constructions. They can have either TN – N2 order, as in *the modern genre of the horror story* (87) and (88)–(89), or N2 – TN order, as in *the horror film genre* (90) and (91).

(87) I would say that this story crosses the obscure border line between a true magical tale and **the modern genre of the horror story.** (WB)

(88) Nevertheless, this awe did not prevent the tortoise from being sacrificed (for divination purpose) in such huge numbers that **the species of tortoise** became totally extinct. (WB)

(89) Many vireyas have very long, narrow tubular flowers, **the species tuba** is well-named. (WB)

---

8 This is why in Brems and Davidse (2010) we referred to the general function of TN/premodifiers as "descriptive modifiers", but we did not relate the TN/premodifying-construction to the TN/postmodifying-construction as we now advocate to do.

(90) How dare you be so disrespectful to the man who basically invented **the horror film genre**? (WB)

(91) To do this they are introducing some genes from other species, particularly **the Fescue species**. (WB)

7.1 Functional-structural assembly

We start with the structural assembly of appositional constructions with TN – N2 order. There is considerable controversy in the literature about the analysis of such appositional complex NPs. A common view is that the two NPs in e.g. *the modern genre of the horror story* in (87) and *the species tuba* in (88) are "identical in reference" (Quirk et al 1985: 130). Huddleston and Pullum (2002: 447), by contrast, analyse complex appositional NPs like *the opera 'Carmen'* in (92) as a head–restrictive postmodifier structure. Their argumentation for this is that "*'Carmen'* restricts the denotation of the nominal headed by *opera*: the opera 'Carmen' contrasts with other operas." (*Ibid.*: 447). They further observe that, but do not really explain why, the matrix NP in (92a) is substituted by the appositive dependent *Carmen* in (92b). We can observe here that we find the same possibility of leaving out the first apposite in TN/appositional constructions, e.g. (87)' as opposed to the impossibility of (87)''.

(92) She sang in [the opera 'Carmen']. (Huddleston and Pullum 2002: 447)

(92)' She sang in 'Carmen'. (Huddleston and Pullum 2002: 447)

(87)' this story crosses the obscure border line between a true magical tale and ~~the modern genre of~~ the horror story.

(87)'' *this story crosses the obscure border line between a true magical tale and the modern genre ~~of the horror story~~.

Van Langendonck (1999, 2007) points out a number of problems with these two analyses of appositional complex NPs. Firstly, he rejects, with Burton-Roberts (1975), the claim that the first segment is a referential NP (contra Quirk et al 1985). Secondly, he points out that it is the second apposite that identifies the actual referent of the complex NP, which, in his view, argues against analysing it as a modifier. This leads him to consider whether appositional constructions like (87)–(89), (92) and (93)–(94) are premodifier–head structures, in which the second NP is obligatorily definite, i.e. either a proper name, definite descriptive NP or bare generic.

(93) the city of London (Van Langendonck 1999: 114)

(94) the poet Burns (Acuña-Fariña 2009: 461)

This alternative is at first sight attractive because it would appear to offer a better explanation of the alternation pattern in (92) and (92)'. *The opera 'Carmen'* could be argued to be substitutable by *'Carmen'* only, because this is the head of the appositional complex NP. We see, however, a major problem with a premodifier–head analysis, and this involves considering the systematic alternation that *the genre of the horror story* allows with *the horror story genre*. As noted in Section 2 on our theoretical premises, we hold with such authors as Gleason (1966), Levin (1993) and Halliday (1994) that systematic alternations of constructions are revealing of their component elements and structural integration. If *the genre* were to be a premodifier in *the genre of the horror story* (87), then one would expect it to also be a modifier in *the horror film genre* (90). However, we argue that *genre* is the head in (90), and also in (87). For its head status in both variants, the following argument can be given. Both alternates allow a demonstrative determiner like *that* to substitute for the identifying information given by *of the horror story* in (87) and *the horror film* in (90): *the genre of the horror story* stands to *that genre* in the same way as *the horror film genre* stands to *that genre*. This shows that *of the horror story* in (87) and *the horror film* in (90) are the dependents while *genre* is the head in both examples.

We propose that the appositional constructions with TNs are TN/head–complement structures.[9] like those construing a superordinate relation between the subtype TN and supertype N2, as in *a rare type of marble* and *a rare marble type*. Just as the possibility of a complementation analysis was overlooked in much of the literature for the latter constructions (except by Keizer 2007). it was overlooked for appositional constructions, which themselves were largely overlooked (but see Umbach (this volume) on appositional TN-constructions in German). The general arguments for this structural analysis are parallel to those given for the superordination TN/head–N2/complement construction. As noted above, the regular alternation between *the modern genre of the horror story* and *the modern horror story genre* shows that the TN is the head. The relational meaning of TNs

---

9 This proposal is strongly indebted to discussion with Alena Kolyaseva (p.c.) and Yuchan Li (p.c.) and would not have been arrived at without their justified criticisms of our earlier analysis.

is compatible only with the conceptually incomplete element in a dependency relation. In appositional constructions this has to be the conceptually dependent head of complementation structures which receives the necessary completion from a complement. As the complement is the conceptually independent element, it can be expected to be able to function on its own, as it does in (80)' above, *the obscure border line between a true magical tale and* ~~*the modern genre of the horror story*~~. The variation between *the modern genre of the horror film* and *the modern horror film genre* can be accounted for in terms of post- and precomplement. We will first further clarify the appositional semantics and then discuss the formal properties of the appositional NPs.

We propose that the semantic relation between the two apposites in TN-constructions like (95)–(98), is one of *specification*, i.e. a variable – value relation (Higgins 1973). It is the same semantic relation as found in a specificational copular clause like (99), in which it is generally accepted that *the problem* is the variable for which the concrete value *Kashmir* is specified.

(95) a. the genre of the horror film
 b. the horror film genre (WB)

(96) a. the species Fescue
 b. the Fescue species (WB)

(97) a. the problem of climate change
 b. the climate change problem

(98) a. the problem of Kashmir
 b. the Kashmir problem

(99) The only problem is Kashmir. (https://www.dawn.com/news/1604303)

(100) ... 23 parties campaigning against India's control over Kashmir. Decentralization is an issue that has absolutely no relevance to **the problem that is Kashmir**. (WB)

The variable, *the problem* in (99), is an attributively used NP, defined by Donnellan (1966) as a description used essentially, which is a weakly referential NP that does not pick out a specific individual. The variable forms the starting point of a specificational relation, which seeks to identify its value, i.e. the more specific entity that corresponds to the variable. We argue that the relation between head and postcomplement in NPs like (95–98a) and between head and precomplement in NPs like (95–98b) is one of specification. For instance, in (98a) and (98b) *the + problem*$_{HEAD}$ is the variable for which *Kashmir*$_{COMPLEMENT}$ specifies the value. This specificational interpretation avoids the problem of viewing the first NP as referential (which is inherent in Quirk et al.'s (1985: 130) 'identity of reference' account), but it does capture the unique relation between the two apposites. A nominal paraphrase that makes this specificational relation explicit is 'the problem that is climate change' and *the problem that is Kashmir*, as in (100). The specificational relation in (98) is condensed in *the problem of Kashmir* (98a) and is condensed even more in *the Kashmir problem* (98b). TN/appositional constructions, we argue, likewise incorporate such a specificational relation: both *the modern genre of the horror story* and *the modern horror story genre* refer to 'the modern genre that is the horror story'.

Let us now turn to the formal properties of the appositional complex NPs. Their basic functional-structural assemblies are the same as those of superordination complementation constructions, as shown for the postcomplement structure in (101) and the precomplement structure in (102). In (101) *modern genre* integrates as head with the postcomplement *of the horror story*.[10] The resulting structure is scoped over by the initial definite determiner. In (102), *genre* first integrates as head with the precomplement *horror film*, which is appositional, not subclassifying. The resulting structure is premodified by *modern*, which, in its turn, is scoped over by the definite determiner. In both (101) and (102) *modern* is non-restrictive and characterizes *genre* as such. Restrictive premodifiers are possible, however, contrasting, for instance, *the modern genre of the Hollywood western* with *the older genre of the Hollywood western*.

(101) [the [[modern$_{premod}$ genre$_{head}$]$_{head}$ [of the horror film]$_{of+NP\text{-}complement}$]]

(102) [the [modern$_{premod}$ [[horror film]$_{precomplement}$ genre$_{head}$]]]

While structurally parallel, the appositional semantics impose more restrictions on the fillers of the elements of structure than the superordinate semantics. The appositional construction with *of*-complement requires a full definite NP in the complement, like *the horror story* in (87), because it has to identify one specific genre. By contrast, the *of*-complement of the superordination type can contain either a noun, as in *a rare type of marble* in (1), or a full NP, as in *some varieties*

---

[10] Both the head and the postcomplement have finer internal structures, which are discussed for the superordination construction of *Anthropological types of Corded Ware and Yamna cultures* visualized in (28).

or chemotypes of the same species in (22). As well, the appositional constructions with both *of*-complement and precomplement require a definite initial determiner because they set up a variable whose value is uniquely specified.

7.2 Referential types

The TN/appositional constructions identify a specific type as the unique value of the variable with TN. Hence, they always operate in the type universe of interpretation, like the discussion of literary or film genres or of biological taxonomies, as illustrated in (87)–(91). They are obligatorily definite and realize generic reference in the sense of reference to genres, species, etc. They cannot realize dual reference. In (103a), *the obligatory "epic"* refers, via the mechanism of dual reference to an 'obligatory', i.e. expected and predictable, instance of the genre "epic". This meaning cannot be conveyed by an appositional TN/construction, as shown by the ungrammaticality of (103b). Neither can a TN/appositional construction be used as a non-referential predicative complement, as shown in (104b). This meaning can only be expressed if *an instance/example/* etc. *of* is added, as in (104a).

(103a) The final track, **the obligatory "epic"** of the album, is thoroughly enjoyable. (https://www.metal-archives.com/reviews/Dream_Theater/Dream_Theater/3815)

(103b) The final track, ***the obligatory genre of the "epic"** of the album is thoroughly enjoyable.

(104a) Halloween is an example of **the horror film genre.** (WB)

(104b) Halloween is ***the horror film genre.**

8 Conclusion

The aim of this chapter was to address the descriptive gaps in the literature on English constructions in which type nouns (TNs) are used in a lexical sense. Semantically, such constructions are concerned with either *taxonomies* in the 'type' universe of interpretation or with the *characterization* of entities. The literature on English TNs has so far concentrated mainly on constructions with the surface order 'TN followed by N2', as in the TN/head construction *a rare type* of marble and TN/modifier constructions like *non-Hodgkin type (of) lymphoma* and *an ordinary sort of (a) guy*. This descriptive focus has been at the expense of TN-constructions with the surface order 'N2 followed by TN', as in *lymphoma of the non-Hodgkin type* and *a model of the plumper kind*. Moreover, little attention has gone to constructions in which the two segments stand in an appositional relation to each other, as in *the modern genre of the horror film* and *the modern horror film genre*. In terms of the surface order of TN and N2, this set of lexical TN-constructions appears as in Table 1.

Table 1: Constructions with lexical uses of TNs classified in terms of surface order of TN and N2.

TN – N2	N2 – TN
a rare type of marble	Nick's rare tissue type
non-Hodgkin type (of) lymphoma	lymphoma of the non-Hodgkin type
an ordinary sort of (a) guy	a model of the plumper kind
the modern genre of the horror story	the modern horror film genre
the species (of) tuba	the Fescue species

Our specific descriptive aim was to analyse these types in terms of Langacker's cognitive construction grammar, which derives the meanings of constructions from the modification and complementation relations of heads at different levels of structural assembly. This analysis has revealed the different constructions lurking under the *prima facie* identical surface sequences of TN – N2 and N2 – TN.

In the resulting typology, visualized in Table 2, the grammatical-semantic contrast between *complementation* and *modification* is central, and, within the former, the semantic difference between superordination versus apposition.

The reference of the superordination TN/head–complement constructions is determined by the article, demonstrative or quantifier + the TN/head. The referents are therefore situated intrinsically in the type universe of interpretation. The referents can be of three types, all involving the 'type'-denotation: generic reference, dual reference to an overt type and pragmatically implied instances, and non-referential predicate nominatives. The referents of the appositional TN/head–complement constructions are likewise situated in the type universe of interpretation. They always refer to a unique type. They cannot realize dual reference or non-referential predicate nominatives. In the TN/modifier–N2/head constructions, the referents are identified by the determiner and N2. Therefore, their unmarked reference is to concrete spatio-temporal referents. They can also realize generic reference and predicate nominatives by using the determiner choices that ordinary NPs (with non-TN heads) use for these types of reference.

Table 2: Constructions with lexical uses of TNs classified in terms of complementation and modification.

Complementation		Modification	
Superordination			
TN/head *of* N2/postcomplement	N2/precomplement + TN/head	N2/head *of* NP/ postmodifier with TN	TN/premodifier *(of)* + N2/head or NP2/head
a rare type of marble	Nick's rare tissue type	lymphoma of the non-Hodgkin type a model of the plumper kind	non-Hodgkin type (of) lymphoma an ordinary sort of (a) guy
Apposition			
TN/head *(of)* + NP2/postcomplement	N2/complement + TN/head		
the modern genre of the horror story the species tuba	the horror film genre the Fescue species		

What is the relevance of this extended typology? We propose that it necessitates the rethinking of synchronic and diachronic studies of English TN-constructions, and provides a better basis for contrastive research of Germanic, Romance and Slavic languages.

Synchronic descriptions such as corpus-based studies of NPs with TNs will have to cast their nets more widely and include data instantiating both TN + N2 and N2 + TN order. In these extended data, linguists will have to analyse not only the lexical TN-constructions discussed in this chapter (Table 2) but also those with grammatical functions such as quantification, e.g. *no tactical success of any kind* (10), and hedging, e.g *comfort of a sort* (9). Corpus study should address this greater constructional variation than hitherto researched from various perspectives such as variationist study and information structure, including the prosodic marking of accents as in Dehé and Stathi (2012). The impact of textual progression on the choices made by speakers and writers might be of particular interest. The 'pre' and 'post' alternatives available for the main lexical TN-constructions offer a denser and a less compact variant. For instance, *the modern horror film genre* is more compact than *the modern genre of the horror film*. For the complementation constructions, there is the additional possibility of presupposing and eliding the supertype expressed by N2, once it has been introduced, as in *The Royal Fruit Company produces two types of fruit drinks. The first type is 25% pure fruit juice, and the second type is 75% pure fruit juice.* Halliday and Martin (1993) have drawn attention to progressive 'compacting' of referent descriptions in scientific texts. The diachronic development of this variation, whereby in English prehead dependents came to do more and more work (Halliday 1967b), may be an example of change driven mainly by practices in written registers such as science and advertising.

The scope of diachronic research of English TN-constructions likewise has to be broadened and reconceptualized. So far trajectories of change have been hypothesized solely on the basis of examples in which the TN precedes N2, with the two typically linked to each other by *of*. Examples with this surface realization appeared in Middle English (Denison 2002; Brems and Davidse 2010). The assumption was that the TN/head construction, as in (1) *a rare sort of marble*, was the only source construction, from which all other NP-internal constructions derived through a head–modifier reversal, i.e. reanalysis from head/TN–*of*-postmodifier/N2 into premodifier/TN–head/N2. Thus, Brems and Davidse (2010) viewed TN/premodifying constructions like *an ordinary sort of a guy*, *a pop and lock kind of guy* and *a West European-type democracy* as deriving from the TN/head construction, which we wrongly viewed as a modification structure rather than as a complementation structure. However, we now crucially distinguish TN/head–N2/complement constructions from TN/modifier–N2/head constructions and have shown that both have variants with a pre- and postdependent as visualized in Table 2 above, and repeated in Table 4 below.

Table 3: TN-constructions with lexical functions in Present-day English.

	predependent + head	head + postdependent
NP with TN/head + superordinate complement	*a rare marble*$_\text{PRECOMPLEMENT}$ *type*$_\text{HEAD}$	*a rare type*$_\text{HEAD}$ *of marble*$_\text{POSTCOMPLEMENT}$
NP with TN/head + appositional complement	*the horror film*$_\text{PRECOMPLEMENT}$ *genre*$_\text{HEAD}$	*the genre*$_\text{HEAD}$ *of the horror film*$_\text{POSTCOMPLEMENT}$
NP with TN/modifier + superordinate N2/head	*pop and lock kind*$_\text{PREMODIFIER}$ *(of) dance moves*$_\text{HEAD}$	*dance moves*$_\text{HEAD}$ *of the pop- and-lock kind*$_\text{POSTMODIFIER}$.

This requires us to investigate whether in earlier stages of English there were multiple source constructions, which contrasted with each other in terms of complementation and modification. The diachronic data presented in Davidse, Brems, and Van linden (this volume) reveal that in Old English there were indeed two different basic source constructions. In that early stage of English, the head–dependent relations were marked by genitive coding of the dependent, thus unambiguously showing up the N2/genitive complement–TN/head construction, illustrated in (105) and (106), and the TN/genitive modifier–N2/head construction, as in (107). The genitive typically preceded the head.

(105) *Feower synt **muneca cyn**.* (c960, *Rule St. Benet*, OED)[11]
four are monk$_{\text{GEN.PL}}$ kind$_{\text{NOM.PL}}$.
'There are four kinds of monks.'

(106) *Him biþ beforan andweard **eal engla cynn & manna cynn**.* (971 Blickl. Hom, OED)
Him$_{\text{DAT}}$ is before present all angel$_{\text{GEN.PL}}$ kind$_{\text{NOM.SG}}$ & man$_{\text{GEN.PL}}$ kind$_{\text{NOM.SG}}$
'Before Him the whole kind of angels and kind of men is present.'

(107) ***ælces cynnes déor*** (?c825, *kin*, n. †6 †b, OED)
each$_{\text{GEN.SG}}$ kind$_{\text{GEN.SG}}$ déor$_{\text{NOM.PL}}$
'animals of each kind'

In (105) the genitive *muneca* is a superordinate N2/complement of the TN/head *cyn*, with the NP referring to 'four kinds of monks' in a 'type' interpretation of reality. In (106), the genitives *engla* and *manna* are appositional N2/complements of the TN/head *cynn*. In (107) the genitive *ælces cynnes* is a TN/modifier and *déor* is the N2/head. The designatum of this NP is hence 'animals of each kind'. In sum, the basic construction types of Present-day English in Table 3 were already present in Old English, but with the dependent coded by the genitive, as visualized in Table 4.

These two constructions with genitive were gradually replaced by NPs expressing the relation between TN and N2 analytically, typically with the linking particle *of*. Each was the source of different paths of change, which are reconstructed in Davidse, Brems, and Van linden (this volume) and which overhaul the received diachronic account of English TN-constructions.

The synchronic account in this chapter and the historical reconstruction in Davidse, Brems, and Van linden (this volume) thus dovetail in showing up two, rather than one, basic constructions, associated with two distinct paths of change. This new historical outline will have to be fleshed out with further close study of historical data, and partly novel assessments of the role of processes such as decategorialization, re-analysis and lexicalization, which have to be revised in particular for the constructions that developed from the source construction with TN/genitival modifier + N2/head.

---

[11] Abbreviations used in the glosses are as follows: ACC – accusative; DAT – dative; GEN – genitive; M – masculine; N – neuter; NOM – nominative; PL – plural; PREP – prepositional case; and SG – singular.

Table 4: TN-constructions in Old English.

	predependent + head	head + postdependent
NP with TN/head + superordinate genitive complement	feower muneca$_{GEN.PL}$ cyn$_{NOM.PL}$ (c960, OED) 'four kinds of monks'	twa cyn$_{NOM.PL}$ þæs$_{GEN.SG}$ martyrhades$_{GEN.SG}$ (c 1050–1099, YCOE) 'two kinds of that martyrdom'
NP with TN/head + appositional genitive complement	eal engla$_{GEN.PL}$ cynn$_{NOM.SG}$ & manna$_{GEN.PL}$ cynn$_{NOM.SG}$ (c971, OED) 'the entire kind of angels and the kind of humans'	wið þa missenlican$_{ACC.PL}$ cynd$_{ACC.PL}$ nædrena$_{GEN.PL}$ (c1000, OED) 'against the various kinds of adders'
NP with genitive TN/ modifier + superordinate N2/head	ælces$_{GEN.SG}$ cynnes$_{GEN.SG}$ déor$_{NOM.PL}$ (?c825, OED) 'animals of each kind'	---

Finally, the proposed new typology of lexical TN-constructions offers a better basis for contrastive research. By revealing the ability of English to put dependents in both pre- and postposition, it shows that its lexical TN-constructions are more *like*, for instance, those in Russian (see Kisiel and Kolyaseva this volume) and *less unlike* those in French than suggested in some earlier work. The N2/genitive complement–TN/head construction, e.g. (105), and the TN/genitive modifier–N2/head construction, e.g. (107), of Old English have exact functional-structural counterparts in Russian, as illustrated by the TN/head–N2/genitive complement construction in (108) and the N2/head–TN/genitive modifier construction in (109).

(108) *Dannyj   avtomobil'   proizvoditsja   i   postavljaetsja*
    this.NOM.M.SG   car.NOM.M.SG   produce.3SG.PASS and   supply.3SG.PASS
    *na   naš   rynok   v   **trex   tipax***
    onto   our.ACC.M.SG   market.ACC.M.SG in   tree.PRP   type-PRP.PL
    kuzovov.
    body.GEN.PL
    'This car is manufactured and supplied to our market in three types of bodies.' (http://auto.obozrevatel.com/news/2006/04/18/450.htm) (Kolyaseva and Davidse 2018: 198)

(109) *Delaetsja   popytka   ocenit'   perspektivy*
      do.3SG.PASS attempt.NOM.F.SG evaluate.INF prospect.ACC.PL
      razvitija   sistem   različnogo   tipa.
      development.GEN.N.SG system.GEN.F.PL various.GEN.M.SG type.GEN.M.SG
      'An attempt is being made to assess the prospects of development of systems of various sort. (2004, *Voprosy statistiki*, RNC) (Kolyaseva and Davidse 2018: 201)

Some of the alleged differences between English and French TN-constructions noted in Davidse et al (2013) turn out to be unfounded in light of the more exhaustive description of English we have now elaborated. We had looked at French through the prism of an incomplete description of English. For instance, we wrongly claimed that the descriptive modifier function was much less common in French than in English except for some examples with postmodifiers, as in (110).

(110) Je songe m'en faire une, mais très discrète, **du genre noire et marron foncée**. (http://www.adojeunz.com/forum/index.php)
      'I'm thinking of making myself one, but very discrete, of the black and dark brown type'.

In fact there is nothing intrinsically marginal about descriptive TN/postmodifier constructions, which are also part of the English inventory of TN-constructions, as shown in this chapter. We also wrongly claimed that predicative complements like *être du genre* 'be of the kind' as in (111) are found in French, but not in English, which is belied by examples like (66) *Dan's thinness ... was of the skinny sort*. (WB).

(111) je ne suis pas **du genre "groupie"**. (http://www.adojeunz.com/forum/index.php)
      'I'm not of the "groupie" type'

We conclude that the analysis of lexical TN-constructions in terms of pre- and postcomplementation and pre- and postmodification opens promising perspectives to construct more complete synchronic typologies and diachronic trajectories of English TN-constructions and to carry out sounder comparison across language families such as the Germanic, Romance and Slavic languages.

References

Acuña-Fariña, Juan Carlos. 2009. Aspects of the grammar of close apposition and the structure of the noun phrase. *English Language and Linguistics* 13. 453–481.
Adamson, Sylvia. 2000. *A lovely little example*. Word order options and category shift in the premodifying string. In Olga Fischer, Anette Rosenbach & Dieter Stein (eds.), *Pathways of change*, 39–66. Amsterdam: Benjamins.
Aijmer, Karin. 2002. *English discourse particles: Evidence from a corpus*. Amsterdam: Benjamins.
Bolinger, Dwight. 1968. Entailment and the meaning of structures. *Glossa* 2. 119–127.
Bolinger, Dwight. 1977. *Meaning and form*. London & New York: Longman.
Brems, Lieselotte. 2003. Measure noun constructions: an instance of semantically-driven grammaticalization. *International Journal of Corpus Linguistics* 8. 283–312.
Brems, Lieselotte. 2011. *Layering of size and type noun constructions in English*. Berlin: De Gruyter Mouton.
Brems, Lieselotte. 2012. The establishment of quantifier constructions for size nouns: a diachronic case study of *heap(s)* and *lot(s)*. *Journal of Historical Pragmatics* 13. 202–231.
Brems, Lieselotte & Kristin Davidse. 2010. The grammaticalization of nominal type noun constructions with *kind/sort of*: chronology and paths of change. *English Studies* 91. 180–202.
Burton-Roberts, Noel. 1975. Nominal apposition. *Foundations of Language* 13. 391–419.
Carlson, Greg. 1978. *Reference to kinds in English*. Bloomington: Indiana University Linguistics Club.
Carlson, Greg. 2005. Generic reference. In Keith Brown (ed.), *The encyclopedia of language and linguistics*, 14–18. Oxford: Elsevier.
Carlson, Greg & Francis Pelletier (eds.). 1995. *The generic book*. Chicago/London: The University of Chicago Press.
Davidse, Kristin. 1998. Agnates, verb classes and the meaning of construals: the case of ditransitivity in English. *Leuvense Bijdragen* 87. 281–313.
Davidse, Kristin. 1999. The semantics of cardinal versus enumerative existential constructions. *Cognitive Linguistics* 10. 203–250.
Davidse, Kristin. 2004. The interaction of quantification and identification in English determiners. In Michel Achard & Suzanne Kemmer (eds.), *Language, culture and mind*, 507–533. Stanford: CSLI.
Davidse, Kristin. 2011. Alternations as a heuristic to verb meaning and the semantics of constructions. In Pilar Guerrero (ed.), *Morphosyntactic alternations*, 11–37. London: Equinox.
Davidse, Kristin. 2018. Complex NPs with third-order entity clauses: towards a grammatical description and semantic typology. In Alex Ho-Cheong Leung & Wim van der Wurff (eds.), *The noun phrase in English: Past and present*, 11–46. Amsterdam: Benjamins.
Davidse, Kristin, Brems, Lieselotte & Liesbet De Smedt. 2008. Type noun uses in the English NP: A case of right to left layering. *International Journal of Corpus Linguistics* 13. 139–168.
Davidse, Kristin, Lieselotte Brems, Peter Willemse, Emeline Doyen, Jessica Kiermeer, Elfi Thoelen. 2013. A comparative study of the grammaticalized uses of English *sort (of)* and French *genre (de)* in teenage forum data. In Emanuele Miola (ed.), *Languages go Web. Standard and non-standard languages on the Internet*, 41–66. Alessandria: Edizioni dell' Orso.

Declerck, Renaat. 1988. *Studies on copular sentences, clefts, and pseudo-clefts*. Leuven: Leuven University Press.
Dehé, Nicole & Katerina Stathi. 2015. Grammaticalization and prosody: the case of English sort/kind/type of constructions. *Language* 92. 911–947.
Denison, David. 2002. History of the *sort of* construction family. Paper presented at the Second International conference on Construction Grammar, Helsinki, September 6–28, 2002.
De Smedt, Liesbet, Lieselotte Brems & Kristin Davidse. 2007. NP-internal functions and extended uses of the 'type' nouns *kind*, *sort*, and *type*: Towards a comprehensive, corpus-based description. In Roberta Facchinetti et al. (eds.), *Corpus Linguistics 25 years on*, 225–255. Amsterdam: Rodopi.
Donnellan, Keith. 1966. Reference and definite descriptions. In Aloysius Martinich (ed.), *The philosophy of language*, 265–277. New York/Oxford: Oxford University Press.
Gleason, Henry. 1966. *Linguistics and English grammar*. New York: Holt, Reinhart & Winston.
Goldberg, Adele. 1995. *Constructions. A Construction Grammar approach to argument structure*. Chicago. University of Chicago Press.
Goldberg, Adele. 2002. Surface generalizations: An alternative to alternations. *Cognitive Linguistics* 13. 327–56.
Goldberg, Adele. 2006. *Constructions at work: The nature of generalization in language*. Oxford: OUP.
Halliday, Michael. 1967a. Notes on transitivity and theme in English. Part 2. *Journal of Linguistics* 3. 199–244.
Halliday, Michael. 1967b. Grammar, society and the noun. Lecture given at University College London on 24 November 1966. H. K. Lewis (for University College London).
Halliday, Michael. 1968. Notes on transitivity and theme in English. Part 3. *Journal of Linguistics* 4. 179–215.
Halliday, Michael. 1985. *An introduction to Functional Grammar*. London: Arnold.
Halliday, Michael. 1994. *An introduction to Functional Grammar*. 2nd edn. London: Arnold.
Halliday, Michael & Jim Martin. 1993. *Writing science. Literacy and discursive power*. London: The Falmer Press.
Halliday, Michael & Christian Matthiessen. 2004. *An introduction to Functional Grammar*. 3rd edn. London: Arnold.
Higgins, Francis. 1973. The pseudo-cleft construction in English. Doctoral dissertation, MIT.
Hjelmslev, Louis. [1943] 1961. *Prolegomena to a theory of language*. Revised English edition of original Danish version 1943. Madison: University of Wisconsin Press.
Huddleston, Rodney & Geoffrey Pullum. 2002. *The Cambridge grammar of the English language*. Cambridge: CUP.
Hudson, Richard. 1984. *Word Grammar*. Oxford: Basil Blackwell.
Keizer, Evelien. 2007. *The English noun phrase. The nature of linguistic categorization*. Cambridge: CUP.
Kennedy, Christopher & Louise McNally. 2005. Scale structure, degree modification, and the semantics of gradable predicates. *Language* 81. 345–381.
Kolyaseva, Alena. 2021. The nominal uses of the Russian *rod* ('genus', 'genre', 'kind') and *tip* ('type'): the starting point of desemanticization, *Slovo a Slovesnost* 82. 3–44.
Kolyaseva, Alena & Kristin Davidse. 2018. A typology of lexical and grammaticalized uses of Russian *tip*. *Russian Linguistics* 42. 191–220.
Kruisinga, Etsko 1932. *A handbook of Present-day English*. 5th edition. Groningen: Noordhoff.

Kuno, Susumu. 1970. Some properties of non-referential noun phrases. In Roman Jakobson & Kawamoto Shigeo (eds.), *Studies in general and Oriental linguistics presented to Shiro Hattori on the occasion of his sixtieth birthday*, 348–373. Tokyo: TEC.

Langacker, Ronald. 1987. *Foundations of Cognitive Grammar*. Vol. 1: *Theoretical preliminaries*. Stanford: Stanford University Press.

Langacker, Ronald. 1991. *Foundations of Cognitive Grammar*. Vol. 2: *Descriptive application*. Stanford: Stanford University Press.

Langacker, Ronald. 1999. *Grammar and conceptualization*. Berlin: Mouton de Gruyter.

Langacker, Ronald. 2002. Deixis and subjectivity. In Frank Brisard (ed.), *Grounding: The epistemic footing of deixis and reference*, 1–27. Berlin & New York: Mouton de Gruyter.

Langacker, Ronald. 2009. Cognitive (Construction) Grammar. *Cognitive Linguistics* 20.167–176.

Langacker, Ronald. 2021. Functions and assemblies. In Kazuhiro Kodama & Tetsuharu Koyama (eds.), *The forefront of Cognitive Linguistics*, 1–54. Tokyo: Hituzi Syobo.

Levin, Beth. 1993. *English verb classes and alternations: A preliminary investigation*. Chicago: University of Chicago Press.

Li, Yuchan. 2022. Russian *tip* in appositive modifier construction. A tentative exploration. Term paper. Linguistics Department: University of Leuven.

Lumsden, Michael. 1988 *Existential sentences. Their structure and meaning*. London: Croom Helm.

McGregor, William. 1997. *Semiotic Grammar*. Oxford: Clarendon.

McGregor, William. 2003. The nothing that is, the zero that isn't. *Studia Linguistica* 57. 75–119.

Mihatsch, Wiltrud. 2016. Type-noun binominals in four romance languages. *Language Sciences* 53. 136–159.

Nunberg, Geoffrey, Ivan Sag & Thomas Wasow. 1994. Idioms. *Language* 70. 491–538.

Perek, Florent. 2012. Alternation-based generalizations are stored in the mental grammar: Evidence from a sorting task experiment. *Cognitive Linguistics* 23. 601–635

Perek, Florent & Adele Goldberg. 2017. Linguistic generalization on the basis of function and constraints on the basis of statistical preemption. *Cognition* 168. 276–293.

Sinclair, John et al. 1987. *Collins COBUILD English language dictionary*. London/Glasgow: Collins.

Van Langendonck, Willy. 1999. Neurolinguistic and syntactic evidence for basic level meaning in proper names. *Functions of Language* 6. 95–138.

Van Langendonck, Willy. 2007. *Theory and typology of proper names*. Berlin: Mouton de Gruyter.

Voghera, Miriam. 2013. A case study on the relationship between grammatical change and synchronic variation: the emergence of *tipo*[–N] in Italian. In Anna Giacalone Ramat, Catarina Mauri & Piera Molinelli (eds.), *Synchrony and diachrony. A dynamic Interface*, 283–312. Amsterdam: Benjamins.

Ward, Gregory & Betty Birner. 1995. Definiteness and the English existential. *Language* 71. 722–742.

Karin Aijmer
4 Type nouns in some varieties of English

Abstract: This article expands research on type nouns by looking at varieties of English other than British and American English. It investigates if the various uses of type nouns established in previous descriptions are also attested in other varieties and with what frequency. It does so by comprehensive corpus research of data extracted from the ICE-corpora and COCA. Special attention will go to the formal as well as semantic characteristics of the various uses of type nouns, their collocational patterns and the division of labour between the various type nouns, i.e. *sort*, *kind* and *type*. Differences and similarities between American English and other varieties are studied and results show, for instance, that the nominal qualifier use of *sort/kind of* is absent in the other varieties. The corpus study also reveals new patterns like *kinda of* which have to be considered as non-standard at this point. In addition, it seems that *all manner of* is making a recovery. Outer and inner circle varieties show differences in terms of the use of *sort* and *kind*, such that in outer circle varieties the binominal and postdeterminer uses are more frequent. However, in inner circle varieties, these type nouns are most frequently used as an adverbial modifier or discourse marker. The study confirms the general tendency that elements typically shift from propositional uses to non-propositional ones and argues that taking a global view is necessary in type noun research.

1 Introduction

The type nouns *sort, kind, type* provide a number of challenges both syntactically and semantically.[1] They may, for example, be difficult to describe because the same surface structure or syntactic pattern can have several different interpretations depending on the context. Specifically, it has been shown that it is difficult to distinguish between uses where constructions with type nouns are used for categorization and where they have an approximative meaning. Tied to this fuzziness between the uses is the fact that it is sometimes unclear if the meanings associated with a form or structure are coded or only an implicature or side-

---

[1] The nouns have been referred to as the SKT-nouns in the literature. They will be discussed in the order *sort (of)*, *kind (of)*, *(type) of* and not alphabetically.

Karin Aijmer, University of Gothenburg, e-mail: karin.aijmer@sprak.gu.se

https://doi.org/10.1515/9783110701104-004

effect of a more established meaning. As a result of the fuzzy boundaries between different patterns, there is also much uncertainty about the number of different subtypes we need to distinguish.

Previous research has discussed type nouns both synchronically and diachronically in different theoretical frameworks including Construction Grammar (e.g. Denison 2002). Synchronically, the focus has been on their semantic-pragmatic properties as adverbials or pragmatic markers and on their multifunctionality (e.g. Holmes 1988; Aijmer 2002; Kirk 2015; Beeching 2016). Diachronically, the relations between different uses of the type nouns have been studied from a grammaticalization perspective showing how new forms and uses emerge while the old uses remain (e.g. Denison 2002; Margerie 2010; Brems 2011). Thus, it has been argued that the binominal *sort of / kind of / type of* have changed in the direction of adverbial intensifying and discourse marker uses and that the synchronic meanings of the type nouns represent various stages of the grammaticalization process using a Construction Grammar approach (see Brems 2011; Traugott 2008; Denison 2011).

The English type nouns have been most completely described for British (and American) English. The aim of the present chapter is to extend the analysis of the uses of type nouns to more varieties of English in order to describe the relationship between their forms and functions from a more global perspective. The larger theoretical issue is whether the type nouns develop the same uses in different languages and varieties of the same language and what the implications are of a cross-linguistic perspective for pragmatic theory. Extending the study of the type nouns to more varieties also provides an extra lens through which we can make detailed observations about the relation between the semantic, pragmatic and discoursal aspects of the type nouns and their formal properties.

The research questions are both quantitative and qualitative:
- how widespread are the type nouns across varieties of English?
- how many uses (nominal and non-nominal) of the type nouns should be distinguished?
- what are the collocational patterns or constructions with type nouns in the corpora and how should they be characterized in terms of syntax, semantics and pragmatic function?
- what are the mechanisms explaining the similarities and differences between their frequencies and uses in the varieties?
- how do the specific type nouns differ from each other? *Type (of)* has, for example, been shown to be rather marginal while *sort of* and *kind of* are used more broadly in many different functions.

The article is organized as follows. Section 2 describes the methodology followed. In Section 3, I will present an overview of the frequencies of the type nouns in the data. Sections 4 to 6 will describe the type nouns with regard to their syntactic structure, collocations and semantic or pragmatic functions. In the concluding section I will return to a discussion of the similarities and differences between *sort of* and *kind of* (and *type of*) in varieties of English and how they should be explained.

2 Methods

The empirical study of type nouns in varieties of English is based on comparable corpora designed and collected in the same way within the International Corpus of English project http://ice-corpora.net/ice/. The aim is to compare the frequency and use of the nouns both in varieties where English is the standard and in varieties where it is spoken as the second language. The corpora selected therefore represent both inner circle varieties of English (British English, Canadian English, New Zealand English) and outer-circle varieties (Philippine English, Hong Kong English, Singapore English). Each corpus consists of one million words of spoken and written English produced after 1989. The occurrences of the type nouns have been retrieved from the spoken part of the corpora consisting of face-to-face conversations (c.180,000 words from each variety). The absence of a comparable ICE-corpus for American English has been compensated for by the use of the Santa Barbara Corpus of Spoken American English (SBCSAE) which contains 249,000 words of "naturally spoken interaction from all over the United States" (http://www.linguistics.ucsb.edu/research/santa-barbara-corpus). In addition, I have used the Corpus of Contemporary American English (COCA) to illustrate recent uses of the type nouns in American English. The COCA corpus contains data from transcripts of unscripted speech from television, movies subtitles, blogs and other web pages from the 1990s to the present (Davies 2008). Because of its large size (520 million words of speech and writing) it can be expected to contain uses which are not found in the smaller Santa Barbara Corpus and which can foreshadow new developments.[2]

One hundred instances of *sort of* and the same number of tokens of *kind of* and *type of* were extracted from each corpus.[3] *Kinda* was included as a separate

---

[2] All the examples will be quoted in the form they were printed in the corpora. For example, the corpora contain special conventions for transcribing contracted forms which have been retained. It is generally difficult to distinguish linguistic features of a variety of English from errors. No attempt has therefore been made to correct errors in the examples.
[3] If there were fewer examples of either *sort of* or *kind of*, all examples were included.

lexical item although it was only found in American (and Philippine) English. The occurrences (1,616 in all) were coded for information about the constructions in which they were found, their pragmatic function and the choice of type noun.

3 The frequency of the type nouns in the selected varieties

Sort (of), *kind (of)* and *type (of)* are so-called type nouns referring to a subtype or subcategory of a larger category. Table 1 shows the raw numbers and frequencies per 10,000 words for the three type nouns in the selected varieties of English in this study:

Table 1: Frequencies of *sort of (sorta)*, *kind of (kinda)* and *type of* in selected varieties of English normalized to 10,000 words.

	ICE-GB	SBCSAE	ICE-CAN	ICE-NZ	ICE-HK	ICE-SIN	ICE-PHIL
Sort of	639 (35.5)	65 (2.61)	280 (15.56)	512 (28.44)	58 (3.22)	104 (5.78)	37 (2.06)
Sorta	–	10 (0.40)	–	–	–	–	–
Kind of	175 (9.72)	160 (6.43)	348 (19.33)	111 (6.17)	138 (7.72)	218 (12.11)	211 (11.72)
Kinda	–	167 (6.71)	2 (0.11)	–	1 (0.06)	–	65 (3.61)
Type of	14 (0.78)	22 (0.89)	22 (1.22)	9 (0.05)	6 (0.33)	28 (1.56)	11 (0.61)
Total	828 (46)	424 (17.03)	652 (36.22)	632 (35.11)	203 (11.27)	350 (19.44)	324 (18)

Figure 1 presents the frequencies of the type nouns *sort of, kind of* and *type of* as a bar chart:

The type nouns occurred most frequently in ICE-GB, ICE-CAN and ICE-NZ with the highest frequency in British English. The low frequency of type nouns in American English may be due to the fact that the corpus contains data from many different situations where people use spoken language such as classroom lectures, sermons, etc. In the Asian varieties the type nouns were relatively infrequent.

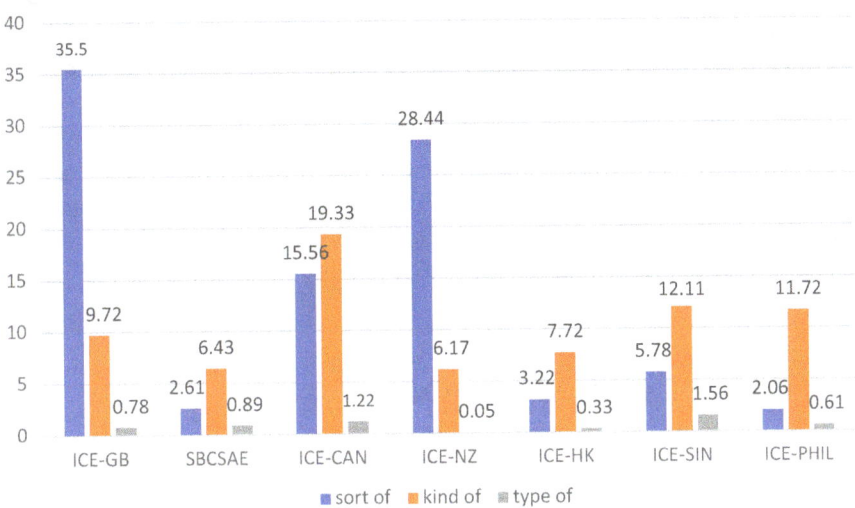

Figure 1: Frequencies of *sort of, kind of* and *type of* in varieties of English normalized to 10,000 words.

The choice of a specific type noun is associated with the particular variety. *Sort of* was more frequent than *kind of* in ICE-GB and ICE-NZ. The reduced form *kinda* was more frequent than *kind of* in SBCSAE, and was also found in Philippine English. *Sorta* was only attested in SBCSAE (and only in a few instances). *Type of* was found in all the varieties but only with a low frequency.

The distribution of *sort of* and *kind of* in ICE-GB and the SBCSAE is in line with previous work. Biber et al. (1999) (referring to *sort of* and *kind of* as epistemic adverbials of imprecision) found that *kind of* was used 400 times per million words in American conversation and less than 50 times per million words in British conversation. On the other hand, *sort of* was more frequent in British conversation with 300 times per million words compared with 100 times per million words in American English conversation. The findings from a study comparing *sort of* and *kind of* in a variety of spoken corpora of British and American English by Miskovic-Ludovic (2009) confirm the preference for *kind of* in American English: "*Sort of* occurred more frequently in the British corpus, while *kind of* was more typical of the American corpus" (Miskovic-Ludovic 2009: 619). She also concluded that *sort of* occurred in more formal contexts in her data while *kind of* (*kinda*) was more linked to slang.

More recently, Beeching (2016: 172) compared *sort of* and *kind of* in the British National Corpus and the Corpus of Contemporary American English (COCA). The conclusion from her study was that British speakers favoured *sort of* more strongly than *kind of* while American speakers favoured *kind of* over *sort of*. Zámečnik and Denison (2018) also found a preference for *kind of* rather than *sort of* in comparable corpora of British and American English. They also showed that the frequency of *kind of* has increased over time accompanied by an overall decline of both *sort of* and *type of*.

The high frequency of *sort of* in New Zealand English has been observed by De Klerk (2005: 89) in a study comparing intensifiers in Xhosa and New Zealand English.[4] In the Wellington Corpus (500,000 words) *sort of* was found in 1138 examples (22.76 tokens per 10, 000 words) and *kind of* in 273 examples (5.46 tokens per 10,000 words).

4 The uses of the type nouns

Previous work (e.g. Denison 2002; Brems 2011) has demonstrated that a large number of factors play a role in the categorization of type nouns, such as the preceding indefinite or definite article, the use of demonstratives, collocations with verbs, adjectives and nouns, and number agreement. On the basis of the syntactic and functional criteria which have been proposed, I have distinguished the following main categories: (a) nominal uses with type nouns as head words and modifiers, (b) approximating (qualifying) uses, and (c) discourse markers. The discussion of the nominal uses of type nouns heads includes cases where it is uncertain which noun in the construction 'Type Noun + of + Noun' is the head.

4.1 Type nouns as heads and modifiers

Kind in (1) is a head noun followed by a postmodifier introduced by *of*. It has the function of referring to a subtype of the larger category indicated by the second noun. The speakers are discussing how dirty trains are depending on whether the passenger has got a ticket for a hard or a soft bed.

(1) That depends **what kind of** uhm **ticket** you got. (icehkv2:S1A-002)[5]

---

4 Australian English may be similar to British and New Zealand English with regard to the preference for *sort of*. According to Mulder et al. (2019), *sort of* occurred more often in their Australian corpus of television panel discussions than in comparable data of British and American English in the *Longman Grammar of Spoken and Written English*.
5 S1A refers to the sub-category Private Conversation in the spoken component of the ICE-corpora.

The syntactic criteria distinguishing the original meaning of the type noun from its other meanings involve number agreement. In (2) the demonstrative pronoun agrees with the following noun.

(2) I like having more like little alcoves and **those types of things** but. (icecan-v2:S1A-079)

Number mismatch between the demonstrative and the type noun may occur, as in (3).

(3) So maybe the the TO themselves can can check some of **those type of details** (icesingv2:S1A-015)

The form *type* is potentially erroneous in this example. However, the lack of number agreement may indicate that this type noun construction should be given a different functional and formal analysis (see Section 4.1.3).[6]

Table 2 shows the distribution of type nouns (both singular and plural forms) with the function of denoting a subcategory. We can observe that *sort of* has an unusually low frequency compared with *kind of* (and *type of*) in all the varieties (including ICE-GB). *Kind of* did not occur at all in Canadian English (although *kinds of* did) but was frequent in Hong Kong English. *Type of* and *types of* occurred more often in Singapore English than in the other varieties.

Table 2: The frequencies of type nouns as head nouns in constructions.

	ICE-GB	SBCSAE	ICE-CAN	ICE-NZ	ICE-HK	ICE-SIN	ICE-PHIL	Total
Sort of	2	2	2	1	2	3	3	15
Kind of	7	5	–	3	17	10	5	47
Sorts of	3	1	1	9	–	6	2	22
Kinds of	7	2	13	1	6	2	11	42
Type of	1	5	–	5	4	16	5	36
Types of	2	–	5	2	2	6	6	23
Total	22	15	21	21	31	42	32	185

---

[6] Number mismatch may not be a reliable criterion that change has taken place especially if the examples occur in varieties where English is spoken as a second language. The psychological process of learning a second language may result in errors or overextension of a certain lexical item or grammatical pattern. Speakers use strategies such as simplification in situations where number agreement is required. In a language using English as a second language the simplified or erroneous patterns may even be conventionalized.

The type nouns in their head use occur in a wide range of constructions where they are modified by adjectives, or preceded by demonstratives or quantifiers. However, it is often uncertain whether in the construction 'Type noun + of + N2' it is the type noun or the N2 which functions as the head of the construction. Moreover, there is no consensus about the number of patterns (sub-variants) which need to be distinguished (see Brems 2011). For instance, it has been suggested that type nouns preceded by adjectives can have two different interpretations. This matter will be pursued further in the following section.

4.1.1 Type nouns preceded by adjectives

Surface strings where type nouns are preceded by adjectives can be argued to have multiple functions. A distinction can be made between three kinds of constructions: type nouns preceded by classifying adjectives, type nouns preceded by descriptive (attributive) adjectives and semi-suffix type constructions (with and without *of*).

4.1.1.1 Type nouns preceded by classifying adjectives

Adjectives which collocate with the type noun are either classifying or descriptive. In (4) the head noun, *type*, is preceded by an adjective with the function of referring to a subclass of the superordinate category.

(4) I bet it's a Cantonese dish in those easter uh no **western eastern type of cookbooks** right (icesingv2:S1A-019)

The reference is to *western eastern* types or styles of cookbooks. According to Brems (2011: 278), "adjectives premodifying TN [type noun] head consist mainly of a small cohesive set of adjectives that are very frequently used in English as such, e.g. *rare, new, right, special, wrong* and *different*." Examples (5) to (9) illustrate adjectives premodifying a head noun from different varieties in my material.

In (5), the beads have been categorized as being of the *right* kind.

(5) [And that's] the **right kind of beads**, (SBCSAE)[7]

---

[7] The transcription used in SBCSAE has been simplified in the examples given in the text.

Different picks out a subgroup of people or personalities:

(6) I do n't know how to contact with **different kind of people** who would have **different kinds of personalities**. (icehkv2:S1A-022)

In (7) the speaker describes a person as belonging to a traditional kind (subgroup) of Chinese people (because she shares their beliefs).

(7) I think she is **a kind of traditional kind of Chinese** to believe in something like uhm it was I I do n't know how to say just I think she she thinks uhm (icehkv2:S1A-001)

In (8) the adjective *alternative* singles out certain kinds of housing which are less prototypical.

(8) ... She .. deals a lot with .. **alternative kinda housing**, and co-housing, and .. housing .. for the sake of people and stuff. (SBCSAE)

Compare also: *standard kind of physiology* (ICE-GB), *every single sort of foreign cuisine* (ICE-GB), *a royal type of family* (SBCSAE), *the classic type of prostitutes* (SBCSAE) where the adjectives describe a particular aspect of or a subclass of a category.

4.1.1.2 Type nouns preceded by descriptive adjectives
The type noun can also be preceded by an adjective describing the characteristic properties of an individual, place or object.

(9) We try you know I love my cousin and we played a lot as kids but I guess I'm **an introvert kind of person** I I you know (icephiv2:S1A-016)

(10) He looked like a ....kind of **a sloppy kind of guy**. (SBCSAE)

The adjective before the type noun has the function of characterizing a person rather than categorizing them (Brems 2011: 284 "the attributive modifier use"). When the adjective is descriptive it refers to an instance of the noun phrase describing the subclass rather than the whole subclass. Pursuing this analysis further would entail that *kind of* (*sort of, type of*) was no longer the head of the construction. According to Davidse et al. (2008: 142), *sort of* and *kind of* could be said to have been "demoted from head to modifier status".

An observation we can make is that the adjectival material preceding the type noun with a descriptive function is typically prominent or foregrounded (cf. Beeching 2016: 175).

In (11) the type noun is preceded by a combination of adjectives.

(11) I think it's **a very deep or enriching kind of book** is n't it (icephiv2:S1A-062)

In (12) the use of two adjectives results in greater emphasis on characterization.

(12) Are they talkative or they're **the strong silent type of guy** (icephiv2:S1A-096)

The adjective is more distinctive when intensified by an adverbial:

(13) Would n't that be **a pretty odd sort of proposition** like have a look to see if it's going round would always be a good one. (icegbv2:s1a-008)

(14) Ya and it ended up that they've had **some really bad kind of results** (icecanv2:S1A-023)

The comparative form can also make the adjective more prominent, as in (15).

(15) I mistook you for **a more intelligent kind of man.** (icegbv2:s1a-041:s1a-041)

In (16) *huge* has an expressive ring to it, making it more emphatic:

(16) i wonder do they really live like that the middle of the wops **these huge sort of plains** just flat plains with one like (icenzv2:S1A-026)

The type noun is usually singular. There was one occurrence of the plural *sorts of* preceded by adjective with an attributive function, as in (17).

(17) Uhm I mean **in the oddest sorts of ways** I mean they're really very proper and very sober and very conscientious hard-working little bunch (icegbv2:s1a-054)

Sorts of ways can be regarded as a variant of the semi-fixed *sort of way*.

The construction with an attributive modifier is described by Brems as "having a rather limited application in present-day English" (Brems 2011: 288). In my analysis the pattern was found in all varieties but was infrequent, as shown in Table 3.

Table 3: The frequency of type nouns preceded by a descriptive modifying adjective.

	ICE-GB	SBCSAE	ICE-CAN	ICE-NZ	ICE-HK	ICE-SIN	ICE-PHIL	Total
Sort of	1	1	4	1	–	3	1	11
Kind of	5	1	4	6	1	1	4	22
Type of	–	2	2	–	–	–	1	6
Total	6	4	10	7	1	3	6	38

4.1.1.3 The semi-suffix construction

Instances containing a longer string of words modifying the type noun have been described as having a semi-suffix use (see Brems 2011: 288). Brems and Davidse (2010: 188) describe the semi-suffix use as "an ad hoc, and often very creative classifier". (18)–(21) illustrate the ad hoc nature of this use.

(18) So he went from like the romantic .. sexual getaway, to, you know, **a soul searching .. (SNIFF) bond with nature .. type of deal.** (SBCSAE)

(19) But I still think that it's it's still nicer than what we are having here in Singapore you know at the Metro stores where they're having **those back to sixties kind of clothes.** (icesingv2:S1A-003)

(20) Well my experience uhm first semester of teaching I was like **this uh very uh strict Hitler type of a teacher.** (icephiv2:S1A-020)

(21) But with **a sort of lovely sort of shortbready kind of taste** to it. (icegb-v2:s1a-057)

The semi-suffix use is similar to the attributive use of descriptive adjectives in the sense that the N2 is the headword of the construction. In (19) and (20) where the type noun is preceded by a demonstrative pronoun it also functions as a postdeterminer (see Section 4.1.3).

Zámečnik and Denison (2018) describe the semi-suffix pattern as hybrid "depending on the example, not easily distinguishable from binominal, attributive modifier or postdeterminer". The following example illustrates that the same pattern is also difficult to distinguish from patterns where *sort of / kind of* has a hedging and qualifying meaning. Contextual clues are essential to show how the type noun pattern should be interpreted:

(22) They are they are because I mean even if you okay do we we do have **Chinese** uhm **sort of pilots** but they are not real they are not really the pilots yet. (icehkv2:S1A-094:S1A-094:1:388:B)

The context makes it clear that the Chinese pilots the speaker is referring to are not yet real pilots but perhaps amateur or unqualified pilots.

Table 4 shows the frequencies of the type nouns in semi-suffix constructions:

Table 4: Type nouns in semi-suffix constructions in the varieties.

	ICE-GB	SBCSAE	ICE-CAN	ICE-NZ	ICE-HK	ICE-SIN	ICE-PHIL	Total
Sort of	1	–	–	3	1	4	1	10
Kind of	1	–	1	3	–	6	2	13
Type of	–	3	2	1	–	–	3	9
Total	2	7	6	2	–	10	7	34

4.1.1.4 Patterns without *of*

With the loss of the following preposition the type noun becomes (even) more suffix-like although it still retains head status (Denison 2011). Only *type* was found in this pattern. The reference is to different types of medicine, food, furnaces or wood:

(23) I do n´t know how to explain just just a kind of uhm **Chinese type medicine**. (icehkv2:S1A-001: 364)

(24) And uh anyways uhm and we will have this sort of **buffet type food** so it´s like European in style uh whatever Western yeah (icehkv2:S1A-100)

(25) I know there's **pulse type furnaces**,
which evidently are kinda loud (SBCSAE)

(26) now when when i saw her putting it in the oven i thought it was going to come out **sort of like a lasagne type thing** but it did n´t. (icenzv2:S1A-003)

In (27) the speakers are discussing whether to buy a breadbox in maple type wood.

(27) DARLENE: ... And so,
but all the ones <X in X> the paper were showing,
the early American,
the lighter ... **maple type wood**. (SBCSAE)

Adjectives or nouns appearing before *type* are generally classifying in nature. However, in (28) the adjective is descriptive rather than classifying.

(28) And [what's] his name,
      PATRICK: [Mm].
      CORINNA: that other guy?
      PATRICK: .. Mhm.
      CORINNA: ... Did happen to him.
                    ... Cause they're like **weaker type men**.
                    ... You know in prison they'd never survive. (SBCSAE)

This pattern is uncommon, with the highest frequency attested in SBCSAE (SBCSAE 5 examples, ICE-NZ 1 example, ICE-HK 2 examples, ICE-SIN 1 example).

Variants of the semi-suffix function are *sort of thing (kind of thing, type of thing)*. These can also be regarded as general extenders although they are less frequent than more prototypical ones (e.g. *and that sort of thing*) (see Beeching 2016: 259). General extenders are multifunctional and it is often difficult to distinguish between usages such as metacomments, qualifier, pause-fillers and face-threat mitigators (see Section 6.4).

4.1.2 *All kinds of / all sorts of / all types of*: The quantifying function

All kinds/sorts of contains the universal quantifier 'all' but it can also be interpreted as referring to quantity ('many', 'a large quantity') and to diversity ('different', 'various') (see Brems and Davidse 2010: 182). The construction is close both to the postdeterminer (Section 4.1.3) and to variants where *all kinds/sorts/types of* would refer to different subclasses of a superordinate category. In (29) the derived quantifying interpretation is most likely.

(29) You want uh ah nice uh seasoned wood that uh is not twisted into **all kinds of funny shapes**. (icecanv2:S1A-012)

In example (29), *all kinds of* does not involve identification of all types of funny shapes but can be replaced by 'many'. The proposal is that "the constructional meaning shifts away from pure head noun status to quantifier-(like) status via the implicature 'all the different kinds of'> 'instances of many kinds' > 'many instances" (Brems 2011: 281). However, as in the occurrences with a preceding descriptive adjective the type noun has an uncertain head noun status.

Table 5 represents the frequencies of the type nouns with a quantifying function:

Table 5: The frequency of *all sorts of / all kinds of / all types of* in their quantifier uses.

	ICE-GB	SBCSAE	ICE-CAN	ICE-NZ	ICE-HK	ICE-SIN	ICE-PHIL	Total
All sorts of	10	2	3	17	1	3	2	38
All kinds of	5	10	13	1	–	3	2	34
All types of	–	–	–	–	–	1	1	–
Total	15	12	16	18	1	7	45	74

The preference for *sorts of* rather than *kinds of* in ICE-GB and ICE-NZ is to be expected from the general frequency of this form in those varieties. *All types of* was only found in two examples (ICE-SIN 1 example, ICE-PHIL 1 example). The low frequency of quantifiers with *all types of* is confirmed by Brems (2011: 283) who found only two examples, both in (written) corpus data from The Times sub-corpus of the Collins Wordbanks corpus consisting of texts from the London newspapers *The Times* and *The Sunday Times* from the 1990s.

4.1.2.1 *All manner of*

The diachronic account of type nouns also discusses *manner of* which is not found in the ICE-corpora or in SBCSAE (see Zámečnik and Denison 2018). However, the COCA corpus contained instances of both the lexicalized pattern *all manner of* with a singular head noun and *all manners of* where the head noun agrees with *all*. *All manner of* and *all manners of* were used to refer to distinct types of a superordinate category (the binominal use) and with reference to a large amount of instances (the quantifier use). In (30) the speaker is referring to several different types of unorthodox therapists.

(30) They are being taken to naturopaths, acupuncturists, shamans and **all manner of completely unorthodox "therapists"**. (COCA BLOG 2012, original punctuation)

In (31) the speaker makes it clear that she sewed many (or a variety of) dresses of a particular style.

(31) She may have had the ideas down pat, not so much the execution as she sewed us **all manner of Little House on the Prairie style dresses** while my father went off to work (COCA BLOG 2012)

The plural *all manners of* is used with a quantifier function.

(32) He is a good man who always means well. Yet somehow he finds himself in **all manners of ridiculous and awful situations.** (COCA BLOG 2012)

In addition to the complex *all manner of* there was one instance of the collocation '*many manner* + Noun' in COCA:

(33) **Many manner districts in California** require college guidance counseling on principal school sophomores, while some districts in Wisconsin ask for sessions during the freshmen year. (COCA BLOG 2012)

Such examples which can be regarded as 'American English' may foreshadow changes which can be expected to take place more generally especially as 'manner' has a history as a type noun in earlier English.

4.1.3 *The/that/this sort of/kind of/type of*: Identifying and intensifying functions

In (34) *the kind of . . . current theoretical literary cultural theory* is most likely interpreted in a propositional way where the speaker is referring to types of current literary theory on identity.

(34) Uhm I think he knows a bit about **the kind of** you know **current theoretical literary cultural theory** uhm **on this sort of thing on identity**. (iceh-kv2:S1A-047)

However, other patterns with *the (that, this) sort of, kind of* and *type of* may better be regarded as non-head uses with the function of pointing deictically to a following noun broadening its reference to other, similar things. This usage has been described as a special postdeterminer construction: "Together with the primary determiner it forms a complex determiner that can express more intricate identifying and phoric relationships than a simple determiner can" (Brems and Davidse 2010: 184).

A noticeable feature of the construction is the agreement mismatch (Denison 2002) where the type noun (singular) is preceded by a plural anaphoric determiner:

(35) The whole interior of the apartment was completely dark No skylights no windows nothing And uh just really you know **those kind of places** that have uhm phone wire kind of painted and crusted to the baseboards (icecanv2:S1A-007)

Kinda can also be found as a postdeterminer with an identifying function:

(36) on the door of this little shacky building,
it's all around this big square,
there are **these kinda beat-up little buildings**.
And,
... painted on one,
a big, the circle with the triangle (SBCSAE)

It has been claimed that the phrase *that sort of / kind of* "may well be in complementary distribution with anaphoric *such*" (Denison 2002), and that it intensifies more effectively than the simple determiners *this* and *that* (van der Auwera and Coussé 2016: 15). We also find *such kind of* and *these such kind of* with *such* preceding the type noun. The combination of *such* and *kind of* is not accidental but suggests that they belong to the same semantic area of identification and intensification.

The postdeterminer construction can intensify or emphasize the speaker's negative evaluation of an item or person. *Such translators* in the example below refers to Japanese translators who translate into English without having a good command of the language.

(37) That s why uh **such kind of** uh **translators** may become very popular very uhm well demanded by the movie. (icehkv2:S1A-006)

In (38) *this type of this kind of work* conveys the speaker's negative attitude to 'this kind of work' (it is tiring, involves a lot of effort, etc.).

(38) Uhm management uhm management trainee or but I don't like **this type of this kind of work** actually. (icehkv2:S1A-092)

In (39), *these such kind of silly things* intensifies the speaker's annoyance with film-makers.

(39) You know **these such kind of silly things** and then their the I mean the mother have to stop her stop the daughter so it create a rather uhm kind of entertain. (icehkv2:S1A-016)

In addition to its subjective use, the postdeterminer can be regarded as intersubjective since it implies that the hearer is able to ascertain the identity of the referent. The intersubjective or interpersonal function is particularly clear in examples where *this sort/kind of thing* is used with a generalizing function. The speaker refers to a more general category which can be understood by the hearer, thereby establishing common ground.

(40) yeah you rely on your mum for **that kind of thing**. (icenzv2:S1A-096)

The postdeterminer identifying construction can also contain *any* followed by a type noun:

(41) and I enjoy **any kind of physical exercise** that is you know stretching or uhm working out building on muscle. (icegbv2:s1a-003)

According to Brems (2011: 302), the noun modified by *any kind of* can convey a quantitative implied meaning associated with size or effort rather than (negative) evaluation as in (38) and (39). In (41) the speaker makes it clear that she enjoys *any possible kind of exercise* (even if it implies a great deal of effort).

In addition to the simple pattern, the COCA corpus contained one example with *any such type of* where the postdeterminer is both intensifying and identifying:

(42) what advice can you give to the general public to make people confident again, or can you offer **any such type of advice**? (COCA SPOK1991)[8]

Table 6 states the frequencies of type nouns as postdeterminers.[9] Some constructions are only found in a few varieties.

That/this/the kind of with the type noun *kind* was the most frequent combination (even in varieties which usually prefer *sort*).

Such kind of represents another pattern not found in the standard varieties. It was not found in the SBCSAE but occurred in the COCA corpus with the variants *such kinda* and *such kinds of*. Other combinations only found in the COCA corpus are *such sort(s) of* and *such type of / such types of*:

---

[8] The texts in the corpus represent different genres such as blogs (BLOG), spoken (SPOK), fiction (FIC), web pages (WEB), TV (TV), movies (MOV), newspapers (NEW).
[9] Examples with the plural *sorts, kinds* and *types* have been classified as examples having the noun as a head word.

Table 6: The frequency of postdeterminer usage of the type nouns.

	ICE-GB	SBCSAE	ICE-CAN	ICE-NZ	ICE-HK	ICE-SIN	ICE-PHIL	Total
That/this/the/what sort of	11	1	5	14	3	18	4	58
That/this/the /what/ kind of	17	10	20	21	33	47	34	182
That /this/the type of	1	13	6	–	–	6	2	28
These/those sort of	–	–	1	1	1	–	–	3
These/those kind of	2	–	1	2	1	3	3	12
Such kind of /these such kind of	–	–	–	–	3	–	–	3
What/these kinda	–	2	–	–	–	–	–	2
Any kind of	2	–	3	2	–	–	–	7
Total	33	26	36	40	41	74	43	295

(43) I doubt very much that the Americans would elect somebody to become their president who has performed **such kind of rituals** for decades (COCA BLOG 2012)

(44) still think Google Maps is more functional . . but singling out apple in **such kinda childish way** is just pathetic. (COCA BLOG 2012)

(45) Park, the KOGAS executive, said, referring to the protest. "Anyhow, we have to work together with the central government and provincial government to solve or prevent **such kinds of incidents**." (COCA NEWS 2010)

(46) But, like, you know, I've talked to his friends who've been on the receiving end of **such sort of statements** and said, you know, he talked to you like that because it was real. (COCA SPOK 2019)

(47) "I thought they didn't do **such sorts of things**." (COCA FIC 2014)

(48) We also find the evidence for **such type of behavior** in two climate simulations using a state-of-the-art model. (COCA WEB 2012)

(49) Perhaps she could be selected as the VP on the Edwards ticket, **such types of such types of deals** are not uncommon. (COCA WEB 2012)

Such kind(s) of was also attested in a few examples in the Corpus of Historical American English (COHA) indicating that this is a latent pattern in English which can be revived if needed. The first example of *such kind of* in COHA comes from 1830.

4.1.4 *A sort/kind of* and *some sort/kind of* with a nominal qualifying function

A sort/kind of and *some sort/kind of* have the function of qualifying the following noun in an approximative way "but this can be done for various reasons and further meanings can be added to this core meaning" (Brems 2011: 311). This is illustrated in (50).

(50) She had her hair kind of down in **a kind of** I do n`t know **net**. (icegb-v2:s1a-037)

The qualifying construction is concerned with the relation of the referent to the categorization used in the N2 position ('net'). *A kind of* has an approximative function which adds uncertainty to the categorization of the referent.

There were also instances where an indefinite article both precedes and follows *kind of* or *sort of* with an approximating function:

(51) So so I had to I had to uh parang you know lay low and then and go on **a sort of a retreat** because I was so depressed. (icephiv2:S1A-098)

Where the surface string has the form *a sort/kind of a* with an indefinite article before both nouns 'the indefiniteness may trigger the inference that because the class membership is not uniquely identifiable, it is not exact. In this kind of context NP2 [N2] came to be reanalyzed as the head and *a sort of* became a degree modifier conveying the speaker's assessment that the entity referred to is not an adequate or prototypical exemplar (Traugott 2008: 229). In (51) the speaker is not referring to a 'prototypical exemplar of N2' but to an entity which only approximates a retreat. The inference that the relationship between the referent and how it is categorized is not exact can also be made if the indefinite article is missing as in (52):

(52) The rhetoric that would have been appropriate to liberalism has now become appropriate to **a kind of conservative outlet**. (icecanv2:S1A-025)

The situation is complicated by the existence of occurrences where the indefinite article before *sort of* or *kind of* is missing:

(53) Uhm well it was **kind of a related field.** (icegbv2:s1a-034)

Kind of clearly has less scope over the following noun and is best described as a discourse marker in such uses (see Section 6).

The hedging nature of *sort of* is also evident in *some sort of (a)*. Following Margerie (2011: 336) it can be claimed that *some* does itself reinforce the idea of hedging or approximation associated with *sort of*:

(54) So are you saying that this is **some sort of an experimental research** wherein you will use your classes (icephiv2:S1A-052)

By means of *some sort of a* the speaker questions the appropriateness of the term *experimental research*.

In (55), *some sort of (like)* highlights the fact that the reference is to something which only vaguely resembles a book.

(55) They start from scratch but they do n't have **some sort of like a book.** (icesingv2:S1A-084)

A/some sort of / kind of can combine with *(a) bit of (a)* for downtoning effect. (56) contains *some sort of bit of* before the noun and (57) the longer string *a bit of a sort of a*.

(56) Oh you told me about her she had **some sort of bit of a physical thing.** (icecanv2:S1A-095)

(57) And they're having **a bit of a sort of a sale** on that might not apply to that but. (icegbv2:s1a-040)

A type of is unusual as a nominal qualifier with only a few tokens in the corpus data. The examples are:

(58) they put,. . . **a type of** uh . . **base** on it that needs water (SBCSAE)

(59) and uh it was uhm **a type of department store** but uhm for tourists in that they had English speaking uh clerks as well (icecanv2:S1A-055)

(60) And I think that is **a type of burden.** (icehkv2:s1a-032)

In addition, *some type of* occurred in a few instances:

(61) I'll be studying and uh,
 ... but in a sense,
 I need uh,
 ... **some type of steady income.** (SBCSAE)

An additional pattern is provided by *such a sort / kind of*. Example (62), from the COCA corpus, illustrates the use of hedging *a sort of* together with intensifying *such* (Denison 2002: 6).

(62) I think it would -- in the first place, the first trial just seemed **such a sort of fiasco**, and this trial was run so well, and I think seeing Simpson on the stand was one of the most fascinating things that I ever saw in my life (COCA SPOK 1997)

However, the surface string is ambiguous and (63) must be given a different meaning where *sort* is the head:

(63) Cezanne would have found colour for the figure and the background and everything else and not **such a sort of tonal** uhm **device** that you've used. (icegbv2:s1b-008)

Such a sort of tonal device represents a head noun use as suggested by the context (a type of tonal device like the one you've used).

Table 7 shows the frequencies of the type nouns in nominal patterns with the indefinite article or *some*.

Table 7: The frequencies of the type nouns in constructions with a nominal qualifying use.

	ICE-GB	SBCSAE	ICE-CAN	ICE-NZ	ICE-HK	ICE-SIN	ICE-PHIL	Total
A sort of (a)	9	–	1	5	2	–	4	21
A kind of (a)	3	–	4	4	17	2	5	35
Some sort of (a)	2	1	5	3	1	4	3	19
Some kind of (a)	6	5	6	1	15	13	7	53
A type of	1	1	–	–	1	–	–	3
Some type of	–	2	–	–	–	–	1	3
Total	21	9	16	13	36	19	20	134

Some sort of / some kind of / some type of are generally more frequent than nominal qualifiers introduced by the indefinite article.[10] The low frequency of *a sort/kind of* in some varieties is striking. In SBCSAE there was not a single example of the nominal qualifier (*a kind of / a sort of / a kinda* + noun). The following example is taken from the COCA corpus:

(64) "Little daughter... "She sat stone-still and waited. "There's **a kinda mist**... but I see a well... (COCA FIC1990)

A kinda was never followed by the indefinite article but we find *a kinda of a*:

(65) Hi. Excuse me. I got **a kinda of a long shot** here for you. (COCA MOV 2008)[11]

5 The adverbial qualifying function

Sort of and *kind of* can also modify verbs and adjectives and a few other categories such as numerals and prepositional phrases in an 'adverbial-like' way. The ability to modify verbs and adjectives can be interpreted as a sign of Himmelmann's syntactic context expansion (Himmelmann 2004: 32–33). *Sort of* and *kind of* are extended from their uses in the binominal construction to strings where they modify nouns, adjectives, verbs, and numerals. In its adverbial use the type noun string can also come at the end of the utterance or be used on its own. Syntactic expansion accompanies shifts in meaning and usage. *Sort of* and *kind of* as adverbials are used with pragmatic functions such as metacommenting and hedging. *Type of* was not found with an adverbial function in my data.

Quirk et al (1985) analyse *sort of / kind of* as an adverbial (a subjunct) with a downtoning function. As such it has "a generally lowering effect on the force of the verb or predication" (Quirk et al 1985: 597). The authors also suggest that different subgroups of downtoning adverbials such as approximator, compromiser (e.g. *quite,rather*), minimizer can be distinguished, providing a guide to the hearer's interpretation of the following element. Quirk et al. predominantly discuss downtoning adverbials before verbs. However, the grammatical unit after the adverbial type string can also be an adjective.

In this section, I will first discuss *sort of / kind of* in their qualifying function before adjectives. This will be followed by a discussion of their functions when

---

10 In addition, there were seven instances of *some kinda* in SBCSAE.
11 See also Section 5.6 for more discussion of *kinda of*.

they are followed by verbs, by numerals and by preposition phrases. Finally, I will discuss *sort of* and *kind of* in their qualifying function at the end of the utterance and as response markers.

5.1 *Sort of* and *kind of* as adverbial qualifiers of adjectives

Sort of and *kind of* as downtoning adverbials before adjectives co-occur with *rather, quite, slightly,* and *particularly*.

In (66), the adverbial ('a sort of rather sort of slightly') reduces the potentially offensive properties of 'taking a cynical view of a certain theoretical framework' (the approximator function).

(66) You know but but taking **a sort of rather sort of sort of slightly cynical view of terms like that** but basically it s it is that kind of theoretical framework that he is operating in. (icehkv2:S1A-047:S1A-047:1:236:A)

Downtoning adverbials allow speakers to be cautious or over-cautious in the way they express themselves. *Sort of* can combine with *a bit* to express 'a low or moderate degree of intensification', 'to some extent' (Quirk et al's 1985 'compromiser' function). In (67) *a bit sort of* combines with a coined adjective *nothingy* which has both a downtoning and approximating function:

(67) in a lot of other contact-based dance work you can actually cheat and not give your weight fully or uhm take weight fully and it becomes **a bit sort of nothingy** whereas with this you've really got to put your whole body into it (icegb:sa-022)

It is generally difficult to distinguish between cases where the type noun construction is an adverbial with a subjective function and other more intersubjective uses where the type noun is oriented towards politeness. In (68), the speaker shows her awareness that she may be threatening the hearer's face by asking if something is factually incorrect and uses *sort of (like)* as a mitigator to soften the potential threat:

(68) And uh is n`t that **sort of like factually incorrect** and should it be allowed on a poster. (icegbv2:s1a-069)

In addition to its downtoning use, *sort of / kind of* can be used as a booster emphasising an adjective. In (69) this interpretation is conveyed by the context.

The speaker thinks that something sounds like quite a lot of fun except for the sweaty part of the activity:

(69)   Well that sounds **kind of fun** except for the sweaty part do n`t you think. (icephiv2:S1A-034)

In (70) *sort of* is best analysed as having a booster function indicated by the focusing *particularly* and the intensifying *smashing:*

(70)   But actually at the moment we've got **a particularly sort of smashing selection of dialects on tape.** (icegbv2:s1a-012:s1a-012:1:8:A)

Use in combination with *really* can suggest that *sort of* has a boosting rather than an approximating value:

(71)   The night before and then you wake up feeling **really sort of dopey kind of whatever.** (icehkv2:S1A-100)

Brems (2010: 314) regards the boosting or intensifying function of *sort of / kind of* as an implicature, while Margerie (2010:323) argues that *kind of / kinda* will need to be used with a boosting function on a wider scale before it becomes entrenched in language. However at least in some, highly emotional, contexts with adjectives *kind of* seems to be on its way to acquiring a new booster meaning in addition to its downtoning and hedging functions.

An observation shared by Gries and David (2007) is that *kind of* appears frequently with subjective adjectives expressing an emotion or evaluative judgment. In my data this tendency was particularly obvious for the American data. In SBCSAE all the adjectives (after both *kind of* and the few examples with *sort of*) expressed the speaker's emotion or evaluation of a situation, person or object. The semantic prosody of the adjective collocating with the adverbial *kind of* was generally negative: *annoyed, bad, boring, crazy, crude, cheesy, dense, embarrassing, frustrated, gross, pushy, risky, sad, silly, smelly, stupid, surly, terrible, tough, weird, worthless.* Positive collocating adjectives were *fun, neat* and *weird.* (72)– (74) illustrate the use of *kind of* with evaluative adjectives (from SBCSAE).

(72)   And once, it was **kind of funny** cause uh,
         . . . it was like, all these cops are like . . . there.
         . . You know they're like driving,
         they don't do anything. (SBCSAE)

(73)
  WALT: and a little damp. You know?
      That's **kind of gross,**
      isn't it. (SBCSAE)

(74) ROY: I don't know if you've seen either of those
  PETE: No
  ROY: They're **kind of neat.** (SBCSAE)

Table 8 shows the distribution of *sort of* and *kind of* as adverbials before adjectives in the varieties studied.

Table 8: The frequency of *sort of* and *kind of* as adverbials before adjectives.

	ICE-GB	SBCSAE	ICE-CAN	ICE-NZ	ICE-HK	ICE-SIN	ICE-PHIL	Total
Sort of	14	6	11	11	11	5	4	62
Kind of	7	22	18	15	8	6	16	92
Total	21	28	29	26	19	11	20	154

In the adverbial qualifying function *kind of* competes with *kinda*. There were 28 occurrences of *kinda* before adjectives in a comparable sample of 100 occurrences from SBCSAE.

5.2 *Sort of* and *kind of* as qualifiers of verbs

Table 9 shows the frequency of *sort of* and *kind of* before verbs in the varieties studied.

Table 9: The frequency of the adverbial *sort of* and *kind of* before verbs.

	ICE-GB	SBCSAE	ICE-CAN	ICE-NZ	ICE-HK	ICE-SIN	ICE-PHIL	Total
Sort of	26	29	26	25	15	43	5	169
Kind of	12	23	19	15	–	3	10	82
Total	38	52	45	40	15	46	15	252

Sort of and *kind of* were generally more frequent before verbs than before adjectives in all varieties (with the exception of ICE-PHIL and ICE-HK).

The larger number of occurrences of the adverbial qualifier before verbs in American English in comparison with the other varieties is noteworthy. We can also note that *kinda* was even more frequent than *kind of* before verbs in the comparable sample from SBCSAE (36 occurrences compared to 23).

Depending on the type of collocating verb *sort of* and *kind of* receive different functions. In (75) *sort of* expresses approximation, reducing the force of the verb while indicating that *finished* expresses more than is relevant since no revision has been carried out ('one could almost say that she has finished but that would be to say too much, since she hasn't revised yet').

(75) She has **sort of finished** but she has n't revised it. (icesingv2:S1A-030)

Similar instances where *sort of* can be paraphrased by 'almost' (Quirk et al.'s 'approximator') expressing approximation or hedging are (76) and (77).

(76) The clock just **sort of like fades away** like <unclear> word (icesingv2:S1A-021)

(77) You know you dig into your toe nails when you watch TV Aiyoh then I suddenly look at myself from outside **sort of like distance myself** from (icesingv2:S1A-028)

Sort of and *kind of* as a compromiser reducing the force of the verb are typically used with verbs such as quotative *say* or *go*, the mental verbs *think* and *know*, and *like* and *want*. In (78) *kind of say* is followed by a quotation and is almost a set phrase (see also Section 6.4 on the quotative function of *kind of* as a discourse marker).

(78) Well he is **kind of saying** it's too late (SBCSAE)

In (79) *kind of* minimizes the force of the verb and is associated with politeness. The speaker is afraid of appearing conceited when speaking about herself and about her life:

(79) You know what I mean uhm with O levels and A levels and stuff like that I got to a point where I was **kind of thinking** for myself about my life. (icegbv2:s1a-034)

Kinda / kind of is both mitigating and hedging in function:

(80) Well for next year just to **kinda kind of know** just to **kinda kind of know** what you have to do (icecanv2:S1A-026)

Sort of renders a suggestion less forceful and more polite:

(81) he and I decided that,
 well we'd **sort of wanna** do something more adventuresome (SBCSAE)

The speaker can also describe a situation in a less precise way by using *kind of* or *sort of* (paraphrases are 'more or less', 'so to speak', 'as it were' and 'what you might call'). The paraphrases show the close association between *sort of / kind of* and metacommenting in the sense of using the marker to establish a distance from the lexical item (Beeching 2018: 128). *Sort of* and *kind of* are, for instance, used before metaphors and idiomatic expressions to mark them as special in some way.

In (82) *kind of* signals that the description by the predication 'nods her head' may not be the most appropriate expression and that there may be alternative expressions which fit the situation better (cf. Andersen 2001: 248).

(82) ALINA: She just looks at me,
 she **kind of nods her head**,
 LENORE: She's terrified
 ALINA: and she's going, Ah,
 shit. (SBCSAE)

Kind of (kinda) and *sort of* are subjective and emphasise that the speaker is uncertain about the choice of appropriate expression in (83) and (84).

(83) So we had that little talk and it **kinda** you know it **kinda stuck in my mind**. (SBCAE)

(84) And I worked I dabbled into uh Buddhist scriptures also and some theosophical books and I **sort of toyed around** with uh different forms of meditation. (icephiv2:S1A-054)

5.2.1 *Kinda of* and *sorta of* as adverbial qualifiers

Kinda has the variant form *kinda of* found in a single example in ICE-CAN. However, the sequence *kinda of* is found more frequently in the COCA Corpus which suggests that it is mainly American. It did not occur in ICE-GB and there was only one example in the spoken British National Corpus 2014. The occurrences are therefore recent and come mainly from social media. New non-standard uses documented in this type of medium can make their way into the standard language and therefore provide a possible clue to ongoing change and conventionalization (see Denison 2008).

Syntactically *kinda of* is adverbial. It is used before adjectives, verbs and nouns with a downtoning (or boosting) function, as in (85).

(85) It's **kinda of frustrating** to not see the scale moving much sometimes not at all from one week to the next (COCA TV 2008)

The adjectives modified by *kinda of* convey negative connotations (*crazy, depressing, disappointing, frustrating. ironic, lost, odd, sad, scary, stupid, weird*) except for *funny. Kinda of* is also used to boost a following verb phrase as shown by the collocation with *really*:

(86) i really **kinda of do nt like this website** that much i cant look the sreen and keys fast anough it gets on but it **kinda of helps me** but i like typing web better. (COCAWEB 2012)[12]

In (87) *kinda of* appears before a verb with a hedging (or qualifying) function.

(87) You can **kinda of accomplish** this in Indesign, by creating a radio button (COCA WEB 2012)

In (88) the emotional context suggests that *kinda of a* is used as a booster.

(88) Note that some places used for this concert series have an extremely bad acoustic quality, so it's **kinda of a shame** the band chose for instance the' bunker' on the people, ideas and companies that drive the region's innovation economy. (COCA BLOG 2012)

The less frequent *sorta of* is illustrated in (89) and (90). In (89), *sorta of* has a downtoning function.

(89) When I first read the item, I **sorta of thought**, ehh, they're going a bit far. # (COCA WEB 2012)

---

[12] The large number of errors in this example (from web pages) can perhaps be explained by the fact that the speaker is demonstrating that s/he is learning to type.

In (90) it has a metacommenting function before a prepositional phrase.

(90) Craig Knox # I'm **sorta of with and against you.** (COCA BLOG 2012)

5.2.2 *Kinda sorta* (also *sorta kinda*)

Sort of kind of was found in ICE-NZ (1 example) and in ICE-PHIL (1 example). It was also found in the COCA corpus (with the variants *kind of sort of, sorta kinda, sort of kind of*. Examples (91) and (92) illustrate the phrase qualifying an adjective and a verb respectively:

(91) And I'm really sorry I lied to you, but you're **kinda sorta super cute**, but (COCA MOV 2012)

(92) (Um, yeah, actually, we **kinda sorta do need** you. (COCA MOV 2015)

As a response marker it can be regarded as covering the area between yes and no. The Urban Dictionary describes it as "really a cover-up avoiding the true answer 'yes'".

(93) # So what you're telling us is that Internal Affairs was in on it the whole time? #**Kinda sorta.** I don't think any positive review ever started with " Its like sex and the city for nerd (COCA WEB 2012)

5.3 *Sort of / kind of* with an utterance-qualifying meaning at the end of the utterance

Sort of / kind of can also be placed utterance-finally with scope over the whole of the preceding utterance or an element in the preceding utterance.

(94) I think you know when you've found a name **kind of.** (icecanv2:S1A-008)

In (95) *kind of* is used on its own. In this function it could also have been analysed as a discourse marker or as a separate 'response marker' signalling that the answer to the question is fuzzy (neither yes nor no).

(95) Mary: ... Did they all hit each other?
              Or just,
       Alice: .. **Kind of.** (SCBSAE)

5.4 Approximation and numerals

Sort of and *kind of* also modify numerals. In their approximative or hedging function preceding numerals, *sort of* and *kind of* can be replaced by *about, roughly* or *approximately:*

(96) but I actually remember getting a whole series of uhm books that'd been in a sort of 2 basement and were **sort of one pound fifty** each. (icegbv2:s1a-013)

Sort of indicates that *one pound fifty* (£1.50) is close to but not exactly the amount indicated. *Sort of* can collocate with *about* in this function:

(97) that's one thing i did n`t understand they just had **these sort of about twenty cows** and a few horses and a few goats he goes into town. ICE9V2_T6571 (icenzv2:S1A-026)

Only eight examples with *about* were found, most frequently with *sort of* (*sort of* ICE-GB 2 examples, ICE-CAN 2 examples, ICE-NZ 2 examples; *kind of* ICE-GB and ICE-SIN 1 example each).

5.5 Approximation and prepositional phrases

The modified element can also be a prepositional phrase (20 examples with *sort of*; 3 examples with *kind of*). *Sort of* and *kind of* have a hedging or metacommenting function, as in (98):

(98) but uh **sort of in my late teens and twenties** I suppose every Saturday one of my pleasures was to go to the local bookshop and buy another volume in the Everyman Library or whatever. (icegbv2:s1a-013)

The speaker is not confident about what age he was when he used to go to the local bookshop.

6 Discourse marker use

Discourse markers can be defined as non-propositional elements with the procedural function of providing a clue to the hearer about how an utterance should be interpreted. They are optional elements which can be deleted from the utterance without any syntactic or semantic consequences. They have little meaning but operate on the pragmatic level serving textual and interpersonal functions. Denison (2002: 4) refers to a discourse marking use in which *sort of* is becoming increasingly bleached and has lost "even its (semantic) downtoner function", coming to resemble the popular discourse marker *like*.

However, the relationship between pragmatic or discourse function and propositional (usually qualifier meaning) is complex. Formal criteria such as the absence of either the indefinite article or a demonstrative pronoun before the type noun are insufficient to define them as discourse markers, and there is a great deal of possible ambiguity between uses or indeterminacy where different meanings cannot be distinguished. Moreover, metacommenting, hedging and approximating functions cannot be used as criteria since these are not unique to discourse markers but also characteristic of the qualifying uses of *sort of* and *kind of (kinda)* before adjectives or verbs. As pointed out by Brems (2011: 325), "there is no clear-cut boundary between the hedging semantics expressed by qualifying uses, with scope over various types of predicate, and the broader scope and further detachment from NP or clause structure typical of the discourse marker use".

The strategy followed here has been to distinguish between qualifying uses and the discourse marker use based on the possible 'omissibility' of *sort of / kind of* as a pragmatic marker and the presence of other pragmatic markers in the immediate environment.

Sort of / kind of / kinda have a number of pragmatic marking functions. They can express approximation, also associated with the related discourse marker *like* with which it often collocates. They can also fulfil a hesitation function where the markers co-occur with planning or speech management problems. Finally, they can function as quotative markers and are used in a suffix-like way in the combination *sort/kind/type of thing* with an interpersonal function.

6.1 Hedging and metacommenting

Discourse markers have hedging or metalinguistic commenting as one of their chief functions. In (99) the speaker is unsure whether to refer to what she has been doing as a job and chooses to preface it with 'kind of':

(99) It was just **kind of a job** I was n't really interested in doing anyway so. (icegbv2:s1a-034)

Sort of / kind of often collocates with *like* signalling a non-literal interpretation:

(100) It's like **sort of ticket touts** over here or something. (icegbv2:s1a-014)

6.2 Hesitation and planning

Sort of and *kind of* have strategic speech management functions to resolve, or prevent, communication problems motivated by cognitive factors such as the speaker's need to find time to search for words, or production problems in the communicative context.

Sort of uh accompanies a restart, as in (101).

(101) No there is another theory that you **can not sort of** uh you **can not sort of** uh dig what. (icesingv2:S1A-100)

In (102) *kind of* coincides with a false start.

(102) In fact I was too eager to go to his place uhm but then during our conversation I mean on the phone when we re talking on the phone uhm he was **kind of** I think he decided not to. (icephiv2:S1A-031)

Kind of and *sort of* were also found in collocations such as *(and) it's kinda (like)*, *it was kind of, and (but) I kinda*, and *they're like sort of* where their function is not only hesitational but *kinda* also provides a link to a new utterance or topic.

Sort of / kind of / kinda also co-occur with *like* in this function:

(103) fifth form you're **sort of like** you're no one man
you're not not a junior but you're not a senior (icenzv2:S1A-070)

In (104) *(it was) kinda* marks the speaker's hesitation (or on-going planning) before starting on a new utterance or topic:

(104) It was you know when you're **kinda** drunk and and you ca n't get your footing right. (icephiv2:S1A-007)

The collocation with *you know* indicates that *sort of* has an interpersonal function in addition to marking hesitation and linking discourse.

The speaker's hesitation or planning difficulties can be more or less obvious. In example (105), (*but*) *sort of* has the primarily textual function of introducing a following argument.

(105) But **sort of** you know I do n't think that's probably unreasonable. (icecan-v2:S1A-012)

In (106) *well yeah sort of* signals the speaker's planning problems and also has the function of linking an utterance to the preceding context and following context.

(106) And uh I think it's one way of expressing myself
B>Yeah that's why your masteral's in relation to that
A>Well yeah **sort of** but uh you know I really want to pursue a kind of uh further studies in theater arts (icephiv2:S1A-066)[13]

6.3 *Sort of/kind of/kinda* with a quotative function

There are also functions that the markers were found to fulfil only occasionally and not in all varieties. This is coherent with the tendency of certain functions associated with *sort of* and *kind of* to develop later (or not at all). In (107) *kind of* co-occurs with *I said* followed by an utterance in direct speech:

(107) PAMELA: and then she said,
... and then she said well,
who fills the stockings.
... And I **kind of**,
I said,
... love fills the stockings. (SBCSAE)

In example (108), *and sort of* is used before a representation of the speaker's thoughts:

(108) oh when i was at the pub all i kept thinking was oh i just want to go home to my bed and **sort of** oh i can't cos there was all these people round. (icenzv2:S1A-022)

---

[13] 'Masteral' in the example is a Philippine word for Master's degree.

In (109) *sort of like* is followed by a representation of what the speaker would say to somebody sharing a place to live:

(109)   You know if I had uhm somebody sharing the place I mean there'd be enough money to pay somebody top **sort of** like okay you do that (icecanv2:S1A-036)

In (110) I have regarded *kind of* as a qualifier of *said* (see Section 5.2). However, such examples may contribute to the use of *kind of* as a quotative marker.

(110)   And then you know my husband you know he **kind of said** well you know next time we're not going to take your mother (icecanv2:S1A-062)

6.4 Utterance-final *sort of / kind of thing*

The utterance-final *sort of / kind of thing* has similarities with the semi-suffix use of type nouns but has developed new pragmatic functions separate from the semi-suffix use. According to Beeching (2016: 182), *sort of thing/kind of thing* is "by its very nature, implicit and uncoded, pragmatic, and not semantic". As a discourse marker the utterance-final *sort of / kind of / type of thing* functions as a mitigator which can serve "to hedge and downplay any perceived conceitedness and thus serves as a face-threat mitigator" Beeching (2016: 158–159).

(111)   I don't mind doing **some classical music sort of thing** you know. (icesingv2:S1A-046)

The speaker refers to *some classical music sort of thing* rather than *classical music* because it makes her sound more friendly and less abrupt.

In (112) the speaker is anxious not to sound angry or annoyed and therefore uses the mitigated *it irks me kind of thing you know*.

(112)   And strangely enough we ve had to go on to canvass and discuss with certain uh avenues like uh uh the canteen and uh that s why I really uh uhm not that uh it angers me but it **it irks me kind of thing** you know. (icephiv2:S1A-026:S1A-026:1:103)

According to Denison (2002: 14), this semi-formulaic use is perhaps the only context in which *type* occurs in a hedging construction. Utterance-final *type of thing* was found in ICE-GB and SBCSAE:

(113) not a painter's ladder of course,
but **a a tower of Babel type of thing** (SBCSAE)

This use of type *of thing* is similar to the semi-suffix construction but serves the interpersonal function of establishing common ground.

(114) So I mean she came in as **sort of while you were around type of thing** or. (icegbv2:s1a-081)

The utterance-final pragmatic marker has a rich potential for implicatures or side-effects. It can also convey 'humour and irony' as in (115) where the reference to *becoming a real person* is probably meant ironically (see Brems 2011: 292):

(115) and I'll sort of uh live in a council flat quite into the idea of that of just actually getting out of the whole scene and **becoming a real person kind of thing** and just working in a chip shop or something like that. (icegbv2: s1a-034:1:134:B)

Tables 10 and 11 represent the frequencies of the functions of *sort of* and *kind of* as pragmatic markers in different varieties.

Table 10: The different functions of pragmatic marker *sort of*.

	ICE-GB	SBCSAE	ICE-CAN	ICE-NZ	ICE-HK	ICE-SIN	ICE-PHIL	Total
hedging/metacommenting	–	6	6	5	6	5	2	30
hesitation/discourse-linking	9	5	6	2	1	3	2	28
quotative	1	–	1	1	–	–	–	3
sort of thing	1	–	–	4	–	1	–	6
Total	11	11	13	12	7	9	4	67

What we can conclude is that the vast majority of uses of both *sort of* and *kind of* have a hedging or hesitational function. *Kind of thing* is also frequent in its pragmatic usage.

Kind of can be compared with *kinda*. *Kinda* (in SBCSAE) was used as a discourse marker in 17% of the sample examples compared with only 9% of occurrences of *kind of*.

Table 11: The different functions of pragmatic marker *kind of*.

	ICE-GB	SBCSAE	ICE-CAN	ICE-NZ	ICE-HK	ICE-SIN	ICE-PHIL	Total
hedging/metacommenting	4	8	–	2	–	–	1	15
hesitation/discourse-linking	7	1	–	2	1	–	2	13
quotative	–	–	–	3	–	–	–	3
kind of thing	6	–	1	2	–	5	2	16
Total	17	9	1	9	1	5	5	47

7 Conclusion

An illuminating way of comparing type nouns across the varieties is to describe the degree to which they have developed the same spectrum of new meanings or functions. *Type of* does not occur in functions related to approximation but is mainly associated with categorization. On the other hand, *sort of* and *kind of* develop in parallel and can be expected to function in the same way.

Table 12 represents the uses of *sort of* and *kind of* / *kinda* in their major functions in the corpora.

Table 12: The frequencies of *sort of* and *kind of* in nominal, adverbial and discourse uses.

	ICE-GB	SBCSAE	ICE-CAN	ICE-NZ	ICE-HK	ICE-SIN	ICE-PHIL
Nominal	93 (46.5%)	40 (24.2%)	87 (43.5%)	97 (45%)	104 (65.8%)	120 (60%)	92 (67.2%)
Binominal	19	10	16	6	26	13	21
Descriptive	6	2	8	7	1	4	5
Semi-suffix	2	–	1	6	1	10	3
Post-determiner	32	11	30	40	41	69	41
Quantifier	15	12	16	18	1	5	3
Nom. qualifier	19	5	16	13	34	19	19
Adverbial/qualifying	63 (31.5%)	83 (50.3%)	85 (42.5%)	80 (40%)	37 (23.4%)	64 (32%)	40 (29.2%)
Before verbs	38	52	45	40	15	46	15
Before adjectives	21	28	29	26	19	11	20
Before numerals	2	–	2	2	–	1	–
Utterance-final/response marker	2	2	4	7	1	4	5

Table 12 (continued)

Before preposition phrase	–	1	5	5	2	2	–
Discourse marker	27 (13.5%)	20 (12.1%)	14 (7%)	24 (12%)	8 (5.1%)	15 (7.5%)	12 (8.8%)
Hedging/ metacommenting	4	14	6	7	6	5	3
Hesitation/ Linking	15	6	6	7	2	3	4
Quotative	1	–	1	4	–	1	3
Sort/kind of thing	7	–	1	6	–	6	2
Unclear	17 (8.5%)	22 (13.3%)	14 (7%)	6 (3.4%)	19 (12.0%)	1 (0.5%)	12 (8.8%)
Total	200	165	200	200	158	200	137

The table highlights the similarities and differences between the varieties and shows the importance of studying the type nouns from a global perspective. The number of binominal uses is highest in the outer circle varieties where *sort of* and *kind of* are frequent both with a binominal function and as postdeterminers. On the other hand, the adverbial and discourse marker functions represent the most frequent uses of *sort of* and *kind of* in the inner circle varieties.

The major patterns which have been established on the basis of the association between form and function are found in all the varieties of English. In line with what we know about the diachronic developments of the type nouns it can be assumed that grammaticalization applies in the same way in all the varieties in line with universal tendencies of how lexical items shift from propositional meaning to discourse-oriented meaning. *Sort of* and *kind of* have developed the same range of functions from their basic type noun meaning including fully pragmatic functions concerned with speech management and textual or interpersonal functions.

At a more detailed level we can notice several differences between the type nouns in the different varieties. The developments in American English may be different from those which have been demonstrated for other varieties. In American English the type noun (especially *kind of*) was, for example, predominantly used as an adverbial qualifier. When the type noun construction was used before adjectives it seems to be on its way to becoming a booster with emotional and evaluative adjectives. A noticeable difference between American English and the other varieties is the absence of *a kind of* and *a sort of* as nominal qualifiers.

A finding in line with the meaning-creating and dynamic properties of the type nouns is the occurrence of innovative or non-standard patterns which may then spread to the standard language. Prior research would indicate that the new patterns emerging on the Internet in American English are likely to foreshadow changes which may affect the standard language as well as other varieties of English (See Tagliamonte and Roberts 2005; Quaglio 2009; Denison 2008). The pattern *kinda of* is in variation with *kinda* and *kind of* in the COCA corpus which suggests that it is emerging in natural spoken conversation.

In the second-language varieties we also find *such kind(s) of, all manner(s) of* which are not represented in standard English. However, they are attested in older stages of English and on the internet indicating that they are latent features in the language.

References

Aijmer, Karin. 2002. *English discourse particles. Evidence from a corpus*. Amsterdam & Philadelpha: John Benjamins.

Andersen, Gisle. 2001. *Pragmatic markers and sociolinguistic variation*. Amsterdam & Philadelphia: John Benjamins.

Beeching, Kate. 2016. *Pragmatic markers in British English. Meaning in social interaction*. Cambridge: Cambridge University Press.

Beeching, Kate. 2018. Metacommenting in English and French: A variational pragmatics approach. In Kate Beeching, Chiara Ghezzi & Piera Molinelli (eds), *Positioning the self and others*, 127–153. Amsterdam & Philadelphia: John Benjamins.

Biber, Doug, Stig Johansson, Geoffrey Leech, Susan Conrad & Edward Finegan. 1999. *The Longman grammar of spoken and written English*. London: Longman.

Brems, Lieselotte. 2011. *Layering of size and type noun constructions in English*. Berlin & Boston: Mouton de Gruyter.

Brems, Lieselotte & Kristin Davidse. 2010. The grammaticalization of nominal type noun constructions with *kind/sort of*: Chronology and paths of change. *English Studies* 91(2). 180–202.

Davidse, Kristin, Lieselotte Brems & Liesbeth De Smedt. 2008. Type noun uses in the English NP: A case of right to left layering. *International Journal of Corpus Linguistics* 13(2). 139–168.

Davies, Mark. 2008.The Corpus of Contemporary American English. 425 million words. 1990– present. Available online at http:// corpus.byu-edu/coca.

de Klerk, Vivian. 2005. Expressing levels of intensity in Xhosa English. *English World-wide* 26(1). 77–95.

Denison, David. 2002. History of the *sort of* construction family. Paper presented at the Second International Conference on Construction Grammar, University of Helsinki, 7 September 2002, http://lings.In.man.ac.uk/staff/dd/papers/sortof_iccg2.pdf.

Denison, David. 2008. Clues to language change from non-standard English. *German life and letters*. 61(4). 537–545.

Denison, David. 2011. The construction of SKT. Paper presented at Second Vigo-Newcastle-Santiago-Leuven International Workshop on the Structure of the Noun Phrase in English (NP2), Newcastle upon Tyne.

Gries, Stefan & Caroline David. 2007. *This is kind of/sort of interesting.* Variation in hedging in English. In Päivi Pahta, Irma Taavitsainen, Terttu Nevalainen & Jukka Tyrkkö (eds.), *Towards multimedia in corpus studies.* Vol. 2. Varieng E-series *Studies in variation, contacts and change in English,* Helsinki: University of Helsinki, http://www.helsinki.fi/varieng/journal/volumes/02/gries_david/.

Himmelmann, Nikolaus. 2004. Lexicalization and grammaticalization: Opposite or orthogonal? In Walter Bisang, Nikolaus Himmelmann & Björn Wiemer (eds.), *What makes grammaticalization? A look from its fringes and components,* 21–42. Berlin: Mouton de Gruyter.

Holmes, Janet. 1988. *Sort of* in New Zealand women's and men's speech. *Studia Linguistica* 42(2). 85–121.

Kirk, John. 2015. *Kind of and sort of*: Pragmatic discourse markers in the SPICE-Ireland Corpus. In Carolina Amador-Moreno, Kevin McCafferty & Elaine Vaughan (eds.), *Pragmatic markers in Irish English,* 89–113. Amsterdam & Philadelphia: John Benjamins.

Margerie, Hélène. 2010. On the rise of (inter)subjective meaning in the grammaticalization of *kind of /kinda.* In Kristin Davidse, Lieven Vandelanotte & Hubert. Cuyckens (eds.), *Subjectification, intersubjectification and grammaticalization,* 315–346. Berlin & Boston: De Gruyter Mouton.

Miskovic-Lukovic, Mirjana. 2009. *Is there a chance that I might kinda sort of take you to dinner?*: The role of the pragmatic particles *kind of* and *sort of* in utterance interpretation. *Journal of Pragmatics* 41. 602–625.

Mulder, Jean, Cara Penry Williams & Erin Moore. 2019. *Sort of* in Australian English: The elasticity of a pragmatic marker. *Journal of Asian Pacific Communication* 29(1). 9–32.

Quaglio, Paolo 2009. *Television dialogue. The sitcom* Friends *vs. natural conversation.* Amsterdam & Philadelphia: John Benjamins.

Quirk, Randolph, Sidney Greenbaum, Geoffrey Leach & Jan Svartvik. 1985. *A comprehensive grammar of the English language.* London: Longman.

Tagliamonte, Sali & Chris Roberts. 2005. So weird; so cool; so innovative: The use of intensifiers in the television series *Friends. American Speech* 80(3). 280–300.

Traugott, Elizabeth Closs. 2008. Grammaticalization, constructions and the incremental development of language: Suggestions from the development of degree modifiers in English. In Regine Eckardt, Gerhard Jäger, Tonjes Veenstra (eds.), *Variation, selection. development: Probing the evolutionary model of language change,* 219–250. Berlin: De Gruyter Mouton.

Van der Auwera, Johan & Evie Coussé. 2016. *Such* and *sådan* – The same but different. *Nordic Journal of English Studies* 15(3). 15–32.

Van Olmen, Daniel. 2019. A diachronic corpus study of prenominal *zo'n* 'so a' in Dutch: Pathways and (inter)subjectification. *Functions of Language.* 26. 216–247.

Zámečnik, Jiří & David Denison. 2018. *A quantitative exploration of SKT constructions.* Paper presented at *ICEHL.* Edinburgh, August 2008.

Evelien Keizer

5 The function and use of NP-external *sort/kind of*: The case of *sort/kind of DEF NP*

Abstract: Over the last two decades a considerable amount of research has been conducted on *sort/kind/type of* constructions in English, both on their NP-internal uses (e.g. nominal qualifier uses like *a sort of holiday*) and on their external uses (e.g. adverbial qualifier uses like *sort of personal, sort of understand*). The aim of this paper is to provide further insight into the meaning and use of *sort/kind/type of* constructions by investigating a very specific use of *sort of* and *kind of*, namely those instances where they immediately precede a definite NP (e.g. *sort of the enemy of Trump, kind of the pageant world*). It will be shown that these instances which, given their NP-external status, resemble the adverbial qualifier or discourse marker use of *sort/kind of* while, due to their pre-NP position, differing only minimally from the NP-internal qualifying use (*the sort of enemy of Trump; the kind of pageant world*), are characterized by a unique combination of functional (in terms of assumed familiarity and scope) and formal (distributional) features. In addition, it is shown that the two forms *sort of* and *kind of* are developing in different directions, each establishing their own preferred contexts of occurrence. Finally, a brief analysis of the use of these constructions in different text types (spoken, fiction, newspaper) seems to confirm this conclusion.

1 Introduction

In recent years considerable attention has been paid to *sort of/kind of/type of* constructions in English (pioneering work by Aijmer 2002 and Denison 2002, 2005, 2011; followed by contributions by, for example, De Smedt, Brems, and Davidse 2007; Keizer 2007; Brems and Davidse 2010; Margerie 2010; and Brems 2011). This paper intends to contribute to the description and analysis of these constructions by focusing on a very specific use of *sort of* and *kind of*, namely those cases where they occur NP-externally, more particularly those cases where they immediately precede a definite NP. Some examples are given in (1):

Evelien Keizer, University of Vienna, English departments, Spitalgasse 2, 1060 Vienna, Austria, e-mail: evelien.keizer@univie.ac.at

https://doi.org/10.1515/9783110701104-005

(1) a. Because it seems to me they've already set themselves up as **sort of** the enemy of Trump. (COCA, spoken)
  b. As a young girl, I grew up in **kind of** the pageant world, but I always wanted to be a lawyer and took social justice and politics very seriously. (COCA, spoken)
  c. The 6-foot-3, 200-pound Livingston is described by his coach, Latrell Scott, as "a very special kid" and "**kind of** the true student-athlete." (COCA, newspaper)
  d. And there was **kind of** this fear (COCA, spoken)

The reason for looking at these uses in particular is that they may be regarded as hybrid uses. On the one hand, as NP-external uses of *sort/kind of* they may be taken to represent the adverbial qualifier use (comparable to *sort/kind of* preceding adjectives and verbs (see De Smedt, Brems, and Davidse 2007: 245–247), but now scoping over the NP) or to fulfil a more bleached discourse-marker function (indicating tentativeness or hesitation; cf. De Smedt, Brems, and Davidse 2007: 247–249). On the other hand, the expressions in (1) differ only minimally from the NP-internal qualifying use of *sort/kind of* (e.g. *the sort of enemy of Trump*; see also example (2b)). The questions to be answered are therefore whether these specific NP-external occurrences differ in any way from other, by now well-described, uses of *sort/kind of*, and if so, what specific functional, formal and distributional features they exhibit.

In what follows, these questions will be addressed by investigating the various discourse-pragmatic functions of these NP-external uses of *sort/kind of*, as well as the role of the definite determiner (in terms of the familiarity of the referent and the concept evoked; Prince 1981; Diessel 1999), the scope of the determiner (Hengeveld and Keizer 2011: 1971–1972) and the distribution of these instances of *sort/kind of* (in terms of sentence type, e.g. their occurrence in copular or existential constructions). In all these respects, a comparison will be made between the NP-external and the NP-internal use of *sort/kind of*; between, for instance, examples (2a) and (2b):

(2) a. But I will say, what's interesting about attacking the press is if you adhere to old political ideology and campaigning, and, you know, **sort of** the old rules of politics, blaming the media means you're losing. (COCA, spoken)
  b. So you know, these hurricanes, these storms that we've seen this season are an indicator that, you know, we're moving into this sort of new age when *the* **sort of** *old rules of how our climate works* are off the table. (COCA, spoken)

In addition, a comparison will be made between the use of *sort of* and *kind of* in this position in terms of frequency, preferred discourse-pragmatic functions, their distribution, and their occurrence in different types of text (spoken, newspaper, fiction). Although this study will be based on synchronic data, taken from the Corpus of Contemporary American English (COCA; Davies 2008), it will be argued that the data suggest that a change is taking place in this particular use of *sort/kind of*, with *sort of* and *kind of* developing their own specific discourse functions.

The paper is structured as follows. Section 2 is devoted to a brief discussion of the use of *sort/kind of* constructions in definite NPs. Subsequently, Section 3 investigates the specific features of the NP-external use of *sort/kind of DEF-NP* sequences. In Section 4 the use of *sort/kind of* before a (singular) demonstrative NP is examined, while Section 5 focuses on the difference between NP-external *sort of* and *kind of*. Section 6 summarizes and concludes.

2 Definite NP-internal *sort/kind of* constructions

When *sort* and *kind* function as the head of a complex NP, indicating a subcategory of the category denoted by the embedded NP, there are no constraints on the form of the first determiner: it can be a definite or indefinite article, demonstrative determiner, possessive pronoun, numeral, or quantifier, etc., as shown in example (3):

(3) a. ... making sure it's *the right **kind of** white* to match with the snow. (COCA, spoken)
 b. And we have the Senate Intelligence Committee investigation, which is *a different **kind of** investigation*, a counterintelligence investigation. (COCA, spoken)
 c. And when they were asked whether or not they would put *this **kind of** software* on their own computers, they unanimously said no. (COCA, spoken)
 d. The kids are listening because he's singing *their **kind of** music*. (COCA, spoken)
 e. Well, there are *two **kinds of** subsidies* in the Affordable Care Act. (COCA, spoken)

In those cases where the noun is no longer used referentially, with the sequence *sort/kind of* having taken on a modifying or qualifying use, the NP as a whole is typically indefinite, taking the indefinite articles *a/some*, as well as discourse topic-introducing, conversational *this* ("new-*this*" or "introductory this"; e.g. Prince 1981; Wald 1983: 98; Chen 1990: 142–143; Biber et al. 1999: 274; Diessel 1999: 109; Stirling and Huddleston 2002: 1510):

(4) a. He is ***a sort of*** *artist photographer* (ICE-GB, spoken)
    b. That's why I thought it was a good idea to try and apply – ***some sort of*** *a model* (ICE-GB, spoken)
    c. And she said you know he spent all his time, on ***this sort of*** *ego trip* this power trip (ICE-GB, spoken)
    (Keizer 2007: 154, 164, 167)

However, there are exceptions. Definite NPs with *sort/kind of* are often used anaphorically or cataphorically, especially with demonstrative determiners (see examples (5a) and (5b), respectively). Such instances are analysed as post-determiner uses by De Smedt, Brems, and Davidse (2007: 239–241) and Brems (2011: 292–307); Keizer (2007), on the other hand, regards most of these instances as referential uses, reserving the post-determiner use, as first introduced by Denison (1998; see also Denison 2002, 2005, 2011) only for those (far less frequent) cases in which a plural determiner does not agree in number with the first noun, but only with the second (example (6)).

(5) a. "The days in the palace of art were over, and before the busy harassed idealist there now stretched an unsuspected wilderness of inner desolation and pain." *This **kind of** hyperbolic writing does Morris no favours.* (CW-Times) (Brems 2011: 295)
    b. If the war reignited, it could spread and spark ***the kind of*** *conflict that has drawn Americans into two larger wars this century.* (CW-Times) (Brems 2011: 300)

(6) And then we can also use the same feedback to help them to produce ***those kind of*** *pitch changes* in their speech (ICE-GB, spoken) (Keizer 2007: 170)

When part of a definite NP, *sort/kind of* can also have a modifying use. Thus, *sort/kind of* can occasionally be found in what has been referred to as the "attributive modifier use" (e.g. Denison 2002; De Smedt, Brems, and Davidse 2007: 234–236; Brems 2011: 284–288), with *sort/kind of* modifying a preceding adjective (e.g. *biggish looking* in (7)). Examples can also be found of the "semi-suffix use", where *sort/kind of* functions as a kind of suffix to a preceding phrase (as in example (8); De Smedt, Brems, and Davidse 2007; Brems 2011: 288–292):

(7) You know... *the biggish looking **kinda** one*. (COLT) (Brems 2011: 286–287)

(8) He was like in prison and he worked himself up in *the peak no pain **kind of** thing*. (COLT) (Brems 2011: 290)

Furthermore, definite *sort/kind of* constructions can be used as "nominal qualifiers" (Denison 2002; Aimer 2002; Keizer 2007; De Smedt, Brems, and Davidse 2007: 244–245; Brems 2011: 307–313). In that case, *sort/kind of* is typically used to indicate approximation, imprecision, or a lexical gap (example (9a) and (9b)), or as a hedge or mitigator (example (9c)).

(9) a. Gosh, you know, I have to say this sounds like a metaphor for the – you know, *the **kind of** psychological neglect of the victims here*, that you've got people at the hospital consoling each other. (COCA, spoken)
 b. We just didn't want *the **kind of** responsible wife character*, you know, frowning at his mistakes (COCA, spoken)
 c. And right now I'm very worried about the – *the **sort of** decimation of the State Department* and the departure of many, many senior diplomats, (COCA, spoken)

Finally, definite determiners can be found in those cases where *sort/kind of* has a meta-level use, serving as the marker of a style shift preceding, for instance, the use of a rather formal description (example (10a)), a creative expression (example (10b)) or a well-known idiom (example (10c)) (see Aijmer 2002: 195; Brems 2011: 311).

(10) a. And Senator Diaz, a Democrat, he said I'm a democrat but my Democratic governor said there is no place for me as a pastor. That's *the **sort of** liberal intolerance*. (COCA, spoken)
 b. ... to imagine that these spaces which are about *the **kind of** cultivation of one's inner-life, of one's soul*, if you want to call it that, (COCA, spoken)
 c. ... to communicate to people that we wanted to know, which was the human story of the war, not the big propaganda narrative and *the **sort of** conventional wisdom*, (COCA, spoken)

Let us now turn to the role of the definite article in the non-head uses of *sort/kind of* constructions. Interestingly, the article typically does not have its normal anaphoric or deictic use; in other words, the entities denoted are not retrievable from the previous discourse (co-text) or immediate context, nor does the definite article serve to indicate that the referent is inferable from entities evoked in the previous discourse or present in the immediate situation. Instead, the NPs in question are always first-mention definites. If we apply Prince's (1981) terminology, the referents of these NPs are not (textually or situationally) "evoked"; in other words, their entity is not "already in the discourse-model" (Prince 1981: 236). In terms of Hawkins' (1978) classification of definite expressions, these NPs do not represent the "anaphoric use" or "immediate situation use". Nor do we find what Prince refers to as "non-containing inferables", i.e. NPs referring to discourse entities that "the speaker assumes the hearer can infer [. . .], via logical – or, more commonly, plausible – reasoning, from discourse entities already Evoked or from other Inferables" (Prince 1981: 236), as in *a house: the door*; *a party: the music* (see Hawkins's [1978] "associative anaphoric use").

What we do find are "containing inferables", a special subclass of inferables "where what is inferenced off of is properly contained within the Inferable NP itself" (Prince 1981: 236). These NPs typically contain an *of*-complement (e.g. *the purpose of this chapter*; Prince 1981: 248), or a clausal complement (as in *the incredible claim that the devil speaks English backwards*; Prince 1981: 237), but may also be inferable on the basis of information provided in a relative clause (see Hawkins's "unfamiliar" and "unexplanatory modifier" uses of the definite article).[1] Occasionally we also find what Prince calls "unused" NPs, which are used when the hearer is assumed to be already familiar with an entity that is, however, newly introduced into the discourse (cf. Hawkins's [1978] "larger situation definites"). Some examples are given in (11):

(11) a. . . . and then uhm the vicar totally ignoring *the **sort of** moral danger they're in* (ICE-GB, spoken; Keizer 2007: 166)
 b. And while we're folding that in what – that's what kind of makes it light and airy, *the **sort of** marquise* (COCA, spoken)

In (11a) we have a containing inferable, where *sort of* qualifies the following nominal (*moral danger*), which itself is postmodified by a restrictive relative clause containing an evoked entity (the pronoun *they*), allowing the hearer to link the overall referent to the context (see also Prince 1981: 249). Interestingly, the more typical kind of containing inferable, where the head noun is followed by a complement, does not seem to be found in combination with this use of *sort/kind of* (compare Section 3.3). In (11b), we find an unused definite NP: no marquises have been entered into the discourse, but the hearer is assumed to be familiar

---

[1] Note that for Prince, 'containing inferables' can also be indefinite, as in the case of partitives (*one of the eggs*); however, this is not relevant to the current discussion.

with the unique notion of "the marquise". Thus, in both cases, despite being discourse-new, the concept evoked by the NP ("moral danger", "marquise") is presented as familiar to the hearer, which explains the use of the definite article. In all these cases, reference is made to a discourse-new entity (non-phoric/non-deictic use), while the concept denoted by the following nouns (and in those cases where they are followed by a modifier, by the combination of noun and modifier) is presented as familiar (hearer-old; Prince 1992).

When it comes to the use of demonstratives, qualifying *sort/kind of* constructions, as already mentioned, can be determined by "new-*this*"; in that case, we are dealing with a non-anaphoric, non-deictic use of the proximate demonstrative, typically used to introduce new discourse topics, as illustrated in example (4c) (repeated here for convenience):

(4c) And she said you know he spent all his time, on **this sort of** *ego trip* this power trip (ICE-GB, spoken)

In addition, it turns out that qualifying *sort/kind of* constructions can also take "old-*that*", or "recognitional *that*", a non-anaphoric/non-deictic use of the distal demonstrative (e.g. Wald 1983: 97; Chen 1990: 143; Diessel 1999: 105–109; Himmelmann 1996: 230–239; Stirling and Huddleston 2002: 1510; see also Cornish 2004: 137). As in the case of new-*this*, the entity referred to by these constructions has not been previously mentioned in the discourse, nor is it present in the immediate situation; however, the hearer is expected to be able to identify the referent on the basis of specific shared knowledge. In this respect, old-*that* thus differs crucially from new-*this*: where new-*this* introduces hearer-new information into the discourse, old-*that* indicates that the newly introduced information is, in fact, hearer-old (Diessel 1999: 109). Rather than relying on previous discourse or the immediate situation, these "old-*that*" constructions "appeal to cultural knowledge" (Wald 1983: 97), and are used to activate information that "speaker and hearer share due to common experience in the past" (Diessel 1999: 106); as Himmelmann (1996: 233) puts it, "[r]ecognitional use of demonstratives ... draws on specific, 'personalized' knowledge that is assumed to be shared by the communicating parties due to a common interactional history or to supposedly shared experiences". In addition, they are often used to indicate that "speaker and hearer share the same view or that they sympathize with each other" (Diessel 1999: 106). Some examples are given in (12); in all these cases, the speaker uses *that* to indicate that she expects the hearer not only to know the entity referred to, but also to share the view expressed:

(12) a. We have got to instill *that **sort of** go-for-the-jugular attitude* in our players (COCA, newspaper) [approximation, idiomaticity]
 b. But in my case, you know, if I was out with my father alone, people would say, who are you with, little girl? And if I was out with my mother alone, they would say, who are you with, little girl? So it's *that **kind of** strange double sense of alienation.* (COCA, spoken) [creative expression]
 c. Obviously there are a lot of people inside the White House who are not fans of Bannon. He clashed with a lot of president's top advisors. Clearly you have General John Kelly coming in as the new chief of staff wanting to clean up shop, wanting to stop leaks, wanting to get rid of a lot of *that **sort of** infighting that's going on.* (COCA, spoken) [hedging, mitigation]

Note that the function of *sort/kind of* in these constructions is the same as that of qualifying *sort/kind of* constructions with the definite article, indicating approximation or imprecision, functioning as a hedge or mitigator, filling a lexical gap, or serving as a marker of meta-language.

3 A study of definite NP-external *sort/kind of*

3.1 Data and methodology

The Corpus of Contemporary American English (Davies 2008) was searched for occurrences of *sort of* and *kind of* followed by a definite determiner to compose a representative and manageable sample of the expression under investigation. As shown in Table 1, this sample consisted of the first 100 examples of "*sort of* + definite article" and "*kind of* + definite article" in the spoken section of the corpus, the first 50 examples of "*sort of* + definite article" and "*kind of* + definite article" in the newspaper section, and all examples of "*sort of* + definite article" and "*kind of* + definite article" in the fiction section; in addition, the sample included 200 examples of "*sort/kind of* + demonstrative determiner" from the spoken section only (distributed as indicated in the table).[2]

---

[2] For a more detailed overview of the frequencies of different constructions with the nouns *sort* and *kind*, see Table 2 in Section 4.1.

5 The function and use of NP-external *sort/kind of*: The case of *sort/kind of DEF NP* — 189

Table 1: Sample of "*sort/kind of* + definite determiner" constructions.

	the	DEM (*this/that*)	Total
sort of DEF-NP	100x spoken 50x news 39x fiction	100x spoken (50x *this* / 50x *that*)	289
kind of DEF-NP	100x spoken 50x news 46x fiction	100x spoken (50x *this* / 50x *that*)	296
Total	385	200	585

All instances were subsequently tagged for the following properties:
- the discourse-pragmatic function of *sort/kind of* (approximation, imprecision, filling a lexical gap, hedging, mitigation, idiomatic/creative use, hesitation, etc.)
- the presence of pre- or postmodifier or complement
- their use before an NP in post-copular position (in a classificational copular construction)
- the presence of a proper name or other unique description in the following NP (as typical representatives of unused NPs)
- their use within a PP (e.g. *in kind of the pageant world* in (16a)); relevant for establishing the scope of *sort/kind of*)
- the presence of other discourse markers/particles (e.g. *just, you know, like*) or repetition of *sort/kind of*
- their occurrence in a frequently used, more or less fixed expression (e.g. *That is kind of the point*).

3.2 The discourse functions *sort/kind of* + definite article

3.2.1 Subtypes of *sort/kind of* constructions

Since *sort/kind of* in the sequences investigated here are not part of the NP, they cannot have any of the NP-internal uses identified for *sort/kind of* constructions, i.e. they do not function as the head of a complex NP, nor can they function as attributive modifiers, semi-suffixes, post-determiners or nominal qualifiers (for examples, see Section 2).

The only uses of *sort/kind of* available for the NP-external instances discussed here are the adverbial qualifier use and the discourse marker use. Note that when used as adverbial qualifiers, *sort/kind of* are normally taken to scope over adjectives (or adjectival phrases), verbs (or verb phrases) or prepositional phrases (examples (13a), (13b) and (13c), respectively); however, in the examples discussed in this chapter, *sort/kind of* takes scope over an NP (as in example (14)), and not just a noun, as in the nominal qualifier use.

(13) a. She's **sort of** broad in the chest and she's sort of stocky (ICE-GB, spoken)
b. ... and then they **kind of** snap back shut again (ICE-GB, spoken)
c. It was **sort of** between Leicester Square and Piccadilly Circus (ICE-GB, spoken)
(Keizer 2007: 163)

(14) Because it seems to me they've already set themselves up as **sort of** the enemy of Trump. (COCA, spoken) (=example (1a))

The NP-external uses of *sort/kind of* examined in this paper can, of course, also be used as discourse markers (e.g. Aijmer 2002; Keizer 2007: 164; De Smedt, Brems, and Davidse 2007: 247–249; Brems 2011: 317–325). In that case, they do not scope over (i.e. modify or qualify) the following NP (or indeed any syntactic unit), but "apply more diffusely to the discourse" (De Smedt, Brems, and Davidse 2007: 247). As subjectified, semantically bleached versions of the adverbial use (Denison 2002: 4, 14; De Smedt, Brems, and Davidse 2007: 247), they function as hesitation markers, fillers or planners. Some examples are given in (15):

(15) a. So it's a tough place to be and, you know, just *kind of* that concept of, will I love you to death? (COCA, spoken)
b. You were there for the *sort of* the end of the daily era *kind of* the – it was a beginning to unravel a little bit toward the end of his life. (COCA, spoken)
c. Mm-hmm. And – and yet, at the same time, because I had that date, if you will, *kind of* that – that safe place or an end, if you will, in sight, where I didn't have to take it anymore... (COCA, spoken)

Naturally, it is not always easy to determine which function the expression performs in each individual case. In this study, the presence of other hesitation markers (self-repair, repetition, pauses, multiple discourse markers) has been used as a criterion.

3.2.2 Discourse-pragmatic functions

Given the fact that the NP-external *sort/kind of* occurrences under investigation here typically have a qualifying function, it will come as no surprise that they tend to serve the functions identified in the literature for non-head (nominal or adverbial qualifying) uses of *sort/kind of*. Some examples illustrating some of these functions are given in (16):

(16) a. As a young girl, I grew up in **kind of** *the pageant world*, but I always wanted to be a lawyer and took social justice and politics very seriously. (COCA, spoken) [approximation/lexical gap] (= example (1b))
   b. We're not there yet. Keep in mind there are a couple different ways we address disaster relief funding in this country. And right now we're still *at* **sort of** *the emergency*, making sure people have drinking water, making sure people have electricity. (COCA. spoken) [hedging]
   c. Or if he continues to, in terms of the – the tweets and – and just **kind of** *the debasing statements that he's made* and – and also on the foreign stage, we need to be incredibly careful about what we're doing. [mitigation]
   d. Plus, I have some lovely Christmas cons that take about six weeks to put the partridge in the pear tree, which makes Halloween **sort of** *the kickoff to the Christmas scamming season* (COCA, fiction) [creative expression]
   f. The troop strength question is **sort of** *the cart before the horse*. (COCA, spoken) [idiomatic expression]

In all these cases, *sort/kind of* has an additional focalizing function, resulting in increased emphasis on the following noun (reflected in the presence of a clear movement in pitch; see also Margerie 2010: 327–328). This is illustrated by the example in (17), taken from the Santa Barbara Corpus of Spoken American English (SBC-SAE; Du Bois et al. 2000–2005) (capital letters indicate emphatic stress, underlining regular stress):

(17) that's kind of the .. the meCHANics of the .. of the flow of funds. (SBA-SAE, 014, 1555.95 1559.41)

3.3 The role of the definite article

As in the case of the NP-internal use of *sort/kind of*, the definite article in these sequences does not have an anaphoric or deictic use, i.e. the entities denoted are not given in the (previous or following) discourse or context; nor does it serve to indicate that the referent is inferable from the entities evoked in the previous discourse or context. Thus, here too, the NPs following *sort/kind of* are always first-mention definites, i.e. unused definite NPs (Prince 1981; see Hawkins [1978] "larger situation definites") and containing inferables (see Hawkins's [1978] "unfamiliar use" and "unexplanatory modifiers").

Unused NPs (in general) typically do not include a postmodifier. However, in some cases they may include a complement PP or complement clause, when these are part of a unified concept assumed to be present in long-term knowledge (as with Hawkins's [1978] "unexplanatory modifiers", where the postmodifier does not link the referent to the hearer's knowledge base, but nevertheless helps the hearer to identify a set of objects in which the hearer can (uniquely) locate the referent [Hawkins 1978: 167]). Some examples are given in (18):

(18) a. But I will say, what's interesting about attacking the press is if you adhere to old political ideology and campaigning, and, you know, **sort of** *the old rules of politics*, blaming the media means you're losing. (COCA, spoken) (= example (2a))
   b. We are going to dig in to **sort of** *the question of truth*, and accountability. (COCA, spoken)
   c. They were repositioning the building, and they wanted us as **sort of** *the flagship first deal*. (COCA, newspaper)

Containing inferables (Hawkins's "unfamiliar uses"), as we have seen, always include a postnominal complement or modifier linking the referent to the hearer's knowledge base, usually by linking it to another, identifiable referent (*the process* in (19a), *her op-ed* in (19b), etc.). Note that unlike the containing inferables found with the internal use of *sort/kind of* discussed in Section 2 (see example (11a)), here we do find plenty of cases with an *of*-complement:

(19) a. My concern is not so much the disagreement with the outcome, but rather the attack on **sort of** *the legitimacy of the process*. (COCA, spoken)
   b. To take control of the situation, which is really a fantasy because you don't have any. I was surprised at **sort of** *the tone deafness of her op-ed*, because she talked a lot about physical beauty (COCA, spoken)
   c. It's a complicated place, because Steve Bannon, in that "60 Minutes" interview, portrayed himself as **sort of** *the flame keeper of what is Trumpie*. (COCA, spoken)
   d. And we were right next door to a lab that studied how proteins move along microtubules, so this is considered **kind of** *the highway of the cell*. (COCA, spoken)

In all these cases, the NPs preceded by *sort/kind of* introduce new referents into the discourse (present discourse-new information); at the same time, these referents (or the concepts evoked by the NPs) are assumed to be familiar to the hearer (are assumed to be hearer-old). We will come back to the notion of hearer-old (assumed familiarity) in Section 3.5 below. This explains why these definites can easily occur in existential sentences: these do not allow anaphoric definite expressions, but do allow discourse-new, referent introducing, definites:

(20) We haven't heard that he's really directly threatened people. There's been **sort of** the suggestion that Trump voters may not be pleased if members don't go. (COCA, spoken)

3.4 The use of NP-external *sort/kind of* in post-copular position

One noticeable feature of NP-external *sort/kind of* is that it frequently occurs before a post-copular NP in a classificational copular construction, i.e. copular constructions where the post-copular expression is used non-referentially to indicate class-membership (or class inclusion) of the referent of the subject (as opposed to identification; see, for example, Declerck 1988: 55; Dik 1997: 204–206; Hengeveld 1992: 81; Keizer 1992: 46–53; Halliday and Matthiessen 2014: 262; cf. Bolinger 1972; Lyons 1977);[3] examples are given in (21) and (22):

(21) a. We're **sort of** the featured attraction. (COCA, fiction)
 b. So this portion is **sort of** the technology and math portion (COCA, spoken)
 c. His title was shellfish constable, he really was **sort of** the police of the fish in the area. (COCA, spoken)

---

3 Although some authors use the term "classificational" only for copular constructions with an indefinite post-copular NP (e.g. Dik 1997: 204; Hengeveld 1992: 77–91), others allow for the post-copular NP in classificational sentences to be indefinite (see, for example, Declerck 1988: 55–66; Keizer 1992: ch. 2; cf. Hengeveld's [1992: 88] "identification-characterizing" constructions). In the examples given here the post-copular NPs are clearly non-referential: they do not identify or specify the referent of the subject NP (i.e. they do not answer an (implicit) *wh*-question, do not consist of a presupposed constituent (variable) and a focal constituent (value), and the post-nominal NP does not receive a contrastive accent; nor are the two NPs reversible (e.g. Declerck 1988: 5–54). Instead, the post-copular NPs are used predicatively, assigning a property to the referent of the subject NP (Declerck 1988: 55).

(22) a. That's **kind of** the dream scenario. (COCA, newspaper)
 b. So when you say support, was there ever any – look, I was **kind of** the pariah. I was the guy who wanted to legalize pot. (COCA, spoken)
 c. This is **kind of** the fruit of that rhetoric. (COCA, spoken)

As demonstrated in Table 2, in the COCA as a whole, *sort/kind of* followed by a definite NP occurs about twice as often in post-copular position as a definite NP containing *the sort/kind of*. Moreover, the difference is greater with *kind* than with *sort*.[4]

Table 2: *sort/kind of the* in copular constructions (COCA as a whole, all sections).

		all	post-copular
NP-external	sort of the	2,555	1,124 (43.9%)
	kind of the	1,986	1,164 (53.6%)
NP-internal	the sort of	7,560	1,697 (22.4%)
	the kind of	29,818	7,055 (23.7%)

Given the nature of the classificational function of these copular constructions, it is not surprising that *sort/kind of* often occurs in post-copular position; *sort/kind of* here can be regarded as commenting on the classification process coded in the copular construction. Note that *sort/kind of* in these constructions may either be used to signal that the entity does not really fit the description (in the case of a well-defined category, e.g. **sort of** the featured attraction in (21a)),[5] or to indi-

---

4 With the indefinite article, too, an increase can be found in post-copular position, but the difference is much smaller: *sort of a* (36.6%) against *a sort of* (19%); *kind of a* (31.6%) against *a kind of* (21.2%).

5 As pointed out by one of the reviewers, example (21a) (as well as other instances in examples (21) and (22)) could also involve irony ("we're like a circus attraction") or focus ("we're like the main attraction"). Although I do not deny that such interpretations are possible, I do not believe that they are triggered by the presence of *sort/kind of*. In all these cases, it would be very difficult not to have a focal reading of the post-copular expressions (with or without *sort/kind of*) since they are all in focus position, providing new, salient information. Furthermore, if we look at the context in which (21a) is used (given in (i)), it is clear that the description provided is not meant ironically, but simply indicates the presence of a lexical gap (whereby the specific choice of alternative description may create a special effect, ranging from self-aggrandizement to self-deprecation):
(i) Terrell Lee: Guess we ought to go to graduation. John: They aren't going to start without us. We're **sort of** the featured attraction. (COCA, fiction)

cate either that the (ad hoc) category itself is not clearly established or that the description may not really capture the category in question (e.g. **sort of** the police of the fish in (22c)), or both.

3.5 Scope and familiarity

The next question to be answered concerns the exact difference between qualifying NP-internal *the kind/sort of* and NP-external *sort/kind of the*. The difference is clearly not in their discourse-pragmatic functions, as these seem to straddle the NP boundary. In what follows, it will be argued that there is a subtle difference in meaning between the two uses, which can be captured in terms of scope (Hengeveld and Keizer 2011: 1971–1972).

– *the kind/sort of* (NP-internal; qualifying use):
The speaker may have a clear idea of what the referent of the expression is (and can categorize it conceptually), but lacks a straightforward means of describing or pinpointing it linguistically; in other words, the imprecision/approximation/hedging function concerns the relation between the concept evoked and the linguistic description used:

(23)   referent – concept ≈ description

In these cases, *sort/kind of* can be said to have scope over only the noun,[6] which is the element providing the linguistic description, as reflected by its NP-internal position.

– *sort/kind of the* (NP-external; qualifying use):
The speaker is uncertain as to how to categorize the referent in the first place; in other words, the imprecision/approximation/hedging concerns the relation between the referent and the concept evoked (and, possibly, the linguistic expression as well; see below).

(24)   referent ≈ concept – description

Here, *sort/kind of* may be regarded as scoping over the NP as a whole, as the expression used to refer to a particular entity.

---

6 Or rather, to have scope over the extended nominal, i.e. noun + modifiers (as in *the sort of old rules of how our climate works*, example (2b)).

Using Ogden and Richards's (1923) semiotic triangle, we may represent the difference between the two uses as in Figure 1a-b:

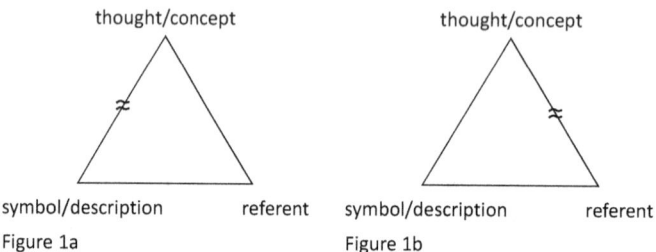

Figure 1a-b: Locating the focus of NP-internal and NP-external uses of *sort/kind of* in the semiotic triangle.

As already mentioned, the difference is a very subtle one; moreover, there may be very little by way of linguistic (or other) evidence to substantiate its existence. What one would expect, however, is for NP-external *sort/kind of* to somehow involve a higher degree of uncertainty/imprecision; after all, the uncertainty in this case is of a more fundamental nature, affecting an earlier stage of the language production process. And although far from conclusive, the minimal pairs provided in (25)–(27) seem to confirm this intuition, with the a-examples communicating a higher degree of uncertainty concerning the applicability or appropriateness of the description used than the b-examples.

(25) a. And the inaugural itself is the beginning of a presidency, it's imbued with enormous symbolism as *the **sort of** kickoff for what a president clearly hopes will be a successful four years.* (COCA, spoken)
 b. Plus, I have some lovely Christmas cons that take about six weeks to put the partridge in the pear tree, which makes Halloween ***sort of** the kickoff to the Christmas scamming season* (COCA, fiction) (= example (16d))

(26) a. So you know, these hurricanes, these storms that we've seen this season are an indicator that, you know, we're moving into this sort of new age when *the **sort of** old rules of how our climate works* are off the table. (COCA, spoken) (= example (2b))
 b. But I will say, what's interesting about attacking the press is if you adhere to old political ideology and campaigning, and, you know, ***sort of** the old rules of politics*, blaming the media means you're losing. (COCA, spoken) (= example (2a))

(27) a. a lot of people anticipated for PayPal to accept it's (sic) fate as *the **kind of*** *"Founding Father."* (Internet)[7]
b. he would have been thinking much more in terms of the reputation of Van Dyck *as **kind of** the founding father of English painting* (Internet)[8]

This also shows that, importantly, the notion of familiarity may be applied to various stages involved in a single reference. Thus, in analysing both the NP-internal and the NP-external use of *sort/kind of*, a distinction needs to be made between assumed familiarity (on the part of the hearer) with the referent, the concept and the description. More specifically, definite NPs containing or following *sort/kind of* are characterized by the following levels of (un)familiarity:

1. The referent is discourse-new (non-anaphoric; hearer-new [Prince 1992]); see Sections 1 and 2.3.
2. The concept evoked is assumed to be familiar (hearer-old [Prince 1992]); hence the use of a definite expression.
3. The description provided is either new/creative or familiar/idiomatic. However, in both cases, there is no perfect match between description and concept; hence *sort/kind of* is used to express approximation:
   a. with regard to categorization (speaker uncertain which category the referent belongs to) (e.g. examples (21a) and (27))
   b. (occasionally) also with regard to the appropriateness of the description provided (in the case of new/creative descriptions: speaker creates a new category/concept, but lacks a conventionalized description for this category) (e.g. examples (19c) and (21c)).

4 The use of *sort/kind of* + demonstrative

The 200 examples of *sort/kind of* followed by a demonstrative NP (introduced by the demonstrative determiners *this* or *that*) were all taken from the spoken section of the corpus (there were no hits in the fiction section and only a few in the newspaper section). Here, too, it turns out that in the great majority of cases, the demonstrative NP following *sort/kind of* is not used anaphorically (or deicti-

---

[7] From a website (blog) on travel (https://madeofmiles.com/index.php/2018/04/19/max-out-the-q2-2018-chase-freedom-bonus/, accessed 9 April 2019).
[8] From the transcript of a documentary on Buckingham Palace (https://subsaga.com/bbc/documentaries/history/the-queens-palaces/1-buckingham-palace.html, accessed 9 April 2019).

cally). In only 14 out of the 200 examples has the referent of the demonstrative already been introduced (2x *this sort/kind of*; 12x *that sort/kind of*), and in only a handful of cases was the reference purely (unequivocally) anaphoric. Two examples are given in (28):

(28) a. But *that message on Thanksgiving eve about unity and healing the divisions and I'm going to be the president for all of the people* – he is making it really tough for his critics, right, because he's not providing the kind of ammunition that they expected him to. BOOTHE# Something tells me they'll still find things to criticize him for. But you're right, Monica. he sort of set the groundwork. He's set the tone. . . . when he gave his first speech as president-elect, he really set the groundwork and set the tone for the kind of president that he wants to be and **sort of** *that unifying message.* (COCA, spoken)
b. If anything, I just was surrounded by a lot of police officers, and I actually wished that there was *someone there to kind of coach me through what I was feeling,* And my co-worker, Chris Ann, actually was **kind of** *that person for me that day.* (COCA, spoken) (specificational construction)

In the vast majority of cases, however, the demonstrative NPs are used neither anaphorically nor deictically; instead, they are instances of "new-*this*" and "old-*that*". In the latter case, as we have seen in Section 1, the speaker assumes the hearer to be able to identify the referent on the basis of some shared experience or knowledge (e.g. Wald 1983: 97; see also Chen 1990; Diessel 1999; Himmelmann 1996; Stirling and Huddleston 2002: 1510; see examples in (29)). In many cases, this use of *that* is also used to indicate that the speaker assumes the hearer to share his/her attitude towards the referent; this is particularly clear in examples (29c) and (29d). Given the fact that the referent is assumed to be familiar to the hearer, *sort/kind of* in these cases serve to indicate that the description chosen is new or creative, and may not be entirely appropriate.

(29) a. I know right after Desperate Housewives you moved back to where your wife is from, Minneapolis– JAMES-DENTON# Yeah. KATHIE-LEE-GIFFORD# –just to escape **sort of** *that L.A. scene* with your kids, right? (COCA, spoken)
b. But, you know, the Beatles were a good representation of that. the Beatles really – they could write songs that were sweet and melancholic but definitely rooted in **sort of** *that Tin Pan Alley* and early pop tunes. (COCA, spoken)

c. In Iowa, they're slow to commit, but once they commit, they stay with you through thick or thin. It's **sort of** *that Midwestern sensibility*. (COCA, spoken)
d. Or it's just – you kind of learn, I guess, in the town that I grew up in, like, secrecy is the key to keeping everyone happy and making it look like it's still **kind of** *that small, hometown feeling*. (COCA, spoken)

The specific function of "new-*this*" (Wald 1983: 98; Chen 1990: 142–143) – as opposed to the indefinite article – is to indicate that a newly introduced referent will play a role in the subsequent discourse, i.e. that it will become a topical referent (e.g. Prince 1981), or that it "persists" in the discourse (Wald 1983: 97). Chen (1990: 143) takes a somewhat broader view, suggesting that the NP introduced by *this*, rather than introducing a topical referent, provides information that "is of further interest or relevance to the present discourse" (hence the use of a proximate marker). Examples of this use of *this* in combination with *sort/kind of* can be found in (30). In this case the function of *sort/kind of* could be either to comment on the appropriateness of the description (e.g. example (30b)) or to indicate the speaker's problems in categorizing the referent in the first place (e.g. example (30a)):

(30) a. I thought she was saying, maybe I'm not as charismatic as these other people, but I'm **sort of** *this policy wonk*. (COCA, spoken)
b. the way it hurts Cruz is that he's **sort of** *this anti-elite candidate*, a populous candidate, and a place against that. Because when you look at Ted Cruz, he went to Princeton, he went to Harvard Law. He was a Supreme Court Law Clerk, he worked for George W. Bush. So you know, this guy came from a very elite establishment lane. His wife works at Goldman Sachs or worked at Goldman Sachs. And so it's sort of placed against type. (COCA, spoken)
c. And it's just that he got caught up, like a lot of other folks, including Governor Bush did, in **sort of** *this Trump anti-establishment wave*. (COCA, spoken)

Finally, both new-*this* and old-*that* can be found in presentational *there*-sentences, where they can readily be preceded by *sort/kind of*. This is, of course, not surprising, given the fact that these sentences typically serve to introduce new referents into the discourse:

(31) a. And there was **kind of** *this fear* (COCA, spoken) (= example (1d))
b. Even the players who didn't use a decade ago, there was **kind of** *this code of silence*. No one said anything. And the leaders of the Players

Association were complicit in taking the game down the drain, ... (COCA, spoken)

c. There's always **sort of** this backdrop, this underpinning of tension between animals. Whale-on-whale aggression was just part of your – you know, the daily existence. (COCA, spoken)

d. Certainly there's **kind of** that multitude of different views held by Arab countries. (COCA, spoken)

5 Differences between *sort* and *kind* in *sort/kind of DEF-NP* sequences

5.1 Overall frequency patterns

Let us begin by considering some overall frequencies for the use of *sort of* and *kind of* in combination with a preceding or following determiner (i.e. for all uses in all sections of the corpus). Some of the relevant frequencies are given in Table 3:

Table 3: Frequencies of some *sort of/kind of* sequences in COCA.

COCA	N = *sort*	N = *kind*	total
N *of*	91,333 (30.50%)	208,078 (69.50%)	299,411
a N *of*	7,932 (27.72%)	20,680 (72.28%)	28,612
N *of a*	5,732 (32.59%)	11,854 (67.41%)	17,586
the N *of*	7,560 (20.23%)	29,818 (79.77%)	37,378
N *of the*	2,555 (56.27%)	1,986 (43.73 %)	4,541
N *of* DEM	352 (57.42%)	261 (42.58%)	613

These rough numbers allow for a number of general observations. First of all, the frequencies in Table 3 confirm that (unlike British English) American English, generally speaking, prefers *kind of* over *sort of* (e.g. Biber et al. 1999). This holds across the board for all sections of the corpus (although there are, as we will see in Section 5.3, differences between the different sections). However, in those cases where *sort of* is immediately followed by a definite NP (introduced by *the* or a demonstrative), the pattern changes: *sort of* is much more frequent than *kind of*.[9] On the whole, there thus seems to be a shift in the distribution of *sort of* and

---

[9] In the British National Corpus (Davies 2004), the use of *sort of* is also considerably more frequent.

kind of in the pattern investigated in this study;[10] a shift which, as we will see, this is mainly due to a change in spoken language.[11]

In what follows, we will look at some differences between the use of *sort of* and *kind of* when followed by the definite article. These differences concern their specific discourse functions and their use in certain fixed expressions (Section 5.2), as well as their occurrence in the different sections of the corpus (in particular in post-copular position) (Section 5.3).

5.2 The discourse functions of NP-external *sort of* and *kind of*

The first important difference between *sort of* and *kind of* when followed by a definite NP concerns their use as discourse markers, as it transpires that *kind of* is used much more often as a discourse marker than *sort of*: among the spoken examples, only 4% of *sort of* constructions were used as discourse markers, compared to 11% of *kind of* constructions. This difference is even larger in those cases where *sort of* and *kind of* are followed by a demonstrative (11% *sort of* vs. 36% *kind of*).[12]

---

[10] This could be interpreted as indication that *kind* more frequently occurs in the head use than *sort*. This, however, would not explain the prevalence of *kind* in *kind of a* and *DET kind of a*, nor does it fit in with the finding that in the sequences investigated here *kind of* is more likely to be used as a discourse marker (see below).

[11] It is, however, important to realize that the spoken section of the COCA consists of transcripts of one particular type of spoken language, namely unscripted conversation from TV and radio programmes, which may have an influence on the result. A brief look at the LDC Fisher Corpus of spoken American English (Cieri, Miller, and Walker 2004), which consists of telephone conversations, however, reveals a similar pattern when it comes to the distribution of *sort/kind of* in general and the sequence *sort/kind of the*, although not as pronounced as in the COCA.

[12] This would also explain why *kind of the* is more frequent in the LDC Fisher Corpus than in the spoken section of the COCA (see fn. 9): the telephone conversations of the LDC Fisher Corpus can be expected to be more "messy" than those in COCA, which contains spoken language from TV and radio programmes where people are to some extent prepared and know what the topic of the conversation is going to be (which is also typically something they are knowledgeable about). In the LDC Fisher Corpus, on the other hand, two strangers talk about a subject they agree on at the beginning of the conversation. This means that there are more instances of hesitation, false starts, self-repair, and with it more use of discourse markers.

In addition, it turns out that *kind of* occurs much more often than *sort of* in a number of frequently used, (semi-)fixed constructions, such as *kind of the same N*, *kind of the opposite*, *kind of the way that* . . ., *kind of the point/idea/problem*): no fewer than 26.4% (47 out of 178) of the *kind of* occurrences could be found in such expressions, against 9.09% (16 out of 176) of the *sort of* examples. As shown in Table 4, this holds for both copular constructions and non-copular constructions, and across all sections of the corpus. Note also that for both *sort of* and *kind of* the percentage of fixed combinations in fiction is particularly high (see also Section 2.5).

Table 4: The occurrence of *sort/kind of the* in fixed expressions in all sections.

	section	sort of the	kind of the
copular	spoken	2 (44)	10 (62)
	fiction	6 (25)	18 (35)
	newspaper	3 (40)	10 (44)
	total	11 (109)	38 (141)
non-copular	spoken	0 (44)	3 (23)
	fiction	4 (13)	6 (9)
	newspaper	1 (10)	0 (5)
	total	5 (67)	9 (37)
total		16 (176)	47 (178)

Finally, as we have seen above, NP-external *sort/kind of* tend to perform the kinds of discourse functions previously identified in the literature for qualifying *sort/kind of*: indicating approximation/imprecision or the presence of a lexical gap; hedging and mitigation; marking ad-hoc categorization; and signalling the use of a special idiom (meta-level use). This invariably holds in the case of *kind of the* sequences. However, in the case of *sort of the*, a number of additional functions can be found, in particular in those cases where *sort of* precedes an argument (i.e. in non-copular constructions). Consider the examples in (32):

(32) a. I'm bearish, in general, about the Congress getting really anything done just because I don't see the President focusing in a sustained way and delivering a kind of public pressure campaign on legislative issues the way he does on **sort of** the NFL or, I mean, we saw the Gold Star family this week. (COCA, spoken)

5 The function and use of NP-external *sort/kind of*: The case of *sort/kind of DEF NP* — 203

b. The fact that it is a counterintelligence case and **sort of** *the FBI and the Justice Department's spy hunters*, does that make it different? (COCA, spoken)
c. and particularly, obviously, the national security team will be under pressure to answer for **sort of** *the Trump worldview, ISIS, what are his plans for Russia's involvement in Syria, and on and on*. (COCA, spoken)
d. But so there will be questions here about **sort of** *the timeline and the decision-making, the thinking and the rational* (sic) *that went into the decision-making over the course of the last couple weeks about how to talk about this to the American people*. (COCA, spoken)

In these examples, *sort of* seems to have the function of exemplification (paraphrasable as "such things as" + approximation; see Mihatsch [2018: 168–169] for Spanish; Kolyaseva and Davidse [2018: 193, 204] for Russian). Note in particular the use of unique expressions / proper names in (32a) and (32b); these uses were exclusively found with *sort of* (in the current sample).

Another additional function found with *sort of the* in non-copular environments is that of specification, as illustrated in example (33), where *sort of* introduces an NP providing a more specific description of a generic or vague expression in the immediately preceding discourse (*turmoil* in (33a), *inside look* in (33b) and *yummy brown* in (33c)):

(33) a. Is this any way an acknowledgment that the turmoil and **sort of** *the back-and-forth that you saw with the House Intelligence Committee trying to investigate this*, that they just could not handle this, that you had to turn to someone, an outsider like this? (COCA, spoken)
b. So we're getting an inside look into all kinds of – **sort of** *the voyeuristic thing*. (COCA, spoken)
c. He turned his gaze on me. Those were yummy brown eyes, **sort of** *the color of brown M&Ms*. I like M&Ms. (COCA, fiction)

Overall, we can conclude that there are clear differences in use between the two nouns, with *kind of* being used more often as a discourse marker, while *sort of* seems to be developing additional discourse functions (exemplification, specification). However, these new uses are less frequent and, given the previous literature on *sort/kind of* in English, rather unexpected, or at least less conventionalized. As we will see in the next section, this appears to be confirmed by a comparison between the use of NP-external *sort of* and *kind of* in different sections of the corpus.

5.3 Text type

In the COCA as a whole, there is a difference in the NP-external use of *sort of* and *kind of* between the spoken language, fiction and newspaper sections of the corpus, in that it is only in the spoken language section that *sort of* is more frequent than *kind of* (although also in the other sections the use of *sort of* is clearly higher compared to its use in other positions or configurations). This is shown in Table 5.

Table 5: Distribution of *sort of the* and *kind of the* in three sections of the corpus.

	sort of + *the* (per mil)	*kind of* + *the* (per mil)
spoken	2291 (19.62)	1632 (13.98)
fiction	41 (0.37)	49 (0.44)
newspaper	123 (1.09)	182 (1.61)

When we distinguish between the use of NP-external *sort of* and *kind of* in copular and non-copular sentences, some further interesting differences emerge. In the newspaper and fiction sections we find higher percentages of NP-external *sort of* and *kind of* in classificational copular constructions than in the spoken section (newspaper 84.85%; fiction 73.17%; spoken 61.27%; see Table 6). Moreover, in the newspaper and fiction sections all qualifying *sort of the* and *kind of the* constructions have the basic discourse-pragmatic functions of approximation, hedging etc.; any additional uses (found exclusively with *sort of*) can only be found in the spoken section of the corpus.

Table 6: Distribution of *sort/kind of the* in copular and non-copular constructions over three sections.

	copular	non-copular	total
spoken	106 (61.27%)	67 (38.73%)	173
fiction	60 (73.17%)	22 (26.83%)	82
newspaper	84 (84.85%)	15 (15.15%)	99

$\chi^2 = 17.204$, df $= 2$, $\chi^2/df = 8.60$, p $= 0.0002$

It further turns out, not unexpectedly perhaps, that in the newspaper section almost all examples of the sequences of NP-external *sort of the* and *kind of the* appear in (edited) reported or scripted speech. The fact that these occur predominantly in copular constructions (84.85%) shows that this use has become more or less accepted. The fact that the non-copular use is significantly more frequent in the spoken section (38.73%) than in the newspaper section (15.15%) suggests that this particular use is more acceptable in spontaneous speech than in newspapers, where it still seems to be avoided, presumably because language users are more careful in their speech when being interviewed (or when their speech is scripted), or because their speech has been edited.

In terms of occurrence of *sort/kind of the* in copular sentences, the fiction section is situated in between spoken and newspaper; this is to be expected, as here informal speech is often being emulated. However, there is still a considerable difference in distribution between the fiction and the spoken sections, in the sense that the non-copular use is more frequent in spoken language.

Finally, looking at the frequency of *sort of* and *kind of* separately, we see that the tendencies described above can be found for both sequences. In addition, we see that there are interesting differences between the two nouns in the sense that *sort of* is used more in non-copular constructions than *kind of*, not only overall (38.1% vs. 20.8%; Table 7), but also in all three sections separately (see Tables 7a and 7b). This may, to some extent, offer an explanation of the higher frequency in the use of *sort of* observed in these NP-external contexts.

Table 7: Distribution of *sort of the* and *kind of the* in copular and non-copular constructions.

	copular	non-copular	total
sort of the	109 (61.9%)	67 (38.1%)	176
kind of the	141 (79.2%)	37 (20.8%)	178

$\chi^2 = 12.739$, df = 1, $\chi^2/\text{df} = 12.74$, p = 0.0004

Table 7a: Distribution of *sort of the* in copular and non-copular constructions in three sections.

	sort of the copular	sort of the non-copular	total
spoken	44 (50%)	44 (50%)	88
fiction	25 (65.8%)	13 (34.2%)	38
newspaper	40 (80%)	10 (20%)	50

$\chi^2 = 12.477$, df = 2, $\chi^2/\text{df} = 6.24$, p = 0.0020

Table 7b: Distribution of *kind of the* in copular and non-copular constructions over three sections.

	kind of the copular	*kind of the* non-copular	total
spoken	62 (72.9%)	23 (27.1%)	85
fiction	35 (79.5%)	9 (20.5%)	44
newspaper	44 (89.8%)	5 (10.2%)	49

χ^2 = 5.366, df = 2, χ^2/df = 2.68, p = 0.0683

5.4 Summary

On the basis of the evidence presented above, it may be concluded that there is a trend (a) for the non-copular use of *sort/kind of DEF-NP* to be most frequent in spoken language, followed by fiction and newspapers (for *sort of* and *kind of* together and separately); and (b) for the non-copular use to be more common with *sort of* than with *kind of*. This seems to confirm that the copular use is more generally accepted, whereas the non-copular use is a new development largely restricted to spontaneous speech. This goes hand in hand with the development in spoken language of new discourse functions of NP-external *sort of* in non-copular constructions (exemplification, specification). These findings may go some way in explaining the overall increase in *sort of the* at the expense of *kind of the* compared to other uses of *sort of* and *kind of*.

6 Conclusions

The aim of this paper has been to make a contribution to the description and classification of English *sort/kind of* constructions by investigating one particular subgroup of these constructions, namely those preceding a definite NP starting with the definite article or the demonstratives *this* and *that*. It has been shown that *sort/kind of* in these positions differ from both their nominal qualifying (NP-internal) use and their use as adverbial qualifiers (preceding verbs, adjectives or prepositional phrases), and are characterized by a unique combination of functional and formal properties. Thus, we have seen that although *sort/kind of* in these positions fulfil the same discourse-pragmatic functions of approximation, hedging and mitigation, ad-hoc categorization, and signalling changes in style, *sort of* seems to be developing the additional functions of exemplification and specification. Similarly, although the role of the definite determiner in the NPs following *sort/kind of* is the same as in definite NPs containing qualifying *sort/kind of*, signalling a combination of discourse-new referents and hearer-old concepts (i.e. unused NPs or containing inferables in the case of the definite article, "new-*this*" and "old-*that*" in the case of demonstratives), it has been argued that there is a difference in scope between the internal and external uses of *sort/kind of*, with the former qualifying the appropriateness of the linguistic description used, and the latter the categorization of the referent. In addition, and related to the difference in scope, it has been shown that NP-external *sort/kind of* differs from NP-internal *sort/kind of* in that it occurs much more often in a post-copular position.

Finally, it has been shown that there are also differences between NP-external *sort of* and *kind of*. First of all, there is an interesting difference in overall frequency, with *sort of* being more frequent than *kind of*, which is surprising given that in American English, in general as well as in the NP-internal use, *kind of* clearly outnumbers *sort of*. It has been argued that this unexpected difference in frequency may to some extent be explained by the fact that *sort of* and *kind of* develop in different ways. Thus, *sort of* is used more often in non-copular constructions than *kind of*, and it is here that *sort of* seems to be developing its own, specific discourse functions of exemplification and specification. However, these uses have not become fully established and can as yet only be found in spoken language (not in newspapers or fiction). *Kind of*, on the other hand, tends to the functions normally associated with qualifying or adverbial *kind of*; moreover, it functions more often as a discourse marker than *sort of* and is more often found in more or less fixed phrases. These uses are more established and can also be found in other genres (newspapers and fiction), where they tend to occur in post-copular position.

References

Aijmer, Karen. 2002. *English discourse particles: Evidence from a corpus*. Amsterdam & Philadelphia: John Benjamins.
Biber, Douglas, Stig Johansson, Geoffrey Leech, Susan Conrad & Edward Finegan. 1999. *Longman grammar of spoken and written English*. Harlow: Longman.
Bolinger, Dwight. 1972. A look at equations and cleft sentences. In Evelyn S. Firchow (ed.), *Studies for Einar Haugen*, 96–114. The Hague: Mouton.
Brems, Lieselotte & Kristin Davidse. 2010. The grammaticalisation of nominal type noun constructions with *kind/sort of*: Chronology and paths of change. *English Studies* 91. 180–202.

Brems, Lieselotte. 2011. *Layering of size and type noun constructions in English*. Berlin: De Gruyter Mouton.
Chen, Rong. 1990. English demonstratives: A case of semantic expansion. *Language Sciences* 12 (2/3). 139–153.
Cieri, Christopher, David Miller & Kevin Walker. 2004. The Fisher Corpus: a resource for the next generations of speech-to-text (2004). In *Proceedings 4th International Conference on Language Resources and Evaluation*. Available at https://pdfs.semanticscholar.org/a723/97679079439b075de815553c7b687ccfa886.pdf.
Cornish, Francis. 2004. Focus of attention in discourse. In J. Lachlan Mackenzie & María de los Ángeles Gómez-González (eds.), *A new architecture for Functional Grammar*, 117–150. Berlin: Mouton de Gruyter.
Davies, Mark. 2004. BYU-BNC. (Based on the British National Corpus from Oxford University Press). Available online at http://corpus.byu.edu/bnc/.
Declerck, Renaat. 1988. *Studies on copular sentences, clefts and pseudoclefts*. Leuven: Leuven University Press/Fortis Publications.
Denison, David. 1998. Syntax. In Susanne Romaine (ed.), *The Cambridge history of the English language*, Vol. IV: 1776–1997, 93–329. Cambridge: Cambridge University Press.
Denison, David. 2002. History of the sort of construction family. Paper presented at the Second International Conference on Construction Grammar, University of Helsinki, 7 September.
Denison, David. 2005. The grammaticalizations of sort of, kind of and type of in English. Paper presented at NRG 3 (New Reflections on Grammaticalization 3), Santiago de Compostela, 17–20 July.
Denison, David. 2011. The construction of SKT. Paper presented at the Second Vigo-Newcastle-Santiago-Leuven International Workshop on the Structure of the Noun Phrase in English (NP2), Newcastle upon Tyne, 15–16 September.
De Smedt, Liesbeth, Lieselotte Brems & Kristin Davidse. 2007. NP-internal functions and extended uses of the 'type' nouns *kind*, *sort*, and *type*: Towards a comprehensive, corpus-based description. In Roberta Facchinetti (ed.), *Corpus linguistics 25 years on*, 225–255. Amsterdam: Rodopi.
Diessel, Holger. 1999. *Demonstratives. Form, function and grammaticalization*. Amsterdam/Philadelphia: John Benjamins.
Dik, Simon C. 1997. *The theory of Functional Grammar. Part I: The structure of the clause*. 2nd revised edition. Edited by Kees Hengeveld. Berlin & New York: Mouton de Gruyter.
Halliday, M.A.K. & Christian M.I.M. Matthiessen. 2014. *An Introduction to Functional Grammar*. 4th edition. Revised by Christian M.I.M. Matthiessen. London: Routledge.
Hawkins, John A. 1978. *Definiteness and indefiniteness*. London: Croom Helm.
Hengeveld, Kees. 1992. *Non-verbal predication. Theory, typology, diachrony*. Berlin & New York: Mouton de Gruyter.
Hengeveld, Kees & Evelien Keizer. 2011. Non-straightforward communication. *Journal of Pragmatics* 43. 1962–1976.
Himmelmann, Nikolaus. 1996. Demonstratives in narrative discourse: A taxonomy of universal uses. In Barbara Fox (ed.), *Studies in anaphora*, 205–254. Amsterdam/Philadelphia: John Benjamins.
Keizer, Evelien. 1992. *Reference, predication and (in)definiteness in Functional Grammar. A functional approach to English copular sentences*. Amsterdam: Vrije Universiteit Amsterdam doctoral dissertation.

Keizer, Evelien. 2007. *The English noun phrase: the nature of linguistic categorization*. Cambridge: Cambridge University Press.

Kolyaseva, Alina & Kristin Davidse. 2018. A typology of lexical and grammaticalized uses of Russian *tip*, *tipa*, *po tipu*. *Russian Linguistics* 42. 191–220.

Lyons, John. 1977. *Semantics*. Cambridge: Cambridge University Press.

Margerie, Hélène. 2010. On the rise of (inter)subjective meaning in the grammaticalization of *kind of/kinda*. In Kristin Davidse, Lieven Vandelanotte & Hubert Cuyckens (eds.), *Subjectification, intersubjectification and grammaticalization*, 315–346. Berlin: De Gruyter Mouton.

Mihatsch, Wiltrud. 2018. From ad hoc category to ad hoc categorization: The proceduralization of Argentinian Spanish tipo. In Caterina Mauri & Andrea Sansò (eds.), *Linguistic strategies for the construction of ad hoc categories: Synchronic and diachronic perspectives*. Folia Linguistica Historica special issue 39(1). 147–176.

Ogden, Charles K. & Ivor A. Richards. 1923. *The Meaning of meaning*. New York: Harcourt, Brace & Company.

Prince, Ellen. 1981. Toward a taxonomy of given/new information. In Peter Cole (ed.), *Radical Pragmatics*, 223–254. New York: Academic Press.

Prince, Ellen. 1992. The ZPG letter: subjects, definiteness, and information-status. In William C. Mann & Sandra A. Thompson (eds.), *Discourse description: Diverse linguistic analyses of a fund-raising text*, 295–325. Amsterdam: Benjamins.

Stirling, Lesley & Rodney Huddleston. 2002. Deixis and anaphora. In Rodney Huddleston & Geoffrey Pullum (eds.), *The Cambridge grammar of the English language*, 1449–1564. Cambridge: Cambridge University Press.

Wald, Benji. 1983. Reference and topic within and across discourse units: Observations from current vernacular English. In Flora Klein-Andreu (ed.), *Discourse perspectives on syntax*, 91–116. New York: Academic Press.

Corpora

The Bergen Corpus of London Teenage Language (COLT). 1993.
The British component of the International Corpus of English (ICE-GB). 1990–1998.
Collins WordbanksOnline, Times subcorpus (CW-Times). 1990–.
The Corpus of Contemporary American English (COCA). 1990–2015. Mark Davies. 2008. http://corpus.byu.edu/coca.
Santa Barbara Corpus of Spoken American English, Parts 1–4, Philadelphia, Linguistic Data Consortium. Du Bois, John W., Wallace L. Chafe, Charles Meyer, Sandra A. Thompson, Robert Engelbretson & Nii Martey. 2000–2005. http://www.linguistics.ucsb.edu/research/santa-barbara-corpus.

Carla Umbach
6 Ways of classification: German *Art* and *Typ*

Abstract: In this paper, the meaning and use of the two taxonomic nouns *Art* and *Typ* in German is examined from the point of view of semantics/pragmatics. It is hypothesized that *Art* and *Typ* differ in their way of classification: Classification by *Art* refers to (natural) kinds, and thus individuals belonging to an *Art* share essential properties that are closely connected to lexical meanings. Classification by *Typ*, on the other hand, refers to classes in arbitrary (artificial) systems, and tokens of a *Typ* match a model or prototype represented by the *Typ*. This entails that while classification by *Art* makes use of linguistic knowledge in a broad sense, classification by *Typ* tends to be based on expert-knowledge. The hypothesis was successfully tested against lexicographic data and corpus data and was, moreover, subject of an online experiment. The experimental results not only confirmed the hypothesis, but in addition provided insight into subtle differences between classification by *Art* and by *Typ* in cases in which, at first sight, both ways of classification appear equally appropriate. The findings on the difference in meaning of *Art* and *Typ* are finally considered against the background of the notions of *kind* and *type* as used in formal semantics, highlighting their respective role in semantic theory.

1 Introduction

There are nouns in many languages expressing classification, for example in English *sort*, *class*, *kind* and *type*. They are called *taxonomic nouns*; see Mihatsch (2016). Although from a broader perspective all taxonomic nouns fulfil the same

---

Acknowledgements: I would like to express my gratitude, first, to two anonymous reviewers for their detailed and helpful comments, to the editors of the volume for their patient assistance, and to my former student assistant Julia Otterpohl, who developed the stimuli and implemented the experimental study. Furthermore, I am most grateful to Louise McNally for organizing the workshop on "*Types, tokens, roots, and functional structure*" that sparked my interest in the topic and for providing valuable comments on the first draft of this paper. I would also like to thank the audience of the workshop, in particular Fabienne Martin, for detailed feedback. The research reported in this paper was funded by the Deutsche Forschungsgemeinschaft, DFG, UM 100/1-3.

Carla Umbach, Institut für deutsche Sprache und Literatur (ISDL 1), Universität Köln,
e-mail: carla.umbach@uni-koeln.de

https://doi.org/10.1515/9783110701104-006

task, that is, classification, there are at a closer look differences in meaning and usage which are interesting beyond matters of style, since they reveal differences in their way of classification. The focus in this paper is on the German taxonomic nouns *Art* ('kind'/'species'/'manner') and *Typ* ('type'/'model') which are, at first sight, nearly synonymous, as in the example in (1).

(1) Kapitalismus lässt sich verschieden klassifizieren. Der rheinische **Typ des Kapitalismus**/die rheinische **Art des Kapitalismus** zeichnet sich beispielsweise durch viel Mitbestimmung und durch eine funktionierende Zivilgesellschaft aus.
'Capitalism can be classified differently. The Rhenish *Typ/Art* of capitalism, for example, is characterized by a lot of codetermination and a functioning civil society.'

While the example in (1) seems to suggest that there is no difference between *Art* and *Typ*, substitution of one by the other is hardly acceptable in the examples in (2) – (6).[1]

(2) Die alten Streifenwagen haben ausgedient. Ab 2004 werden die ersten drei Streifenwagen **vom Typ (*von der Art) Opel Vectra** in Betrieb genommen.
'The old patrol cars have had their day. From 2004, the first three patrol cars of the *Typ/Art* Opel Vectra C will be put into operation.'

(3) Frau Däubler-Gmelins Gegner werfen ihr gern vor, dass sie kompromissunfähig sei. Sie wolle "das deutsche Recht umkrempeln", behauptet die FAZ, die wohl eine weibliche Version **des Typs (?? der Art) Lafontaine** in ihr fürchtet.
'Ms. Däubler-'Gmelin's opponents like to accuse her of being incapable of compromise. She wanted "to revise German law," claims the FAZ, which probably fears a female version of the *Typ/Art* Lafontaine in her.'[2]

---

[1] Most examples in this paper are taken from the DEWAC corpus provided by the corpus linguistics group at Humboldt-University Berlin, with grateful thanks for access permission. Examples are often slightly simplified. English translations are intended to clarify the structure of the examples and are not always optimal due to structural differences between German and English.
[2] Hertha Däubler-Gmelin and Oskar Lafontaine are German politicians, FAZ (Frankfurter Allgemeine Zeitung) is a German newspaper.

(4) Fledermäuse stoßen Laute aus, die sehr schnell hintereinander folgen und sich hinsichtlich ihrer Lautstärke unterscheiden. **Die Art (*der Typ) "Große Hufeisennase"** stößt Ortungslaute aus, deren Schalldruck der Lautstärke eines Presslufthammers entspricht.
'Bats emit sounds that follow each other very quickly and differ in their volume. The *Art/Typ* "Big Horseshoe Nose" emits location sounds whose sound pressure corresponds to the volume of a jackhammer.'

(5) Das Ausmaß und die Intensität des Antisemitismus in Europa haben sich stets verändert. Unterschiedlich waren auch der Grad und **die Art (?? der Typ) von Diskriminierung der Juden.**
'The extent and intensity of anti-Semitism in Europe has always changed. The degree and *Art/Typ* of discrimination against the Jews has also differed.'

(6) Jandl, der zu den führenden Vertretern der experimentellen Literatur in der Nachkriegszeit gehörte, verstarb im Juni 2000. **Die Art (?? der Typ) seiner Vorträge** war für seine wortmalerische Lyrik von besonderer Bedeutung.
'Jandl, one of the leading exponents of post-war experimental literature, passed away in June 2000. The *Art/Typ* of his presentations was of particular importance for his lyrics.'

As a first guess one might think that *Typ* is used in technical domains, while *Art* is used to refer to biological classification, i.e., species, as in (2) and (4). This idea is refuted by the example in (3), which is about a type of politician, and the examples in (5) and (6), in which *Art* refers to a kind of discrimination and a manner of presentation. One might think, then, that the use of *Art* and *Typ* is selected by the particular noun or name: the noun *Vortrag* 'talk' selects *Art* and the proper name *Lafontaine* selects *Typ*. This is refuted by (1) as well as (7) where both *Typ* and *Art* are licensed. However, while the alternatives in (1) appear synonymous, the example in (7) exhibits a subtle difference between the *Typ* and the *Art* alternative: *Typ des Handys* seems to refer to different models, say, *iPhone 3* as opposed to *Nokia Lumina* and *Moto G*, while *Art des Handys* refers to, for example, the difference between a classical feature phone, an outdoor phone and a smartphone.

(7) Per Fernbedienung wird die Sendeleistung jedes Handys individuell geregelt. Je nach *Typ/Art* des Handys beträgt die maximale Sendeleistung zwischen 1W und 20W.
'Depending on the *Typ/Art* of mobile phone, the maximum transmission power is between 1W and 20W.'

The difference in meaning between the *Typ* variant and the *Art* variant in (7) provides evidence that the two taxonomic nouns have not, at least not in the first place, specialized in a particular domain, but rather employ different ways of classification: classes referred to by *Art* differ from those referred to by *Typ*, which raises the question of how to characterize the difference.

The research on *Art* and *Typ* described in this paper grew out of a talk that argued against the widely held supposition that kinds and types – more precisely, the notion of *kind* and the notion of *type* as employed in semantics – are roughly the same. The main argument in that talk addressed the different roles of kinds and types in the semantic analyses: while kinds in many semantic frameworks are considered as basic ontological entities in addition to (regular) individuals, types are part of the framework as such ensuring the well-formedness of composition and consistency of representations. Different from the talk, the perspective in this paper is an empirical one. The focus will be on the comparison of the meaning and, in particular, the classificatory potential of the German taxonomic nouns *Art* and *Typ* on the basis of lexicographic, distributional and experimental data. The question to what extent the findings match with the roles of kinds and types in semantic theory is only addressed at the end of the paper.

The first hypothesis in comparing *Art* and *Typ* will be that classification by *Art* does what it is expected to do, i.e., refer to kinds – natural kinds and beyond. Kinds are generally assumed to be associated with essential properties as opposed to accidental ones, though it is meanwhile understood that such properties are not strictly necessary. For example, a dog is four-legged in virtue of being a dog, even though an accidentally three-legged dog still counts as a dog. For ease of presentation these properties will be called *essential* in this paper without implicating that they are necessary. They are properties that entities have simply because they are the kind of things they are; they accommodate exceptions and, most importantly, they are part of what speakers acquire when learning a language. It may be argued that knowledge of these properties is encyclopedic rather than linguistic as such. Still, it is knowledge associated with words and must be acquired when learning the meaning of the words. Therefore, the assumption that the taxonomic noun *Art* refers to kinds entails that classification by *Art* relies on linguistic knowledge (in a broad sense).

In the case of *Typ* it is more difficult to formulate a clear hypothesis. There seems to be no generally established idea of what a type is apart from the distinction between *type* and *token* (Peirce 1931) according to which types are abstract entities and tokens are particular instances. Types occur in a wide variety of contexts and there is no indication that they are rooted in essential properties of the objects they classify. They seem to be defined instead by models or prototypes provided by a community of experts, independent of general linguistic knowledge.

Here is an example illustrating this idea: when I am asked what kind of heating system (*welche Art von Heizung*) we have in our house, I may answer that it is gas operated and supplies heat as well as hot water and was installed just two years ago (and was fairly expensive). I know that these features are relevant because I am familiar with the meaning of the word *Heizung* 'heating 'system' and with what counts as essential properties of heating systems. However, if you asked me for the type (*Typ*) of the heating system in our house, I would be lost and refer you to our heating engineer. I might of course try the same answer as in the case of *Art* (gas-operated, heat as well as water, etc.) and run the risk that this was not what you wanted to know. At the same time, it would be infelicitous if I were to answer the *Art* question by naming a *Typ* telling you, e.g., that we have a *B-2248 Weishaupt Eco*.[3] The hypothesis pursued in this paper is therefore as follows:

***Art*&*Typ* hypothesis**

Classification by *Art*	(i)	refers to (natural) kinds,
	(ii)	indicates that individuals share essential properties, and
	(iii)	is based on general linguistic knowledge (in a broad sense).
Classification by *Typ*	(i)	refers to classes in arbitrary systems,
	(ii)	indicates that individuals match a model or blueprint or prototype, and
	(iii)	is based on expert knowledge.

In the remainder of this paper, this hypothesis will be tested against three different sets of data. In section two, *Art* and *Typ* will be examined from a lexicographical point of view exploring synchronic as well as diachronic data. In section three, distributional characteristics will be considered, based on corpus data. In section four, an experimental study will be presented testing preferences in usage. In section five, we will finally address the role of kinds and of types in semantics.

Finally, there is a caveat: throughout the rest of this paper the focus will be on German *Art* and *Typ*. English *kind* and *type* are close in meaning but not fully equivalent to the German terms. For nouns corresponding to *type* across Romance languages see Mihatsch (2016).

---

[3] Many thanks to one of the reviewers for pointing out the infelicity of answering the *Art* question in this way.

2 Lexical meaning

In this section, *Art* and *Typ* will be examined from a lexicographical point of view. We start with their entries in the *Duden* (lexicon of modern German), look at their provenience in the *Grimm* (Grimm and Grimm 1854–1969, etymological lexicon of German) and briefly consider the English counterparts *kind*, *species*, *manner* and *type* in the Oxford English Dictionary (OED). In concluding this section, the implications for the *Art&Typ* hypothesis will be considered.

2.1 *Art*

The *Duden* lists five senses of *Art*:[4]

(8) a. *angeborene Eigenart / Wesen / Natur*
 'innate nature', 'character';
 b. *(Art und) Weise*
 'manner';
 c. *gutes Benehmen*
 'good manners';
 d. *Einheit im System der Tiere und Pflanzen, in der Individuen zusammengefasst sind, die in allen wesentlichen Merkmalen übereinstimmen und die untereinander fruchtbare Nachkommen hervorbringen können*
 'unit in the system of animals and plants including those individuals which are consistent in all essential characteristics and which can produce fruitful offspring among each other.' (English *species);*
 e. *eine besondere, bestimmte Sorte von etwas* ('sort', 'kind').

The sense in (8e) is the general taxonomic one. Since the paraphrase by *Sorte* ('sort') is not very helpful, we refer to the more informative entry in Adelung (1811) which is a High German dictionary from the nineteenth century:

Adelung entry on *Art*

(9) *Die Ähnlichkeit einzelner Dinge in wesentlichen Eigenschaften, und solche Dinge zusammen genommen*
 'The similarity of individual things in essential properties, and the collection of these things'

---

4 Dudenredaktion (o. J.): „Art", Duden online; https://www.duden.de/node/8848/revision/8875.

The etymology of the word *Art* is not fully transparent. Following the *Grimm* dictionary, a Slavic root *roditi* meaning *give birth* or *generate* seems to be relevant.

English translations of the taxonomic meaning of German *Art* are *kind* or *species*, and also *sort* or *type*. *Species* is a technical term in biology. *Kind*, like German *Art*, refers to "the essential quality [...] as determining the class or type to which a thing belongs".[5] Note that the Oxford English Dictionary includes *type* as a sense of *kind* indicating a less strict division line between *kind* and *type* than that between German *Art* and *Typ*.

2.2 *Typ*

The *Duden* lists five senses of German *Typ*:[6]

(10) a. *durch bestimmte charakteristische Merkmale gekennzeichnete Kategorie; Art (von Dingen oder Personen)*
'category characterized by characteristic features; kind of things or persons';
b. *Modell oder Typ einer Konstruktion*
'model or type of a construction';
c. *Urgestalt, Grundform, Urbild, das ähnlichen oder verwandten Dingen oder Individuen zugrunde liegt*
'basic form or archetype underlying similar or related things or individuals';
d. *als klassischer Vertreter einer bestimmten Kategorie von Menschen gestaltete, stark stilisierte, keine individuellen Züge aufweisende Figur*
'highly stylized figure, designed as a classical representative of a certain category of human beings, without individual features';
e. *männliche Person* 'male person' (as in *einen Typen kennenlernen* 'get to know a guy').

In (10a) the *Duden* lists a sense of *Typ* that is equivalent to *Art* in being defined by characteristic features, which will be discussed in section 2.4 below. The senses in (c) and (d) are synonymous with *Typus*, which is a common term in philosophy and literature studies. The sense in (e) is very colloquial. According to the etymo-

---

[5] Oxford English Dictionary (OED) https://www.oed.com/viewdictionaryentry/Entry/103444 (accessed Nov 15, 2020).
[6] Dudenredaktion (o. J.): „Typ", Duden online; https://www.duden.de/node/187038/revision/187074.

logical *Grimm* dictionary, the origin of *Typ* is the Greek verb for *strike/ beat* suggesting a connection to minting and printing. The latter is still visible in the printing sector where movable metal letters are called *Typen* (and *types* in English).[7]

English *type* is also rooted in the Greek verb for *strike/beat*. It has a taxonomic use analogous to German *Typ*, denoting either a class or kind, or a prototype – note that the Oxford English Dictionary also lists *kind* as a synonym of *type*, see (11a).

Oxford English Dictionary, *type*[8]

(11) a. A kind, class, or order as distinguished by a particular character;
    b. A person or thing that exhibits the characteristic qualities of a class; a representative specimen; a typical example or instance.

2.3 *Unterart* and *Untertyp*

The core idea of taxonomic nouns is two-fold. Firstly, there is the dichotomy between class and instance – *set* vs. *element*, *Art* vs. *Individuum*, *type* vs. *token*, etc. On the other hand, there is the idea of a taxonomy establishing a hierarchy such that a subordinated class inherits the features of the superordinated class. This idea is found in biology, but also in mathematics and computer science. Accordingly, there are in English the notions of *subspecies* and *subkind* and, in mathematics and computer science, the notion of *subtype*. In German, there is *Unterart* covering *subspecies* and *subkind*, as in (12). However, while *Unterart* is found in various contexts, the expression *Untertyp* occurs nearly exclusively in the context of diseases, as in (13a); it is rarely found in other contexts and, if so, appears marked, see (13b). This is surprising since in mathematics and computer science *type* is translated into German by *Typ*, and the prefix *Unter-* is fully productive in German.

(12) Der in verschiedenen Unterarten vorkommende Besenginster wird meist bis zu 2 m hoch.
    'The common broom, which occurs in different subspecies, is usually up to 2m high.'

---

[7] However, the singular forms are different; a movable letter is called *die Type*, with feminine gender, whereas the classification noun is masculine – *der Typ*.
[8] OED Online. https://www.oed.com/view/Entry/208330?rskey=rALWIs&result=2&isAdvanced=false (accessed November 15, 2020).

(13) a. Wie die Krankheit verläuft, hängt davon ab, mit welchem Untertyp des Erregers der Patient sich angesteckt hat.
'How the disease progresses depends on the subtype of the pathogen the patient has been infected with.'
b. Die Auswahl der Panzer ist beeindruckend: Fast jeder Panzertyp und Untertyp, der damals aus den Rüstungsfabriken rollte, steht auch in *Panzer Elite*[9] zur Verfügung.
'The choice of tanks is impressive: almost every type and subtype of tank that rolled out of the arms factories is also available in *Panzer Elite*.'

2.4 Implications for the *Art&Typ* hypothesis

The dictionary entries support the *Art&Typ* hypothesis in many ways. The core part where *Art* is concerned – individuals share essential properties – is provided as a defining characteristic in the entry in Adelung, see (9). Furthermore, the Slavic root *roditi* (*give birth* or *generate*) mentioned in the *Grimm* suggests that *Art* is diachronically connected to descent and inheritance, which is additional support for the constitutive role of essential properties.

The entry for *Typ* in the *Duden* highlights the role of a model or basic form (10b and 10c), which is the core part of the hypothesis concerning *Typ*. The origin of *Typ* in the Greek word for *beat* and its use to denote movable letters in printing confirms the idea that a *Typ* is specified by a prototype. In fact, the word *Typ* developed into a common term from the eighteenth century on, that is, only after movable type printing had become established as a technique.[10] It does not seem too speculative to assume that the taxonomic noun *Typ* is still connected to the idea of types in printing – produce any number of indistinguishable tokens – which is strong evidence that the idea of a prototype is at the core of its meaning.

The constitutive role of the prototype is the key point distinguishing classification by *Typ* from that by *Art*. Note that unlike a stereotype, a prototype is not just a collection of properties but an actual individual. In *der Typ Lafontaine* in (3) the actual politician Oscar Lafontaine serves as a prototype characterizing the tokens of this type. By contrast, the *Art Große Hufeisennase* is not constituted by a prototypical exemplar – bats of this species are related by descent. The role of the prototype is taken to the extreme when *Typ* no longer denotes a class but a

---

9 Computer game.
10 Mihatsch (2016) also observes for Romance languages that type nouns appeared later than the other taxonomic nouns.

man: *Sie hat einen Typ kennengelernt* ('She has met a guy'); see (10e). This usage is colloquial and derogative, and it seems to be saying that the guy she met is a prototypical male lacking other relevant properties.

However, the *Duden* entry of *Typ* includes in addition a sense in which a *Typ* is established by characteristic features, see (10a), entailing that the dividing line between *Art* and *Typ* is not as clear-cut as suggested by the *Art&Typ* hypothesis. An example for this sense is *Fehler dieses Typs* (listed in the *Duden*) which appears equivalent to *Fehler dieser Art* ('errors of this *Typ/Art*'). We have already seen in the heating example in the introduction that a question addressing the *Typ* may be answered in the same way as a question addressing the *Art*, by naming characteristic features. But we also noted that this is only true in one direction: a question addressing the *Art* cannot adequately be answered by naming a *Typ*. We will return to overlapping interpretations in section 4.3.

In English, the dividing line between *kind* and *type* appears even more vague. The Oxford English Dictionary mentions *type* as (one) synonym of *kind* and vice versa. That might indicate that in English the prototype characteristic is less distinctive. The fact that *type* is not used as a synonym of 'man' or 'guy' also points to the less prominent role of the prototype in English.

The almost complete absence of *Untertyp* in German is a puzzle. It might be considered to support the *Art&Typ* hypothesis, namely that the use of *Typ* is strongly related to the concept of a prototype. The fact that a "sub-prototype" is hard to conceive of thus explains why *Typ* might not readily support the inheritance of properties from a superordinated to a subordinated class. This would again point to a less prominent role of the prototype in English where *subtype* is highly frequent and indicates inheritance of properties.[11]

3 Distribution

In this section, DPs headed by *Art* and *Typ* will be examined with respect to grammatical form and meaning. The analysis is based on a corpus study (*DEWAC* corpus, see footnote 1). There are two major constructions. In the first, the taxo-

---

[11] Janebová, Martinková, and Gast (2023) explore the contrast between two major type nouns in Czech, *druh* and *typ*, by means of statistical analyses of their distribution in discourse. The meanings of *druh* and *typ* appear close to German *Art* and *Typ*: While *druh* denotes a group of individuals sharing the same characteristics, *typ* refers to a model, example, or prototype. The authors note that *typ* is a 19th-century borrowing which came into Czech via German and, as in German, can be used with the meaning of 'a strange man' in addition to its taxonomic uses.

nomic noun is combined with another noun by juxtaposition while in the second the taxonomic noun is complemented by a partitive genitive or a *von* ('of') PP.

Art+N, Typ+N	*die Art Große Hufeisennase,* *der Typ Opel Vectra, Bundesschatzbriefe Typ A,* *Politiker des Typs Lafontaine* 'the species Big Horseshoe Nose', 'Opel Vectra type [of car]', 'Type A federal saving bonds', 'politicians of the type of Lafontaine';
Art+von/des+N, Typ+von/des+N	*eine besondere Art von Wald, (der viel Wasser speichert),* *eine Art [von] Gegengift,* *der rheinische Typ des Kapitalismus,* *der Typ der ultraviolett leuchtenden Galaxien,* *der Typ des Kleinkriminellen* 'a special kind of forest (that retains a lot of water)', 'a kind of antidote', 'the Rhenish type of capitalism', 'the type of ultraviolet luminous galaxies', 'the petty criminal type';

The two forms will be demonstrated below. The focus will be on how the denotation of the taxonomic DP relates to that of the embedded noun, by identity or by subsumption. Cases with a hedging interpretation are discussed at the end of the section.

3.1 *Art+N, Typ+N*

Art and *Typ* can both be combined with nouns by mere juxtaposition which is a form of apposition (see *Duden Grammatik* 2006). In the case of *Art* we have to distinguish between combinations that block a partitive genitive or *von* ('of') prepositions and those that do not. The former (strict) variety requires the noun to be the name of a species, e.g., *Große Hufeisennase*.[12] Other nouns are blocked even if they allow for a kind reading: **Die Art Batterie / Die Batterie wurde von Volta erfunden* ('The kind of battery / The battery was invented by Volta'). Moreover, the strict variety of *Art*+N requires a definite article which is explained by the fact that

---

[12] *Große Hufeisennase* is the name of a species, not a combination of adjective and noun.

names of species are unique – there is exactly one kind of *Große Hufeisennase*. The semantics of these Art+N constructions is such that the denotation of the full DP is identical to that of the noun (on a kind reading): *die Art Große Hufeisennase* and *die Große Hufeisennase* denote the same kind of bat.

Art+N constructions may also occur with nouns other than species names and with an indefinite article if they allow for a partitive genitive or the preposition *von* ('of') without change of meaning, as in *eine Art [von] Smartphone* 'a kind of smartphone'. For this reason they are subsumed under the form *Art+von/ des+N* (see below).

When *Typ* is combined with a noun by juxtaposition, the noun is always a proper name. In *der Typ Opel Vectra* the term *Opel Vectra* is the name of the type. Similarly, in *Bundesschatzbriefe Typ A* ('type A federal saving bonds') and *Politiker des Typs Lafontaine* ('politicians of the type of Lafontaine') the terms *A* and *Lafontaine* are names of types. Even in *Autofahrer vom Typ "Hauptsache ich"* ('"Me first" type of car drivers') the phrase *Hauptsache ich* is understood to be the name of the type.

Type names are less commonly known and exhibit a high degree of freedom compared to the names combined with *Art*. This corresponds to the idea that types classify artefacts or refer to prototypes, and are not conventionalized, whereas names of species adhere to the conventions of biological classification.

From the semantic point of view, phrases of the form *Typ+N* are identical in reference to that of the name alone, provided that the name is interpreted as the name of a type. This can be tested with the help of predicates that block a token reading.[13] In (14a) *Der Opel Vectra* must have a type reading because the verb *produzieren* ('produce') along with the time span blocks a token reading, and in this reading (14a) is equivalent to (14b). In (14c) only the token reading is possible since a type cannot be owned by a person, which is confirmed by the unacceptability of (14d).

(14)   a. Der Opel Vectra wurde von 1988 bis 2008 produziert.
       b. Der Typ Opel Vectra wurde von 1988 bis 2008 produziert.
         'The [type] Opel Vectra was produced from 1988 to 2008. '
       c. Der Opel Vectra gehört meinem Bruder.
       d. *Der Typ Opel Vectra gehört meinem Bruder.
         'The [type] Opel Vectra is owned by my brother.'

---

[13] We adopt this test from a test for kind readings: Kind readings can be tested with the help of kind level predicates like *extinct* which cannot be predicated of (regular) individuals, see Krifka et al. (1995). Compare the individual reading in (a) to the kind reading in (b):
a. Die Große Hufeisennase ist ausgeflogen. ('The Big Horseshoe Nose flew away.')
b. Die Große Hufeisennase ist ausgestorben. ('The Big Horseshoe Nose is extinct.')

In cases like *der Typ Opel Vectra* the type name is primary in the sense that the type/model existed before an instance was generated. This is different in cases like *der Typ Lafontaine* in which the politician Lafontaine is used as a prototype generating the type/model. When occurring without the taxonomic noun a type reading of *Lafontaine* is licensed only if combined with an indefinite article, as in (15b); (for proper names combined with indefinite articles see von Heusinger 2010).

(15) a. Der neue Vorsitzende ist vom Typ Lafontaine.
 b. Der neue Vorsitzende ist ein Lafontaine.
 'The new chairman is the Lafontaine type / is a Lafontaine.'

The ambiguity of proper names between a token and a type reading may lead to the idea that a phrase of the form *Typ+N* denotes a superclass including two individuals, the subject of the classification and the one serving as a prototype (for example in 15a the new chairman and Oskar Lafontaine).[14] This seems reasonable if a prototype is provided by the name of a person. We nevertheless remain with the analysis such that the proper name has a type reading in *Typ+N* constructions because type readings of proper names with indefinite articles are attested.

3.2 *Art+von/des+N, Typ+von/des+N*

Art and *Typ* can both be combined with nouns in the form of a partitive genitive or *von* 'of' PP.[15] *Art* phrases of this form are not restricted to species but instead combine with all sorts of everyday domains including abstract entities, see (16). They may occur with indefinite as well as definite articles (provided uniqueness is guaranteed), and also with quantifiers, see (17). We subsume here cases of the form *Art+N* which allow for insertion of genitive or prepositional marking without change of meaning, as in (18), where we assume a covert preposition *von* 'of'.

(16) eine Art von Fledermäusen, eine (besondere) Art von Baumwollstoff, eine (neue) Art von Vampiren, eine (neue) Art von Abschreckung
 'a kind of bat', 'a (special) kind of cotton fabric', 'a (novel) kind of vampire', 'a (novel) kind of deterrence'

---
14 Many thanks to an anonymous reviewer for pointing out this possibility.
15 Lawrenz (1993) argues that *Art* is a relational noun such that the subsequent nominal or prepositional phrase has the status of a complement instead of an adjunct.

(17) a. eine / die (neue) Art von Wald (die die dem Klimawandel standhalten kann)
'A / the (novel) kind of forest that can withstand climate change.'
b. jede Art von Wald
'every kind of forest'

(18) eine/die Art [von] Handy, die den Benutzer als Künstler ausweist
'a/the kind of mobile phone that identifies the user as an artist'

The relation between the kind denoted by the *Art* phrase and the domain denoted by the nominal complement is that of subsumption – *eine neue Art von Wald* ('a novel kind of forest') denotes a subkind of the kind forest. If combined with indefinites, *Art+von/des+N* phrases preferably include information distinguishing the subkind from the superordinated kind, as in 'a novel kind of forest', otherwise they tend to be understood as a form of hedging; see section 3.3.

Finally, there is a form of *Art* phrase that does not pattern with either *Art+N* or *Art+von/des+N*. In these cases, *Art* has the meaning of manner and is specified by a relative clause headed by *wie* ('how'); see (19a). The relative clause may also occur without being headed by *Art* with the same meaning, as in (19b). These cases express identity of the *Art* phrase and its complement. There is no corresponding construction with *Typ*.

(19) a. Die Art, wie sie sich mit ihm unterhielt, erinnerte mich an frühere Zeiten.
b. Wie sie sich mit ihm unterhielt, erinnerte mich an frühere Zeiten.
'The way/How she talked to him reminded me of earlier times.'

Moving on to *Typ*, phrases of the form *Typ+von/des+N* prefer artefacts and also diseases[16] as their domain of classification, see (20a), while everyday domains and abstract notions occur only rarely, see (20b).

(20) a. ein (neuer) Typ von aufladbarer Batterie, drei Typen von Fibromyalgie
'a novel type of rechargeable battery', 'three types of fibromyalgia'
b. der zweite Typ des fortgeschrittenen Trainings, der rheinische Typ des Kapitalismus
'the second type of advanced training', 'the Rhenish type of capitalism'

---

[16] The use of *Typ* when classifying diseases is not surprising taking into account that diseases are frequently classified by way of "clinical pictures", that is, by way of prototypical appearance.

In other respects, *Typ+von/des+N* phrases exhibit the same characteristics as in the case of *Art*. They can be indefinite or definite or quantified, as shown in (21). The relation between the denotation of the *Typ* phrase and the denotation of the nominal is that of subsumption: *Ein neuer Typ von Hybridfahrzeug* ('a novel type of hybrid vehicle') denotes a subtype of hybrid vehicles.

(21) Ein/der (neue)/jeder Typ von Hybridfahrzeug
'a/the (novel)/every type of hybrid vehicle'

There are also *Typ+von/des+N* phrases expressing identity instead of subsumption. In (22a), for example, *der Typ der ultraviolett leuchtenden Galaxien* ('the type of ultraviolet luminous galaxies') does not denote a particular subtype of ultraviolet luminous galaxies but instead a type that is described as ultraviolet luminous galaxies. Likewise, in (22b) the *Typ* phrase does not denote a subtype but the type as such.

(22) a. Entdeckungen, die zum Typ der ultraviolett leuchtenden Galaxien gehören.
'Discoveries that belong to the/a type of ultraviolet luminous galaxies.'
b. Eigentlich ist er nicht der Typ des Kleinkriminellen.
'He is not the petty criminal type.'

3.3 Hedging via *Art*

It was observed above that indefinite *Art+von+N* phrases preferably include information distinguishing the subkind from the superordinated kind, as in *eine Art von Wald, die dem Klimawandel standhalten kann* ('a kind of forest that can withstand climate change').[17] Without distinguishing information, indefinite *Art+von+N* phrases and also indefinite *Art+N* phrases tend to be understood as a form of hedging: when the speaker uses the expression *eine Art [von] Smartphone* ('a kind of smartphone') instead of *ein Smartphone* she seems to be reluctant to call the referent a smartphone even though this term is the closest she can think of. The same effect is shown in (23): *eine Art Gegengift* is something close to an antidote but not what is usually meant by this term and *eine Art von Dialog* differs

---

17 Information distinguishing the subkind from the superkind might also be hinted at by accenting the indefinite article – *EINE Art von Smartphone* – thereby indicating that the distinguishing property will be subsequently mentioned (such indefinites are analyzed as cataphors in Umbach 2004).

from a real dialogue – you cannot have a proper dialogue with your tools and medium.

(23) a. [In seiner Übertreibung ist diese Erzählung] eine *Art* Gegengift zu Gaarders Innerlichkeit.
'[In its exaggeration, this narrative is] a kind of antidote to Gaader's inwardness.'
b. Sicher steht ein Künstler in einer Art von Dialog mit seinem Werkzeug und seinem Medium.
'Certainly, an artist stands in a (particular) kind of dialogue with his tools and his medium.'

The puzzle with this form of hedging is the following: why call something *eine Art von Smartphone* if it is not a smartphone in the first place? In fact, these phrases appear ambiguous in an elusive way, because there seems to be no clear difference between the regular (subkind) interpretation and the hedging interpretation. One might test whether speakers agree that *eine Art von Smartphone* is a smartphone. The prediction will be that they agree and at the same time argue that *eine Art von Smartphone* is not a genuine smartphone.

There is no room in this paper to do justice to the broad literature on hedging (beginning with Lakoff 1973). However, for the *Art* variety there is a straightforward semantic explanation as to how the hedging effect comes about. First, assume that inheritance in taxonomies is a default: by default, every subkind of smartphone inherits the features of the kind smartphone, but there may also be exceptional subkinds. Secondly, the Gricean maxim of manner allows us to reason as follows: if the speaker uses the expression *Art von Smartphone* instead of the simpler expression *Smartphone* without explicating the distinctive features of the kind she has in mind, the hearer will wonder why she not simply calls this thing a smartphone. Therefore, the hearer concludes that it is a smartphone (because it is a subkind of smartphone), but it is not a smartphone (because it is not called that, although there seems to be no better term available), and solves the dilemma by concluding that it is an exceptional smartphone (not inheriting all of the smartphone features).[18]

From this point of view, hedging via *Art* is not a matter of fuzzy boundaries of a concept but instead a matter of non-strict taxonomic inheritance (from a logical

---

[18] Manfred Bierwisch (p.c.) argues that even though *eine Art Smartphone* is clearly a hedging expression, *eine Art von Smartphone* need not be. A similar observation is reported for English in Anderson (2013): "A sort of fairytale is a type of fairytale, but a sorta fairytale can be taken to mean something that is only like a fairytale in some respect." These observations seem to indicate that the intonation and information structure of the phrase play a role.

point of view, it is not a matter of indeterminate truth values but of non-monotonic inference). This explanation for the hedging use of *Art* is supported by the observation that the hedging flavour is lost as soon as *Art* is modified: *eine neue Art von Smartphone* ('a novel kind of smartphone') denotes a subkind of smartphone without any trace of hedging (see also Kolde 2004 on the grammar of the German *Art* when used for hedging).

Finally, unlike *Art* phrases, *Typ* phrases never license a hedging interpretation. Similarly, English *kind* is used as a hedging device, but not English *type*. However, in many languages, the word corresponding to *type* is a prominent hedging device, for example Swedish *typ* (see Rosenkvist and Skärlund 2013) and Italian *tipo* (for Romance languages see Mihatsch 2010).[19]

4 Empirical study

Summarizing the results of section two and three, the dictionary entries in section two provided evidence that the taxonomic nouns *Art* and *Typ* are notably different in origin: *Art* is diachronically connected to descent and inheritance, whereas *Typ* appears connected to minting and printing. This supports the general hypothesis in this paper that classification by *Art* is based on essential properties whereas classification by *Typ* is based on a model or prototype.

In section three, the analysis of *Art* and *Typ* phrases provided evidence that they are either combined with a name (or an expression that functions as a name) by juxtaposition (*Art+N, Typ+N*), or they are combined with a genitive or *von*-PP (*Art+von/des+N, Typ+von/des+N*). The former express identity of the denotation of the taxonomic phrase and the referent of the name, while the latter express subsumption – the denotation of the taxonomic phrase is subsumed by the denotation of the complement nominal phrase. Regarding lexical content, it was found that *Typ* is preferred with artefacts and diseases and also with humans, while *Art* is used in biological domains but more importantly (and more frequently) in classifying everyday items and abstract issues.

These results raise the question as to what extent the taxonomic nouns *Art* and *Typ* are specialized. The idea that *Art* makes use of essential properties while *Typ* makes use of prototypes predicts that *Art* is more suitable for use in biology and *Typ* is more suitable for technology. However, it does not predict that classi-

---

19 For Czech, Janebová, Martinková, and Gast (2023) observe that *druh* 'kind' may function as hedge when occurring in a non-head position determined by a reflexive pronoun. *Typ*, on the other hand, was not attested in a hedging function.

fication by *Art* and classification by *Typ* exclude each other. Why should it not be possible to classify a domain on the basis of essential properties and, alternatively, classify it on the basis of models or prototypes? In fact, such a case was presented in the example in (7) in the introduction which was evidence that the same domain may be subject to classification by *Art* and by *Typ* and that, moreover, the two ways of classification yield different results.

4.1 Experimental design

The experiment described below aims at detailing the differences between classification by *Art* and by *Typ*. We used (slightly simplified) corpus examples with *Art* or *Typ* phrases as stimuli. Each example occurred in two variants: the original one and one in which *Art* and *Typ* was substituted with the other term. The variants were presented simultaneously in a forced choice acceptability design, with one or two sentences of preceding contexts. Participants were informed that they would see texts from newspapers and blogs with two different final sentences. They were instructed to decide which of these was the original one, assuming that they consider the more acceptable version to be the original. In (24) and (25) two experimental items are shown, the first occurred originally with *Art* and the second with *Typ*. Judgments for these two items were in agreement with the original variant: in (24), around 90% of the participants decided in favour of *Art* while in (25), around 90% chose *Typ*.

(24) (originally *Art*)
Schäuble vertrat [...] die Auffassung, dass das Instrumentarium der internationalen Gemeinschaft nicht mehr ausreicht, um den Herausforderungen der Gegenwart zu begegnen.
a. Er forderte eine neue *Art* von Abschreckung.
b. Er forderte einen neuen *Typ* von Abschreckung.
'Schäuble proposed [...] that the means of the international community were insufficient to meet present challenges. He called for a novel *Art/Typ* of deterrence.'

(25) (originally *Typ*)
Das Ziel der Militäroperation "Grand Slam" war ein sowjetisches Raketentestgelände, das die Piloten jedoch nie erreichten.
a. Abfangjäger fingen das US-amerikanische Aufklärungsflugzeug des *Typ*s U-2 kurz vor Erreichen des Ziels ab.

b. Abfangjäger fingen das US-amerikanische Aufklärungsflugzeug der *Art* U-2 kurz vor Erreichen des Ziels ab.

'The target of the military operation "Grand Slam" was a Soviet missile test site which the pilots never reached. Interceptors caught the US reconnaissance aircraft of *Typ/Art* U-2 shortly before reaching its goal.'

The predictions resulting from the previous section are:

For phrases of the form *Art+N* and *Typ+N*
(i) if N is a biological name, *Art* is preferred (*die Art Große Hufeisennase*);
(ii) if N is the name of a technical device, *Typ* is preferred (*der Typ Opel Vectra*);
(iii) if N is the name of a person, *Typ* is preferred (*der Typ Lafontaine*);

For phrases of the form *Art+des/von+N, Typ+des/von+N*
(iv) if N denotes entities created in mass production, *Typ* is preferred (*ein neuer Typ von Batterie*);
(v) if N denotes schemata imposed by definitions, *Typ* is preferred (*der rheinische Typ des Kapitalismus, der klassische Typ der Depression*);
(vi) if N is an abstract noun, *Art* is preferred (*die Art von Abschreckung/Kommunikation*);
(vii) in all other cases, *Art* is preferred (*die Art der Nahrungsmittel / des Materials);*

These predictions relate to preferences in certain domains for *Art* over *Typ* or vice versa. The main hypothesis of our experiment is, however, that there are *equal preference items*, that is, cases where neither *Art* nor *Typ* is preferred, but classification by *Art* and by *Typ* yields different results.

The experiment included ten *Art* and ten *Typ* items of the form *Art/Typ+des/von+N*, as well as ten *Art* and ten *Typ* items of the form *Art/Typ+N*. We also added five items of the form *Art+N* for which we assumed an implicit *von*-phrase, as in (18). The items were presented online in a forced choice acceptability design. We had 25 participants. For equal preference items we conducted informal post-hoc interviews.

4.2 Results

The results agree with some but not all of the predictions listed above. Since the main hypothesis relates to the equal preference items, we did not perform a full statistical analysis and the percentages mentioned below describe tendencies. Starting with the *Art* items, (i) was fully confirmed: in the case of biological names (e.g. *Großer Brachvogel, Crassula brevicaule*), more than 80% of the participants preferred *Art*, although, surprisingly, the preference for *Art* was never absolute. Prediction (vi) was confirmed to a large extent: nouns denoting abstract entities like *Erfolg* 'success', *Variation* 'variation', *Diskriminierung* 'discrimination', *Reaktion* 'reaction' etc. yielded a preference for *Art* of more than 75%. This included combinations of the form *Art+des/von+N* with implicit *von*-phrases.

For *Typ* items results were more diverse. On the one hand, prediction (ii) and (iii) were fully confirmed: technical names yielded a preference of more than 90% for *Typ* and personal names a preference of more than 80% for *Typ*. However, predictions (iv) and (v) failed: most of the *Typ+des/von+N* items yielded no *Typ* preference and sometimes even a slight *Art* preference. This included nouns like *Hörgerät* 'hearing aid', *Persönlichkeitsstörung* 'personality disorder', *Schlaganfall* 'stroke' and *Dokument* 'document'. Cases like these will be discussed in the next section.

Summing up the results, the predictions for constructions of the form *Art/Typ+N* have been confirmed. Moreover, for those of the form *Art/Typ+des/von+N* there were a number of equal preference items. Equal preference results might be explained by assuming that the domains of classification in these items are insensitive to the choice between *Art* and *Typ*. However, if classification by *Art* and by *Typ* are two distinct ways of classification, the participants may opt for either way depending on what they consider more relevant in the context.

4.3 Equal preference items

In this section, selected equal preference items will be discussed. We asked some of the participants post-hoc why they chose a particular alternative and what they thought was the difference between, for example, *eine Art von Smartphone* ('a kind of smartphone') as opposed to *ein Typ von Smartphone* ('a type of smartphone'). The interviews were conducted orally and informally with a limited number of participants. The most interesting results are discussed below.

Handy

The equal preference item shown in (7) in the introduction is repeated in (26). It occurred in the corpus with *Typ*. The text is about the regulation of transmission power, which is highly technical topic. Post-hoc assessments provide evidence that *Art* and *Typ* convey slightly different meanings which are, nonetheless, both reasonable in this context. *Art von Handy* classifies mobile phones according to form and function, e.g., smartphones, children's phones, slider phones, flip phones, outdoor phones, etc. By contrast, *Typ von Handy* refers to a classification imposed by the manufacturer, e.g., *Samsung Galaxy iPhone 3, Nokia Lumina* and *Moto G*. The results of classification are distinct: when classifying by *Art* there is, for example, a class of outdoor phones including a wide range of phones sharing outdoor fitness as an essential property. When classifying by *Typ* there is, for example, a class named *Samsung Galaxy* including instances of this model. Two exemplars may differ in their date of manufacture and in colour and traces of use, but otherwise, they are clones – tokens of the same type.

(26) (originally *Typ*)
Per Fernbedienung wird die Sendeleistung jedes Handys individuell geregelt.
a. Je nach Typ des Handys beträgt die maximale Sendeleistung zwischen 1W bis 20W.
b. Je nach Art des Handys beträgt die maximale Sendeleistung zwischen 1W bis 20W.
'The transmission power of each mobile phone is individually controlled by remote control. Depending on the *Typ/Art* of mobile phone, the maximum transmission power is between 1W and 20W.'

The semantic difference between *Art* and *Typ* found in the above example is supported by examples like (27)–(30) (which were not part of the study). In (27), smartphones are said to be the preferred *Art* of mobile phones implying that a smartphone is in fact considered an *Art* of mobile phone. Using *Typ* in (27) would not be unacceptable but less appropriate. In (28), the fact that mobile phones are in general banned on the factory site is expressed by quantifying over *Art*. Quantifying over *Typ* would not fulfil the intention of the ban, which is (presumably) to prohibit simple feature phones as well as smartphones with cameras, irrespective of manufacturer and model.[20] Finally, the coordination of *Art* and *Typ* in (29) would not be acceptable if there were no semantic difference, and in (30), which is taken from a technical data sheet, the notions of *Geräteart* and *Gerätetyp* ('kind

---

[20] An anonymous reviewer argued that a ban of any *Typ von Handy* (including, for example, *Galaxy S8, iPhone 10, Huawei P3* . . .) would essentially mean the same thing as with *Art*, namely that mobile phones in general are banned on the factory site. However, this view does not take into account differences when it comes to exceptions. It might make sense to allow a particular kind of mobile phone, for example, one without a camera. But it would not make sense to allow a particular model, e.g., a *Galaxy S8* while banning an *iPhone 10*.

vs. type of device') are used side by side. *Geräteart* refers to the function of the device, in this case a TV, while *Gerätetyp* refers to the model.

(27) Smartphones sind inzwischen ohne Zweifel die bevorzugte *Art* von Handy.
 'Smartphones are undoubtedly the preferred *Art* of mobile phone.'

(28) Außerdem gibt es auf dem Werksgelände bestimmte Bereiche, zu denen der Zutritt mit jeder Art von Handy untersagt ist.
 'In addition, there are certain areas on the factory site to which access is prohibited with any *Art* of mobile phone.'

(29) [...] Fahrzeuge, die von der Art und vom Typ her generell nicht gewerblich genutzt werden.
 '[...] vehicles that are generally not used commercially in terms of their *Art* and *Typ*.'

(30) Geräteart : LCD TV 'kind of device'
 Hersteller : Sony 'manufacturer'
 Gerätetyp : KDL 46xxx 'type of device'

Depression

We saw in the previous section that variants of a disease are usually classified using *Typ*. The item in (31), however, does not exhibit preference for either *Typ* or *Art*. In post-hoc interviews participants indicated that the use of *Art* is closer to everyday language than that of *Typ*: "*Typ* klingt technischer, oder medizinischer, *Art* eher umgangssprachlich" ('*Typ* sounds more technical or medical, *Art* more colloquial'). This suggests that the notion of depression licenses classification by *Art* because the disease is sufficiently well-known for participants to be able to think of essential properties of depression. At the same time, half of the participants opted for classification by *Typ*, pointing to the idea of a clinical picture as a prototype.

(31) (originally *Typ*)
 Eine endogene Depression ist nicht durch erkennbare körperliche Erkrankungen oder einen äußeren seelischen Anlass begründbar.

a. Sie ist der klassische Typ der Depression.
b. Sie ist die klassische Art der Depression.

'Endogenous depression is not due to recognizable physical disease or external mental illness. It is the classic *Typ/Art* of depression.'

Windkraftanlage

The item in (32) refers to a technical device, as in the case of mobile phones, and it yielded a slight *Typ* preference (around 70%). This preference appears plausible when thinking about what *Art der Windkraftanlage* ('kind of wind power plant') might refer to. Unlike mobile phones, wind power plants are not everyday objects, and German native speakers are not normally familiar with their essential properties. Therefore, *Arten von Windkraftanlagen* are difficult to conceive of by non-expert speakers. Speakers are, of course, not familiar with *Typen von Windkraftanlagen* either, but they know that a wind power plant is a technical device and, moreover, the context in (32) is a technical one. So, when opting for *Typ*, participants presumably presuppose that there is a classification scheme defined by experts that they may not know.[21]

(32) (originally *Typ*)
Bei der Entscheidung, neue Windkraftanlagen zu bauen, steht der Referenzertrag der Anlage im Fokus.
a. Das ist die für den jeweiligen Typ der Windkraftanlage spezifische Strommenge, die in fünf Betriebsjahren erbracht wird.
b. Das ist die für die jeweilige Art der Windkraftanlage spezifische Strommenge, die in fünf Betriebsjahren erbracht wird.

'When deciding to build new wind power plants, the focus is on the plant's reference yield. This is the amount of electricity specific to each *Art/Typ* of wind power plant, which will be provided over five years of operation.'

Hörgerät

Surprisingly, there are a number of items showing a slight preference for *Art* even though the original was a *Typ* sentence. Examples are *Typ des Hörgeräts* 'hearing

---

[21] It would be interesting to see whether experts familiar with wind power plants would rate items like (32) differently.

aid', *Typen von Persönlichkeitsstörungen* 'personality disorders', *Typ von Schlaganfall* 'stroke' and *Typ des Dokuments* 'document'. These terms are familiar in everyday language and, moreover, the items included non-expert contexts, such as (33). The results support the tendency we saw above: in the case of everyday terms, when speakers are familiar with their meaning and essential properties, *Art* is a good choice, and in a non-expert context may even be the preferred one.

(33) (originally *Typ*)
Menschen mit Hörgeräten können unter Umständen Störgeräusche wahrnehmen, wenn in deren Nähe schnurlose Geräte verwendet werden.
a. Der Grad der Störung ist abhängig vom Typ des Hörgeräts und dem Abstand zur Störungsquelle.
b. Der Grad der Störung ist abhängig von der Art des Hörgeräts und dem Abstand zur Störungsquelle.
'People with hearing aids may experience noise when cordless devices are used nearby. The degree of interference depends on the *Typ/Art* of the hearing aid and the distance to the source of the interference.'

Vampir

The item in (34) originally contained *Art*. The term *Vampir* 'vampire' belongs to everyday language and speakers of German are familiar with vampires and their essential properties, which would support classification by *Art*. The equal preference result may be explained by taking into account that the context is about the presentation of vampires in animated film which is an expert context, and the vampire in question is an animation instead of a "real" one.

(34) (originally *Art*)
Michael hat mit seiner Freundin einen Animationsfilm über Vampire gesehen und freut sich über die Darstellung: "Sie sind robuster und haben einen netten Unterkiefer. Sowas habe ich echt noch nicht gesehen und es ist auch einfach zu genial, wie sich das Gesicht öffnet, eine Zunge hervorkommt und den Anderen aussaugt." ...
a. "Ich finde diese neue Art von Vampiren wirklich äußerst gelungen."
b. "Ich finde diesen neuen Typ von Vampiren wirklich äußerst gelungen."
'Michael saw an animated film about vampires and is pleased with the presentation: "They are more robust and have a nice jaw, something I've really never seen, and it's just too awesome when the face opens, a tongue comes out and sucks the other out. I really like this new *Art/Typ* of vampire."'

Herrscher

Finally, the item in (35) originally contained *Art*. Since the term *Herrscher* 'ruler' belongs to everyday language and the context is a non-expert one, the question arises as to why we do not find a clear preference for *Art*. A possible explanation is as follows: recall that *Typ* is not only preferred with technical items but also with persons (*Typ Lafontaine*). When choosing *Art*, the sentence is about classifying behaviour – the manner of ruling. When choosing *Typ* it is about classifying persons on the basis of prototypical rulers. But even though the ways of classification differ, the outcome will be the same: in the case of *Art* the president belongs to a class comprising rulers that came to power in a particular manner, namely in a coup d'état, whereas in the case of *Typ* the president belongs to a class of rulers matching a prototype who came to power in a coup d'état.

(35) (originally *Art*)
Der damalige Präsident von Togo machte sich das Konzept der ethnischen Zugehörigkeit zunutze.
   a. Er war die Art Herrscher, die durch Staatsstreich an die Macht gekommen das Land mit Terror überzieht.
   b. Er war der Typ Herrscher, der durch Staatsstreich an die Macht gekommen das Land mit Terror überzieht.
'The former president of Togo took advantage of the concept of ethnicity. He was the *Art/Typ* of ruler who came to power in a coup d'état covering the country with terror.'

5 Kinds and types in semantics

As mentioned in the introduction, the research on *Art* and *Typ* described in this paper grew out of a talk that argued against the widely held supposition that kinds and types – more precisely, the notions of kinds and types employed in semantic theory – are roughly the same. While in the talk the theoretical status of these notions was considered, this paper took an empirical approach to comparing the meaning, and in particular the classificatory potential, of the German taxonomic nouns *Art* and *Typ*. The question as to what extent the findings in the paper match with the notions of kinds and types in semantic theory will be addressed in this section.

Kinds

The concept of kinds as a theoretical notion in semantics is rooted in the philosophical notion of natural kinds (Putnam 1975) and plays a major role in the analysis of generic expressions; see Carlson (1980) and Krifka et al. (1995). In English and German (and many other languages), kinds can be denoted by bare plurals. The bare plural in (36a) refers to a plural individual of whales (say, a group of whales), while the same expression in (36b) refers to the kind *Cetacea*. The fact that kind-denoting terms must be distinguished from individual-denoting terms is obvious in (36c): the predicate *be an endangered species* cannot be applied to a (plural) individual. This observation led to the idea that kinds are basic ontological entities, in addition to (regular) individuals. This step provides a straightforward interpretation of taxonomic phrases using *kind/Art*, as in (36d) or (36e).

(36) a. There are whales to be seen.
b. Whales are mammals.
c. Whales are an endangered species.
d. Die Art 'Wal' ist eine gefährdete Spezies. / The kind 'whale' is an endangered species.
e. Zwei Unterarten des Wals, nämlich der Blauwal und der Finwal, wurden unter Artenschutz gestellt. / Two subkinds of whale, namely the blue whale and the fin whale, were put under protection.

In philosophy as well as psychology there is a longstanding debate about the question of whether kinds (or concepts)[22] are associated with so-called essential properties. Recent research in the area of genericity shows that there are in fact particular properties associated with kinds, although contrary to what was long thought, such properties are not necessary but allow for exceptions. Greenberg (2003) refers to them as "in virtue of" properties. For example, a dog is four-legged in virtue of being a dog, even though an accidentally three-legged dog still counts as a dog. Likewise, Prasada and Dillingham (2006) present a series of experiments showing that there are principled connections between kinds and properties – so-called *k-properties* – which differ from merely statistically correlated properties and nevertheless allow for exceptions. Carlson (2010) argues that Greenberg's "in virtue of" properties and Prasada and Dillingham's k-properties are in fact the same.

---

22 I follow Carlson (2010) in assuming that kinds correspond to labeled concepts.

These properties play a core role in classification by *Art/kind* because entities have these properties simply by virtue of being the kind of entities they are. They are learned when learning the meaning of a word, that is, the kind (or concept) denoted by a word. Even if this is encyclopedic rather than core linguistic knowledge, it is something speakers of a language are in command of. This is why classification by *Art/kind* feels more colloquial.

The notion of kinds in semantics has meanwhile been subject to further specification. There are *well-established kinds*, which in English allow for singular definite generic expressions; compare *the Coke bottle* as opposed to **the green bottle*, see (Krifka 1995).[23] Furthermore, Rothstein (2013) distinguishes *taxonomic kinds*, which are expressed by bare singulars in Hebrew, from general intensional kinds. She argues that while intensional kinds are provided by regularities across worlds taxonomic kinds are particular individuals (and rigid designators in the sense of Kripke 1972).[24]

Another variety of kinds are those that are generated ad hoc by the use of similarity demonstratives like German *so* and English *such/like this* (see Umbach and Gust 2014). Suppose that the speaker points to a table while uttering the sentence in (37a). The nominal phrase *so ein Tisch* will denote a set of tables similar to the one the speaker points to. This set constitutes a kind ad-hoc created by similarity, which is evidenced by the fact that (37b) is equivalent to (37a).[25]

(37) a. So einen Tisch hat Berta auch.
          'Berta has a table like this, too.'
      b. Diese Art von Tisch hat Berta auch.
          'Berta has a table of this kind, too.'

The core issue raised by similarity-based kinds is the question of which properties of the target of the pointing gesture, i.e. the table being pointed to in (37), are suitable in determining similarity. Consider (38). In (38a), being a diesel as well as being a Japanese car leads to the interpretation that Berta has a Japanese car and a diesel, respectively. By contrast, in (38b) being a new car does not qualify as a

---

23 From the point of view of this paper, *the Coke bottle* might be more of a type than a kind.
24 Hebrew bare singulars are primarily used to denote species and sub-species as well as "types of machines such as cellular phones, food processors and so on" (Rothstein 2013: 36). The latter characteristic is strongly reminiscent of types in the sense of this paper.
25 Kinds ad-hoc created by similarity are also observed with verbal expressions, but not with adjectives: *Diese Art zu laufen* 'this way of running' vs. ?? *Diese Art groß (zu) sein* 'this kind of being tall'.

feature of comparison for determining similarity – the second sentence cannot be understood such that Berta has a new car.

(38) a. Anna fährt ein japanisches Auto / einen Diesel. Berta fährt auch so ein Auto (nämlich ein japanisches Auto / einen Diesel).
'Anna drives a Japanese car / a diesel. Berta drives such a car, too (namely a Japanese car / a diesel).'
b. Anna fährt ein neues Auto. Berta fährt auch so ein Auto (*nämlich ein neues Auto).
'Anna drives a new car. Berta drives such a car, too (namely a new car).'

Umbach and Stolterfoht (in preparation) present a sequence of experimental studies testing these restrictions and argue that properties suited in kind-formation by similarity have to be "in-virtue-of" properties in the sense of Greenberg (2003) and Prasada and Dillingham (2006). Their findings confirm the idea that classes generated by similarity demonstratives (combined with nominal and verbal expressions) are kinds, even if ad hoc kinds. It is thus predicted that the expressions including *Art* phrases are subject to the same restrictions as found for similarity demonstratives, which appears plausible, see (39).[26]

(39) Anna fährt ein japanisches/ein neues Auto. Berta fährt auch diese Art von Auto. (nämlich ein japanisches Auto/*nämlich ein neues Auto).
'Anna drives a Japanese car/a new car. Berta also drives this kind of car (namely a Japanese car/a new car).'

By contrast, it is predicted that expressions including *Typ* phrases should not be picked up by similarity demonstratives, which seems to be refuted by the fact that the *so* phrase in (40) is fully acceptable. On a closer look, however, the *so* phrase does not pick up the type Opel Vectra – Berta need not have the same type of car. Instead, it picks up Opel Vectra features in creating a kind of car (medium size,

---

[26] Janebová et al. (2023) observe for Czech *typ* that it has a non-taxonomic use when combined with individuals (*Neni to typ Pavarottiho* 'He is not the Pavarotti type'). They suggest that this use of *typ* evokes similarity to certain properties of the individual, creating an ad hoc category, as argued above for (the deictic use of) German *so*. This idea appears plausible when presuming that the individual (Pavarotti) takes over the role of the target of the pointing gesture. Janebová et al. furthermore observe a correlation between Czech similarity demonstratives (*takový*) and *typ*. This points to an interaction of similarity demonstratives and taxonomic nouns the nature of which needs to be clarified in future work.

small motor, etc). This is evidenced by the fact that the *Art* continuation but not the *Typ* continuation is congruent with the *so*-phrase.

(40) Anna fährt einen Opel (vom Typ) Vectra. Berta fährt auch so ein Auto. (nämlich ein Auto derselben Art/?? ein Auto desselben Typs).
'Anna drives an Opel Vectra. Berta drives such a car, too (namely a car of the same kind/ namely a car of the same type).'

Types

Types play a major role in semantics as an analytical tool. They provide a *regime* (Chatzikyriakidi and Cooper 2018) for structuring the universe and safeguarding semantic representations. Their role as semantic objects depends on the respective semantic theory. Standard Montague-style semantics makes use of *simply typed λ-calculus* where types are built from two basic types, e(ntities) and t(ruth values) and functions thereof, and guide the denotations of natural language expressions in order to avoid inconsistencies. The other strand of semantic theory is oriented towards *constructive type theory* (Martin-Löf 1984). One of these systems is *Type Theory with Records* (Cooper and Ginzburg 2015, Cooper in preparation) in which basic types can be freely chosen. In this system, types may themselves serve as denotations of, e.g., nouns and verbs (for an overview see Chatzikyriakidi and Cooper 2018).

Setting formal issues of type theory aside, the notion of types in semantics goes back to Peirce's distinction between *type* and *token* (Peirce 1931). Following Peirce, types are abstract entities and tokens are particulars instantiating or exemplifying types. Even though the relation between a type and a token is similar to that between a set and an element, the perspective is reversed. While the idea of sets is to collect distinct objects into a single unit, the idea of types is to generate arbitrarily many clone-like tokens. This is why the classificatory capacity of a type is not determined by common origin or common characteristics but is instead rooted in the type itself – the prototype or model – independent of whatever tokens there are.

6 Conclusion and future prospects

We started out with the idea that the German taxonomic nouns *Art* and *Typ* denote two distinct ways of classification: classification by *Art* makes use of essential properties shared by the instances of a kind while classification by *Typ* makes use of models or prototypes being a blueprint for the tokens of a type. Essential properties of a kind are associated with the meaning of the corresponding word and are thus part of what speakers learn when they learn a language. Models or prototypes, on the other hand, are specified by expert communities and need not be familiar to non-expert speakers of a language. This idea was stated in the *Art&Typ* hypothesis in the introduction.

Support for this idea was found in dictionaries (section two), in corpus data (section three) and in the results of an experimental study (section four). While the dictionary entries of *Art* highlight the sharing of essential properties, the entries of *Typ* point to the role of a model or prototype. From a diachronic point of view, *Art* and *Typ* notably differ in origin: while *Art* is connected to descent and inheritance, *Typ* is connected to minting and printing.

The corpus search showed that there are two basic forms of *Art*/*Typ* phrases in which the specified noun is either juxtaposed or embedded in a genitive or *von*-phrase. If the noun is juxtaposed, *Art* phrases preferably denote biological species whereas *Typ* phrases refer to technical devices, diseases, or persons. In genitive or *von*-phrases, *Art* occurs with terms from everyday domains as well as abstract entities while *Typ* still prefers technical issues and diseases.

The experimental study confirmed the division of domains between *Art* and *Typ* to some degree. However, the main result is the existence of equal preference items for which classification by *Art* is as acceptable as classification by *Typ* while showing subtle differences in meaning.

Languages other than German have not been taken into consideration in this paper. English *kind* and *type* appear close in meaning to *Art* and *Typ*, but they are not equivalent. One hypothesis that could be explored in future work is that languages cross-linguistically include taxonomic expressions denoting classification based on linguistic knowledge and also expressions denoting classification by language-independent expert knowledge.

The original interest in the topic of this paper was not so much about the semantic difference between the expressions *Art* and *Typ* but rather about the difference in the role of kinds and types in semantic theory. This question was addressed in the final section. Even though the semantics of the lexical expressions *Art* and *Typ* is not decisive in theory formation, the empirical results provide some evidence challenging the idea that kinds and types are roughly the same.

References

Adelung, Johann Christoph. 1811. *Grammatisch-kritisches Wörterbuch der hochdeutschen Mundart*. Wien: Bauer, https://lexika.digitale-sammlungen.de.
Anderson, Curt. 2013. Inherent and coerced gradability across categories: manipulating pragmatic halos with 'sorta'. In Todd Snider (ed.) *Proceedings of the 23rd Semantics and Linguistic Theory Conference (SALT 23)*, University of California, Santa Cruz, May 3–5, 2013, https://journals.linguisticsociety.org/proceedings/index.php/SALT/issue/view/85
Carlson, Gregory. 1980. *Reference to kinds in English*. New York & London: Garland.
Carlson, Gregory. 2010. Generics and concepts. In Francis Jeffrey Pelletier (ed.), *Kinds, things and stuff*, 16–36. Oxford: Oxford University Press.
Chatzikyriakidis, Stergios & Robin Cooper. 2018. Type theory for natural language semantics. In Mark Aronoff (ed.), *Oxford research encyclopedia of linguistics*. Oxford: Oxford University Press, https://doi.org/10.1093/acrefore/9780199384655.013.329.
Cooper, Robin & Jonathan Ginzburg. 2015. Type theory with records for Natural Language Semantics. In Shalom Lappin & Chris Fox (eds.), *The handbook of contemporary semantic theory*, 375–407. Oxford: Wiley-Blackwell.
Cooper, Robin (in preparation) Type theory and language. From perception to linguistic communication.
Duden Grammatik. 2006. Dudenverlag Mannheim, https://www.duden.de.
Duden Lexikon online (o. J.) Dudenverlag Mannheim, https://www.duden.de.
Greenberg, Yael 2003. *Manifestations of genericity*. New York & London: Routledge.
Grimm, Jacob & Wilhelm Grimm. 1854–1960. *Deutsches Wörterbuch*; digitalisierte Version im digitalen Wörterbuch der deutschen Sprache, www.dwds.de.
Heusinger, Klaus von. 2010. Zur Grammatik indefiniter Eigennamen. *Zeitschrift für Germanistische Linguistik* 38(2). 88–120.
Janebová, Marketa, Michaela Martinková & Volker Gast. 2023. Czech type nouns: Evidence from corpora. In Wiltrud Mihatsch, Inga Hennecke, Anna Kisiel, Alena Kolyaseva, Kristin Davidse & Lieselotte Brems (eds.), *Type noun constructions in Slavic, Germanic and Romance languages – Semantics and pragmatics on the move*, 571–617. Berlin/Boston: De Gruyter.
Kolde, Gottfried. 2004. Gehört der Heckenausdruck (so)(ei)n(e) Art (von) X ins Valenzwörterbuch? In Speranta Stanescu (ed.), *Die Valenztheorie – Bestandsaufnahme und Perspektiven*, 133–146. Frankfurt am Main: Peter Lang.
Krifka, Manfred, Francis Jeffrey Pelletier, Gregory Carlson, Alice ter Meulen, Godehard Link & Gennaro Chierchia. 1995. Genericity: An introduction. In Gregory Carlson & Francis Jeffrey Pelletier (eds.), *The generic book*, 1–124. Chicago: University of Chicago Press.
Kripke, Saul. 1972. Naming and Necessity. In Donald Davidson & Gilbert Harman (eds), *Semantics of natural language*, 253–355. Dordrecht: Reidel.
Lakoff, George. 1973. Hedges: A study in meaning criteria and the logic of fuzzy concepts. *Journal of Philosophical Logic* 2. 458–508.
Lawrenz, Birgit 1993. *Apposition. Begriffsbestimmung und syntaktischer Status*. Gunter Narr Verlag: Tübingen.
Martin-Löf, Per. 1984. *Intuitionistic Type Theory*. Naples: Bibliopolis.
Mihatsch, Wiltrud. 2010. *"Wird man von Hustensaft wie so ne art bekifft?" Approximationsmarker in romanischen Sprachen*. Frankfurt am Main: Klostermann (Analecta Romanica 75).

Mihatsch, Wiltrud. 2016. Type-noun binominals in four Romance languages. *Language Sciences* 53.1 136–159.
Oxford English Dictionary (OED), including the *Historical thesaurus of the OED*. Oxford University Press. (http://dictionary.oed.com).
Peirce, Charles S. 1931. *Collected papers of Charles Sanders Peirce*. Edited by Hartshorne and Weiss. Cambridge, MA: Harvard.
Pfeifer, Wolfgang. 1993. *Etymologische Wörterbuch des Deutschen*. Digitalisierte Version im *digitalen Wörterbuch der deutschen Sprache*. www.dwds.de.
Prasada, Sandeep & Elaine Dillingham. 2006. Principled and statistical connections in common sense conception. *Cognition* 99. 73V112.
Putnam, Hilary. 1975. *Mind, language and reality*. (Philosophical papers Vol. 2). Cambridge: Cambridge University Press.
Rosenkvist, Henrik & Sanna Skärlund. 2013. Grammaticalization in the present – The changes of modern Swedish typ. In Ramat, Anna Giacalone; Mauri, Caterina & Molinelli, Piera (eds.), *Synchrony and diachrony: A dynamic interface*, 313–338. Amsterdam: Benjamins (Studies in Language Companion Series 133).
Rothstein, Susan. 2013. Some cross-linguistic aspects of bare noun distribution. Modern Hebrew and Brazil Portuguese. In Kabatek, Johannes & Wall, Albert (eds.) *New perspectives on bare noun phrases in Romance and beyond*, 35–61. Amsterdam: Benjamins.
Umbach, Carla. 2004. Cataphoric Indefinites. In Cécile Meier & Matthias Weisgerber (eds.) *Proceedings of Sinn und Bedeutung 8*, 301–316. held in Vienna in 2003, https://doi.org/10.18148/sub/2004.v8i0.765
Umbach, Carla & Helmar Gust. 2014. Similarity demonstratives. *Lingua* 149. 74–93.
Umbach, Carla & Britta Stolterfoht (in preparation) Ad-hoc kind formation by similarity.

Part 2: Type noun constructions in Romance languages

Wiltrud Mihatsch

7 A panoramic overview of the extended uses of taxonomic nouns in Romance languages

Abstract: The articles of this section focus on the extended functions of taxonomic nouns in four of the major Romance languages, i.e. French, Italian, Portuguese and Spanish. The aim of the present survey is to compare and contrast the functions originating from these nouns in these four languages as well as in other Romance languages. The synchronic and, wherever possible, diachronic observations of this chapter are partly taken from the contributions to this volume as well as previous analyses, particularly in the case of Romanian. In order to obtain a broader picture, new observations on further Romance languages were collected in a pilot study combining lexicographic and complementary corpus data with a small selection of non-representative speakers' judgments for Galician, Catalan and Romanian. From the linguistically highly diversified Rhaeto-Romance languages Romansh has been taken into account. For Sardinian observations from Campidanese and Logudorese have been included, and, to a far lesser extent, complementary lexicographical data from Occitan and Franco-Provençal. This overview starts with an inventory of taxonomic nouns in the above-mentioned Romance languages and their etymological sources and then proceeds to a comparative presentation of the most important functions derived from subtype binominals (such as *a type of NP*), i.e. attributive modifier and semi-suffix uses which support nominal modification, emerging postdeterminers where the taxonomic noun unites with determiners or quantifiers, and nominal qualifier or approximator (or qualifying) uses. The chapter closes with a survey of the pragmaticalized expressions based on taxonomic nouns, including mitigators, quotative markers, focus markers and other pragmatic marker functions. While the derived functions based on subtype binominals can be observed to a greater or lesser degree in all the Romance languages presented and start to arise very early on, the more recent pragmaticalized uses seem to be restricted to the standardized national Romance languages, however, in some cases start to spread to other Romance languages.

Wiltrud Mihatsch, University of Tübingen, e-mail: w.mihatsch@uni-tuebingen.de

https://doi.org/10.1515/9783110701104-007

1 Aims and scope of this overview

The aim of this chapter is to give a broad overview of the functions derived from TNs in Romance languages as described in the general introduction. The observations herein are predominantly based on previous research, including the contributions to this volume in the case of the well-studied national languages French, Italian, Portuguese, Romanian and Spanish. The comparative perspective draws on Mihatsch (2007, 2010, 2016, 2020b), complemented by new corpus data. There will necessarily be some asymmetries in the treatment of the different languages due to varied intensity of research activities in this domain and also differences in (lexicographic) documentation. In order to obtain a broader picture, new observations on Romanian and a selection of "minor" Romance languages have been collected in a pilot study combining lexicographic and complementary corpus data with speakers' judgments. I have obtained data for Galician, Catalan and Romanian. From the linguistically highly diversified Rhaeto-Romance languages I selected Romansh (both the supra-regional variety Rumantsch Grischun and the regional variety Sursilvan), which is heavily influenced by German and thus likely to show differences from other Romance languages; to these are added some data from Ladin. Additionally, I have obtained data from Sardinian including observations from Campidanese and Logudorese, and, to a lesser extent, complementary lexicographical data from Occitan and Franco-Provençal, which are today both of rather limited vitality (see Polzin-Haumann 2017 for an overview).

In February and March 2021 I contacted native speakers with a professional and/or institutional linguistic background and a particular focus on their mother tongue asking explicitly for approximative uses of TNs corresponding to *sort of* and *kind of* as well as possible pragmaticalized uses of TNs equivalent to English *like*. I provided the native speakers with Spanish examples in the case of Galician and Catalan, English, Italian and German examples (as far as available) for Romansh, examples from the Romanian literature as well as English examples for Romanian, and Italian examples for Sardinian.

Their observations, additional examples and bibliographic information made this very broad overview possible. I would like to thank them all for thinking about taxonomic nouns in their respective mother tongues, for discussing them with other speakers and for kindly sharing their insights with me. Of course, in many respects this overview remains explorative and further data will be required for a nuanced picture and a statistically significant and sociolinguistically refined analysis, but their introspective judgments and observations on usage in their linguistic communities, backed up with corpus examples, hopefully provide a good starting point for further research.

2 An inventory of taxonomic nouns in Romance languages

A glance at the inventory of established taxonomic nouns in Romance languages[1] shows that they share the same, mostly Latin- and Greek-based, loanwords (see Table 1 below), which are also found in Germanic languages and in some Slavic languages. However, in the Romance languages in particular, cognates of *genus* and *species* are more integrated into everyday usage than in English or German. Cognates of *sort* are pan-Romance, too, although in some languages such as Spanish the etymologically older meaning 'fate', 'luck' is more common than the taxonomic sense. Spanish *suerte* is today more commonly used with the sense 'lot, fate, destiny, luck' (s. MOL, DLE, s.v. *suerte*), as in the case of Campidanese Sardinian *sorte/sorti* (p.c. Stèvini Cherchi). Catalan *sort* seems rather marginal today, its taxonomic meaning is not mentioned in the dictionary Vox, but in the DIEC. Romanian *sórt* is now only accepted with a taxonomic reading in its plural form (p.c. Cristina Bleorțu and DEX, s.v. *sórt*).[2] Cognates with a taxonomic meaning of *type*, *form*, *class* and *category* are also found across all the Romance languages.

The taxonomic nouns are not entirely synonymous; there are subtle differences, for instance, as for the preferred taxonomic level and super- or subordination of *genus* and *species*, but also concerning the preferred domain of classification and the degree of integration into everyday language, aspects often found in dictionaries and which will not be addressed in detail in this overview.[3]

In Catalan, Occitan, Romansh, Sardinian and Romanian there are well-established TNs with different etymological origins, which will be sketched out below.

Of course, this inventory is not exhaustive. Some nouns have developed or are currently developing secondary meanings close to TNs, in particular those referring to 'manner' or 'way (of being/doing)' or those referring to 'rank' or 'degree of importance' as in the case of Romanian *calíbru* 'calibre', which also has the colloquial meaning 'sort' (DEX 2009), similar to tendencies of cognates within and beyond the family of Romance languages. Other quasi-taxonomic nouns which in some cases show similar derived uses may be found in the domain of 'quality' or 'style' and related domains.

---

[1] In most cases the standard and general colloquial language has been considered; however, further studies are needed to take into account the full sociolinguistic and dialectal diversity in this very dynamic domain.
[2] For information found on the lexicographical platform DEX, I also indicate the respective dictionary; complete references are provided on the DEX website.
[3] The dictionary resources and corpora are listed in the References section.

Table 1: Overview of cognates of TNs in Romance languages.[4]

Cogn. of:	Ibero-romance				Gallo-romance			Rhaeto-Rom. (Rum. Gr.) / Sursilv.	Italo-Romance			Balkan Rom.
	pt.	gl.	es.	ca.	fr.	oc.	Franco-Prov.		it.	sc.[5]		ro.
genus	género	xénero	género	gènere	genre	genre	genro	gener	genere	genia (C) zenía/genía (L)		gen
species	espécie	especie	especie	espècie	espèce	espècia	èspèce	spezia	specie	spétzia (C) (i)spètzia (L)		spetă specie
sort	sorte	sorte	(suerte)	sort	sorte	sòrta	sôrta	sort	sorta	/ (C) sorta (L)		(sort)

---

4 The language abbreviations follow ISO 639-1:

pt. = Portuguese
gl. = Galician
es. = Spanish
ca. = Catalan
fr. = French
oc. = Occitan
it. = Italian
sc. = Sardinian
ro. = Romanian

5 C = Campidanese Sardinian, L = Logudorese Sardinian.

type	tipo	tipo	tipo	tipus	type	tipe	tipo tipe	tip	tipo	tipu (C, L) tipízu (L)	tip
form	forma	forma	forma	forma	forme	fòrma forma	fòrma	furma	forma	forma (C) froma (L)	formã
cate-gory	cate-goria	cate-goria	cate-goria	cate-goria	caté-gorie	cate-goria	catè-goria/e	cate-goria	cate-goria	categoria[6]	cate-gorie
class	classe	clase	clase	classe	classe	classa	cllàssa/e	classa	classe	/ (C)[7] crasse (L)	clasã

---

6 According to Stèvini Cherchi this is an Italian loanword not commonly used by native speakers.
7 Again, according to Stèvini Cherchi this is an Italian loan not commonly used by native speakers.

3 Etymological sources of TNs in Romance languages

Remarkably, all or nearly all TNs are loanwords from Latin or Greek, either via Latin or indirectly via other Romance languages (for Italian *sorta* DELI specifies direct inheritance from Latin; similarly FEW (s.v. *sors*) for French *sorte*, DCECH for Spanish *suerte* and DCLIC for Catalan *sort*). The lexicographical data point to a tendency for loans from the major, standardized Romance languages to the minor ones, which have a weaker written tradition. Here are a few examples: in the case of Romansh, *gener* and *tip* are loanwords from Italian, and *sort* could be a loan from Italian or German (HWR, NVS, s.v. *gener, sort, tip*), whilst Sursilvan *gatti* and *stagl* (NVS, s.v. *gatti* and *stagl*) are German loanwords. Romanian is particularly interesting, since neighbouring Slavic languages as well as non-Indo-European languages Turkish and Hungarian have provided loans. In some cases, multiple sources are possible – *clasă* might have originated from German, French or Russian (RDW, s.v. *clasă*). This explains the shared cognates, but possibly also the great conceptual uniformity of the sources due to calques, since the Romance TNs share not only the cognates themselves but also their principal conceptual sources with the Germanic and Slavic TNs (see Ch. 1, this volume).

3.1 Family, clan, rank and other groupings based on similarity relations

The taxonomic meaning of the cognates of *genus*, *sort* and *class* derives from the general idea of 'family, clan, social group', which tends to assemble subkinds into a common superordinate. Latin *genus* 'birth, race, stock, kind, genus' goes back to Classic Greek γένος, *genos*, and was shaped by Aristotelian philosophy (DHLF, s.v. *genre*). The taxonomic meaning of the cognates of *class* is also derived from a meaning in the domain of social groups from the Latin sense 'draft, levy, fleet, class of citizens' (DELL, s.v. *genus*) via 'rank, class'.[8] The Romance equivalents of *genus* and *class* are mostly medieval Latin loanwords (see also Stefenelli 1983: 891–892), while the inherited form of *genus* survived as a negative reinforcer in Catalan and Old French (see Section 4.1). Indirect loans via other Romance lan-

---

8 Both for Latin *classis* and *sors*, the taxonomic reading develops rather late; for *sors* the meaning of 'rank, class, order' appears in Late Latin, for *classis* in post-Augustan texts (Lewis and Short 1879).

guages are quite plausible too, as in the case of the possible Italian origins of Romansh *gener* (DRG and NVS, s.v. *gener*).

The cognates of *sort* can be traced back to Lat. *sors* 'lot, destiny', then 'rank, category'. As mentioned above, these seem to be rather directly inherited in many Romance languages, while English *sort* as well as German *Sorte* are French loanwords (or in the case of German, possibly also with an Italian influence, EWD, s.v. *Sorte*, OED, s.v. *sort*).

Sursilvan Romansh has a Swiss German loanword *gatti* related to German *Gattung*, which in turn is based on the idea of ‚family, clan' (NVS, s.v. *gatti*). Perhaps conceptually related to the idea of genealogy is Sursilvan *stagl*, a Germanic loanword with the meaning of 'place' 'position', but perhaps via 'stable' to 'stock' and 'stud' (compare Italian *stallone* or French *étalon* 'stallion'(GDWB, s.v. *Stall*)) and on to 'breed' of horses or cattle. Romanian *soi* 'kind, sort, category' is a Turkish loanword going back to *soĭ*, 'race, family, kind, nation' (RDW, s.v. *soi*). Also related to 'race' are Logudorese Sardinian *ratza* and Campidanese *arratza*, related to Italian *razza*, and 'rank' in the case of *casta/crasta* related to Spanish *casta* 'ancestry, descent'. Logudorese *pàru* shows a polysemic structure including 'family, lineage, herd' pointing to a similar etymology (compare the entries for *pàru* in DLCS and VSLI). Campidanese and Logudorese *crèze* translating Italian *genere* (p.c. Vittorio Pinna-Sindia) show a similar relation to the meaning 'herd' (DLCS, s.v. *crèze*, VSLI, s.v. *grèze*).

Also possibly belonging to this conceptual domain of grouping together is Romanian *seamă* from Hungarian *szám* 'number, order' (DEX 2009); similarly Gascogne Occitan *ordi* (Dicod'Òc, s.v. Fr. *genre*) is related to 'order' and 'arrangement'.

3.2 *Distinctive features* (differentia specifica)

TNs translating 'species' are often semantically derived from 'outer appearance, shape', based on the Aristotelian distinction between *genus* and the *differentia specifica* subdividing the genus and stressing the differences within one category and its division into subkinds. This is the second important conceptual source of TNs, notably from Lat. *spěcĭes* 'look, outer appearance' and then 'species, kind' translating Classic Greek *eidos* (DHLF, OED, Ernout and Meillet 1994). The philosophical origins are also visible in the sources of the earliest attestations, as in the case of the works of Ramon Llull for Catalan *espècie* and *gènere* (DCECH, s.v. *espècie* and *gènere*).

The same conceptual basis underlies *form* and its cognates, which do not designate any specific levels of scientific categorization, but rather general categories and also 'manner of being'. In Scholastic philosophy, the older sense is 'shape, configuration, mould' (DHLF, OED), then 'essential property'; early meanings also include 'way', 'manner' and 'manifestation'. In addition to these older meanings, today these nouns are also used to designate categories in everyday language. According to Lewis and Short (1879, s.v. spěcĭes), Latin fōrma was also used in the sense of 'species' in Cicero's time instead of spěcĭes. Further etymological research on the taxonomic nouns in Latin and Greek and their uses may shed light on the general European etymological tendencies of TNs.

Romanian has a conceptually equivalent TN with a non-Romance origin, i.e. chip, originally from Hungarian, based on 'image, likeness, kind, manner' (RDW, s.v. chip). Possibly also belonging to this type of source based properties of subkinds is the taxonomic reading of French based Caribbean creoles' kalté/kalité 'sort, kind' (DUFC, s.v. sorte) and Sardinian calidàde, a Spanish loan, for which DLCS (s.v. calidàde) gives the meaning 'quality', 'property', but which according to my informants is also used as a taxonomic noun.

Also concerned with the idea of shape are the cognates of type, which ultimately stem from Classic Greek τύπος meaning 'impression, imprint, matrix, engraving, cast or replica made in a mould, sketch, model, outline' from the root of τύπτειν, typtein 'to beat, strike' (LSJ), with the categorizer meaning of type arising relatively late (see Table 2). Here the immediate source of the taxonomic reading is that of a prototypical representative category member. French-based Caribbean creoles also have a TN model ‚sort' (DUFC, s.v. sorte).

The Romanian loan teapă 'kind', probably taken from Old Slavonic, is related to the notion of 'beating' and 'imprint' (RDW, s.v. teapă). The cognates of style, not (yet) strictly taxonomic, have acquired some derived uses ('way of being' via 'style of writing', see OED [s.v. style]) and also belong here.

3.3 Manner, way of doing

The third path described in the general introduction, which shows the close relation between 'type or category of thing', and 'manner, way of being or doing something', is certainly relevant to Romance languages. Interestingly, taxonomic meanings of nouns of manner tend to be obsolete now as in the case of French manière, Spanish manera, Italian maniera and possibly others (as a look at the etymological and contemporary dictionaries in the References section shows; see also Moline 2011). French manière and equivalents in other Romance languages derive from classical Latin manuārius 'operated by hand', 'tractable', 'skilful'. Cognates of manner are now mostly used in the sense 'way of being or doing something'.

Catalan and Languedoc Occitan *mena* are well established everyday TNs (and being different from its Spanish equivalent, *mena* is normatively preferred in Catalan; see Vox, s.v. *tipus*). According to DCLIC *mena* goes back to a Celtic origin 'mine', 'type of mineral or metal', attested from the twelfth century onwards with the senses 'kind', 'manner of being or doing something'. However, the latter subsense may point to a Latin origin sharing the path of the manner cognates. FEW (s.v. *mĭnare*) relates Occitan *mena* to the Latin verb *mĭnare* 'drive, lead, guide', from which nouns such as Middle French *menée* 'way of acting' and Old Provençal *mena* 'manner of being' are derived, while the senses given for the lexical units derived from the Celtic **meina* are related to 'mine, metal', but not to the taxonomic senses.

A similar origin related to 'manner of making' is Latin *factiōnem*, acc. de *factiō* 'power, way of doing' (TLFi, s.v. *façon*, OED, s.v. *fashion*) which, with a tendency to give up an earlier taxonomic sense, has given us English *fashion*, with a now obsolete kind reading, and similarly French *façon* meaning 'way of doing or making something' and also with a now rather rare sense of 'sort' or 'kind'. Catalan *faiçó*, Italian *fazione* and Portuguese *facção* seem to have become archaic (see the respective entries in VOX, DLE and Houaiss).

The obsolete loans from Germanic cognates of *wise* identified in Spanish *guisa* and French *guise* (and other Romance languages) go back to a root reminiscent of the etymology of *spĕcĭes*: 'to see' via 'appearance' then 'way of doing', 'character' and, marginally, 'kind'. Sursilvan Romansh *uisa* is provided as a synonym of *sort* and *spezia*, not only *maniera* (NVS, s.v. *uisa*). The two most common Romanian TNs *fel* (see 3.4 below) and *soi* show both meanings, 'manner' and 'kind'. Also belonging to the periphery of taxonomic nouns closer to 'way of being made' are Spanish *corte* 'cut' and related nouns in other languages, or the cognates of English *mode* from classical Latin *modus* 'measure, size, limit of quantity, manner, method, musical mode' (OED, s.v. *mode*).

The rather frequent polysemy and diachronic transitions combining the senses 'kind' and 'manner' point to a close conceptual relation between the two domains (see also Martinique and Gouadeloupe Creole *jan* 'manner' from French *genre* 'kind', DUFC, s.v. *manière*). However, there is a certain tendency to abandon such polysemic structure and to distinguish these domains lexically; in some cases, fixed expressions preserve a now otherwise obsolete taxonomic meaning (see Section 3, Ch. 1, this volume).

Spanish *suerte*, today rather secondary as a TN, has both senses, 'manner' and 'kind', beside the now prevailing sense of 'fate, luck, destiny' (DLE, s.v. *suerte*), and the French fixed expressions *de sorte que* 'so that' or *de la sorte* 'that way' also point to earlier manner senses.

It would be certainly worth studying the thus far understudied nouns designating 'manner' and their dynamics in greater detail in the vein of Stosic and

Moline (2016), who offer the first comprehensive onomasiological overview of linguistic expressions of manner.

3.4 Further sources of taxonomic nouns

The uniformity of semantic paths leading to taxonomic nouns is rather striking and can be partly explained by a common European source, Greek philosophy; studies of taxonomic nouns in languages outside Europe (and where loans can be excluded) may help to investigate this point in the future. However, there other more idiosyncratic sources, such as Languedoc Occitan and Franco-Provençal *merça* plausibly derived from the sense 'goods, commodities' (a sense which is still preserved; see Dicod'Òc). This does not seem to be a unidirectional path, since cognates of *genus* and *species* also develop senses related to 'goods, commodities' and more specifically 'spices' for *species*, and 'cloth, fabrics' for *genus* (see for example the respective entries in DCECH and FEW).

At first sight rather particular is Romanian *fel*, a loanword from Hungarian based on 'part' (DEX, DER 1958–1966) and now possibly the most common Romanian TN with many derived uses. This in turn is reminiscent of Latin *pars* 'part', used as a synonym for *spěcĭes* (Georges 1910, s.v. *spěcĭes*). Romanian also has a colloquial taxonomic noun *calibru* (DEX '09 2009), with cognates in many European languages which have a quasi-taxonomic reading in particular constructions, showing a meaning shift from 'internal diameter or bore of a gun' to 'degree of social standing or importance, quality, rank' (OED, s.v. *caliber*), a sense already found in sixteenth century French.

A further special case is *category* and its cognates, originating from Greek κατηγορία, *katīgoría*, 'accusation, assertion, predication' via Latin *catēgoria* (OED, s.v. *categoria*). It can be traced back to Aristotle's ten most general categories or predicaments, which are also at the root of current debates about top ontologies (OED s.v. *category*), now adopted for a class or division in general, although still not part of colloquial vocabulary or still showing at least some learned connotation in Romance languages.

3.5 Timeline of first attestations as TNs

The following table indicates first attestations of the taxonomic reading of each TN according to DHLF and FRANTEXT for French, DEI, DELI and Zingarelli for Italian, DNFLP and CDP for Portuguese, DCLIC for Catalan, and DCECH and CORDE for Spanish. The corpora point to earlier appearances of some of the nouns when compared to the dates proposed in Mihatsch (2007) and (2010). Romanian is a special case and has not been included in the table below, since the earliest written document in Romanian is from the sixteenth century (similarly in Romansh; see DRG).

First attestations of taxonomic uses are sometimes hard to pin down, especially if there are closely related meanings such as 'manner' and in many cases after some hapax attestations it takes time for a TN to enter common parlance (see Voghera, Ch. 9, this volume, for a careful examination of Italian TNs).

Table 2: First attestations of taxonomic nouns with their taxonomic reading.

12th century and earlier	13th century	14th century	15th century	16th century	17th century	18th century	19th century
fr. *forme*	ca. *espécie*	es. *especie*	es. *suerte*	ca. *classe*	fr. *classe*	fr. *type*	ca. *categoria*
fr. *genre*	ca. *gènere*	fr. *sorte*	es. *tipo*	es. *clase*	it. *classe*		ca. *tipus*
	es. *forma*	it. *sorta/sorte*	pt. *forma*	fr. *catégorie*	pt. *tipo*[9]		es. *categoría*
	es. *género*		pt. *género*	it. *categoria*	pt. *classe*		
	fr. *espèce*	pt. *espécie*		it. *tipo*			
	it. *forma*						
	it. *genere*						
	it. *specie*						
	pt. *sorte*						

This overview shows a general tendency for the taxonomic readings of type and class cognates to appear later than those of the other noun.

4 Uses derived from binominals

Similar to the Germanic and Slavic languages (and probably other language families), the Romance languages have developed a variety of new functions from the binominal construction Det TN of N2, in most cases expressing a subkind relation. For the Romance languages, the uses of TNs in determiner and quantifier complexes as well as in the context of modification have been addressed rather briefly in the existing literature so far, usually within rather more general anal-

---

9 Few occurrences are attested in the fourteenth and fifteenth centuries according to CDP, after which there is a long gap; from the nineteenth century onwards a great number of attestations can be observed.

yses of TNs, for instance, by Voghera on Italian, Ch. 9, this volume, and in more detail by Chauveau-Thoumelin (2020) on French *genre* and *espèce*. Mihatsch (2010, 2016) gives a comparative overview and some diachronic observations for French, Italian, Portuguese and Spanish. Approximation (or qualifier uses) have been studied in greater detail; see Section 4.3. In what follows I will summarize these studies and will try to add some rather general observations based on rough corpus analyses as well as complementary data from the lesser studied Romance languages for a more complete picture and in order to point out some tendencies that could be investigated further in future research.

4.1 Emerging postdeterminer or complex determiner uses

In binominal constructions with quantifying expressions and identifying determiners or determiner-like adjectives, the taxonomic reading can become backgrounded as a consequence of the frequent conflation of type and instance, and the taxonomic noun may then become an enclitic of the preceding determiner (Denison 2002). As I argue in the general discussion in section 4.1.2, the communicative strategy behind the uses of emerging universal, negative and free-choice quantifier complexes is expressivity, with the subkind reading heightening the quantificational force via implicature. In the following example the verb *rendir* 'yield' takes *encanto* ‚charm', formally embedded in a complex NP with a taxonomic head, as its argument:

(1) Spanish
*Coralina no amó jamás a nadie, ni se rindió a **ninguna especie de** encantos varoniles.* (CDE, Torrente Ballester (1972): La saga/fuga de J. B.)
'Coralina never loved anyone, nor did she yield to **any kind of** virile charms.'[10]

In the case of identifier uses with determiner-like adjectives (see Davidse, Brems, and De Smedt 2008) and also interrogative determiners and phoric expressions, notably demonstratives, such as *which type, the same kind of, such a kind of, another kind of, different kinds of,* and *that kind of,* the discursive source is rather an explicit reference to ostensibly careful, conscious categorization and lexical selection. In both cases, it is not always easy to detect unambiguously reanalysed uses. The identifying uses are also commonly employed to establish ad hoc

---

10 Morpheme-by-morpheme glosses are only given if relevant for the analysis. Here and in the following examples the bold typeface is mine.

superordinates (as discussed by Mauri 2017) by pointing to subkinds or exemplars usually present in the prior text or discourse. Phoric uses often lead to general extender constructions, as in French *et ce genre de chose* 'and that kind of thing'.[11]

In most cases, postnominal type noun uses (as in Det NP *of this type / of all sorts*) may have an equivalent function to the preposed variant with an original type noun head. These do not require a loss of head status of the type noun. However, the interchangeability can give us a clue as to the loss of head status of the construction. The following phoric uses show both positional variants sharing the same reference:

(2) French
*A la fin de la soirée, les Yéménites interviewés ont tous insisté sur le succès **du concert** et ont exprimé leur joie de découvrir pour la première fois le groupe français. Certains ont même évoqué l'importance de **ce genre d'évènement** pour l'ouverture sur les autres cultures du monde. Un Français qui travaille au Yémen et qui a fait trois heures de route pour assister au concert de Noir Désir, était encore sous l'émotion quand il a déclaré : « J'ai été emballé ! Un **concert de ce genre**, c'est unique au Yémen ! »*
'At the end of the evening, the Yemenis interviewed all insisted on the success of **the concert** and expressed their joy at discovering the French band for the first time. Some even mentioned the importance of **this type of event** for opening up to other cultures in the world. A Frenchman who works in Yemen and who drove three hours to attend the Noir Désir concert was still moved when he said: "I was thrilled! **A concert of this kind** is unique in Yemen!"'
(https://musique.rfi.fr/musique/20020411-noir-desir-yemen, accessed 22 February 2019)

Despite sharing the same reference, the variants are not completely synonymous, since the postposed variant cannot be interpreted as primarily taxonomic with a taxonomic head, while a lexical N2 may (with some restrictions) or may not become head in the preposed variant as can be seen in the restrictions on anaphors in (3):

---

11 A similar tendency towards fusion with emphatically used quantifiers and identifiers can be found with manner nouns, generally resulting in adverbial constructions such as English *anyway* or *no way*, French *de toute façon* 'in any case' and Spanish *de ninguna manera* 'in no way'. Such prepositional uses are attested for all the Romance languages and are typically listed in dictionaries (a good example is ct. *manera* in Vox). Typical Germanic uses without prepositions can be found in medieval texts, particularly in Spanish alongside the Germanic loan *guisa* 'manner' (Hernández González 1992: 499), as in *nulla guisa* 'in no way' and *otra guisa* 'otherwise' (Spanish *guisa* and en. *wise* are cognates) See Mihatsch (2019) on such adverbial uses in Spanish.

(3) a) *There is a student of that type in the class. She does better than most.*
    b) There is that type of student in the class. ??She does better than most.
    (Zamparelli, 2000: 90)

The asymmetry becomes visible with TNs showing preferences for either super- or subordination, correlated with preferences for lower or higher taxons, as in the case of most Romance cognates of *genus* for more general inclusive categories and *especies* establishing subcategories.[12] Since the variant with a postposed TN places the first noun into a category, this construction shows a move towards a more general category, and TNs specializing in taxonomic subdifferentiation are barely acceptable:

(4) French
    cette espèce de dossier / ? Un dossier de cette espèce.[13]
    'this kind of file / ? A file of this kind'

A cursory purely quantitative search in frTenTen17 (top-level domain .fr) shows 0.87 per million tokens for N *de cette espèce* and 5.85 per million tokens for N *de ce genre*.[14] According to Mihatsch (2016) there is no clear tendency as for the preferred position with phoric determiner constructions in general. However, with *genre*, the preposed variant is clearly preferred (22.49 per million words), while *cette espèce de* N (0.5 per million words) seems to lead to purely taxonomic or approximative uses (preferring indefinite articles; however, see section 4.3 below) rather than postdeterminer uses.

In principle all taxonomic nouns should be able to create expressive quantifying and emphatic identifying uses. In reality, some TNs seem more established than others with differences between the Romance languages, but also common trends. In Mihatsch (2016) I combine a small-scale comparative analysis of oral data with a large scale Google search (restricted to pages from France, Italy, Portugal and Spain in French, Italian, Portuguese and Spanish, respectively, and retrieved in March and April 2012 and not attempting to disambiguate uses with and without taxonomic heads). The present study involves a similar although more controlled search using CQL in the huge web corpora of the TenTen family (via Sketchengine), again merely looking for surface strings (and again restricted

---

12 Unlike colloquial English, where *kind* and *sort* do not specialize in higher or lower level taxons.
13 This example has been adapted from Rosier (2002a: 82), who gives an example with *genre* ‚kind, genus' allowing both constructions.
14 The rough search did not exclude superficially similar strings based on a different cosntruction such as *L'extinction de cette espèce* ‚the extinction of this species'.

to the domains .fr, .it, .pt and .es, respectively).[15] The TenTen search largely confirms the earlier Google search and shows clear tendencies. The TNs given in Table 3 are the most frequently used TNs in the respective construction type; the second most frequent one is given in brackets. I have also indicated differing results for the TenTen and the Google search:

Table 3: Prevailing TNs in postdeterminer constructions.[16]

	French	Italian	Portuguese	Spanish
Possible identifier uses 'the same TN of NP'	type (genre) (1.07)	tipo (genere) (0.93)	tipo (forma) (2.44)	tipo (forma) (1.09)
Possible quantifier uses 'all TN of NP'	sorte (type) toutes sortes de (9.39)	tipo (forma) ogni tipo de (12.22)	tipo (forma) todos os tipos de (5.82)	tipo (clase) todo tipo de (47.75)
Possible phoric uses with demonstratives 'this TN of NP'	genre (type) (21.61)	tipo (génere) (30.95)	tipo (espécie) (40.41)	tipo (forma/clase) (78.81)

This first rough search shows that quantifying and phoric uses are more frequent than identifying uses equivalent to *the same* TN *of* N2, and also points to differences between the languages. Cognates of *type* clearly prevail except for French.

These constructions are typically mentioned in dictionary entries of TNs, which is a good indicator for the importance of the constructions generally, including with TNs that are not particularly frequent today, while the ones with *type* cognates might be more recent and less entrenched and tend to show up less prominently in the dictionary examples (for example, they are absent in Houaiss and ZVI). The dictionaries indicate constructions with the universal quantifier, as in French *de toute espèce* (PR, s.v. *espèce*), *toutes sortes de* (PR, s.v. *sorte*), Italian

---

[15] The purely formal search leads to very rough results, since polysemy or syntactic ambiguities were not considered. This might distort the picture for the cognates of *class* ('social class', 'lesson').

[16] I consulted frTenten17, itTenTen16, ptTenTen11 and esTenTen18, all available at https://app.sketchengine.eu/. The normalized occurrences per million tokens indicate the frequencies for the most frequent TNs in each respective construction and for the most frequent combination of a singular TN with a following N2 (both singular and plural nouns) except for the quantifier uses, where I checked different constructions and noted the most frequent one indicated in the table. Further studies of phoric uses should differentiate between different types of demonstratives for those languages which make distinctions: Italian *quel* and *questo*, Portuguese *esse, este* and *aquele*, and Spanish *ese, este* and *aquel*. In this search I checked only proximal demonstratives.

ogni sorta di, NP *di ogni sorta* (ZVI, s.v. *sorta*; see also Voghera, Ch. 9, this volume), and Portuguese *todo gênero de* (ADLP, s.v. *gênero*); they also include negative expressions, as in French *aucune espèce de* (PR, s.v. *espèce*), and obsolete forms such as *en nulle sorte* and *en aucune sorte* (PR, s.v. *sorte,* DHLF, s.v. *sorte*). DUFC mentions a universal quantifier use for *kalté* in Caribbean French-based creoles in a dictionary which unfortunately does not give many examples.

In what follows I will have a look at such determiner and quantifier uses in the other Romance languages mostly on the basis of dictionary entries, which may not be the most frequent ones in current usage.[17]

In Galician, these constructions appear in the DRAG for several TNs in their respective entries, such as *Sempre anda con problemas dese tipo* 'He/she always has problems of this kind', or *Que tipo de sal prefires?* 'What type of salt do you prefer?', *Xentes de toda especie* 'people of all sorts', *diferentes especies de libros* 'different kinds of books', *Neste edificio non vive ese xénero de xente.* 'In this building there are no people of that sort' and *Nestas fértiles veigas cultívanse toda sorte de hortalizas* 'On these fertile plains they grow all kinds of vegetables'.

For Catalan we find the negative expression *espero no trobar cap mena de problema.* 'I hope I will not have any kind of problem', followed by the normative advice not to use the Spanish calque **cap tipus* 'no type'. We also find *moltes menes de gent* 'many kinds of people' (DIEC) and *gent de tota espècie* 'people of all sorts' and *Quina espècie d'home és?* 'What kind of man is he?' (DIEC)

In Occitan and Franco-Provençal we find similar examples, for instance, the translation of *nous avons vu toutes sortes d'animaux* 'we saw all kinds of animals' as *que vedom bèstias de tot ordi* using Gascogne Occitan *ordi* in the entry for French *sorte* in the Dicod'Òc; for Franco-Provençal we have *de toute sorte* 'of all kinds' translated as *de tota sòrta, de tota mena* and in particular for nouns designating objects *de tota merça*, and we find a postposed example with *éspésse* (against the general trend not to use cognates of *species* here), translated by French *sorte*:

(5) Franco-Provençal, Bressan dialect
*Vou cognète byè de payi, in. O bin zh'me doutou bin ari que vouz éte byé vyë de payi **de toute éspésse**.* [St.Cyr2]
'You know many countries. I can imagine that you have seen many countries **of all kinds**.' (DicoFranPro, s.v. *sorte*)

---

17 Here and in the following sections after describing the well-studied languages French, Italian, Spanish and Portuguese, I will present data from the other Romance languages from West to East, i.e. from Galician to Romanian.

Romansh has analogous dictionary entries. The entries for *stagl* and *gatti* in Sursilvan offer numerous examples in the NVS, such as *Per negin stagl* 'no way, not at all', *Stagl buc, ni stagl bucca* 'not at all', *Negin gatti* 'not a bit, not at all' or *Da quei gatti* 'in that way', *da quella specia* 'of such kind, such' and a nice example of a general extender:

(6) Romansh
 . . . *meila salvadia e gloigns, tschareschas salvadias **e da quei gati*** (Cud. instr. I 69)
 'wild apples and acorns, wild cherries **and so on**' (literally 'and of those kinds')

Here is a corpus example of a list extender with *geners*:

(7) Romansh
 . . .*operas, teaters e concerts **da tut ils geners**.* (www.rtr.ch, collected on 26/04/2012, https://corpora.uni-leipzig.de/)
 '. . .Operas, theatre plays and concerts **of all kinds**'

For Sardinian, VSLI mentions *Fruttos de dogn'ispessia* 'fruits of all types' and *De dogni genia* 'of all kinds' in the respective entries; further uses of the TNs can be found in DLCS.

Romanian dictionaries (consulted via the platform DEX) also offer a wealth of quantifying and identifying constructions, even for the rather limited TN *sórt* (restricted to the plural), possibly fossilized in *Toate sorturile de fructe* 'all kinds of fruits' (DEX, Sinonime 2002); also listed are *nici un fel de* ,no kind of' , *fel de fel* and *de tot felul* 'diverse' (DEX '09 2009), *ce fel* 'what kind', and *de tot soiul* 'all kinds of', 'a variety of'. A similar picture holds for the TN *chip*, where we find *fel și chip de* 'literally ,kind and sort of', meaning 'all kinds of' and *În* (or *cu) chipul acesta/în acest chip* 'of this kind, manner', *În* (or *cu) nici un chip* lit. 'in or with no way/kind', 'no way' (DEX, DLRLC 1955–1957).

While the dictionary examples show postdeterminer uses of only the older TNs, the web corpora also reveal uses with the less established TNs. This suggests that throughout the centuries TNs have been employed in determiner complexes. In fact, Denison (2002, 2005); Keizer (2007); and Davidse, Brems and De Smedt (2008) demonstrate for English that these uses arise very early and not long after the first attestations of a lexeme with a taxonomic sense. This also seems to be true for Romance languages (see Voghera (2013, 2017) for Italian and Mihatsch (2010, 2016) from a comparative Romance perspective). Although Willemse, Brems, and

Davidse (2008) argue that the complex determiner uses are generally less developed for French than English, such uses are attested in all the Romance languages I considered for this overview. Here, further comparative studies are needed for a crosslinguistic picture as for the degree of entrenchment and discursive preferences, since TNs in determiner or quantifier complexes are not referentially necessary and can be easily replaced by NPs without taxonomic elements, as the following bilingual dictionary example shows, where the Latin expression *omne iuramentum*, either with a sort or an instance reading, is translated by a more expressive type binominal in Spanish:

(8) Latin
Hereges. Valdensium sunt factionis. Respuunt omne iuramentum. [. . .]
[*Son de la facción de los valdenses. Rechazan* **todo tipo de juramento**.]
'They are of the faction of the Valdense people. They reject any kind of oath'
(CDE, Covarrubias (1611): *Suplemento al Tesoro de la lengua española castellana*)

However, the quantifying uses are by no means a seventeenth century invention, since they are attested in Latin too, as in *omne genus* 'any kind' (Bambeck 1959: 25); additionally, *nullā parte* 'not at all' and *omni parte* 'in every respect, entirely' could be attributed to the meaning 'kind' of the noun *pars* (Lewis and Short 1879; Georges 1910, s.v. *pars*). The high productivity of these constructions[18] is due to the ubiquity of the implicatures involved and also to the ambiguity or hybridity as to the kind vs. instance readings found in most type binominals. Therefore the early attestations are hardly surprising. Here some examples, both with type nouns preceding and following a quantified noun:

(9) French
(. . .) les hommes ont plus de manieres de delectations que **quelconque espece de beste**. (DMF, Oresme (1370): *Le livre de ethiques d'Aristote* (Commentaire), 513)
'human beings have more kinds of pleasure than **any kind/species of animal**'[19]

---

18 As Voghera (Ch. 9, this volume) points out, in the Middle Ages Italian *ogni sorta* and *ogni sorta di* N represent half of the uses of *sorta* and conventionalize in the meaning 'various N'.
19 In the first example, the taxonomic reading might still prevail.

(10) Spanish
*Porque **ningun género de locura hai maior**, que (. . .).* (CDE, Mondragón (1598): *Censura de la locura humana y excelencias della*)
'Because there is **no kind of madness** greater than . . .'

(11) French
*sont tellement abandonnez à toute vilainie et ordure, à **toute espèce de crime et de turpitude**, qu'ils ressemblent plustost à des monstres qu'à des hommes* (FRANTEXT, Calvin (1560): *Institution de la religion chrestienne*)[20]
'are so surrendered to all wickedness and filth, to **every kind of crime and vice**, that they look more like monsters than men'

(12) Italian
*da **ongna specie di male** v'astenete* (OVI, Anonimo (1288): *Trattati di Albertano da Brescia. . .*)
'abstain from **any kind of evil**'

(13) Portuguese
*asy mesmo vam desta cidade chamada Calecut mujtas **pedras preciosas de toda sorte*** (CDP, Vasco da Gama (1498): *O descobrimento das Indias*)
'so from that city called Calcutta come many **gems of all kinds**'

The attested cases show a certain affinity with learned texts or discourse, which favour the strategy of explicit classification. This is also true for identifier uses (Mihatsch 2016), although they are generally less frequent, as the search results in Table 3 suggest. Identifier, quantifier and phoric uses develop time and again, as in the case of rather recent TNs with a similar timeline for Portuguese, French, Italian and Spanish (Mihatsch 2016; Voghera, Ch. 9, this volume); the cognates of *type* arising in the nineteenth century in several Romance languages now even prevail in these uses.

As dictionary entries show, all the Romance languages considered here have fixed expressions fossilizing or at least showing entrenchment of determiner and quantifier uses. Fused (and reduced) forms observed in Norwegian, German or English (see General introduction, 4.1.3) such as Middle English *alkin, nakin, whatkin* (OED, s.v. *kind*) seem rare, but do exist, as in Romanian *astfel* 'this way/kind', 'thus' and very remarkably also exist in a series of Sursilvan expressions

---

[20] Interestingly, this use occurs in a list after a coordinated quantified NP without the TN, so the quantification with and without the TN seems to be regarded as equivalent here.

such as *ninstagl*, literally 'no kind' (NVS, s.v. *stagl*) and a whole adverbial series with *uisa* 'kind, manner' but without prepositions, as in *autruisa* 'otherwise, else', *quelluisa* 'such way', 'so, thus', *taluisa* 'such way', and *tschelluisa* 'otherwise, else'. It is possibly no coincidence that such fused expressions are found with loans from German possibly copying the Germanic pattern; perhaps they were even borrowed in such constructions, although the determiners and quantifiers are of Romance origin. This is reminiscent of Old Spanish adverbial uses of *guisa* without a preposition (DCECH s.v. *guisa*) functioning as a 'true adverbial suffix' according to Hernández González (1992: 499), who lists rather literary uses with quantifying and identifying adjectives, such as *nulla guisa* and *otra guisa*.

Signs of clear semantic reanalysis, although without formal evidence of grammaticalization, are Negative Polarity Items, originally positive constructions with TNs that have acquired negative polarity or can even be used as negative expressions by themselves, as in Italian *di sorta*, literally 'of sort', meaning 'no way, not at all' (ZVI, s.v. *sorta*) and Romanian *de fel*, also literally 'of sort', meaning 'no way, not at all' (DEX, DLRLC (1955–1957).

Clearly grammaticalized negative markers are Old French *gens*, *giens* (LDAF, FEW, s.v. *gĕnus*) and ca. *gens* (DCLIC, s.v. *gens*; see also Stefenelli 1992: 171), both showing the medieval bare noun construction.

4.2 Modifier uses in Romance languages

A function related to the derivation of enclitics attaching to determiner-like and quantifier expressions is the one of the emerging complex with an adjective or another type of modifier in English with a backgrounded taxonomic reading of the TN. Modifier uses are based on binominals with a TN-head which is modified by an adjective. This use can be reinterpreted as a modifier construction with the adjective modifying N2, not the TN, which then loses its head status.

Denison (2002, 2005) and subsequent analyses assume two subtypes of modifier constructions. The first construction type is the **attributive modifier use** with rather unexpected or unusual characterizing adjectives, as in *a very dramatic sort of person*. Apart from highlighting deliberate categorization in the context of a strong subjective evaluation the type noun construction may secondarily help to overcome the selection restrictions of adjectives (Mihatsch 2016). The second more entrenched construction type according to Davidse, Brems and De Smedt (2008) is the **classifying semi-suffix use,** as in *Quick reaction type missions* or *a keeping–up-with-the-Joneses sort of person*, which facilitates modification by possibly unusual or ad hoc classifying adjectives and also other constituent types, often with subjective connotations.

The general impression is that uses of TN with modifiers exist in all the languages studied in this volume, however, uses where the modifiers refer to N2 and not the TN are very limited and rather marginally possible in most languages discussed in this volume, while they seem most established in English (see Chauveau-Thoumelin (2020) on French, Odden (2019) on Norwegian, Mihatsch (2016)) on Romance languages and the Introduction to Slavic by Kolyaseva and Kisiel, Ch. 12 (this volume) for general observations of these uses in Slavic languages.

In addition to an emphasis on modification, as mentioned above there might be another motivation to use this construction, i.e. the accommodation of adjectives not usually selected to modify a particular N2. In *a very dramatic sort of person* the N2 designates (a) human being(s), while the adjective or modifier rather modifies abstract nouns. The TN-construction leads to an indirect modification of the N2. The expression *a dramatic person* is not straightforward, although not impossible. The entry for *dramatic* in the OED only marginally relates the adjective to persons as in *dramatic soprano*. The use of the premodifier unambiguously points to a character type. This flexibilizing function is even more obvious for the semi-suffix uses with non-adjectival modifiers. Such uses are known to be well established in English and not intensively studied for Romance languages. Indeed, first observations suggest that they are less entrenched here. Willemse, Brems and Davidse (2008) find no semi-suffix occurrences for French *espèce* and *sorte* and only one token as an attributive modifier use in their data, while in English they find these uses to be very frequent. The authors argue that in French such modifier usage is not possible because of the prevalence of adjectival postposition. They point out that only anteposed adjectives allow reanalysis (via syntactic ambiguity) and that only in this position can the taxonomic noun be reinterpreted as a suffix of the adjectival phrase, which can then acquire scope over the second noun. This should be true for all Romance languages, where the generally unmarked adjectival position in a noun phrase is after the noun, except for a small number of emphatic and subjective adjectives as well as most determiner-like adjectives translating 'another', 'same', etc.

This general tendency leads not to one different position in a binominal, but a whole series of options. There is of course the position preceding the TN as in English with subjective emphatic adjectives, possible with a relatively small class of preposed evaluative adjectives then showing scope ambiguity between narrow scope over just the TN or over the binominal TN of N2:

(14) French
   *C'est **une excellente sorte de nuit** pour fumer dehors en regardant les étoiles.*
   (FRANTEXT, Déon (1960): *La carotte et le bâton*)
   'It's an **excellent sort of night** for smoking outside while watching the stars'

Then we have the majority of Romance adjectives immediately following the TN:

(15) French
l-a charade incit-e à un
DET.DEF-F.SG charade.F.SG elicit-PRS.3SG to DET.INDF.M.SG
genre très subtil de commutation
sort.M.SG very subtle.M.SG of commutation.F.SG
'the charade elicits **a very subtle sort of commutation**' (FT, Willemse, Brems, and Davidse 2008)

(16) French
... l-e sentiment **d'un-e sorte délicieus-e**
DET.DEF-M.SG feeling.M.SG of DET.INDF-F.SG sort.F.SG delicious-F.SG
de connaissance immédiat-e
of knowledge.F.SG immediate-F.SG
'the feeling of **a delicious sort of immediate knowledge**' (FRANTEXT, Valéry (1944): *Cours de poétique*)

Although attested, these constructions do not show scope ambiguity and I would agree with Willemse, Brems and Davidse (2008) that the lack of scope ambiguity of these constructions blocks further entrenchment. However, there are two further possible adjectival positions in Romance TN-binominals – the one immediately preceding the N2 can be disregarded, since the adjectives are restricted to a small class and the scope is clearly N2. However, postposition after N2 may be the best candidate for reanalysis as a modifier, since here the adjective ambiguously refers either to the N2 alone or to [TN of N2] with the TN as head:

TN of [N2 Adj]
[TN of N2] Adj

The greater semantic plausibility (depending on the data prosody may also give clues as in (21) below) of the following example points to the latter interpretation in the following transcription:[21]

---

21 In some cases, use of the TN may lead to approximation with a metalinguistic distancing flavour, overlapping with the premodifier use.

(17) Spanish
    ...el   caso   de   l-a-s   deshesa-s /   que   es
    DET.DEF.M.SG   case.M.SG   of   DET.DEF-F-PL pasture.F-PL   which   is
    un   tipo   de paisaje   muy optimizad-o/
    DET.INDF.M.SG   kind.M.SG   of landscape.M.SG very optimised-M.SG
    eh?
    eh?
    '...the case of the pastures, which is [sic] **a highly optimised kind of landscape**.' (C-ORAL-ROM, enatte01)

Premodifier uses are based on binominals with a TN-head. In such uses agreement should be able to disambiguate scope as it does indeed in the following Galician dictionary example in the entry of *forma* (DRAG), where the feminine adjective *autoritaria* agrees with the feminine TN *forma*, not the masculine N2 *goberno*:

(18) Galician
    A   ditadura   é   unh-a   forma   de
    DET.DEF.F.SG   dictatorship.F.SG   is   DET.INDF-F.SG   form.F.SG   of
    goberno   autoritari-a
    government.M.SG   authoritarian-F.SG
    'a dictatorship is **an authoritarian type of government**'
    (DRAG, s.v. *forma*)

Nevertheless it is easy to find occurrences which show agreement with the second noun, although the semantic scope is clearly the binominal complex [TN of N2]:

(19) Spanish
    Pero   hay   un   tipo   de   persona   muy
    But   there is   DET.INDF.M.SG   type.M.SG   of   person.F.SG very
    específic-a   que...
    specific-F.SG who...
    'But there is **a very specific type of person** who...'
    (http://ciegaacitas.tv/, accessed 24 April 2012)

In (20) the list of adjectives would be awkward after the TN, separating TN and N2, which explains the postposed adjectives following the binominal:

(20) Spanish
otr-o **tipo** de ciudad más eficiente, más
another-M.SG **type.M.SG** of city.F.SG more efficient.SG more
racional más **ciudadan-a,** aunque también, originariamente
rational.SG more **civic-F.SG** although also, originally
a-l menos, más **campesin-a.**
at-DET.DEF.M.SG least more **rural-F.SG.**
'another **more efficient, more rational, more civic,** although also, at least originally, **more rural type of city**'
(CORDE, Díez del Corral, Luis [1953 – 1974]: *El rapto de Europa. Una interpretación histórica de nuestro tiempo*)

The next example again shows a short break (/) after N2 suggesting a modification of [TN of N2]:

(21) Italian
con un tipo di **regolarizzazione / divers-a**
with DET.INDF.M.SG type.M.SG of **regulation.F.SG different-F.SG**
'with a different type of regulation'
(C-ORAL-ROM, inatte03)

Such cases seemingly violate constituency and show the effects of adjacency disregarding hierarchical constituency relations comparable to Corbett's example *the illiteracy level of our children are appalling* (George Bush, Washington, 23 January 2004, cited in Corbett 2006: 223).[22]

All in all my data from C-ORAL (Mihatsch 2016) rather confirm Willemse, Brems and Davidse (2008), who observe that modifier uses (adjectives, but also participles and relative clauses) preceding an NP do not appear frequently in Romance languages, at least not in French, Italian, Portuguese and Spanish.

In order to translate the English semi-suffix uses, in Romance languages as well as Slavic languages (at least Polish and Russian, see Kolyaseva and Davidse 2018, Kolyaseva and Kisiel, Ch. 12, this volume), a different construction is required. Here the functionally equivalent construction is a binominal with a postposed TN, which in turn is modified by an adjective or a PP or another appos-

---

22 However, according to Corbett, this is a case of attraction and not due to word order; see also Dikken (2001: 23 note 4) and Corbett (2006: 279–281)).

itive element (Mihatsch 2010: 178–187). Postpositions of TNs with modifiers are awkward in English and German (except for idiomatic uses such as *encounters of the third kind*), while postposition is certainly more in line with the general Romance tendency towards modification to the right of the head.

Postposed TN constructions with a modified TN often appear with classifying predicates, often nouns, especially brand names and proper names, nonce expressions and adjectives, i.e. we find them with exactly the same group of words or long and idiosyncratic phrases that accompany semi-suffix uses of TNs in English (see De Smedt, Brems and Davidse 2007: 237–238).

(22) French
*de-s   entreprise-s   publiqu-e-s   **genre**   SNCF*
DET.INDF-PL company.F-PL public-F-PL **type.M.SG** SNCF
'**SNCF-type** state companies'
(ELICOP, Corpus Tours, file faf01gb6.txt)

(23) Spanish
*un-o-s   conocimiento-s /   **de   tipo** /   Helénic-o /   de*
some-M-PL knowledge.M-PL **of   type.M.SG**   Hellenic-M.SG of
l-o-s /   grieg-o-s /   y /   de   l-o-s /   Alejandrin-o-s
DET.DEF-M-PL Greek- M-PL and of DET.DEF-M-PL Alexandrian-M-PL
'**Hellenic type** of knowledge of the Greeks and of the Alexandrians'
(C-ORAL-ROM, emedsc04)

(24) Italian
[…] l-a   guerra   divenne   un-a   guerra   di
[…] DET.DEF-F.SG war.F.SG became DET.INDF-F.SG war.F.SG of
*civiltà,   un-a   **guerra   tipo**   Crociate*
civilisation.F.SG DET.INDF-F.SG **war.F.SG kind.M.SG** Crusade
'[…] the war became a war of civilisation, **a Crusade-kind of** war.' (Voghera 2013)
(A. Gramsci, *Quaderni del carcere*, 1937).

As in the case of the identifier and quantifier constructions there is an adverbial counterpart to the nominal premodifiers with manner nouns not only in the Romance languages, but also in English and German, stressing reflected modification, but also facilitating adverbialization:

(25) Spanish
en   l-a   que/   se   evidenciaba/   un-a [/]
in   DET.DEF-F.SG   which   REFL.3   was evident   DET.INDF.SG
langosta /   corta-d-a   **de forma   muy   bonit-a**
lobster.F.SG cut-PST.PTCP- F.SG   **in way.F.SG   very   pretty-F**
'in which you could see a lobster/cut **in a very pretty way**'
(C-ORAL-ROM, efammn05)

Remarkably, we also find semi-suffixes in English (and in German) creating new adverbials such as –*wise* and German equivalents (see, for instance, Lenker (2002) and Paraschkewoff (1976: 176)), which are partly based on manner nouns (see Mihatsch (2019) on Spanish, but with a look at Germanic languages). These may originally have suggested careful modification, but syntactically serve as an adverbializer of nouns otherwise impossible to transform into adverbs. Next to the fossilized identifying form *otherwise* we can create new adverbs such as *stylewise*. Partly grammaticalized forms creating such adverbials in Romance languages are again emerging postpositional expressions, for instance, Spanish *a nivel de, al estilo de, en (el) plan* and the formally reduced prepositions in French *côté* and *niveau* (Noailly 2006, Mihatsch in press).[23]

The parallels and overlaps between the domain of verbal manner and the domain of nominal taxonomies are striking and deserve further studies.

4.3 Nominal qualifier or approximator uses

Although the approximator or qualifier uses that some taxonomic nouns acquire can be traced back to binominal subkind constructions, there are some important properties that set approximators apart from postdeterminer and quantifier uses as well as premodifier uses. In approximator constructions, the taxonomic noun loses its head status and acquires a supporting function and the second noun becomes the head. The approximator itself loses its head status, but also semantically affects the interpretation of the N2 by loosening the categorial boundaries of the N2. Furthermore, unlike the premodifier and quantifier uses, there is no tight relationship between a determiner and the former TN. Although indefinite articles prevail, since approximation is often tied to rhematic positions (Mihatsch

---

[23] Some of these Spanish expressions develop uses partly equivalent to the pragmatic markers based on type cognates and English *like* (for Spanish *en plan* see Jørgensen (2009) and Borreguero Zuloaga (2020); see Section 5.

2010; Chauveau-Thoumelin 2020), in principle approximators can be found with any other determiner. Furthermore, approximation neither seems to belong to the inventory of grammatical categories, nor is the new function purely pragmatic, so it is not clear whether this is a case of grammaticalization.

As for the communicative trigger of this change, neither careful categorization (even if used as a subterfuge) nor expressivity leads to approximation. Rather, we have a case of the "wear and tear" of a category frequently employed for peripheral or doubtful category members, in the same way that frequently wearing clothes that are actually too tight makes the clothes become baggy in the long run. In the case of the formerly taxonomic nouns, peripheral categorization leads to a blurred distinction between hyponymy and cohyponymy. In (26) *poree* is used as a superordinate, which has a subkind *poree commune*.[24] Remarkably, we have both an assignment to a superordinate and a comparison with a cohyponym (*poree commune*):

(26) French
 Une espece de poree *que l'en dit espinars et ont plus longues feuilles, plus gresles et plus vers, que poree commune.* (FRANTEXT, Anonymous (1394): *Le Menagier de Paris*)
 '**A kind of leek** which is called spinach and which has longer, finer and greener leaves than the common leek.'

Semantic imprecision tends to be employed for other communicative needs such as distancing, hedging or other metalinguistic comments which accompany approximation in the Romance languages (Mihatsch 2007, 2010). However, in the Romance languages such approximators are (still) bound to positions to the left of an NP, while by comparison English *sorta* and *kinda* are both functionally and syntactically more flexible (see Aijmer (2002) and Section 4.1.4 in Ch. 1, this volume).

In what follows I will give an overview of approximators derived from binominals with TNs in Romance languages, drawing from existing analyses, but also dictionaries and corpora, and for Galician, Catalan, Romanian, Romansh and Sardinian also considering speakers' judgments. All in all, there are not many dedicated studies focusing on these approximators in comparison to the very recent upsurge of analyses of pragmatic markers derived from TNs, discussed in

---

24 *Poree* 'leek' also had a general meaning 'vegetable' according to Godefroy (1881–1902, s.v. *poree*); it may represent an intermediate level between 'leek' and 'vegetable'.

Section 5.2. More subtle patterns such as constraints on the N2, differences as to entrenchment or particular pragmatic effects will not be addressed here.

Within the family of Romance languages French has most studies on TN-derived approximators.[25] In French, three taxonomic nouns have been clearly reinterpreted in this way: *genre de, espèce de* and *sorte de* (Fleischman 1998; Rouget, 1997; DHLF). *(Un) type de* and *forme de* (restricted to abstract nouns) appear occasionally in contexts of approximation, but *classe* does not (Mihatsch 2010: 146). Thus, TNs are not equally established as approximators. Chauveau-Thoumelin (2020) shows that qualifying *espèce de* is more frequent than *genre de*. According to Mihatsch (2010), qualifying *espèce de* is more frequent than *sorte de*, followed by *genre de* and *forme de*, which, however, do not only differ in frequency, but also as to their constraints on the N2 and their semantic and pragmatic effects. *(Une) manière de* also has approximative uses (Moline 2011; Gréa and Moline 2013; Petraş 2014):

(27) French
 . . .*la jolie story d'un certain Daniel Rose, bohème natif de San Francisco, débarqué dans la peau d'un étudiant à Paris et devenu, en quelques saisons,* **une manière de vagabond des casseroles** (frTenTen17, Emmanuel Rubin, 30.08.2010, Figaro)
 'the charming story of a certain Daniel Rose, a bohemian native of San Francisco, who arrived in Paris as a student and became, in a few seasons, **a kind of vagabond of the pot and pan**'

Curiously, the noun *manière* today designates 'way/manner' rather than 'kind' or 'sort', and is archaic in the taxonomic sense today (TLFi, s.v. *manière*), preserving only the derived qualifier use.

For Acadian French (Nova Scotia) Petraş (2014) shows striking adverbial uses of *manière (de)* rather reminiscent of the flexible adverbial uses of English *kinda* and *sorta:*

(28) *ça c'est* **manière** *intéressant*
 'that's **kinda** interesting'

(29) *quoi-ce que vous avez* **manière de** *planifié pour l'année*
 'what have you **kinda** planned for the year?'

---

[25] See for instance, Blanche-Benveniste et al. (1991); Rouget (1997); Fleischman (1998); Landheer and Dostie (2003); Moline (2011); Gréa and Moline (2013); Flaux (2015); Chauveau-Thoumelin (2020); Rosier (2002a); and Vassiliadou et al. Ch. 17, this volume)

(30)   tu peux **manière** assayer [sic]
       'you can **kinda** try'

Petraş (2014) suggests a source based on a subkind binominal *une manière de* + N. However, I think we cannot completely exclude another origin, namely the construction "X of the kind of Y", as discussed in Section 5.

French-based creoles also deserve a closer look, specifically to address the question of how far qualifying uses are inherited from French, as in the case of *espes*, or possibly evolve in a creole, as in the case of the TN *kalté*, which has developed its taxonomic sense from French *qualité*.

DCM (s.v. *espes*) gives an approximative example for *espes* in the French-based creole of Martinique, while DUFC (s.v. *bloquer*) offers a plausible qualifying use in the same creole language with *kalté*:

(31)   French-Creole
       *I ka tann an boug ka bat **an espes dè tanbou*** (I. Césaire, C.N.J.)
       'He hears someone banging **a kind of drum**'

(32)   French-Creole
       *Epi **an kalté lafos** té ka koré mwen.* (R. Confiant, Bitak)
       'And **a sort of force** stopped me'

For Spanish, the literature with a clear focus on approximators derived from binominals is scarce (for a comparative study see Mihatsch (2007, 2010)). Again *especie de* seems the best-established approximator reliably mentioned in dictionaries such as MOL or DLE. Qualifying uses can be found for *tipo de* and *clase de* as well as *forma de*, the latter being restricted to abstract nouns (Mihatsch 2010). Spanish *suerte* is today a rather secondary TN, as in the case of French *manière* the preserved approximating uses testifies to an erstwhile taxonomic use:

(33)   Spanish
       *¿Pero, es cierto que cuando el niño nace es **una suerte de hoja en blanco**, un campo virgen, sobre el que comienza a imprimirse la experiencia?* (esTen-Ten2018)
       'But is it true that when the child is born it is **a kind of blank sheet of paper**, a virgin territory, on which experience begins to be imprinted?'

For Portuguese, there are observations on European Portuguese in Franco (1998) and on Brazilian Portuguese in Morães de Castilho (1991). Again *espécie* is the only TN for which some dictionaries indicate approximative uses (for example,

ADLP but not Houaiss). *Forma de* is used in combination with abstract nouns. There are also attestations for qualifying *género* (Mihatsch 2010):

(34) Portugese
   Eu não sou um músico, sou **um género de músico**, *a minha formação prende-se mais com o cinema e o audiovisual* (. . .) (http://www.ccb.pt/ccb/cgi-bin/magazine/magazine.php, 29.12.2005)
   'I am **a kind of musician**; my background is more related to cinema and the audiovisual sector'

Like Spanish *suerte*, Portuguese *sorte de* is a rather secondary TN with other prevailing senses, but also with qualifying uses:

(35) Portugese
   Esplêndido retrato do indomável Jim Morrison interpretado por Val Kilmer. Para muitos é **uma sorte de** *Deus (. . .)*
   (http://www.dvdpt.com/t/the_doors_o_mito_de_uma_geracao.php, 02.01.2007)
   'A splendid portrayal of the indomitable Jim Morrison played by Val Kilmer. For many he is **a kind of god**'

For Italian, we have detailed analyses by Voghera (Ch. 9, this volume and the references therein). As in the other Romance languages *specie di* is a conventionalized approximation marker documented in dictionaries such as ZVI, and *sorta di* and *tipo di* can also be used as qualifiers (Voghera, Ch. 9, this volume, Mihatsch 2010), but no such uses seem to exist for *genere di* and *classe di*. Curiously, *sorta di* has been subject to prescriptive stigmatization (see the extract from http://www.homolaicus.com/linguaggi/traduzioni_testi.htm, 01.02.2007 in Mihatsch (2010)), which points to an increased use. And again, qualifying *forma di* is restricted to abstract nouns.

In Galician, we find a similar picture with *unha especie de* as an established approximator, also *tipo de* and to a lesser extent *clase* 'class' and *sorte* 'sort' (Xosé Luís Regueira Fernández, p.c.). Vanesa Rodríguez Tembrás and Alba Romero add *xeito* and *modo*, both meaning 'manner'. Alba Romero also suggests that *maneira* 'manner' and *estilo* 'style', but not *xénero* 'kind, genus' can be used as approximators, and again, *forma* tends to be used with abstract nouns. Quotation marks are relatively reliable indicators of approximative uses:

(36) Galician
*Non se trata de inxerir **un tipo de** « representatividade profesional »* (...)
(TILG, Xente 1972)
'It is not a question of adopting **a kind of "professional representation"**'

Similarly in Catalan, the qualifying use of *una espécie de* is mentioned in dictionaries, as is the well established TN *mena*; the DIEC (s.v. *mena*) gives a very concise description of its pragmatic overtones such as irony, and derogatory uses. To the dictionary-attested approximators Maria Burguera Mas (p.c.) adds *una classe de* and *un tipus de*. A corpus search also brings to light approximative uses of *sort de* and *forma de* with abstract nouns:

(37) Catalan
*Promocionats com **una sort de Pet Shop Boys espanyols** (poques vegades he vist comparacions més desencertades)* (caTenTen14 v2, https://productes12.rssing.com/chan-35122381/all_p2.html, accessed 6 August 2021)
'Promoted as **a sort of Spanish Pet Shop Boys** (I have rarely seen more misguided comparisons)'

(38) Catalan
*Així com hi ha una "esperança" —**una forma d'"esperança"**— que permet de pensar en la salvació eterna, també n'hi ha una altra referida o referible a la condemnació eterna.* (CTILC, Fuster, Joan 1964)
'Just as there is a "hope" —**a form of "hope"** —that allows us to think of eternal salvation, so there is another that refers to eternal condemnation'

For Romansh (Sursilvan and the unified Rumantsch Grischun) Marietta Cathomas Manetsch (p.c.) accepts *gener, specia/spezia, sort, tip, stil* and *fuorma/furma* as approximators. Andri Casanova points out that in the case of *sort* the construction without a preposition where the N2 directly follows the TN is most common.

(39) Romansh
*Il vegl ruver da Gernika è tschentà en **ina sort tempel**.* (ROH, www.rtr.ch, collected on 26.04.2012)
'The old holm oak of Gernika has become **a sort of temple**.'

Ina sort N2 is followed by the less common *ina spezia da*, which tends towards a taxonomic reading according to Andri Casanova, who proposes purely taxonomic readings for Sursilvan *in tip da, ina fuorma da, ina classa da, ina categoria da* and the now partly obsolete *in gener da* (still common in the Engadin region).[26]

The differing judgments might point to individual differences of usage, since TNs may gradually acquire approximative functions. Typical for Romansh, we find structures adopted from German, namely the juxtaposition of *sort* and the following noun without an intervening preposition, a structure also observed with (pseudo-)partitive constructions such as Sursilvan *mantun sablun* or *migliac sablun* 'a heap of sand' (Andri Casanova, p.c.). It is remarkable that this structure applies to *sort*, possibly a direct loan (HWR, NVS, s.v. *sort*) also adopting the typical German binominal construction with direct juxtaposition (see Ch. 1, section 4.1.6, this volume).

Sardinian too has several approximators based on TNs. Stèvini Cherchi (p.c.) indicates common approximative uses for Campidanese *na spécia/spétzia de*, *zenia/genia de* and *un'arratza de*, while stating that other TNs tend to be taxonomic. Here is an example with *arratza*:

(40) Sardinian
*(. . .) inghitzat a torrai agoa in su tempus cun **un'arratza de arrelògiu de brùscia*** (www.bideas.org, accessed 6 August 2021)
'starts to come back to his/her time with a kind of witch clock'

For Logudorese, Vittorio Pinna (p.c.) gives the following translation of the English sentence below using *una calidade de*, a quasi-TN:

(41) Logudorese
*Issa at comintzadu s'isperimentu poninde umpare bìculos de roba e nd'at fatu **una calidade de bunnedda**.*
'She started to experiment with putting together pieces of fabric and made **like a skirt**'

As in the other languages, less established qualifying uses with other TNs are certainly possible, too.

In Romanian, *fel* and *soi* are given as approximators in dictionaries (see the entries in DEX). My three informants agree on the approximative uses of *fel*, *formă*, *gen*, *soi* and *tip*, examples are easy to find. The following attestations are taken from the corpus COROLA; as in the other Romance languages, *formă* modifies abstract nouns:

---

[26] See also Pledari, s.v. *spezia*.

(42) Romanian
*anume acela de a se ajunge în punctul de acceptare a crimei de către comunitatea globală ca pe **o formă de "normalitate" existenţială**.* (COROLA, http://confluente.ro/magdalena_albu_1460208777.html, accessed 6 August 2021)
'namely to reach the point of acceptance of crime by the global community as **a form of existential "normality"**'

(43) Romanian
*Acolo se simţea Mira într-o lume boemă. Scara interioară îi provoca **un gen de frică plăcută**.* (COROLA, http://confluente.ro/mirela_stancu_1459038217.html, accessed 6 August 2021)
'There Mira felt [as if] in a bohemian world. The inner staircase caused him **a kind of pleasant fear**.'

(44) Romanian
*Acest Ionică Mitroi pe care l-am cunoscut mai bine că locuiam pe aceeaşi uliţă, era **un tip de haiduc**'* (COROLA, http://confluente.ro/Caseta_cu_amintiri_iii.html, accessed 6 August 2021)
'This Ionică Mitroi, whom I knew better because I lived on the same street, was **a kind of outlaw**'

Two further informants add *clasă* and *categorie*, and one of my three informants adds *chip, seamă, specie* and *teapă* to the list of Romanian approximators. Further studies will show whether these are established as approximators.

Although Romanian inflects nouns for case, since case is tied to determiners, the bare N2 is not marked for case and therefore does not give any indication as to the loss of head status similar to German *Art* 'kind' (see Ch. 1, section 4.1.6, this volume).

For Occitan and Franco-Provençal I have found approximative dictionary examples with cognates of *sort* and *species* as well as *mena* (Dicod'Òc and DicoFranPro, s.v. *espèce* and *sorte*)

Generally speaking, these approximators are not particularly colloquial nor stigmatized. Since they coexist with the oldest TNs as well as now obsolete TNs and also recent additions to this domain, there is evidence that the change from TN to approximator takes place repeatedly in the history of the Romance languages.

4.4 Summary and a glimpse at the timeline of evolving approximators

As a rule of thumb, the oldest taxonomic nouns with a preference for those expressing subordination are well established approximators; in most Romance languages these are cognates of *species*. Cognates of *sort* are also attested as approximators, although the taxonomic meaning of these nouns tends to be secondary with respect to meanings in the domain of 'fate' or 'destiny'. As for the more recent taxonomic nouns, informants seldom agree, but qualifying uses are often not hard to find, which points to a fairly productive path from TN to approximator, the only condition being that the TN is not restricted to special learned domains, as in the case of *category* and its cognates, which do not yet seem to have developed qualifying uses. Cognates of *form* can be found in all the Romance languages studied; these uses seem less established, but are easy to find and seem restricted to uses with abstract nouns.

The best established approximators are also among the oldest TNs in the respective language; this function arises early, although slightly later than the postdeterminer uses. Approximative uses of *species* cognates arise from the sixteenth century in French, Italian, Portuguese and Spanish (Mihatsch 2010, DHLF, s.v. *espèce*, Voghera, Ch. 9, this volume), and qualifying uses of Spanish *suerte* appear in the sixteenth century:

(45) Spanish
 *Y, en después, han sacado otro entremés que parrescen todos patos, que se ponen en los pies **una suerte de çapatos**, no sé cómo, que ni es de punta, ni romo.*
 (CDH, Huete, Jaime de (**1535**): *Comedia Vidriana*)
 'And, then, they brought out other *entremés* that all look like ducks, who put on their feet **a kind of shoe**, I don't know how, which is neither pointed nor blunt'

Qualifying French *sorte de* is attested from the seventeenth century onwards (DHLF, s.v. *sorte*), while the equivalent appears in the eighteenth century in Italian (Voghera, Ch. 9, this volume) and in the nineteenth century in Portuguese, according to a corpus search in CDP (Mihatsch 2010).

Since more recent TNs also develop approximator uses, this kind of functional change is not restricted to any particular period of time but keeps occurring with TNs sufficiently integrated into the general lexicon. Further studies are required to investigate the timelines of the more recent approximators.

4.5 Formal signs of grammaticalization of originally binominal TN constructions

As TN binominals acquire new functions, the former TNs lose their head status and with time also their nominal properties, becoming enclitics of determiners, quantifiers and adjectives or approximative modifiers of nouns.

The loss of head status arguably becomes visible first in external agreement with the N2 and not the former head to its left. This phenomenon does not necessarily demand a very advanced stage of grammaticalization. For French *genre* and *espèce* Chauveau-Thoumelin (2020: 78–87) shows that NP-external agreement is generally more frequent than internal agreement with the N2, although external agreement is more frequent with approximative than with postdeterminer uses.

Such agreement phenomena are not hard to find, even in cases where a taxonomic reading is still available, although somewhat backgrounded:

(46) Italian
 allora **quel** **tipo** di borsa/ è necessariamente
 so DEM.M.SG type.M.SG of bag.F.SG is necessarily
 morbid-a
 soft-F.SG
 'so that **kind of bag** is nessarily **soft**'
 (C-ORAL-ROM ifamdl04)

(47) Spanish
 a mi **es-e** **tipo** de persona-s así/ no
 for me DEM-M.SG type.M.SG of person.F-PL like that not
 me/ **gusta-n**//
 me pleasePRS-3.PL
 'that type of persons don't please me'
 [C-ORAL-ROM efamdl04]

Internal agreement seems more restricted and the fossilization of the former TN as a singular form (as in *these sort of people*) doesn't seem to exist in the Romance languages, the determiner always agrees in number (not gender!) with the former TN. However there is a very subtle pattern of number marking that might point to a reorganization of agreement and the loss of autonomous agreement of the two nouns of the binominal.

In the purely lexical uses with a TN as a head referring to a taxonomy, the grammatical number of the TN and the second noun should be determined by the intended meaning and in principle, N2 should rather show singular forms, since

N2 designates the superordinate which may then be subdivided into subkinds. However, if the TN appears in the plural, a plural N2 seems more natural (?*two types of apple*), thus, already in the lexical uses, there seems to be some internal agreement and the unmarked form is *two types of apples* in English (Keizer 2007: 160). This is also true in Romance languages; for French the Banque de dépannage linguistique (http://bdl.oqlf.gouv.qc.ca/bdl/gabarit_bdl.asp?id=1596) explicitly gives the following rule:

> *On peut néanmoins retenir quelques principes. Après les mots genre, espèce, variété, classe, forme, sorte, catégorie, type, etc., au pluriel, le complément est généralement au pluriel s'il se réfère à une réalité concrète ou que l'on peut compter, et au singulier s'il désigne une valeur abstraite non dénombrable.*
>   *Cette entreprise ne fabrique que deux* **sortes de chaises**. *(Le complément désigne une réalité concrète: chaises.)* (http://bdl.oqlf.gouv.qc.ca/bdl/gabarit_bdl.asp?id=1596, accessed 6 August 2021)
>
> 'Nevertheless, some principles can be noted. After the words *genus, species, variety, class, form, kind, category, type*, etc., in the plural, the complement is generally in the plural if it refers to a concrete or countable reality, and in the singular if it designates an uncountable abstract value.
>   This company makes only **two kinds of chairs**. (The complement designates a concrete reality: chairs.)'

A cursory Google search (in April 2012) for nouns equivalent to *type* (with a numeral in order to exclude postdeterminer uses such as *these kinds of*) shows a preference for identical number marking in all four languages studied (Mihatsch 2016). For instance, in French we find 110,000 cases of *deux types de problèmes* but only 9,970 cases of *deux types de problème*; in Italian, we find 529,000 cases of *due tipi di problemi* but 107,000 cases of *due tipi di problema*; in Portuguese we observe 11,800 cases of *dois tipos de problemas* but 487 cases of *dois tipos de problema*; and in Spanish pages located in Spain we find 54,500 cases of *dos tipos de problemas* but only 7,190 cases of *dos tipos de problema*. These frequencies may very well show plural agreement even in the clearly taxonomic or hybrid, and thus ungrammaticalized, readings.

I have checked the combinatory possibilities of an unambiguous taxonomic noun in Spanish, *categoría*, in esTenTen18, where I find the following normalized frequencies (per million tokens). The combination of a plural TN with a following plural lexical noun is 2.93, thus slightly higher than the combination with a singular form, which has 2.74 per million tokens; however, here we find many examples such as *categorías de riesgo* 'risk categories' or *categorías de control* 'control categories' as well as mass nouns, so the actual frequency of plural TNs with a singular N2 in a subkind binominal should be much lower. This pattern might reflect agreement resembling a modifier-noun relation.

In colloquial English, derived uses of *kind of* and *sort of* tend to fossilize a singular form of the TN, while the determiner agrees with the N2. There is yet another possible pattern of fossilization, i.e. the preference for a singular TN with a preceding singular determiner even with a plural N2. Again, having checked the frequencies for Spanish *categoría* in esTenTen18, the most frequent combination is that of a singular TN with a singular N2 (10.26 per million tokens), but the combination of a singular TN with a plural N2 (4.39) is still considerably higher than the one combining a plural TN with a plural N2.

In Mihatsch (2016) I compared agreement results of the rather small oral Corpus C-ORAL-ROM with a rough Google search. In order to get a more accurate picture I have searched frTenTen17, itTenTen16, ptTenTen11 and esTenTen18, which offer PoS-tagging and a greater control of the data, although again I have not disambiguated the attestations, only counting formal surface strings. I have restricted my search to the respective European national domains in order to reduce dialectal variation. Table 4 shows the frequencies (normalised per million tokens) for the most frequent TNs in phoric uses and with the identifier 'same'. Italian has been excluded here, since there is no available PoS-tagging for grammatical number.

Table 4: Grammatical number preferences of TN binominals in the TenTen corpora.

	French	Portuguese	Spanish
Possible identifier uses 'the same TN of NP'	*type*	*tipo*	*tipo*
TN sg N2 sg	**0.82**	**1.7**	**0.8**
TN sg N2 pl	0.27	0.74	0.29
TN pl N2 sg	0.03	0.01	0.03
TN pl N2 pl	0.09	0.05	0.06
Possible phoric uses 'this TN of NP'	*genre*	*tipo*	*tipo*
TN sg N2 sg	**14.59**	19.34	21.51
TN sg N2 pl	7.02	**21.07**	**57.3**
TN pl N2 sg	0.02	0.14	0.25
TN pl N2 pl	0.05	0.34	0.59

The construction where both the former TN and the N2 are singular forms clearly prevails in most cases except for phoric Spanish and Portuguese *tipo*; however, this construction is followed in frequency by the combination of a singular TN and a plural N2, so it may be that we are observing a certain fossilization of the singular TN (with a singular determiner).

The picture might be different for the qualifier uses, particularly in French, where we often find pluralized approximators with a plural N2:

(48) French
   et   qu'on   av-ai-t   pris/
   and   that we. PERS.PRON.3.SG have-IMPRF-3.SG   take.PST.PTCP.M.SG
   ce-s [/] # ce-s   espèce-s d'embarcation-s là /   pour y
   DEM-PL DEM-PL   kind.F-PL of boat.F-PL   there to   there
   all-er //
   go-INF
   'and we had taken **those those kinds of boats** there to go there'
   (C-ORAL-ROM, ffamdl12)

For French, a cursory TenTen search allows us to differentiate between singular and plural indefinite articles, which in turn correlate with qualifier uses, at least for the established approximators *espèce de*, *genre de*, *sorte de* and *forme de*. The picture diverges from the identifier and phoric uses in Table 4 above:

Table 5: Grammatical number preferences for qualifying French TN binominals with indefinite articles.

Possible approximative uses (with the indef. article)	sorte de	forme de	espèce de	genre de
TN sg N2 sg	*19.36*	*9.36*	*2.68*	*0.89*
TN sg N2 pl	*0.24*	*0.1*	*0.11*	*0.09*
TN pl N2 sg	*0.08*	*1.83*	*0.27*	*0.04*
TN pl N2 pl	*0.67*	*0.42*	*0.56*	*0.06*

First of all, the the most frequently used TNs in Table 5 diverge from the phoric and identifying uses, which show a clear difference in the evolution of postdeterminers and approximators. We can observe, at least for French, that the plural agreement pattern prevails in plural uses of approximative *sorte de* und *espèce de*, while *forme de* mostly modifies abstract nouns which tend to be mass nouns, which explains the prevailing TN pl N2 sg-pattern.

If we turn to gender agreement – all the Romance languages have two grammatical genders except for Romanian, which has three – we can detect a pattern comparable to the English mismatch between plural determiners and the TN where the determiner agrees with the N2 (*these sort of people*), a pattern documented as early as the seventeenth century for qualifying *espèce de* (DHLF s.v. *espèce*), although still stigmatized today. According to Rouget (1997: 292) this is most frequent with *espèce* due to its vocalic onset. The degree of entrenchment and the dominance of the unmarked masculine gender in French (where feminine agreement such as *une genre de* is rare) might be further factors (Mihatsch

2010). Mihatsch (2010) discusses analogous cases for Italian, Portuguese and Spanish. Chauveau-Thoumelin (2020) shows isolated cases of agreement with the N2 for postdeterminer and quantifier uses, but very frequent cases for approximator uses.

My own purely formal search in TenTen tentatively confirms this picture: identifying uses ('the same TN of N2') and phoric uses with the cognates of *species*, *genus*, *type*, *form*, *sort* and *class* only present isolated cases of agreement with the N2, except for *cet espèce de* N.masc, where the masculine demonstrative agrees with N2 in 0.07 cases per million. Indefinite NPs with a probable qualifier interpretation do appear showing gender agreement with the N2, although the proportion is low; compare the 2.68 per million tokens of French *une espèce de* + N with the 0.2 per million uses of *un espèce de* N.masc.sing.

Determiner use might also be an indicator of reanalysis of the former TN. In the case of the postdeterminers and postquantifiers the determiners or quantifiers are, of course, an integral part of the construction and may in time agglutinate, such as in cases like Romanian *astfel* 'this way/this kind' > 'thus'. Agglutination has not been attested with approximating uses, possibly due to the fact that, theoretically, any determiner can appear in front of the former TN, although, due to the rhematic status of many occurrences, the indefinite article is the most frequent determiner (Mihatsch 2010: 171).

Equivalents of the approximative English variants (DET) *kind of a* or *sort of a*, where the approximating expression precedes the second determiner belonging to the N2 (Keizer, Ch. 5, this volume), are not frequent and have been hardly studied, but do exist in Romance languages and can be found in TenTen (Mihatsch 2010):

(49) Spanish
como si el juego no fue-se suficientemente
as if DET.DEF.M.SG game.M.SG not were enough
un-a especie de un sueño
DET.INDF-F.SG kind.F.SG of DET.INDF.M.SG dream.M.SG
diurn-o new-age, *un-a enorme y espectral*
diurnal-M.SG new-age DET.INDF-F.SG huge.SG and spectral.SG
ballena (…) aparece ante nosotros.
whale.F.SG (…) appear.PRS.3.SG before us
'As if the game were not enough of **a kind of a new-age daydream**, a huge, spectral whale (…) appears before us'
(http://www.eurogamer.es/articles/child-of-eden-avance?page=2, accessed 6 August 2021)

For Brazilian Portuguese Morães de Castilho (1991) also discusses some cases:

(50) Portuguese
então foi **um** *tipo* de um
so was DET.INDF.M.SG type.M.SG of DET.INDF.M.SG
rumo d-o inicio d-a
direction.M.SG of-DET.DEF.M.SG beginning.M.SG of-DET.DEF.F.SG
industrialização japones-a totalmente *diferente*
industrialization.F.SG Japanese-F.SG totally different.SG
'so it was **a completely different kind of a direction from the beginning of Japanese industrialization**' (EF RJ 379:184)

(51) Portuguese
eles fazem assim **um-a** *espécie* de **um-a**
they make so DET.INDF-F.SG kind.F.SG of DET.INDF-F.SG
un *melado*.
DET.INDF.M.SG honeydew.M.SG
'they make like **a kind of a honeydew**'
(DID RJ 328:128)

Future analyses will be required to study the distribution of these constructions in the other Romance languages.

5 Pragmatic markers derived from a "trinominal" construction

5.1 Origins and functions

At first sight the following uses of French *genre* seem to be formal variants with an identical function, that of approximation, in both cases metalinguistically signalling a creative metaphor:

(52) French
Ça moutonnait le long des boutiques. Le tramway, **un genre de girafe obèse**, il dépassait les bicoques, il laminait la cohue, il godaillait dans les vitres...
(FRANTEXT, Céline, Louis-Ferdinand [1936]: *Mort à crédit*)

'people pushed along the shops. The tramway, **a kind of obese giraffe**, passed the shacks, it toppled the crowd, it dug into the shop windows'

(53)   French
*Mais je vous promets pas que ce soit super compréhensible, la fiscalité française c'est **genre un labyrinthe aux murs qui bougent**....* (FrTenTen12, freegan.fr)
'But I can't promise you that it's super understandable, the French tax system is **like a labyrinth with moving walls**'

However, the uses can be traced back to different source constructions and only the case shown in (53) with a bare TN preceding an NP with a determiner, based on a trinominal construction, has so far led to further processes of pragmaticalization in many Romance languages. There are now very recent studies of the derived pragmatic functions of these constructions for Portuguese, Spanish and Italian *tipo*, French *genre* and Romanian *gen*.[27] Equivalents of these pragmatic markers also exist in Swedish and Norwegian, in Russian and other Slavic languages; however, not in English and German (see Ch. 1, 4.3.2, this volume). They can generally be translated by the equally pragmaticalized colloquial English *like*.

Unlike the rather grammatical postdeterminers and the truth-functional approximators, these markers overwhelmingly operate on the pragmatic illocutionary level, as the following mitigator or hedging use of Spanish *tipo* illustrates:

(54)   Spanish
*sí pero ponéte m% **tipo** más acá* (COLA Buenos Aires)
'yes, but stand **like** closer'

Although this use looks like a syntactically flexible pragmatic marker derived from only a bare noun, its origins are more complex and originate from a "trinominal" construction 'X of the type of Y' which can be paraphrased as 'X of the same category as Y'. Here, the superordinate tends to be implicit, often created ad hoc (Mauri 2017). (55) shows an early attestation of that underlying construction in French:

---

27 See, for instance, Isambert 2016; Vladimirska 2016; Voghera 2017; Terian 2018; Borreguero Zuloaga 2020; Mondaca Becerra 2020; Mihatsch 2020 a and b, 2021; as well as the contributions to this section of the volume.

(55) French
Du haut de l'escarpement qui offre cette vue, on descend dans le précipice **par un chemin du genre de celui de Kander-Steg**, *et que l'on a fort bien nommé les galleries; c'est un long zig zag taillé dans le roc perpendiculaire.* (FRANTEXT, Ramond de Carbonnières, Louis (1781): *Lettres de M. William Coxe à M. W. Melmoth sur l'état politique, civil et naturel de la Suisse*)
'From the top of the escarpment which offers this view, one goes down into the precipice **by a path of the kind of that of Kander-Steg**, and that people have very well named the galleries: it is a long zigzag cut into the perpendicular rock'

The complex cognitive operation via an implicit superordinate can be simplified as a relation of comparison, 'X like Y', directly linking two cohyponyms without requiring a superordinate. Semantically, the element linking X and Y is reinterpreted as a similative expression, which can then also link concepts not belonging to the same taxonomic domain. The construction may become formally reduced to 'X TN Y' (Mihatsch (2018a, 2018b); Kornfeld, Ch. 11, this volume; Rosier (2002a); Voghera, Ch. 9, this volume). The taxonomic noun or rather the simplified construction is then prepositional and may also directly modify a VP:

(56) Spanish
Sugiero que puedan comer el pescado crudo agregandole un poco de Limon y aderezarlo **tipo un ceviche**(*plato tipicodel Perú) [sic]* (esTenTen18, https://www.biomanantial.com/raw-food-comer-de-forma-crudivegana-a-2460-es.html, accessed 6 August 2021)
‚I suggest that you can eat the raw fish adding a bit of lemon and season it **like a Ceviche**'

Similative comparison is always approximative, this function may then be foregrounded.[28] The prepositional construction may then get reanalyzed as an adverbial, as becomes clear when it appears introducing a direct object:

(57) Spanish
porque querían creo que en la universidad querían hacer **tipo charlas** (COLA Buenos Aires)
'because they wanted I think at university they wanted to have **like chats**'

---

[28] Many established grammatical comparison markers also undergo this development, English *like*, but also most if not all Romance languages (Mihatsch 2009).

Truth-functional lexical approximation or imprecision usually carries pragmatic overtones and may further evolve into purely pragmatic mitigation on the illocutionary level, but also numerical approximation (arguably via metalinguistic distancing) and focus marking via an association with rhematic positions. The following examples are all taken from the Argentinian subcorpus of the COLA-corpus with teenage Spanish from the beginning of the millennium:

a) Lexical approximation

(58) *no es **tipo** un tapado es **tipo** un no un sweater tipo montgomery*
 'no it's like a coat it's **like** a no a duffle coat-type sweater (lit. sweater of the type of a duffle coat)'

b) Mitigation (metadiscursive/illocutionary)

(59) *sí pero ponéte m% **tipo** más acá*
 'yes, but stand **like** closer'

c) Numerical approximation (rounder)

(60) *volvemos. volvemos **tipo** a las once menos cuarto o menos diez*
 'we come back we come back **like** at a quarter to eleven or ten to eleven'

d) Focus marking

(61) *porque es **tipo** así re linda*
 'because she is **like** so very pretty'

The similative preposition is also employed as an exemplification marker and leads to a second path of pragmaticalization producing quotative uses and connector uses with functions such as illustration, explanation, narrative progress, and punctuation (Chauveau-Thoumelin 2018, Mihatsch 2018a, 2018b):

e) Exemplification

(62) *después **tipo** por ejemplo en inglés es the boy*
 'then **like** for example in English it's the boy'

f) Quotative marking

(63) *conversando en el colegio oh eh ah **tipo** hola hola quién sos'*
 'talking at college oh eh ah **like** hi hi who are you'

g) Connecting (clauses)

(64) *entonces era un viernes y **tipo** llega a su casa y va a arreglar todo*
'then it was on a Friday and **like** she arrives at home and prepares everything'

As I argue in the general introduction (Ch. 1, this volume), the syntactically most flexible functions, connecting clauses and focus marking, represent the most advanced stage of pragmaticalization and tend to arise later than the other functions.

Such pragmatic markers evolve in many of the Romance languages with a nearly identical array of functions, depending on the degree of pragmaticalization. An advanced stage of pragmaticalization can be observed in detached uses separated by pauses or commas from the host sentence (see Hennecke and Mihatsch, in press, for a prosodic analysis of *genre* in different functions; see also Isambert (2016) for examples), and in sentence-initial and particularly sentence-final position, in addition to uses as autonomous constituents in short answers in some languages. As the pragmatic markers acquire sentence scope they often combine with a complementizer, as in French *genre que* (Beeching, Ch. 18, this volume), but also in Italian (Voghera, Ch. 9, this volume) and Spanish and Portuguese (Mihatsch 2010, 2020b).

5.2 Pragmaticalized TNs in the different Romance languages

In what follows I will sketch the state of the art in most Romance languages and additionally in some dialects. For the minor Romance languages and Romanian, I have collected new material by asking speakers and consulting corpora wherever possible in order to complete the picture.

Both in Brazilian and European Portuguese, *tipo* now occurs in all the functions listed above. There are now several studies of Brazilian Portuguese,[29] often covering the combination *tipo assim*, along with similar, incipient markers *género* and *estilo* (Mihatsch 2010, 2020b); studies of European Portuguese are more scarce (Marques 2015, Ch. 10, this volume; Mihatsch 2020b). *Tipo* competes with the originally deictic expression *assim* and the comparative preposition *como*

---

29 See for example Bittencourt (1999, 2000); Lima Hernandes (2005); Castelano and Luquetti (2014), Castelano (2013), Luquetti and Castelano (2012).

(Mihatsch 2020b). (65) is a sentence-connecting example which also contains the complementizer *que*:

(65) Portugese
Pediram para eu falar sobre minha infância. Para mim foi uma fase muito difícil. ***Tipo assim que*** *me marcou para o resto da vida.* (Bittencourt 2000: 267)
'I was asked to talk about my childhood. For me it was a very difficult phase. **Like** it marked me for the rest of my life'

Tipo (assim) has been described as a highly colloquial and stigmatized teenage phenomenon in Bittencourt (1999) and still seems to be typical of young people, although it now does not seem restricted to adolescents any longer. Teixeira, Ribeiro, and Salgado (2016) find the same clear preference in European Portuguese, where it might be a more recent phenomenon.

As for a timeline, Lima Hernandes (2005) points out first uses by the Brazilian journalist and cartoonist Henfil during the military dictatorship 1964–1985. I found some partly pragmaticalized uses in the NURC-corpus in conversations from the mid-seventies:

(66) Portugese
então a quantidade vai crescendo . . . e você entã:o se arma de uma lista que: já não parece mais nem uma . . . lista de material já é um jornal dominical assim Estado **tipo** *Estado de São Paulo o negócio começa e não acaba mais nunca . . .* (NURC, 1973, teacher and lawyer, 33 years old, male)
'so the quantity keeps growing . . . and you then arm yourself with a list that no longer seems like one . . . the list of materials is already a Sunday newspaper like Estado **like** Estado de São Paulo, the thing starts and never ends.'

Brazilian Portuguese *tipo* seems syntactically quite flexible and appears sentence-initially, sentence-finally and as an autonomous constituent (commonly followed by *assim*)

(67) Portugese
estou construindo uma página pelo espaço grátis do "vilabol", bom sei alguns pequenos códigos e para que servem, ***tipo.*** (ptTenTen11, http://www.linhadecodigo.com.br/dica/390/Como-escolher-fontes-para-sites.aspx)
'I am building a page for the free site of "vilabol", well I know some simple code and what it is for, **like**.'

(68) Portugese
O Século XXI inaugurou-se com a Escola Inclusiva e Promotora da autoestima e da aceitação social de todos. **"Tipo assim. . ."**
'The twenty-first century opened with the School of Inclusivity promoting self-esteem and social acceptance of all. **"Kinda. . ."**' (ptTenTen11, http://www.usinadeletras.com.br/exibelotexto.php?cod=59275&cat=Artigos)

Xosé Luís Regueira (p.c.) states that such uses of *tipo* are unknown in Galician; however, there are functionally equivalent uses of *en plan*, with examples going back to the middle of the nineties. There are uses of *tipo* with a comparative function attested in the *Corpus de Referencia do Galego Actual* (CORGA):

(69) Galician
Sempre estou aforrando para mercar algo grande, **tipo** *un pedal para a guitarra ou así.*
'I am always saving to buy something big, **like** a guitar pedal or something like that'

The following usage is possibly a contamination of *tipo* and *en plan*:

(70) Galician
é que o que pasa é que María Xosé primeiro falábanos así en **en tipo** *broma da da das croquetas con cuncha* (CORGA, [I have eliminated the pauses])
'what happens is that María Xosé we first talked like that as **like a** joke of croquettes with scallops'

Alba Romero, 25 years old, and Vanesa Rodríguez Tembrás, only a few years older, are both familiar with pragmaticalized uses of *tipo* in Galician; while Vanesa Rodríguez Tembrás only admits a smaller selection of functions, Alba Romero accepts all functions attested for Spanish *tipo*. Both are also familiar with the marker *en plan*, which according to Vanesa Rodríguez Tembrás is a loan from Spanish showing some increase in use. *Estilo, como* and to some extent *modo* show rather comparative uses corresponding to the early stages of TN pragmaticalization.

Spanish also has *tipo*, although with differing degrees of pragmaticalization in the diatopic varieties: use of *tipo* as a pragmatic marker seems more established in American varieties, although with differing degrees of conventionalization, and it seems there are more recent and less established uses in Spain (Mihatsch 2020a). Most studies to date look at Argentinian Spanish and notably the region of Buenos Aires.[30] Spanish *tipo* has variants with *que*, notably with sentential scope (Camacho 2011), but *tipo* cannot appear sentence-finally or as an autonomous constituent (Kornfeld 2013).

There are several analogous markers derived from quasi-taxonomic nouns (along with the less pragmaticalized *como* 'like') in nearly equivalent constructions, notably *onda* in some varieties in Latin America, particularly in Chile (Mondaca 2020), from *onda* 'vibes'.[31] In Buenos Aires, some groups of young people employ *corte (que)* (Rojas 2012); Kaplan (2012: 51) comments that this marker is the lower class equivalent of the rather upper class *tipo que*.

In Spain, *en plan* is far more common among young people than TN-based markers, although uses of *tipo* currently seem to become more established with younger speakers, as with *rollo*, derived from a meaning related to 'vibes' (Mihatsch 2020a, 2020b). *En plan* originates in an adverbial construction closer to 'manner' than to 'kind' (Borreguero Zuloaga 2020; Rodríguez Abruñeiras 2020).

As for the timeline, according to Kornfeld (Ch. 11, this volume) *tipo* seems to be the oldest marker, followed by *onda* and *corte* (see also Mihatsch (2020a) for early attestations of the source construction):

> *Tipo* is the more generalized marker of mitigation among people in their sixties and under, while *onda* seems to be more restricted to speakers between 25 and 50, but it is also attested in other nearby countries, such as Paraguay or Chile. As for *corte*, it was originally employed among people under 40 belonging to lower social classes of the *Conurbano* (i.e., the peripheral metropolitan areas near Buenos Aires) (Kornfeld, Ch. 11, this volume)

Rollo as a pragmatic marker seems rather recent since it does not appear in the COLA-corpus containing teenage data from the beginning of the millenium (Mihatsch 2020a). Source constructions are attested somewhat later than the data in the COLA-corpus:

(71) Spanish
 *baterías crudas y hasta algunas **guitarras rollo Fugazi*** (CORPES, Alsedo, Q. (2008): «Electric President y Enon suenan a hoy», España)
 'raw drums and even some **Fugazi-type guitars**'

While the source construction of *tipo* ('X of the same category as Y') emerges in the late nineteenth century, (sparse) corpus data and speaker's comments

---
30 See for instance Huseby (2010); Kornfeld (2013); Fernández (2017); Mihatsch (2018a, 2018b); and Bregant (2019).
31 See further in Rojas Inostroza et al. (2012); Kornfeld (2013); San Martín Nuñez et al. (2016); San Martín Núñez (2017); Mihatsch (2020a); and Mondaca (2020).

(Mihatsch 2018a and b, 2020a) point to an incipient pragmaticalization from the sixties onwards, possibly related to the countercultures of the time.

For Catalan, Maria Burguera Mas (p.c.) comments that *rotllo* and *tipus* are quite common in Catalan especially for some of the rather less pragmaticalized functions of type nouns, as is *en pla(n)*, and to a lesser extent the similative *del pal*, in addition to *com* 'like'. (72) and (73) are two comparative examples from caTenTen14 v2 (see also the examples in Magraner Mifsud 2018):

(72) Catalan
imagino mes aviat un futur semblant al de "la maquina del tiempo" **rotllo** *cataclisme i tal. . .* (caTenTen14 v2, http://propde40.blog.cat/2006/09/17/mes_enlla_dorio/)
'or I imagine rather a future resembling „time machine" **like** cataclysm and so on'

(73) Catalan
Disposa, a més, d'una ferramenta de missatgeria instantània anomenada Jabber, integrada en la barra de comunicacions **tipus** *Facebook* (caTenTen14 v2, http://www.viu.es/va/la-viu/)
'It also has an instant messaging tool called Jabber, integrated into the Facebook-**type** communication bar.'

Maria Burguera Mas suggests that these uses might be calques from Spanish (see Bernal and Sinner 2009 on *rotllo* and other expressions of Catalan youth language), since the pronunciation (as in her own case) is mostly Spanish, including *tipo* instead of Catalan *tipus*, although there are also phonetically adapted pronunciations as *tipu* or *rollu*. In fact, criticism of derived uses of *tipus* copying Spanish patterns is rather common (VOX, s.v. *tipus*, Marquet 2003).

French has an established pragmatic marker, *genre*,[32] while *comme* 'like' is less flexible, similarly the preposition *style*, here illustrated in combination with *genre*:

(74) French
D'un autre côté, en relisant Nietzsche – quand je suis en vacances, je relis toujours Nietzsche – je vois qu'il a écrit un truc **style genre** *"ne dépouillez*

---

[32] Among the pragmaticalized TNs in Romance languages *genre* has been studied most extensively (see, for instance, Danon-Boileau and Morel (1997); Fleischman (1998); Rosier (2002a and b); Dufaye (2014); Isambert (2016); Chauveau-Thoumelin (2020), Ch. 8, this volume; Beeching, Ch. 18, this volume; and others).

pas la femme de son mystère" (oui, **style genre**, *parce qu'il l'a dit en allemand, et en allemand ça ne donne pas du tout la même chose....*) (http://alinea.hautetfort.com/archive/2007/02/22/mystery-girl.html, accessed 12 March 2007)
'On the other hand, when I reread Nietzsche – when I'm on holiday, I *always* reread Nietzsche – I see that he wrote **something like,** [style genre] "Don't strip the woman of her mystery" (yes, **like** [style genre], because he said it in German, and in German it doesn't mean the same at all....)'

Genre is strongly pragmaticalized and may appear as an autonomous constituent:

(75) French
*Attends elle va revenir sousou tu vas voir! – Oui Oui **genre**!* (http://www.comlive.net/sujet-134631-2166.html, in Davidse, Brems, Willemse, Doyen, Kiermeer & Thoelen (2013)
'Just you wait, you'll see that she'll come back all tipsy! – Yeah yeah, **right**!'

The combination with the complementizer in *genre que* seems to be rather recent. Beeching (Ch. 18, this volume) suggests a process of reobligatorification or regrammaticalization. Quite often, in all uses, but particularly where we have a hedging effect, *genre* may be separated from its host sentence by commas or comma intonation:

(76) French
*Les iraniens sont un peuple inventé ? Typés européens, pour des européens, c'est un peu, **genre**, normal.* (Isambert 2016, http://forum.ados.fr/actu/actualites/combattants-racontent-ciruler-sujet_24709_6.htm, accessed 27 November 2020, I have slightly widened the context)
'The Iranians are a made-up people? European types, for Europeans, that's a bit, **like,** normal'

First scattered uses of the source construction with a prepositional phrase following *genre* (NP1 *du/dans le genre de* NP2) creating an ad hoc superordinate start appearing towards the end of the 16th century in FRANTEXT (Mihatsch in press), as in (55), and the first reduced constructions of the form *X genre Y* appear in the middle of the nineteenth century (Mihatsch 2010: 205, in press). Early reanalyzed uses are attested in the later seventies and early eighties (Isambert 2016). While (77) is still close to the similative prepositional use, (78) is clearly adverbial:

(77) French
*une petite agence euh **genre dix quinze personnes*** (corpus CLAPI, 1960/1970)
'a little agency uh **like ten fifteen people**'

(78) French
*Mais c'est bizarre, il y a pas des, il y a pas **genre un parti 'ecolo** ou euh?* (corpus PFC, 1976)
'But it's strange, there is no there isn't **like an ecological party** or uh?'

Yaguello (1998) points to a typical teenage use as in the case of English *like*, with a more recent quotative function; see also Davidse, Brems, Willemse, Doyen, Kiermeer & Thoelen (2013) whose data show a connection to teenage language.

In Canadian French varieties today, the more recent *genre* used by teenagers competes with a strongly pragmaticalized *comme* rising in the eighties and nineties (see Beeching, Ch. 18, this volume), for which a calque from English seems plausible (on *comme* and *genre* in Canadian varieties of French see Beeching, Ch. 18, this volume, Chevalier (2001); Hennecke (2014); Sankoff et al. (1997) and Vincent (2005)). Just like *comme*, *genre* (and *style*) may appear sentence-finally in Quebec, but are also found sentence-finally in European French (81):

(79) A: *Qu'est-ce que vous aviez à faire comme travail ?*
B: *Ben, i fallait faire des réparations **genre/style*** (Dostie 1995: 247)
'A: What kind of work did you have to do?
B: Well, I had to do some fixing **like**'

(80) A: *(. . .) y en a plein qui viennent pas parce qu'ils ont pas cours alors ils ren- ils s'rendorment mais*
B: *non mais y a aussi la la pression des parents **genre*** (CFPP2000)
'A: (. . .) many of them don't come because they don't have classes, so they go back to sleep but
B: no, but there's also pressure from parents **like**'

For Acadian French in Nova Scotia, Petraș (2014) shows uses of *manière* that are partly equivalent to *genre* (see section 4.3), and proposes a binominal origin for these constructions.

Occitan doesn't seem to have equivalent pragmaticalized TNs (p.c. Myriam Bras).

In Romansh (Rumantsch Grischun and Sursilvan), spoken in a contact zone characterized by German and Romansh bilingualism, we only find the rather lexical uses 'X of the type of Y' with *dal gener, da la sort, dal tip, dal stil*. This is according to Marietta Cathomas Manetsch (p.c.), who also points to a very interesting recent quotative use in young people's language with *uschia* 'so', very certainly a calque from German *so,* and equally typical of youth language in Germany:

(81) Romansh
*Ed jau **uschia**: "Tge diavel . . ."*
(German: Und ich **so**: "Was zum Teufel") (Example provided by Marietta Cathomas Manetsch)
'And I **like**: "What the hell"'

For Sursilvan, Andri Casanova (p.c.) points out similar uses with *sco* 'like, as', the similative marker reminiscent of the origins of the marker *like* and the German approximator *wie* (from *wie* 'like').

Fiorentini (2016) offers data on the use of reformulation markers in a language contact situation between Ladin and Italian (with speakers from the Fassa Valley, Trentino South-Tyrol, Italy). Her data present several cases of the Italian marker *tipo* in some of its typical functions, here a strongly pragmaticalized connector use:

(82) Ladin-Italian
*ela la cianteva cianter tant'è che l'ultim l'ultim an / **tipo** me sà un'ora dant che che st'encantesim l'aesse a:* / (Fiorentini 2016)
'she sang, she sang, she sang so much that the last year, the last year, **like** I think it was about an hour before this spell had. . .'

Since her data show numerous cases of code-switching, *tipo* may not necessarily have been borrowed.

Italian *tipo* covers all the functions mentioned above (see Voghera (2017), Ch. 9, this volume; Benigni, Ch. 16, this volume, on Italian vagueness markers in general, see Ghezzi (2013)). Competing but less established expressions are *genere, stile* and *come* (Mihatsch 2010); *stile* seems to to be developing functions related to 'manner' rather than 'kind' (see Masini and Mauri (2020) on new functions of *stile*). As in French and Spanish the Italian source construction for *tipo* and competing *genere* arises in the nineteenth century (Voghera 2017).

Tipo is strongly grammaticalized: it has a recent variant with the complementizer *tipo che*, can appear sentence-finally and may appear as an independent constituent in short answers (Voghera, Ch. 9, this volume).

From the second half of the twentieth century onwards its usage diversifies and it expands (Voghera, Ch. 9, this volume); similarly to Spanish, Portuguese and French, emerging uses can be found starting in the mid-twentieth century:

(83) Italian
la luna questa notte è scura scura come me, sono certo che la canteranno tutti perché è ottimista e c'è la speranza, **tipo** *torna io t'aspetto lo sai , so che mi porterai cieli limpidi mari limpidi, . . .* (DiaCORIS, Cederna, Camilla (1963): Il re del tangaccio, L'ESPRESSO)
'The moon tonight is dark, dark like me, I'm sure everyone will sing it because it's optimistic and there's hope, **like** come back I'm waiting for you, you know, I know you'll bring me clear skies clear seas, . . .'

For Sardinian, Stèvini Cherchi indicates some full prepositional constructions translating prepositional Italian *tipo* such as *a tipu de/a trassa de*. According to my Sardinian informants, who are all over 50 years old, there are no Sardinian equivalents to the pragmatic uses of *tipo* and even the expression *a tipu* is a recent Italian calque not used by older generations.

Colella and Blasco Ferrer (2016: 519) analyse Sardinian youth language and provide a pragmaticalized example of Italian *tipo che* in an Italian dialogue with Sardinian elements, produced by two 21-year-old students of the University of Cagliari, but with origins in Nuoro:

(84) Sardinian
B: *No vabbè lui non è così furbo, ma. . .* **tipo che** *gliel'ha detto a mia madre bette preda* (literally 'molto pietra' = 'troppo scemo').
'B: No, he's not that smart, but. . . . **like** he told my mom too dumb'

The authors also present a Sardinian extract ending with the Italian marker *fissu* and, more unexpectedly, English *like* (not Italian *tipo*):

(85) Sardinian
E cussu m'at agiuntu a su facebook e mi ponit fissu **like** (Colella and Blasco Ferrer 2016: 519)
'and he has added me to Facebook and writes me all the time **like**'

Remarkably, in Romanian *gen*, not *tip*, is pragmaticalized in all functions described above, in colloquial and youth language; initial comments can be found in Zafiu (2001), further studies are Zafiu (2012), and very recently Terian (2018) and Popescu and Ionescu (2019). My Romanian informants have confirmed the very colloquial character of the more pragmaticalized uses as well as a strong association with young people's slang. Cristina Bleorțu (p.c.) points out that uses meaning ‚as if', such as in the following example, are generally accepted, while mitigating uses and other pragmaticalized uses are sociolinguistically restricted to young people:

(86) Romanian
Mă uitam **gen** *nu îmi vine să cred.*
'I was looking **[like/as if]** I can't believe it.'

Elena Faur (p.c.) estimates that pragmaticalized uses of *gen* are restricted to speakers between 11 and 30 years old and are not used by children under 10 or 11, which points to teenagers as the innovators and also as those who employ this marker most frequently. *Gen* can appear sentence-finally, often separated by a comma, both of which are indicators of a high degree of pragmaticalization. Popescu and Ionescu (2019) assume an English influence for this position, since the younger speakers using this construction tend to be in touch with the anglophone language and culture:

(87) Romanian
Ce ai făcut în weekend? Am fost la film, **gen** (http://glasulploiestean.ro/adolescenta-vazuta-intr-un-stilcool-gen-periculoszic/, in Popescu and Ionescu (2019: 110)
'What have you done this weekend? I went to see a movie, **like**'

If *gen* is followed by a noun, it is not inflected (Popescu and Ionescu 2019).
Zafiu (2012) also suggests a possible influence of English *like*; however, the evolution of *gen* starts relatively early in Romanian according to Terian (2018). It was first used to designate scientific categories in the nineteenth century, spreading to other domains outside science and academia followed by initial steps of (inter-)subjectification in the context of literary or artistic criticism in the early twentieth-century as part of the construction *de genul* 'of the kind', which competed with the learned construction *în genul* for some time and was ousted (or rather, restricted again to a more technical sense) during the communist period by the more colloquial *de tipul* (Terian 2018).[33] *De genul* returned after the fall of

---

33 According to Terian (2018) the highly successful 1934 book *În genul . . . tinerilor* "In the genre . . . of young people" by N. Steinhardt under the pseudonym Antistihus might have played an important role in increasing the popularity of *de/în genul*. In this book, the author parodies man-

communism and started to prevail from the nineties onwards, outing *de tipul* and, being a simpler and syntactically more flexible construction, also *în genul*, which requires a following genitive.

5.3 Concluding remarks on pragmaticalised TNs

Pragmaticalized uses derived from an 'X of the type of Y' construction have developed in all the standardized national Romance languages, with a divide between those languages selecting cognates of *type* (Portuguese, Italian, Spanish) and those selecting cognates of *genus* (French and Romanian). The taxonomic sense of *type* cognates develops late, starting in the eighteenth century, while the source constructions seem to get established in the nineteenth century. Terian (2018) explicitly comments on the competition between *tip* and *gen* in Romanian, and a look at other Romance languages confirms that both TNs have been used in the source construction. Why exactly one or the other has been selected remains unclear (although Terian 2018 provides some possible explanations for Romanian). A look at early frequencies may shed light on which period was decisive for the selection. To this end, I conducted a search on possible source constructions using *genus* and *type* cognates in French (FRANTEXT) and Spanish (CORDE) for the periods 1850–1899 and 1900–1949 and calculated normalized frequencies per 35 million words, very close to the actual sizes of the selected subcorpora. As figure 1 shows, the early dominance of French *genre* is clear, while in Spanish the construction with *género* is far less frequent, although increasing over time. In the nineteenth century, French *type* and Spanish *tipo* were both far less frequent than the constructions with French *genre* and Spanish *género*, they show a sharp increase in the twentieth century in both languages, considerably higher in Spanish, however.

Diachronic data are scarce and hard to come by since pragmatic uses are all highly colloquial and we lack a colloquial oral corpus from the mid-century to the seventies and eighties. However, evidence from metacommentaries and written colloquial texts as well as some early oral data in Portuguese, Spanish and French point to an evolution that might have started in the eary sixties and seventies, possibly related to the countercultures laying the foundations of youth cultures. The fact that there seems to be a certain association with middle and upper classes might establish a link between the rather learned origins of the

---

ners ("genres") of young people of his time and thus may have contributed to the playful dimension of the expression, which has been preserved until today according to Terian (2018).

Figure 1: The competition between *type* and *genus* cognates in prepositional constructions.

TNs and their later colloquial uses, a link to the intellectual strain of mid-century countercultures.

The international tendencies and contexts of youth cultures, and possibly similar communicative tendencies in the uses of hedging or quotatives, might also explain the very similar chronology in the different languages, not only the Romance languages.

Language contact, either direct calques or grammaticalization triggered by contact (Heine and Kuteva 2005), is a possible factor, too, both between Romance languages and varieties and also under English influence. The phenomenon is highly dynamic, as the very recent and ongoing changes (particularly in minority languages) show. Clear evidence for borrowing can be seen particularly in Romance minority languages spoken by bilinguals, as in the case of Catalan, Galician, Romansh, Ladin and Sardinian, a tendency which points to the urban youth cultures dominated by the national languages (and English) as an important factor.[34]

---

[34] Walters (in preparation) shows a comparable picture for the English loanword *type* undergoing pragmaticalization in Hindi, competing with a similative demonstrative.

6 Conclusion

Functions derived from type nouns show a very similar picture in the different Romance languages, with postdeterminer and quantifier uses arising early on and evolving repeatedly as new TNs are integrated into the respective lexicon. Modifier uses supporting adjectival modification do exist, but due to adjectival postposition in Romance languages an alternative construction with a postposed TN seems to be preferred. Further studies should indicate the degrees of conventionalization in the different Romance languages. Approximative uses also arise early; in many Romance languages *species* cognates are most established, but again approximative uses are continually developing from TNs.

Pragmatic markers equivalent to English *like* originate from a different construction type ('X of the type of Y'). Although there are competing TNs (and quasi-TNs), here too *genus* and *type* cognates have reached an advanced status of pragmaticalization. While the source construction has emerged by the nineteenth and twentieth centuries, pragmaticalization, originating in youth cultures, sets in in the second half of the twentieth century, and some recent developments in Spain show that this type of pragmaticalization is still productive (although processes of analogy cannot be excluded either).

For all derived uses, future studies are needed to analyse the relationship between general cognitive and communicative mechanisms leading to these functional changes and external factors such as particular discourse traditions or language contact which might explain the striking similarities between the different languages.

Acknowledgements: For the Galician data I would like to thank Xosé Luís Regueira Fernández, chair of Galician and Portuguese Philology at the Department of Galician at Santiago de Compostela, director of the *Instituto da Lingua Galega* (https://ilg.usc.gal) and member of the *Real Academia Galega*. Vanesa Rodríguez Tembrás, PhD student at the Heidelberg Center for Ibero-American Studies (HCIAS) and Alba Romero also contributed valuable insights on Galician data.

Maria Burguera Mas, lecturer of Catalan from the Romance department of Tübingen University at the time oft he study, now in Berlin, kindly provided me with detailed observations on Catalan TNs.

I would also like to thank Marietta Cathomas Manetsch, editor and translator at the Lia Rumantscha (http://www.liarumantscha.ch/ao) and Andri Casanova, documentalist of the *Dicziunari Rumantsch Grischun* (https://www.drg.ch/) for their very helpful comments on Rumantsch Grischun and Sursilvan.

Stèvini Cherchi, coordinator of the *Collegio Scientifico Acadèmia de su Sardu* (https://www.academiadesusardu.org) and Giuanni Spano shared their insights on Campidanese Sardinian TNs with me. Bolentina Pulina, member of the *Acadèmia de su Sardu* and coordinator of the editorial team of the work of reference on the Sardinian standard *Su Sardu Standard* and Vittorio Pinna, also a member of the *Acadèmia de su Sardu*, kindly provided valuable observations and comments on Logudorese data.

Elena Faur, researcher at the *Academia Romana Institutul de lingvistica si istorie literara "Sextil Puscariu"* at Cluj-Napoca (http://www.inst-puscariu.ro/index.html), Cristina Bleorțu, postdoc from the Romance department in Zurich, as well as Lucia Calapis and Daniela Meile contributed insightful observations on Romanian TNs.

References

Dictionaries

ADLP = Ferreira, Aurélio Buarque de Holanda. 1999 [1988]. *Novo Aurélio Século XXI: o dicionário da língua portuguesa* [The new 21st century Aurélio: the dictionary of the Portuguese language] . 3rd edn. Rio de Janeiro: Nova Fronteira.

DCECH = Corominas, Joan and José A. Pascual. 1980–1991. *Diccionario crítico etimológico castellano e hispánico*. 6 Bde. Madrid: Gredos (Biblioteca románica hispánica 5. Diccionarios 7).

DCLIC = Coromines, Joan. 1991 [1980]. *Diccionari etimològic i complementari de la llengua catalane* [Etymological and complementary dictionary of Catalan], 9th edn. Barcelona: Curial.

DCM= Confiant, Raphaël. 2007. *Dictionnaire créole martiniquais-français*. Matury, Guyan: Ibis Rouge Editions.

DEI = Olivieri, Dante. ²1965. *Dizionario etimologico italiano : concordato coi dialetti, le lingue straniere e la topo-onomastica*. 2nd edn. Milano: Ceschina.

DELI = Cortelazzo, Manlio and Paolo Zolli. 1979–1988. *Dizionario etimologico della lingua italiana*. Bologna: Zanichelli.

DELL = Ernout, Alfred and Antoine Meillet. 1994. *Dictionnaire étymologique de la langue latine*. 4 ed. Paris: Klincksieck.

DES = Wagner, Max Leopold. 1960–64. *Dizionario etimologico sardo*. 3 Vol. Heidelberg: Ilisso.

DEX = Frâncu, Cătălin. 2004–2021. *Dicționare ale limbii române* [Dictionaries of the Romanian language]. https://dexonline.ro/ (accessed 13 April 2021).

DHLF = Rey, Alain. 1998. *Dictionnaire historique de la langue française*. Paris: Dictionnaires Le Robert.

Dicod'oc = Lo Congrès permanent de la lenga occitana. *Dictionnaire occitan*. https://locongres.org/fr/applications/dicodoc-fr/dicodoc-recherche (accessed 13 April 2021).

DicoFranPro = Université de Montréal. *Dictionnaire Français/Francoprovençal.* https://dicofranpro.llm.umontreal.ca (accessed 13 April 2021).
DIEC = Institut d'Estudis Catalans. *Diccionari de la llengua catalana* [Dictionary of the Catalan language]. https://dlc.iec.cat/ (accessed 13 April 2021).
DLCS = Puddu, Mario. 2016–2021. *Ditzionàriu in línia de sa limba e de sa cultura sarda.* [Online Dictionary of the Sardinian language and culture]. http://ditzionariu.sardegnacultura.it/ (accessed 13 April 2021).
DLE = Real Academia Española. 2014. *Diccionario de la lengua española,* 23rd ed. https://dle.rae.es (accessed 8 April 2021).
DLRLC = Macrea, Dimitrie, Petrovic, Emil (eds.). 1955–1957. *Dicţionarul limbii romîne literare contemporane.* Bucharest: Editura Academiei Republicii Populare Române.
DNFLP = Cunha, Antônio Geraldo da. 1982. *Dicionário etimológico Nova Fronteira da língua portuguesa.* [Etymological dictionary Nova Fronteira of the Portuguese language]. Rio de Janeiro: Editora Nova Fronteira.
DRAG = Real Academia Galega. 2012. *Dicionario da Real Academia Galega* [Dictionary of the Galician Royal Academy]. https://academia.gal/dicionario (accessed 13 April 2021).
DRG = Institut dal Dicziunari Rumantsch Grischun. *Dicziunari Rumantsch Grischun* [Dictionary of Rumantsch Grischun]. http://online.drg.ch/ (accessed 13 April 2021).
DUFC = Confiant, Raphaël. *Dictionnaire universel français-créole.* https://www.potomitan.info/dictionnaire/diko_universel.php (accessed 13 April 2021).
Ernout, Alfred & Antoine Meillet (eds.). 1994. *Dictionnaire étymologique de la langue latine: Histoire des mots.* Paris: Klincksieck.
EWD = Kluge, Friedrich. 1999. *Kluge etymologisches Wörterbuch der deutschen Sprache.* Berlin/New York: de Gruyter.
FEW = von Wartburg, Walther. 1922–2002. *Französisches Etymologisches Wörterbuch. Eine darstellung des galloromanischen sprachschatzes.* 25 Vol. Bonn/Heidelberg/Leipzig–Berlin/Basel: Klopp/Winter/Teubner/Zbinden.
GDLL = Encyclopedia.com. 2019. *Gran diccionari de la llengua catalana* [Great dictionary of the Catalan language]. www.enciclopèdia.cat (accessed 13 April 2021).
GDWB = Grimm, Jacob & Wilhelm Grimm. 1854–1893. *Deutsches Wörterbuch.* Leipzig: Hirzel. http://dwb.uni-trier.de/de/ (accessed 06 August 2021).
Georges, Karl Ernst. 2004. *Kleines deutsch-lateinisches Handwörterbuch.* Nachdr. d. 7., verb. u. verm. Aufl. 1910 / von Heinrich Georges, Darmstadt: Wiss. Buchges.
Godefroy, Frédéric. 1881–1902. *Dictionnaire de l'ancienne langue française et de tous ses dialectes du IXe au XVe siècle.* Paris: F. Vieweg.
Houaiss, Antônio. 2009. *Dicionário Houaiss da língua portuguesa* [Houaiss dictionary of Portuguese]. Rio de Janeiro: Objetiva.
HWR = Bernardi, Rut. 1994. *Handwörterbuch des Rätoromanischen.* Zürich: Società Retorumantscha.
LDAF = Greimas, Algirdas Julien. 1992. *Dictionnaire de l'ancien français. Le Moyen Âge.* Paris: Larousse.
Lewis, Charlton T. and Short, Charles. 1879. *A Latin Dictionary.* Founded on Andrews' edition of Freund's Latin dictionary. revised, enlarged, and in great part rewritten by. Charlton T. Lewis, Ph.D. and. Charles Short, LL.D. Oxford: Clarendon Press. https://www.perseus.tufts.edu/hopper/text?doc=Perseus%3Atext%3A1999.04.0059%3 (accessed 13 December 2021).
LSJ = Thesaurus Linguae Graecae. The *Online Liddell-Scott-Jones Greek-English Lexicon.* http://stephanus.tlg.uci.edu/lsj/#eid=1 (accessed 13 April 2021).

MOL = Moliner, María. 1998. *Diccionario de uso del español*. Madrid: Gredos.
NVS = Decurtins, Alexi. *Niev Vocabulari Sursilvan* [New Sursilvan vocabulary]. https://www.vocabularisursilvan.ch/ (accessed 13 April 2021).
OED = Oxford University Press. 2021. *Oxford English Dictionary*. http://dictionary.oed.com (accessed 13 April 2021).
Pittau, Massimo. 2003. *Dizionario Della Lingua Sarda: Fraseologico Ed Etimologico*. Cagliari: Ettore Gasperini Editore.
Pledari. *Deutsch-Romanisches Wörterbuch*. http://www.pledari.ch/meinpledari/ (accessed 13 April 2021).
PR = Rey-Debove, Josette & Alain Rey. 1993. *Le Nouveau Petit Robert. Dictionnaire alphabétique et analogique de la langue française*. Paris: Dictionnaires Le Robert.
RDW = Tiktin, Hariton. 1989. *Rumänisch-deutsches Wörterbuch*. 2. 3. Bde. Wiesbaden: Otto Harrassowitz.
TLFi = ATILF – CNRS and Université de Lorraine. *Trésor de la Langue Française informatisé*. http://atilf.atilf.fr/ (accessed 13 April 2021).
Vox = Vox and Larousse Editorial. 2000. *Diccionari Manual llengua catalana Vox* [Manual dictionary of Catalan Vox]. https://www.diccionaris.cat/diccionari/catala/tipus/0 (accessed 13 April 2021).
VSLI = Istituto Superiore Etnografico della Sardegna. 2011. *Vocabolario Sardo logudorese-Italiano*. http://vocabolariocasu.isresardegna.it/ (accessed 13 April 2021).
ZVI = Zingarelli, Nicola. 1999. *Vocabolario della lingua italiana*. Bologna: Zanichelli.

Corpora

CDE = Davies, Mark. *Corpus del Español [en línea]* http://www.corpusdelespanol.org/ (accessed 14th April 2021).
CDH = Instituto de Investigación Rafael Lapesa de la Real Academia Española (2013). *Corpus del Nuevo diccionario histórico [en linea]*. http://web.frl.es/CNDHE (accessed 14 April 2021).
CDP = Davies, Mark & Ferreira, Michael J. *Corpus do português [en línea]* http://www.corpusdoportugues.org/ (accessed 14 April 2021).
CFPP = Branca-Rosoff, Sonia, Serge Fleury, Florence Lefeuvre & Mat Pires. 2013. *Corpus de Français Parlé Parisien des années 2000* (Version 1). Langage et langues : description, théorisation, transmission; Fédération CLESTHIA; Systèmes Linguistiques, Énonciation et Discursivité. https://doi.org/10.34847/COCOON.8BC96A4E-9899-30E4-99BE-C72D216EB38B (accessed 14th April 2021).
CLAPI = Bruxelles, Sylvie, Carole Etienne, Emilie Jouin-Chardon, Justine Lascar, Sandra Teston-Bonnard & Véronique Traverso, *Corpus de Langues Parlées en Interaction* http://clapi.ish-lyon.cnrs.fr/ (accessed 14 April 2021).
COLA = Jørgensen, Annette Myre & Esperanza Eguía Padilla. *Corpus Oral de Lenguaje Adolescente [en línea]*. http://www.colam.org/ (accessed 14 April 2021).
C-ORAL-ROM = Cresti, Emanuela & Massimo Moneglia (eds.). 2005. *C-ORAL-ROM: integrated reference corpora for spoken Romance languages*. CD-ROM. Amsterdam & Philadelphia: John Benjamins Publishing Company.

CORDE = Real Academia Española. *Banco de datos (CORDE) [en linea]. Corpus Diacrónico del Español* http://www.rae.es (accessed 14 April 2021).
CORGA = Centro Ramón Piñeiro para a investigación en humanidades. *Corpus de Referencia do Galego Actual (CORGA) [en linea] [3.2]* http://corpus.cirp.gal/corga/ (accessed 14 April 2021).
COROLA = *Corpus computațional de referință pentru limba română contemporană [en linea]* [Computational reference corpus for contemporary Romanian] https://corola.racai.ro/ (accessed 14 April 2021).
CORPES] = Real Academia Española. *Corpus del Español del Siglo XXI* (CORPES). http://web.frl.es/CORPES/ (accessed 14 April 2021).
CREA = Real Academia Española. *Banco de datos (CREA) [en línea]. Corpus de Referencia del Español Actual* http://corpus.rae.es/creanet.html (accessed 8 April 2021).
CTILC = Rafel i Fontanals, Joaquim. *Corpus textual informatitzat de la llengua catalana [en linea]* [Digital text corpus of Catalan]. https://ctilc.iec.cat/scripts/CTIL (accessed 14 April 2021).
DiaCORIS = *Corpus diacronico dell'italiano scritto [en linea]* http://dslo.unibo.it/DiaCORIS/ (accessed 14 April 2021).
DMF = Corpus du *Dictionnaire du Moyen Français*, version 2020 (DMF 2020). ATILF – CNRS & Université de Lorraine. Site internet : http://www.atilf.fr/dmf. (accessed 14 April 2021)
ELICOP = Debrock, Mark, Piet Mertens, Frederick Truyen & Veerle Brosens.1997–2000. *Etude linguistique de la communication parlée.* Katolieke Universiteit Leuven. http://bach.arts.kuleuven.be/pmertens/corpus/search/s.html (accessed 14 April 2021).
FRANTEXT = Boulton, Alex. *FRANTEXT [en línea].* http://zeus.inalf.cnrs.fr/ (accessed 14 April 2021).
LCC = Leipzig Corpora Collection. *Leipzig Corpora Collection [en linea]* https://corpora.uni-leipzig.de (accessed 14 April 2021).
OVI = Opera del Vocabolario Italiano. *Banca dati dell'italiano antico [en linea]* http://www.ovi.cnr.it/itnet intro.htm (accessed 14 April 2021).
PFC = *Phonologie du Français Contemporain* (PFC). https://www.projet-pfc.net (accessed 14 April 2020)
ROH = *Leipzig Corpora Collection:* Romansh news corpus based on material crawled in 2011. Leipzig Corpora Collection. Dataset. https://corpora.uni-leipzig.de?corpusId=roh_newscrawl_2011 (accessed 14 April 2021).
TenTen-webcorpora = Sketchengine. *TenTen-Webcorpora* https://app.sketchengine.eu/ (accessed 14 April 2021).
TILG = Santamarina, Antón. *Tesouro Informatizado da Lingua Galega* [Digital archive of the Galician language]. http://ilg.usc.gal/TILG/gl/tilg (accessed 14 April 2021).

References

Aijmer, Karin. 2002. *English discourse particles: Evidence from a corpus.* Amsterdam: John Benjamins.
Bambeck, Manfred. 1959. *Lateinisch-romanische Wortstudien.* Wiesbaden: Steiner.
Bernal, Elisenda & Carsten Sinner. 2009. *Al seu rotllo*: aproximació al llenguatge juvenil català ["Al seu rotllo": an approach to Catalan teenagers' language]. *Zeitschrift für Katalanistik* 22. 7–36.

Bittencourt, Vanda de Oliveira. 1999. Gramaticalização e discursivação no Português oral do Brasil: o caso "tipo (assim)" [Grammaticalization and discursivization in oral Brazilian Portuguese: the case of „tipo (assim)"]. *Scripta* 2 (4). 39–53.

Bittencourt, Vanda de Oliveira. 2000. *Tipo (assim) como Delimitador de Unidades de Informação* ["Tipo (assim) as a demarcator of information units]. *Estudos Lingüísticos* 29 (1). 264–269.

Blanche-Benveniste, Claire, Mireille Bilger, Christine Rouget, & Karel van den Eynde. 1991. *Le Français parlé*. Paris: Éditions du Centre National de la Recherche Scientifique.

Borreguero Zuloaga, Margarita. 2020. Los marcadores de aproximación (en el lenguaje juvenil): it. *tipo* vs. esp. *en plan*. In Miguel Ángel Cuevas Gómez, Fernando Molina Castillo & Paolo Silvestri (eds.), *España e Italia: Un viaje de ida y vuelta. Studia in honorem Manuel Carrera Díaz*, 53–78. Sevilla: Editorial Universidad de Sevilla.

Bregant, Lucía. 2019. Marcadores de reformulación en adolescentes bonaerenses. In Dora Riestra, Nora Múgica (Ed.), *Estudios SAEL 2019*, 9–22. Bahía Blanca: Editorial de la Universidad Nacional del Sur, Ediuns.

Brems, Lieselotte & Kristin Davidse. 2010. The grammaticalization of nominal type noun constructions with *kind/sort of*: chronology and paths of change. *English Studies* 91 (2). 180–202.

Camacho, José. 2011. La estructura de la secuencia "como que". In María Victoria Escandell Vidal, Manuel Leonetti, Cristina Sánchez López (eds.), *60 problemas de gramática*, 31–36. Madrid: Ediciones Akal.

Castelano, Karine Lôbo & Eliana Crispim França Luquetti. 2014. Uma abordagem dos vocábulos 'assim', 'tipo' e 'tipo assim' e sus implicações para o ensino de língua portuguesa [An approach to the expressions 'assim', 'tipo' and 'tipo assim' and its implications for the teaching of Portuguese] *Revista Científica Interdisciplinar* Nº 1, volume 1, artigo nº 5, Julho/Setembro 2014 D.O.I: 10.17115/2358-8411/v1n1a5 (accessed 17 January 2022)

Castelano, Karine Lôbo. 2013. *Uma abordagem dos vocábulos 'assim', 'tipo' e 'tipo assim' e sus implicações para o ensino de língua portuguesa* [An approach to the expressions 'assim', 'tipo' and 'tipo assim' and its implications for the teaching of Portuguese]. Rio de Janeiro: Universidade Estadual do Norte Fluminense, thesis.

Chauveau-Thoumelin, Pierre. 2018. Exemplification and ad hoc categorization: The *genre*-construction in French. *Folia Linguistica* 52 (39/1). 177–199. https://doi.org/10.1515/flih-2018-0004, (accessed 17 January 2022).

Chauveau-Thoumelin, Pierre. 2020. *Une approche constructionnelle des enclosures genre et espèce*. Lille: Université Charles de Gaulle–Lille III doctoral thesis.

Chevalier, Gisèle. 2001. Comment *comme* fonctionne d'une génération à l'autre. *Revue québécoise de linguistique* 30 (2). 13–40.

Colella, Gianluca & Eduardo Blasco Ferrer. 2016. 7.3 I linguaggi giovanili. In Eduardo Blasco Ferrer, Peter Koch & Daniela Marzo (eds.), *Manuale di linguistica sarda*, 508–526. Berlin & New York: Mouton de Gruyter.

Corbett, Greville G. 2006. *Agreement*. Cambridge: Cambridge University Press.

Danon-Boileau, Laurent & Mary-Annick Morel. 1997. *Question, point de vue, genre, style...*: Les noms prépositionnels en français contemporain. *Faits de Langues* 9. 193–200.

Davidse, Kristin, Lieselotte Brems & Liesbeth De Smedt. 2008. Type noun uses in the English NP. A case of right to left layering. *International Journal of Corpus Linguistics* 13 (2). 139–168.

Davidse, Kristin, Lieselotte Brems, Peter Willemse, Emeline Doyen, Jessica Kiermeet & Elfi Thoelen. 2013. A comparative study of the grammaticalized uses of English "sort of" and French "genre (de)" in teenage forum data. In Emanuele Piola (ed.), *Languages go web. Standard and non-standard languages on the internet*, 41–66. Alessandria: Edizione dell'Orso.

De Smedt, Liesbeth, Lieselotte Brems & Kristin Davidse. 2007. NP-internal functions and extended uses of the 'type' nouns *kind, sort*, and *type*: towards a comprehensive, corpus-based description. In Roberta Facchinetti (Ed.), *Corpus Linguistics 25 Years on*, 225–255. Amsterdam & New York: Rodopi.

Denison, David. 2002. History of the *sort of* construction family. Paper presented at the Second International Conference on Construction Grammar, University of Helsinki, 7 September.

Denison, David. 2005. The grammaticalisations of *sort of*, *kind of* and *type of* in English. Paper presented at New Reflections on Grammaticalization 3, University of Santiago de Compostela, 17–20 July.

Dikken, Marcel den. 2001. Pluringulars. *Linguistic Review* 18. 19–41.

Dostie, Gaétane. 1995. *Comme, genre* et *style* postposés en français du Québec: une étude sémantique. *Linguisticae Investigationes* 19 (2). 247–263.

Dufaye, Lionel. 2014. GENRE ou le scenario d'une grammaticalisation. *Linx* 70–71, 51–65.

Fernández, Julieta. 2017. The language functions of *tipo* in Argentine vernacular. *Journal of Pragmatics* 114. 87–103.

Fiorentini, Ilaria. 2016. Segnali discorsivi italiani in situazione di contatto linguistico. Il caso degli indicatori di riformulazione. *Quaderns d'Italià* 21. 11–26.

Flaux, Nelly. 2015. Les noms d'approximation et les noms d'idéalités. Paper presented at the International Colloquium on *L'expression de l'imprécision dans les langues romanes*, Université de Bucarest, 22–23.

Fleischman, Suzanne. 1998. Des jumeaux du discours: *genre* et *like*. *La linguistique* 34 (2), 31–47.

Franco, António. 1998. ,Uma Espécie (de)' Nem Sempre E uma Espécie: Marcadores de Gradação Variável e os Dicionários [A kind (of) is not always a kind: variable degree markers and dictionaries]. In María Teresa Fuentes Morán & Reinhold Werner (eds.), *Lexicografías iberorrománicas: Problemas, propuestas y proyectos*, 81–95. Frankfurt am Main/Madrid: Vervuert/Iberoamericana.

Ghezzi, Chiara. 2013. *Vagueness markers in contemporary Italian. Intergenerational variation and pragmatic change*. Pavia: Università di Pavia doctoral dissertation.

Gréa, Philippe & Estelle Moline. 2013. Une manière de construction/un mode de construction: classification floue et classification hyperonymique. *Le Français Moderne* 81 (2), 215–229.

Heine, Bernd & Tania Kuteva. 2005. *Language contact and grammatical change*. Cambridge: Cambridge University Press.

Hennecke, Inga & Wiltrud Mihatsch. In press. From taxonomic to pragmatic uses of French *genre*: Degrees of prosodic prominence as an indicator of pragmaticalization. In Hélène Vassiliadou & Marie Lammert (eds.), *Clear versus approximate categorization: A crosslinguistic perspective*. Cambridge: Cambridge Scholars.

Hennecke, Inga. 2014. *Pragmatic markers in Manitoban French: a corpuslinguistic and psycholinguistic investigation of language change*. Bochum: Ruhr-Universität Bochum Ph.D. Thesis. https://hss-opus.ub.ruhr-uni-bochum.de/opus4/frontdoor/index/index/year/2018/docId/4051 (accessed 17 January 2022)

Hernández González, Carmen. 1992. Contribución al estudio de los adverbios largos españoles formados con los sustantivos "guisa", "cosa" y "manera". *Actas del II Congreso Internacional de Historia de la Lengua Española* 2, 497–504. Madrid: Pabellón de España.

Huseby, Stine. 2010. *Las funciones de tipo como marcador del discurso en el lenguaje juvenil de Buenos Aires: Un estudio descriptivo*. Bergen: Universitetet i Bergen MA thesis.

Isambert, Paul. 2016. *Genre*: une mode récente mais qui vient de loin. *Journal of French Language Studies* 26, 85–96.

Jørgensen, Anette Myre. 2009. *En plan* used as a hedge in Spanish teenage language. In Anna-Britta Stenström& Annette Myre Jørgensen (eds.), *Youngspeak in a multilingual perspective*, 95–115. Amsterdam & Philadelphia: Benjamins.

Kaplan, Carina V. 2012. Mirada social, exclusión simbólica y auto-estigmatización. Experiencias subjetivas de jóvenes de educación secundaria. In Carina V. Kaplan, Lucas Krotsch & Victoria Orce (eds.), *Con ojos de joven. Relaciones entre desigualdad, violencia y condición estudiantil*, 15–78. Buenos Aires: Editorial de la Facultad de Filosofía y Letras Universidad de Buenos Aires.

Keizer, Evelien. 2007. *The English noun phrase. The nature of linguistic categorization*. Cambridge: Cambridge University Press.

Kolyaseva, Alena & Kristin Davidse. 2018. A typology of lexical and grammaticalized uses of Russian *tip, tipa, po tipu*. *Russian Linguistics* 42 (2). 191–220.

Kornfeld, Laura Malena. 2013. Atenuadores en la lengua coloquial argentina. *Lingüística* 29 (2), 17–49.

Landheer, Ronald & Gaétane Dostie. 2003. Quelques observations sur trois classifieurs français: *espèce, genre* et *sorte*: un cas d'espèce du phénomène de la grammaticalisation. In Fernando Sánchez Miret (ed.), *Actas del XXIII Congreso Internacional de Lingüística y Filología Románica 2001*. Vol. II/1, 291–301. Tübingen: Niemeyer.

Lapteva, Olga Alekseevna. 1983. *Tipa* ili *vrode* [*Tipa* or *vrode*]. *Voprosy jazykoznanija* [Topics in linguistics] 1. 39–51.

Lenker, Ursula. 2002. Is it, stylewise or otherwise, wise to use *-wise*? Domain adverbials and the history of English *-wise*. In Teresa Fanego, María José López-Couso & Javier Pérez-Guerra (eds.), *English historical syntax and morphology*. Selected Papers from 11 ICEHL, Santiago de Compostela, 7–11 September 2000, 157–180. Amsterdam & Philadelphia: John Benjamins.

Lima Hernandes, Maria Célia. 2005. *A interface sociolinguística / gramaticalização: estratificação de usos de tipo, feito, igual e como – sincronia e diacronia* [The interface sociolinguistics /grammaticalization: stratification of the uses of *tipo, feito, igual* and *como* – synchrony and diachrony]. Campinas: Unicamp doctoral dissertation.

Luquetti, Eliana & Castelano, Karine Lôbo. 2012. As trajetórias de mudança dos vocábulos "assim" e "tipo" [The paths of change of the words „assim" and „tipo"]. *Revista e-scrita* 3 (3), 42–52.

Magraner Mifsud, Àngela. 2018. Estudi comparatiu de l'atenuació pragmàtica en la llengua catalana: converses col·loquials prototípiques-converses col·loquials perifèriques [Comparative study of pragmatic mitigation in Catalan: prototypical colloquial conversations- peripherical colloquial conversations]. *Textos en Proceso* 3 (2), 166–197.

Marques, Maria Aldina. 2015. 'Tipo'. Référenciation et modalisation dans des interactions verbales orales. In Maria Helena Araújo Carreira (ed.), *Faits de langue et de discours pour l'expression des modalités dans les langues romanes. Travaux et documents* 60, 249–260. Paris: Université Paris 8-Vincennes-Saint-Denis.

Marquet, Lluís. 2003. "Mena" i "tipus", mots no sinònims ["Mena" and "tipus", words which are no synonyms]. *Llengua nacional: publicació de l'Associació Llengua Nacional* 43. 20.

Masini, Francesca & Caterina Mauri. 2020. Questione di stile. L'espressione analitica della maniera indessicale. *Testi e Linguaggi* 14, 259–271.

Mauri, Caterina. 2017. Building and interpreting ad hoc categories: a linguistic analysis. In Joanna Blochowiak, Stephanie Durrleman, Cristina Grisot & Christopher Laenzlinger (eds.), *Formal models in the study of language. Applications in Interdisciplinary Contexts*, 297–326. Berlin: Springer.

Mihatsch, Wiltrud. 2007. The construction of vagueness: 'Sort of' expressions in Romance languages. In Günter Radden, Klaus-Michael Koepcke, Thomas Berg & Peter Siemund. (eds.), *Aspects of meaning construction*, 225–245. Amsterdam & Philadelphia: John Benjamins.

Mihatsch, Wiltrud. 2009. The approximators French *comme*, Italian *come*, Portuguese *como* and Spanish *como* from a grammaticalization perspective. In Corinne Rossari, Claudia. Ricci, & Adriana Spiridon (eds.), *Grammaticalization and pragmatics: Facts, approaches, theoretical issues*, 65–91. Bingley: Emerald.

Mihatsch, Wiltrud. 2010. *Wird man von Hustensaft wie so ne art bekifft? Approximationsmarker in romanischen Sprachen*. Frankfurt am Main: Klostermann.

Mihatsch, Wiltrud. 2016. Type-noun binominals in four Romance languages. In Lieselotte Brems, Bernard De Clerck & Katrien Verveckken (eds.), *Binominal syntagms as a neglected locus of synchronic variation and diachronic change: Towards a unified approach*. Special issue in Language Sciences, 136–159.

Mihatsch Wiltrud. 2018a. De la escritura científica a la conversación coloquial adolescente. El caso de *tipo*. *Spanish in Context* 15 (2). 281–303.

Mihatsch, Wiltrud. 2018b. From ad hoc category to ad hoc categorization: The proceduralization of Argentinian Spanish *tipo*. *Folia Linguistica* 52. 147–176.

Mihatsch, Wiltrud. 2019. *De manera, de forma, de modo*: construcciones adverbiales de manera en tres variedades del español. In Franz Lebsanft & Sebastian Greußlich (eds.), *El español, lengua pluricéntrica. Discurso, gramática, léxico y medios de comunicación masiva (Sprache in kulturellen Kontexten 4)*, 431–459. Göttingen: V & R unipress.

Mihatsch, Wiltrud. 2020a. Los orígenes discursivos de los atenuadores procedimentalizados 'tipo', 'onda', 'corte' y 'rollo': Una exploración microdiacrónica. *Revista Signos* 53 (104). 686–717.

Mihatsch, Wiltrud. 2020b. A semantic-map approach to pragmatic markers: the complex approximation/mitigation/quotation/focus marking. (Peninsular Spanish (*tipo, así, como*) and European Portuguese (*tipo, assim, como*) based on a corpus analysis of C-ORAL-ROM). In Isabel Margarida Duarte & Rogelio Ponce de León (eds.), *Marcadores Discursivos. O Português como Referência Contrastiva*, 137–162. Bern: Peter Lang.

Mihatsch, Wiltrud. 2021. French type-noun constructions based on *genre*: From the creation of ad hoc categories to ad hoc categorization. In Caterina Mauri, Ilaria Fiorentini & Eugenio Goria (eds.), *Building categories in interaction: linguistic resources at work. Studies in Language Companion Series*, 373–413. New York & Amsterdam: John Benjamins.

Mihatsch, Wiltrud. In press, The evolution of complex and simple comparative prepositions based on French *genre*. In Dejan Stosic, Myriam Bras, Chiara Minoccheri & Océane Abrard (eds.), *Les prépositions complexes en français : théories, descriptions, applications*. Paris: L'Harmattan.

Moline, Estelle. 2011. Une manière d'article en manière d'hommage. *Sur les tournures en* une manière de N. In Dany Amiot Walter de Mulder, Estelle Moline & Dejan Stosic. (eds.), *Ars Grammatica. Hommages à Nelly Flaux*, 389–402. Bern: Peter Lang.
Mondaca Becerra, Lissette. 2020. Aproximación al estudio de las funciones pragmáticas y a la atenuación en la partícula 'onda' en el español de Chile. *Revista Signos* 53 (104), 718–743.
Morães de Castilho, Célia Maria. 1991. *Os delimitadores no português falado no Brasil* [Demarcators in spoken Brazilian Portuguese]. Campinas: IEL/UNICAMP1 MA Thesis.
Noailly, Michèle. 2006. Quoi de neuf côté préposition?. *Modèles linguistiques* 53, http://journals.openedition.org/ml/521 (accessed 17 January 2022)
Odden, Oda Røste. 2019. *North Scandinavian type noun constructions: Patterns with slags, SORTs and TYP(E)*. Oslo: University of Oslo doctoral dissertation.
Paraschkewoff, Boris. 1976. Zur Entstehungs- und Entwicklungsgeschichte der Bildungen auf -weise (Teil 1). *Beiträge zur Geschichte der deutschen Sprache und Literatur* 97, 165–201.
Petraş, Cristina. 2014. "Noms métalinguistiques" et grammaticalisation: *manière (de)* en français acadien. *Faits de langues* 43, 115–135.
Polzin-Haumann, Claudia. 2017. Pays occitan et francoprovençal. In Ursula Reutner (ed.), *Manuel des francophonies*, 89–112. Berlin, Boston: De Gruyter.
Popescu, Cecilia-Mihaela & Alice Ionescu. 2019. Étude comparative des marqueurs métadiscursifs *gen* du roumain et *genre* du français. Distribution et valeurs pragmatiques. *Studii de lingvistică* 9 (2). 93–112.
Rodríguez-Abruñeiras, Paula. 2020. Outlining a grammaticalization path for the Spanish formula *en plan (de)*: A contribution to crosslinguistic pragmatics. *Linguistics* 55 (6). https://doi.org/10.1515/ling-2020-0229 (accessed 17 January 2022)
Rojas Inostroza, Cristian, Rubio Núñez, Alejandra, San Martín Núñez, Abelardo & Guerrero González, Silvana. 2012. Análisis pragmático y sociolingüístico de los marcadores discursivos de reformulación en el habla de Santiago de Chile. *Lenguas Modernas* 40, 103–123.
Rojas, Edgardo Gustavo. 2012. Caracterización pragmático discursiva de la partícula conversacional "corte/corte que" en la variedad juvenil del español metropolitano. Paper presented at I Congreso de la Delegación Argentina de la Asociación de Lingüística y Filología de América Latina (ALFAL) y V Jornadas Internacionales de Filología Hispánica, La Plata, Argentina. http://sedici.unlp.edu.ar/bitstream/handle/10915/42397/Documento_completo__.pdf?sequence=1&isAllowed=y (accessed 14 December 2021).
Rosier, Laurence. 2002a. *Genre*: le nuancier de sa grammaticalisation. *Travaux de Linguistique* 44 (1), 79–88.
Rosier, Laurence. 2002b. Des "profileurs" de l'énonciation : les constructions avec *genre, sorte et espèce*. *Linx* 12. http://journals.openedition.org/linx/1313 (accessed 17 January 2022)
Rouget, Christine. 1997. *Espèce de, genre de, sorte de*: Approximatifs ou sous-catégorisateurs?. In Paulo de Carvalho & Olivier Soutet (eds.), *Psychomécanique du langage. Problèmes et perspectives. Actes du 7ᵉ Colloque International de Psychomécanique du langage (Cordoue, 2–4 juin 1994)*. 289–298. Paris: Champion.
San Martín Núñez, Abelardo, Christian Rojas Inostroza & Silvana Guerrero González. 2016. La función discursiva y la distribución social de los marcadores *por ser y onda* en el corpus del PRESEEA de Santiago de Chile. *Boletín de Filología* 51 (2). 235–254.
San Martín Núñez, Abelardo. 2017. Análisis sociolingüístico de los reformuladores de explicación en el español hablado de Santiago de Chile. *Revista SIGNOS* 50 (93), 124–147.

Sankoff, Gillian, Pierrette Thibault, Naomi Nagy, Hélène Blondeau, Marie-Odile Fonollosa & Lucie Gagnon. 1997. Variation in the use of discourse markers in a language contact situation. *Language Variation and Change* 9 (2), 191–217.
Stefenelli, Arnulf. 1983. Latinismen im Spanischen und im Französischen. In José Manuel López de Abiada & Titus Heydenreich (eds.), *Iberoamérica. Historia – sociedad – literatura. Homenaje a Gustav Siebenmann*. vol. 2, 883–901. München: Fink (Lateinamerika-Studien 13).
Stefenelli, Arnulf. 1992. *Das Schicksal des lateinischen Wortschatzes in den romanischen Sprachen*. Passau: Wissenschaftsverlag Richard Rothe.
Stosic, Dejan & Estelle Moline. 2016. *L'expression de la manière en français*. Paris: Éditions Ophrys (collection L'essentiel en français).
Teixeira, Cristiana Filipa Silva, Elisabete Pinto Ribeiro & Sara Raquel da Silva Salgado. 2016. Marcadores discursivos na oralidade [Discourse markers in spoken language]. *Revista eletrónica de Linguística dos Estudantes da Universidade do Porto* (5). http://ojs.letras.up.pt/index.php/elingUP/index (accessed 14 December 2021)
Terian, Simina-Maria. 2018. (Inter)subiectificare și gramaticalizare: *gen* în limba română contemporană [(Inter)subjectification and grammaticalization: *gen* in contemporary Romanian]. *Transilvania review* (11–12). 129–134.
Vincent, Diane. 2005. The journey of non-standard discourse markers in Quebec French: Networks based on exemplification. In Maj-Britt Mosegaard Hansen & Corinne Rossari (eds.), *The evolution of pragmatic markers*, Special issue of *Journal of Historical Pragmatics* 6 (2), 188–210.
Vladimirska, Elena. 2016. Entre le dire et le monde. Le cas du marqueur discursif *genre*. In Hava Bat-Zeev Shyldkrot, Silvia Adler & Maria Asnes (eds.), *Nouveaux regards sur l'approximation et la précision*, 195–209. Paris: Honoré Champion.
Voghera, Miriam. 2013. A case study on the relationship between grammatical change and synchronic variation: The emergence of *tipo*[-N] in Italian. In Anna Giacalone Ramat, Caterina Mauri & Piera Molinelli. (eds.), *Synchrony and diachrony: A dynamic interface*, 283–312. Amsterdam: John Benjamins.
Voghera, Miriam. 2017. La nascita delle costruzioni non nominali di *specie, genere, sorta* e *tipo*: uno studio basato su corpora. In Maria Grossmann & Paolo D'Achille, P. (eds.), *Per la storia della formazione delle parole in italiano: un nuovo corpus in rete (M.I.DIA.) e nuove prospettive di studio*, 277–307. Florenz: Franco Cesati.
Walters, Emma (manuscript). Semantic innovation and grammaticalization of the English loanword *type* in colloquial *Hindi*. PhD-thesis. London: Birkbeck College, University of London.
Willemse, Peter, Lieselotte Brems & Kristin Davidse. 2008. Synchronic layering of type nouns in English and French. Paper presented at the 41st Annual Meeting of SLE (Languages in Contrast: Grammar, Translation, Corpora), University of Bologna at Forlì, 17–20 September.
Yaguello, Marina. 1998. *Genre*, une particule d'un genre nouveau. *Petits Faits de Langue*, Paris: Le Seuil, 18–24.
Zafiu, Rodica. 2001. Tip și gen [Tip and gen]. *România literară* 12. http://www.romlit.ro/index.pl/tip_i_gen (accessed 25 April 2021).
Zafiu, Rodica. 2012. Gen. Sau ceva de genul. . . . [gen. Or something like that] *Dilema veche* 460. https://dilemaveche.ro/tag/cuvinte-nepotrivite?page=33 (accessed 25 April 2021).
Zamparelli, Roberto. 2000. *Layers in the determiner phrase*. New York: Garland.

Pierre Chauveau-Thoumelin

8 Classification, qualification, typification: Categorizing with *genre de* and *espèce de* 'kind of' in French

Abstract: The French nouns *genre* 'genus; kind' and *espèce* 'species; kind' belong to a paradigm of taxonomic nouns, i.e. nouns denoting taxonomic ranks. These nouns have developed other uses, notably as approximators. In this paper, I consider three constructions, i.e. form-meaning pairings, with the apparent same structure [DET N_{TAX} *de* N]. Taking a synchronic perspective, I show how each of these constructions is used in French to categorize in a different way. The first one, the classifying construction, provides a means of demarcating one or more subclasses within a bigger category. This corresponds to the original scientific taxonomic use which has subsequently spread to everyday language. The second one, the qualifying construction, blurs the membership relation between an individual and a category or between two categories; it works as an approximator. I particularly focus on the third one, the typifying construction, whose status is not as well established. This construction helps create a category on the basis of individuals usually previously mentioned in the discourse. The category thus referred to is often an ad hoc category, created on the fly, on the basis of some properties shared by the set of individuals selected. I show how this construction takes after both the classifying and qualifying constructions, considering the formal and semantic properties of each. Special attention is given to type of determiner, agreement patterns, type of noun in the N-slot, and constraints with regard to modifiers in each construction. My analyses are based on a corpus of recent written examples involving several types of discourse (newspapers, literature, law, encyclopaedia, online forums).

1 Introduction

The French nouns *genre* 'genus; kind' and *espèce* 'species; kind' belong to a paradigm of taxonomic nouns, i.e. nouns denoting taxonomic ranks. These nouns have developed other uses, notably as approximators (Mihatsch 2007, 2016). In this paper, I will consider three constructions, i.e. form-meaning pairings (e.g.

Pierre Chauveau-Thoumelin, Université de Lille, e-mail: p.chauveau.thoumelin@gmail.com

Goldberg 2006), with the apparent same structure [DET N$_{TAX}$ *de* N][1] (see e.g. Rosier 2002; Mihatsch 2007, 2016; Doyen and Davidse 2009):

(1) Il y a **deux genres de fraude**, celles commises en aval du vote et celles en amont. (LEM,[2] 02/03/2016)
 'There are **two types of fraud**, that committed after the vote and that committed ahead of the vote'

(2) Il a une connaissance livresque unique au monde. Il est **une espèce d'encyclopédie magique**. (LEM, 15/07/2016)[3]
 'He has a book knowledge that is unique in the world. He is **a kind of magical encyclopaedia**.'

(3) Mais, pour prévoir **ce genre de mission**, il faut du temps. (LEM, 14/02/2013)
 'But, in order to plan **this kind of mission**, time is needed.'

The classifying construction, as in (1), provides a means to define one or more subclasses within a larger category. This corresponds to the original taxonomic use (e.g. *un genre de mammifère* 'a genus of mammal') which has spread to everyday language (Mihatsch 2007, 2016). Here, *deux genres de fraude* defines two subcategories within the FRAUD category.

The qualifying construction, as in (2), blurs the membership relation between an individual and a category (or between two categories); it works as an approximator. Here, a man is metaphorically identified as belonging to the MAGICAL ENCYCLOPAEDIA category.

The typifying construction helps create a category on the basis of individuals usually previously mentioned in the discourse. In (3), the phrase *ce genre de mission* 'this kind of mission' comes after a number of such missions have been mentioned in the article. Through a kind of resumptive anaphora (Maillard 1974), encapsulating several elements of the previous discourse, the construction loosely identifies a category of space missions whose objective is to deflect the trajectory of asteroids threatening to crash into the Earth.[4] Instances of this construction are often seen as borderline cases of the classifying and qualifying

---

[1] N$_{TAX}$ refers here to *genre* and *espèce*, even though most of the analyses presented could also apply to other nouns (e.g. *sorte, type, style*).
[2] See the rest of this section for a short presentation of the corpus used. For a full description, see Chauveau-Thoumelin (2020).
[3] In this example, *Il* 'he' refers to Sébastien Clergue, close collaborator of David Copperfield.
[4] For a more detailed analysis of these constructions see Chauveau-Thoumelin (2020, chap. 2 to 4).

constructions (see e.g. Rouget 1997). I will show however that this construction possesses unique characteristics, both formal and semantic, that clearly differentiate it from the other two.

By examining their syntactic and semantic properties, I will show how these constructions differ from one another, and that they do not constitute three interpretations of the same structure, but three different constructions on their own. The constructional approach (Goldberg 2006) adopted here allows us to focus on the whole construction rather than on the taxonomic nouns themselves. This approach is particularly useful for better understanding how these constructions are related.[5]

The analyses are based on a corpus composed of data from five different sources (see Chauveau-Thoumelin 2020): articles from the newspaper *Le Monde* (LEM),[6] literary texts from the Frantext database (FRA),[7] official documents from the Digital Corpus of the European Parliament (EUR),[8] articles from Wikipédia (WIK),[9] and messages from the Doctissimo online forums (DOC).[10] Although not exhaustive, the diversity of sources makes it possible to give an overview of these constructions in the language and to cover a variety of fields, taking into account both journalistic, literary, legal, technical and scientific texts written in controlled language and messages from online forums written in more orally-oriented, less controlled language.

Section 2 gives an overview of the distribution of the constructions in the corpora. Each of the following sections is devoted to one of these constructions (see Sections 3–5), the first subsection of which details some of the construction's formal properties (i.e. types of determiner, agreement within and outside of the construction, behaviour of modifiers towards N_{TAX} and N; see Sections 3.1, 4.1, and 5.1). A subsequent subsection deals with more semantic aspects, the semantics of N where relevant, as well as the categorization processes at work in the construction (see Sections 3.2, 4.2, and 5.2).

---

[5] For lack of space, the hierarchical organization of the constructions will not be dealt with in this paper.
[6] https://www.lemonde.fr (accessed 31st May 2019).
[7] https://www.frantext.fr (accessed 31st May 2019).
[8] https://ec.europa.eu/jrc/en/language-technologies/dcep (accessed 31st May 2019).
[9] https://fr.wikipedia.org (accessed 31st May 2019).
[10] http://forum.doctissimo.fr/ (accessed 31st May 2019).

2 Distribution of the constructions

Before getting into the specifics of each of these constructions, it is insightful to see how they are distributed in the corpora. Table 1a shows the distribution of interpretations among [DET N_{TAX} *de* N] constructions involving either *genre* or *espèce*.[11]

Table 1: Distribution of the constructions of the [DET N_{TAX} *de* N] kind.
Table 1a: [DET N_{TAX} *de* N] constructions.

	LEM	FRA	EUR	WIK	DOC	ALL	ALL (%)
CLA	53	36	38	262	16	405	26.16
QUA	45	256	0	6	232	539	34.82
TYP	126	186	34	18	240	604	39.02
Total	224	478	72	286	488	1548	100

Table 1b: [DET *genre de* N] constructions.

	LEM	FRA	EUR	WIK	DOC	ALL	ALL (%)
CLA	7	12	0	86	3	108	14.54
QUA	5	13	0	4	9	31	4.17
TYP	126	186	34	18	240	604	81.29
Total	138	211	34	108	252	743	100

Table 1c: [DET *espèce de* N] constructions.

	LEM	FRA	EUR	WIK	DOC	ALL	ALL (%)
CLA	46	24	38	176	13	297	36.89
QUA	40	243	0	2	223	508	63.11
TYP	0	0	0	0	0	0	0
Total	86	267	38	178	236	805	100

According to the data, the classifying construction represents slightly over 26% of the occurrences of [DET N_{TAX} *de* N]-type constructions. The frequency of the classifying construction is, as can be expected, very much dependent on the type of text. In the WIK corpus, more than 91% of occurrences of the structure

---

[11] The quantifying construction, as in *aucune espèce d'importance* 'no importance at all', will be left out (see for example Mihatsch 2016; Chauveau-Thoumelin 2020, chap. 5).

[DET N$_{TAX}$ *de* N] are instances of the classifying construction, as this corpus deals quite a lot with classification of genera and species. On the contrary, the classifying construction is rare in the DOC corpus, for instance, where it represents only about 3.3% of cases.

The qualifying construction appears in about one third of cases. A closer look at the data shows a significant difference in frequency depending on the noun the construction involves. Contrary to the intuition I had when I started this study, the construction [DET *genre de* N] is rarely interpreted in a qualifying way (just over 4% of cases; see Table 1b). Conversely, the qualifying construction [DET *espèce de* N] is frequent (over 63% of cases; see Table 1c).

In slightly more than 39% of cases, the structure [DET N$_{TAX}$ *de* N] has a typifying interpretation. It should be immediately noted that this construction is not attested with *espèce* in the corpora (see Table 1c), an interesting observation in that it provides the first argument in favour of a typifying construction distinct from the classifying and qualifying constructions.[12] Conversely, the typifying interpretation is the preferred interpretation of the structure [DET *genre de* N] with 81.29% of occurrences (see Table 1b). It would seem that there is a certain distribution of interpretations between *genre* and *espèce*: *genre* for the typifying interpretation and *espèce* for the qualifying interpretation.[13] Except in the WIK corpus where the typifying interpretation represents only 16.67% of the occurrences of the structure [DET *genre de* N], this interpretation is largely predominant in the other corpora (92.28% excluding the WIK corpus).

3 The classifying construction

The classifying construction provides a means to extract one or more subclasses within a bigger category. This corresponds to the original taxonomic use which has spread to everyday language (Mihatsch 2007, 2016). Example (1) illustrates this construction, as does the following:

---

[12] Despite the absence of *espèce* in the construction, I will maintain the more inclusive [DET N$_{TAX}$ *de* N] notation, as other nouns than *genre* can be used in the construction; this is the case, for example, for *sorte*, *style*, or *type*, which will not be discussed in this work, although it will be clear that most of the analysis proposed here could easily be applied to them (see Mihatsch 2007, 2016).
[13] This trend is confirmed by the typifying construction [X (*du*) *genre* Y] from which *espèce* is also excluded (see Chauveau-Thoumelin 2018, 2020, chap. 4).

(4) Nous distinguons **trois espèces principales d'adverbes**, du point de vue sémantique. (BU, § 956: 1233).
'We distinguish **three main kinds of adverbs**, from a semantic point of view'

Here too, the construction offers the possibility of defining three subcategories within the ADVERB category.

In the first half of this section, I will outline the formal properties that characterize the classifying construction (determination, agreement, modification; Section 3.1) before, in the second half, focusing on the types of classification that emerge in the corpora (Section 3.2).

3.1 Formal properties

3.1.1 Determination

Each of the [DET N_{TAX} de N] constructions shows preferences concerning the types of determiners it can host. The classifying construction, unlike the other two, does not exhibit any real constraints; the qualifying construction favours the indefinite (see Section 4.1), and the typifying construction the demonstrative (see Section 5.1).

Table 2: Types of determiners attested in the classifying construction.

DET		LEM	FRA	EUR	WIK	DOC	ALL	ALL (%)
Definite	Article	10	2	20	12	6	50	12.35
	demonstrative	3	1	0	2	2	8	1.97
Indefinite	Possessive	0	1	0	0	0	1	0.25
	Article	15	16	5	221	4	261	64.44
	numeral	16	8	2	13	1	40	9.88
	other indefinites	6	7	7	9	3	32	7.90
Ø		3	1	4	5	0	13	3.21
Total		53	36	38	262	16	405	100

Table 2 shows that the definite determiner appears in about 15% of cases, the indefinite in about 82%, and no determiner in slightly more than 3%. Within the definite determiner category, the definite article is the most frequently occurring; definite demonstratives and possessives are quite rare. Indefinites appear either as the article, the numeral, or other indefinites (e.g. *plusieurs* 'several', *certains* 'some', *différents* 'various').

Looking closely, the WIK corpus distinguishes itself from the other four: the indefinite article appears in 84.35% of cases in the WIK corpus, while it appears in an average of only 27.97% of cases in the other corpora. This can be explained by the very frequent presence of the following structure in the encyclopaedia: "X_N *est {un, une} {genre, espèce} de* Y_N *de la famille des* Z_N" 'X_N is a {genus, species} of Y_N in the Z_N family'. These analytic statements (Martin 1985) are true by definition and a comparison with reality is not needed to specify their truth conditions, contrary to synthetic statements such as *it is starting to rain*, which demand empirical verification in order to state whether they are true or false.

3.1.2 Agreement patterns

The three constructions under study behave differently with regard to agreement. Be it internal to the noun phrase (agreement of determiners, adjectives, etc.) or external (agreement of verbs, predicative adjectives, etc.), agreement patterns are stable for the classifying construction and do not show specificity: N_{TAX} is the head of the noun phrase, and, as expected by French syntactic norms, DET always agrees with it:

(5) Jo Haineaux. **Un autre genre de noblesse**. Celle des barons, des princes de l'arnaque et des rois de l'embrouille. (FRA, Patrick Pécherot, *Les Brouillards de la Butte*, 2001)
'Jo Haineaux. **Another kind of nobility**. That of barons, of fake princes and carry-on kings.'

Another argument backs up this analysis of N_{TAX} as head: the possibility of removing the sequence ⟨*de* N⟩ without rendering the sentence ungrammatical, provided the context is clear:

(6) Son efficacité chute au bout de quelques dizaines de minutes [...] et se limite à **certaines espèces (de moustiques)**. (LEM, 29/07/2015)
'Its effectiveness drops after about ten minutes [...] and is limited to **certain species (of mosquitos)**.'

Finally, and here again unsurprisingly, constituents external to the noun phrase also agree with N_{TAX}:

(7) **Une_F nouvelle_F espèce_F de dinosaure_M carnivore_M** datant d'environ 90 millions d'années a été découverte_F en Patagonie (Argentine) (LEM, 14/07/2016)
'**A new species of carnivorous dinosaur** has been discovered in Patagonia (Argentina)'

The fact that the determiner systematically agrees with N_{TAX}, that any external constituent also agrees with N_{TAX}, and that the sequence ⟨de N⟩ can be deleted, make N_{TAX} incontrovertibly the head of the noun phrase. This distinguishes the classifying construction from the qualifying and typifying constructions as will become clear in the following sections.

3.1.3 Modification

N_{TAX} can be easily modified. This is linked, once again, to N_{TAX}'s head status in the construction. In this respect, N does not behave differently.

(8) **Une nouvelle espèce de petit requin préhistorique** [. . .] a été découverte [. . .] (LEM, 22/01/2019)
'**A new species of small prehistoric shark** [. . .] has been discovered [. . .]'

Here, both N_{TAX} and N are modified.

These few remarks on the syntactic organization of the construction may seem obvious. Nevertheless, it is important to mention them here because, whether regarding determiners, agreement phenomena or modification, the functioning of the qualifying and typifying constructions studied in Sections 4 and 5 proves to be very different.

3.2 Types of classification: Specialized *vs* everyday language

The classifying interpretation of *genre* and *espèce* found in scientific taxonomies has spread widely in non-specialized language, and these two nouns –this is especially true for *genre*– are often found whenever there is a need to put entities into categories or classes. Considering the five corpora, the classifying construction is unsurprisingly predominantly used to classify living things (c. 87% of cases). In nearly 3% of the uses, the classification is related to the arts (literature,

cinema, painting, etc.).[14] Finally, in slightly more than 10% of the occurrences, the classification is neither scientific nor artistic but represents common classification. In order to identify and more precisely analyse the types of classification in the corpora, I have created two subcorpora:
- A specialized language subcorpus (SPE) made up of the WIK and EUR corpora which both favour scientific classification as they deal with genera and species. The former describes them, while the latter legislates about them (see Section 3.2.1).
- A general language subcorpus (GEN) made up of the LEM, FRA, and DOC corpora, which, even though they sometimes deal with scientific topics (zoology especially), contain texts written in non-specialized language (see Section 3.2.2).[15]

3.2.1 Classification in specialized language

In standard taxonomy, the genus and the species constitute the two lower ranks of the hierarchy. The species (e.g. *Canis lupus*) is a division of the genus (e.g. *Canis*), the genus a division of the family (e.g. *Canidae*), and so on until the kingdom (e.g. *Animalia*). *Genre* and *espèce* are naturally very frequent in the WIK corpus with a classifying interpretation (97.33% of cases). There is another classifying use, specific to *genre* this time, which concerns aesthetic genres: literature, cinema, painting, etc. This use represents 6 of the 86 occurrences of the classifying [DET *genre de* N] construction:

(9) Un *Immram* [...] est **un genre de contes** de la mythologie celtique irlandaise [...] (Wikipédia, s.v. Immram)
'An immram is **a genre of tales** from Irish Celtic mythology [...]'

This use does not represent a scientific classification of the same nature. Nevertheless, the genres, whether literary, cinematographic or pictorial, correspond to precise definitions; they are codified by their practitioners and commentators, and in this respect, differ from the common classification found in everyday language.

---

14 This use is specific to *genre*.
15 I do not consider either the SPE subcorpus or the GEN subcorpus to be representative of specialized and general language respectively. The subdivision of corpora is somewhat arbitrary but nevertheless convenient for the demonstration made here.

3.2.2 Classification in everyday language

Needless to say, in the GEN subcorpus, there are uses that pertain to scientific classification and the arts (literature, music, painting, etc.). However, contrary to the SPE subcorpus, no occurrences of [DET *genre de* N] are related to scientific classification; the construction is used exclusively for the arts and for common classification. Except with the arts, the classifying construction [DET *genre de* N] always correspond to non-scientific classification, which makes it potentially arbitrary, as in (1) where *genre* provides a means of creating two categories of fraud. The speaker could have used *type* or even *sorte* to achieve the same goal. *Espèce* can also be used to classify in non-specialized language, but this usage is much rarer:

(10) Or, Diesel fait partie de **cette nouvelle espèce de labels** qui fait figure d'alternative entre luxe et petits prix. (LEM, 07/04/2014)
'Now, Diesel has become part of **this new kind of label** that is an alternative between luxury and low prices.'

This view on taxonomies is undoubtedly partial, as it is limited to the five sources of my corpus. The following observations may nevertheless be made:
– Scientific classification with *espèce* is present in both specialized and non-specialized language (e.g. *cette espèce de macaque* 'this species of macaque'); with *genre*, the classification of living things seems to be limited to the specialized language (e.g. *un genre d'insectes lépidoptères* 'a genus of lepidopterous insects'), while classification in the field of arts –specific to *genre*– is found in both types of discourse (e.g. *un genre de contes* 'a genre of tales').
– Non-scientific classification is mainly the prerogative of *genre* (e.g. *deux genres de fraude* 'two types of fraud'). It is much rarer with *espèce* (e.g. *diverses espèces d'orchestres* 'various kinds of orchestras'; *trois espèces principales d'adverbes* 'three main kinds of adverbs').

Generally speaking, whether in the scientific field with *genre* and *espèce*, or in the artistic fields with *genre*, the classes pre-exist; the genera, genres and species in question are precisely defined and belong to a larger taxonomy. It seems that with common classification, classes do not pre-exist, but that it is the structure that creates the class, and, at the same time, allows it to be defined (e.g. *deux genres de fraude* 'two types of fraud').

Let us now move on to the qualifying construction where N_{TAX} plays the role of an approximator – an adaptor more specifically – by blurring the membership relation between an entity and a category.

4 The qualifying construction

The qualifying construction, as in (2), is the archetypal hedge. It constitutes a prominent linguistic strategy for speakers to make their discourse vague. Here is another example:

(11) c'est peut etre une sous couche pour empecher l'humidité! **un genre de peinture poreuse** qui permet au mur de respirer (DOC, 14/07/2010)
'It migt be an undercoat to prevent dampness! **a kind of porous paint** that allows the wall to breathe'

The construction signals that *porous paint* may not be the appropriate term, as the nature of the coating in question has not been identified with confidence.

In this section, I will focus on the formal properties of the qualifying construction, thereby distinguishing it from the classifying one. I will then make some comments on the semantics of N in this construction, particularly its frequent association with metaphor.

4.1 Formal properties

4.1.1 Determination

As can be seen in Table 3, which shows the frequency of the various types of determiners in the qualifying construction, DET is most of the time an indefinite (77.74% of cases):

(12) [...] il reste **des espèces d'auréoles** sur la plaque que je viens d'utiliser et qui ne part que difficilement. (DOC, 30/09/2009)
'[...] there are **some sort of stains** remaining on the hob after use and they are difficult to remove'

Table 3: Types of determiners attested in the qualifying construction.

DET		LEM	FRA	EUR	WIK	DOC	ALL	ALL (%)
Definite	Article	1	26	0	0	18	45	8.35
	demonstrative	6	32	0	0	12	50	9.28
	possessive	1	4	0	0	5	10	1.85
	Article	37	188	0	6	185	416	77.18

Table 3 (continued)

DET		LEM	FRA	EUR	WIK	DOC	ALL	ALL (%)
Indefinite	Numeral	0	0	0	0	2	2	0.37
	other indefinites	0	0	0	0	1	1	0.19
Ø		0	6	0	0	9	15	2.78
Total		45	256	0	6	232	539	100

To a lesser extent, the definite is also found (19.48%), be it the article,

(13) J'ai eu droit à la pesé sur 2 balances : une à l'ancienne avec **les espèces de barres** et une qui donne le gras et l'eau contenu dans le corps. (DOC, 09/04/2012)
'I got myself the weighing on two scales: one old-fashioned with **the kinds of bars** and one that gives the fat and water contained in the body.'

the demonstrative,

(14) Il est toujours là, l'arrêt du 96, avec son panneau, immuable. L'habituel poteau surmonté de **cette espèce de petite barrique**, [...] (FRA, Marie Sizun, *Éclats d'enfance*, 2009)
'It's still there, the 96 stop, with its sign, immutable. The usual pole surmounted by **this sort of small barrel**, [...]'

or the possessive:

(15) j'ai essayé plusieurs fois les papillottes jusqu'au jours où je suis tombée sur la bonne recette à force d'expérimenter (à chaque fois le poisson gardait **son espèce de gout de poisson cru** mais plus maintenant) (DOC, 26/05/2007)
'[...] (each time the fish kept **its kind of raw fish taste** but not anymore)'

In the data, the definite article does not have a specific value, but has "une présupposition existentielle de totalité" 'an existential presupposition of totality' to take up Kleiber's (1983) phrase, that is to say, the referent denoted by the construction is (i) identified within a set, and (ii) assumed to be known by the addressee. It is worth noting that the definite is possible with *genre* but only if it is a possessive; the definite article and the demonstrative in combination with *genre* always lead to a typifying interpretation (see Section 5.1.1). Finally, in specific syntactic contexts, DET is missing; this is particularly the case when the construction is a complement of certain prepositions, especially *en*,

(16) dans les magasins de bricolage il y en a **en espece de papier maché** a decorer [...] (DOC, 28/05/2009)
'In DIY shops, some of them are **made of some sort of papier-mâché** to be decorated [...]'

or is in apposition:

(17) [...] on voyait de loin sa baraque au bout de la route, sur la plaine de Waterloo, **espèce de chalet de sorcière illuminé comme un Magritte fameux**, et authentique celui-là. (FRA, Olivier Rolin, *Tigre en papier*, 2002)
'[...] we could see his hut from afar at the end of the road, on the Waterloo plain, **a kind of witch's cottage lit up like a famous Magritte**, and an authentic one.'

4.1.2 Agreement patterns

The study of agreement patterns allows to better identify the head of the construction, which tends to no longer be N_{TAX}, as with the classifying construction, but N. I will particularly focus on agreement within the noun phrase, a distinctive feature of this construction.

The presence of a masculine determiner in front of the feminine noun *espèce* is a well-known phenomenon. It has been attested since the very beginning of the 18th century by reference books (DHLF; BU), or even earlier, considering example (18). This use is very frequent in modern spoken French but is also well attested in writing. Nonetheless, it is considered wrong by traditional grammars and regularly condemned in articles with such titles as "5-top-grammatical-errors-you-need-to-stop-making". Here is a quick overview of agreement "mistakes" in the French literature:

(18) [...] je les menai avec **un$_M$ espèce$_F$ de triomphe$_M$** à l'hôtel de ville. (FRA, Jean-François de Retz, *Mémoires*, 1679)
'[...] I led them with **some kind of triumph** to the town hall.'

(19) [...] un lacis de cordes de roseau forme, dans la partie inférieure, **un$_M$ espèce$_F$ de filet$_M$** où l'on place les malles et les paquets. (FRA, Théophile Gautier, *Voyage en Espagne*, 1843)
'[...] a network of cords made of reeds form, in the lower part of it, **a sort of net** in which the trunks and packages are stowed.'

(20) Je fis état de mon extase devant l'œuvre Go-Tobaienne [...] en **un$_M$ espèce$_F$ de sonnet$_M$ en prose maladroite mais réfléchie** [...] (FRA, Jacques Roubaud, *La Bibliothèque de Warburg. Version mixte*, 2002)
'I stated my ecstasy in front of the Go-Tobaian works in **a kind of sonnet written in clumsy but well-thought-out prose**'

This use is so frequent, that many other examples could be given; here is one more of them, heard on the radio:

(21) Elle [George Sand] [...] va ajouter à la lettre **une$_F$ espèce$_F$ de un$_M$ espèce$_F$ de petit texte$_M$ qu'elle a composé**, comme ça, [...] (France Culture, 16/06/2016)[16]
'[...] very often she would add to the letter **a kind of small text** she composed, like that, [...]'

It is interesting to note that in (21), the speaker corrects himself, not to rectify an alleged agreement mistake, but on the contrary to make the indefinite determiner *un* agree with the noun *texte*, so that the speaker self-corrects in the direction of the "faulty" variant.

Despite its ubiquity, this use is held in contempt by purists, who see it as an unacceptable agreement mistake. The Académie française, ambassador of linguistic conservatism if ever there was one, makes this very clear. In a blog article about *espèce* under the heading "*Emplois fautifs*" 'faulty uses' one can read:

> Le mot *Espèce* est féminin, et doit le rester lorsqu'il est suivi d'un complément (*Espèce de...*), quel que soit le genre de ce complément. On dira *Une espèce de camion* comme *une espèce de charrette*, *Une espèce de voyou* comme *une espèce de canaille*. (*Dire, ne pas dire*, blog de l'Académie française, s.v. *espèce*) (http://www.academie-francaise.fr/espece; accessed 1st May 2019).

---

[16] "George Sand : Dix-huit mille lettres !", *La Compagnie des auteurs*, France Culture, 16/06/2016. https://www.franceculture.fr/emissions/la-compagnie-des-auteurs/george-sand-44-dix-huit-mille-lettres (accessed 02 February 2022).

[The word *Espèce* is feminine and must remain so when followed by a complement (*Espèce de*. . .), whatever the gender of this complement. We will say *Une*$_F$ *espèce*$_F$ *de camion*$_M$ 'a kind of truck' like *une*$_F$ *espèce*$_F$ *de charrette*$_F$ 'a kind of cart', *Une*$_F$ *espèce*$_F$ *de voyou*$_M$ 'a kind of thug' like *une*$_F$ *espèce*$_F$ *de canaille*$_F$ 'a kind of scoundrel'.]

The *Banque de dépannage linguistique*, published by the Office québécois de la langue française,[17] makes a similar pronouncement.[18] This would be true if *espèce* were a noun and the sequence ⟨*de* N⟩ its complement (e.g. *une espèce de portail* 'a kind of gate'). However, it is hard to see how this could be possible. If it were the case, we should be able to,

i) insert a modifier (of *espèce*) between *espèce* and *de* (see Section 4.1.3):

(22) #on voyait une espèce nouvelle de portail
      'one could see a new kind of gate'

ii) make an adjective or a participle agree with *espèce*:

(23) a. #on voyait une$_F$ espèce$_F$ de portail$_M$ très brillante$_F$
          'one could see a very bright kind of gate'
      b. #une$_F$ espèce$_F$ de portail$_M$ a été découverte$_F$
          'a kind of gate has been discovered'

iii) remove the sequence ⟨*de* N⟩:

(24) #on voyait une espèce qui brillait
      'one could see a kind that shined'

iv) refer to N$_{TAX}$ anaphorically:

(25) #on voyait une$_F$ espèce$_F$ de portail$_M$; celle-ci$_F$ brillait
      'one could see a kind of gate; it shined'

Conversely, if *espèce* were a noun and ⟨*de* N⟩ its complement, we should not be able to,

---

17 Quebec Board of the French Language.
18 http://bdl.oqlf.gouv.qc.ca/bdl/gabarit_bdl.asp?t1=1&id=2743 (accessed 24 April 2019).

i) remove the sequence ⟨*espèce de*⟩:

(26) on voyait un portail qui brillait
'one could see a gate that shined'

ii) refer to N anaphorically:

(27) on voyait un$_M$/une$_F$ espèce$_F$ de portail$_M$; celui-ci$_M$ brillait
'one could see a kind of gate; it shined'

Examples (22) to (25) while being well-formed do not elicit the correct interpretation, whereas in examples (26) and (27) the meaning is preserved.

The Académie makes *espèce* the head of the noun phrase, even though in the construction [DET N$_{TAX}$ de N] it is N that undoubtedly takes on this function. It is clear that within a qualifying interpretation the sequence ⟨*espèce de*⟩ forms a unit resulting from a lexicalization process whose role is to modify N. The "noun" *espèce* has lost its nominal status and with the preposition forms a kind of "adjectival phrase" (*locution adjectivale*; Dufaye 2014). The same phenomenon can be observed in English (e.g. Doyen and Davidse 2009; Brems and Davidse 2010; Brems 2011), except that the lexicalization process, much more advanced, materializes graphically: *kind of* and *sort of* can be written as *kinda* and *sorta* respectively:

(28) The world-famous Queen show, **It's A Kinda Magic**, is back, bringing you the best of the band's legendary music. (https://randfonteinherald.co.za/)

(29) But the spicy vinegar sauce is a must if you want **a sorta 'real' Carolina BBQ taste**. (https://fr.foursquare.com)

In French, this agreement phenomenon is not peculiar to *espèce* but rather extends to the whole qualifying construction. Authors like Roché (1997), Rouget (1997), or Mihatsch (2016) mention this agreement when other nouns than *espèce* are involved in the construction:

(30) ... **le$_M$ sorte$_F$ de puzzle$_M$** que constitue ... (France Musique, 16/09/1994, quoted by Roché [1997: 71])
'**the kind of puzzle** constituted by ...'

(31) [...] c'est **une**~F~ **genre**~M~ **de double contrainte**~F~ qui peut vous faire glisser sous votre douche. (France 2, 05/03/2016)[19]
 '[...] this is **a kind of double bind** that can make you slip in your shower.'

This phenomenon is very delicate to identify in written texts where we may wonder whether we are dealing with typing errors or intentional agreements, as in the following examples:

(32) Dans la chambre, **un**~M~ **espèce**~F~ **de bleu**~M~ **moche**, vieillot à souhait... [...] Et dans la salle de bain, je crois qu'il y a **un**~M~ **espèce**~F~ **de papier peint**~M~ qui a été peint justement lol, [...] (DOC, 07/09/2007)
 'In the bedroom, **a kind of ugly blue**, incredibly quaint... [...] And in the bathroom, I think there is **a kind of wallpaper** (lit. painted paper) which precisely has been painted lol, [...]

(33) Mais, il y a 10ans, je mangeais très mal, resto, junk ect... et je me suis tappé **une**~F~ **genre**~M~ **de gastro**~F~ qui m'a mis à terre, suivi d'**une**~F~ **genre**~M~ **de dépression**~F~ du à une anémie, [...] (DOC, 12/12/2006)
 'But, 10 years ago, I used to eat very badly: restaurants, junk food, etc. and I had **a kind of gastroenteritis** that knocked me down, followed by **a kind of depression** due to anaemia, [...]'

Typing errors are never to be excluded but considering the high frequency of this kind of agreement in the spoken language, we can safely assume these are intentional agreements.

While gender agreement between DET and N is considered wrong by purists, at least it is logical: it is only possible within the qualifying construction.[20] It is important to keep in mind that this phenomenon does not affect only *espèce*. Even though it is true that *espèce*'s initial vowel often leads to the blurring of grammatical gender, other N~TAX~ like *genre* or *sorte*, which start with a consonant sound, are also affected by this phenomenon.[21] Despite the relative low frequency of the qualifying construction with *genre* (see Table 1b), I am not convinced

---

19 Utterance pronounced without any hesitation. It was about the hospitalisation of the Minister of Labour following a domestic accident; she reportedly fell in her shower.
20 Agreement is also found in the quantifying construction omitted from this paper: *aucun espèce de remords* 'no remorse at all' (see Chauveau-Thoumelin 2020, chap. 5).
21 In many cases, the initial vowel of *espèce* causes the elision of the article or a liaison, thus blurring word boundaries and erasing its grammatical gender. For example, the feminine article *la* becomes *l'* in front of *espèce*, thus taking the same form as the elided masculine article *le*.

that gender agreement is less frequent with nouns like *genre* or *sorte* than with *espèce*. However, in order to check this, recent, voluminous and spontaneous oral corpora would be needed to identify the proportion of agreement between DET and N in non-ambiguous contexts, that is when the gender of N is different from the one of N_{TAX}, taking into account the overall frequency of these nouns in the constructions.

These observations about determination tend towards a strong argument to make N the head of the noun phrase, and the sequence ⟨N_{TAX} *de*⟩ a modifier of N. The study of modification within the construction tends to support this analysis.

4.1.3 Modification

According to my data, it seems that N_{TAX} is never pre- nor postmodified in the qualifying construction; a modifier on N_{TAX} always changes the interpretation:

(34) a. Je fais davantage appel à **une espèce de conscience supérieure**. (LEM, 22/05/2016)
      'I appeal more to **a kind of higher consciousness**.'
   b. Je fais davantage appel à **une nouvelle espèce de conscience supérieure**.
      'I appeal more to **a new kind of higher consciousness**.'

(35) a. Ils [les enfants] sont souvent pris d'**une espèce de vertige** quand [. . .] (LEM, 21/03/2016)
      'Children are often affected by **a kind of vertigo** when [. . .]'
   b. Ils sont souvent pris d'**une espèce encore inconnue de vertige** quand [. . .]
      'Children are often affected by **a still unknown kind of vertigo** when [. . .]'

Examples (34a) and (35a) have a qualifying interpretation. What it refers to is similar to a superior consciousness or a vertigo without being prototypical exemplars of these categories. With a modifier on *espèce* –examples (34b) and (35b)–, the reading becomes classifying; the construction thus refers to a subcategory of superior consciousness or vertigo.

Similarly, the demonstrative in front of a vowel, although spelled differently, is pronounced in the same way (i.e. [sɛt]) whether it is feminine (i.e. *cette*) or masculine (i.e. *cet*).

Unlike N_{TAX}, N can easily be modified:

(36) [Il] se rendit à la boulangerie et acheta toute la fournée de croissants. Enfin. . . de ce que la vendeuse, encore pétrie de sommeil, appelait des croissants. . . Un Parisien aurait dit « **vos genres de petites brioches courbées.** . . » (FRA, Anna Gavalda, *La Consolante*, 2008)
'He went to the bakery and bought the whole batch of croissants. Well. . . what the saleswoman, still asleep, called croissants. . . A Parisian would have said **"your kind of little curved brioches. . . ."**'

These examples seem to confirm that in the qualifying construction N_{TAX} can never be modified. The presence of a modifier on N_{TAX} always triggers a classifying reading of the construction. This backs up the analysis of N as head of the noun phrase; the sequence ⟨N_{TAX} de⟩ takes on the role of a kind of modifier of N and its possible complements.

4.2 Semantics of N and categorization

In the qualifying construction, two main types of use of N can be distinguished: non-metaphorical uses and metaphorical uses.

4.2.1 Non-metaphorical uses

In the case where N is not used metaphorically, it denotes a category with which the referent designated by the construction shares a certain number of properties; the sequence ⟨N_{TAX} de⟩ thus indicates that membership of the category is only partial. Very often, the non-prototypical nature of the referent is made explicit by N itself:

(37) [. . .] il existe **des espèces de palmes pour les mains** [. . .] qui réduisent la pression de l'eau et donc les douleurs. (DOC, 29/06/2011)
'there are **some kind of flippers for the hands** [. . .] which reduce the water pressure and therefore the pain'

The modifier *pour les mains* cancels an essential property of the flippers, that of being designed for the feet. The presence of N_{TAX} makes it easier to match N with the reality it designates.

4.2.2 Metaphorical uses

As for metaphorical uses, the metaphor can concern both the proper noun and the common noun:

(38) L'expression « coureur de bois » est bien connue au Québec, où elle évoque **une espèce de Jack Kerouac** avant l'heure, sillonnant l'Amérique en canot. (LEM, 17/02/2016)
'The expression "coureur de bois" (trapper, lit. runner of the woods) is well known in Quebec, where it refers to **a kind of Jack Kerouac** before his time, travelling across America in a canoe.'

(39) Ce sont des questions qui parfois tournent dans ma tête. **Des espèces de mouches** que je repousse. (FRA, Mathieu Simonet, *Les Carnets blancs*, 2010)
'These are questions that sometimes turn in my head. **Some kind of flies** I push away.'

According to *Le Monde*, *coureur de bois* 'lit. runner of the woods' appeared around 1672; it was then used to refer to a wanderer. The link between the two becomes obvious. It is the hedge *espèce de*, which conveys approximation, that facilitates the comparison between the wanderer of the 17th century and the author of *On the Road*, a book that relates his American peregrinations. The same is true in (39), where the interpretation that the referent denoted by the construction is not really a N is already available. Here again, *espèce de* only makes the connection between the two easier.

The last construction, the typifying construction, is interesting as it displays characteristics of both the classifying and qualifying constructions.

5 The typifying construction

Similar to the classifying construction, the typifying construction helps define a category; similar to the qualifying construction, the borders of the category prove to be fuzzy, thus leading to an approximative reading. Example (3) is one instance of the typifying construction; example (40) is another:

(40) Sinon pour le magnétiseur je demanderais à ma mère très portée sur *la médecine genre ostéophate et compagnie* pour qu'elle me conseil une bonne adresse de magnétiseur. [...] Ma mère est très portée sur **ce genre**

de pratique, elle tiens ça de ma grand mère qui est à fond dedant... (DOC, 11/01/2006)[22]

'As for the magnetic healer, I'll ask my mother, who is very fond of *medicine like osteopath and the like*, to advise me on a good magnetic healer. [...] My mother is very fond of **this kind of practice**; she gets it from my grandmother who is really into it.'

From this example, two characteristics of the typifying construction emerge:
- Identification of a category (here, ALTERNATIVE MEDICINE) on the basis of one or more individuals explicitly or implicitly mentioned in the context (here, magnetism and osteopathy, through the use of the practitioners' title, i.e. magnetic healer and osteopath). These individuals, de facto members of the category, are identifiable from the context, and because they share a number of salient properties, contribute to the emergence of the category.
- Approximation as to the extension of the category: in addition to magnetism and osteopathy implicitly mentioned in the context, the other members of the category remain undetermined, although inferable, at least in part, by the reader (e.g. acupuncture, homeopathy).

Through a kind of resumptive anaphora (Maillard 1974), encapsulating several elements of context (i.e. medicine, magnetic healer, osteopath) under the label *practice*, the construction identifies a category of alternative medicine. The following sections show how this semantic functioning is accompanied by formal characteristics that are specific to the construction and thus distinguishes the typifying construction from the other two.

5.1 Formal properties

5.1.1 Determination

As far as types of determiners are concerned, the typifying construction is the most restrictive of all (see Table 4). The only determiners encountered in the corpora are the demonstrative *ce* 'this', the definite article *le* 'the', and the interrogative *quel* 'what, which'. The majority of examples involve the demonstrative; the definite article and the interrogative are proportionally much less frequent.

---

[22] *la médecine genre ostéophate et compagnie* is an example of another typifying construction involving *genre*, the [X (*du*) *genre* Y] construction (see Chauveau-Thoumelin 2018, 2020, chap. 4).

Table 4: Types of determiners attested in the typifying construction.

DET		LEM	FRA	EUR	WIK	DOC	ALL	ALL (%)
Definite	Article	16	32	0	2	15	65	10.76
	Demonstrative	107	146	28	16	204	501	82.95
Indefinite		0	0	0	0	0	0	0
Interrogative	*quel* 'what, which'	3	8	6	0	21	38	6.29
Ø		0	0	0	0	0	0	0
Total		**126**	**186**	**34**	**18**	**240**	**604**	**100**

Ce

The use of the demonstrative *ce* 'this' is the most frequent in the data (c. 83% of cases):

(41) Adamsberg s'agenouilla et enfonça le portable dans l'oreille du chat. Il avait connu un berger qui téléphonait à sa brebis de tête pour maintenir son équilibre psychologique et, depuis, **ce genre de choses** ne le surprenait plus. (FRA, Fred Vargas, *Dans les bois éternels*, 2006)
'Adamsberg knelt down and stuck the phone into the cat's ear. He had known a shepherd who used to phone his head ewe to maintain her psychological balance and, since then, **this kind of thing** no longer surprised him.'

In example (41), *ce genre de choses* 'this kind of thing' refers to a category of extravagant behaviours such as that of the cat owner who insists on speaking to her cat on the phone, or the shepherd who used to phone one of his ewes, concerned with her psychological balance. This use of *ce genre* 'this kind' can be easily substituted by anaphoric *tel* 'such' when it is placed immediately before the noun phrase (Van Peteghem 1995; Riegel 1997):

(42) a. Jean est un étudiant zélé. Un **tel** étudiant ne peut qu'obtenir des succès. (Van Peteghem 1995: 63)
'Jean is a zealous student. Such a student can only be successful.'
b. **Ce genre d'étudiant** ne peut qu'obtenir des succès.
'**This kind of student** can only be successful.'

However, the presence of both the demonstrative *ce* and *genre* is not on its own a strong enough criterion to identify the typifying construction and exclude the classifying construction:

(43) Il s'adonna d'abord à la peinture à l'huile, puis à la fresque ; mais la nécessité où l'on est dans **ce dernier genre de peinture** de terminer très vite, [. . .] (WIK, *s.v.* Joseph Werner)
'He first devoted himself to oil painting, then to fresco; but the necessity in **this latter genre of painting** to finish very quickly, [. . .]'

This is an instance of the classifying construction: a subcategory FRESQUE 'fresco' is identified within the bigger category TECHNIQUE PICTURALE 'pictorial technique' which also subsumes the subcategory PEINTURE À L'HUILE 'oil painting'. Here, *ce genre de peinture* 'this kind of painting' is not used to refer to "paintings like that" but rather to the fresco as a pictorial genre. The fact that there is an adjective (i.e. *dernier* 'last') modifying *genre* is a good indication of the classifying reading.[23]

Le

The structure involving the definite article differs slightly from that of the demonstrative. The presence of the definite article almost always goes hand in hand with a restrictive relative clause or with the preposition *à* introducing an infinitive:

(44) En même temps, à la base, je n'étais pas **le genre de mec qui aime se mettre en avant, ou affronter la presse**, donc cela m'a permis de faire mon chemin tranquillement. (LEM, 22/05/2014)
'On the other hand, basically, I wasn't **the kind of guy who likes to put himself forward, or face the press**, so it allowed me to make my way quietly.'

(45) Selon Sandy Guerra-Cline, éditrice au *Star-Telegram* et cliente régulière du restaurant, « il n'était pas **le genre de personne à parler d'armes à feu ou de choses violentes** ». (LEM, 17/09/2013)
'According to Sandy Guerra-Cline, *Star-Telegram* editor and regular restaurant customer, "he wasn't **the type of person to talk about guns or violent things**".'

Contrary to the anaphoric value of *ce genre de*, *le genre de* introduces a number of properties (i.e. *qui aime se mettre en avant* 'who likes to be in the forefront', *affronter la presse* 'to face the press'; *à parler d'armes à feu* 'to talk about firearms',

---

23 A parallel should be noted between [*ce genre de* N], e.g. *ce genre d'opérations* 'these kinds of operations', and [DET N *de ce genre*], e.g. *les opérations de ce genre* 'operations of this kind' (Rosier 2002; Mihatsch 2016). The semantic difference between the two is subtle, but both have the same typifying interpretation (see also Chauveau-Thoumelin 2020, chap. 4).

de choses violentes 'about violent things') allowing the speaker to describe more precisely the category already set by the nouns *mec* 'guy' and *personne* 'person'.[24]

Quel

Finally, instances of the construction with the interrogative *quel* 'what, which' have an ambiguous function. The question *quel genre de* N ? almost always offers two interpretations: either one questions the subclass (classifying interpretation), or one questions the type (typifying interpretation). The choice for one of these readings is left to the addressee, even though most of the time the scales are tipped in favour of the typifying interpretation. The expected answer is not so much the mention of a well-defined subclass, as the mention of examples from which it will be possible to deduce a category:

(46) A : Pour le son d'avoine on en trouve dans **quels genres de magasins** ?
B : en mag bio, t'en trouves a coup sur, et aussi svt dans les rayons diététiques des grandes surfaces (DOC, 29/12/2006)
'A: As for the oat bran, in **what kinds of shops** can you find it?
B: In organic shops you'll find some for sure, and also often in the health-food departments of supermarkets'

Here, A is looking for places where he or she may find oat bran. Organic shops and the health-food departments of supermarkets are two possibilities suggested by B. These are examples of places where A may certainly find oat bran, but at the same time, identify a "type" of shop; the health-food or organic department of a mini-market, or the market stall of an organic cereal grower are in principle not ruled out. The following example is even clearer:

---

24 The sequence ⟨*de* N⟩ can be removed if N is recoverable from the context: *Or Ida Rubinstein est formidable, c'est **le genre de fille** qui part chasser le lion en Afrique quand elle s'ennuie, **le genre** qui vous appelle en pleine nuit d'Amsterdam pour vous dire à quel point, ce matin, vu de l'avion qui la ramenait de Bali, le soleil se levait élégamment sur l'Acropole, **le genre** qui embarque sur son yacht vers l'autre bout de la terre en compagnie de ses singes et de sa panthère apprivoisée* [. . .]
'Now, Ida Rubinstein is fantastic, she is **the kind of girl** who goes lion-hunting in Africa when she is bored, **the kind** who calls you in the middle of the night from Amsterdam to tell you how elegantly, seen from the plane taking her back from Bali this morning, the sun was rising on the Acropolis, **the kind** who sets sail on her yacht towards the other side of the world, accompanied by her monkeys and her tamed panther [. . .]' (FRA, Jean Echenoz, *Ravel*, 2006).

(47) Vu ce qui précède, je voudrais poser à la Commission les questions suivantes :
   1. La Commission a-t-elle l'intention de procéder à la mise à jour et à la valorisation des données existantes relatives aux îles, aux régions montagneuses et aux régions à faible densité de population dans un avenir proche ?
   2. **Quel genre de mesures** envisage-t-elle de proposer par la suite pour ces régions ? (EUR, 11/07/2006)
   'In the light of the above, I would like to ask the Commission the following questions:
   1. Does the Commission plan to proceed with the update and development of the existing data relative to islands, mountain regions and sparsely populated regions in the near future?
   2. **What kind of measures** is the Commission planning to propose afterwards for these regions?'

It is very likely that the member of Parliament asking this question is looking for examples of practical measures: the setting-up of a dedicated team out in the field, additional subsidies granted to local authorities, etc. These examples expected as an answer never exclude any other convergent measures, nor that measures selected at the start may be replaced by more appropriate ones when the project gets under way; the main thing is that the aim remains the same: "update and development of the existing data relative to islands, mountain regions and sparsely populated regions".

Without trying to make [*quel genre de* N ?] a typifying construction at all costs (from this point of view, the constructions [*ce genre de* N] and [*le genre de* N] are more clearly so), the fact remains that a typifying interpretation is always possible, and that outside a context in which there is an established classification, it is even the only one that holds. By asking the question *quel genre de N* ?, one is trying to obtain answers, exemplary answers in a way, and all these examples chosen by the speaker because of certain shared properties offer the necessary elements for the identification of a category.[25]

---

[25] It is interesting to note that *quel* and *tel* answer each other, the first being the interrogative counterpart of the second, which, as we have seen, constitutes a gloss of choice to render the typifying value of [*ce genre de* N] (see Section 5.1.1, § *Ce*): one questions the type with *quel* (e.g. *Quel genre de mesures envisagez-vous ?* 'What kind of measures are you considering?') and one refers to it anaphorically with *tel* (e.g. *De telles mesures sont nécessaires* 'Such measures are necessary').

5.1.2 Modification

In the data, *genre* is very seldom modified. Among the 604 instances of the typifying construction, I counted only 11 cases of modification (1.82%), 10 of which were of the structure [*le genre de* N]. The modifier applied to *genre* is invariably *même* 'same'. (48) is the only example in my corpus with the demonstrative *ce* combined with the use of *même*, while (49) illustrates the modification with the definite article *le*.

(48) Je comprends que tu aies des problèmes et c'est bien que tu te fasses aider, seulement si les autres ont **ce même genre de problème** et posent des questions, laisse les faire, [...] (DOC, 10/10/2005)
'I understand that you have problems and it's fine that you want help, but if others have **the same kind of problem** and ask questions, let them do so, [...]'

(49) Le nom de la société, présentée comme « un agent de change et une chambre de compensation », avait déjà été évoqué dans le cadre de l'affaire Bettencourt, où elle aurait réalisé **le même genre de « service »** pour la milliardaire, héritière de L'Oréal. (LEM, 19/11/2014)
'The name of the company, which was presented as "a stockbroker's and a clearing house", had already been mentioned in the Bettencourt case, where she reportedly performed **the same kind of "service"** for the billionaire, L'Oréal's heiress.'

In (48), the analysis is not any different from above (e.g. 41): *ce même genre de problèmes* points to a category of problems educed on the basis of examples given by a net surfer –weight problems, to be specific. The anaphoric reference is clear. A difference should be noted between example (49) and examples of *le genre de* N seen above. Here, *le genre de* N appears without a relative clause. It is the presence of *même* which gives this usage an anaphoric value: *ce (même) genre de service* would have been equally acceptable without modifying the utterance meaning.

In traditional grammar, *même* belongs to the category of indefinite determiners-adjectives. For the detail of its syntactic and semantic properties, I refer the reader to Van Peteghem (1997a, 1997b). Let us keep in mind that:
- *même* is not a "true" determiner as it cannot be used on its own as such: *Jean n'a lu aucun livre* 'Jean has not read any book' vs **Jean et Luc ont lu même livre* '*Jean and Luc read same book' (Van Peteghem 1997b: 62);

- *même* is not a "true" adjective either (Van Peteghem 1997a, 1997b; Noailly 1999): it cannot be predicative (**Elles sont mêmes '*They are same'), and can only be placed in front of the noun in this use;
- Finally, *même* is not a true indefinite as it does not express quantification as indefinites usually do (e.g. *un* 'a, one', *deux* 'two', *plusieurs* 'several', *quelques* 'some, a few').

Let us take a moment to consider modification in all three constructions. First, it should be recalled that N_{TAX} in the classifying construction can easily be modified, whereas in the qualifying construction it is never modified. In this respect, the typifying construction can be found in between, allowing for N_{TAX} to be modified but in a very restrictive way. As for N, nothing prevents it from being modified: regardless of the construction (classifying, qualifying, typifying) and even though N is not always the head of the phrase, it always behaves as a "true" noun, and can thus be easily accompanied by modifiers. On the other hand, what is important to note is that this modification does not occur to the same extent for each of these constructions. Modification is quite common in the classifying construction (25.06% of modified N) and very frequent in the qualifying construction (54.83% of modified N). However, in the typifying construction, N is only modified in 16.33% of cases. The fact that N is seldom modified in the typifying construction is interesting. It seems that the use of a modifier is, in a way, rendered superfluous by the actual functioning of the construction: it does not have a denominative function; its role is merely to refer, under a label (N), to a certain number of individuals mentioned in the discourse. Conversely, the qualifying construction makes great use of modifiers; its function has to do with vague denomination. Compare (50) and (51):

(50) François-Marie-Louis-Alexandre Gobinet, connu sous le nom de Franck, photographie la place Vendôme, avec les débris de la colonne écrasée, comme **une espèce de grand corps monstrueux et tronçonné**, à côté de son socle. (FRA, Michelle Grangaud, *Calendrier des poètes*, 2001)
'François-Marie-Louis-Alexandre Gobinet, known as Franck, photographs Place Vendôme with the remains of the crushed column, as **a kind of large, monstrous and cut-up body**, next to its base.'

(51) Jeudi 13 octobre, lors d'un meeting de soutien à Hillary Clinton, et évoquant les propos obscènes de Donald Trump, qui assurait dans une conversation de 2005 que sa position d'homme riche et célèbre l'autorisait à « tout faire aux femmes » y compris « les saisir par la chatte », la première dame des

États-Unis s'est inquiétée de voir « nos enfants entendre **ce genre de chose** quand on allume la télé ». (LEM, 21/10/2016)

'On Thursday, October 13th, at a meeting in support of Hillary Clinton, and referring to the obscene remarks of Donald Trump, who assured in a 2005 conversation that his position as a rich and famous man allowed him to "do anything to women" including to "grab them by the pussy," the first lady of the United States worried that "our children would hear **this kind of thing** when we turn on the TV'.

Example (50) shows an instance of the qualifying construction. Wishing to best describe Franck's photographic reproduction of the Vendôme Column (or at least what is left of it after its destruction ordered by the Commune in 1871),[26] the author uses the noun phrase *une espèce de grand corps monstrueux et tronçonné* 'a kind of large, monstrous and cut up body' in which the noun *corps* is accompanied by the approximator *espèce de* and no fewer than three adjectives. In example (51) which illustrates the typifying construction, the abjection of Donald Trump's behaviour towards women does not require any adjectives; the phrase *ce genre de chose* is enough to refer to the demonstration of his extreme and obscene behaviour mentioned in the previous context. Even the noun does not communicate much; *chose* works as a mere "shell", to borrow Schmid's (2000) metaphor, which helps build the anaphora. The use of this kind of noun is characteristic of the typifying construction; I return to this issue in Section 5.2.1.

5.1.3 Agreement patterns

The study of agreement patterns, both internal and external to the noun phrase, clearly shows how the typifying construction differentiates itself from the classifying and qualifying constructions.

5.1.3.1 Internal agreement

In 411 cases out of 604 (68.04%), it is impossible to determine if DET agrees with N_{TAX} or N: either because the whole phrase is in the masculine singular (e.g. *ce genre de trouble* 'this kind of trouble'), in the plural (e.g. *ces genres de mobilisations* 'these kinds of mobilizations'), or because N is invariable (e.g. *ce genre de cas* 'this kind of case'). Out of 192 occurrences (31.62%) where agreement is clear, DET

---

[26] See https://commons.wikimedia.org/wiki/File:Franck,_Colonne_Vendôme,_1871.jpg for Franck's photography (accessed 27 April 2019).

agrees with *genre* in 191 of them. In English, Denison (2002, 2005, 2011) observes cases of a plural agreement between the determiner and the second noun even though the type noun remains singular (e.g. *these sort of skills, those sort of creatures, these kind of reasonings*). He makes this number mismatch the main criterion to identify what he calls the postdeterminer construction, which is very similar to the typifying construction under study.[27] This example of number mismatch occurs only once in the data:

(52) **Quels genre de soins** *font-ils ?* (DOC, 08/04/2005)
 '**What kind of care** do they offer?'

Doyen and Davidse (2009) also found *ces genre de conneries* 'this kind of bullshit' in their corpus, but these two examples are too rare to show any tendency. Oral corpora would not help us either, insofar as *genre* and *genres* are both pronounced [ʒɑ̃ʁ].

5.1.3.2 External agreement

The external constituent (e.g. verb, adjective, participle) sometimes agrees with N_{TAX}, as in (53), and sometimes with N, as in (54):

(53) **Ce$_{SG}$ genre$_{SG}$ de bourrasques$_{PL}$** rend$_{SG}$ la visibilité nulle durant moins de 30 minutes en général. (*Wikipédia, s.v.* bourrasque de neige)
 '**This kind of gust** brings down visibility to zero for less than 30 minutes in general'

(54) Je pense quand même que **ce$_{SG}$ genre$_{SG}$ de boutons$_{PL}$** sont$_{PL}$ une sorte d'acné dépuratif. (DOC, 22/07/2011)
 'I do think that **these kind of spots** are some kind of depurative acne'

In (53), it is clearly the gusts that reduce the visibility. However, the verb agrees with *genre* in the singular. Agreeing with *bourrasques* would have been equally fine (i.e. *rendent$_{PL}$*). This is the case in (54) where *être* agrees with the noun *boutons* in the plural. Conversely, an agreement in the singular with N_{TAX} (i.e. *est$_{SG}$*) would have been perfectly acceptable and would in fact be the norm in this case.

Out of 604 occurrences of the typifying construction, there are only 163 cases in which there is an external constituent that undergoes agreement (verb, predic-

---

[27] Other authors have extended the definition of the postdeterminer construction (see Brems and Davidse 2010; Brems 2011 amongst others).

Table 5: External agreement in the typifying construction.

Agreement	Frequency
with N_{TAX}	26
with N	31
Undecidable	106
no explicit agreement	441
Total	**604**

ative adjective, etc.), but in most cases (106 out of 163; 65.03%), it is impossible to establish whether it is N_{TAX} or N that triggers the agreement (cf. Table 5):

(55) En dépit de ce que tu prétends, Jack, **ce**$_{SG}$ **genre**$_{SG}$ **de recherche**$_{SG}$ ne m'apprendra$_{SG}$ rien. (FRA, Anne-Marie Garat, *Programme sensible*, 2012)
'In spite of what you are claiming, Jack, **this kind of research** won't teach me anything.'

(56) Depuis 2001, les autorités publiques ont imposé aux teufeurs – de « teuf », fête en verlan – des mesures répressives pour encadrer **ce**$_{M.SG}$ **genre**$_{M.SG}$ **d'événement**$_{M.SG}$, venu$_{M.SG}$ d'Angleterre, arrivé$_{M.SG}$ en France en 1993. (LEM, 02/05/2016)
'Since 2001, public authorities have imposed repressive measures on *teufeurs* (= merrymakers) –from "*teuf*", *fête* in back slang– in order to supervise **this kind of event**, coming from England, [which] arrived in France in 1993'

In these two examples, neither number nor gender help identify what triggered the agreement, and in each case both analyses are tenable (agreement with N_{TAX} or N). There are only 57 cases (34.97%) in which there is an indication allowing us to identify the trigger: N_{TAX} in 26 cases out of 57, and N in the 31 remaining cases.

This analysis confirms the in-between status of the typifying construction compared to the classifying and qualifying constructions: in the majority of cases (547 out of 604; i.e. 90.56%), there is no agreement or the absence of an identifiable agreement, and among these 57 cases where agreement is clear, the difference in distribution is not clear enough to establish a true tendency.

Le Bon Usage (BU) ventures to suggest a rule accounting for these agreement variations. Two scenarios are considered:

I. "Quand ce complément représente l'idée principale, l'expression qui précède fonctionne plus ou moins comme un adjectif, jusqu'à signifier seulement "qq. ch. comme" [...] " (BU: 560, § 431a 1o)
'When this complement represents the main idea, the preceding expression functions more or less as an adjective, until it only means "something like".'

II. "Si *espèce, genre*, etc. ont leur signification ordinaire, si l'attention se porte sur eux, ce qui est particulièrement le cas quand ces mots sont précédés du déterminant démonstratif, le complément n'a pas d'effet sur l'accord" (BU: 560, § 431a 1o)
'If *espèce, genre*, etc. have their ordinary meaning, if the focus is on them, which is particularly the case when these words are preceded by the demonstrative determiner, the complement has no effect on the agreement.'

Analysis (I) corresponds to that proposed for the qualifying construction in which the sequence ⟨N_{TAX} de⟩ is viewed as a linguistic unit playing the role of modifier of N (see Section 4.1.3). The description given in (II) seems rather to correspond to the cases under study here (presence of the demonstrative determiner, agreement). From these distinctions, it is quite hard to understand what led the authors to distinguish the functioning of (57) which they associate with analysis (I), from the one in (58) which they relate to analysis (II):

(57) **Ce**$_{SG}$ **genre**$_{SG}$ **d'amitiés**$_{PL}$ finissent$_{PL}$ autrement qu'on ne pense (Oldenbourg, quoted by BU, § 431a 1°)
'These kind of friendships end differently from what one usually thinks'

(58) **Ce**$_{SG}$ **genre**$_{SG}$ **d'exercices**$_{PL}$ vous fera$_{SG}$ du bien (Dict. contemp. quoted by BU, § 431a 1°). (Dubois *et al.* (1966). *Dictionnaire du français contemporain*. Paris : Larousse.)
'These kind of exercises will do you good'

In these two examples, the noun phrases *ce genre d'amitiés* and *ce genre d'exercices* follow the same interpretation (paraphrase with *tel* 'such', Section 5.1.1; anaphora, introduction to Section 5). About example (59), the authors note: "Vu les ex. de Beauvoir qui ont été cités plus haut [i.e. (60) et (61)], on peut se demander si dans celui-ci on n'a pas une faute contre la règle générale de l'accord du participe passé employé avec avoir." (§ 431, R1, p. 560) [Considering Beauvoir's examples quoted above (i.e. (60) and (61)), one may wonder whether in this one we do not have a mistake against the general rule of the agreement of the past participle when used with *avoir*.] (my translation).

(59) Ce n'est pas le$_{M.SG}$ genre$_{M.SG}$ de réponse$_{F.SG}$ qu'il aurait fait$_{M.SG}$ l'année dernière (Simone de Beauvoir, quoted by BU, § 431a 1o)
'This is not **the kind of answer** he would have given last year'

(60) Voilà bien le$_{SG}$ genre$_{SG}$ de questions$_{PL}$ qui ne servent$_{PL}$ à rien (Simone de Beauvoir, quoted by BU, § 431a 1o)
'Here are **the kind of questions** that are useless'

(61) Ce n'était pas exactement le$_{M.SG}$ genre$_{M.SG}$ de vacances$_{F.PL}$ qu'il avait rêvées$_{F.PL}$ (Simone de Beauvoir, quoted by BU, § 431a 1o)
'This was not exactly **the kind of holiday** he had dreamt of.'

In trying to blame Simone de Beauvoir, the authors admit that (II) proves inadequate for the analysis of example (59), which, the agreement of the verb aside, works in every respect like examples (60) and (61), analysed according to (I). It is through examples such as this one that the necessity of considering a third interpretation, different from the classifying and the qualifying interpretations, clearly appears. That is what Rouget (1997) does, somewhat at her own expense, since in addition to the "subcategorizing" (*sous-catégorisatrice*) interpretation (i.e. classifying here) and the "approximate" (*approximative*) interpretation (i.e. qualifying here), she introduces a third category named "undecidable" (*indécidable*) in which she places all examples including demonstratives (Rouget 1997: 295) for lack of being able to put them in the two categories previously mentioned. This undecidable category corresponds more or less to my typifying construction which also groups occurrences with the interrogative determiner (i.e. *quel genre de* N ?) and the definite article (i.e. *le genre de* N).

The highly justified hesitation shown by scholars in dealing with the typifying construction clearly illustrate its ambivalent nature, taking after both the classifying construction and the qualifying construction.

5.2 Semantics of N and categorization

5.2.1 N as a general noun?

As mentioned above (see Section 5.1.2), N frequently appears without any modifier. The nouns that appear in this context are all the more interesting since they often carry vague semantic content, which led me to consider the category of general nouns (Halliday and Hasan 1976; Mahlberg 2005), a class of nouns characterized by "la pauvreté du contenu descriptif et la très large application

référentielle des noms concernés." (Huyghe 2015: 20) [the poverty of the descriptive content and the very broad referential application of the nouns involved] (my translation). The nouns *chose* 'thing', *endroit* 'place', *problème* 'problem' and *situation* 'situation' are general nouns. Other similar classes of nouns have been identified in the literature: container nouns (Vendler 1968), anaphoric nouns (Francis 1986), carrier nouns (Ivanič 1991), shell nouns (Schmid 2000), *noms sous-spécifiés* 'underspecified nouns' (Legallois 2008).[28] All these classes are not identical but sometimes overlap. There is no unique list of general nouns; Schmid (2000) considers that shell nouns are not shell nouns intrinsically but only because they are used as such. Without attempting to precisely define the class of general nouns, a task that is outside the scope of this paper, let us keep in mind the following characteristics that they share:
- general nouns are frequent in the language;
- they bear a vague meaning which requires a context to be correctly interpreted;[29]
- they are known for the importance of their role in discourse cohesion, more specifically as phoric mechanisms.[30]

Instead of deciding for each noun used in the typifying construction whether it belongs to the class of general nouns or not, I examined a list of the 25% most frequent nouns used as N in the construction (see Table 6).

Table 6: The 25% most frequent N in the typifying construction.

noun	TYP	CLA	QUA
chose 'thing, thingy'	48	0	0
problème 'problem'	22	0	0
situation 'situation'	15	0	0
truc 'thing, thingy'	11	0	4
produit 'product'	10	0	0
personne 'person'	9	1	0
pratique 'practice'	8	0	1

---

28 One could also mention Channell's (1994) placeholder words, e.g. *thingy, thingummy, whatsisname*; and Mihatsch's (2006) all-purpose nouns (*noms passe-partout*), e.g. *machin, truc, chose*. On space general nouns, see Huyghe (2009); on human general nouns, see Schnedecker (2018).
29 Besides, Ivanič (1991) entitled his study on carrier nouns "Nouns in search of a context". This idea is also found in the metaphor of the shell in Schmid (2000).
30 This idea is found in the denomination *anaphoric nouns* adopted by Francis (1986).

Table 6 (continued)

noun	TYP	CLA	QUA
propos 'words'	8	0	0
maladie 'disease'	7	0	1
homme 'man'	6	5	0
souci 'worry, concern'	5	0	0
service 'service'	5	0	0

The results are striking: of the 25% most frequent nouns, the majority are general nouns. In comparison, most of these nouns never appear in the classifying and qualifying constructions.[31] These nouns fully play their role of "shell", triggering, often by means of anaphora, the rebuilding of a category:

(62) Ensuite, Draap[32] a revendu le cheval à la société française Spanghero, qui l'a fait venir à Castelnaudary (Aude). A son tour, Spanghero a cédé la marchandise à la Cogimel, dont l'usine se trouve au Luxembourg. Ainsi, au lieu d'aller directement de Breda à Luxembourg (310 km), la viande de cheval roumaine a fait un détour de 2 100 km par le sud de la France. En chemin, elle s'est transformée en bœuf. [...] « **Ce genre de choses** arrive, c'est la conséquence du libre commerce au sein de l'UE. [...] » (LEM, 12/03/2013)
'Draap then sold the horsemeat to the French company Spanghero, which brought it to Castelnaudary. In turn, Spanghero sold the goods to Cogimel, whose factory is located in Luxembourg. Thus, instead of going directly from Breda to Luxembourg (310 km), Romanian horsemeat made a 2,100 km detour to the south of France. On the way, it turned into beef. [...] « **This kind of thing** happens, it's the consequence of free trade within the EU. [...] »'

In this example, *ce genre de choses* 'this kind of thing' refers to both absurd distances travelled by the meat between the cattle farm, its place of processing and its point of sale, and to what is known as the "horsemeat scandal" which was in the news a few years ago: horsemeat was sold to consumers as beef (even halal beef sometimes) after multiple resales from corrupt trader to corrupt trader. The

---

[31] As a side note, the sequence ⟨*ce genre de* N⟩ with unmodified N might be a good test for detecting general nouns.
[32] Trading company. *Draap* is an anagram of *paard*, which means 'horse' in Dutch.

noun *chose* holds, in this context, all of this referential detail, even though it remains descriptively empty.

5.2.2 Ad hoc categorization

In the previous example, *ce genre de choses* builds up, by anaphora, a category we could name EXCESSES OF THE FOOD INDUSTRY. This category does not have a stable and shared mental representation outside of the context of the *Le Monde* article and would need to be explained before being used.[33] This kind of category is an ad hoc category, and I will refer to the categorization process leading to the emergence of such categories as ad hoc categorization.

Barsalou (1983) is the first to suggest the existence of ad hoc categories. According to him, an "ad hoc category is a novel category constructed spontaneously to achieve a goal relevant in the current situation" (Barsalou 2010: 86).[34] In the seminal works by Rosch and her team (see Rosch 1973, 1975; Rosch et al. 1976) which gave birth to prototype theory, only common categories, also known as 'natural' categories, were considered, that is categories like FLOWER, BIRD, or FURNITURE. The main difference between natural and ad hoc categories is that the former are well entrenched into long-term memory while the latter are created on the fly to satisfy a precise communication need.[35] As Barsalou (1983, 1985, 2010) showed, both natural and ad hoc categories are structured in an identical way: some members are better exemplars of the category than others (they are prototypes), and category borders are fuzzy.[36] Two main characteristics distinguish natural and ad hoc categories. Unlike natural categories, ad hoc categories, i) are completely context-dependent, and ii) are not well-entrenched in the memory.

It seems that the typifying construction provides a means to create an ad hoc category on the basis of some properties shared by a set of individuals men-

---

[33] This ad hoc category might be losing its "ad hocness" as we are becoming more familiar with this kind of excess. In Barsalou's (1985: 632) terms this is more of a goal-derived category, i.e. a category of categories that includes both ad hoc categories and former ad hoc categories that have become entrenched into memory.
[34] The equivalent notion of covert categories is found in Cruse (1986: 148).
[35] Smith and Samuelson (1997), for instance, reject this distinction between two types of categories. They consider all categories ad hoc, claiming that no category has a stable mental representation which is shared by speakers.
[36] Here again, this is a point that is not shared by all linguists; for example, Mauri and Sansò (2018) consider, following Croft and Cruse (2004), that it is not the category borders that are blurred but our degree of knowledge of these borders.

tioned in the context and a vague category established by N. The noun phrase that constitutes the construction is usually vague on its own (e.g. *ce genre de situation, d'évènement, de chose* 'this kind of situation, event, thing'); it thus points to a category that is highly context-dependent and whose extension is to be inferred by similarity to known members more or less explicitly mentioned in the context.

6 Conclusion

Under the appearance of the same structure [DET N_{TAX} *de* N], three distinct constructions can be clearly distinguished by their formal and semantic properties. As we have seen, determination, modification and agreement patterns are three discriminating features which facilitate the identification of the three constructions: classifying, qualifying and typifying. These criteria make it possible to identify the head of the noun phrase in each of the constructions with more or less clarity. Semantically, while the classifying construction offers the means to subclassify (scientific and non-scientific classification), the qualifying construction allows the vague categorization of an entity in relation to a category of which it does not constitute a prototypical member. The typifying construction, in the form of resumptive anaphora, triggers the phenomenon of ad hoc categorization, based both on elements of the context, as well as on the (often vague) category denoted by N. It is interesting to compare the functioning of these three constructions to the quantifying construction (e.g. *aucune espèce d'importance* 'no importance at all') –left out in the present paper– which does not have a categorizing function but works more as a reinforcer of a quantification process (see Mihatsch 2016; Chauveau-Thoumelin 2020). Finally, I have only scratched the surface of the specificities related to the choice of N_{TAX} (*genre* or *espèce*), and in particular for the typifying interpretation which of these two options is specific to *genre*.[37] The typifying construction would benefit from further investigation by extending the analysis to other N_{TAX} *(style, sorte, type, forme,* etc.).[38]

---

[37] For a comparative analysis of the typifying constructions [DET *genre de* N] and [X (*du*) *genre* Y], both involving *genre*, see Chauveau-Thoumelin (2020, chap. 4).
[38] See for example Mihatsch's (2016) study which analyses a wider range of nouns in the Romance languages.

References

Barsalou, Lawrence W. 2013. Ad hoc categories. *Memory & Cognition* 11. 211–227. https://doi.org/10.3758/BF03196968 (Accessed 03 December 2021).
Barsalou, Lawrence W. 1985. Ideals, central tendency, and frequency of instantiation as determinants of graded structure in categories. *Journal of Experimental Psychology: Learning, Memory, and Cognition* 11(4). 629–654. https://doi.org/10.1037/0278-7393.11.1-4.629 (Accessed 03 December 2021).
Barsalou, Lawrence W. 2010. Ad hoc categories. In Patrick Colm Hogan (ed.), *The Cambridge encyclopedia of the language sciences*, 86–87. Cambridge: Cambridge University Press.
Brems, Lieselotte. 2011. *Layering of size and type noun constructions in English*. Berlin & Boston: Mouton de Gruyter.
Brems, Lieselotte & Kristin Davidse. 2010. The grammaticalisation of nominal type noun constructions with *kind/sort of*: chronology and paths of change. *English Studies* 91(2). 180–202. https://doi.org/10.1080/00138380903355023 (accessed 03 December 2021).
BU = Grevisse, Maurice & André Goose. 2011. *Le Bon Usage*. 15th edn. Bruxelles: De Boeck Duculot.
Channell, Joanna. 1994. *Vague language*. Oxford: Oxford University Press.
Chauveau-Thoumelin, Pierre. 2018. Exemplification and ad hoc categorization: the *genre*-construction in French. *Folia Linguistica Historica: Linguistic strategies for the construction of ad hoc categories. Synchronic and diachronic perspectives* 52(39–1). 177–199. Berlin & Boston : Walter de Gruyter.
Chauveau-Thoumelin, Pierre. 2020. *Une approche constructionnelle des enclosures* genre et espèce. Lille : Université de Lille dissertation.
Croft, William & D. Alan Cruse. 2004. *Cognitive linguistics*. Cambridge: Cambridge University Press.
Cruse, D. Alan. 1986. *Lexical semantics*. Cambridge: Cambridge University Press.
Denison, David. 2002. History of the *sort of* construction family. Paper presented at the Second International Conference on Construction Grammar (ICCG2). Helsinki.
Denison, David. 2005. The grammaticalisations of *sort of*, *kind of* and *type of* in English. *New Reflections on Grammaticalization*. Santiago de Compostela: University of Santiago de Compostela.
Denison, David. 2011. The construction of SKT. Second Vigo-Newcastle-Santiago-Leuven International Workshop on the Structure of the Noun Phrase in English (NP2). Newcastle upon Tyne.
DHLF = Rey, Alain (ed.). 2012. *Dictionnaire historique de la langue française*. Paris: Dictionnaires Le Robert.
DOC = http://forum.doctissimo.fr (accessed 31st May 2019).
Doyen, Émeline & Kristin Davidse. 2009. Using e-data for the study of language change: a comparative study of the grammaticalized uses of French *genre* in teenage and adult forum data. In Iñaki Alegria, Igor Leturia & Serge Sharoff (eds.), Proceedings of the fifth Web As Corpus workshop (WAC5), 17–25. San Sebastián: Elhuyar Fundazioa.
Dufaye, Lionel. 2014. *Genre* ou le scénario d'une grammaticalisation. *Linx* 70–71. 51–65. https://doi.org/10.4000/linx.1567 (Accessed 03 December 2021).
EUR = https://ec.europa.eu/jrc/en/language-technologies/dcep (accessed 31st May 2019).
FRA = https://www.frantext.fr (accessed 31st May 2019).

Francis, Gill. 1986. *Anaphoric nouns*. (Discourse Analysis Monographs 11). Birmingham: English Language Research, Department of English, University of Birmingham.

Goldberg, Adele. 2006. *Constructions at work: The nature of generalization in language*. Oxford: Oxford University Press.

Halliday, Michael A. K. & Ruqaiya Hasan. 1976. *Cohesion in English*. London: Longman.

Huyghe, Richard. 2009. *Les noms généraux d'espace en français: Enquête linguistique sur la notion de lieu*. Bruxelles: De Boeck Duculot.

Huyghe, Richard. 2015. Les typologies nominales : présentation. *Langue française* 185. 5–27. https://doi.org/10.3917/lf.185.0005 (Accessed 03 December 2021).

Ivanič, Roz. 2009. Nouns in search of a context: a study of nouns with both open- and closed-system characteristics. *International Review of Applied Linguistics in Language Teaching* 29(2). 93–114. https://doi.org/10.1515/iral.1991.29.2.93 (Accessed 03 December 2021).

Kleiber, Georges. 1983. Article défini, théorie de la localisation et présupposition existentielle. *Langue française* 57. 87–105. https://www.persee.fr/doc/lfr_0023-8368_1983_num_57_1_5158 (Accessed 03 December 2021).

Legallois, Dominique. 2008. Sur quelques caractéristiques des noms sous-spécifiés. *Scolia* 23. 109–127.

LEM = https://www.lemonde.fr (accessed 31st May 2019).

Mahlberg, Michaela. 2005. *English general nouns: a corpus theoretical approach*. Amsterdam: John Benjamins.

Maillard, Michel. 1974. Essai de typologie des substituts diaphoriques (supports d'une anaphore et/ou d'une cataphore). *Langue française* 21. 55–71. https://www.jstor.org/stable/41558486 (Accessed 03 December 2021).

Martin, Robert. 1985. Aspects de la phrase analytique. *Langages* 79. 40–54. https://www.jstor.org/stable/41682035 (Accessed 03 December 2021).

Mauri, Caterina & Andrea Sansò. 2018. Linguistic strategies for ad hoc categorization: theoretical assessment and cross-linguistic variation. *Folia Linguistica Historica: Linguistic strategies for the construction of ad hoc categories. Synchronic and diachronic perspectives* 52(39-1). 1–35. https://doi.org/10.1515/flih-2018-0001 (Accessed 03 December 2021).

Mihatsch, Wiltrud. 2006. *Machin*, *truc*, *chose* : la naissance de marqueurs pragmatiques. In Martina Drescher & Barbara FrankJob (eds.), *Les marqueurs discursifs dans les langues romanes*, 153172. Frankfurt: Peter Lang.

Mihatsch, Wiltrud. 2009. L'approximation entre sens et signification : un tour d'horizon. In Dominique Verbeken (ed.), *Entre sens et signification. Constitution du sens : points de vue sur l'articulation sémantique-pragmatique*, 125–143. Paris: L'Harmattan.

Mihatsch, Wiltrud. 2007. The construction of vagueness. "sort of" expressions in Romance languages. In Günter Radden, Klaus Michael Köpcke, Thomas Berg & Peter Siemund (eds.), *Aspects of meaning construction*, 225–245. Amsterdam &Philadelphia: John Benjamins Publishing Company.

Mihatsch, Wiltrud. 2016. Type-noun binominals in four Romance languages. *Language Sciences* 53. 136–159. https://doi.org/10.1016/j.langsci.2015.05.009 (Accessed 03 December 2021).

Noailly, Michèle. 1999. *L'adjectif en français*. Paris: Ophrys.

Riegel, Martin. 1997. *Tel* adjectif. Grammaire d'une variable de caractérisation. *Langue française* 116. 81–99. https://www.jstor.org/stable/41558845 (Accessed 03 December 2021).
Roché, Michel. 1997. *La variation non flexionnelle du genre des noms. Diachronie, diatopie, diastratie*. (Cahiers d'Études Romanes). Toulouse: Université de Toulouse II Le Mirail.
Rosch, Eleanor. 1973. On the internal structure of perceptual and semantic categories. In Thimothy E. Moore (ed.), *Cognitive development and the acquisition of language*, 111–144. New York: Academic Press.
Rosch, Eleanor. 1975. Cognitive representations of semantic categories. *Journal of Experimental Psychology: General* 104. 192–233. https://doi.org/10.1037/0096-3445.104.3.192 (Accessed 03 December 2021).
Rosch, Eleanor, Caroline B. Mervis, Wayne D. Gray, David M. Johnson & Penny BoyesBraem. 1976. Basic objects in natural categories. *Cognitive Psychology* 8. 382–439. https://doi.org/10.1016/0010-0285(76)90013-X (Accessed 03 December 2021).
Rosier, Laurence. 2005. Genre : le nuancier de sa grammaticalisation. *Travaux de linguistique* 44. 79–88. https://doi.org/10.3917/tl.044.0079 (Accessed 03 December 2021).
Rouget, Christine. 1997. *Espèce de*, *genre de*, *sorte de* : approximatifs ou sous-catégorisateurs ? In Paulo de Carvalho & Olivier Soutet (eds.), *Psychomécanique du langage. Problèmes et perspectives*. Actes du 7ᵉ colloque international de psychomécanique du langage, 289–198. Paris: Honoré Champion.
Schmid, Hans-Jörg. 2000. *English abstract nouns as conceptual shells. From corpus to cognition*. Berlin & New York: Mouton de Gruyter.
Schnedecker, Catherine. 2018. Le nom d'homme est-il un nom général ? *Linx* 76. 23–56. https://doi.org/10.4000/linx.2506 (Accessed 03 December 2021).
Smith, Linda B. & Larissa K. Samuelson. 1997. Perceiving and remembering: category stability, variability and development. In Koen Lamberts & David Shanks (eds.), *Knowledge, concepts and categories*, 161–195. Hove: Psychology Press.
Van Peteghem, Marleen. 1995. Sur les emplois anaphoriques de tel. *Sémiotiques* 8. 57–78. http://www.revue-texto.net/1996-2007/Parutions/Semiotiques/SEM_n8_4.pdf (Accessed 03 December 2021).
Van Peteghem, Marleen. 1997a. Mécanismes anaphoriques sous-jacents aux "indéfinis" *autre* et *même*. In Walter De Mulder, Liliane Tasmowski-De Ryck & Carl Vetters (eds.), *Relations anaphoriques et (in)cohérence*, 187–200. Amsterdam &Atlanta: Rodopi.
Van Peteghem, Marleen. 1997b. Sur un indéfini marginal : *même* exprimant l'identité. *Langue française* 116. 61–80. https://www.jstor.org/stable/41558844 (Accessed 03 December 2021).
Vendler, Zeno. 1968. *Adjectives and nominalizations*. The Hague &Paris: Mouton.
WIK = https://fr.wikipedia.org (accessed 31st May 2019).

Miriam Voghera
9 The network of *specie, genere, sorta, tipo* constructions: From lexical features to discursive functions

Abstract: This paper provides a study on the network of the non-nominal head constructions (TNCxs$_{[-N]}$) developed by the Italian taxonomic nouns (TNs) *specie, genere, sorta* and *tipo* (SGST). The analysis is focused on the relationship between the semantic development of SGST and their diffusion in various types of text, as well as the frequency and productivity of the TNCxs$_{[-N]}$. In order to assess whether and how their distribution in different texts has affected the course of their development, data derived from diachronic and synchronic Italian corpora will be analysed. The corpus-based analysis demonstrates that TNs have developed different types and numbers of Cxs$_{[-N]}$ due to a strong interrelationship between lexical, constructional and textual factors. Firstly, the increase in frequency of the abstract taxonomic meaning of the nouns was the first step towards a possible determinologization of the TNs in specific constructional contexts. Secondly, the differing nature of the lexical sources resulted in partially different semantic operations for the various TNCxs$_{[-N]}$, such as categorization and analogical comparison, approximation, exemplification and focusing. This process favoured some constructions, which spread and in turn occupied syntactic spaces of different mobility. If we rank the TNs according to the number and variety of Cxs$_{[-N]}$, *tipo* occupies the first position, followed by *genere, sorta* and *specie*. It seems possible to attribute these differences to constructional factors, i.e. to the greater flexibility of the *Tipo*Cxs$_{[-N]}$ at both a formal and semantic level. As a final point, the relationship between the formation of new functions and their use in new contexts is very close and they are mutually reinforcing. This encourages the diachronic study of textual pathways as a source of new knowledge.

Acknowledgements: I would like to thank Wiltrud Mihatsch, who, by planning and hosting the workshop *Pragmatic functions of type nouns: a crosslinguistic perspective* at the University of Tübingen, created a stimulating and enriching opportunity to discuss many of the topics developed in this article. I also thank the two anonymous referees for their suggestions. Special thanks to Lorenza Raponi and Alex Andò.

Miriam Voghera, Università di Salerno, e-mail: voghera@unisa.it

1 Introduction

In recent years, numerous studies have been carried out on taxonomic nouns (TNs) and their development of non-nominal head constructions (TNCxs$_{[-N]}$)[1] with very different meanings and functional values. This phenomenon affects many languages, which also belong to different families, and the more the number of languages investigated increases, the more common elements are found.[2] The interlinguistic data, on the one hand, show the existence of a paradigmatic series of TNs from which TNCxs$_{[-N]}$ originate in many languages.[3] On the other hand, both interlinguistic and intralinguistic data reveal that not all nouns develop the same types of constructions and are therefore not always interchangeable in any context. In other words, there is no two-way correspondence between the semantic traits of taxonomic lexical units and the types of Cxs$_{[-N]}$ they can develop.

In this paper I propose a study on the network of TNCxs$_{[-N]}$ developed by the Italian TNs *specie*, *genere*, *sorta* and *tipo* (SGST). I will also take into account the development of the various lexical meanings and the type of texts in which the nouns and the constructions have gradually spread, in order to assess whether and how the textual pathway has affected the course of their development (Lindquist and Mair 2004). The analysis is, therefore, focused on the relationship between the semantic development of SGST, their diffusion in the various types of text and the frequency and productivity of TNCxs$_{[-N]}$ which they develop.

The data are predominantly taken from the following diachronic and synchronic corpora of Italian, both written and spoken: OVI is a collection of texts prior to 1375; M.I.DIA. (Iacobini, De Rosa, and Schirato 2017) contains written

---

[1] I assume here the definition of construction by Goldberg (1995: 4): "C is a CONSTRUCTION iff def C is a form-meaning pair <Fi, Si> such that some aspect of Fi or some aspect of Si is not strictly predictable from C's component parts or from other previously established constructions". I will use the following abbreviations: TN= taxonomic noun; Cx= construction; Cxs= constructions; Cxs$_{[-N]}$= non-nominal constructions; TNCxs$_{[-N]}$= non-nominal constructions derived from a taxonomic noun: TN can be replaced by a single taxonomic noun, therefore *Specie*Cxs $_{[-N]}$= non-nominal constructions derived from *specie*.
[2] It is not possible to list here the now very extensive bibliography, for which I refer to all the essays collected in this volume.
[3] I give here some examples: English *sort, kind, type* (Denison 2002, 2005, 2011; Brems and Davidse 2010; Brems 2011); French *genre, espèce, sorte*, (Danon-Boileau and Morel 1997; Fleischman and Yaguello 2004; Mihatsch 2016); Italian *genere, tipo, specie, sorta* (Mihatsch 2007, 2016; Masini 2012, 2016; Voghera 2013a, 2017b), Spanish *tipo, especie* (Mihatsch 2016), Swedish *typ* (Rosenkvist and Skärlund 2013); Russian *tipa* and *vrode* (Kolyaseva and Davidse 2018).

texts from 1200 to 1945; DiaCORIS (Proietti 2008) contains written texts from 1861 to 2001; the *Primo tesoro della lingua letteraria italiana* (De Mauro 2007) contains novels from 1947 to 2006; VoLIP (Voghera et al. 2014) contains spoken texts from the final decade of the 20th century;[4] C-Oral-Rom (Cresti and Moneglia 2005) contains spoken texts from the beginning of the 21st century.

To reconstruct the diachronic textual pathway followed by the TNCxs$_{[-N]}$ I used the corpora M.I.DIA. and DiaCORIS, which present an articulated typology of texts. The two corpora, although not containing the same types of texts, have a comparable common core of texts: scientific and specialized texts; divulgation essays and press reports; fiction and drama. M.I.DIA. also includes personal texts such as letters and poetry. Since the language of the poetic text, especially in its oldest phases, has followed very strong coding rules that concern not only metrical aspects but also canons of composition that are separate from the parameters of textual characterization designed for continuous prose, I decided not to consider poetry in this textual analysis, though the data are still reported in Voghera (2017b).

Although quantitative analyses based on diachronic corpora are valuable, it should be borne in mind that they are inevitably partial because they only capture the written aspect of linguistic reality. This is all the more true in the Italian linguistic context, in which there has been complex relationships between the linguistic varieties and the spoken and written modes of realization (Lepschy, Lepschy, and Voghera 1996). It would therefore not be correct to take the resulting quantitative data as if they were providing a complete picture of a given time period; they are rather to be used as tendential data.

The article is organized in this way. In section 3, I give a summary of the semantic and textual evolution of SGST, presenting qualitative and quantitative data on the emergence of taxonomic meanings, which as we know are not etymologically primary, and their diffusion in the various types of texts; in section 4, I explain some of the questions that arise concerning the relationship between lexical source and TNCxs$_{[-N]}$; in sections 5–6, I present the history, frequency and productivity of the TNCxs$_{[-N]}$, grouping them according to history and common development and highlighting the similarities and differences between them; finally, in section 7, I try to reconstruct the semantic and functional space occupied by each TNCx$_{[-N]}$ in contemporary Italian, assessing the weight of the lexical source and subsequent semantic development, the points of contact between the constructions, their contexts of use, their frequency and their productivity.

---

4 VoLIP is the online version of the LIP corpus (De Mauro et al. 1993) with revised transcriptions and the alignment of text transcription and recorded audio (Voghera et al. 2014).

2 The nouns and their meanings

The four nouns we are considering here do not originally have a taxonomic meaning, nor is there any semantic or formal link between them. They have different etymologies but have in common the fact that they have been, and continue to be, strongly polysemic nouns: Table 1 gives an overview of their most frequently used meanings in the most recent section of the DiaCORIS corpus. An examination of the various meanings of SGST can be found in Voghera (2017b).

Table 1: Frequency of the main meanings of *specie, genere, sorta* and *tipo* in section 1966–2001 of the DiaCORIS corpus.

Meanings	Dia.CORIS 1968–2001			
	Specie	Genere	Sorta	Tipo
category	43%	61%	100%	84%
biological class	51%	14%	0%	0%
artistic genre	0%	23%	0%	0%
un tipo [AN] ('a guy')	0%	0%	0%	9%
model	0%	0%	0%	7%

The taxonomic meaning of SGST emerged at different times in their respective histories. *Specie*[5] (*Latin spěcǐe(m)*, derived from *specěre* «look») occurs initially with the meaning of 'biological class' in the expression 'human species' and then with the taxonomic meaning in scientific and expository texts from the 15th century:

(1) *Bestemmiavano Dio e lor parenti, l'umana spezie e 'l loco e 'l tempo e 'l seme [...]* (D. Alighieri, *Commedia, Inferno*, beginning of XIV century)
'They were cursing God and their relatives, the human species and the time and the seed [...]'.

(2) *[...] è il feltro vilissima spezie di panno, come ciascun sa manifestamente.* (G. Boccaccio, *Esposizioni sopra la Comedia di Dante*, 1374)
'Felt is a very low quality type of cloth, as everyone clearly knows'

---

[5] In ancient Italian *specie* can have other spellings that have been counted under the same lemma (Voghera 2017b).

The meaning of 'category' and that of 'biological class' fight for primacy for centuries, but from the end of the 19th century onwards the first one becomes emphatically the most common, as can be seen from Table 2. The high number of occurrences of the biological meaning in the most recent period is probably due to its use in the press and in popular scientific articles.

Table 2: Distribution (%) of the meanings 'category' and 'biological species' of the total occurrences of the noun *specie* in the DiaCORIS.

	Specie = 'category' and 'biological class' in DiaCORIS				
Meanings	1861–1900	1901–1922	1923–1945	1945–1967	1968–2001
category	78%	70%	90%	68%	43%
biological class	21%	24%	8%	27%	51%

The taxonomic meaning of *specie* is predominantly used in specialized texts, but it also occurs from the beginning in other types of texts. Surprisingly in poetry and drama it is much more frequent in 1220–1375 than in 1847–1947. Tables 3 and 4 show clearly how it gradually spreads from scientific texts to more general texts, so much so that in contemporary Italian the meaning 'category' is distributed almost equally between legal and scientific texts and popular ones, namely press and fiction.

Table 3: Distribution (%) of the meaning 'category' of noun *specie* across the various types of texts in M.I.DIA.

	Specie = 'category' in M.I.DIA.				
Types of text	1220–1375	1376–1532	1533–1691	1692–1840	1841–1947
Legal	8%	9%	6%	32%	34%
Science	23%	61%	19%	22%	34%
Expository	30%	22%	35%	20%	22%
Literary	8%	7%	31%	16%	4%
Poetic	15%	0%	3%	1%	0%
Personal	0%	1%	6%	6%	5%
Drama	15%	0%	0%	3%	1%
Total	100%	100%	100%	100%	100%

The increase in its use in fiction is interesting because these texts are by definition heterogeneous in terms of both structure and content. Stories and novels may contain narrative, and both descriptive and argumentative text, but of course

Table 4: Distribution (%) of the meaning 'category' of noun *specie* across the various types of texts in DiaCORIS.

Type of text	*Specie* = 'category' in DiaCORIS				
	1861–1900	1901–1922	1923–1945	1946–1967	1968–2001
Legal	35%	20%	34%	19%	19%
Essays	30%	36%	24%	36%	26%
Divulgation essays	12%	10%	6%	18%	8%
Press	13%	26%	26%	15%	28%
Fiction	10%	8%	10%	12%	19%
Total	100%	100%	100%	100%	100%

also dialogues and various forms of speech mimesis. Although fiction may not bear much resemblance to everyday language, it bears little resemblance to scientific texts either. In addition, fiction is polyphonic and can express different perspectives and subjectivities. The spread of the taxonomic meaning of *specie* in fiction is therefore a concrete sign of its use in areas that are not necessarily sector-specific. Today, in fact, *specie* is no longer perceived as a specialized word and the *Grande Dizionario dell'uso* (GRADIT 1999), which indicates the levels of use of each lemma, assigns the taxonomic meaning of *specie* to basic vocabulary, that is, to the range of the first two thousand lemmas per frequency of use in contemporary Italian.

Genere (Lat. *genus* cfr. *gignĕre* «give birth»; Gr. *génos, gígnomai* «be born», «ancestry, lineage») has been predominantly used to indicate a category, which can include subclasses or species. Its prevailing uses in philosophical and scientific texts derive from this sense. It is not easy to find the first abstract uses that clearly mean 'category' without other attributes. In the 13th century we find some uses in which the meaning of quality or manner (3) prevails, which are the precursors to the most abstract meaning, but the first clear occurrences appear in the 16th and 17th centuries (4).

(3) *Di ciò nasce cotal questione di questa qualitade: se l'a fatto iustamente o iniustamente, e perciò si è appellata questione di genere, cioè della qualità di un fatto e di che maniera sia.* (Brunetto Latini, *Rettorica*, 59–30, XIII century).
'From here arises a question of this type: if he did it justly or unjustly, and it is therefore called a question of *genere*, that is of the quality of a fact and of its characteristics'

(4) [. . .] *i più pericolosi, e paurosi, che sieno in tutta questa carriera, dove chi tocca non ha nessun genere di rimedio, non vi sendo se non tre, o quattro secche di arenali, dove non è acqua* (Filippo Sassetti, *Lettere*, XVI century)
'the most dangerous and frightful passages are those where if you run aground there is no sort of remedy since there are three or four sandbanks in which there is no water'

As can be seen from Table 5, between the 16th and 17th centuries the taxonomic meaning became more and more frequent and predominant, even beyond scientific or specific-sectorial texts, and began to be used in increasingly diversified types of texts.

Table 5: Distribution (%) of the meaning 'category' of noun *genere* in M.I.DIA.

Types of texts	Genere = 'category in M.I.DIA.				
	1220–1375	1376–1532	1533–1691	1692–1840	1841–1947
Legal	100%	100%	0%	12%	3%
Science	0%	0%	80%	15%	20%
Expository	0%	0%	0%	32%	65%
Fiction	0%	0%	0%	23%	4%
Poetic	0%	0%	0%	1%	2%
Personal	0%	0%	20%	16%	6%
Drama	0%	0%	0%	0%	0%
Total	100%	100%	100%	100%	100%

Expansion into different spheres increased after the 19th century (Table 6), to the point that non-specialist uses became predominant.

Table 6: Distribution (%) of the meaning 'category' of the noun *genere* in DiaCORIS.

Type of texts	Genere = 'category' in DiaCORIS				
	1861–1900	1901–1922	1923–1945	1946–1967	1968–2001
Legal	7%	3%	6%	4%	6%
Essays	40%	73%	21%	24%	18%
Divulgation essays	18%	8%	12%	21%	11%
Press	20%	14%	40%	42%	43%
Fiction	15%	2%	21%	9%	22%
Total	100%	100%	100%	100%	100%

As in the case of *specie*, the taxonomic meaning of *genere* in GRADIT is also assigned to the list of basic vocabulary.

Sorta (Lat. *sŏrte(m)*, cfr. Fr. *sorte*, 1530 *sourte* «lot, share, fortune, condition») is not present in OVI; in M.I.DIA., the first occurrences appear in the 14th century in scientific and legal texts, with the taxonomic meaning already present:[6]

(5) *tucti li maestri dell'Arte minore, o che vendaranno a minuto qualunque sorta di seta [...]* (*L'Arte della seta nei secoli XV–XVI. Statuti e documenti* 1513)
'all the masters of minor arts or those who will sell any type of silk by the yard'

All occurrences of the noun have the meaning of 'category'. Its characteristic is that of being accompanied mainly by universal quantifiers, like *qualunque* ('any') or *ogni* ('every'). By the 14th century the constructions N *di ogni sorta* and *ogni sorta di* N have come to constitute half of the uses of *sorta* and they will absorb almost all the nominal occurrences, rapidly becoming a fixed construction meaning 'various N' (Table 7).

Table 7: Distribution (%) of the meanings 'category' of the total occurrences of the noun *sorta* in the DiaCORIS.

	Sorta = N in DiaCORIS				
	1861–1900	1901–1922	1923–1945	1946–1967	1968–2001
N	20%	20%	37%	5%	4%
ogni sorta di N	57%	49%	48%	75%	70%
N *di ogni sorta*	23%	31%	15%	20%	26%

Also *sorta* is initially used in scientific and legal texts, but by the 17th century its use has spread to other types of texts (Tables 8 and 9). It remains a word of a higher register than *specie* and *genere* and in the GRADIT is not labelled as part of basic vocabulary. It is no coincidence that the occurrences of *sorta* in fiction are half of those of *specie* and *genere*.

---

[6] In M.I.DIA. the tokens of *sorta* are lemmatized under a single lemma *sorte/sorta*. In the earliest texts (1200–1375) we find occurrences of *sorte*, all with the meaning of 'fate'. The taxonomic meaning is attested in the GDLI as early as the 15th century.

Table 8: Distribution (%) of the meaning 'category' of the noun *sorta* in M.I.DIA.

	Sorta = 'category' in M.I.DIA.			
Types of texts	1376–1532	1533–1691	1692–1840	1841–1947
Legal	45%	35%	12%	0%
Science	22%	53%	21%	0%
Expository	0%	0%	30%	23%
Fiction	0%	8%	21%	12%
Poetic	0%	0%	2%	31%
Personal	33%	0%	8%	0%
Drama	0%	4%	6%	34%
Total	100%	100%	100%	100%

Table 9: Distribution (%) of the meaning 'category' of the noun *sorta* in DiaCORIS.

	Sorta = 'category in DiaCORIS				
Type of texts	1861–1900	1901–1922	1923–1945	1946–1967	1968–2001
Legal	3%	5%	1%	0%	0%
Essays	39%	33%	42%	37%	10%
Divulgation essays	13%	10%	7%	13%	17%
Press	18%	24%	34%	31%	48%
Fiction	27%	28%	16%	19%	25%
Total	100%	100%	100%	100%	100%

Let us now come to *tipo* (Lat. *tỹpum*, Gr. *túpos* «print»), whose first occurrences are attested in the 15th century with the meaning of 'model', but which appears with the taxonomic meaning only from the 19th century (Table 10):[7]

Table 10: Distribution (%) of the meanings of the noun *tipo* in DiaCORIS.

	Tipo = N DiaCORIS				
Meaning	1861–1900	1901–1922	1923–1945	1946–1967	1966–2001
category	37%	73%	66%	62%	84%
model	37%	14%	20%	12%	7%

The taxonomic meaning of *tipo* rapidly spreads also in non-specific-sectorial texts, such as press and divulgation texts, as we can see in Table 11 and of which

---

[7] A very recent article by Di Bonito (2022) reports two occurences of *tipo* already in the 14th century.

we report an example in (6). For a detailed diachronic analysis of *tipo* see Voghera (2013, 2014).

(6) *trovò in fondo a un breve corridoio dove un lumicino a petrolio ardeva davanti a parecchi santi, a madonne d'ogni tipo e d'ogni colore* (A. Fogazzaro, *Daniele Cortis*, 1885).
 'At the end of a short corridor where a small petrol lamp was placed in front of various saints, (s/he) found, at the end of a short corridor madonnas of all sorts and colours'

Table 11: Distribution (%) of the meaning 'category' of the noun *tipo* in DiaCORIS.

	Tipo = 'category' in DiaCORIS				
	1861–1900	1901–1922	1923–1945	1946–1967	1968–2001
Legal	1%	1%	4%	9%	14%
Essays	50%	61%	55%	37%	21%
Divulgation essays	9%	4%	2%	7%	20%
Press	28%	24%	34%	33%	34%
Fiction	12%	10%	5%	14%	11%
Total	100%	100%	100%	100%	100%

In conclusion, I present the timeline of the development of the taxonomic meanings of SGST and their distribution across the various types of texts in Table 12.

Table 12: Centuries in which the taxonomic meaning of *specie*, *genere*, *sorta* and *tipo* spread into the various types of text.

	Emergence of Taxonomic Meaning and its distribution in different kinds of texts					
SGST	13th	14th	16th–17th	17th–18th	19th	20th
Specie	Mostly in expository scientific texts		Nearly in all kinds of texts			Nearly equal distribution in every kind of texts
Genere	Legal texts			Nearly all kinds of texts		Mostly in non-specialist texts
Sorta			Mostly in legal, scientific texts	Every kind of text		Mostly in non-specialist texts
Tipo					Nearly all kinds of texts	Mostly in non-specialist texts

Two differences between the four nouns are immediately apparent. The first is related to the attestation period of the taxonomic meaning: the taxonomic meaning of *specie* and *genere* is documented in ancient Italian while *sorta* develops it in the 16th century and *tipo* in the 19th century. The second difference concerns their distribution throughout the texts: in the first centuries, the taxonomic use of *specie*, *genere* and *sorta* is primarily documented in scientific or legal texts and in general in cultured specific-sectorial texts. Only later does the taxonomic meaning gain usage in popular and literary texts. On the contrary, the taxonomic use of *tipo* is documented from its very first attestations in various types of texts, without great distinction between scientific and specific-sectorial texts and more popular texts. To understand if these differences influence the development of TNCxs$_{[-N]}$ or not, in the following sections (3–5) I investigate the ways in which they originated and spread, their points of contact and their functional differences.

3 Nouns and the TNCxs$_{[-N]}$

TNCxs$_{[-N]}$ display many characteristics that are usually attributed to the outcomes of grammaticalization processes: semantic change, reanalysis, transcategorialization, syntagmatic reduction, generalization, increase in structural scope, pragmatically richer value, subjective expressiveness (Hopper 1991; Traugott 1995, 2008; Lehmann 2002, 2004; Hopper and Traugott 2003). However, there is no unanimous agreement on the necessary and sufficient elements to determine grammaticalization. First, the very distinction between lexical and grammatical elements can be interpreted differently, depending on whether the emphasis is on more strictly semantic, formal or functional aspects (Lehman 2002; Hopper and Traugott 2003). Secondly, since processes can have different degrees of granularity, i.e. fusion, and can have multiple and parallel outcomes, there is no agreement on the defining role to be assigned to some features of the process, such as gradualness or unidirectionality (Haspelmath 1999; Hopper and Traugott 2003).

An analysis of the various defining positions on grammaticalization goes beyond the aims of this essay; I shall therefore limit myself to a broad definition of grammaticalization, such as the traditional one proposed by Kuryłowicz: "Grammaticalization consists in the increase of the range of a morpheme advancing from a lexical to a grammatical or from a less grammatical to a more grammatical status" (1965: 43). In this definition, the distinction between lexical and grammatical elements is dynamic and gradual, not only from the diachronic point of view but also from the synchronic one. This allows the conception of a scale of lexicality and/or grammaticality rather than a closed list of criteria that must be necessarily positive in order to define the lexical or grammatical elements. In this regard, I find the distinction between grammatical and lexical morphemes by De Mauro (1982) to be useful. According to De Mauro, lexical morphemes express senses external to the process of production and reception of signs and the grammatical morphemes express "quella parte di significato che definisce i rapporti tra le parti di un segno e i rapporti tra il segno e la situazione in cui viene a collocarsi chi lo realizza e lo riceve [. . .]"(De Mauro 1982: 108)['that part of meaning which defines the relationships between the parts of a sign and the relationships between the sign and the situation, in which the persons who produce it and receive it find themselves.' (Translation M.V.)]. As for this definition, the grammatical elements acquire meaning only as part of the enunciation process. The distinction made in these terms has many advantages because it takes a broad view of grammar that includes among its systemic means the expression of the relationship between the speaker and the utterance. This allows the overcoming of a contrast between purely grammatical and pragmatic meanings, not so much because it denies the existence of pragmatics, but because it identifies a strong integration between two equally systemic levels.

If we accept this definition of grammatical meanings, then it is easy to understand that they, even more than lexical meanings, are dependent on contextual and textual variables. It is no coincidence that in recent years the number of studies that include context as a decisive element in the study of grammatical processes has increased (Diewald 2002; Heine 2002; Heine and Kuteva 2002; Bergs and Diewald 2009; Traugott 2010). The availability of textual data, due to the creation of diachronic corpora, has permitted a wider view of the unfolding of the process, which is not unilateral, but rather resembles a thread that can be composed in turn of woven threads, which can sometimes separate and reunite again, with multiple and parallel outcomes. The use of diachronic corpora is decisive in this respect; it is well known that grammaticalization can be a long-drawn-out process that does not necessarily take place in every context in which its potential conditions exist (Haspelmath 2004).

The TNs seem to be a good example of this, because they have developed constructions which are partly or completely different, with a different diffusion and distribution (Voghera 2017b), thus rendering an interlinguistic comparison interesting. There are cases where the same TN is used with the same functions in different languages: this is the case, for example, of Italian and Russian *tipo* and *tipa*, whose uses present many similarities. However, there is also the opposite case, in which different languages necessarily require different TNs for the same functions: Italian *tipo* and French *genre* are examples of this. Finally, we have cases of TNCxs[-N] that allow multiple TNs: for example, in Italian *una specie/sorta di*. In essence, there is a dynamic relationship between TNs and Cxs[-N].

In contemporary Italian, the nominal taxonomic use of SGST can be synonymous in various contexts, as in (7):

(7) *Alla festa c'era gente di ogni specie/genere/sorta/tipo*
'At the party there was every kind of person'

However, the TNCxs[-N] constitute a functional network with areas of overlap and difference. In the descriptions that follow, the TNCxs[-N] have been grouped according to history and common development in order to help the identification of the web of similarities and differences between them.

4 *In genere e(t) in specie*

The first type of TNCx[-N] that includes *specie* and *genere* precedes the birth of the taxonomic meaning and derives from a construction that was already present in medieval Latin: *in genere e(t) in specie*:

(8) [. . .] *quod omnia simul creata sunt tempore in genere et in specie* (Alexander Halensis, *Quaestiones disputatae,* XII--XIII centuries)
'[. . .] because all things are created at the same time in gender and in species'

The two fixed prepositional phrases *in genere* and *in specie* together form a single construction which over time comes to mean 'in general and in particular'. In ancient Italian, the Latin construction is still present, but we also find the two distinct phrases *in specie* 'in particular' and *in genere* 'generally' fulfilling an adverbial function:

(9) *cose et ciaschuna d'epse in genere et in spetie et in publico et pel publico o privato et contro,* [. . .] (*Riforma e Nuova Riforma della Costituzione fiorentina,* 1494)
'things and each one of them generally and in particular and publicly and for the public or for the individual and against (them)'

(10) *E di quel ch' egli afferma ch' abbia Eurialo Commesso, che né a me né a messer Claudio In specie se ne parli, si può credere Che se ne menta.* (L.Ariosto, *I studenti*, 1474)
'And about what he says Eurialo did, which does not interest either me or Sir Claudio especially, one could think it is all but lies'

(11) *Si perché gli è patron; sì perché in genere M' avete tutti voi di casa in odio;* [...] (L.Ariosto, *Cassaria*, 1533)
'Yes, because he is the boss; yes, because generally all of you here hate me'

The two constructions *in genere* and *in specie* are still used in contemporary Italian, separately, but the second one occurs much more frequently as *specie*:

(12) *Era come se tutti e due, specie quando non c'era la presenza del nonno* [...] (D.Rea 1993)
'It was as if both of them, especially when the grandfather wasn't there [...]'

Since the 17th century, cases in which *genere* can be interpreted as an adjectival modifier of the noun (13) have been attested, a function which developed fully in the 19th century, when, as we shall see, other adjectival constructions with *genere* began to arise:

(13) *Allorché questo abbandono è impedito con la forza si ha la schiavitù non il [dominio [in genere]$_A$]]$_{SN}$* (Alfonso Asturaro, *Il materialismo storico e la sociologia generale*, 1903)
'When one uses strength to stop abandonment, it results in slavery not *in genere* domination'

This construction is not only still current in contemporary Italian in both speech and writing, but it is the most frequent *Genere*Cx$_{[-N]}$ in every kind of text.

5 *Una specie di* and *una sorta di*

As noted for other languages (Mihatsch 2007; Denison 2011), the development of TNCxs$_{[-N]}$ is a complex process which has lasted several centuries and occurred at partially different times for each type noun. Most developments have followed the appearance of the taxonomic meaning of SGST.

The Cxs$_{[-N]}$ of *specie* and *sorta* in Italian originate from a predicative construction in which there is an analogy between two elements or a set of elements. This construction in Italian could have the two forms shown in (14a) and (14b).

(14) a. *X is of a specie/sorta of Y*
    b. *X is a specie/sorta of Y*

The construction in (14a). is marginal and does not in fact evolve. Between the 16th and 17th centuries, constructions appear in which *specie* can be interpreted both as a TN and as part of an emerging adjectival construction whose meaning is no longer that of the original predicative construction, but rather that of (15):

(15) *X is a species of Y = X is analogous to Y, resembles Y*

Analogy is a very flexible procedure because it does not imply identity, but is based on salient similarities between a source and a target domain "grounded in easily retrievable aspects of representations, regardless of whether or not they represent descriptive or relational, perceptual or conceptual properties" (Vosniadou and Ortony 1989: 4). The perception of similarity plays a major role in some of the key processes associated with analogical reasoning, so following Gentner and Markman's (1997) proposal I will consider analogy and similarity as basically equivalent. Since the properties of people's underlying representations may change, analogy is a process more than a stable association. From a functional point of view, the outcome of this process is the realization of adjectival constructions that qualify a certain N, establishing a similarity with the members of a whole. This interpretation naturally involves reanalysis, on the basis of which *specie* loses its nominal value and *una specie di* becomes a single construction modifying the noun [[*una specie di*]$_{AP}$N]$_{NP}$ whose meaning can be paraphrased as 'something like N'.

(16) [. . .] *questa vana gloria è giudicata da Aristotile una spezie di pazzia*
    (G. Giraldi Cinzio, *L'uomo di corte*, 1569)
    '[. . .] this boastfulness is considered by Aristotle to be a sort of madness'

There are many ambiguous contexts in which both interpretation (14) and interpretation (15) are possible. For example, in the following sentence, taken from the same text as example (16), *una spezie* can still legitimately be paraphrased with *un genere di* 'a kind of':

(17) *il servire a grato Signore è quasi una spezie di mercanzia* [...] (G. Giraldi Cinzio, *L'uomo di corte*, 1569)
'to be serving a grateful master is a kind of commerce [...]'

These ambiguous contexts are bridging contexts, which constitute a condition for the transition to and development of new constructions (Heine 2002). Since the beginning of the 19th century, the adjectival construction has been widespread in all types of texts, including popular and literary texts, not only in the scientific and sector-specific texts where the first occurrences are to be found.

(18) *Quando il sipario si alzò, [[una specie di]$_A$ stupore]$_{SN}$ invase gli animi.* (G. D'Annunzio, *Novelle della Pescara*, 1902)
'When the curtain was lifted a kind of amazement filled people's hearts'

Finally, in contemporary Italian, adjectival *una specie di* has lost any specific-sectorial use and is so common that it is much more frequent than the noun in all types of texts.

The same path is partially valid for the Cxs$_{[-N]}$ *una sorta di*, even if the situation in this case is more complex. First, *sorta* is a term that in its taxonomic meaning remains more anchored in formal texts and, in general, does not become as familiar a term as *specie*. Secondly, the *Sorta*Cxs$_{[-N]}$ are more numerous and therefore it is necessary to take their possible reciprocal influences into account.

The Cx$_{[-N]}$ *una sorta di* appears with the same meaning and function as *una specie di* around the 18th century, but struggles to establish itself and so even in the 19th century we find many contexts in which it is difficult to decide whether it has the function of N or of a Cx$_{[-N]}$. Only from the 20th century onwards does *una sorta di* become established as Cx$_{[-N]}$ (19):

(19) *E una sorta di rimorso ci assale* (A. Soffici 1914)
'And a sort of remorse takes hold of us'

The fact that ambiguous contexts are numerous and long-lasting is probably due to the fact that there are two other formally similar constructions, in which the taxonomic meaning of *sorta* is partially recognizable, N *di ogni sorta* and *ogni sorta di* N with the meaning 'varied, multiple N', both of which are documented from the 16th century onwards:[8]

---

[8] In some contexts, the construction N *di ogni sorta* can also have the negative meaning 'worthless, vulgar N'.

(20) que 'legnami, e del bestiame d'ogni sorta (V. Viviani, *Intorno al difendersi da' riempimenti, e dalle corrosioni de' fiumi applicate ad Arno in vicinanza della città di Firenze*, 1687)
'those woods, and cattle of all types'

(21) *Parmi d 'aver parlato di ogni sorta d'ambizione, che allignare possa nella tirannide.* (V. Alfieri, *Della tirannide*, 1777)
'It seems to me [that] I have discussed all types of ambition that can have roots in tyranny'

Additionally, we find the construction [non V [N *di sorta*]] which takes on the meaning 'not V of any N' and which probably derives from constructions in which *sorta* was preceded by the indefinite quantifier, *alcuna sorta*, already present in previous periods:

(22) [. . .] *col quale non hanno analogia di sorta* [. . .] (G. Carmignani, *Una lezione accademica sulla pena di morte detta nella Università di Pisa*, 1836)
'[. . .] with which they have no analogy at all'

The presence of these other constructions has probably slowed down the process of transcategorization of *sorta* as part of the construction *una sorta di*. However, this has not prevented its subsequent diffusion: in fact, in the portion of DiaCORIS from 1966 to 2001, 84% of all *sorta* tokens appear as part of the construction *una sorta di*, as do 100% of *sorta* tokens in the spoken VoLIP corpus.

6 *Genere* and *tipo*

The emergence and spread of TNCxs$_{[-N]}$ with *genere* is strongly intertwined with that of *tipo* from a semantic, formal and functional point of view. However, their pace of development is different, and it is therefore necessary to follow the entire process before being able to identify a suitable interpretative framework.

6.1 The common path of *Genere*Cxs$_{[-N]}$ and *Tipo*Cxs$_{[-N]}$

In the second half of the 19th century the first attestations of non-nominal uses of *tipo* appear, in which *tipo* is an adjectival modifier postponed to a noun and with the meaning of 'exemplary, ideal':

(23) *A diciott'anni è permesso credere ancora all'amore, alla fedeltà, alla donna tipo.* (G. Verga, *Una peccatrice*, 1866)
'At eighteen one is still allowed to believe in love, faithfulness and the ideal woman'

The syntactic role of *tipo* in this case is entirely equivalent to that of a qualifying adjective even if it has not formally acquired the categorical features of most Italian adjectives, i.e. the gender and number agreement with the modified noun. This is a similar case to the use of colour names as nominal modifiers (Thornton 2004). Unlike the majority of Italian adjectives, the singular form of the colour names *viola* ('purple') can function as an adjective of singular or plural nouns remaining unchanged, e.g *gonna viola* ('purple skirt'), /*gonne viola* ('purple skirts'). Although these formations remain in contemporary Italian, in the last portion of DiaCORIS their frequency never exceeds 5% of *tipo* occurrences. Interestingly, they are not restricted to non-fiction, but are from the outset also present in popular texts, in the press and in literary texts. They are still frequent in contemporary Italian, but, congruent with the semantic shift of the nominal uses, the adjective *tipo* that originally meant 'representative of a model or paradigm' now predominantly means 'representative of a category' and therefore 'standard':

(24) *Voglio una bottiglia di spumante: devo festeggiare il compleanno. Questa la richiesta del [consumatore$_N$ tipo$_A$]$_{SN}$ in enoteca, fino a qualche anno fa.* (*La Stampa* 1982)
'I want a bottle of champagne to celebrate a birthday. Such, till a few years ago, was the request of the standard consumer'

At the end of the 19th century both *tipo* and *genere* start to be used in another kind of construction. This is the TNCx$_{[-N]}$ whose starting base consists of an N modified by a complex prepositional phrase, usually introduced by the prepositions *di* ('of') and *su* ('on'), which establishes a comparison or similitude between two elements or sets of elements:[9]

(25) *tutti i giornali, eccetto quelli del genere della «Gazzetta di Mosca»* [. . .] (*Avanti!*, 1881)
'all the newspapers, except those like the "Gazzetta di Mosca"'

---

[9] It is also possible to find, with slight nuances of meaning, prepositional phrases introduced by other prepositions (*a* 'at' and *in* 'in'); since these variations do not affect the process here described, we will not discuss them further.

(26) *[. . .] primeggiano gli scrittori del genere di Harnack e simiglianti.* (A. Labriola, *Discorrendo di socialismo e filosofia*, 1889)
'[. . .] most important are the writers like Harnack and similar'

(27) *non il militare del tipo di Moltke, ma l'avventuriero di guerra, nel senso nobile della parola.* (E. Ferri, *Garibaldi nelle sue Memorie*, 1889)
'not the military of Moltke's type but the war adventurer, in the purest sense of the word'

(28) *Si istituiranno scuole speciali sul tipo della scuola all'aperto (. . .).* (*Regolamento per la difesa contro le malattie infettive nelle scuole*, 1921)
'special schools like the open air schools will be established'

These binominal constructions (Traugott 2008; Mihatsch 2016) encourage a process of reanalysis, on the basis of which the PP *del/sul genere/tipo di* is interpreted as part of a complex preposition that also includes the head preposition of the second PP (Danon-Boileau and Morel 1997; Traugott 2008):

(29) [*gli scrittori*]$_{NP}$ [*del genere*]$_{PP1}$ [*di Harnack*]$_{PP2}$ > *gli scrittori* $_{NP}$ [*del genere di Harnack*]$_{PP1}$
[the writers]$_{NP}$ [of.ART.SING kind]$_{PP1}$ [of Harnack]$_{PP2}$ > the writers $_{NP}$ [of.ART.SING kind Harnack]$_{PP1}$

In these constructions, the prepositional phrase *del/sul genere/tipo di* becomes a mark of similarity and can be paraphrased as 'analogous to/like'.

(30) a. *scrittori*   *del genere di Harnack*
          'analogous to/like Harnack'
     b. *militare*   *del tipo di Moltke*
          'analogous to/like Moltke'

These are analogical (Serianni 1988) or similative (Haspelmath and Buchholz 1998) comparisons, which indicate a generic correspondence between two elements and not equality or equivalence. The constructions tend to be progressively reduced: firstly, the preposition of the second PP, which has become redundant, is eliminated, followed by the preposition of the first PP: *N del genere/tipo di N > N del genere/tipo N > N genere/tipo N*.

(31) [...] *capivo che era un gioco del tipo Robinson* (L. Romano, *Le parole tra noi leggere,* 1969)
'[...] I understood it was a game like Robinson'

(32) *fisicamente repulsivo (genere "maître d'hôtel cerimonioso")* (A. Arbasino, *L'anonimo lombardo,* 1960)
'physically repulsive (like "obsequious maître d'hôtel")'

(33) *le istituzioni tipo collegio* (VoLIP)
'institutions like the college'

If there is a preposition before *genere* and *tipo*, there must also be an article, i.e. the contraction of a preposition and a definite article (*preposizione articolata*), as can be seen from a comparison of the constructions in (34). In fact, when there is no article, as in (34b), *tipo* is interpreted as a TN and *Robinson* becomes an adjectival modifier:

(34) a. [un gioco [del tipo Robinson]$_A$]$_{NP}$
 b. [un gioco]$_{NP}$ [di tipo [Robinson]$_A$]$_{PP}$

In (34a) the meaning approximates 'a game which resembles the adventure of Robinson Crusoe'; in (34b) it is not easy to find the right paraphrase, but we can propose something like 'a Robinsonian game' or 'a game of the Robinson model'.

The same opposition between the presence and absence of the article is also evident in sentences such as:

(35) a. È un tavolo [di tipo moderno]$_{PP}$
 'It is a modern type of table'
 b. È [un tavolo [del tipo moderno]$_A$]$_{NP}$
 'It is a sort of modern table'

The mandatory presence of the article in the attributive constructions is evident also when the modifier is not a noun and therefore the taxonomic interpretation is unlikely:

(36) a. *sì ma una roba del tipo tre contro due* (VoLIP)
 'yes, but something [of.ART *tipo*] like three against two'
 b. **sì ma una roba di Ø tipo tre contro due*
 'yes, but something [of *tipo*] three against two'

In reduced constructions, *genere* and *tipo* can function as adjectival prefixes in a manner comparable to the suffixed uses of *like* and *type* in English, as demonstrated by the fact that most of the examples reported by Biber et al. (1999) can be translated into Italian with the structures *genere/tipo* N:

(37) birthday-type -> *genere/tipo compleanno*

(38) Hollywood-type -> *genere/tipo Hollywood*

The extended construction and the reduced one are not different from a semantic point of view because both introduce an original analogy, created on the fly by the speaker. As Brems (2011: 292) states for the semi-suffix uses of TNs in English:

> Both [semi-suffix use and attributive modifier use of TNs] involve specific collocational patterns in the shape of unusual lexical items and the TN-strings following them have a metalinguistic flavour. Hence, even though both these features tend to be pushed further in the semi-suffix use, the boundaries between attributive modifier and (classifying) semi-suffix use are fuzzy [...]. Consequently, it seems reasonable to consider attributive and semi-suffix uses as the two ends of one internally graded category.

However, in Italian the prefix constructions mainly modify nouns, in contrast to English in which, according to Brems (2011), it is possible to find semi-suffix constructions with adjectives: *European-type film*.

The *genere/tipo* N constructions have both developed in different ways. *Genere* N has a very limited use, and today there are some rare examples in novels. Although it is still perfectly common usage for older people, it has an awkward feeling for the younger generation: its absence in contemporary speech is evidence of this. Moreover, the few occurrences found in the *Primo Tesoro della lingua letteraria italiana* do not fulfil an adjectival function but are rather assigned the function of introducing sentences or expressions quoted as the discourse of others in order to "label" a given expression or behaviour in an expressive way, through sayings, formulas, maxims or clichés. These uses are usually called quotative and interpretative quotative and are widely known for *like* in English and *genre* in French (Romaine and Lange 1991; Fleischman and Yaguello 2004):

(39) *Il cambiamento di tono da parte mia significa poi lasciar perdere il modo di fare da incontro casuale, genere "esaurito il gioco del bel dottore e della bella ammalata" non si ha più niente da dirci* [...]" (A. Arbasino, *Anonimo lombardo*, 1960)
'My change of tone implies that one can set aside the casual behaviour of the type "once the game of the handsome doctor and the pretty patient is over" there is nothing more to say'

Obviously, in such cases *genere* is no longer the part of a nominal modifier but becomes a marker that can introduce whole sentences. *Tipo* is also used in the same way, and with much greater success.

In parallel to these constructions, from the mid-19th century, another adjectival construction N *di genere* is making its mark. This construction, linked to the noun meaning 'artistic genre', progresses over time from the meaning 'belonging to a specific artistic genre' to the meaning 'typical of a situation, responding to expectations' (40):

(40) nei soliti quadretti di genere, osavano raffigurar cardinali con paramenti addirittura spropositati (L.Piradello, *La vita nuda*, 1922)
'in the usual genre of paintings they dared even represent cardinals with exaggerated vestments'

Subsequently, the construction *nel suo genere* comes into use, initially with the meaning 'typical of its category', which is then changed into 'in its own way', if one considers the circumstances' (41) and therefore assumes the function of an adverb:

(41) nella vita vegetale, unica nel suo genere (I. Guareschi, *Jons Jacob Berzelius e la sua opera scientifica*, 1915)
'in the vegetable world, unique in its type'

Both constructions are still possible in contemporary Italian, although absent in the last section of DIaCORIS and in the spoken corpora.

6.2 The different paths of *Genere*Cxs$_{[-N]}$ and *Tipo*Cxs$_{[-N]}$ and their combinations

Since the mid-20th century new and different constructions with *genere* and *tipo* have arisen. Although they are separate from each other in contemporary Italian, some of them are used in combination to form new constructions: for this reason, it is useful to discuss them together.

Another adjectival construction, N *del genere*, establishes analogies and similitudes, even if differently from the constructions described above. In fact, the analogies can vary not only as regards the chosen similarities, but also in their internal structure, i.e. the way in which they treat the analogs. In fact, analogies can vary in relation to a) the type of analogs they employ; b) the relative order of the analogs; c) the degree of explicitness of the relation between analogs; d) the relation between analogs.

(42) *la signorina si riferisce al al bilinguismo per esempio nel Galles / in posti del genere* (VoLIP)
'the young lady is talking about bilingualism for instance in Wales / in places like that'

First, in (42) the target analog is put in second position and matched to the source analog, which is in first position, using an inverse order with respect to the most common one presented in (15):

(43) [*bilinguismo$_i$ nel Galles*]$_{ii}$ [*Ø$_i$ in posti del genere*]$_{ii}$
      Target analog   Source analog

Secondly, while the source analog is defined, the target analog is expressed through an analogy with one or more members considered representative of a whole (*un genere*) which has been previously mentioned or is retrievable from the context. In (42) the target category is a kind of bilingualism, although the similarity with the basic analog is only partially explicit and must be inferred from the shared knowledge and the context. In fact, there is no reference to the properties of bilingualism in Wales, but the speaker assumes that the addressee is able to identify the reference by relying on her encyclopedia. In this case, we can speak of implicit reference or associated anaphora (Channel 1994; Overstreet 1999). Note that the N representing the basic analog, precisely because it represents an indefinite category, cannot be preceded by the determinative article (**nei posti del genere* 'in the places of the sort').

Besides these uses, in the middle of the 20th century, this construction also acquires the function of general extender in the form (*e/o*) N *del genere*, in which N is a vague noun, also appearing in plural form, *cosa/e, roba/e, affare/i del genere*, ('thing/s of the kind, stuff of the kind'), or as an indefinite pronoun such as *qualcosa* ('something') (Channel 1994; Overstreet 1999, 2001; Fiorentini and Sansò 2016). As we know, a general extender is an expression that widens the scope and the meaning of what was previously said. Its function is twofold: on the one hand, it creates an open and potential category of entities, for which there is not perhaps a defined noun and on the other hand, it allows the speaker to choose one or more common properties of some elements to group them together, fulfilling a purpose in the immediate discourse (Barotto and Mauri 2018). This explains why (*e/o*) N *del genere* is very common in speech compared with writing: 37% in VoLIP vs. 4% in the last portion of DiaCORIS, even though it is the only TN that can form a general extender in Italian.

*Tipo*Cxs[$_{-N}$] follow a different path that continues the attributive uses discussed in the previous paragraph. First, the approximate meaning is accentuated: the reduced construction [*tipo* N]~NP~ definitively means 'approximately N'; secondly, it widens its scope and *tipo* can be the head of a phrase, acting as a preposition. In these cases, it assigns the oblique case to its complements when they are expressed by personal pronouns, as is the case in the modified b. versions of the examples (44) and (45).

(44) a. *La trattava [tipo segretaria insomma]*~PP~ (VoLIP)
  's/he treated her like a secretary after all'
 b. *La trattava [tipo lei]*~PP~
  'he treated her~i~ like her~ii~ after all'

(45) a. *non fare [tipo i soliti moralisti]*~PP~ (Twitter)
  'don't be like the usual moralists'
 b. *non fare [tipo loro]*~PP~
  'don't do like them'

Although still limited to informal contexts, the use of *tipo* as a marker of similarity is very common in contemporary Italian, the reason for which seems to be the possibility it affords of expressing an approximate similarity, which could be paraphrased as 'more or less like'.

Italian does not have different markers for equative and similative comparison (Haspelmath and Buchholz 1998), unlike in English, where there is a difference between *as* (equative comparison) and *like* (similative comparison). The comparative marker *come* ('how, as, like') can potentially cover both equative (46) and similative comparison (47), which is "a construction expressing sameness of manner", according to Haspelmath and Buchholz (1998: 278):

(46) *la mia casa è grande come la tua* → equative comparison
 'it is a house as big as yours'

(47) *ti sei vestito come lui* → equative/similative comparison
 'you are dressed as/like he is'

(48) *ti sei vestito tipo lui* → similative comparison
 'you are dressed like him'

The sentences (47) with *come* are ambiguous because the equative interpretation cannot ever be excluded. However, if we substitute *come* with *tipo*, as in (48), the only possible interpretation is the similative one. Only in some particular cases can *come* be interpreted as similative with any certainty, when introducing an adjective or an indefinite NP (Mihatsch 2009; Voghera 2022):[10]

(49)   *era come stordita*
       'she was as if dazed'

(50)   *era come sonnambulo*
       'he was as if sleep walking'

Tipo, therefore, unambiguously expresses similative comparison and occupies a meaning slot that did not have a specific marker in Italian prior to this development.

Tipo also expresses approximation in an adverbial function (Voghera 2013, 2014):

(51)   [...] *cose che noi consumiamo tipo tutti i giorni* (VoLIP)
       'things that we use like every day'

(52)   *questa è una prova//tipo*[11] (conversation)
       'this is a trial//sort of'

In its adverbial function, *tipo* generally has a modal value as irrealis, with varying scope: the phrase, as in (51), or the whole clause, as in (52). In the latter example, in fact, *tipo* has the function of changing the meaning of the entire preceding clause (*this is a trial*). However, it is not so easy distinguishing these uses from those of *tipo* as a discourse marker, because it is not possible to decide in each individual case whether *tipo* should be interpreted as a marker of hypothetical mode or an element that affects the illocutive force of the utterance. One element that can help to distinguish these different uses of *tipo* is its position. In adverbial uses with scope over the entire clause *tipo* is predominantly in the final position and constitutes a tone unit with a lowering of the prosodic contour whose left boundary is often, but not necessarily, marked by a break. As a discourse marker, as we will see, *tipo* usually appears in initial position.

The position of *tipo* at the borders of the clause favours the emergence of two other constructions absent from the corpora consulted but widespread in con-

---

10 Similative uses of *type* can also be expressed by French *comme* and Spanish and Portuguese *como* (Mihatsch 2009; Piot 2009).
11 The double slash // marks the boundary of a tone unit.

temporary Italian, both in speech and in informal web writing. The first is the *tipo che* construction (more rarely *del tipo che*), which works as an interclausal connective (Benigni, Ch. 16, this volume):[12]

(53) *Cerco di cogliere i lati positivi :3 Tipo che domani salto l'interrogazione di Storia! (Twitter)*
'I try and appreciate the positive side :3 *tipo che* tomorrow I'll skip the History test'

(54) *Prima ho avuto un altro attacco di tristezza tipo che stavo per mettermi a piangere nel mezzo della lezione. . . (Twitter)*
'Earlier on I felt very sad *tipo che* I was about to start crying in the middle of the lesson'

Semantically, *tipo che* introduces a proposition that expresses a number of values ranging from illustrative exemplification to argumentative exemplification; the second one provides an exemplification as a kind of justification for the assertion expressed in the previous proposition (Manzotti 1995).[13] These are very common uses in the colloquial register where *tipo che* could be substituted both by *for example* and *in fact* (Voghera 2022). However, these clauses are characterized by intentional vagueness (Voghera 2017a) because the speaker presents their content as a possibility and not as a certain cause. Compare the clauses in (55) and (56) in this regard:

(55) *Il terrazzo è bagnato, infatti piove*
'The terrace is wet; in fact, it's raining'

(56) **Il terrazzo è bagnato, tipo che piove*
'The terrace is wet, like it's raining'

The example in (56) is not acceptable because the use of the present tense suggests that the sentence introduced by *tipo che* asserts a cause: the reason why the terrace is wet. The sentences introduced by *tipo che* can only express a hypothesis, and this is the reason why it rather becomes acceptable, albeit in an informal

---

[12] The examples taken from the web are reported with the original spelling and punctuation.
[13] Manzotti (1995:80) would call these uses *paradigmatizzanti*, because they present examples in comparison to other alternatives.

register, if *tipo che* is followed by a past tense, which can express irrealis and therefore conjecture:[14]

(57) *Il terrazzo è bagnato, tipo che pioveva*
      'The terrace is wet, as if it had been raining'

In some cases, the argumentative exemplification may be given a consecutive value, as in (58) or an adversative one, as in (59), but in this second sense the form *del tipo che* is not acceptable:

(58) *La cassiera della Coop ha sempre delle unghie imbarazzanti, del tipo che ogni volta ti verrebbe da fermarti e dirle: "hai 50 anni, ti prego"* (Twitter)
      'The cashier at the Coop always has terrible nails, *del tipo che* you'd like to stop and say, "Please, you are 50 years old"
(59) *Sto account me l'ha fatto mia cugina nel 2009. Tipo che non l'ho mai usato* (Twitter)
      'My cousin made this account for me in 2009. *Tipo che* I never used it'

The shift at the edge of the clause of *Tipo*Cxs$_{[-N]}$ reaches the full extent of its uses with the function of discourse marker, appearing mainly at the beginning of a sentence or of a conversational turn. As a discourse marker, *tipo* exploits the two main meanings developed by TNCxs$_{[-N]}$: the approximate one and the illustrative one. Uses of *tipo* to delimit the meaning and/or the illocutive force of a statement refer to the approximative meaning because they determine the vagueness level of the utterance, either higher or lower. In these cases, *tipo* is a hedge and expresses an intersubjective, and therefore more properly pragmatic, value (Lakoff 1973; Fischer 2006; Fraser 2010; Aijmer and Vandenbergen 2011). These uses are very frequent in the informal spoken registers. In fact, like most discourse markers, *tipo* is used not only to delimit and segment portions of speech which are textually and pragmatically meaningful but also to cover and fill temporal imbalances between programming and production times, which in speech are in fact overlapping, thus avoiding disfluences. Sometimes this causes, among other things, repetition of the same discourse marker or of clusters of discourse markers:

---

14 It is possible to recognize a similarity with the properties attributed by Manzotti 1995 to *ad esempio*, which is defined as a paradigmizing adverb because it places the example "in the background of other alternatives".

(60) *ma tipo prova a cliccare sul suo nome e riportalo per spam* (conversation)
'but *tipo*, try to click on his name and mark it as spam'

(61) [...] *cioè uno che parte devono dirgli addio cioè sai quelle tipo sai tipo serie Berlinguer* [...] (VoLIP)
'I mean one leaves, they have to say goodbye to him I mean you know, *tipo* you know *tipo* the Berlinguer series'

As stated earlier, *tipo* can have an exemplifying function and this leads to the use of *tipo* as a focusing discourse marker. As already noted by Manzotti (1995), using or introducing an example means more or less explicitly drawing the recipient's attention toward an element within the text that is functionally relevant. The examples are communicatively prominent and therefore the elements that introduce them have a focusing role (Voghera 2022). This explains why *tipo*, as an introducer of examples (optionally followed by complementizer *che*), can develop the function of non-contrastive focus:

(62) *tipo uno di questi giorni giuro che* [...] (VoLIP).
'*tipo* one of these days I swear that...'

Since the focus expressed by *tipo* arises from an implicit exemplification, it actually presupposes a reference to an utterance in the preceding co-text or context, even when it is at the beginning of a conversational turn. This explains the cataphoric uses before a list construction (Voghera 2018) or contexts that presuppose explicit alternatives, for example in a request for information or clarification:

(63) A: *C'erano molti altri possibili regali per le bambine*
'There were many other possible presents for the girls'
B: *Tipo?*
Tipo?
A: *Un gioco da tavola* (Personal conversation)
'A table game'

In B's response in (63), *tipo* is synonymous with *per esempio* ('for example'). It is a case of para-exemplification that allows the comparative identification within a larger set of the subset that the speaker has in mind.

Very recently, although it is not easy to establish when it happened, we have seen the emergence in informal registers, especially in chats and with diatopic differences, of *tipo che* with the function of focuser in the initial position of a sentence and/or conversational turn:

(64) Quanti piercing hai? *Tipo che* ho già risposto 20 volte a questa domanda. (*Twitter*)
'How many piercings do you have? *Tipo che* I have already replied 20 times to this question'

(65) *Tipo che se tu fossi cibo io sarei obesa.* (*Twitter*)
Tipo che if you were food, I would be obese'

These uses have the function of starting a discourse by marking personal involvement, and thus acquire a pragmatic function in addition to the textual one (Waltereit 2006; Voghera 2013).

The expansion of the role of exemplifier *tipo* has allowed the development of new constructions, in which *tipo* introduces what Manzotti (1995) calls restrictive qualification. The construction involves the use of *tipo* after a semantically vague noun, such as *cosa*, to express a concept or a category through one or more exemplary cases:

(66) *La gente lavora troppo di questi tempi, la sera preferisce accendere la televisione e guardare passivamente invece di fare cose tipo andare a un concerto*
'People work too much nowadays; in the evening they prefer to switch on the TV and watch passively rather than doing things like going to a concert'

(67) *Percuote cose tipo pentole, spazzolini elettrici, . . .*
'He beats things like pans, electrical toothbrushes, . . .

From a semantic point of view, while the general extender widens the scope and the meaning of what has been previously said, *cose tipo* narrows the scope of the meaning of the general referent *cosa* through a comparison with a series of specific referents.

Even more interesting are the following two constructions in which it is clear how *genere* and *tipo* have diversified their functions, thus explaining why they can be combined.

(68) *Riparatore del genere tipo fai da te*
'Repairman of the type like do it yourself'

(69) *Mi consigliate uno scrittore del genere tipo Dan Brown [. . .]?*
'Can you suggest me a writer of the type like Dan Brown [. . .]?'

In the previous examples taken from the web, *del genere* functions as an identifier of a category of elements, of which *tipo* introduces the specification. The same construction can occur with vague nouns like *cosa*, obtaining the same effect:

(70)   *Il frigo è un prodotto molto utile in quanto permette di raffreddare piuttosto bene, cose del genere tipo bottiglie d'acqua-bibite ecc.*
'The fridge is a very useful product since it facilitates pretty well the cooling down of things of the sort like bottles of water etc.'

In (70) *cose del genere* should not be interpreted as a general extender, but as meaning 'things belonging to the kind...'; this is confirmed by the fact that after the specification introduced by *tipo* there is the general extender *etcetera*. The whole sentence can then be paraphrased as follows 'things that belong to the vague, approximate category of which I give an example: water bottles and such like'.

Finally, it is possible to combine *tipo* as specifier with the general extender *cose del genere* ('things of the sort'):

(71)   *Per anestetizzare il suo dolore si lasciava andare a cose che le facevano male. Tipo bere, tipo cose del genere...*(Interview)
'To anaesthetise her pain, she allowed things to hurt her. Like drinking, like things of this sort'

The example in (71) is of particular interest because it allows us to observe the flexibility of these constructions. In the first sentence the speaker introduces an unspecified set of things that hurt her, followed by a first occurrence of *tipo*, which works as a specifier, introducing the example of drinking. This is followed by a second occurrence of *tipo*, which, since it is followed by a general extender, rather than specifying fulfils the function of a focuser.

7 The lexical sources, the texts, the constructions

In this final section I would like to outline the functional space occupied by each of the TNCxs$_{[-N]}$ in contemporary Italian, taking into account their grammaticalization processes, the role of their lexical sources, various formal aspects, their frequency and their contexts of use. This, I hope, will allow us to account for their varied productivity.

As we have seen in the previous sections, the $TipoCxs_{[-N]}$ are the most numerous and diversified from the functional point of view. This confirms the absence of correlation between the duration of the process and the number of outcomes: although the development of the $SpecieCxs_{[-N]}$ started five centuries before the development of $TipoCxs_{[-N]}$, their number remains substantially unchanged.

The duration of the process seems instead to have an influence on the frequency ratio of SGST and $Cxs_{[-N]}$. The figures from 1 to 7 show the trend of the frequencies of the $TNCxs_{[-N]}$ in M.I.DIA. and DiaCORIS, and how they are increasingly more frequent than the occurrences of the nouns, except in the case of the $TipoCxs_{[-N]}$.

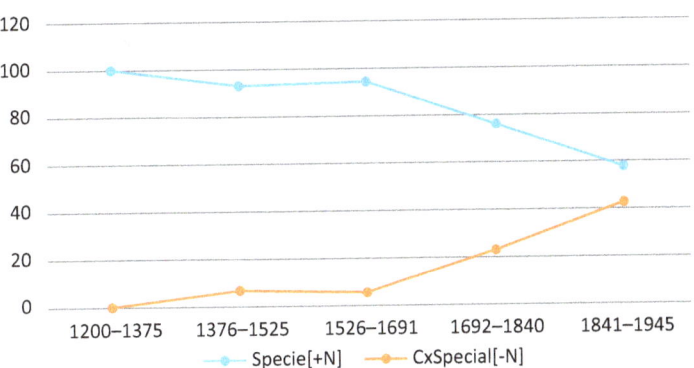

Figure 1: Frequency trend of nominal uses of *specie* and $SpecieCxs_{[-N]}$ in the M.I.DIA. corpus.

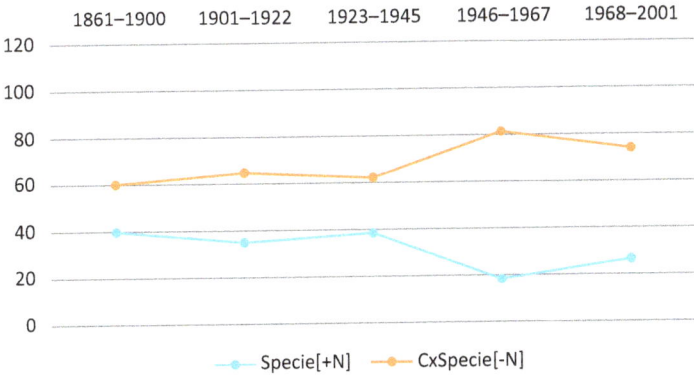

Figure 2: Frequency trend of nominal uses of *specie* and $SpecieCxs_{[-N]}$ in the DiaCORIS corpus.

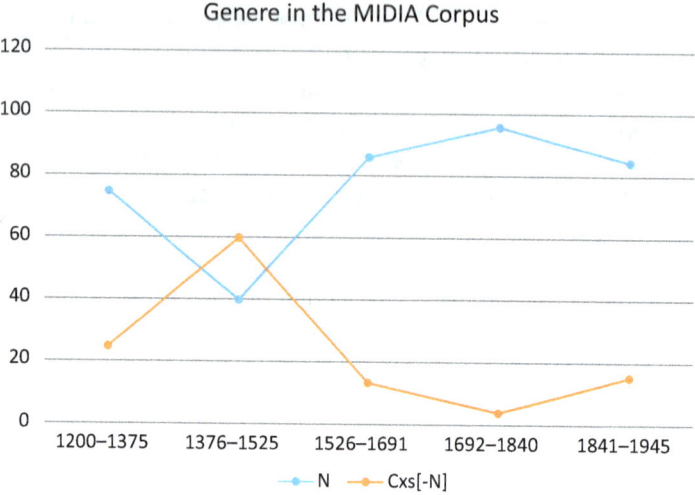

Figure 3: Frequency trend of nominal uses of *genere* and *Genere*Cxs[-N] i in the M.I.DIA. corpus.

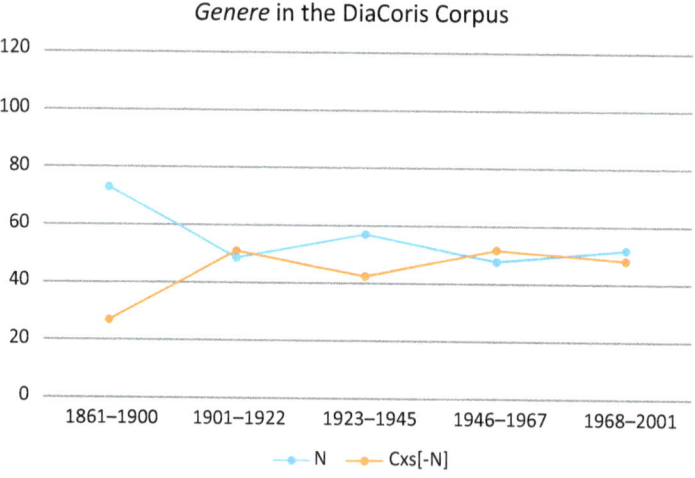

Figure 4: Frequency trend of nominal uses of *genere* and *Genere*Cxs[-N] in the DiaCORIS corpus.

Cxs[-N] are very frequent in speech and this is even more evident when compared to the frequencies of the individual nouns (Figure 8); furthermore, if we compare the LIP and the C-ORAL-ROM we can observe that occurrences of *Tipo*Cxs[-N] are increasing, although they are always lower than those of the noun (Figure 9).

The difference in frequencies between speech and writing highlights the role of different types of texts in the development and diffusion of TNCx[-N]. As predicted, given the meanings of the lexical sources, the texts in which SGST are initially

9 The network of *specie, genere, sorta, tipo* constructions — **383**

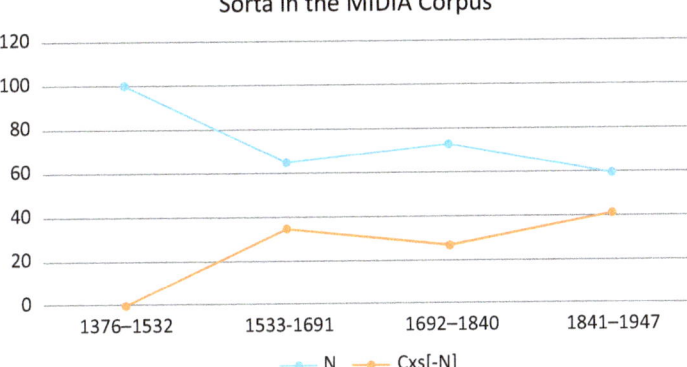

Figure 5: Frequency trend of nominal uses of *sorta* and *Sorta*Cxs[-N] in the M.I.DIA. corpus.

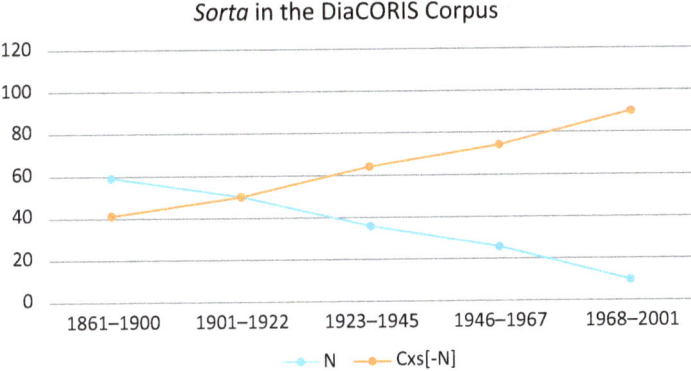

Figure 6: frequency trend of nominal uses of *sorta* and *Sorta*Cxs[-N] in the DiaCORIS corpus.

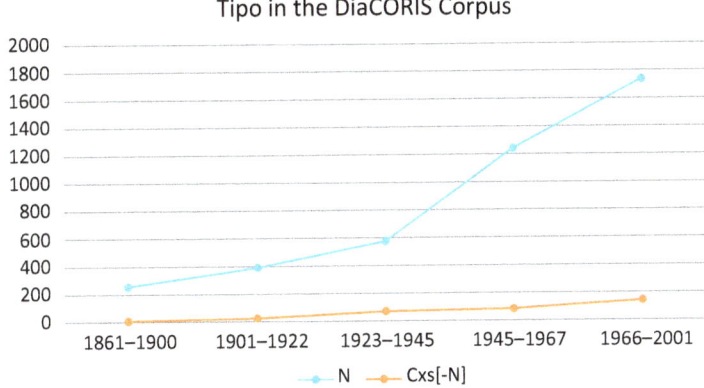

Figure 7: frequency trend of nominal uses of *tipo* and *Tipo*Cxs[-N] in DiaCORIS corpus.

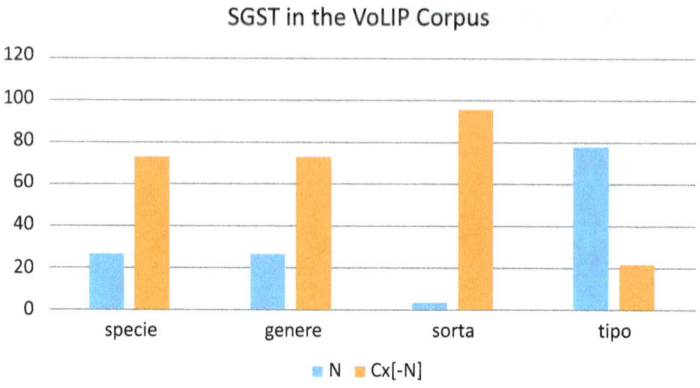

Figure 8: frequency trend of nominal uses and Cs[-N] of SGST in the VoLIP corpus.

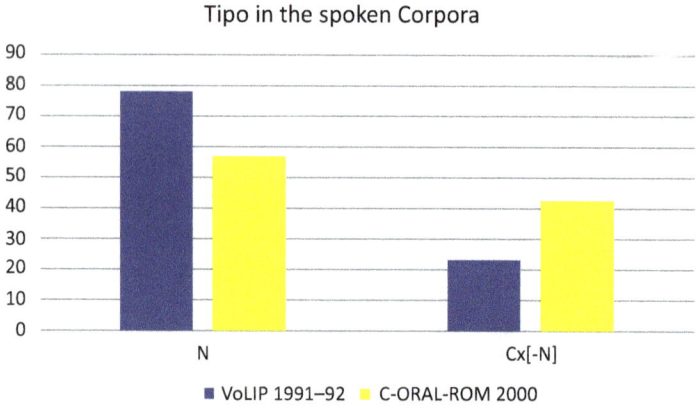

Figure 9: comparison between the nominal uses of *tipo* and *Tipo*Cxs[-N] in the VoLIP and C-ORAL-ROM corpora.

present are the juridical and scientific ones, i.e. texts that are monologual, non-subjective, monologic, and formal par excellence.[15] These are texts in which the author's voice must not be heard because the validity of a statute or of a scientific work lies precisely in their being independent of the person who wrote them. Subsequently, SGST spread into expository texts and essays, which are also in principle monological and formal, but more or less subjective. Essays may in fact contain argu-

---

15 I assume here the distinction by Traugott (2008) between *monologual* and *dialogual*, that indicates the number of producers of a text, and *monologic* and *dialogic*, that indicates instead texts in which a unique authorial point of view is present and texts in which more points of view are expressed.

mentative sections in which the author reveals and expresses him/herself clearly. Moreover, among the expository texts of M.I.DIA. there are three dialogues which, although they are not comparable to a spoken conversation, show greater traces of subjectivity and proximity between the interlocutors compared to a monologic text. From the expository texts SGST move on to literature in M.I.DIA. and to fiction in DiaCORIS, which act as bridging texts for the development of TNCxs$_{[-N]}$ and for their future diffusion in other contexts. The literature within this textual typology represents an open window to less formal and more personal and subjective themes. In these new contexts the decategorialization of TNs takes place and this also accelerates the diffusion of Cxs$_{[-N]}$. The *Tipo*Cxs$_{[-N]}$ have a similar but more compact path to the other TNCxs$_{[-N]}$, even if their increase has only been accelerating since the last decade of the 20th century. Finally, all the TNCxs$_{[-N]}$ spread into all types of texts, and they gain a much higher frequency in both of the spoken corpora considered.

Therefore, the trend of the frequencies of the TNCxs$_{[-N]}$ just described develops along a textual dimension that goes from the expression of a minor to a major level of subjectivity. This is true if one considers the movement from legal texts to literary and fictional texts, but it is also true in the movement from written to spoken texts. Although there is no mechanical relationship between subjectivity and speech, and a spoken text may lack explicit subjectivity markers, for example in the case of a scientific lecture, speech usually implies proximity to the recipient and a greater personal involvement by the speaker than in any traditional writing context (Koch and Oesterreicher 2011; Voghera 2017a). Moreover, in spoken corpora, strictly dialogical texts constitute the majority of the material.

It has been widely observed that the process of grammaticalization often involves a shift from a neutral textual meaning to a meaning that is anchored in the expression of the speaker's attitude (Traugott 1982, 2010). This has been recorded for the English TNCxs$_{[-N]}$ developed by *kind* and *sort* (Brems and Davidse 2010; Beeching 2016) and for those analysed here, which, as we have seen, can express from a minimum to a maximum level of generality (*in specie* vs. *in genere*) and from a minimum to a maximum level of vagueness (*una specie di, una sorta di, tipo*). Interestingly, our investigation has proven that the emergence of this subjective dimension of meaning in the TNCxs$_{[-N]}$ is reflected in their textual distribution in a transparent way, through the progressive increase of their frequency in texts of greater subjectivity and polyphony, such as essays compared to scientific texts and even more so, fiction and speech. The new textual distribution therefore appears as evidence of the new semantic-discursive status of these constructions which have originated from nouns used initially in other contexts.

A cooperation between contextual and textual elements therefore seems confirmed in conditioning the distribution of the *in fieri* constructions. Even though the distribution of any linguistic unit in the various types of texts should always be taken as an indication of a trend rather than as a demonstration of mechanical correspondences, the data presented here have shown a correlation between some formative dimensions of the texts and the meanings and discursive functions of the considered constructions. This shows that the relationship between the formation of new functions and their use in new contexts is very close and that they are mutually reinforcing. This is a result that encourages the diachronic study of textual pathways as a source of new knowledge about the relationship between the process of grammaticalization and its outcomes.

Data on frequency are very different from those on productivity. Table 13 shows clearly that if we rank the TNs according to the number and variety of Cxs$_{[-N]}$, *tipo* occupies the first position, followed by *genere*, *sorta* and *specie*. Besides this, and in contrast to *specie* and *sorta*, *tipo* and partially *genere* are continuing to develop other constructions, or rather, *tipo* and *genere* constructions are continuing to develop in parallel with new combined constructions. It seems possible to attribute these differences to constructional factors, i.e. to the greater flexibility of the *Tipo*Cxs$_{[-N]}$ at both a formal and semantic level.

Diachronic data confirm a strong correlation between the emergence of taxonomic meaning and the emergence of Cxs$_{[-N]}$ (Mihatsch 2007). The meaning that I glossed 'category' and which is assigned to categorization operations is suitable for analogical comparison that allows the attribution of an element to an impromptu category. TNCxs$_{[-N]}$ emerged primarily to form, through analogy, either non lexicalized or extemporaneous categories, that is categories which may have an experiential reality but not a noun to designate them. It can be said that TNs initially develop constructions for taxonomies with opaque borders or, even better, for the spontaneous process of categorizing (Mauri 2017). In fact, they are constructions that predominantly express approximation and vagueness. However, the various Cxs$_{[-N]}$ used in contemporary Italian present multiple differences that can be traced back to their respective evolutionary processes.

Specie and *genere* come into Italian without any interruption from Medieval Latin, in which they were already used in cultivated texts. Yet, although they both identify a category, *genere* had a more abstract and general meaning than *specie*: for example, its use in the construction *in genere et in specie*. In biological taxonomy, for instance, *genere* can be superordinate to *specie*. Although this difference is not perceived in the common use of the two nouns, it has conditioned the development of Cxs$_{[-N]}$. The *Specie*Cxs[$_{-N}$], *una specie di*, basically expresses the analogy between two elements or set of elements. It does not undergo a formal reduction and the approximating analogy is explicitly constructed starting from the target analog and arriving at the source analog.

The situation with *Genere*Cxs[$_{-N}$] is more complicated. Today *del genere* is used to build an a posteriori category, starting from one or more exemplars. The source analog, to which *del genere* refers, is in the previous context and this allows, unique among the TNs in Italian, its use in general extender constructions.

Sorta only entered the Italian language in the 15th century but has undergone a development similar to that of *specie*; in fact, *una sorta di* is synonymous with *una specie di*, although sociolinguistically belongs to a higher register.[16] The other constructions with *sorta*, *ogni sorta* di N and N *di ogni sorta*, have the function of noun modifiers as well.

The taxonomic meaning of *tipo* develops only in the 19th century, without replacing the original 'model' meaning, of which some trace remains also in the *Tipo*Cxs[-N]. They create similarities between an element and an exemplar (model?) of a potential category. This means that although *tipo* has undergone a decategorialization process, the similitude implies a shift through the assignment of an element to a type. It is precisely this semantic residue that allows, as we saw, the expansion of *tipo* as specifier and focuser.

The following semantic map (Figure 10) depicts the development of the prevailing meanings of the TNCxs[-N].

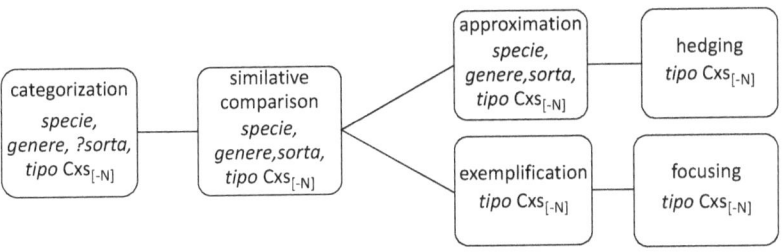

Figure 10: The map of main semantic area express by TNCxs[-N].

The map clearly shows that only *Tipo*Cxs[-N] occupy all the semantic slots. In fact, they can express both approximation and exemplification as well as many other nuances. Approximation often smooths the progression of communication as well as exemplification: both may have the purpose of simplifying the acceptance of an assertion, an opinion or a request by an interlocutor (Manzotti 1998). In other words, an approximation or an exemplification can be a way of giving a hand to the addressee to better participate in the communication, to make the speakers more proximate.

Thus, we can conclude that TNs have developed different types and numbers of Cxs[-N] because of many factors that have affected their formation process. On the one hand, the increase in frequency of the abstract taxonomic meaning of

---

[16] The same differences of register between *sort of* and *kind of* are reported by Beeching (2016).

the nouns was the first step towards a possible determinologization of the TNs in specific constructional contexts. On the other hand, in line with Hopper's principle of 'persistence' (Hopper 1991), the nature of the lexical sources meant that partially different semantic operations were selected for the various TNCxs[-N], such as categorization and analogical comparison, approximation, exemplification and focusing. This spread and favoured some constructions, which in turn occupied syntactic spaces of varying mobility.

*Specie*Cxs[-N] and *Sorta*Cxs[-N] remained substantially part of the NP, occupying mainly the role of noun modifiers; *Genere*Cxs[-N] can have both the function of noun modifier and verb modifier. *Tipo*Cxs[-N] and the new combinations with *Genere*Cxs[-N] can occupy a comparatively wider syntactic space and carry out multiple discursive functions.

Table 13: TNCxs[-N] derived from the Italian nouns *genere, specie, sorta, tipo* in contemporary Italian.

SGSTCxs[-N] in contemporary Italian		
TNCxs[-N]	Function	Meaning
N [*in genere*]	Adjective	*libri in genere* 'non-specific books'
[*una specie di*] N		*una specie/sorta di casa* 'a sort of house'
[*una sorta di*] N		
[*ogni sorta di*] N		*ogni sorta di questioni* 'all questions'
N [*di sorta*]		*senza vincolo di sorta* 'without any constraint'
N [*del genere*]		*strumenti del genere* 'instruments of the kind'
N[*tipo*]		*divano-tipo* 'standard sofa'
[(*del*) *tipo* (*di*) N]	Adjectival Suffix	*tipo intemperanze* 'excess-like'
[(*del*) *genere* (*di*) N]		*genere intemperanze* 'excess-like'
e/o N [*del genere*]	General extender	*e cose del genere* 'and things of the kind'
[*tipo* XP]	Similative marker	*la mia casa è tipo la tua* 'my house is like yours'
[*tipo* N]SP	Preposition	*a trattava tipo segretaria* 'he treated her like a secretary'
in genere	Adverb	*in genere mi piacciono i film* 'generally, I like movies'
(*in*) *specie*		*mi diverto in specie a cucinare* 'I especially enjoy cooking'
[XP]*tipo*		*tipo festa* 'like party'
[clause]*tipo*]		*questa è una prova//tipo* 'this is a trial// sort of'
clause[*tipo*(*che*)] clause	Connective	*teniamoci in contatto tipo che ti chiamo domani* 'let's keep in touch *tipo che* I'll call you tomorrow'
tipo, tipo che	Discourse marker	*faccio un caffè, tipo?; ma se tipo faccio un caffè?* Should I like make coffee?; 'What if I like make coffee?'

As we observe in Table 13, the *Tipo*Cxs$_{[-N]}$ cover the most space, as they do in the semantic map, assuming the role of head modifier of a NP up to that of clausal adverb and discourse marker. In other words, *Tipo*Cxs$_{[-N]}$ display a strong correlation between the breadth of the semantic area and that of the syntactic-functional area which they cover. This shows how the development of the constructions depends equally on semantic and functional factors and, consequently, how this interdependence is a crucial factor for their productivity.

References

Aijmer, Karin & Anne-Marie Simon Vandenbergen. 2011. Pragmatic markers. In Jef Verschueren, Jan-Ola Östman & Eline Versluys (eds.), *Handbook of pragmatics*, 223–247. Amsterdam & Philadelphia: John Benjamins.

Barotto, Alessandra & Caterina Mauri. 2018. Constructing lists to construct categories. *Italian Journal of Linguistics* 30 (1). 95–134.

GDLI. 1961–2002. *Grande dizionario della lingua italiana*. Edited by Salvatore Battaglia. Torino: UTET.

Beeching, Kate. 2016. *Pragmatic markers in British English: Meaning in social interaction*. Cambridge: Cambridge University Press.

Bergs, Alexander & Gabriele Diewald (eds.). 2009. *Contexts and constructions*. Amsterdam & New York: John Benjamins.

Biber, Douglas, Stig, Johansson, Leech, Geoffrey, Conrad, Susan, & Edward, Finegan. 1999. *Longman grammar of spoken and written English*. London: Longman.

Brems, Lieselotte. 2011. *Layering of size and type noun constructions in English*. Berlin & Boston: De Gruyter Mouton.

Brems, Lieselotte & Kristin Davidse. 2010. The grammaticalization of nominal type noun constructions with kind/sort of: Chronology and paths of change. *English studies* 91.2. 180–202. Leuven: University of Leuven.

Caffi, Claudia. 2007. *On mitigation*. Amsterdam & Oxford: Elsevier.

Channell, Joanna. 1994. *Vague language*. Oxford: Oxford University Press.

Cresti, Emanuela & Massimo Moneglia (eds.). 2005. *Integrated reference corpora for Romance spoken languages*. Amsterdam & New York: John Benjamins.

Danon-Boileau, Laurent & Morel May-Annick. 1997. Question, point de vue, genre, style: Les noms prépositionnels en français contemporain. *Faits de langue* (9). 193–200.

De Mauro, Tullio. 1982. *Minisemantica*. Roma–Bari: Laterza.

De Mauro, Tullio. 2007. *Primo tesoro della lingua letteraria italiana*. Torino: Utet.

De Mauro, Tullio, Federico Mancini, Massimo Vedovelli & Miriam Voghera, M. *Lessico di frequenza dell'italiano parlato*. Milano: Etaslibri.

Denison, David. 2002. History of the sort of construction family. Paper presented at the Second International Conference on Construction Grammar (ICCG2), Helsinki, September 6–8.

Denison, David. 2005. The grammaticalization of sort of, kind of and type of in English. Paper presented at New Reflections on Grammaticalization 3, University of Santiago de Compostela, 17–20 July.

Denison, David 2011. The construction of SKT. Paper presented at Second Vigo–Newcastle–Santiago–Leuven International Workshop on the structure of the noun phrase in English (NP2), Newcastle upon Tyne, 15–16 September.
DiaCORIS: http://corpora.dslo.unibo.it/DiaCORIS/ (accessed 02.02.2022)
Di Bonito, C. 2022. Un nuovo tassello per la storia di tipo. *Lingua e Stile* 57.1. 71–81.
Diewald, Gabriel. 2002. A model for relevant types of contexts in grammaticalization. In Ilse Wischer & Gabriele Diewald (eds.), *New Reflections on Grammaticalization*, 103–120. Amsterdam & New York: John Benjamins.
Fiorentini, Ilaria & Andrea Sansò. 2016. Interagire in contesto multilingue e cose così. Il caso dei general extenders. In Cecilia Andorno & Roberta Grassi(eds.), *Dinamiche dell'interazione: testo, dialogo, applicazioni educative*, 189–202. Perugia: Guerra.
Fischer, Kerstin. 2006. Towards an understanding of the spectrum of approaches to discourse particles: Introduction to the volume. In Kerstin Fischer (ed.), *Approaches to discourse particles*, 1–20. Amsterdam: Elsevier.
Fleischman, Suzanne & Marina Yaguello. 2004. Discourse markers across languages: Evidence from English and French. In Carolin Lynn Moder & Aida Martinovic-Zic, *Discourse across languages and cultures*, 129–148. Amsterdam & Philadelphia: John Benjamins.
Fraser, Bruce. 2010. Pragmatic competence: The case of hedging. In Gunther Kaltenböck, Wiltrud Mihatsch & Stefan Schneider (eds.), *New Approaches to hedging*,15–34. Bingley: Emerald Group Publishing Limited.
GDLI = *Grande dizionario della lingua italiana*. 1961–2002. Torino: Utet.
Gentner, Dedre & Arthur B. Markman. 1997. Structure mapping in analogy and similarity. *American psychologist* 52. 1–45.
Goldberg, Adele E. 1995. *Constructions: A construction grammar approach to argument structure*. Chicago: University of Chicago Press.
Haspelmath, Martin. 1999. Why is grammaticalization irreversible? *Linguistics* 37 (6). 1043–1068.
Haspelmath, Martin. 2004. On directionality in language change with particular reference to grammaticalization. *Typological Studies in Language* (59). 17–44.
Haspelmath, Martin & Oda Buchholz. 1998. Equative and similative constructions in the languages of Europe. In Johan van der Auwera (ed.), *Adverbial constructions in the languages of Europe*, 277–334. Berlin: Mouton de Gruyter.
Heine, Bern. 2002. On the role of context in grammaticalization. In In Ilse Wischer & Gabriele Diewald (eds.), *New reflections on grammaticalization*, 83–102. Amsterdam & New York: John Benjamins.
Heine, Bern & Tania Kuteva. 2002. *World lexicon of grammaticalization*, Cambridge: Cambridge University Press.
Hopper, Paul J. 1991. On some principles of grammaticalization. In Traugott Closs, Elisabeth & Bernd Heine (eds.), *Approaches to grammaticalization Volume II. Types of grammatical markers*, 17–35. Amsterdam & New York.
Hopper, Paul J. & Elisabeth Closs Traugott. 2003. *Grammaticalization*. 2nd edn. Cambridge: Cambridge University Press.
Iacobini, Claudio, Aurelio De Rosa & Giovanna Schirato. 2017. Criteri e strategie di classificazione morfo-sintattica dei testi del corpus M.I.DIA. In Maria Grossmann & Paolo D'Achille, P. (eds.), *Per la storia della formazione delle parole in italiano: Un nuovo corpus in rete (M.I.DIA.) e nuove prospettive di studio*, 33–51. Firenze: Franco Cesati.
Koch, Peter & Wulf Oesterreicher. 2011. *Gesprochene Sprache in der Romania: Französisch, Italienisch, Spanisch*. Vol. 31. Berlin: Walter de Gruyter.

Kolyaseva, Alena & Kristine Davidse, 2018. A typology of lexical and grammaticalized uses of Russian *tip, tipa, po tipu*. *Russian Linguistics* 42 (2). 191–220.

Kuryłowicz, Jerzy. 1965. The evolution of grammatical categories. *Diogenes* (13) 51. 55–71.

Lakoff, George. 1973. Hedges: a study in meaning criteria and the logic of fuzzy concepts. *Journal of Philosophical Logic* 2. 458–508.

Lehmann, Christian, 2002. *Thoughts on grammaticalization*. Munich: Lincom.

Lehmann, Christian. 2004. Theory and method in grammaticalization. *Zeitschrift für Germanistik und Linguistik* 32 (2). 152–187.

Lepschy, Anna Laura, Giulio C. Lepschy & Miriam Voghera. 1996. Linguistic Variety in Italy. In Carl Levy (ed.), *Italian Regionalism*, 69–80. Oxford: Berg Publishers.

Lindquist, Hans & Christian Mair (eds.). 2004. *Corpus approaches to grammaticalization in English*. Amsterdam & New York: John Benjamins.

Lo Baido, Cristina. 2018. Mitigation via exemplification in Present-Day Italian: a corpus-based study. In García Ramón, Amparo, Soler Bonafont & María Amparo (eds.), *ELUA: Estudios de atenuación en el discurso*. Anexo IV (67), 11–32.

Manzotti, Emilio. 1995. Aspetti linguistici dell'esemplificazione. *Versus* (70/71). 49–114.

Manzotti, Emilio. L'esempio. Natura, definizioni, problemi. *Cuadernos de Filología Italiana*. 1998 (5). 99–123.

Masini, Francesca. 2012. *Parole sintagmatiche in italiano*. Cesena-Roma: Caissa.

Masini, Francesca. 2016. Binominal constructions in Italian of the N1-di-N2 type: towards a typology of light noun constructions. *Language sciences* (53). 99–113.

Mauri, Caterina. 2017. Building and interpreting ad hoc categories: A linguistic analysis. In Joanna Blochowiak, Cristina Grisot, Stephanie Durrleman & Christopher Laenzlinger (eds.), *Formal models in the study of language*, 297–326. Cham: Springer.

Mihatsch, Wiltrud. 2007. The construction of vagueness: *sort of* expressions in Romance languages. In Günter Radden, Klaus-Michael Köpke, Thomas Berg & Peter Siemund (eds.), *Aspects of meaning construction meaning: From concepts to utterance*, 225–245. Amsterdam & Philadelphia: John Benjamins.

Mihatsch, Wiltrud. 2009. The approximators French *comme* Italian *come*, Portuguese *como* Spanish *como* from a grammaticalization perspective. In Corinne Rossari Ricci, Claudia, Spiridon & Adriana. Bingley (eds.), *Grammaticalization and pragmatics: Facts, approaches, theoretical*, 65–92. Amsterdam: Emerald Group Publishing Limited.

Mihatsch, Wiltrud. 2016. Type-noun binominals in four romance languages. *Language Sciences* (53). 136–159.

Overstreet, Maryann. 1999. *Whales, candlelight, and stuff like that: General extenders in English discourse*. Oxford: Oxford University Press.

Piot, Mireille. 2009. *Come, Comme, Como*: de la modalité de phrase à la modalité discursive. Recueil de contributions scientifiques: "Panorama des études en linguistique diachronique et synchronique". https://halshs.archives-ouvertes.fr/halshs-00365263. (accessed on 1.07.2019)

Proietti Domenico. 2008. Tra DiaCORIS e CORIS: corpora elettronici e storia moderna e contemporanea dell'italiano. In Rema Rossini Favretti (ed.), *Frames, corpora and knowledge representation*, 201–43. Bologna: Bonomia University Press.

Romaine, Suzanne & Deborah Lange. 1991. The use of like as a marker of reported speech and thought: A case of grammaticalization in progress. *American Speech* 66 (3). 227–279.

Rosenkvist, Henrik & Sanna Skärlund. 2013. Grammaticalization in the present-the change of modern Swedish typ. In Anna Giacalone Ramat, Caterina Mauri & Piera Molinelli, (eds.), *Synchrony and diachrony: A dynamic interface*, 313–38. Amsterdam & Philadelphia: John Benjamins.

Serianni, Luca. 1988. *Grammatica italiana. Italiano comune e lingua letteraria*, in collaboration with Alberto Castelvecchi. Torino: Utet.

Thornton, Anna M. 2004. Conversione. In Maria Grossmann & Franz Rainer (eds.), *La formazione delle parole in italiano*, 501–33. Tübingen: Niemeyer.

Traugott, Elisabeth C. 1982. From propositional to textual and expressive meanings: Some semantic-pragmatic aspects of grammaticalization. In Winfred P. Lehmann & Yakov Malkiel (eds.), *Perspectives on historical linguistics*, 245–271. Amsterdam & New York: John Benjamins.

Traugott, Elisabeth C. 1995. *The role of the development of discourse markers in a theory of grammaticalization*. Paper presented at the XII International Conference of Historical Linguistics, Manchester, August.

Traugott, Elisabeth C. 2008. The grammaticalization of *NP of NP* patterns. In Alexander Bergs & Gabriele Diewald (eds.), *Constructions and language change*, 23–45. The Hague: Mouton de Gruyter.

Traugott, Elisabeth C. 2010. (Inter)subjectivity and (inter)subjectification: A reassessment. In Kristin Davidse, Lieven Vandelanotte & Hubert Cuyckens (eds.), *Subjectification, intersubjectification and grammaticalization*, 29–71. Berlin & New York: Walter de Gruyter.

Voghera, Miriam. 2013. A case study on the relationship between grammatical change and synchronic variation: the emergence of $tipo_{[-N]}$ in Italian. In Giacalone Ramat, Mauri, Molinelli (eds.), *Synchrony and diachrony. A dynamic interface*, 283–312. Amsterdam: Benjamins.

Voghera, Miriam. 2014. Da nome tassonomico a segnale discorsivo: una mappa delle costruzioni di *tipo* in italiano contemporaneo. *Studi di grammatica italiana*. XXIII. 197–221.

Voghera, Miriam. 2017a. *Dal parlato alla grammatica*. Roma: Carocci.

Voghera, Miriam. 2017b. La nascita delle costruzioni non nominali di *specie, genere, sorta* e *tipo*: uno studio basato su corpora. In Maria Grossmann & Paolo D'Achille, P. (eds.), *Per la storia della formazione delle parole in italiano: un nuovo corpus in rete (M.I.DIA.) e nuove prospettive di studio*, 277–307. Firenze: Franco Cesati.

Voghera, Miriam. 2018. List constructions: a specialised means of text progression. *Italian Journal of Italian Linguistics* 30 (1). 173–200.

Voghera Miriam. 2022. Building the reference by similarity: from vagueness to focus. In Hélène Vassiliadou & Marie Lammert (eds.), *A Crosslinguistic Perspective on Clear and Approximate Categorization*, 271–298. Cambridge: Cambridge Scholars Publishing.

Voghera Miriam, Claudio Iacobini, Renata Savy, Francesco Cutugno, Aurelio De Rosa & Iolanda Alfano. 2014. VoLIP: a searchable Italian spoken corpus, in complex visibles out there. In Ludmila Veselovská & Markéta Janebová (eds.), *Language use and linguistic structure*, 627–640. Proceedings of the Olomouc Linguistics Colloquium Olomouc: Palacký University.

Vosniadou, Stella & Andrew Ortony. 1989. Similarity and analogical reasoning: a synthesis. In Stella Vosniadou & Andrew Ortony (eds.), *Similarity and analogical reasoning*, 1–17. Cambridge: Cambridge University Press.

Waltereit, Richard. 2006. The rise of discourse markers in Italian: A specific type of language change. In Kerstin Fischer (ed.), *Approaches to discourse particles*, 61–76. Amsterdam: Elsevier.

Maria Aldina Marques
10 Pragmatic functions and contexts of use of TIPO in European Portuguese

Abstract: This paper is the continuation and extension of a previous study on the discourse marker *tipo* 'type' in European Portuguese. Firstly, I will review the semantic and pragmatic characteristics of the uses of *tipo* in spontaneous speech. Next, the characteristics of the contexts in which the discourse marker tipo occurs will be analyzed, including the syntactic structures and, in particular, the clusters of discourse markers with *tipo* and the semantic-pragmatic values that they convey. Concerning the functions of discourse markers (henceforward DMs) in discourse, the findings of studies carried out by other researchers, *inter alia*, provide the foundation for ongoing tipo analysis. The analysis is based on oral data from two corpora, the CRPC-Oral and the corpus *Perfil Sociolinguístico da Fala Bracarense* (Sociolinguistic profile of Braga speech /PSFB). Both data sets are of spontaneous speech, characterized by a colloquial register within a discursive genre, the sociolinguistic interview.

1 *Tipo* as a discourse marker

DMs[1] are a heterogeneous category with pragmatic-discursive functions.[2] Despite theoretical and methodological differences in discourse marker research, it is widely agreed that DMs are multifunctional since they operate on several dis-

---

[1] Discourse marker is a fuzzy category. I adopt the definition by Martín Zorraquino and Portolés Lázaro (1999: 4057): "unidades lingüísticas invariables, no ejercen una función sintáctica en el marco de la predicación oracional-son, pues, elementos marginales- y poseen un cometido coincidente en el discurso: el de guiar, de acuerdo con sus distintas propiedades morfosintácticas, semánticas y pragmáticas, las inferencias que se realizan en la comunicación." [Invariable linguistic units, they do not have a syntactic function in the framework of the sentence – they are therefore marginal elements – and have a coincidental role in discourse: that of guiding, according to their different morphosyntactic, semantic and pragmatic properties, inferences made in communication.] (my translation).
[2] The formal heterogeneity of this category derives from the fact that the DMs are linguistically differentiated forms, that is, they originate in quite different classes of words, verbs, adjectives, conjunctions, adverbs and sentence fragments; taxonomic nouns are another important class.

Maria Aldina Marques, Universidade do Minho, e-mail: mamarques@elach.uminho.pt

https://doi.org/10.1515/9783110701104-010

course levels simultaneously. They are also polysemous (Hansen 1998: 241–242). As Wichmann and Chanet (2009: 24) point out, considering a long process of pragmaticalization of DMs, "the new meanings exist alongside the older meanings." The third feature of these units is their predominantly procedural or instructional meaning; they fulfil a metadiscursive function. One salient feature is their context-dependence.

Thus, the concept of context[3] is a key notion to the analysis of meaning construction in discourse. Due to their procedural meaning, DMs play an important role in discourse construction. The fact that they are context-sensitive produces meaningful effects that may be imprecise or ambiguous. However, DMs are strategic to both discourse local and global goals. Imprecision and efficacy are not incompatible.

The analysis I carried out on the discourse marker *tipo* is informed by the broadest theoretical frameworks of discourse pragmatics. I adopt an empirical and a corpus-based approach grounded in a qualitative method with the aim of describing and explaining the different pragmatic-discursive functions of *tipo*.[4] The analysis is based on oral data from two corpora, the CRPC-Oral and the corpus *Perfil Sociolinguístico da Fala Bracarense* (Sociolinguistic profile of Braga speech /PSFB).[5] Both data sets are of spontaneous speech, characterized by a colloquial register within a discursive genre, the sociolinguistic interview.

---

[3] See further: van Dijk 2001, 2004 and 2012; Kerbrat-Orecchioni 2002; Adam 2006; Koch, Bentes and Morato 2011.

[4] *Tipo* occurs mainly in spontaneous oral language. In written language, mediatic texts for example, as a DM, *tipo* occurs in contexts that simulate an informal register (Marques 2015a).

[5] This corpus consists of interviews, in audio recordings, carried out within the scope of the project *Perfil sociolinguístico da fala bracarense* (Sociolinguistic profile of Braga speech / PSFB), at the University of Minho, Portugal, under the reference FCT PTDC/CLE-LIN/112939/2009. "The C-ORAL-ROM resource is a multilingual corpus of spoken language for the main Romance languages, namely Spanish, Portuguese, French and Italian, constituted by formal and informal speech, in a total of 1,200,000 words (300,000 words for each language)." (Information available on the CLUL website). Some transcription conventions: Tone units with a not terminal contour: / (single slash); terminal prosodic break: //? (double slash or question mark) ; interruption: +; quotation: "..."(Cresti et al. 2002; CLUL website).

Transcription conventions of PSFB: punctuation marks were used with the values established by the orthographic conventions of Portuguese (.,?,!,); all non-linguistic events are transcribed in double brackets (()); all rephrased terms are separated by a slash /; doubtful passage: (I think); all pauses up to 0.3 seconds are transcribed with • • (2 bullets); all pauses over 1 second are transcribed with • • • (3 bullets); All uncertain transcriptions are transcribed in brackets ( ); all repetitions and false starts are transcribed; incomplete sentence: . . .; enumeration. (https://sites.google.com/site/projectofalabracarense).

The main goal of the present study is twofold. In what follows, firstly, *tipo*'s main features on the level of semantics, pragmatics and syntax are presented and discussed and, secondly, its occurrences in clusters of DMs are identified and analyzed. Specifically, the aim is to identify and determine pragmatic effects of this clustering. The following research questions are the starting point of this analysis: (1) with which markers does *tipo* occur? (2) when does this clustering process occur? (3) what pragmatic values emerge from this clustering process?

2 The meanings of *tipo*: Polysemy and multifunctionality

Tipo is a type noun or taxonomic noun,[6] maintaining a general meaning of 'type' or 'subcategory'.[7] According to the existing empirical studies, *tipo* has been known to be polysemous and to have multiple functions. I will distinguish different semantic-pragmatic values of *tipo*, whose polysemy extends to both conceptual and procedural meanings.

Firstly, *tipo* is synonymous with 'guy'. According to the Portuguese dictionary, *Dicionário da Língua Portuguesa Contemporânea* (Casteleiro 2001), it is an "informal way and with some pejorative sense of referring to a person without naming him/her."[8]

(1) *como é que, que os teus, que as tua[. . .], os teus laços de camaradagem se vão desenvolver / com um **tipo** que é/completamente analfabeto?* | (CRPC-Oral)
'how is it, that yours, that yours [. . .], your bonds of camaraderie will develop/ with a *guy* who is/completely illiterate?'

---

[6] See: Davidse, Brems, and De Smeth 2008; Mihatsch 2010 and 2018; Voghera 2014; Voghera and Borges 2017.
[7] On this definition, see, for example, Mihatsch (2018): "The Spanish lexical item *tipo*, like its equivalents in other languages, belongs to the class of taxonomic nouns, i.e., nouns designating categories or (sub)kinds. Other taxonomic nouns are *sort*, *kind*, *class*, *category* and to some extent *form* (in Spanish, *especie*, *género*, *clase* and *forma*, respectively)."
[8] The dictionary definition is a good starting point, in so far as it is a selection of the main uses ratified by the linguistic community. Another meaning of *tipo* referring to a model or prototype is also described, but this usage is not attested in the corpora studied here.

(2) *cinco de abril / correram com o* **tipo** *de lá // | conseguiram correr com o tipo* (CRPC-Oral)
'On April 5th/they fired the **guy**// // | they managed to fire the *guy*'

2.1 The taxonomic use of *tipo*

A second meaning of *tipo* is with a taxonomic function as a categorizer. According to the same Portuguese dictionary, it comprises "a set of common traits that represent and define a class of things", or an "abstract concept that expresses the essence of a set of objects and people and can serve as an example" (Casteleiro 2001). This function draws on the establishment of a subcategory. **Tipo** refers to a subcategory within a general category, and thus marks a semantic relation of hyponymy:

(3) *a cerveja corrente / não se / define que* **tipo** *de cerveja é // | nós aqui temos / eh / tipos* (CRPC-Oral)
'the current beer / it is not / defined what *type* of beer it is // | we have here/ eh/types'

(4) *perguntei para ela / se ela teve algum* **tipo** *de pressentimento / ela falou que não* (CRPC-Oral)
'I asked her / if she had any **kind of** foreboding / she said no'

(5) *disse que / vem gente de* **todo o tipo** *// | e / quais são as dificuldades / os principais* (CRPC-Oral)[9]
'said that / **all kinds** of people are coming // | and / which are the difficulties / the main'

This categorizing function constitutes the prototypical meaning of *tipo*, even though it has divergent discourse functions: from determinacy to indeterminacy, and from reference to a well-defined category to a discursive process of categorization by approximation, an *ad hoc* categorization process.[10] As Mihatsch

---

9 "*todo o tipo de*" is the semantic equivalent of English 'all kind(s) of'. As Brems and Davidse (2010: 182) state for 'all kinds of', and it is also valid for "*todo o tipo de*", "...that is a lexicalized chunk with a quantifier meaning that is not derived compositionally: the expression contains a universal quantifier, but its meaning has shifted to 'many'."
10 On the definition of *ad hoc* categorization, see Mihatsch (2018: 149). Approximation is a complex discourse phenomenon. Mihatsch (2009a: 100) defines approximation as "les moyens

(2018: 153) states about 'sort of', these kinds of hedges "...are rather procedural interpretive instructions that license *unusual processes* of predication or reference." [emphasis mine].

As a discourse marker, *tipo* flags the ongoing process of negotiated construction of meaning in context (Marques 2015a: 95). The analysis highlights *tipo*'s contribution to the discourse construction, combining semantic, enunciative and illocutionary dimensions of meaning in the service of communicative efficacy. These discursive uses of *tipo* will be considered and analyzed in the following sections. The functions listed below co-occur in different contexts, assuming different meanings.

2.2 The quotative function of *tipo*

One of the discursive uses of *tipo* is as a quotation marker (Buchstaller 2002; Marques 2015b). In this role, it introduces direct speech. *Tipo* precedes a quotation and plays the role of a speech verb:

(6) *nós vimos passar um moço / de cabeção / hhh / **tipo** // | hhh / "sabe onde é que é / o* (CRPC-Oral)
 'we saw a boy go through / wearing a short cap / hhh / **like** / and he said) // | hhh/"Do you know where is / the'

(7) *para o outro// | uns para os outros / **tipo** / hhh/ | "coitada / passou-se" hhh// | hhh | ah / hhh/ e pronto/*(CRPC-Oral)
 'to the other// | each other / **like** / hhh/ | "poor thing/gone crazy" hhh// | hhh | ah / hhh / and you know / that's it /'

However, the speech verb fulfils more than simply an introducing function. The act of quoting another person's speech does not entail a presumption of literality or factuality (Marques 2015b: 96–97). It is the relevance assigned by the speaker to quoted material that is important. Hence a quotation is only ever an approximate account of what happened, as a consequence of the speaker's evaluation. In examples (6) and (7), the words quoted are not necessarily the exact words origi-

---

linguistiques explicites qui servent à rendre floues les limites catégorielles de l'élément linguistique qu'ils modifient" [the explicit linguistic means which serve to blur the categorical limits of the linguistic element which they modify] (my translation). Vigara Tauste (1966: 25) defines *approximation* as "algo que '*no es exactamente eso*'" [something that "is not exactly that"](my translation).

nally uttered (in fact, probably not). The quoted text is what the speaker remembers and wants to emphasize, or even something that has never been uttered but is used by the speaker to stress certain aspects of a person or a situation. The words reported are therefore inherently characterized by imprecision.

The imprecise nature of quotation allows the DM *tipo* to report fictive and iterative speeches:

(8) *aquelas coisas de mãe // | sim sim sim// |**tipo** // | "minha filha / tens que seguir isto* ((CRPC-Oral))
'those mother things// | yes yes yes// | **like**// | "My dear/you have to follow this'

(9) • • *É o que eu digo à minha mãe, quando (ouvir) a minha mãe a queixar-se,*
•• *a única coisa que eu digo é **tipo**: • • – Esquece.* (PSFB)
'• • That's what I say to my mother, when (listening) to my mother complaining, •• the only thing I say is like: • • – Forget it.'

The combination of *tipo* with the discourse marker *assim* reinforces the approximative interpretation of direct speech:[11]

(10) *- És assim? • • Mas não é positivo. É um **assim tipo**: • • – Fogo,• • tem calma, sim? • •* (PSFB)
'- Are you like this? But it is not positive. It's something **like that like**: – Dammit, calm down, will you?'

2.3 The function of categorization

Prototypically, the DM *tipo* retains a categorizing meaning as an approximator, i.e, something that *"no es exactamente eso"* [is not exactly that] (Vigara Tauste 1966: 25).[12] This function is regulated by textual, enunciative and pragmatic constraints that co-occur. Depending on the context of the occurrence of *tipo*, those constraints get different discursive relevance that determines the meaning of the DM. The possibility of expressing more than one meaning at a time in a given context is frequently a source of ambiguity.

---

[11] For some references on the DM *assim*, see footnote 24.
[12] Following the seminal work of Lakoff (1972), Trujillo Carreño (1990), Fuentes Rodríguez (2008), Said-Mohand (2008) Mihatsch (2009a, 2009b) and Hengeveld and Keizer (2011), *inter alia*, are key authors in the current research on approximators.

Specifically, *tipo* moves between a function of categorization by hyponymy, presented above, to that of categorization by approximation. These two kinds of precise and imprecise categorization account for gradual and related dimensions of meaning that this DM can express. The following examples demonstrates categorization by hyponymy (11) and categorization by approximation (12):

(11) *acho que ele tem mesmo jeito para aquilo e basicamente é • • é naquele **tipo** de filmes que ele participa.* (PSFB)
'I think he's really good at it and basically it's those **kind of** films that he acts in'

(12) *• • • ((hesitação)) • • Jogos **tipo** da treta,* (PSFB)
'• • • ((hesitation)) • • **sort of** bullshit games'

While examples (11) and (12) illustrate the two poles of the above categorizing function, in the example (13) *tipo* introduces a non-exhaustive list of items belonging to the category named by the speaker as 'the old part of Lisbon' (Alfama, Bairro Alto and Castelo de S. Jorge are some of the old city districts). The enumeration of a few Lisbon districts serves to specify the ongoing referential process.

(13) *conhecer a parte antiga de Lisboa // | hã hã// | **tipo** Alfama/Bairro Alto/ Castelo de são Jorge* (CRPC-Oral)
'to know the old part of Lisbon// | hã hã// | **like** Alfama/Bairro Alto/Castelo de São Jorge'

The following example (14) reinforces the claim of the contextual heterogeneity of the senses of *tipo* in this categorization process:

(14) *um carro óptimo / percebes / grandes férias sempre / **tipo** Caraíbas / ah / pronto//* (CRPC-Oral)
'a great car / you know / always great holidays / **like** the Caribbean/ah/ that's it//'

In fact, taking the Caribbean as a prototype or model of a place for "great holidays", the holidays the speaker is referring to are understood to be close to this model. It is an evaluative judgment based on comparison. The speaker negotiates a sense that is assumed to be approximate. He or she knows and shows that it is not a real destination he is referring to. The focus is not the holiday location itself, but rather the fact that someone indulges in the luxury associated with the

Caribbean. The goal is to approximate the unknown to the known, the abstract to the concrete, using the DM *tipo*.

Those occurrences point to the fact that *tipo* introduces heterogeneous subcategories of meaning, which must be considered in terms of family resemblances.

The inherent uncertainty in this process of ad-hoc categorization is sometimes reinforced by a metadiscursive comment, as '*Como é que hei-de lhe explicar?*' in the following example:

(15) não é? • • E tinha uma cozinha fora, • • e tinha um corredor **assim**, tudo / **tipo**• • ((hesitação)). . . • • ((hesitação)) **Como é que hei de lhe explicar?** (PSFB)
'isn't it? • • And there was a kitchen outside, • • and there was a hallway **like this**, everything/**sort of** • • ((hesitation)). . . • • ((hesitation)) **How can I explain that?**'

The uncertainty can be total, blocking the categorization process, as in this example:

(16) • • ((hesitação)) **Tipo**. . . • • • ((risos)) (PSFB)
'(((hesitation)) **Sort of** . . . • • • ((laughs))'

Other discourse devices take part in this categorization process and contribute to make the category fuzzier.

2.4 The enunciative function

In (17), there is an initial categorization modalized by the epistemic adverb *quase* ("*é quase uma performance*" [It is almost a performance]).[13] The speaker repeats the same modalization strategy in a second reformulation ("tipo teatro quase" [like theatre *almost*]). In terms of providing clear-cut textual information the result is vague, but in terms of the communication it is effective, by leaving the addressee with several hypotheses for what the object of discourse might be:

---

[13] Modality and modalization, as Monte (2011) points out are a theoretical and highly debated issue, central to the enunciative approach of discourse. In a broad sense, used here, modalization is a discursive category, to express the speaker's enunciative position (epistemic, appreciative, axiological, intersubjective. . .) towards the content of his/her utterance and also towards the other, the interlocutor.

(17) *É quasi uma performance • • o que ele está ali a fazer • • **tipo** teatro quase.*
(PSFB)
'It's *almost* a performance • • what he's doing there • • **like** theatre *almost*.'

The metadiscursive comments signal a vague categorization, as seen above, but they also explicitly request that the addressee share responsibility for the ongoing categorization process. In fact, we are dealing with an inter-subjective process of meaning construction. The speaker seeks an adjustment.

Examples (18) and (19) show that the speaker clearly appeals to the addressee through interpersonal discourse structures such as "*estás a ver*" (you see) in (18) and "*estás a imaginar*" (can you imagine this) in (19):

(18) *que eu já te contei// | que era /**tipo** / uma garagenzinha / **estás a ver**//* (CRPC-Oral)
'I already told you// | it was/**like**/a little garage/**you see**'

(19) *mas eram para aí setenta escadas.• • Assim, até. . . **Tipo** uma torre de vigia, **está a imaginar**? Pronto.*[14] (PSFB)
'but there were about seventy steps. • • Just, until . . . **like** a watchtower, **can you imagine this**? You know / That's it'

Since Benveniste's work (1970), it has been understood that the act of enunciation involves both the speaker and the addressee. Benveniste's theory stands up for a dialogical perspective on the negotiation and construction of meaning in discourse. (Marques 2015a: 256).

Categorization by approximation is relevant for the construction of inter-subjectivity in discourse, of which modalization constitutes a central linguistic device, with pragmatic effects on the speaker's enunciative responsibility (Marques 2013):

(20) *portanto/já assim crescidota//| aí assim/**tipo** não sei o quê/assim empregada* (C-ORAL-ROM)
so/[a girl] already grown up//| almost like/**sort of** I don't know what/like an employee

---

14 *Pronto* is polysemous and multifunctional; among other functions, it is an interpersonal marker expressing shared knowledge (Marques 2014: 103).

(21) •*A minha mãe foi lá fazer os seus curativos **tipo** médica.* (PSFB)
'My mother went there to dress the wounds **like** a doctor'

In these examples, the use of *tipo* allows the speaker (the locutor) to distance himself or herself from the expressed point of view (of the enunciator).[15] It is a comment on what is said and simultaneously a strategy of distancing from what is being said (Ducrot 1984; Rabatel 2005).

2.5 The illocutionary function

Closely related to the enunciative function is the illocutionary function of *tipo*. It acts as a softener, allowing the speaker to avoid giving a full commitment to the truth of the propositional content.[16] Therefore, the illocutionary function of *tipo* is related to its epistemic (modal) function. The occurrence of the DM downgrades the epistemic force of the assertive speech act:

(22) *O engenheiro só vai lá, **tipo**, • • tirar umas dúvidas, dizer como é que quer,* (PSFB)
'The engineer just goes there, **like**, • • to clarify some issues, to say what should be done'

The context again emphasizes the strategic mitigation of the assertion. The co-occurrence of *tipo* with propositional/attitude verbs such as *achar* 'think/find' accentuates this process:

(23) *Mas ela ela foi para África para uma institu / para um / tipo a ONU, assim qualquer coisa, para para África e e trabalha e trabalha lá **tipo** em causas humanitárias, **acho** que é isso* (PSFB)

---

[15] Locutor and enunciator are discursive instances of the polyphonic theory of Ducrot (1984). The enunciator is the source of a point of view.
[16] The fuzzy nature of *tipo* and its mitigation effect enable the occurrence of very specific contextual meanings, namely as a trigger of alternative worlds: (a) mesmo naquela faculdade//| e então pronto //| hhh | é *tipo/vamos supor*/o gajo dá aulas (CRPC-Oral) '/(even in that college//| and then you know//| hhh | *it's like/let's suppose/the guy teaches*); (b) as instalações são porreiras/mas é assim/eh/*tipo*/queres alguma coisa/tens que ir lá (CRPC–ORAL)/(the facilities are cool/ but it's like/eh/*kind of/you want something/you have to go there*).'

'But she she went to Africa for an institu/for a/like the UN, something like that, for for Africa and and she works and she works there **kind of** in humanitarian causes, **I think** that's it'

(24) com uma capa de / **acho** que é **tipo** de folhas de jornal / ou uma cena (CRPC-Oral)
'with a cover of/I **think** it's **kind of** newspaper sheets/or something'

Tipo also prevents a Face Threatening Act (FTA),[17] as in this example:

(25) Eu ia utilizar uma expressão muito má, mas não vou estar a ... dizer que é, **tipo**, alimentar burros. (PSFB)
'I was going to use a very bad expression, but I will not ... [you can] say it's, **like**, "casting pearls (before swine)".'

(26) Lá eu e um amigo meu andávamos **tipo** abraçados, os espanhóis a dizer que nós éramos gays (PSFB)
'There, my friend and I, we were walking, **like**, with our arms around each other, the Spaniards saying that we were gay'

In both examples, the speaker intends to soften or attenuate the effects of the negative content of these utterances. The phraseology "*alimentar burros*" is a severe disqualification of the discourse object, as well as the expression "*andávamos tipo abraçados*", reported as a joke but also as something that could identify him as a gay person (a potential FTA to the speaker's positive face, from his perspective on the matter). The speaker uses *tipo* to clearly distance himself from something he diminishes.

2.6 A vague quantificational function

The approximative value of *tipo* stands out when a quantitative approach is involved. The focus of information is the evaluative judgment that the speaker makes, and *tipo* renders the numerical values imprecise.

---

[17] The concept of FTA is a fundamental concept of (Im)Politeness Theory, developed in the seminal work of Brown and Levinson (1987) and subsequently. (Im)Politeness Theory is key to explaining how discourse functions, namely through interpersonal relationships.

In the first example, the focus is placed on the existence of an abnormal gang of thieves while in the second example, it is the poor attendance to the concert that is highlighted. The evaluative judgments, as an inferential process, are based on knowledge shared by the participants in the verbal interaction:

(27) *andam em grupo / e que são assaltados / **tipo** seis/ sete pessoas / que lhes levam tudo (CRPC-Oral)*
 'they walk together/and they are mugged/like six/seven people/who steal everything'

(28) *ver os Durutti | [. . .] // | Column / acho que havia / **tipo** sessenta pessoas a ver o concerto // | (CRPC-Oral)*
 'to see The Durutti | [. . .]//| Column/I think there were/**like** sixty people watching the concert// |'

2.7 The filler function

The filler function of *tipo* is considered a secondary function, and the only one recognized by traditional grammar (related to contexts of non-pathological disfluency).

Currently, it is considered a meaningless word that is linked to particular sociolects of young people: "The term filler is used to designate sounds, syllables or expressions typically used in a linguistic community to fill in silences during the production of utterances. (. . .). Expressions such as 'ah', 'so', and in the younger generation the word 'tipo', are examples of fillers." (Lopes and Rodrigues 2013: 36) [my translation].

This filler function is complete when *tipo* is the only word expressed, as in the following example where the speaker does not know what to say but signals his or her status of cooperative participant in the interaction using *tipo*:

(29) E: *que tipo de posts é que tu nunca farias • • no Facebook?*
 I: • • *((hesitação))* **Tipo** ... • • • *((risos))* (PSFB)
 'E: What kind of things would you never post • • on Facebook?
 I: • • *((hesitation))* **Like** ... • • • *((laughs))*'

Specifically, *tipo* serves as a filled pause, but it is more than that, because it gives the speaker the time to choose the word or the expression he wants to use. *Tipo* participates in the cognitive organization of the verbalization process. It also participates in the organization of the interactional relationship; it makes explicit to the listener how the speaker plans to formulate and complete his or her utterance.

In the following example *tipo* is a filler; there is no reformulation, modalization or recategorization process. The speaker does not modify the discourse: he or she just maintains the same discourse orientation, after a moment of verbalized hesitation signaled by *tipo*:

(30) *então, • • ((hesitação)) ela disse-nos que nós podíamos participar **num num, tipo, num** projeto em que dávamos duas vezes • • • aulas, duas vezes, era conversação* (PSFB)
'then, • ((hesitation)) she told us that we could participate **in a in a, kind of, in a** project in which we would give two • • • classes, twice, it was conversation'

The argumentative and discursive orientation of the expression "*num num tipo num projeto*" does not change when the DM is deleted, as in "*num num num projeto*."

To sum up, it should be stressed that all the functions of *tipo* presented above interact and overlap.

3 Clusters with *tipo* – The combination of DMs

The combination of DMs is an important issue but there is still a lack of research on this matter. According to Fraser (2013: 1), "While Discourse Markers (DMs) have been studied as individual markers (e.g., *but, so, instead*), little work has been done on their ability to combine." The same opinion is reaffirmed by the author in Fraser (2015) and, later, Pons Bordería (2018: 1) laments the insufficient research completed on this subject: "The combination of discourse markers (henceforth, DMs) is perhaps the only point in which the (in other respects) large amount of research on this subject has not yet produced relevant contributions."

It is therefore relevant to study the DM *tipo* in addition to the clusters of DMs in which it occurs.

Above all, a distinction must be made between compound DMs and clusters of DMs. A compound discourse marker is a new linguistic unit made up of at least two additional forms.[18] A cluster of DMs evolves from the co-occurrence and the

---

[18] For example, the Portuguese expression *ora bem* is a compound DM, distinct from the DMs *ora* e *bem*; it is not the sum of *ora* plus *bem* (Marques and Sánchez 2020).

combination of discourse markers in a textual sequence.[19] They have a cohesion and coherence function, but they are distinct pragmatic units.

Considering the examples used above to describe the characteristics of *tipo* as a taxonomic noun and discourse marker, several syntactic structures linked to the different functions listed are found:[20]
a) *Um tipo de* X (a tipo of X) (marker of hyponymy)
b) Y *tipo* X (function of approximative categorization)
c) Y *tipo* X (enunciative function)
d) *tipo* X (illocutionary function)
e) *tipo* X (vague quantification function)
f) *tipo*: (quotative function)
g) *tipo* (filler function)

Focusing on the particular contexts of its occurrence, *tipo's* formal (syntactic) context must be compared to its discursive functions, since there is a syntactic and a semantic-pragmatic interface, as signalled by Mihatsch (2010: 110) and Rosier (2002: 82).[21]

The syntactic construction of the DM *tipo* is part of a larger linguistic unit. In the examples below, the scope of *tipo* goes from different phrases (noun (31), adjective (32) and prepositional phrase (33)) to a clause (finite and non-finite) (34) and (35), respectively.

---

[19] Pons Bordería (2018: 16) distinguishes different combination types: (1) adjacency ("whenever two or more DMs are found together in different incompatible, discourse units"; (2) compound markers ["compound, stressed, polysyllabic markers" (*therefore, as a result, on the other hand, and so on*]).

[20] Some features of prosodic context have been discarded, because only the C-Oral-Rom corpus noted these intonational units (noted between / /). However, the variability of the intonational units deserves a more accurate analysis, since *tipo* can be an intonational unit of its own, separated by // or be part of a larger one, as shown in these examples: (| agora assim // /tipo/ escrito por mulheres //) (CRPC-ORAL) (now like // | like / written by women //); (mar // | percebes? | que / andava assim triangular / *tipo raia* // | hhh / (CRPC-ORAL) (sea // | do you understand? | that / was you see triangular / streak-ike); "baseiam-se muito na / pois / /conversa de homens /*tipo mulheres e "viste aquela"* / ") (CRPC-ORAL) ("based a lot on / you know/ / men talk / like women and "you saw her"). There is a need for more fine-grained prosodic analyses of *tipo*, supported by detailed transcriptions of prosodic data.

[21] However, the uses of *tipo* delineated above are the prototypical ones. As we have already observed, the distinction between them is not always clear-cut, due to the confluence of multiple senses of *tipo* in a single occurrence.

10 Pragmatic functions and contexts of use of TIPO in European Portuguese — 407

(31) *um carro óptimo / percebes / grandes férias sempre /* **tipo** *Caraíbas / ah / pronto // | eh / e pronto é isto /* (CRPC–ORAL)
'a great car / you know / always great holidays / **like** *the* Caribbean / ah / that's it //'

(32) *não sei se vocês conhecem.* • • • *Também é algo* **assim tipo** *fantástico, porque é o mesmo espírito* (PSFB)
'I do not know if you know. • • • It's also **like** *sort* **of** fantastic, because it's the same spirit'

(33) • • • *((hesitação))* • • *Jogos* **tipo** *da treta,* (PSFB)
'• • • ((hesitation)) • • **sort of** bullshit games'

(34) *era só para as pessoas ir lá* • • *e poderem ser quem queriam ser.* • • ***Tipo** ias lá e* • • *não interessa, não interessava se eras um um gestor de um banco* (PSFB)
'it was just to allow people to go there • • and be what they would like to be. • • **sort of** you go there and it doesn't matter, didn't matter if you were a a bank manager'

(35) • • *tirar umas dúvidas, dizer como é que quer* • • **tipo** *fazer alguns reparos.* (PSFB)
'• • to clarify some issues, to say what should be done • • **sort of** making some remarks.'

The linguistic co-text where *tipo* occurs is endowed with strong cohesion. Pauses, filled or unfilled, interruptions, repetitions, reformulations and vague expressions establish relations of contiguity with *tipo*, accentuating its status as an approximator in discourse as well as all the senses to which *tipo* relates. Therefore, it would be useful also to take into account the immediate context, which broadens and fits the vagueness introduced by *tipo*, as in the next example:

(36) *quer dizer, para mim, acho que na no/ na minha infância que era assim,* • • **tipo**, *mais alegre* • • *((hesitação)), portanto* • • *vínhamos ((hesitação))* (PSFB)
'I mean, for me, I think that in my my/in my childhood it was sort of, • • **kind of**, more joyful • • ((hesitation)), so • • we used to come ((hesitation)) ••'

This example illustrates the analysis of the relations that *tipo* establishes with its co-text, given the occurrence of different linguistic units that reinforce the senses it activates as a filler. From the discursive markers that co-occur there, to the modalization processes, to verbal and non-verbal hesitations, pragmatically co-oriented proximity relationships are established. In (36), it is the simultaneity of the processes of cognitive organization and verbalization of a propositional content that becomes particularly difficult for the speaker, who thus accumulates linguistic structures, five categories listed in the table below, to preserve his turn and be communicatively effective:

Table 1: Relations of DM *tipo* with its co-text.

1 Discourse markers	2 Modal expressions	3 Interruption/ repetition	Propositional content	4 Unfilled pause	5 Filled pause
Quer dizer; Assim; Tipo; Portanto;	Para mim Acho que	Na no na	Na minha infância que era [...] mais alegre, vínhamos	• •	((hesitação))
I mean, Sort of; Kind of; so	For me; I think that	In in in	in my childhood it was (...) more joyful (...) we used to come	• • (four occurrences)	((hesitação)) (filled with vocalisations)

The co-occurrence of these discourse devices strengthens the convergence with the semantic-pragmatic values of *tipo*. In this particular case, within a broad process of reformulation, DMs and modals contribute to mitigate the speaker's commitment and to fill the hesitations on the construction of the discourse, a feature that integrates the multifunctionality of *tipo*. Whilst all the elements contribute, the analysis will be restricted to the clustering of DMs with *tipo*.

Tipo often occurs as an isolated DM, but it also combines with other DMs, forming a cluster. The clustering is a discursive process concerning the combination of DMs in the local discourse context, and it is governed by coherence relations of semantic and pragmatic contiguity. The scope of DMs is the central criterion to identify the cluster: they combine, keeping their individual meanings, in order to modify the same linguistic unit.[22]

---

[22] There is, of course, co-occurrence of DMs without any pragmatic combination, such as the sequence "*mas tipo*" in "*ela empresta / tudo // | mas tipo + | a Fabiana / que mora comigo // minha colega.*" (CRPC-ORAL) '/ she lends / everything // | but **kind of** + | Fabiana / who lives with me // my colleague'. *Mas* connects two discursive segments while *tipo* modifies part of the second segment.

Clusters of two or more DMs with *tipo* have been attested. These can be organized into three main types of syntagmatic configurations, illustrated in the examples (37)–(41), below:

DM(s) + *Tipo*: (37); (39); (40)
DM(s) + *Tipo* + DM(s): (38);
Tipo + DM(s): (41)

Judging from the occurrences found in the corpora used here, the first combination prevails.[23] The most frequent combinations occur with the DM *assim* (like this), but *se calhar* (maybe), *pronto* (you know), and *portanto* (so) are also found. All of them convey a salient modalization function, reinforcing the values of *tipo* discussed in section two:[24]

(37) *as instalações são porreiras / mas é **assim** / eh / **tipo** / queres alguma coisa / tens que ir lá* (CRPC-ORAL)
'the facilities are cool / but it's **like** / eh / **sort of** / you want something / you have to go there'

(38) *construção | em altura ? | sim // | OK // | **pronto** // | **tipo** / **se calhar** na Nova são três //* (CRPC-ORAL)
'building | in height? | yes// | OK//| **you know**// /**kind of**/**maybe** at the [university] Nova there are three'

(39) *acidentes, traumatismos cranio-encefálicos, • • **portanto assim tipo** • • ((hesitação)) • • do Angélico • • • •* (PSFB)
'accidents, head injuries, **so you know kind of** • • ((hesitation)) • • of Angélico • • •'

Besides modalization, the occurrence of *tipo* also leads the speaker to explicitly include the hearer as a participant in the process of meaning construction in the discourse by the accumulation of interpersonal DMs:[25]

---

23 Unfilled pauses are not analyzed here.
24 All these Portuguese DMs have already been studied. On the modal value of *assim* in European Portuguese, see Lopes and Carapinha (2004). For the same DM in Brazilian Portuguese, see also Lopes-Damasio (2008) and Bittencourt (2000). (I must thank the anonymous reviewer who sent me these references).
25 This category is similar to Fraser's "attention markers" (2009).

(40) mas **olha** agora/**olha/tipo**/| ah/na política///| tens os elementos do Bloco (CRPC-ORAL)
'but **look** now/**look/sort of**/| ah/in politics///| you have the elements of the Block'

Finally, the DM *pronto* conveys shared knowledge, so it is also other-oriented. It has the function of creating common ground to the enunciation process proposed by the speaker:

(41) nós gostamos daquele tipo de pessoas / **tipo pronto** / cinco estrelas / não é? (CRPC-ORAL)
'we like those kind of people/**sort of you know**/excellent, isn't it?'

Contexts involving hesitation show, in addition, a pause-filler function fulfilled by all the DMs.

The examples listed are clusters of approximating discourse markers. Clustering is a discursive strategy that underlines the *ad hoc* categorization as a nuclear feature of *tipo*.

4 Conclusion

This study delineates the main features of DM *tipo* in European Portuguese from a synchronic perspective. From the analysis of *tipo* uses, some fundamental issues stand out. The first of these is its polysemy and multifunctionality, i.e., the fact that as a DM, *tipo* performs textual, enunciative and pragmatic functions. There is no clear-cut boundary between meanings, and the specific context of occurrence highlights the main pragmatic effects on discursive meaning construction.

As a DM, *tipo* is an approximator introducing imprecision to a categorization process. Such imprecision can be motivated by either the need to modify the certainty of an expression or its illocutionary force due to insufficient information, or in order to avoid being too direct or too committed to the utterance content.

The same (approximative) values are present in uses of *tipo* as a quotation marker. Introducing direct speech, it stresses the non-literal character of the speech reported. *Tipo* also flags contexts of somewhat problematic ongoing discourse construction and verbalization.

Secondly, *tipo* occurs within different syntactic structures that can be related to different semantic and pragmatic meanings. Namely, when occurring with the determiner (*um, o, esse,...*) and the preposition *de* (*um tipo de*), *tipo* is a clear marker of hyponymy. Other constructions signal an approximative function of *tipo* as a DM.

Finally, in addition to these findings, the analysis of the combination of *tipo* with other DMs highlights more characteristics that are important to consider.

Tipo always appears as a single DM and never occurs within a compound DM. However, there is an important process of clustering: *tipo* combines with other DMs such as *assim*, *portanto* or *pronto* (the most frequent partners). These clusters establish coherence relations between the DMs involved and they reinforce the semantic-pragmatic values identified in uses of *tipo*. The main discursive effect of the clustering is the reinforcement of a process of *ad hoc* categorization by approximation.

References

Adam, Jean-Michel. 2006. Texte, contexte et discours en questions. *Pratiques* 129–130. 21–34.

Benveniste, Émile. 1970. L'appareil formel de l'énonciation. *Langages* 17. 12–18.

Bittencourt, Vanda. 2000. *Tipo (assim)* como delimitador de unidades de informação. [Tipo (assim) as delimiter of information units]. *Estudos Lingüísticos* 29. http://www.gel.hospedagemdesites.ws/anais/index.php (accessed 15 May 2020).

Brems, Lieselotte &, Kristin Davidse. 2010. The grammaticalisation of nominal type noun constructions with *kind/sort of*: Chronology and paths of change. *English Studies* 91 (2). 180–202.

Brown, Penelope & Stephen Levinson. 1978. *Politeness: Some universals in language usage*. Cambridge: Cambridge University Press.

Buchstaller, Isabelle. 2002. He goes and I'm like. The new quotations revisited. Proceedings of the University of Edinburgh Postgraduate Conference, University of Edinburgh. http://www.lel.ed.ac.uk/~pgc/archive/2002/proc02/buchstaller02.pdf (accessed 25 January 2019).

Casteleiro, J. M. (coord.). 2001. *Dicionário da Língua Portuguesa Contemporânea*. Vols I & II. Lisboa: Academia das Ciências de Lisboa e Editorial Verbo.

Cresti, Emanuela, Massimo Moneglia, Fernanda Nascimento, António Sandoval, Jean Veronis, Philippe Martin, Kalid Choukri, Valérie Mapelli, Daniele Falavigna, Antonio Cid & Claude Blum. 2002. The C–ORAL–ROM Project. New methods for spoken language archives in a multilingual romance corpus. *LREC*. https://pdfs.semanticscholar.org/67d9/a2c52416cd6740d581b04d9e319820aec743.pdf. (accessed 25 January 2019).

Davidse, Kristin, Lieselotte Brems & Liesbeth De Smeth. 2008. Type noun uses in English NP. A case of right to left layering. *International Journal of Corpus linguistics* 13 (2). 139–168.

Ducrot, Oswald. 1984. *Le dire et le dit*. Paris: Les Editions de Minuit.

Fraser, Bruce. 2009. An Account of Discourse Markers. *International Review of Pragmatics* 1 (2). 293–320. https://www.researchgate.net/publication/233594552_An_Account_of_Discourse_Markers (accessed 5 March 2016).

Fraser, Bruce. 2013. Combinations of Contrastive Discourse Markers in English. *International Review of Pragmatics* 5 (2).
Fraser, Bruce. 2015. The combining of Discourse Markers. A beginning. *Journal of Pragmatics* 86. http://dx.doi.org/10.1016/j.pragma.2015.06.007 (accessed 5 May 2017).
Fuentes Rodriguez, Catalina. 2008. La aproximación enunciativa. *Lea: Lingüística Española Actual* 30 (2). 223–258.
Hengeveld, Kees & Evelien Keizer. 2011. Non-straightforward communication. *Journal of Pragmatics* 43 (7). 1962–1976. https://www.sciencedirect.com/science/article/pii/S0378216611000038 (accessed 15 October 2019).
Kerbrat-Orecchioni, Catherine. 2002. Contexte. In Patrick Charaudeau & Dominique Maingueneau (eds.), *Dictionnaire d'Analyse du Discours*, 134–136. Paris: Seuil.
Koch, Ingedore, Morato, Edwiges & Anna Bentes. 2011. Ainda o contexto: algumas considerações sobre as relações entre contexto, cognição e práticas sociais na obra de Teun van Dijk [Still the context: some considerations on the relationships between context, cognition and social practices in the work of Teun van Dijk] . *ALED* 11 (1). 79–91.
Lakoff, George. 1973. Hedges: A study in meaning criteria and the logic of fuzzy concepts. *Journal of Philosophical logic* 2 (4). 458–508. https://georgelakoff.files.wordpress.com/2011/01/hedges-a-study-in-meaning-criteria-and-the-logic-of-fuzzy-concepts-journal-of-philosophical-logic-2-lakoff-19731.pdf (accessed 25 June 2014).
Lopes, Ana Cristina & Maria da Conceição Rodrigues. 2013. *Texto, Coesão e Coerência* [Text, cohesion and coherence]. Coimbra: Almedina/Celga.
Lopes-Damasio, Lúcia. 2008. *A emergência do marcador discursivo assim sob a óptica da gramaticalização: um caso de multifuncionalidade e (inter)subjetivização* [The emergence of the discursive marker *assim* from the perspective of grammaticalization: a case of multifunctionality and (inter) subjectivization]. São José do Rio Preto: Instituto de Biociências, Letras e Ciências Exatas de São José do Rio Preto, Universidade Estadual Paulista Dissertation. https://repositorio.unesp.br/handle/11449/86593 (accessed 15 May 2020).
Marques, Maria Aldina. 2013. Construir a responsabilidade enunciativa no discurso jornalístico [Constructing enunciative responsability in media discourse]. *REDIS: Revista de Estudos do Discurso* 2, 139–166. https://ojs.letras.up.pt/index.php/re/article/view/3590 (Accessed 15 December 2021).
Marques, Maria Aldina. 2014. Linguagem coloquial e modalização [Colloquial register and modalization]. *REDIS. Revista de Estudos do Discurso*, [Review of Discourse Studies]3. 94–106. http://ojs.letras.up.pt/index.php/re/article/view/3577/3339 (accessed 16 April 2021).
Marques, Maria Aldina. 2015a. "Tipo". Référentiation et modalisation dans des interactions verbales orales. In Maria Helena Carreira (org.), *Faits de langue et de discours pour l'expression des modalités dans les langues romanes*. Travaux et documents 60–2015, 249–260. Paris: Université Paris 8 Vincennes Saint-Denis.
Marques, Maria Aldina. 2015b. O Discurso direto em interações orais coloquiais [Direct reported speech in oral coloquial interactions]. In Maria Aldina Marques & Xosé Manuel Sánchez Rei (eds.), *Novas perspectivas linguísticas no espaço galego-português* [New linguistic perspectives in Galicia-Portuguese space]. 89–109. Corunha: Universidade da Corunha.
Marques, Maria Aldina & Xosé Manuel Sánchez Rei. 2020. De ora e ora bem a ahora e ahora bien: especificidades dos marcadores discursivos e ensino da língua [From ora and ora bem to ahora and ahora bien: specificities of discursive markers and language teaching]. In Antônio

Messias Nogueira, Catalina Fuentes Rodríguez & Manuel Martí Sánchez (eds.), *Aportaciones desde el español y el portugués a los marcadores discursivos (treinta años después de Martín Zorraquino y Portolés)*, 443–465. Sevilla: Editorial Universidad de Sevilla.

Martín Zorraquino, Maria Antonia & José Portolés Lázaro. 1999. Los marcadores del discurso. In Ignacio Bosque Muñoz & Violetta Demonte Barreto (eds.), *Gramática descriptiva de la lengua española*, 4051–4213. Madrid: Espasa–Calpe.

Mihatsch, Wiltrud. 2007. The construction of vagueness: Sort of expressions in romance languages. In Günter Radden, Klaus-Michael Köpcke, Tomas Berg & Peter Siemund (eds.), *Aspects of meaning construction*, 225–245. Amsterdam: John Benjamins. doi: 10.1075/z.136.15mih. (accessed 14 May 2018).

Mihatsch, Wiltrud. 2009a. L'approximation entre sens et signification: un tour d'horizon. In Dominique Verbeken (ed.), *Entre sens et signification – Constitution du sens : points de vue sur l'articulation sémantique-pragmatique*, 100–116. Paris: L'Harmattan.

Mihatsch, Wiltrud. 2009b. The approximators French comme, Italian come, Portuguese como and Spanish como from a grammaticalization perspective. In Corine Rossari, Claudia Ricci & Adriana Spiridon (eds.), *Grammaticalization and pragmatics: Facts, approaches, theoretical issues*, 65–91. Bingley: Emerald Group Publishing Limited. doi: 10.1163/9789004253193_006. (accessed 14 May 2018).

Mihatsch, Wiltrud. 2010. The diachrony of rounders and adaptors: approximation and unidirectional change. In Gunter Kaltenböck, Wiltrud Mihatsch, & Stefan Schneider (eds.), *New approaches to hedging*, 93–122. Bingley: Emerald Group Publishing Limited.

Mihatsch, Wiltrud. 2018. From *ad hoc* category to *ad hoc* categorization: The proceduralization of Argentinian Spanish tipo. Linguistic strategies for the construction of *ad hoc* categories: synchronic and diachronic perspectives. *Folia Linguistica*, 52 (39–1). 147–176.

Monte, Michelle. 2011. Modalités et modalisation: peut-on sortir des embarras typologiques? *Modèles linguistiques* 64. 85–101.

Mosegaard Hansen, Maj-Britt. 1998. The semantic status of discourse markers. *Lingua* 104 (3–4). 235–260. https://www.sciencedirect.com/science/article/pii/S0024384198000035 (accessed 5 March 2016).

Pons Bordería, Salvador. 2018. The combination of discourse markers: Keys to untying a Gordian knot. *Revue Romane. Langue et littérature. International Journal of Romance Languages and Literatures* 53 (1).

Rabatel, Alain. 2005. La part de l'énonciateur dans la construction interactionnelle des points de vue. *Marges Linguistiques* 9. http://www.marges-linguistiques.com (accessed 12 october 2012).

Rosier, Laurence. 2002. *Genre*: le nuancier de sa grammaticalisation. *Travaux de linguistique* 44, 79–88. https://www.cairn.info/revue-travaux-de-linguistique-2002-1-page-79.htm (accessed 14 May 2018).

Trujillo Carreño, Ramón. 1990. Sobre la explicación de algunas construcciones de como. *Verba: Anuario Galego de Filoloxía*, 17.249–266. https://minerva.usc.es/xmlui/handle/10347/3135 (accessed 14 May 2018).

van Dijk, Teun. 2001. Algunos principios de una teoría del contexto. *ALED, Revista latinoamericana de estudios del discurso* 1, 69–81. http://discursos.org/oldarticles/Algunos%20principios%20de%20una%20teor%EDa%20del%20contexto.pdf (accessed 14 January 2013).

van Dijk, Teun. 2004. Text and Context of Parliamentary debates. In Peter Bayley (ed.), *Cross-Cultural Perspectives on Parliamentary Discourse*, 339–372. London: Benjamins.

van Dijk, Teun. 2012. *Discurso e contexto: uma abordagem sociocognitiva* [Discourse and context: a sociognitive approach]. São Paulo: Contexto.
Vigara Tauste, Ana. 1966. Español coloquial. Expresión del sentido por aproximación. In Thomas Kotshi, Wulf Oesterreicher & Klaus Zimmermann (eds.), *El Español hablado y la cultura oral en España e Hispanoamérica*, 15–44. Frankfurt am Main, Vervuert, Madrid: Iberoamericana.
Voghera, Miriam. 2014. Da nome tassonomico a segnale discorsivo: una mappa delle costruzioni di *tipo* in italiano contemporaneo, *Studi di grammatical italiana* XXIII. 187–221. https://www.iris.unisa.it/handle/11386/4416665#.YCvVh2j7Q2w (accessed 14 May 2018).
Voghera, Miriam & Carla Borges. 2017. Vagueness expressions in Italian, Spanish and English in task-oriented dialogues. *Normas* 7 (1). 57–74. doi: http://dx.doi.org/10.7203/Normas.7.10424 (accessed 11 October 2018).
Wichmann, Anne & Catherine Chanet. 2009. Discourse markers: a challenge for linguists and teachers. *Nouveaux cahiers de linguistique française* 29.23–40. https://clf.unige.ch/files/3214/4102/7479/04_Wichmann_nclf29.pdf. (accessed 11 October 2018).

Consulted corpora

Perfil sociolinguístico da fala bracarense (Sociolinguistic profile of Braga speech/ PSFB). http://cehum.ilch.uminho.pt/fala_bracarense (accessed 02 February 2022).
C-ORAL-ROM (CRPC-Corpus de Referência do Português Contemporâneo). https://clul.ulisboa.pt/en/projeto/c-oral-rom-integrated-reference-corpora-spoken-romance-languages (accessed 02 February 2022).

Laura Malena Kornfeld
11 Taxonomic nouns and markers of mitigation in Río de la Plata Spanish

Abstract: This paper presents an analysis of three items, *tipo* ('type'), *onda* ('wave', 'style') and *corte* (lit. 'cut', 'type, style') which may be used as lexical taxonomic or semi-taxonomic nouns (e.g. *Tiene una ideología de tipo/onda/corte marxista*, 'She has a Marxist-type/-style ideology') and at the same time as grammaticalized markers of mitigation (or hedges) with sentential scope (e.g. *Tipo/Onda/Corte que no sé qué hacer con este problema* 'Like I don´t know what to do with this problem') in some colloquial varieties of Río de la Plata Spanish, particularly among young people. The paper describes the grammatical distribution of *tipo*, *onda* and *corte* as lexical nouns, taking into account their (semi-)taxonomic value and discussing some grammaticalized uses in the nominal domain and beyond. It then focuses on the cases in which *tipo*, *onda* and *corte* have sentential scope as markers of mitigation in order to systematize their basic grammatical properties: distribution, compatibility with various modalities, moods and polarities, etc. Finally, the paper aims to sketch out an overview of the processes involved in the grammaticalization of nouns with (semi-)taxonomic meanings into markers of mitigation, contrasting them with other mitigating expressions in colloquial Río de la Plata Spanish (*como que*, 'like-that', *medio*, 'half'm or *un poco*, 'a bit') and the case of English *kind (of)/kinda*. From a theoretical point of view, the paper attempts to relate a grammatical view, especially from a generative perspective, to pragmatic approaches such as studies analyzing mitigation or subjectivization.

1 Introduction

This paper presents an analysis of three items, *tipo* ('type'), *onda* ('wave', 'style') and *corte* (lit. 'cut', 'type, style'), which may be utilized as lexical taxonomic or semi-taxonomic nouns (as in (1)), and at the same time used as grammaticalized markers of mitigation (or hedges) with sentential scope (2) in some colloquial varieties of Río de la Plata Spanish, particularly among young people.

Acknowledgements: I thank the two anonymous reviewers of this paper, who have helped to significantly improve the first manuscript. *Any remaining mistakes* are my sole responsibility.

Laura Malena Kornfeld, Universidad de Buenos Aires – CONICET (Argentina)

https://doi.org/10.1515/9783110701104-011

(1) a. Tiene   una ideología de **tipo** marxista.
       has.3.SG   a   ideology of type Marxist
       'She has a Marxist-type ideology'
   b. Tiene   una ideología de **onda** marxista.
       has.3.SG   a   ideology of style Marxist
       'She has a Marxist-style ideology'
   c. Tiene   una Ideología de **corte** marxista.
       has.3.SG   a   Ideology of type Marxist
       'She has a Marxist-type ideology'

(2) a. **Tipo** soy   un éxito   (Caro Pardiaco)
       Kind   am.1.SG   A success
       'I am kind of a success'
   b. **Onda** que no me   interesa   la medida.
       style that not me.DAT,1.SG interest.3.SG   the arrangement
       'Like [onda], I am not interested in this arrangement'
   c. **Corte** que te   dan   una puñalada por la espalda.
       Kind   that you.DAT give.3.PL   a   stab   for the back
       '(They) kind of give you a stab in the back' (Rojas 2012: 1)[1]

On the basis of these initial data, I will discuss why markers of mitigation in Río de la Plata Spanish so frequently originate from lexical nouns related to taxonomic meaning and how their process(es) of grammaticalization can be characterized.

In order to achieve these goals, the paper is organized as follows. *Section 2* describes the grammatical distribution of *tipo, onda* and *corte* as lexical nouns (see examples in (1)), focusing on their (semi-)taxonomic value and describing their grammaticalized uses in the nominal domain and others. *Section 3* particularly takes into account those cases in which *tipo, onda* and *corte* have sentential scope as markers of mitigation (see examples in (2)), in order to systematize their basic grammatical properties: distribution, compatibility with various modalities, moods and polarities, etc. *Section 4* presents an overview of the processes involved in the grammaticalization of nouns with (semi-)taxonomic meanings into markers of mitigation, contrasting them with other mitigating expressions in colloquial Río de la Plata Spanish (*como que* 'like-that', *medio* 'half' or *un poco* 'a

---

[1] The examples with *tipo* or *onda* as mitigators are taken primarily from web pages and minimally adapted, but a few examples (particularly paradigms such as 7–8, 13, 14, 24–34) are entirely constructed, being myself a native middle-class speaker of Río de la Plata Spanish in the relevant age group (see section 9.2). By contrast, all the examples with *corte* are taken from sources (see, specially, Rojas 2012) or checked with speakers of the relevant social and age distribution.

bit') and with English *kind (of)/kinda*. The conclusion reached is that there are at least two different paths, one going through grammatical values such as 'comparison' or 'exemplification' and the other including a use as quantifiers with adjectives or verbs (Margerie 2010).

From a theoretical point of view, this paper attempts to relate a grammatical view, especially from a generative perspective (which I explicitly assume, for instance, in Avellana and Kornfeld 2019; Di Tullio and Kornfeld 2013), to pragmatic approaches, such as the studies analyzing processes related to mitigation (Caffi 1999; Montecino 2004; Landone 2009; and others) or to subjectivization (Traugott 2003; Davidse, Vandelanotte and Cuyckens 2010; and others.).

2 Nominal domain and first grammaticalized uses

In this section, I characterize the grammatical properties and meanings of *tipo*, *onda* and *corte* in the nominal domain, as well as their first grammaticalized uses, representing the early steps of the path from the lexical nouns in (1) to the mitigating items in (2).

As for their distribution, it may be rather difficult to exactly determine the precise sociolinguistic contexts in which *tipo*, *onda* and *corte* are employed as grammaticalized markers of mitigation, as in (2). They seem more frequent in the big cities of the region where Río de la Plata Spanish is spoken, including Uruguay and the Argentinian provinces of Buenos Aires, Santa Fe, Entre Ríos, La Pampa and the whole of Patagonia. *Tipo* is the more generalized marker of mitigation among people in their sixties and less, while *onda* seems to be more restricted to speakers between 25 and 50, but it is also attested in other nearby countries, such as Paraguay or Chile. As for *corte*, it was originally employed among people under 40 belonging to lower social classes of the *Conurbano* (i.e., the peripheral metropolitan areas near Buenos Aires). In brief, the three markers have different social and age distributions and, correspondingly, different frequencies.[2]

Interestingly enough, the distribution as lexical nouns of *tipo*, *onda* and *corte* is not similar. Although *tipo* originated in scientific discourse, today it appears in

---

[2] These observations are based on my own intuitions as a native speaker of Río de la Plata Spanish. Unfortunately, there is no literature systematizing the sociolinguistic distribution of *tipo*, *onda* and *corte* or even recording their origin; there is also an important delay between the first oral uses and the first writing sources, since these items are previous to the big explosion of secondary oral sources related to Internet, such as emails, chats, blogs, forums, etc.

colloquial varieties of standard Spanish[3] combined with nominal appositions or relational classifying adjectives (as in (1a)) as a taxonomic noun meaning 'type' or 'kind'. Instead, *onda* has to undergo a previous process of lexicalization in order to acquire the semi-taxonomic meaning 'style' (as in (1b)), which has only occurred in some American Spanish colloquial varieties (Cone South, México). Meanwhile, *corte* alternatively means 'type' or 'style' when combined with relational classifying adjectives in standard Spanish, as in (1c), but was used only in a higher register (perhaps only academic discourse) before its process of grammaticalization.

2.1 Taxonomic nouns and nominal domain

Tipo is perhaps the best representative of the three units, a highly polysemic lexical item in Río de la Plata Spanish, with some uses or meanings shared with other varieties. This polysemy may be confirmed in the examples in (3), which undoubtedly do not reflect all the possible meanings of *tipo*:

(3) a. *Pedro es un **tipo** muy excéntrico.*
   Pedro is a guy very eccentric
   'Pedro is a very eccentric guy'
  b. *Vino un **tipo** a buscarte.*
   came.3.SG a guy to look for + you.ACC
   'A guy came looking for you'
  c. *Tiene un lindo **tipo**.*
   has.3.SG a nice look
   'She has a nice look'
  d. *Es un **tipo** de casa muy cómoda.*
   is.3.SG a kind of house very comfortable
   'It is a very comfortable kind of house'
  e. *Es una familia **tipo**.*
   is.3.SG a family prototype
   'It's a prototypical family'

Tipo has several lexical senses. In (3a) *tipo* could be translated as 'guy'; used in this sense, it is an animate noun with gender inflection: *un tipo macanudo* ('a cool guy') vs. *una tipa macanuda* ('a cool girl'). With this meaning *tipo* is frequently

---

[3] The label *standard Spanish* stands for standard phenomena in different dialectal varieties of Spanish.

employed in contexts in which somebody's identity (or proper noun) is unknown, as in (3b). *Tipo* also means 'look' (e.g. (3c)) and 'type' or 'kind' (e.g. (3d)), while in (3e) it appears as an apposition (without concord with the nominal head *familia*), with the semantic values of 'standard', 'average' or 'prototype'.

The most interesting usage for this paper is (3d), where *tipo* has some kind of taxonomic meaning, which could be translated as 'type', 'kind' or 'sort'. As Mihatsch (2018) pointed out, the taxonomic meaning of *tipo* arose from its original meanings of 'model', 'ideal' or 'typical exemplar' in order to support the definition of a species or kind, especially in biological taxonomies. Hence, *tipo* has been employed, since the nineteenth century, as a taxonomic noun in technological, scientific and academic texts, appearing in the construction seen in (3d) as well as an alternative construction in which *tipo* is postposed. The examples in (4) show postposed *tipo* in combination either with different kinds of nominal appositions (e.g., letters, numbers or proper nouns, as in (4a–c)) or with classifying relational adjectives (4d–e):

(4) a. sangre del **tipo** A
    blood of-the type A
    'blood type A' (lit.) 'blood of the type A'
 b. una patología del **tipo** 1
    a pathology of-the type 1
    'a type 1 pathology' (lit.) 'a pathology of the type 1'
 c. un Studio del **tipo** Rorschach
    a Study of-the type Rorschach
    'a Rorschach-type study' (lit.) 'a study of the type *Rorschach*'
 d. una película del **tipo** documental
    a film of-the type documentary
    'a documentary (type of) film' (lit.) 'a film of the type documentary'
 e. una lengua del **tipo** oriental
    a language of-the type oriental
    'an oriental (type of) language' (lit.) 'a language of the type oriental'

In the examples in (4), *tipo* is the head of the complement of a prepositional modifier: *un X del tipo Y* ('an X of the type Y'). However, with less frequency, *tipo* can also appear with the same taxonomic meaning as the head of the nominal complement of the determiner phrase (DP),[4] as in (5) (see also (3d)):

---

4 *Determiner phrase* (DP) is used here (as generative literature does in the last three decades) assuming that nominal constructions are headed by determiners which take noun phrases (NP) as their lexical complements.

(5) el **tipo** 1 de patología
 the type 1 of pathology
 'the type 1 pathology' (lit.) 'the type 1 of pathology'

One further possibility is the omission of preposition *de* from a structure such as *un X del **tipo** Y* ('an X of the type Y'), leading to an apposition headed by *tipo*, as in (6a–c). Bosque (1990) observes that this process of omission is very common in standard Spanish with (semi-)taxonomic nouns, for instance *estilo* ('style') or *modelo* ('model') in appositions such as *una silla estilo Luis XIV* (lit. 'a chair style Louis XIV') or *un auto modelo Twingo* (lit. 'a car model Twingo'). The same omission is possible when the complement of *tipo* is a relational adjective (see (6d–e)):

(6) a. sangre **tipo** A
 blood type A
 'type A blood' (lit.) 'blood (of the) type A'
 b. una patología **tipo** 1
 a pathology type 1
 'a type 1 pathology' (lit.) 'a pathology (of the) type 1'
 c. un studio **tipo** Rorschach
 a study type Rorschach
 'a Rorschach-type study' (lit.) 'a study (of the) type *Rorschach*'
 d. una película **tipo** documental
 a film type documentary
 'a documentary (type of) film' (lit.) 'a film (of the) type documentary'
 e. una lengua **tipo** oriental
 a language type oriental
 'an oriental (type of) language' (lit.) 'a language (of the) type oriental'

The examples in (4a–c) and (6a–c) are still synonymous, while in (6d–e) a subtle value of comparison (absent in (4d–e)) may be recognized.[5] A clearer difference appears when *tipo* has evidently lost its scientific taxonomic meaning and is rather a device used by speakers for ad hoc categorization, as Mihatsch (2018) argues. Therefore, in (7a) *diva* introduces a hyponym (or subcategory) of *actriz* ('actress'), as well as *años '20* ('the 20s') does the same with *fiesta* ('party') in (7b), but the variants without *de* in (7a'–b') have an eminently similative meaning:

---

[5] As a reviewer points out, in fact *un X del tipo de Y* ('an X of the type Y') can also be interpreted as 'X belonging to the same superordinate as Y', a paraphrase which is closer in meaning to comparison, according to Mihatsch (2018).

(7) a. Es   una actriz del **tipo** diva.
        is.3.SG a   actress of-the type diva
        'She is a diva-type actress' (lit.) 'She is an actress of the kind (of a) diva'
    a'. Es   una actriz **tipo** diva.
        is.3.SG a   actress type diva
        'She is a diva-like actress' (lit.) 'She is an actress like (a) diva'
    b. Fue   una fiesta del **tipo** años 20.
        was.3.SG a   party of-the type years 20
        'It was a 20s-type party' (lit.) 'It was a party of the kind (of the) 20s
    b'. Fue   una fiesta **tipo** años 20.
        was.3.SG a   party type years 20
        'It was a party like the 20s'

As usually happens in Spanish, the masculine and singular noun *tipo* does not need to concord in gender and/or number with the noun it modifies nor with its own apposition. Hence, mismatches are found either in gender (e.g., the feminine nouns *actriz*, 'actress', and *diva*, 'diva', in (7a–a') or *fiesta*, 'party', in (7b–b')) or in number (e,g., the plural *años '20*, 'years '20' in (7b–b')).

The possibility of the (double) omission of the preposition *de* is also available when *tipo* is not modifying other noun within a DP (as in (6–7)), but included in a predicative complement with a copulative verb, as in (8):

(8) a. La película es del   **tipo** de Tarantino
        The film   is of-the type   of Tarantino
        'It's a Tarantino style of film' (lit.) 'The film is of the type of Tarantino'
    b. La película es **tipo** Tarantino
        The film   is type   Tarantino
        'The film is like Tarantino's'

The omission of *de* and the corresponding change of syntactic function is a first step in the process of recategorization of *tipo*, which at this stage is ambiguous between lexicalization and grammaticalization. In this first step, attested in different varieties of Spanish, *tipo* keeps (part of) its taxonomic lexical meaning (and in fact could still be translated as 'type' or 'kind) but is also to be interpreted with grammatical values such as 'comparison' or 'approximation'. This change may be observed contrasting the two "near-synonym" variants in the previous examples: *tipo* tends to retain its taxonomic (lexical) interpretation in the presence of *de* (see examples in (4d–e), (7a–b) and (8a)), while the same phrases without *de* (see examples (6d–e), (7a'–b') and (8b)) are more frequently understood with a similative or approximative meaning, as the English translations suggest. As a matter of fact, Mihatsch (2018) analyzes these last cases as a kind of prepositional use of *tipo*, parallel to English *like*.

Examples (8) are still ambiguous between the taxonomic lexical meaning and the grammatical values, as mentioned above. But ambiguity disappears in other contexts: only the grammaticalized meaning of comparison is available when *tipo* is used before a DP (such as *los profesores*, 'the professors') in (9a)) or when the nominal head which *tipo* modifies is elided and has some kind of pronominal interpretation (for instance, 'they do something like talks', in (9b)). Additionally, *tipo* can be utilized as an equivalent to 'for instance' (e.g., (9c)) or as a marker of reformulation in examples such as (9d):

(9) a. *Dice   cosas   **tipo** los profesores.*
       says.3.SG things type   the professors'
       'She says things like the professors'
   b. *Hacen   **tipo** charlas.*
       make.3.PL type   talks
       'They do (something) like talks'
   c. *Me   gustan   las películas bizarras **tipo** Tarantino o   Rodríguez.*
       me.DAT   like.3.PL the films   bizarre   type   Tarantino or Rodríguez
       'I like bizarre films like Tarantino or Rodríguez'
   d. *usa   palabras así medio complicadas **tipo** muchas metáforas.*
       uses.3.SG words   so   half   complicated type   many   metaphors
       '[Cerati] uses words a bit complicated, that is, like many metaphors.'
       (Bregant 2018)

Onda (lit. 'wave') has quite a different meaning to *tipo* in standard Spanish: 'Each one of the curves, in the form of S, which are formed naturally or artificially in some flexible things, such as hair, fabric, etc.' (according to the *Dictionary* of the Real Academia Española (RAE), Spanish Royal Academy). There are some variants related to physics (see (10a–d)), and *onda* also supports metaphorical extensions (see (10e)).

(10) a. *longitud de **onda** de rayos luminosos*
         length   of wave   of rays   light
         'wavelength of light rays'

b. *frecuencia de **onda***
   frequency of wave
   'wave frequency'
c. *emisiones de **onda** corta/media/larga*
   emissions of wave short/medium/long
   'short/medium/long wave emissions'
d. *una **onda** de choque de gran velocidad*
   a wave of shock of high speed
   'a high-speed shock wave'
e. *Dejó una **onda** de terror y muerte alrededor del*
   left.3.SG a wave of terror and death across of-the
   mundo.
   world
   'It left a wave of terror and death worldwide'

Argentinian Spanish (as well as other South American varieties: Chilean, Paraguayan, Mexican or Venezualan Spanish) adds other lexical senses, making *onda* a polysemic noun. The lexical meanings of *onda* derived from (10) are varied and may be translated (very approximately) as 'spirit' or 'vibe' (see (11a–b)), but *onda* is also part of many fossilized expressions, such as *qué onda* (translated as 'what's up?' (11c) or 'how was X?' (11d)) and *de onda* (equivalent to 'just because' (11e) or 'hip' (11f)).[6]

(11) a. *Hoy estoy en una **onda** de regalos.*
        today am.1.SG in a wave of gifts
        'Today, I'm in the spirit of (giving) gifts'
     b. *Tiene buena/mala/la mejor **onda**.*
        Has.3.SG good/bad/the best wave
        'He has good/bad/the best vibe'
     c. *¿Qué **onda**?*
        what wave
        'What's up?'
     d. *¿Qué **onda** la fiesta?*
        what wave the Party
        'How was the party?'

---

[6] *Onda* also forms other prepositional (*con onda* ('cool')) and verbal idioms (*tener onda*, 'be cool', *tirar onda*, 'seduce', *poner onda*, 'make an effort', *pegar onda*, 'hit it off').

e. *Lo   hizo   de **onda**.*
   it.ACC made.3.SG of wave
   'She made it just because'
f. *Es   un lugar   de **onda** de Miami.*
   is.3.SG a place of wave of Miami
   'It is a hip place in Miami'

These lexical definitions are not at all similar to those of *tipo*. A more obviously related sense arises when *onda* is lexicalized (only in some South American varieties, as mentioned before) with the meaning of 'style', probably derived from examples such as (11). In these cases, *onda* is usually followed by a qualifying or relational adjective (12a–b), but can also be followed by nouns (12c–d) or infinitive clauses (12e):

(12) a. *Tiene   una **onda**   tranquila.*
        has.3.SG a style quiet
        'It has a quiet style'
   b. *Es   un local   con **onda** tropical.*
        is.3.SG a local with wave tropical
        'It is a club with a tropical vibe'
   c. *Tiene   una **onda** (de) nave espacial.*
        has.3.SG a style (of) aircraft
        'It has the appearance of an aircraft'
   d. *ambiente caribeño   **onda** Key West*
        ambience Caribbean style Key West
        'Caribbean ambience in the style of Key West'
   e. *Diferentes agrupaciones comparten la   **onda** de andar   por*
        different groups   share.3.PL the style of walking through
        las calles   como Dios los   trajo   al   mundo.
        the streets as God them.ACC brought.3.PL to-the world
        'Different groups share the trend of walking by the streets as God brought them into the world'

The lexical contrast between 'type, sort, kind' (*tipo*) and 'style' (*onda*) explains why *onda* cannot replace *tipo* in certain terminological taxonomic contexts: for instance, sequences as ??*sangre onda A* (lit. 'blood style A') (in contrast to (6a)) or ??*patología onda 1* (lit. 'pathology style 1') (see (6b)) are not possible, while *lengua onda oriental* (6d) and *película onda documental* (6e) only could be interpreted as 'a language in the style of [similar to] an oriental language' and 'a film in the style of [similar to] a documentary', and not as a type or kind of language or film. This explains why the label "semi-taxonomic" is useful in order to describe the lexical meaning of *onda*.

However, when examining the relevant contexts, it may be observed that *onda* also becomes easily grammaticalized. As already claimed for *tipo*, the first process of recategorization of *onda* (ambiguous between lexicalization and grammaticalization) occurs when *onda* is the complement of a prepositional phrase headed by *de*, as in (13a–b). This is the construction from which other uses omitting the preposition *de* are derived, as in (13a'–b'), with a similative or approximative meaning (see the parallel examples in (4) vs. (6) and (8a) vs. (8b) for *tipo*):

(13) a. Es   una   actriz   de   la   **onda**   diva.
         is.3.SG a   actress of   the   style   diva
         'She is a diva-style actress' (lit.) 'She is an actress of the style diva'
     a'. Es   una   actriz   **onda**   diva.
         is.3.SG a   actress style   diva
         'She is a diva-like actress' (lit.) 'She is an actress (of the) style diva'
     b. La   película   es   (de la)   **onda**   (de)   Tarantino.
        The   film   is.3.SG   Of the   style   of   Tarantino
        'It's a Tarantino-style film' (lit.) 'The film is of the style of Tarantino'
     b'. La   película   es   **onda**   (de)   Tarantino.
         The   film   is.3.SG   style   of   Tarantino
         'The film is like Tarantino's' (lit.) 'The film is (of the) style (of) Tarantino'

In (13a–b), *onda* is the complement of a prepositional modifier (*un X (de) onda (de) Y*, 'an X of the style (of the) Y'), although *onda* could alternatively be seen as the head of a NP (*una onda Y de X*, a style Y of X'), exactly as observed previously about *tipo*. For instance, both sentences could be paraphrased inverting the word order, without semantic changes, as in *La onda diva de esa actriz* ('The diva style of this actress') or *La onda Tarantino de la película* ('The Tarantinoesque style of the film').

When the preposition *de* is omitted, *onda* becomes an apposition and can be rendered with a similative interpretation: 'it's like (a spacecraft, a diva, Tarantino)' (see examples (12c), (13a'–b')). The approximative meaning is easily derived from these examples and the structures with *tipo* in (9) could be exactly replicated with *onda*. Thus, *onda* can combine with DPs (such as *los profesores*, 'the professors', in 14a) and, when the "original" nominal head disappears, it is understood with a very general interpretation: 'they do something like talks', in (14b). It may also be utilized as an equivalent to 'for instance' (14c) or as a reformulation resource (14d):

(14) a. *Dice   cosas **onda** los profesores.*
        says.3.SG things style the professors'
        'She says things like the professors'
   b. *Hacen   **onda** charlas.*
        make.3.PL style talks
        'They do (something) like talks'
   c. *Me gustan   las películas bizarras **onda** Tarantino o*
        me like.3.PL the films   bizarre   style   Tarantino or
        Rodríguez.
        Rodríguez
        'I like bizarre films, like Tarantino or Rodríguez'
   d. *Usa   palabras así medio complicadas **onda** muchas*
        uses.3.SG   words   so   half   complex   style   many
        metáforas.
        metaphors
        '[Cerati] uses somewhat complex words, that is, many metaphors.'

As can be seen, the process of grammaticalization of *onda* is almost identical to that of *tipo*, although as a marker of comparison, approximation, exemplification or mitigation it is more novel and less widespread in its distribution throughout the generations, only being utilized productively by some people aged between 25 and 50 years.

The last item with a similar meaning and distribution as *tipo* and *onda* is *corte*. It seems to have originated in the '80s in the language of young lower class people in the peripheral metropolitan areas (or *Conurbano*) of Buenos Aires, according to Rojas (2012) and my own intuitions. *Corte* has been increasingly popularized by the music style of *cumbia villera* ('ghetto cumbia') and in recent decades it can be found in informal written texts (chats, 'fotologs', blogs, forums) of young middle-class speakers.

In standard Spanish, *corte* is also a polysemic noun. The relevant lexical definitions originate in the nominalization of *cortar* ('to cut'), as in (15a). With this meaning, *corte* heads fixed expressions such as *corte de pelo* ('haircut'), *corte de luz* ('electrical power outage'), *corte de agua* ('water failure'), *corte de carne* ('meat cut') or *corte del vestido* ('dress cut/design'), utilized often without the PPs, as in (15b–c):

(15) a. *Tiene   un   **corte** en   la   mano.*
        has.3.SG   a   cut   in   the hand
        'He has a cut on his hand'

b. *El* **corte** *más*   *buscado* *es*   *el* *lomo.*
    The cut   more looked-for is.3.SG the loin
    'The more desired cut is loin'
c. *El* *vestido* *tiene*   *un* **corte** *que* *le* *queda* *bien.*
    The dress   has.3.SG a   cut   that her suits   well
    'This dress has a cut which suits her well.'

Other metaphorical uses seem to have developed from the (more or less) literal contexts in (15). In a formal register in writing (and still retaining the relationship with its verbal origin), *corte* can be combined with PPs (16a) or with relational adjectives (16b) with a meaning linked to 'edge' or 'limit':

(16) a. *Se*   *ha buscado*   *el*   *mejor* *punto* *de* **corte** *de* *edad.*
         3.SG.PAS has looked-for the   best   point   of   cut-off   of   age
         'The best age limit has been sought after'
     b. *El* **corte** *social* *de* *su* *audiencia* *es*   *clarísimo.*
         the range   social   of   his   audience   is.3.SG.   clear.AUM.
         'The social range of his audience is absolutely clear.'

In standard Spanish, the taxonomic meaning (related to 'type') arose precisely from these contexts, and extended to other combinations of *corte* with classifying relational adjectives:

(17) a. *una* *literatura* *de* **corte** *tradicional*
         a   literature   of   type   traditional
         'a traditional type of literature'
     b. *un* *discurso* *de* **corte** *Fascista*
         a   discourse of   type   Fascist
         'a fascist-type discourse'
     c. *los* *partidos* *de* **corte** *social-burgués* *de* *la* *II Internacional*
         the parties   of   type   social-bourgeois of   the   II International
         'the social-bourgeois-style parties of the Second International'
     d. *...que* *no* *se*   *utilice*   *como* *trampolín*   *de* **corte**
         that   not 3.SG.PAS utilize.3.SG   as   springboard of   style
         político-electoral
         political-electoral
         '...that should not be utilized as a political-electoral kind of springboard'

As for its grammatical distribution, *corte* can only replace *tipo* in some contexts, mainly when combined with relational adjectives in a formal written register,[7] for instance, *ideología de tipo/corte marxista* ('Marxist-type/-style ideology') (see (1)), *película de tipo/corte documental* ('documentary type of film') (see (4c)), *literatura de tipo/corte tradicional* ('traditional type of literature') (see (17a)), *discurso de tipo/corte fascista* ('fascist-type discourse') (see (17b)). But the equivalence is not uniform, since *corte* cannot replace *tipo* in the nominal appositions characteristic of scientific taxonomies: ?? *sangre corte A* (lit. 'blood style A') (see (6a)), ?? *patología corte 1* (lit. 'pathology style 1') (see (6b)). Moreover, in some cases (e.g., (17d)), its meaning tends to be semi-taxonomic, related to 'style', as with *onda*.

Beyond these subtle differences restricted to the lexical uses, *corte* could replace *tipo* or *onda* in all the paradigms in (7–9) and (13–14), which already imply a certain degree of grammaticalization. Hence, starting from the standard Spanish contexts illustrated in (17), in Río de la Plata Spanish *corte* can have scope over nominal constructions (NPs or DPs), with meanings of approximation (18a) and comparison (18b):

(18) a. *Había un montón de libros **corte** librería.* (Rojas 2012: 6)
there-was.3.SG a lot of books style bookshop
'There were a lot of books like in a bookshop'
b. *Marisa usa polleras **corte** los tenistas.* (Rojas 2012: 6)
Marisa wears.3.SG skirts style the tennis players
'Marisa wears skirts like the tennis players'

2.2 Other category domains

As previously shown, the uses of *tipo*, *onda* and *corte* in the nominal domain systematically develop a set of grammatical (not lexical) meanings, such as 'comparison', 'exemplification' and 'approximation'.

The approximative meaning also dominates when *tipo* and *onda* are employed in other category domains, for instance quantification:

---

[7] It could seem strange that young people in peripheral areas create a mitigating marker starting from an item of a (very) formal written register. However, notice that a representative unit in Río de la Plata youth language is the elative adjective *alto/a* (as in *alto libro*, *alta campera*, lit. 'high', 'great book/jacket'). *Alto/a* is also based on a relatively formal use in standard Spanish: e.g., *un alto funcionario*, *altas responsabilidades* ('a high commissioner', 'high responsibilities') (Resnik 2013).

(19) a. Voy   **tipo/onda** 4.
       go.1.SG kind   4
       'I'm going around 4'
   b. Había   **tipo/onda** dos   personas.
      there-was.3.SG   kind   two   persons
      'There were like two people'

As the English translations show, in examples such as (19) *tipo* or *onda* do not have lexical meanings and cannot be rendered as 'type', 'kind' or 'style'.

Tipo and *onda* also appear in the adjectival domain, particularly in combination with qualifying (or unbound) adjectives, as in (20a). Qualifying adjectives are modifiable by degree quantifiers, with which *tipo* and *onda* may coappear without problems, as (20b) illustrates. As examples (20c–d) show, a similar phenomenon occurs with adverbs, especially in the case of so-called "adjectival adverbs" such as *rápido* ('fast') and *despacio* ('slowly'):

(20) a. Es   **tipo/onda** malo.
        is.3.SG kind   bad
        'He is kind of bad'
   b. Es   **tipo/onda** re/muy/demasiado   malo.
      is.3.SG kind   very/too (much)   bad
      'He is kind of very/too bad'
   c. Va   **tipo/onda** rápido.
      Goes.3.SG   kind   fast
      'He goes kind of fast'
   d. Me   daba   besitos   **tipo/onda** despacio.
      me.DAT   gave.3.SG   little kisses   kind   slowly
      'He gave me little kisses kind of slowly'

Though with a different sociolectal range, *corte* has the same grammatical distribution as *tipo* and *onda*. Thus, it can have scope not only over nominal constructions (NPs or DPs) (e.g., (18)), but also over APs (21a) and PPs (21b), where speakers use *corte* as a synonym of *tipo* ('kind') or *como* ('like') (see Rojas 2012: 6):

(21) a. Tengo   una   moto   así   **corte** chopera   pero   sin
        have.1.SG   a   motorcycle   like that   style   chopper   but   without
        espejos. (Rojas 2012: 6)
        mirrors
        'I have a motorcycle like that, kind of a Chopper, but without mirrors'

b. El   guacho estaba   para darle   pero
   the   man   was.IMP.3.SG for   give + him.DAT but
   de lejos, viste,   **corte** con   una   varita, con   una
   afar   see   style   with a   wand   with a
   cañita de pescar (Rojas 2012: 3)
   fishing rod
   'The man was nice to do it with him, but from afar, see, kind of with a wand, with a fishing rod'

However, it must be noted that the productivity of *tipo*, *onda* and *corte* with APs, AdvPs and PPs is not comparable with the productivity of the English item *kind (of)*, which adopts a semantic value of degree quantification (as in *kind of interesting/loudly*), as Margerie (2010) argues (and subsection 4.2 discusses in detail).

Finally, *tipo*, *onda* and *corte* can have sentential scope, with or without the complementizer *que* (as the sentences in (22) show), resulting in a mitigating interpretation.

(22) a. **Tipo** que no   me   interesó.
        Kind that not   me.DAT   interested.3.SG
        'Like it didn't interest me'
     b. **Onda** que yo   soy   más   espiritual.
        kind   that I   am.1.SG   more spiritual
        'I am kind of more spiritual'
     c. Sí,   **corte** que si   te   mascás   400   árboles, te
        Yes   kind   that if   you.REFL   chew.2.SG 400   trees   you.REF
        das vuelta.
        turn.2.SG
        'Yes, kind of if you chew 400 trees, you are high.' (Rojas 2012: 3)

2.3 Summary

In this section, we have shown the transformation of *tipo*, *onda* and *corte* from lexical words into grammatical items. There are some subtle differences in the lexical meanings of the three units, with *tipo* being the only possibility in real scientific taxonomies. Since *onda* and *corte* are sometimes interpreted as 'style', there are some contexts in which they cannot replace *tipo* (e.g., (23a–b)) and other contexts in which the meaning significantly changes (note that the interpretation of *corte* and *onda* in (23c–d) is not classificatory, but rather similative):

(23) a. *una patología* **tipo/*onda/*corte** 1
       a   pathology type   1
       'a type 1 pathology' (lit.) 'a pathology (of the) type 1'
   b. *Sangre* **tipo/*onda/*corte** A
       blood   type   A
       'blood type A' (lit.) 'blood (of the) type A'
   c. *un estudio* **tipo/onda/corte** *Rorschach*
       a   study   type/style   Rorschach
       'a Rorschach-type/-style study' (lit.) 'a study (of the) type/style (of) Rorschach'
   d. *una película* **tipo/onda/corte** *documental*
       a   film   type/style   documentary
       'a documentary-type/-style film' (lit.) 'a film (of the) type/style (of) documentary'

Despite the heterogeneity of their origins, once started, the process of grammaticalization of *tipo, onda* and *corte* becomes absolutely uniform in meaning (with the values of 'approximation', 'comparison', 'exemplification' and even 'reformulation') and in their grammatical properties. As some examples in subsection 2.1 (see (7–9), (13–14), (18)) and the entire subsection 2.2 clearly show, they can freely alternate in the same contexts.

The process of grammaticalization of *tipo, onda* and *corte* may be conceived as an instance of subjectification and intersubjectification (Traugott 2003; Davidse, Vandelanotte and Cuyckens 2010), as Margerie (2010: 342) also states for *kind (of)* and other similar expressions: "they have evolved along a continuum leading it towards the more (inter)subjective pole of language." With their lexical meanings, they are employed (especially *tipo*) in "objective" intellectual operations, such as proposing hyperonyms both in scientific or popular classifications. Instead, as markers of modality with scope over the entire sentence (as in (22)), they are grammatical items, but their meanings become more (inter)subjective, expressing basically mitigation. Mitigation (or attenuation) is a strategy typical of politeness, useful for regulating the interpersonal and social relations between interlocutors (Landone 2009), since it "reduces risks for participants at various levels; e.g., risks of self-contradiction, refusal, losing face, conflicts and so on" (Caffi 1999: 882).

The next section concentrates precisely on the mitigating uses of *tipo, onda* and *corte*.

3 Sentential scope: markers of mitigation

As discussed in the previous section, when *tipo, onda, corte (que)* have scope over the sentential domain, as in (22), they exhibit a modal interpretation related to mitigation. Markers of mitigation have been characterized by the pragmatic literature as a set of expressions employed to weaken the locutionary content (i.e., the meaning of a word, a phrase or the whole sentence) or the illocutionary force of a statement (see, for example, Caffi 1999, Montecino 2004).

This section aims to determine the grammatical properties of *tipo, onda* and *corte* when they have scope over a whole sentence. The analysis follows the approach taken by Di Tullio and Kornfeld (2013) and considers the words in relation to their basic distribution (syntactic autonomy and position in the sentence) and their interaction with other elements (positive and negative polarity items, modalities, moods, and subordination).

3.1 Grammatical distribution and properties

Tipo, onda and *corte* share a property concerning their distribution: the *absolute impossibility of expressing an independent statement*. The most representative context is the possibility of being answers to closed questions; the ungrammaticality of *tipo, onda* and *corte* in (24a) contrasts with the fact that epistemic markers of certainty (24b) or doubt (24c) function perfectly well as complete answers (Di Tullio and Kornfeld 2013):

(24)   A: –¿Al final viste la película?
Finally saw.2.SG the film?
'Did you see the film in the end?'
  a. **B: –*Tipo/onda/corte.**
Like
*–Like!
  b. **B: –Posta/de una.**
for sure
–For sure!
  c. **B: –Capaz/por ahí.**
maybe/perhaps
–Maybe!

On the other hand, *tipo, onda* and *corte* have a very restricted possibility of varying their syntactic position. When modifying the whole sentence, they are almost always initial (sentence-final position being ungrammatical, as (25b) shows), although topicalized elements are admitted before them, as in both sentences of (26):

(25) a. **Tipo/onda/corte** que no sé.
Kind that not know.1.SG
'Like I don't know'
b. *No sé, *tipo/onda/corte*
Not know-1.SG kind

(26) a. Vos **tipo/onda/corte** que ni lo viste.
You kind that not him.ACC saw.2.SG
'Like you didn't see him.'
b. Con él *tipo/onda/corte* (que) no sé
With him-ABL kind that not know.1.SG
Qué hacer.
What to do
'With him like I don't know what to do.'

Tipo, onda and *corte* may also be characterized according to their combination with different modalities (exclamative, imperative, interrogative), with subjunctive and conditional moods and with certain periphrasis, as well as their possibility of appearing in subordinate clauses.

With regard to modal contexts, there is a clear incompatibility between *tipo, onda* or *corte* and the exclamative (27a), imperative (27b) and interrogative sentences (27c).

(27) a. *¡**Tipo/onda/corte** (que) vino!
kind that came.3.SG
'Like he came!'
b. *¡**Tipo/onda/corte** (que) vení!
kind that come.IMP.2.SG
'Like come!'
c. *¿**Tipo/onda/corte** (que) venís?
kind that come.IND.2.SG
'Like you come?'

Concerning (27c), it is relevant to note that *tipo, onda* and *corte* can appear in confirmation questions:

(28) ¿Vos **tipo/onda/corte** (que) no te la bancás?
    You kind (of) that not you.REFL her.AC tolerate.2.SG
    'You kind of don't tolerate her?'

Sentence (28) is equivalent to *Vos tipo/onda/corte (que) no te la bancás, ¿no?* ('You kind of don't tolerate her, do you?'), which is also not a real question, but a confirmation question.[8] Notice that the scope of the marker of mitigation in (28) is referring to the implicit assertion, not to the speech act 'question' itself. It is important to differentiate *tipo, onda* and *corte* from markers of mitigation allowed to modify different speech acts, such as orders (29a), questions (29b) or pieces of advice (29c), as it is the case with *un poco* ('a bit') or *nomás* (lit. 'no more', 'just') in Río de la Plata Spanish:

(29) a. Entrá **nomás** que tengo algo para decirte.
        get-in.IMP just that have.1.SG something to say + you.DAT
        'Just get in because I have something to say you.'
   b. ¿Me decís **un poco** qué te pasa?
        me.DAT say.2.SG a bit what you.DAT happens.3.SG
        'Are you going to tell me a bit what's wrong with you?'
   c. Me parece que deberías ir **nomás**.
        me.DAT seems.3.SG that should.2.SG go just
        'It seems to me that you should just go.'

On the other hand, *tipo, onda* and *corte* are compatible with different verbal moods: they can coappear with the indicative as a "realis mood" (e.g., (30a)), but also with "irrealis moods" implying a lesser degree of probability attributed to the event, such as subjunctive (30b), conditional (30c) and the "future", when it expresses a hypothetical event (30d):

(30) a. **Tipo/onda/corte** (que) quiero no ir.
        kind that want.1.SG not go
        'I kind of want not to go.'
   b. **Tipo/onda/corte** (que) quisiera no ir.
        kind that want.SUBJ.1.SG not go
        'I would kind of want not to go.'

---

8 Actually, *¿no?* ('don't you?') is another lexical-phrasal resource with a mitigation meaning, used to manage the speaker's relationship with the hearer (Landone 2009).

11 Taxonomic nouns and markers of mitigation in Río de la Plata Spanish — 435

c. ***Tipo/onda/corte*** *(que) le gustaría no ir.*
kind that him.DAT like.COND.3.SG not go
'He would kind of like not to go.'

d. ***Tipo/onda/corte*** *(que) pensará no ir.*
kind that think.FUT.3.SG not go
'He will kind of think not to go.'

Besides, *tipo, onda* and *corte* can appear when the main verb of the sentence is a modal periphrasis with the epistemic auxiliaries *deber* and *poder* (31a), as well as the conditional or future compound forms (31b):

(31) a. ***Tipo/onda/corte*** *(que) debe/ puede haber venido antes.*
Kind that must/ can have come before
'I kind of must/could have come before.'

b. ***Tipo/onda/corte*** *(que) no habría/ habrá venido.*
kind that not would have will have come
'She kind of would/will have come.'

Notice that *tipo, onda* and *corte* admit both the emphatic negation and affirmation (Laka 1990):

(32) ***Tipo/onda/corte*** *(que) Sí/ no lo entendí.*
kind that yes/ not him.AC understood.1.SG
'I kind of did/didn't understand him.'

Finally, *tipo, onda* and *corte* are compatible with different kinds of subordinate clauses (completive clauses as in (33a–b) or relative clauses as in (33c)), as long as the semantic-pragmatic context accommodates a marker of mitigation; consequently, they are impossible in subordinate clauses presupposing the veracity of the statement or involving an absolute degree of certainty (see (34)):

(33) a. *Preguntó si **tipo/onda/corte** (que) conviene ir la semana*
asked.1.SG if kind that suit.3.SG go the week
próxima.
next
'She asked if like we need go (there) next week.'

b. *Contó que **tipo/onda/corte** (que) había venido para*
tell.PAS.3.SG that kind that had.3.SG come for
vernos.
see + us.AC
'She told [us] that like she had come to see us.'

c. Le   regalé   una novela que **tipo/onda/corte** *(que)*
   him.DAT   gifted.1.SG a   novel that kind   that
   eligieron como   la mejor de   Roth.
   chose.3.PL as   the best   of   Roth
   'I gave him a novel which like was chosen as the best one of Roth.'

(34) a. *No   me   explico   cómo* **(*tipo/onda/corte*)**
        not me.REFL explain.1.SG how   Kind
        te   querés   marchar ya.
        you.REFL   want.2.SG   to go   now
        'I don't understand why you (*kind of) want to go now.'
    b. *Te   aseguro   que* **(*tipo/onda/corte*)** *lo*
        you.DAT   ensure.1.SG   that kind   him.AC
        voy a comprar.
        buy.FUT.1.SG
        'I ensure you that I will (*kind of) buy it.'

Besides all these grammatical contexts, *tipo* and *onda* also serve as fillers in the speech of some young *porteños* (i.e., Buenos Aires natives) from upper or upper-middle classes. Some humorous characters satirizing their way of speech, such as Caro Pardiaco (of the group Cualca) or Martín Revoira Lynch (Fernando Peña) show representative uses of this *tipo*, which can virtually appear in any part of the sentence, as long as phrases are not interrupted:[9]

(35) a. **Tipo** *me   acuerdo   de la   democracia.*
        kind   me.REFL remember.1.SG   of the democracy
        'I kind of remember the democracy.'
    b. *Como* **tipo** *una fruta.*
        eat.1.SG kind   a   fruit
        'I kind of eat a fruit.'
    c. *No   ahora, pero* **tipo** *a los 30.*
        not now   but   kind   at   30
        'Not now, but kind of at 30 (years old)...'

---

9 Some of these uses are ambiguous and could be also analyzed as a focus marker or a *marker of reported speech or thought* (Margerie 2010: 327–328), such as (36a) or (36d), since the sentences could be supplemented with some manual gestures of "air quotes".

(36) a. Esos   son   **tipo**   mis   top   artists.
       These are.3.PL kind my   top   artists
       'These are kind of my top artists.'
   b. Me   fijo   **tipo**   las   entrevistas.
       me.REFL watch.1.SG kind the   interviews
       'I kind of watch the interviews.'
   c. La gente   **tipo**   quiere   saber   quién   soy   yo.
       people   kind   want.3.SG to know   who   am.1.SG   I
       'People kind of want to know who you are.'
   d. No   estoy   tampoco   **tipo**   contenta   lo que   se   dice.
       not am.1.SG   either   kind   happy   as   3.SG.PAS   say.3.SG
       'I am not, like, happy either, as they say.'

3.2 Summary

In Río de la Plata Spanish, *tipo*, *onda* and *corte (que)*, when having sentential scope, are typically combined with assertions, independent of whether these are affirmative or negative (see (32)) and of the verbal mood employed (indicative, subjunctive or conditional, see (30)).

Unlike other markers of mitigation in Río de la Plata Spanish, such as *nomás* (lit. 'no more', 'just') or *un poco* ('a bit', 'a little') (see (29)), *tipo*, *onda* and *corte* cannot combine with speech acts other than assertions: this allows us to explain their incompatibility with imperative, exclamative and interrogative modalities (see (27)). Hence, *tipo*, *onda* and *corte* never mitigate the speech act 'question', though they may appear in confirmation questions mitigating an assertion which could be perceived as "too strong" or "shocking" for the hearer (see (28)).

In pragmatic terms, *tipo, onda* and *corte* are not bushes (following the terminology of Caffi 1999), but hedges, since they do not undermine the propositional content of assertions, but rather mitigate their illocutionary force.[10] However, they should be carefully distinguished from epistemic markers of doubt pointing out the speaker's distance or lack of commitment to the truth of his/her statement (as in colloquial Río de la Plata Spanish *por ahí* or *capaz* ('maybe, perhaps'), Di Tullio and Kornfeld 2013), which Caffi would also classify as instances of hedges. *Tipo, onda* and *corte* never affect the truth value of the proposition, so they should

---

[10] Instead, when having a more restricted scope, as in some of the examples in section 2 (see 18–21, for instance), *tipo, onda* and *corte* could be seen as bushes in the terminology of Caffi (1999), since they mitigate the semantic content of a word or a phrase (see also Montecino 2004).

be thought of as modifiers of the implicit speech act verb (*'tipo/onda/corte (que) afirmo que* X', 'I kind of assert that X'). (For a detailed distinction between both groups of modal markers, see Kornfeld 2013 and Kornfeld and Avellana 2019).[11] This also explains why they cannot be answers to closed questions (see (24)), since they can modify the speech act 'assertion' only if something is asserted.

4 An overview of processes of grammaticalization

Sections 2 and 3 presented a motivated argument that taxonomic nouns *tipo, onda* and *corte* are grammaticalized as mitigation markers in Río de la Plata Spanish, via the intermediate steps of the grammatical values 'comparison' and 'approximation'. In order to test the robustness of this pattern, in this section *tipo, onda* and *corte* are contrasted with other markers of mitigation: standard Spanish *como que* ('like that') and English *kind*. These present a slightly different distribution (Margerie 2010), which happens to parallel other expressions in Río de la Plata Spanish (*medio,* 'half', and *un poco,* 'a little, a bit').

4.1 A shortcut in the path of grammaticalization: The case of *como que*

Other common markers of mitigation in Río de la Plata Spanish, *como (que)* ('like (that)') and *casi (que)* ('almost (that)'), sound less informal and are usually attested in different age groups and registers, including writing (Kornfeld 2013). *Como (que)* is common to most Spanish varieties, as may be verified in the *Diccionario Panhispánico de Dudas* [Panhispanic Dictionary of Doubts] of the Royal Spanish Academy (RAE 2005). The case of *como (que)* is especially relevant for this paper, since, as (37) shows, it exhibits a clear meaning of approximation alongside adjectives (e.g., *triste,* 'sad', *cansado* 'tired'), adverbs (e.g., *lejos,* 'far', *cerca,* 'close') and verbs (e.g., *es,* 'is'):

---

11 Following the system in Di Tullio and Kornfeld (2013), the mitigating items would be placed up in the tree (in the position of specifiers of Force Phrase, tightly related to the speech act, according to Rizzi 1997). In this position, they can only modify assertions and are not compatible with other modalities, but do not have any (formal or semantic) conflict with positive or negative polarity contexts.

(37) No   estoy   triste.   Estoy   **como**   triste.   No   estoy   cansado.
      not   am.1.SG sad   am.1.SG like   sad   not   am.1.SG   tired
      Estoy   **como**   Cansado.   Nada   está   lejos.   Está
      am.1.SG   as   tired   nothing   is.3.SG   far   is.3.SG
      como lejos.   Nada   está   cerca.   Está   **como**   cerca (. . .)
      like   far   nothing   is.3.SG   close   is.3.SG   like   close
      El   ser   no   es,   es   **como que**   es.   Hoy,
      the   being   not   is.3.SG is.3.SG   like-that   is.3.SG   today
      aquí,   Parménides   habría   dicho   "El   ser   es   **como que**
      here   Parménides   would have   said   the   being   is.3.SG like-that
      es,   el   no ser   es   **como que**   no   es.
      is.3.SG   the   not being   is.3.SG   like-that   not   is.3.SG
      (J.P.Feinmann, "Como mucho", *Página 12*, https://www.pagina12.com.ar/
      diario/elpais/1-61450-2006-01-08.html)
      'I am not sad. I am like sad. I am not tired. I am like tired. Nothing is far. It
      is like far. Nothing is close. It is like close. (. . .) Being is not, it's like it is.
      Today, here, Parménides would have said: *Being is like it is, not being is like
      it isn't.*'

Unlike *tipo*, *onda* and *corte*, which are nouns with a lexical meaning (as analyzed in section 2), *como (que)* is an exclusively grammatical item and appears in different category domains with diverse functions and semantic values.

The cases in which *como* functions as a relative pronoun or a causal connector should be set aside in order to discover how it is transformed into a marker of mitigation. Instead, its use as marker of comparison in the nominal domain (38a) is relevant, as well as the case in which it introduces a proposition headed by *si* ('if') (38b):[12]

(38) a. Vi   a   una flor   **como**   una   luna.
          saw.1.SG   to.ACC   a   flower   like   a   moon
          'I saw a flower like a moon'

---

12 The comparison value disappears in constructions with a prepositional value, in which *como* could be translated as 'of' or 'as', in the nominal domain (i.a), or when it heads predicatives (i.b):
i. a. *Tiene un uso **como** muletilla en el habla de los jóvenes porteños de clase alta* ('It has a use as [*como*] a filler in the speech of young high class *porteños*')
    b. *Siempre lo presenta **como** un ejemplo de vida* ('She always presents him as [*como*] an example of life')

b. Lo   planteó   **como** si   fuera   muy   difícil.
    it.ACC   showed.3.SG like   if   is.SUBJ.3.SG   very difficult
    'She stated it as if it was very difficult'

In order to function as a marker of mitigation with sentential scope, *como* undergoes a process of secondary grammaticalization when its similative meaning (as in (38)) develops a value of 'approximation'. It can thus mitigate the propositional content of a word or phrase in different category domains, including the whole sentence (when it acts as a bush, according to Caffi 1999) or, alternatively, it can have scope over the illocutionary force of the assertion, as a hedge.[13] The following examples display different pairs including *como* + XP and a more explicit paraphrase; for instance (39a) shows an adjective and (39a') the extended paraphrase with the verb *ser* ('be') and the same can be observed concerning adverbs (cf. (39b) vs. (39b')), prepositional phrases ((39c) vs. (39c')), quantifiers (((39d) vs. (39d')) and ((39e) vs. (39e'))) and the whole sentence ((39f) vs. (39f')):

(39) a. Es   **como** tímido.
         is.3.SG like   shy
         'He is kind of shy'
     a'. Es   **como** si   fuera   tímido.
         is.3.SG like   if   was.SUBJ.3.SG   shy
         'He is as if he was shy'
     b. Es   **como** lejos.
         is.3.SG like   far
         'It is kind of far'
     b'. Es   **como** si   fuera   lejos.
         is.3.SG like   if   was.SUBJ.3.SG   far
         'It is as if it was far'

---

13 Even for normative texts such as the *Diccionario Panhispánico de Dudas* (RAE 2005), it is not easy to determine at which moment *como* lost its "legitimate" meaning of comparison and started to be used with approximation and mitigation values: **"como b)** When preceding an expression of quantity, it has approximation value: *Te estuve esperando como una hora* ('I was waiting for you *como* one hour'); *Esa calle está como a tres cuadras de aquí* ('That street is *como* 300 metres from here'). From this approximation meaning it is easy to derivate a mitigating value, which happens to be admissible when the goal of the speaker is to downgrade the degree of certainty with respect to the following idea: *Tu hijo es un chico como muy tímido* ('Your son is a boy *como* very shy') (it is intended to express that "he seems very shy", not to assert that he is really shy). However, the use of *como* should be avoided when it is clearly superfluous, which is not infrequent in colloquial registers: *La comida estaba como muy sabrosa* ('The food was *como* very tasty); *Me siento como muy cansada* ('I feel *como* very tired')" (see rae.es/dpd/como, my translations).

c. Lo   golpeó   **como** con   delicadeza
    him.ACC   hit.PAS.3.SG   like   with   delicacy
    'He hit him kind of delicately'

c'. Lo   golpeó   **como** si lo   hiciera
    him.ACC   hit.PAS.3.SG   like   if it.ACC   does.SUBJ.3.SG
    con   delicadeza
    with   delicacy
    'He hit him as if he was doing it delicately'

d. Te   esperé   **como** una   hora.
    you.ACC   waited.1.SG   like   one   hour
    'I waited for you like one hour'

d'. Te   esperé   **como** si   fuera   una   hora
    you.ACC   waited.1.SG   like   if   was.SUBJ.3.SG one   hour
    'I waited for you as if it was one hour'

e. Vino   **como** a   las 5.
    came.3.SG   like   at   (the) 5
    'It's like at 5'

e'. Vino   **como** si   fuera   a   las 5.
    came.3.SG   like   if   was.SUBJ.3.SG at   (the) 5
    'It's as if it was at 5'

f. Lo   presenta   **como que** es   un   ejemplo.
    him.ACC   presents.3.SG like-that   is. 3.SG a   example
    'She presents him like he is an example'

f'. Lo   presenta   **como** si   fuera   un   ejemplo.
    him.ACC   presents.3.SG like   if   does.SUBJ.3.SG an   example
    'She presents him as if he was an example'

When having scope over the whole sentence, *como que* (*que* being in this case obligatory) shows exactly the same distribution as *tipo*, *onda* and *corte*, according to the data reviewed in section 3 (see examples 24–31): it cannot form autonomous statements (for instance, functioning as an answer to closed questions, as in (40)); it is placed in initial position of the sentence (41), except with topicalized phrases (42); it is incompatible with imperative, exclamative and interrogative sentences (43); and it can appear not only with indicative but also with subjunctive and conditional moods (44) and with different periphrasis (45):

(40) **A:** –¿Al final   viste   la   película?
     Finally   saw.2.SG   the   film?
     'Did you see the film in the end?'

B: *–*Como*.
Like
'Like.'

(41) a. ***Como que*** *no sé.*
like-that not know.1.SG
Like, I don't know.
b. **No sé,* ***como que***
Not know.1.SG like that
Like, I don't know.

(42) a. *Vos* ***como que*** *ni lo viste.*
you.NOM like-that not him.ACC saw.2.SG
'You like didn't see him'
b. *Con Él* ***como que*** *no Sé qué hacer.*
with him.ABL like-that not know.1.SG what to do
'With him, like, I don't know what to do.'

(43) a. **¡**Como que** *vino!*
like-that came.3.SG
'Like, he came!'
b. **¡ **Como que*** *vení!*
like-that come.IMP.2.SG
'Like, come!'
c. **¿**Como que*** *venís?*
like-that come.IND.2.SG
'Like, you come?'

(44) a. ***Como que*** *quiero no ir.*
like-that want.1.SG not go
'I kind of want not to go.'
b. ***Como que*** *quisiera no ir.*
like-that want.SUBJ.1.SG not go
'I kind of would want not to go.'
c. ***Como que*** *pensará no ir.*
like-that think.FUT.3.SG not go
'He kind of will think not to go.'
d. ***Como que*** *Le gustaría no ir.*
like-that him.DAT like.COND.3.SG not go
'He kind of would like not to go.'

(45) a. **Como que** debe/ puede haber venido antes.
      like-that   must/ can   have come   before
      'I kind of must/could have come before.'
   b. **Como que** no habría/ habrá venido.
      like-that   not would have will have come
      'She kind of would/will have come.'

Additionally, *como que* is compatible with *subordination*, as long as the semantic-pragmatic context enables the occurrence of a marker of mitigation, as in (46). Exactly like *tipo, onda* and *corte* (see (32–34)), it cannot appear in subordinate propositions presupposing the truth of the statement or involving a total degree of certainty (see (47)):

(46) a. Creo   que **como que** conviene ir la semana próxima.
      believe.1.SG that like-that   suit.3.SG go the week   next
      'I think that, like, we need to go (there) next week.'
   b. Contó   que **como que** había venido para vernos.
      tell.PAS.3.SG that like-that   had.3.SG come for   see + us.AC
      'She told [us] that, like, she had come to see us.'
   c. Le   regalé   una novela que **como que** eligieron
      him.DAT   gave.1.SG a   novel that like-that   chose.3.PL
      Como la   mejor de Roth.
      As   the best of Roth
      'I gave her a novel that, like, was chosen as the best one of Roth.'

(47) a. No me   explico   cómo (***como que**) te
      Not me.REFL   explain.1.SG how like-that   you.REFL
      querés   marchar ya.
      want.2.SG to go   now
      'I don't understand how you (*like) want to go now.'
   b. Te   aseguro   que (***como que**) lo   voy a comprar.
      you.DAT   ensure.1.SG that like-that   him.AC   buy.FUT.1.SG
      'I ensure you that I (*like) will buy it.'

Finally, *como que* can coappear with negative or affirmative polarity items (Laka 1990, Bosque 1994), since it admits both emphatic negation and affirmation (see (48)):

(48) **Como que** sí/ no lo   entendí.
      like-that yes/ not him.AC understood.1.SG
      'I kind of did/didn't understand him.'

In sum, as a sentential marker of mitigation, *como que* presents almost the same grammatical properties observed for *tipo*, *onda* and *corte* in section 3, although it comes from standard Spanish and consequently has a more extended distribution across registers and age groups. Its process of grammaticalization is also shorter: it starts directly from a relevant grammatical value, 'comparison', which *tipo*, *onda* and *corte* must first acquire by means of grammaticalization.

4.2 Some contrastive notes about grammaticalization

After our research in sections 2 and 3, it may be assumed that the recurrence of (semi-) taxonomic nouns such as *tipo, onda* and *corte* being utilized as mitigators in Río de la Plata Spanish is not random. Because of their lexical meaning, they easily acquire other values of a more grammatical nature, such as 'comparison', 'exemplification' and 'approximation' (often almost indistinguishable), always within the nominal domain. The approximative meaning in other category domains then lead to the mitigating interpretation over phrases or a whole sentence, as the use of *como* examined in subsection 4.1 illustrates.

The same sequence of semantic values could also be found for Italian (see Voghera, Ch.9, this volume) and Brazilian and European Portuguese *tipo* (see e.g. Bittencourt 2007; Marques, Ch. 10, this volume). The fact that different varieties and languages replicate this connection between taxonomic nouns and markers of mitigation suggests the existence of a cognitive (not only linguistic) pattern. However, it must be remembered that there is arbitrariness in some phenomena. For instance, the concrete choice of the lexical item undergoing the process of grammaticalization is arbitrary. Thus, other taxonomic or semi-taxonomic nouns, such as *modelo* ('model') or *estilo* ('style'), are not grammaticalized in Spanish outside the nominal domain, though both may be occasionally used within the DP with the grammatical values 'comparison', 'approximation' and even 'exemplification' (as (49) illustrate), in the same way as *tipo, onda* and *corte* (cf. examples as 7, 13, 18, 19 in section 2):

(49) a. Un mentiroso **modelo** Macri
         A   liar   model   Macri
         'a liar after the model of Macri'

b. *Traé   alguna   bebida   **estilo** Campari.*
   bring.IMP.2.SG some   beverage style   Campari
   'Bring some Campari-style drink'
c. *Voy   **estilo** 4.*
   come.1.SG style   4
   'I go, like, at 4'

On the other hand, there are some subtle differences in the intermediate processes of grammaticalization between Río de la Plata Spanish *tipo, onda* and *corte* and English *kind of*. According to different researchers (see Margerie 2010; Aijmer, Ch.4, this volume), *kind of* has special lexical or grammatical uses other than taxonomic noun and marker of mitigation. Margerie (2010) recognizes the following primary uses for *kind of*: it can express category membership (50) and approximation (51) within the nominal domain, while (52) shows a first significant step in the grammaticalization process, with the absence of any determiner, *kind of* being used as a nominal qualifier:

(50) the **kind** of college

(51) a. *A/some/this **kind** of reddish-brown colour* (Margerie 2010: 318)
     b. *It's a **kind** of a big interdisciplinary thing.* (MICASE) (Margerie 2010: 339)

(52) *It was **kind** of a surprise.* (Margerie 2010: 340)

The context of (52) enables *kind (of)* to be transposed to other category domains (verbal, adjectival or adverbial) in order to acquire values of degree (53) and pragmatic meaning (or hedges, according to Margerie) (54):

(53) *It's not flat, but it's **kind** of deflated.* (Margerie 2010: 319)

(54) *It's **kind** of fucking important.* (Margerie 2010: 327)

As can be seen, the structure from which *kind* is grammaticalized has the form D + **kind** + of + NP/DP.[14]

---

14 As a reviewer points out to me, this is also the position occupied by the Spanish taxonomic noun *especie* (lit.'species', 'kind, sort'), which is an approximator (e.g., *Es una especie de radiador* 'It is a kind of radiator'), but has not acquired further pragmaticalized functions.

Interestingly, in Río de la Plata Spanish it is possible to replicate the contexts in (50) and (51a) with *tipo* in place of *kind* (e.g., (55a–b)). However, in cases analogous to (51b) or (52), this is not possible (55c–d):

(55) a. un/ algún/ ese **tipo** de colegio
       A some this kind of college
       'a/some/this kind of college'
    b. El **tipo** de colegio que le venga bien
       The kind of college that him.DAT come.SUBJ.3.SG well
       'the kind of college that suits him'
    c. *un **tipo** de un colegio bueno
       a kind of a college good
       'a kind of a good college'
    d. *era **tipo** de una sorpresa
       was.IMP.3.SG kind of a surprise
       'It was kind of a surprise'

These differences seem to be due to the fact that in Río de la Plata Spanish, *tipo*, *onda* and *corte* do not start their grammaticalization processes from the position of head of the complement of the DP. Rather, the original position of *tipo* is the place of a nominal modifier (PP or apposition): D + N (+ de) + **tipo** +Modif (as mentioned in section 2):

(56) a. Una película del **tipo** de Tarantino
       A film of-the type of Tarantino
       'a film of the kind of Tarantino's'
    b. Una película de(l) **tipo** Tarantino
       A film of(-the) type Tarantino
       'a film of (the) kind Tarantino'
    c. Una película **tipo** Tarantino
       A film type Tarantino
       'a film kind (like) Tarantino'

The different structures could be formalized in this way:

(57) a. [$_{DP}$ [$_{D'}$ D [$_{NP}$ [$_{N'}$ **kind** [$_{PP}$ [$_{P'}$ of [$_{DP/NP}$ [$_{N'}$ N]]]]]]]]
    b. [$_{DP}$ [$_{D'}$D [$_{NP}$ [$_{N'}$ N [$_{PP}$ [$_{P'}$ de [$_{DP}$ l [$_{NP}$ **tipo**[$_{PP}$ de [$_{DP/NP}$ [$_{N'}$N]]]]]]]]]]]]

The structural distinction between (57a) and (57b) has multiple consequences and explains why *tipo* (*onda* and *corte*) have different syntactic properties to *kind*, although they share meanings and functions as taxonomic nouns and as markers of mitigation.

Hence, the first steps of grammaticalization of *tipo, onda* and *corte* in Río de la Plata Spanish (i.e., with grammatical values of 'comparison' and 'approximation') are produced from the function of nominal appositions schematized in (57b), representing the case in which the preposition and the determiner are omitted, as in (56c). There, the use of the items is prepositional, as Mihatsch (2018) remarks. By contrast, *kind* is grammaticalized from the structure in (57a), and not (57b), explaining why it never gets meanings such as 'comparison' or 'exemplification' within the nominal domain.

Particularly striking are the differences related to the case of *kind* as a quantifier of degree in adjectival, adverbial and verbal domains, as in (53). As discussed earlier, Margerie (2010) identifies three different uses of *kind* as a quantifier in these category domains: 1) as a "booster" (or intensifier), especially when combined with *really*, as in (58); 2) as a "compromiser", when "the speaker indicates by means of the compromiser *kind of/kinda* that the notion conveyed by the verb or adjective pre-modified by the intensifier applies to some degree, but not fully" (Margerie 2010: 319) (e.g., (59)); 3) as "diminisher" (see (60)):

(58) *I mean isn't this a gorgeous thing? I'm really **kinda** pleased how well these, show up.* (MICASE) (Margerie 2010: 323)

(59) a. *I **kind** of like that sort of colour.* (COLT)
b. *"Are they scary?" "**Kind** of."* (COLT) (Margerie 2010: 319)
c. *I **kind** of rather felt sick and went away.* (COLT) (Margerie 2010: 320)

(60) *It's **kinda** squiggly, it's not straight but it's analogous to something straight, it's very close to being straight.* (MICASE) (Margerie 2010: 324)

In Río de la Plata Spanish *tipo, onda* or *corte* (and even *como*) can never be interpreted with a meaning of degree quantification when combined with verbs, adjectives or adverbs. Hence, the relevant examples of *tipo, onda* and *corte* with adjectives or adverbs show semantic/pragmatic values of approximation or mitigation (as in (20a–d), reproduced in (61)), but never quantification:

(61) a. Es   **tipo**   malo (=20a)
       is.3.SG kind   bad
       'He is kind of bad'

b. *Es* **tipo** *re/muy/demasiado malo* (=20b)
   is.3.SG kind very/too (much) bad
   'He is kind of very/too bad'
c. *Va* **tipo** *rápido* (=20c)
   goes.3.SG kind fast
   'He goes kind of fast'
d. *Me daba besitos* **tipo** *despacio* (=20d)
   me.DAT gave.3.SG little kisses kind slowly
   '(He) gave me little kisses kind of slowly'

In (61), *tipo* does not quantify in any way the property denoted by the adjective or the adverb (as Margerie (2010: 319) describes for (59) and (60)): it only has an approximative (or mitigating) meaning. In fact, as (61b) illustrates, *tipo* can coappear with "real" quantifiers such as *muy* ('very') or *demasiado* ('too'), showing they are not in a complementary distribution.

Moreover, *tipo* (and *onda* or *corte*) can never take scope exclusively over the VP (as *kind (of)* does in (59a)), but is systematically interpreted as modifying the whole sentence in cases such as (62):

(62) a. # *Pedro* **tipo** *va rápido.*
        Pedro kind goes.3.SG fast
        'Like, Pedro goes fast'
     b. # *Jimena* **tipo** *sabe inglés.*
        Jimena kind knows.3.SG English
        'Like, Jimena speaks English'

Instead, the meanings related to degree quantification expressed by *kind* in (59–60) (but not 58) may be conveyed by other Río de la Plata Spanish items which can also be used as mitigators, as *medio* ('half') and *un poco* ('a little, a bit'). These items do appear as quantifiers in combination either with adjectives (63a–c) or verbs (63d–f): *medio* is more related to the idea of a compromiser, following Margerie's labels (e.g., (63a, d, e)), while *un poco* seems to work as a diminisher in (63b, c, f):[15]

---

[15] By contrast, *medio* and *un poco* cannot normally be used as boosters, that is, as true intensifiers, except in occasional ironical uses (*Me pareció un poquito desubicado*, 'It seemed to me a bit out of place').

(63) a. Es   **medio**   grande.
         is.3.SG. half   big
         'It's half big'
    b. **A:** –¿*Estás*   *cansado?*
         is.2.SG   tired
         'Are you tired?'
         B: –*Un poco*
         a bit
         'A bit'
    c. *Está*   **un poco/un poquito**   *torcido.*
         is.3.SG   a bit   twisted
         'It is a bit/a little twisted'
    d. **Medio**   *me*   *empujó.*
         Half   me.ACC   pushed.3.SG
         'Like he pushed me'
    e. **Medio**   *se*   *enojó.*
         Half   3.SG.REFL   get.PAS.3.SG angry
         '(He/she) got a bit angry'
    f. **A:** –¿*Te*   *empujó?*
         you.ACC   pushed.3.SG
         'Did he push you?'
         B: –*Un poco.*
         a bit
         'A bit'

Un poco and *medio* in (63) express a 'low degree' meaning, either applied to a quality (in the case of adjectives and adverbs) or an event (in verbs). Notice that *un poco* can appear as an independent statement when it is used as a quantifier (as in (63b, f)), exactly like *kind (of)* (see (59b)), while *tipo, onda* and *corte* are absolutely forbidden in this syntactic context (see (24e)).

As explained above, *medio* and *un poco* can also have scope over the sentence as markers of mitigation, in cases such as (64), developed from the cases of VP scope, as in (63d–f):

(64) a. **Medio/ un poco (que)**   *no*   *le*   *gustó.*
         half   a bit   (that)   not   him.DAT   liked.3.SG
         'Like, he didn't like him'
    b. **Medio/ un poco (que)**   *no*   *se*   *notó.*
         half   a bit   (that)   not   3.SG.PAS   noted.3.SG
         'Like, it didn't show it'

Therefore, the Río de la Plata Spanish units *medio* and *un poco* show other way to develop markers of mitigation, including a grammaticalization step as degree quantifiers, exactly as occurs with English *kind*.

4.3 Summary

This study has highlighted two different paths of grammaticalization going from the taxonomic nouns to the markers of mitigation.

English *kind* and Río de la Plata Spanish *tipo/onda/corte*, besides being lexical taxonomic nouns, share uses as nominal approximators and as mitigating pragmatic particles (i.e., the extremes of the chain of grammaticalization), but not the intermediate steps. As Path 1 schematizes in (65), *tipo, onda* and *corte* are first grammaticalized in the nominal domain, where they acquire the values of 'comparison' and 'exemplification', also linked to 'approximation' (as seen in subsection 2.1). Then, they extend their scope as approximators to other category domains, such as adjectival, adverbial or quantificational (subsection 2.2) ("non-nominal approximation" in (65)), and, finally, to the whole sentence with a mitigation value (section 9.3):

(65) PATH 1: taxonomic nouns → comparison/exemplification → nominal approximation → non-nominal approximation → sentential mitigation

By contrast, *kind* takes other path of grammaticalization. From the value of 'approximation' in the nominal domain, it jumps to the adjectival, adverbial and verbal domains with different degree quantification meanings, as in examples (58–60), which could not be replicated by *tipo, onda* or *corte* (as we have seen in (61–62)). In these non-nominal domains, the quantificational meanings of *kind* alternates with an approximative interpretation, as in Margerie's examples (53–54), which finally enables its use as a sentential mitigator, as Path 2 illustrates in (66):

(66) PATH 2: taxonomic nouns → nominal approximation → degree quantification → non-nominal approximation → sentential mitigation

The difference between the two languages may be attributed to a structural difference in the original position of the taxonomic noun (head of the complement of the DP vs. modifier of this head, as (57) illustrates). This explains why, in intermediate stages, Río de la Plata Spanish *tipo* is treated as a preposition (Mihatsch 2018), while *kind* rather functions as a quantifier.

Finally, some grammatical items display the same sequences of uses either as Path 1 or as Path 2. Thus, standard Spanish *como*, as English *like*, follows a shortened Path 1, since it originates from the grammatical value of 'comparison' in the nominal domain, as seen in subsection 9.4.1. At the same time, in Río de la Plata Spanish *medio* or *un poco* show a synthetic version of Path 2, since they start as quantifiers expressing low degree, either referring to a quality or an event (63) (compromiser and diminisher, following Margerie's labels (2010)), before being used as mitigators of the whole sentence (64).

5 Conclusion

This paper aimed to characterize the process of grammaticalization transforming the taxonomic nouns *tipo, onda* and *corte* into markers of mitigation. The initial stimulus for this paper was undoubtedly the large number of markers of mitigation in Río de la Plata Spanish, differentiated only by semantic subtleties and by their distribution according to registers, social classes or age groups. Their grammatical properties were focused on here, although it is impossible to ignore that beyond grammar there are many historical, social, cultural and pragmatic factors influencing this variation. Indeed, it is not universal to regard mitigation of the speech act 'assertion' as a form of politeness.

We can conclude that *tipo, onda* and *corte* have many points of contact not only in their lexical meanings (section 2) and in their grammatical properties as markers of mitigation (section 3), but also in the intermediate common grammatical values they hold (e.g., 'comparison', 'exemplification', 'approximation'). Section 4 described the path followed by standard Spanish *como* ('as, like'), a grammatical item sharing an intermediate grammatical meaning ('comparison') with *tipo, onda* and *corte*. By contrast, the English taxonomic noun *kind* follows an alternative path of grammaticalization, through degree quantification of adjectives, adverbs or verbs. This value is not expressible by Río de la Plata Spanish *tipo, onda* or *corte*, but other grammatical items (*medio*, 'half', or *un poco*, 'a little', 'a bit') are able to convey not only mitigation but also quantification of adjectives, adverbs and verbs, expressing low degree.

The robustness of the two patterns producing markers of mitigation and going through the grammatical values 'comparison' + 'exemplification' (65) and 'degree quantification' (66) suggests that these are cognitive (rather than exclusively linguistic) phenomena. However, this should not be taken as a prediction: the sequences of grammatical values discussed in this chapter (and particularly in subsection 4.2) are not the only ways of creating markers of mitigation by means of grammaticalization. Occasionally, other paths are enabled, as may be demonstrated by cases such as peninsular Spanish *en plan* ('in mode', 'like') (Borreguero 2019), Spanish in contact with Guarani *lento* (lit. 'slow', 'kind (of)') (Avellana & Kornfeld 2019) or German *so* ('so') (Umbach, Ch.6, this volume).

References

Avellana, Alicia & Laura Kornfeld. 2019. Sobre la atenuación: el caso de *lento* y *un poco* en español paraguayo. *Lenguas Modernas* 52 (2018).187–213.

Bittencourt, Vanda de Oliveira. 2000. *Tipo (Assim)* como delimitador de unidades de informação. *Estudos Linguísticos* 29. 264–269.

Borreguero Zuloaga, Margarita. 2019. Los marcadores de aproximación (en el lenguaje juvenil): esp. *en plan* vs. it. *tipo*. In Miguel Ángel Cuevas Gómez, Fernando Molina Castillo & Paolo Silvestri (eds.), *España e Italia: Un viaje de ida y vuelta. Studia in honorem Manuel Carrera Díaz*, 53–78. Sevilla: Editorial Universidad de Sevilla.

Bosque, Ignacio. 1990. *Las categorías gramaticales. Relaciones y diferencias*. Madrid: Síntesis.

Bosque, Ignacio. 1994. La negación y el principio de las categorías vacías. In Violeta Demonte (ed.) *Gramática del español*, 167–199. México: El Colegio de México.

Bregant, Lucía. 2018. Reformulación de metáforas en interacciones entre adolescentes rioplatenses. Ms., Universidad de Buenos Aires.

Caffi, Claudia. 1999. On mitigation. *Journal of Pragmatics* 31. 881–909.

Davidse, Kristin, Lieven Vandelanotte & Hubert Cuyckens (eds.). 2010. *Subjectification, intersubjectification and grammaticalization*. Berlin/New York: Walter de Gruyter.

Di Tullio, Ángela & Laura Kornfeld. 2013. Marcas de modalidad epistémica en el registro coloquial. In Ángela Di Tullio (ed.), *El español de Argentina: estudios gramaticales*, 83–103. Buenos Aires: EUDEBA.

Kornfeld, Laura. 2013. Atenuadores en la lengua coloquial argentina. *Lingüística* 29(2). December 2013. 17–49.

Laka, Itziar. 1990. *Negation in syntax: On the nature of functional categories and projections*. Cambridge: MIT PhD thesis.

Landone, Elena. 2009. *Los marcadores del discurso y la cortesía verbal en español*. Bern: Peter Lang.

Margerie, Hélène. 2010. On the rise of (inter)subjective meaning in the grammaticalization of *kind of/kinda*. In Kristin Davidse, Lieven Vandelanotte & Hubert (eds.), *Subjectification, intersubjectification and grammaticalization*, 315–346. Berlin & New York: De Gruyter Mouton.

Mihatsch, Wiltrud. 2018. From ad hoc category to ad hoc categorization: The proceduralization of Argentinian Spanish *tipo*. In Caterina Mauri & Andrea Sansò (eds.), *Linguistic strategies for the construction of ad hoc categories: Synchronic and diachronic perspectives*, Special issue of *Folia Linguistica Historica* 39, 1. 147–176. Berlin & Boston: Walter de Gruyter.

Montecino, Lésmer A. 2004. Estrategias de intensificación y de atenuación en la conversación coloquial de jóvenes chilenos. *Onomázein* 10, 9–32. Santiago de Chile: Facultad de Letras de la Pontificia Universidad Católica de Chile.

[RAE] Real Academia Española. 2005. *Diccionario Panhispánico de Dudas*. Madrid: Espasa Calpe, online: rae.es/dpd.

[RAE] Real Academia Española. 2014. *Diccionario de la Lengua Española*. https://dle.rae.es/ (accessed 20 December 2021).

Resnik, Gabriela. 2013. Gramaticalización de adjetivos en español rioplatense: el caso de los elativos. In Laura Kornfeld & Inés Kuguel (eds.) *El español rioplatense desde una perspectiva generativa*, 53–70. Mendoza: Editorial FFyL-UNCuyo & SAL.

Rizzi, Luigi. 1997. The fine structure of the left periphery. In Liliane Haegeman (ed.), *Elements of grammar*, 281–337. Dordrecht: Kluwer.

Rojas, Edgardo G. 2012. Caracterización pragmático discursiva de la partícula conversacional 'corte/corte que' en la variedad juvenil del español metropolitano, paper presented at the *I Congreso de la Delegación Argentina de la Asociación de Lingüística y Filología de América Latina* (ALFAL) and *V Jornadas Internacionales de Filología Hispánica*, La Plata: FaHCE-UNLP, available in http://sedici.unlp.edu.ar/bitstream/handle/10915/42397/Documento_completo__.pdf?sequence=1&isAllowed=y (accessed 20 December 2021).

Traugott, Elizabeth Closs. 2003. From subjectification to intersubjectification. In Raymond Hickey (ed.), *Motives for language change*, 124–139. Cambridge: Cambridge University Press.

Part 3: Type noun constructions in Slavic languages

Alena Kolyaseva & Anna Kisiel
12 Taxonomic nouns in Slavic: An overview

Abstract: This chapter offers a general overview of type nouns and their uses in Slavic languages. Setting off with a discussion of a non-exhaustive inventory of lexical roots and their etymological sources across West, East and South Slavic languages, it attests a considerable uniformity of the TN roots across the language branches. Yet it also demonstrates a difference as to which of these roots have become entrenched in non-terminological settings, which of them express the general taxonomic meaning 'kind, sort, type' and which of them have developed grammaticalized uses. Based on available lexicographic data, the chapter draws a timeline with the first attestations of TNs and the grammaticalized strings containing them. It also outlines the most distinctive functions developed by Slavic TNs, typical of their intranominal and extranomical uses. The former comprise the postdeterminer uses serving as quantifying, phoric reference and hedging expressions, and the nominal qualifier use signalling approximation or mitigation. The latter function as prepositions, particles or conjunctions. Although most of the discussed functions are also characteristic of TNs in Germanic and Romance languages, there are some specific uses that, to our knowledge, are either not attested in other languages or are not as pronounced.

1 TNs in Slavic languages: Word roots and lexical meanings

TNs are largely uniform across Slavic languages in terms of word roots, with minor variation. All analysed languages have borrowed cognates of *type* and *sort* from Western European languages such as French, German or Italian, though the corresponding resulting items are used with disparate frequency. The counterparts of *species* and *genus* are, on the other hand, mostly a continuation of roots already present in Old Slavonic that have acquired taxonomic meanings. For instance, the taxonomic *rod-* which is the equivalent of *genus* as a biological or logical term in all Slavic languages is a semantic calque of the Ancient Greek γένος (*genos*) combining the classificatory meaning with those related to family, descent and birth

---

Alena Kolyaseva, KU Leuven, e-mail: alena.kolyaseva@kuleuven.be
Anna Kisiel, KU Leuven, e-mail: anna.kisiel@kuleuven.be

(*rod-* < PSl. **ordъ-/rodъ-* < PIE **Hordh-* 'grown, upright'; see Greek ὀρθός *(orthós)* and Latin *arbor* [Vasmer, v. 3, 1987: 491]).[1] *Vid/vyd*, a lower-level taxon referring to biological or logical *species* in the East and Eastern South branches, is another semantic calque, interestingly from its own cognate, Ancient Greek εἶδος *(eîdos)*, which coalesced the meanings of 'species' and 'appearance, look' (PSl. **vid-* < PIE **weid- *woid- *wīd-* 'to see, to look'; see Latvian *veids* 'form, kind', Latin *videre* [Shaposhnikov, v.1, 2010: 115]).[2] The West and Western South languages developed the corresponding meaning based on other Slavic nouns, *vrsta* in the Western South branch and *druh* in the Czech-Slovak branch (*vrsta* < PSl. **vьrsta* 'age, time of life, generation, person of the same age, turn', fem. sg. past participle of **vьrtěti* < PIE **wert- *wer-t-, *wor-t-, *wr-t-* 'to rotate, to spin', as in Russian *versta* and Polish *wiorsta*, an old measure of distance, or Russian *sverstnik* 'a person of the same age', Czech *vrstva* 'a layer, social class' and Latin *versus* 'a line, verse' [Snoj 2016: 858], [Skok, v. 3, 1973: 629], [Shaposhnikov, v. 1, 2010: 104–105]; *druh* < PSl. **drugъ* 'companion, follower, friend, comrade' < PIE **dhroughos*, from **dhreugh-* 'to follow, campaign together, war'; see Gothic *driugan* 'to war' [Rejzek 2009: 147], [Králik 2015: 135–136], [Shaposhnikov, v. 1, 2010: 247]). The new taxonomic meaning of Czech and Slovak *druh* currently appears to dominate over the original 'companion' meaning. It is listed first in dictionaries (SSJ 1959; ISSČ n.d.), whereas its cognates in other Slavic languages (Polish *druh*, Croatian *drug*, Macedonian *drugar*, Russian *drug*, etc.) are used primarily with the 'friend' or 'partner' meaning and have not developed taxonomic homonyms (see Table 1).

In view of the tendency to use Slavic roots for *species*, an interesting exception is Polish *gatunek* which can be traced back to German *Gattung* (Brückner 1927: 136) related to *Gatte* 'husband', formerly 'partner, companion, comrade, comrade-in-arms' (Pfeifer et al. 1993), see the acquisition of taxonomic meaning by the noun *druh* with a similar meaning in Czech and Slovak. The German root was imported, and the suffix *-ung* was transformed into *-unek* following the Slavic model of nouns with the suffix *-ek* (**-ъkъ*) (ESUM v. 1, 1982: 482). Note that the German source word refers to biological genus, not species like the Polish loanword. From Polish, it was further adopted as Ukrainian *gatunok* and Belarusian

---

[1] The 'family' meaning ('clan, a set of generations descending from the same ancestor') has been preserved in *rod-* by most Slavic languages (Russian, Ukrainian, Czech, Slovak, Bulgarian, Slovenian, Macedonian and Croatian). By contrast, in Polish, which distinguishes between the taxonomic *rodzaj* and *ród* 'family', the latter is outdated and is not even mentioned in *Wielki słownik języka polskiego* (WSJP ER).
[2] The same is true for Latin *species* 'appearance, form' < *specere* 'to look'.

Table 1: TN correspondences in Slavic languages.

	West Slavic				East Slavic			South Slavic			
	Lekhitic	Czech-Slovak						Eastern subgroup		Western subgroup	
	Pol.	Cze.	Slo.	Rus.	Ukr.	Bel.	Bul.	Mac.	Srp.	Hrv.	Slv.
Eng. type, Fr. type	typ	typ	typ	tip	typ	typ	tip	tip	tip	tip	tip
Eng. genus, Fr. genre (biol., log. term)	rodzaj	rod*	rod	rod	rid	rod	rod	rod	rod	rod	rod
Eng. species, Fr. espèce (biol., log. term)	gatunek	druh	druh	vid	vyd	vid	vid	vid	vrsta	vrsta	vrsta
Eng. sort, Fr. sorte	gatunek, rodzaj, sort[3]	sorta[4]	sorta	sort	sort gatunok	sort hatunak	sort	sorta	sorta	sorta	sorta
Eng. form, Fr. forme	forma	forma	forma	forma	forma	forma	forma	forma oblik	forma oblik	forma oblik	forma oblika
Eng. category, Fr. catégorie	kategoria	kategorie	kategória	kategorija	katehorija	katěhoryja	kategorija	kategorija	kategorija	kategorija	kategorija
Eng. class, Fr. classe	klasa	třída[5]	klasa, trieda	klass	klas	klas	klas	klasa	klasa	klasa	klasa

3 rare, informal
4 rare
5 In present-day Czech *klasa* functions either as a slang term for something excellent (uncommon) or has an archaic meaning 'classroom'. Similar uses can be observed in Polish, however, without any stylistic marking. In Russian, the former meaning is colloquial, and the latter is stylistically neutral.

hatunak (ESUM v. 1, 1982: 482; ESBM v. 3, 1985: 72) but with a meaning identical to *sort*[6] (the taxon for *species* is occupied in East Slavic languages by *vid/vyd*).

While Ukrainian *gatunok* and Belarusian *hatunak* may refer to varieties of plants, e.g. Belarusian *hatynak buraka "Zalaty"* 'beet variety "Golden"', this meaning should not be confused with the biological term *species*. *Sort/sorta* in Slavic languages (except for Polish) can refer, inter alia, to the *cultivar* (a cultivated variety) of plants, e.g. a variety/sort of apple, rose or wheat. This is another level of classification within species; consider, for example, the definition of this meaning in Ukrainian SUM (v.9. 1978: 467): "cultivated plants that differ from other plants of the same species by certain biological and economic properties", or similar definitions in Slovenian SSKJ (ER), Russian MAS (v. 4, 1999: 204), and Bulgarian RBE (ER). Interestingly, the meaning of a variety of cultivated plant in Macedonian *sorta* (e.g. *nekolku sorti titun* 'several varieties of tobacco') is marked as colloquial in DRMJ (ER), but as an agricultural term in Serbian, e.g. *sorta krušaka* 'variety of pear' (RSJ 2007: 1252), a "technical" term in Slovak, e.g. *včasná sorta* 'early sort' (SSJ ER), and a botanical term in Czech (SSJČ ER). However, in some of these languages the variety meaning is outdated. For instance, despite appearing in the SSJČ, Czech *sorta* is not used as a botanical term anymore, and *odrůda* (< *od* 'from' + *rod* [Rejzek 2009: 442]), *kultivar* or *varieta* are used instead. Similarly, *hatunak* is preferred with this meaning in Belarusian real use, though *sort* may be still found in textbooks (which tend to opt for wordchoices that are closer to Russian).

Often, *sort/sorta* imply a value at the top or bottom of a quality scale. Just as varieties of crops are characterized by their level of fertility, taste, etc., the same is true for the recurring meaning 'a category or rank of something, often goods, by quality or price' (MAS 1999: 204; SUM 1978: 467; DRMJ ER; SSJ ER; WSJP ER),[7] e.g. Russian *čaj pervogo sorta* 'first grade tea', Ukrainian *muka druhoho sortu* 'second grade flour', Macedonian *pološa sorta* 'the worst variety', Bulgarian *stoka părvi sort!* 'first-class goods!', Slovak *najdrahšia sorta cigariet* 'the most expensive sort of cigarette', Czech *nejlepší sorta vína* 'the best sort of wine',[8] and Polish *pośledniego sortu* 'of inferior quality'. Due to such specific meanings, Slavic loanwords *sort/sorta* reveal considerable similarity to German *Sorte* in which both meanings

---

[6] See almost identical definitions of *gatunok* and *sort* in the Ukrainian academic explanatory dictionary (SUM v. 9 1978: 467; v.2 1971: 42).

[7] This meaning originated in commercial jargon, see for example Rejzek (2009: 622) and Bezlaj (v. 3 1995: 292).

[8] *Sorta* is not the lexeme of first choice for expressing inherent quality in Czech (quality is strongly implied in another TN, *třída*, e.g. colloquial *ten člověk je třída* 'the person is exceptionally good').

('a part of a larger whole that has uniform features in terms of its quality' and 'a specific cultivated form of a crop') are present (DWDS ER). Nonetheless, etymological dictionaries recognize Slovak, Czech, Croatian, Serbian and Slovenian *sorta* as borrowings from Italian *sorte* 'kind, variety' < Vulgar Latin *sorta* < Classical Latin *sors* (Králik 2015: 547; Rejzek 2009: 622; Skok 1973: 307; Snoj 2016: 705). Russian, Ukrainian and Polish dictionaries tend to trace *sort* back to French *sorte* (Vasmer v. 3, 1987: 725; Shaposhnikov v. 2, 2010: 358; ESUM, v. 5, 2006: 358; WSJP ER), though Preobraženskij (v. 2, 1910–1914: 359) proposes German *Sorte* as the direct source. Belarusian and Bulgarian sources report that it was borrowed via Russian (ESBM v. 12, 2008: 253; BER v. 7, 2010: 345).

As part of the language used for special purposes, terminological meanings of the TNs are strictly defined. For instance, *rod/rodzaj/rid* and *vid/vyd/vrsta/druh* refer to different stages in biological or logical taxonomy, and *sort/sorta* or *hatunak/gatunok* may refer to the agricultural classification of varieties of cultivated plants. They are also used as grammatical terms, with *rod* referring to gender (and in some languages, like Czech and Serbian, also to voice), *vid/vyd* to verbal aspect (Russian, Ukrainian, Czech, Slovak, Bulgrian, Macedonian, Slovenian and Serbian), *druh* and *vrsta* to part of speech (Slovak *slovný druh*, Czech *slovní druh*, Serbian *vrsta reči* and Slovenian *besedna vrsta*), and *forma* or *oblika* to a word form as a means of expressing grammatical categories (e.g. Slovenian). But in their general taxonomic meaning the TNs often substantially overlap, e.g. *sort* can be explained in a dictionary through *vrsta* (Slovenian SSKJ), *rod* and *vid* (Macedonian DRMJ), *druh* and *typ* (Slovak SSJ), and different equivalents are observed in parallel corpora depending on the specific context.

Despite the considerable uniformity of the TN roots across Slavic languages, it must be emphasized that they differ as to (i) which roots are used in the non-terminological settings and (ii) which of the TNs express the general taxonomic meaning 'kind, sort, type'. For instance, though terminological *rod* is present in all Slavic languages, not all of them have developed a general taxonomic meaning from this root. In Polish and Russian, *rod-* corresponds to both English *kind* and *genus* (in this regard, note the etymological link of English *kind* to *kin*). By contrast, in Czech and Slovak *rod* corresponds to *genus* and is only used as a (biological, logical, linguistic) term besides the family-related meanings, whereas the 'kind' meaning is expressed by *druh*. Similarly, taxonomic *vid* does in principle exist in Czech and Slovak, but as a technical or linguistic term (other meanings, i.e. related to appearance, are archaic). The general taxonomic meaning is mentioned for Croatian and Serbian *rod* in RSHKJ (v. 5 1973: 551) but not in ŠRHJ (ER), which suggests it is not typical in these languages either. *Vid* is also attested in Serbian (*razni vidovi škola* 'various types of schools', RSJ 2007: 145) but the taxonomic use of *vrsta* 'kind' appears to be prevailing. In Russian, on the other hand, the general taxonomic meaning 'kind' is shared by both *rod* and *vid*. However, based on a corpus study Kolyaseva (2021b) reports that head referential use is not typical for Russian *rod*: such a structure accounted for only 10% of the occurrences of the lexeme in the sample, and out of those almost 40% were lexically bound collocations, such as *rod dejatel'nosti* 'occupation' lit. 'kind of activity' or *rod vojsk* 'armed service' lit. 'kind of army'. Interesingly, Serbian and Macedonian dictionaries also illustrate the general taxonomic meaning of *rod* with *rod vojske* 'armed service', *rod oružja* 'arm of the service' lit. 'kind of weapon' (RSJ 2007: 1170) and *rod (na) oružje, rod (na) vojska* (DRMJ ER) respectively. Bulgarian RBE (ER) also mentions *rod vojski* as a set phrase but does not list the 'kind' meaning for *rod* at all. Indeed, our Bulgarian informant[9] confirmed that while *vid kăšta* 'kind of house' is correct, **rod kăšta* is not. In the light of such uneven distribution of meanings across Slavic languages, Polish stands out as one in which *rod-* has not only developed the 'kind' meaning but is also the only root with such a meaning.

Furthermore, particular elements of meaning, such as quality ranking associated with *sort/sorta*, often make them unsubstitutable in certain contexts by TNs with broader semantics. For instance, Russian *pervyj sort* lit. 'first sort' characterizes something as of superior quality as opposed to *vtoroj sort* lit. 'second sort', but *pervyj tip/vid* 'first type/kind' and *vtoroj tip/vid* 'second type/kind' do not imply any ranking and tend to be employed for the purposes of phoric reference to maintain textual coherence, as 'the former and the latter types of something'. In Polish, Ukrainian and Belarusian both *sort* and *gatunek/gatunok/hatunak* can be employed with this meaning (e.g. Belarusian *muka peršaha sortu* 'first-grade flour', *tytun' najvyšèha hatunku* 'tobacco of the highest grade'[10]) but not the more general *rodzaj/rid/rod*. In Slovenian, both *sorta* and *zvŕst* can be used to refer to cultivated varieties of plants, generally with an adjective, e.g. *krompir zgodnje sorte* 'early variety of potato' and *kakovostne zvrsti jabolk, pšenice* 'quality varieties of apples, wheat' (SSKJ: ER). In Serbian not only is *razred* 'class, grade' possible but also *vrsta*, e.g. *brašno prvog razreda* 'first-grade flour' and *umetnička vrednost prve vrste* 'first-class artistic value' (RSJ 2007: 174). It needs to be mentioned, nonetheless, that although *sort/sorta* are attested in all Slavic languages, they are exceedingly rare in some of them, like Polish or Czech. In Czech, for example,

---

[9] We are grateful to all our informants (Yurii Ganoshenko, Katsiaryna Holzapfel-Varazhun, Markéta Janebová, Uladzimir Koshchanka, Daniela Konstantinova, Michaela Martinková, Wirginia Mirosławska, Elena Nikolashchenko, Karmen Oristil, Anastasiya Surinava, Anastasia Shytskova, Katarzyna Taczyńska, Roman Tymoshuk) for their time and the patience they showed answering our many questions. All possible misinterpretations of their answers are ours.

[10] Like with the meaning referring to a cultivated variety of plant, Bel. *hatunak* predominates over *sort* in such contexts.

třída 'class' is more common with the ranking meaning (*mouka první třídy* 'first-grade flour'), and *odrůda* with the 'cultivar' meaning.

The languages also differ as to which TNs grammaticalize/pragmaticalize and to what extent. For instance, *rod* grammaticalizes in Russian into the preposition and particle *vrode* (< *v rode* lit. 'in the kind', see also French *dans le genre de* and German *in der Art von* based on the same structure) and acquires a plethora of new functions, both grammatical and pragmatic (see Kolyaseva 2021a, Kolyaseva 2022). However, in Bulgarian or Czech it has not given rise to new units, except for the infrequent Czech prepositional phrase *z rodu* 'from the kind' in similative use, as in (1),[11] and the somewhat obsolete Bulgarian *ot roda na* 'similar to, like' (lit. 'from the kind of'), as in (2). By contrast, Polish *rodzaj* develops similar prepositional meanings to Russian *vrode* but none of its pragmaticalized particle uses. This potential to form new linguistic units should not be seen as an inherent characteristic of a certain language nor of units based on a certain root but should rather be associated with particular words. For example, Russian does not show a greater potential for developing TN constructions than any other Slavic language. Some Russian TNs, such as *sort* and *vid*, do not reveal irrefutable signs of change. The grammaticalized sequence *v vide* 'in the form of, as, by way of' is attributed in MAS (v. 1 1999: 172) to the homonymous non-taxonomic *vid* 'appearance'. Perhaps, *iz sorta* 'from the sort' can be tentatively analysed as a preposition, but one can argue that it is still a compositional prepositional phrase with a noun, i.e. a lexical use, while in Polish we can observe a multitude of grammaticalized uses such as *w stylu* < *w* 'in' + *styl* 'style', *na kształt* < *na* 'for' + *kształt* 'shape', *z cyklu* < *z* 'from' + *cykl* 'cycle' and *spod znaku* < *spod* 'from under' + *znak* 'sign, shibboleth, pennon'); see also Ukrainian *na kštalt*, *na zrazok* and Belarusian *nakštalt*. Bulgarian *vid* has given rise to new functions, as in (3).

(1) Cze. *Pro obyčejné lidi měl Dubček*
for ordinary-ACC people-ACC have-PST.M.3SG Dubček-NOM.M.SG
*charisma **z rodu** mesiášů typu Ježíše*
charisma-ACC from kind-GEN.M.SG messiah-GEN.PL TYPU Jesus-GEN.SG
Krista nebo Jana Husa.
Christ-GEN.M.SG or John-GEN.M.SG Huss-GEN.M.SG
'For ordinary people, Dubček had charisma **like messiahs** such as Jesus Christ or John Huss'

---

[11] The example is courtesy of Janebová and Martinková, whose chapter (this volume, chapter 15) offers more details on the matter.

(2) Bul. *Ukraina šte săzdade ekip **"ot roda na***
Ukraine FUT set.up-3SG team OT RODA NA/from kind-M.SG.DEF of
Mosad" za zalavjaneto na Janukovič
Mosad for capture-GRD GEN Yanukovych
'Ukraine will set up a **"Mossad-like** team" to capture Yanukovych' (https://www.actualno.com/europe/ukrajna-shte-syzdade-ekip-ot-roda-na-mosad-za-zalavjaneto-na-janukovich-news_690870.html, accessed 5 February 2021)

(3) Bul. *Mnogo prostranno objasneno s fakti*
much extensively explained-N.SG with fact-PL
ot vida na: *mnogobrojni narušenija v*
OT VIDA NA/from kind-M.SG.DEF of numerous-PL violation-PL in
glasuvaneto; razčita izključitelno na DPS za podkrepa,
vote-N.SG.DEF rely-PRS.3SG exclusively on MRF for support-F.SG
kojato izvaršva množestvo dokumentirani
which-F.SG perform-PRS.3SG multitude-N.SG documented-PL
narušenija (nenakazani) vključitelno i dvojno
violation-PL inpunished-PL including and double-N.SG
glasuvane (...)
voting-N.SG
'This has been very extensively explained by facts **such as**: numerous voting violations; relying exclusively on the MRF for support, which has carried out a number of documented violations (unpunished) including double voting (...)' (BulNC)

The TNs discussed in this section in some level of detail do not comprise by any means an exhaustive list of the taxonomic lexemes to be found in Slavic. Among other word roots, both native and borrowed, are Russian *razrjad*, Ukrainian *rozrjad*, Belarusian *razrad*, Serbian, Croatioan, Slovenian, Macedonian and Bulgarian *razred* 'category, class', Czech *třída* and Slovak *trieda* 'class', Russian *raznovidnost'*, Ukrainian *riznovyd*, Belarusian *raznavidnasc'*, Polish *różnorodność* and Bulgarian *raznovidnost* 'variety', Czech *odrůda* and Slovak *odroda* 'variety', Macedonian, Serbian and Croatian *oblik*, and Slovenian *oblika* 'form', Polish *kształt* and Ukrainian and Belarusian *kštalt* 'form', etc. Characteristically, TNs that have developed a 'form' meaning based on inherited Slavic roots are related to words with the meaning 'appearance, looks', e.g. Serbian, Croatian and Macedonian *oblik* (PSl. **likъ* 'face' [Shaposhnikov v. 2 2010: 40]), consider also Russian, Ukrainian, Bulgarian, Macedonian *vid*.

2 First attestations of TNs: A timeline

The scarcity of available linguistic data from early periods cautions against firm conclusions and allows for only a tentative timeline of taxonomic meanings across Slavic languages. The search for first attestations is further complicated by the necessity to separate out other meanings, a task which is especially relevant when native roots were used as a foundation for calques and the distinction between different meanings is not unequivocal. For instance, in the *Materials for the Old Russian* (Old East Slavic) *Dictionary based on Manuscripts* Sreznevskij (v. 3, 1912: 135–138) lists a rather broad range of meanings for *rodъ*, including 'descent', 'family', 'generation', 'a set of generations originating from one ancestor' and, inter alia, 'a group of people with common distinctive features', as in *rodъ pravъdenyxъ* 'the righteous', *rodъ nevěrьnъ* 'the infidels'. The latter example comes from the *Ostromir Gospels* (1056–1057), the oldest dated East Slavic manuscript book. However, it is debatable whether such a meaning could be interpreted as taxonomic per se (equally with Eng. *mankind*). The first undeniably taxonomic occurrences of *rod* and *vid* in the 'genus' and 'species' meanings are attested in *Sviatoslav's Miscellany* (1073), a compendium of translated theological, philosophical, rhetorical and historical works by Greek authors.[12]

To be precise, both manuscripts were written in Old Russian recension of Church Slavonic.[13] In general, "the conversion of Kievan Rus' [into Christianity] did not lead to the introduction of Byzantine Greek culture, but to the transfer *en masse* of the results of over a century of Bulgarian efforts to receive and adapt that culture to Bulgaria's own needs" (Thomson 1989: 214). *Sviatoslav's Miscellany* as well is an East Slavic manuscript copy of the *Florilegium* which was translated from Greek into Old Church Slavonic for the Bulgarian tsar Simeon at the beginning of the tenth century. Though this Bulgarian codex is known only from later copies created by East Slavic and Serbian scribes (with *Sviatoslav's Micellany* (1073) being the earliest extant copy) the semantic calques *rod* and *vid* should be attributed to early tenth-century Bulgaria at the latest, from which they spread to other territories, sometimes through modern languages. For example, ESBM (v. 2, 1980: 124) does not trace the 'kind, variety, type' meaning of Belarusian *vid* to the Old East Slavic sources common to Russian, Ukrainian and Belarusian but

---

12 (. . .) *vidъ že jestъ podъčinęjemoje po rodъ* 'species (vid) is subordinate to genus (rod)', *Sviatoslav's Miscellany* 1073, p. 227, from Sreznevskij (v. 3, 1912: 138).
13 Diglossia in Kievan Rus: Old East Slavic as an oral and business language and Church Slavonic as the language of worship and church literature. Old Church Slavonic, the all-Slavic literary language based on Eastern South Slavic dialects, was a counterpart of Latin in the West.

reports that it was borrowed from Russian *vid*.[14] It is worth mentioning that in early texts *vid* is already being used in quantifying contexts, e.g. *vsjaku vidъ zlobě* 'every kind of evil', an example from a thirteenth- to fourteenth-century Russian manuscript copy of the *Chronicle of George Hamartolus* translated into Slavic in the eleventh century (SRJ 11–17vv. v. 2 1975: 177).

Rod and *vid* as grammatical terms appear in the treatise *O vos'mi častjax slova* 'On the eight parts of speech' (Sreznevskij v. 3, 1912: 138, v. 1. 1893: 255; Cyganenko 1989: 58, 358), the earliest extant grammar in Slavic, sometimes referred to as the *Pseudo-Damaskin Grammar*. Largely based on the Greek linguistic tradition, it is argued to have been written in ca. fourteenth-century Serbia or Bulgaria (Nikolskij 1999). The grammar enjoyed exceptional authority in the Orthodox Slavic literacy, with the earliest extant Serbian copy dating from the fifteenth century and the East Slavic copies dating from the sixteenth to seventeenth centuries (Xaburgaev 1986: 269).

The older Western Slavic data are rather limited. According to Boryś (2005: 515), Polish *rodzaj* has been used with a taxonomic meaning since the fourteenth century, as found in the translation of Latin *Simile est regnum celorum sagene misse in marę et ex omni genere piscium congreganti* (4), a 1420 example from Brückner's *Kazania średniowieczne*. As far as Czech *druh* is concerned, dictionaries of Old Czech do not register uses outside the 'companion' meaning. Machek (1968: 130) posits that its taxonomic meaning arose on the basis of phrases like *toho* 'of that' *druh*, *těch* 'of those' *druh*, *mého* 'of mine' *druh*, *jiného* 'of a different one' *druh*, as in (5), which were common in Middle Czech, i.e. between 1500 and 1775. However, Zubatý (1918) provides evidence of such uses of *druh* from ca. 1450. Rejzek (2009: 147) comments that in such phrases a certain thing is considered a 'companion' to other similar things. When the combinations ceased to be transparent, *togo druh* '*druh*$_{NOM}$ of that$_{GEN}$' transformed into *togo druhu* 'of that$_{GEN}$ *druh*$_{GEN}$' from which the new meaning 'kind' was abstracted (Machek 1968: 130). According to Králik (2015: 136), Slovak *druh* featured the 'type, sort' meaning from the sixteenth century, presumably following its Czech counterpart.

---

[14] Most likely, not earlier than in the nineteenth century, as the taxonomic meaning of Belarusian *vidъ* is not mentioned in the HSBM (v. 3 1983: 257–258), which reflects sixteenth to eighteenth century Belarusian vocabulary at an exceptional level of scrutiny.

(4) Pol. *y sze ffszego   pocolena,   rodzaiw,*
         i self every-ACC.SG generation-GEN.SG kind-GEN.PL
     rodu   ryb   szgromadzagączemu
     kin-GEN.SG fish-GEN.PL gather-PTCP.DAT.SG
     'and gathering all generations, kinds and families of fish' (from Brückner 1895)

(5) Cze. *ten   nůž   je   **mého***
         the knife-NOM.M.SG be-PRS.3SG mine-GEN.M.SG
     druh   = *takový*   *jako   můj*
     companion-NOM.M.SG such-NOM.M.SG like mine-NOM.M.SG
     'this knife is **such as/like** mine' (from Machek 1968: 130).

It is not entirely clear when the inherited lexemes *vrsta* and *oblik* developed the taxonomic meanings 'kind' and 'form' characteristic of the Southern Slavic languages. According to Bezlaj (v. 1 2005: 362–363), in the sixteenth and seventeenth centuries Slovenian *verſta* still meant 'a line, a verse' but in the eighteenth century the meaning 'a class, a series' is mentioned. Slovenian *oblika* is explained as a nineteenth-century calque from Latin *forma* (Snoj 2016).

From the fifteenth century, Slavic languages begin to borrow TNs from Western European languages (or through the medium of these languages). One of the earliest attestations of such loanwords is Old Polish *kstałt* (< Middle High German *gestalt*) which is dated as a fifteenth-century borrowing by Boryś (2005: 269), but is attributed to the fourteenth to sixteenth centuries by Bańkowski (v. 1, 2000: 843).[15] After the establishment of the Polish-Lithuanian Commonwealth in 1569 and the subsequent gradual polonization of Ruthenian territories, *kštalt* appeared in Old Ukrainian (1582) and Old Belarusian (1596) sources (ESUM v. 3, 1989: 172; HSBM v. 16, 1997: 262).[16] Another Polish borrowing followed a similar path: with a first attestation of Polish *gatunek* (< German *Gattung*) in 1629 (Bańkowski v. 1, 2000: 413), Ukrainian *khatunok"* is attested shortly after in 1656 (Rudnyc′kyj

---

15 In the sixteenth century the new spelling *ksztalt* appears in line with the new German pronunciation but *kstałt* was still more common in the second part of the century (Bańkowski v. 1 2000: 843).

16 Both Old Ukrainian and Old Belarusian are also referred to as Old Ruthenian. By the end of the seventeenth century the lexeme had also reached Russian in the form of *kštalt/kyštalt*; however, it went out of use during the eighteenth century (SRJ 18v. v. 11: 96). Also see Czech archaic *křtalt* (< Old Czech *kštalt*) 'form' (Machek 1968: 302), sixteenth- to eighteenth-century Slovenian *štalt* (Besedje 2011: ER; Kastelec and Vorenc 1680–1710: ER), and seventeenth-century Serbian/Croatian *štalt* (Bezlaj v. 4, 2005:105), all reportedly derived from Middle High German *gestalt*.

v. 1, 1972: 808; ESUM v. 1, 1982: 482).[17] However, Belarusian HSBM (v. 15, 1966: 33) reports an even earlier attestation: *kotlov rozmoitoho khatunku* 'cauldrons of different sorts' which comes from a judicial register dated 28 June 1578 (IJuM 1906 issue 32: 214, # 473). This suggests that *gatunek* had appeared in Polish in the sixteenth century at the latest.

Another early attestation is *forma*, found in fifteenth-century sources of the Serbo-Croatian continuum (borrowed via Italian, Skok v. 1, 1971: 525–526) and in a Belarusian text, also attributed to the end of the fifteenth century (HSBM v.36, 2016: 8). In many other languages, this word is not attested before the sixteenth century. In particular, in Ukrainian sources *forma* is attested only from 1627 (Ohienko v. 4, 1994: 433) and is indeed not mentioned in dictionaries specific to earlier periods, such as *SSUM 14–15vv*. However, as with *gatunek*, this may be due to a greater number of preserved Belarusian sources or a more detailed registry thereof, rather than being a conclusive indication of a later borrowing of *forma* by other languages. In any case, there are records of old Slovenian *furm/fúrem* as early as in 1577 (see Croatian *fûrma* from the same period, the sixteenth century), borrowed from Bavarian Austrian, Carinthian German and Tyrolean *Furm/furm* (Bezlaj v. 1, 1977: 133; Besedje 2011: ER; Snoj 2016: 185). As for Western Slavic languages, *forma* is attested in an electronic dictionary of Old Czech (mid-fifteenth century) with the meaning of 'manner' (ESSČ); Polish and Slovak document *forma* in the sixteenth century, with the first Polish attestation from 1560 (Brückner 1927: 125).

The available data on the first attestations of TNs in Slavic languages are summarized in Table 2. Note that most non-inherited Russian TNs pertain to the late seventeenth and early eighteenth centuries. This surge reflects massive linguistic borrowing associated with the drastic reforms of the Russian society by Peter the Great, aimed to transfer European science, knowledge and lifestyles to Russian soil. The earliest reported attestation of Russian *sort* (< French *sorte* or German *Sorte*) dates back to 1711 (*sidr dvux sortej* 'cyder of two sorts', from Černyx v. 2, 1999: 189), *kategorija* (possibly via German *Kategorie* or French *catégorie*, Vasmer v. 2, 1986: 210) to 1722 (SRJ 11–17vv. v. 7 1980: 90), and *forma* (via Polish [Vasmer v. 4, 1986: 203] or through books directly from Latin *forma* [Černyx v. 2, 1999: 321]) to 1704 (Shaposhnikov v.2, 2010: 483). *Klass* (< French *classe* [Vasmer v. 2, 1986: 244; Černyx v. 2, 1999: 399]) is found in a text dated at the turn of the seventeenth and eighteenth centuries (SRJ 11–17vv. v. 7, 1980: 153) and is mentioned in dictionaries starting from 1762 (Černyx v. 2, 1999: 399). Later, languages like Belarusian

---

17 Attestations of the spelling *gatunok"* from the eighteenth century (Rudnyc'kyj v. 1, 1972: 808). '*Kh*' (*кг*) served initially to mark the implosive character of the consonant, in contrast to the fricative sound in Ruthenian.

Table 2: First attestations of TNs in Slavic languages.

10th c.	11th c.	12th c.	13th c.	14th c.	15th c.	16th c.	17th c.	18th c.	19th c.	20th c.
Bulgaria: rodъ, vidъ (Old Church Slavonic, *Simeon's Florilegium*)	Kievan Rus: rodъ, vidъ (Old Russian recension of Church Slavonic, Sviatoslav's Miscellany 1073)			Pol. rodzaj (Boryś 2005)	Bel. forma (HSBM v 36, 2016: 8)	Slo. druh (Králik 2015)	Pol. gatunek (Bańkowski 2000)	Rus. sort	Slo. kategoria (Králik 2015)	Bel. sort (ESBM 2008)
				Bulgaria or Serbia: rodъ, vidъ as grammatical terms (Pseudo-Damaskian Grammar)	Pol. kstatt (Boryś 2005)	Slo. forma (Králik 2015)	Ukr. kgatunokъ (ESUM 1982)	Rus. klass (Černyx 1999)	Slo. trieda (Králik 2015)	Slv. klasa (Snoj 2016)
					Hrv./Srp. forma/furma (Skok 1971)	Bel. kštalt (HSBM 1997)	Rus. forma (Vasmer 1987)	Rus. kategorija (SRJ 11–17vv. 1980)	Slv. kategorija (Snoj 2016)	Ukr. klas (Rudnyc'kyj 1982)
					Cze. druh (Zubatý 1918)	Ukr. kštalt (ESUM 1989)	Slo. sorta (Králik 2015)	Pol. klassa (Bańkowski 2000)	Slv. oblika (Snoj 2016)	
					Cze. forma (ESSČ ER)	Slv. sorta (Bezlaj 1995)	Ukr. forma (Ohienko 1994)		Bul. klas/ klasa (BER 1979)	
						Slv. furm/furem (Bezlaj 1977; Snoj 2016)	Pol. kategoria (Trotz 1764)			
						Pol. forma (Brückner 1927)	Cze. třída (Cvrček and Vondřička 2011)			
						Bel. kgatunokъ (HSBM 1966)				

and Bulgarian reportedly borrowed some TNs via Russian, e.g. Bulgarian *kategorija*, *klas/klasa* and *sort*, and Belarusian *vid* and *sort* (BER v. 2, 1979: 271, 424, v. 7, 2010: 345; ESBM v. 2, 1980: 124, v. 12, 2008: 252). In Soviet Ukrainian as well, *klas* reflected Russian *klass*, although the word had been previously known as *kljasa* (Rudnyc'kyj v. 2, 1982: 693).

Counterparts of *type* deserve a special mention. Though etymological sources provide information on the period when the word was borrowed, they do not always refer to the meaning of interest. For instance, in the early eighteenth century Russian *ti*p"* was known with the meaning 'typography, print, typeface' (Polikarpov 1704: 136), from French *type* 'imprint, prototype' which came via Latin *typus* from Ancient Greek τύπος (*túpos*) 'impression, trace from a hit' (Shaposhnikov v.2, 2010: 416). Though the corpus data of the earlier periods are rather scarce, a search in RNC yields uses as 'imprint' or 'image' at the end of the eighteenth century, and also as 'prototype, epitome, ideal model, typical or exemplary representative' at the beginning of the nineteenth century, often in contexts referring to human appearance, or (literary) characters representing social groups, etc. (similar to *les grands types littéraires* in French, TLFi). Given the role of French as the language of the Russian nobility in the eighteenth and early nineteenth centuries, it is not surprising that Russian *tip* initially followed the semantic development of French *type*. Consider for instance example (6) in which *tip* has the same meaning as French *type* in (7). This meaning in French is marked in TLFi as developed "by extension".

(6) Rus. *Semenova prelestna: soveršennyj*
Semenova-NOM.F.SG charming-F.SG perfect-NOM.M.SG
tip drevnej grečeskoj krasoty
type-NOM.M.SG ancient-GEN.F.SG Greek-GEN.F.SG beauty-GEN.F.SG
'Semenova is charming: the perfect **epitome (type) of the ancient Greek beauty**' (RNC, 1806–1809).

(7) Fr. [Madame Parangon] *c'est, pour ainsi-dire,* **le type de la beauté** (Restif de La Bret., Le Paysan perverti, t. 1, p. 197: 1776, from TLFi)

The 'typography, print', 'epitome', and 'prototype' meanings were eventually lost in Russian *tip* and replaced by the taxonomic meaning 'type, kind, category'. Structures that can be interpreted in this latter taxonomic sense (and not referring to human appearance, character, social status, or a literary character embodying these traits, as in most of the examples from this period) start to appear in the mid-nineteenth century, notably in zoology texts, as in (8).

(8) Rus. *Očevidno, v suščestve **tipa***
Evidently in essence-PRP.N.SG type-GEN.M.SG
***obrazovanija** každogo orudija naxoditsja*
formation-GEN.N.SG every-GEN.N.SG tool-GEN.N.SG be.located-PRS.3SG
odin èlement, odna
one-NOM.M.SG element-NOM.M.SG one-NOM.F.SG
žiznedejatel'nost', kotorye sostavljajut
vital.function-NOM.F.SG which-NOM.PL make.up-PRS.3SG
suščnost' ego (...).
essence-ACC.F.SG its-GEN.M.SG
'Evidently, in the core of **the formation type** of each tool, there is one element, one vital function that constitutes its essence (...).' (RNC, 1850).

In Ukrainian and Belarusian sources, *ti*p″* meaning 'print, typeface' is mentioned even earlier, in 1627 and 1653 (Ohienko v. 4, 1994: 363; HSBM v.33, 2013: 305), but there are no records available of other meanings in the period between the seventeenth and eighteenth centuries. According to ESBM (v.14: 301), it was borrowed via Polish. In its turn, late seventeenth-century Polish features examples of *typ* meaning 'pattern, example', like the one from 1688 in (9).

(9) Pol. *Zakon też nà tablicàch spisàny*
law-NOM.M also on board-LOC.PL write-PTCP.NOM.M.SG
*kàmiennych, ktory był **typem przyszłych***
stone-ADJ.LOC.PL which-SG.M be-PST.3SG.M type-INS.SG future-GEN.PL
***tàiemnic** zbawiennych, dał nà*
secret-GEN.PL salvation-ADJ.GEN.PL give-PST.3SG.M on
gorze Synài.
mount-LOC.SG Sinai
'Also, the law on stone tablets that was **a pattern of the future mysteries** of salvation, was given on Mount Sinai.' (M. Kulig, *Król*, 1688 in the card index of *The dictionary of 17th and 1st half of 18th century Polish*)

For Slovak, Králik (2015: 636) similarly records *typ* from the seventeenth century, but no indication is given of the timeline of emergence of the taxonomic meaning. Rejzek (2009: 725) posits that Czech *typ* was borrowed through German but does not define a period either. There is no occurrence of *typ* in the Old or Middle Czech database, but Jungmann (1838: 687) documents the noun *typičnost* 'typicality' in nineteenth-century Czech. Finally, in nineteenth-century Slovenian, *tip*, also borrowed via German, meant both 'characteristic of products of the same kind' and 'a man with certain (negative) characteristics' (Snoj 2016: 788). Since Western

European languages enjoyed considerable popularity in Slavic countries during this period, it is plausible that the development of the taxonomic meaning of Slavic *typ/tip* was affected by language contact and followed the lead of those languages.

As for the new, grammaticalized structures with various TNs, some of them were attested remarkably early. For instance, Polish *na kształt* (lit. 'on+shape') appeared as a translation of Latin *ad instar, in morem* and was used as early as the fifteenth and sixteenth centuries to mark similarity (Bańkowski 2000: 843). An example *na krzatał ad modum* given in *Słownik staropolski* (The dictionary of Old Polish) dates back to 1438 (Lucjan Malinowski, *Glosy polskie*). This item also enters Polish lexicography very early: the entry *na kształ* appears in Troc (1779) with the definition 'wie; auf art; à l'instar de; comme; à la maniére de; de la sorte de; à la façon de'. An analogous use marking similarity is found in a sixteenth-century example from a Belarusian source in (10):

(10) Ruth. (Old Bel.) koli   by   xto   listy   abo
                    if   COND   anyone-NOM.SG sheet-ACC.PL   or
pečati   n̄šy   Өalšoval   abo   **nakštaltъ**
stamp-ACC.PL   our-ACC.PL   forge-COND.M.SG or   NAKŠTALTЪ
ruki   našoe   podpisoval (...)
hand-GEN.F.SG our-GEN.F.SG   sign-COND.M.SG
'If anyone forged our sheets or stamps or **similarly to our hand** ... signed ...'
(*Statute of Lithuania* 1566, from HSBM v. 19 2000: 108)

Prepositional phrases with cognates of *rod* start to lose their nominal features and grammaticalize into functional items during the nineteenth century. For instance, Čerkasova (1967) observes that bridging contexts with Russian string *v rode/vrode* lit. 'in the kind of' were common throughout the first half of the century, e.g. *bolezn' vrode katalepsii* lit. 'disease in the kind of catalepsy' in (11).[18] Such structures could be interpreted in two ways: (i) "as a lexical means to express the relation of the individual (*catalepsy* as a kind of disease) and the general (*disease* as a generic denomination of any illness)" and (ii) "as a grammatical means of expression of attributive-comparative relations (a disease *like* catalepsy)" (Čerkasova 1967: 94–96). The lexical interpretation by Čerkasova is based on what she

---

18 Such ambiguous contexts can be also found later: *Trexletnjaja devočka bol'na* (...) **čem-to v rode influèncy** 'A three-year-old girl is ill (...) with **something in the nature of / like influenza**.' (Leo Tolstoy, *O golode* [On famine] (manuscript №5), 1891.

describes as the figurative meaning of *rod* 'semblance of something', see contexts like (12) which are discussed as qualifying uses in Kisiel and Kolyaseva (this volume, chapter 13). Besides the meaning of 'variety, sort, type', *rod* also refers to 'a group, category of objects, phenomena, concepts, etc., united by common essential features' (MAS v. 3, 1999: 722–723). In this sense, the example in (11) can also be interpreted as the disease in question belonging to the group of illnesses for which catalepsy is selected as a standard of reference.

(11) Rus. *On lečilsja ot kakoj-to*
   he-NOM treat-REFL.PST.M.SG from some-GEN.F.SG
*udivitel'noj bolezni, **vrode***
curious-GEN.F.SG disease-GEN.F.SG VRODE/in kind-PRP.M.SG
***katalepsii** (...)*
catalepsy-GEN.F.SG
'He was treated for some outlandish disease, **something like catalepsy** (...).' (RNC, 1835).

(12) Rus. *Pokojnyj deduška, skol'ko ja*
   late-NOM.M.SG grandfather-NOM.M.SG how.much I-NOM
*pomnju, byl **rod***
remember-PRS.1SG be-PST.M.SG kind-NOM.M.SG
babuškina dvoreckogo.
grandmother's-ADJ.POSS.GEN.M.SG butler-GEN.M.SG
'The late grandfather, as far as I remember, was **kind of grandmother's butler.**' (RNC, 1833)

Čerkasova (1967: 95) propounds that the second, prepositional interpretation of *v rode/vrode* expressing grammatical relations of comparison started to prevail from the second half of the nineteenth century. Furthermore, the adverbal use of the string acquired a conjunctional function with the meanings 'as, as if', e.g. ***trevožat** soznanie vsex obitatelej temnogo carstva,* ***vrode dalekogo prividenija,** ili košmara* '[they] **disturb** the consciousness of all the inhabitants of the dark kingdom, **like a distant ghost**, or a nightmare', i.e. disturb in the way that a distant ghost would disturb.

Similarly, instances of new uses of Polish *w rodzaju* lit. 'in the kind of' are found in NCP from the nineteenth century onwards. The earlier examples in the corpus occur only with *coś* 'something' in the left-hand slot, i.e. *coś w rodzaju Y* 'something of the Y kind', while nouns are first attested in this position only in 1900. First occurrences of *coś w tym rodzaju* 'something like this' are dated the same year, and the quotative use in 1932. The prevalence of *coś* in structures with *w rodzaju* is confirmed by *Słownik warszawski* (1900–1927), the first Polish dictionary providing an example of the grammaticalized structure: preposition + *rodzaj* (13). However, we can assume that *w rodzaju* had in fact grammaticalized earlier, as indicated by a 1772 example from Korba, the corpus of seventeenth- and eighteenth-century texts (14). In the parallel Polish structure *z rodzaju* lit. 'from the kind', exemplification use is found from 1986 and quotative use only from 2000 onwards. This represents an evolution of the nominal *X z rodzaju Y* 'X from the genus (of) Y' in reference to family or kind which was very frequent in sixteenth-century texts, especially in dictionary definitions, as in (15) from Mączyński (1564). The relation to family/kind is preserved in the current *z rodzaju* preference for collocations with a descriptive phrase *tych, które...* 'those that...'. A very similar path can be presented for the parallel *z gatunku* lit. 'from the species'. Even though it has been very frequently used in definitions in reference to species from the sixteenth century onwards, it is grammaticalizing rather slowly and shows a preference for collocations with a descriptive phrase *tych, które...* 'those that...'. In NCP it is found in an exemplification function from 1936, in para-quotative contexts from 1957 and in quotative ones from the end of the twentieth century (although isolated uses).

(13) Pol. *Naraz usłyszeliśmy* **coś w rodzaju**
suddenly hear-PST.1PL something like
skrzeczenia żab.
croak-GRND.GEN.SG frog-GEN.PL
'Suddenly we heard **something like** frogs croaking.' (Korba)

(14) Pol. *Z Polskich Ziemiopisów co prawda*
from Polish-GEN.PL work-in-geography-GEN.PL in fact
nieliczemy wielu, wszakże licznych zastąpić
not.count-PRS.1PL many-GEN however numerous-ACC.PL replace-INF
może choć jedna, **w rodzaju** *Ziemiopisma*
can-PRS.3SG even one-F.SG W RODZAJU work-in-geography-GEN.M.SG
Politycznego po całym Narodzie od
political-GEN.M.SG over all-LOC.M.SG nation-LOC.M.SG from
wszystkich wzięta Książka, pod tytułem
everyone-GEN take-PTCP.NOM.F.SG book-NOM.F.SG titled
Geografia czasów teraźniejszych.
gepgraphy-NOM.F.SG times-GEN present-GEN.PL
'It is true that there are not many Polish geographical works, but the many can be replaced by one **like** *The Political Geography of the Nation*, a joint publication titled *The Geography of Present Times*.' (Korba)

(15) Pol. *Otus,   Nieyaki   ptak   **z rodzáyu***
         Otus   some-NOM.M.SG   bird-NOM.M.SG   of the genus-GEN.SG
     ſów   *podobno   lelek.*
     owl-GEN.PL   supposedly   lelek-NOM.SG
     'Otus, a sort of bird **of the genus of owls**, supposedly a nightjar.' (Mączyński, 1564)

Interestingly, neither Belarusian, nor Ukrainian (which for geographic and historical reasons were in close contact with both Polish and Russian) developed or adopted such functional units based on the TN *rod/rid*. As mentioned in Section 1, Czech *z rodu* lit. 'from the kind of' and Bulgarian *ot roda na* lit. 'from the kind of' can acquire a relator role (in addition to contexts like 'X from the genus/family (of) Y'), but to a lesser degree than the Russian and Polish examples discussed here.

Finally, *tip/typ* has grammaticalized in many Slavic languages, but pinning the change to a timeline is not an easy task, despite the availability of rich linguistic evidence. What can be said with confidence is that the process accelerated in the second half of the twentieth century. For instance, Lapteva (1983) referred to the drastic expansion of *tipa* in Russian spoken discourse as a recent phenomenon, and, importantly, attested the technical connotation of the item, which allowed for ridicule of its excessive use in overly mundane contexts in 1970s parodies. This connotation has since been lost. On the other hand, isolated instances of structures with *tipa* surrounded by nouns in both the right and left slots, which would now be interpreted as prepositional, can be found as early as the end of the nineteenth century but might not have been classified as such by contemporaries. Consider example (16) whose possible dual interpretation in the late nineteenth and early twentieth century is discussed by Lazareva (2016: 548): "In the case of lexical understanding, *tipa* serves as a lexical means of expressing taxonomic relations where the right component of the three-membered noun phrase refers to the general, and the left – to a particular concept." In this sense, *žurnalisty tipa Citoviča* lit. 'journalists of the type of Tsitovich' with the genitive form of the noun *Tsitovich* marking possessive relations (genetivus possessivus) is equivalent in meaning to 'journalists belonging to the same class as Tsitovich', or 'journalists of the Tsitovich type'. The structure, as Lazareva maintains, could possibly be considered an elliptic modification of structures like *žurnalisty togo tipa, k kotoromu prinadležit Citovič* 'journalists of the kind to which Tsitovich belongs'. Whereas in the lexical interpretation *tipa* serves accuracy, in the grammatical one *tipa* is reanalysed as a means to establish comparative-similative relations: 'journalists like/similar to Tsitovich (with their typical traits)'.

(16) Rus. ...v Rossii   ne   najdetsja   mnogo
          in   Russia-PRP.F.SG not find-REFL.FUT.3SG many
     žurnalistov   tipa   Citoviča
     journalist-GEN.PL type-GEN.M.SG Tsitovich-GEN.M.SG
     '...there are not many **journalists of the type of/like Tsitovich** in Russia
     ...' (RNC, 1886)

In Polish, contexts with *typu* in which a prepositional interpretation (of similarity) is possible are found from the early 1920s and with the exemplification function from the mid-twentieth century (as in an earlier example from Czech in (17)). Quotatives appear in the early 1980s when spoken language enters newspapers; a dictionary from the mid-twentieth century calls quotative uses "frequent in the texts of older writers", but this is not registered in dictionaries. *W typie* develops slightly later with the first similarity context attested in 1934; exemplification starts to appear only in 1990 (including para-quotation) and the quotative function was first attested in 2008. Both exemplification and quotative units first appear in dictionaries in the twenty-first century (also including examples of *typ* usage not noted before).

(17) Cze. *Verocchio*   *má*   *také   o*
           Verrocchio-NOM.M.SG   have-PRS.3SG   also   about
           *vypěstění   **typu**   florentské*
           cultivation-LOC.N.SG   type-GEN.M.SG   Florentine-GEN.F.SG
           Madonny   (...) největší   zásluhu.
           Madonna-GEN.F.SG   greatest-ACC.F.SG   merit-ACC.F.SG
           'Verrocchio also takes the most credit for the cultivation of the Florentine-type Madonna.' (Šimáčkův čtyrlístek, 1909–1910)

3 Functions

In this section, we provide a brief overview of the most distinctive functions developed by Slavic TNs. Most of these functions are also characteristic of TNs in other languages such as English or Romance languages, but there are some specific uses that, to our knowledge, are either not attested in other languages at all or at least are not as pronounced.

Obviously, due to disparities in how grammatical meanings are expressed in various languages, some of the functions of TNs are associated with structures that are different from those observed in Germanic and Romance languages, or seemingly alike sequences might have different functions. For instance, Davidse et al. (2013) distinguish the attributive modifier marker use for English TN expressions 'descriptive modifier + TN + of + N2', as in (18), in which 'TN + of' has been reanalysed as "a suffixal marker of the descriptive modifier, on which it conferred degree modification or approximative value", and N2 as a head of the entire premodifier string. In Slavic languages, constructions with adjectives to the right of the TN are possible but as binominal referential structures in which N2 complements the TN which is functioning as head.

(18) Eng. *This is but **a scandalous sort of an Office**.* (from Davidse et al. 2013)

Though there is no direct structural correspondence, the English semi-suffix use in which "the TN-string functions as a subjectified marker indicating that the preceding (nonce) expression has to be interpreted as a subjective classification by the speaker of the instance referred to" (Davidse et al. 2013) has a functional equivalent. Consider (19) and (20) in which *typu* and *z rodzaju* are grammaticalized items yet cannot be considered semi-suffixes. Unlike in English, they follow the N2 and precede the (descriptive) modifier. However, functionally, as in the English example, they allow the reader to classify an item using a subjective expression.

(19) Pol. *relacja* **typu** *„twarzą* *w* *twarz"*
　　　　relation TYPU face-INS.SG in face-ACC.SG
　　'face-to-face **kind** of relation' (NCP)

(20) Pol. *patriarchalizm* **z rodzaju** *„gdzie* *są*
　　　　patriarchalism Z RODZAJU where be-PRS.3PL
　　moje　　*skarpetki"*
　　my-NOM.PL sock-NOM.PL
　　'"where are my socks" **kind** of patriarchalism' (NCP)

We will first briefly discuss extended uses in which TNs form part of a determiner complex (§3.1) and the nominal qualifier use (§3.2). We will then pass to extra-nominal uses, e.g. those in which the new TN-based items grammaticalized into prepositions or particles (§3.3).

3.1 Postdeterminer uses: Quantifying, phoric reference and hedging expressions

In their non-head uses, Russian *rod*, Polish *rodzaj* and Czech *druh* prefer adjectives with pronominal or numeral semantics, also referred to as determiners, over fully semantic adjectives. In this case, the whole modifier complex 'DET GEN + TN GEN' serves the purposes of quantification (21)–(22), phoric reference (23)[19] or hedging (24)–(25), depending on the semantics of the adjectival component (determiner). A quantitative study in Kolyaseva (2021b) estimates that for Russian *rod*, modifier structures with a lexical adjective are rather exceptional, accounting for only 0.4% of the modifier structures, which in their turn constitute three quarters of all intra-nominal constructions with the TN *rod*. In other words, the adnominal genitive modifier in combination with a determiner (the postdeterminer use) is the most typical use of Russian *rod*. A similar tendency for uses with quantifiers and indefinite pronouns is observed in Czech *druh*.

(21) Cze. tam je spousta těch **supermarketů**
there is lots those supermarket-GEN.PL
všeho druhu
all-GEN.SG kind-GEN.SG
'[T]here are a lot of **supermarkets of all kinds**' (ORAL_07A68N)

(22) Rus. **vsjakogo roda** podkovernye
any-GEN.M.SG kind-GEN.M.SG under-the-carpet-NOM.PL
intrigi
intrigue-NOM.PL
'**All kinds of under-the-carpet intrigues**' (RNC)

(23) Rus. A esli vser'ëz, to ja ne osobenno verju v
and if seriously then I not particularly believe-PRS.1SG in
takogo roda statistiku.
such-GEN.M.SG kind-GEN.M.SG statistics-ACC.F.SG
'But speaking seriously, I don't particularly believe in **these kind of statistics**.' (RNC)

---

[19] Interestingly, similar structures in Polish with *typ* receive a dismissive meaning, as in *Nie podejrzewałem ciebie o tego typu sympatie*. 'I did not think you would have these kinds of affections.'

(24) Pol. *Zazdrość   stała się   **pewnego***
          jelousy-NOM.F become-PST.3SG.F some-GEN.M.SG
     rodzaju   "*sygnałem   alarmowym*"
     kind-GEN.M.SG   signal-INS.M.SG   alarm-ADJ.INS.M.SG
     'Jealously has become **a kind of alarm**.' (NCP)

(25) Cze. *ty   koncerty   beru   jako poklidnou víkendovou*
          the   concerts   take-PRS.1SG as   relaxed   weekend
     *záležitost, jako **svýho**   **druhu***
     affair   as   its.own-POSS.REFL.GEN.M.SG   kind-GEN.M.SG
     čundr
     camping-ACC.SG
     'I treat the gigs as a relaxed weekend affair, like **some sort of camping trip**.' (SYN7_ rockpop:383:83:3)

However, this does not imply that other TNs cannot be used in the same constructions. Interestingly, the similative demonstrative *takový* 'such' is associated in Czech with *typ* (as in (26)) while in Russian *ètot* 'this' more typically collocates with *tip*, and *takoj* 'such' with *rod* (Kolyaseva 2021b).

(26) Cze. ***Rozhodnutí   takového   typu***   *nikdy není*
          decisions   such-GEN.M.SG   type-GEN.M.SG   never   not.be-PRS.3PL
     zcela   jednotné.
     entirely   uniform-NOM.PL
     '**Such decisions** are never entirely uniform.'

In Russian, some postdeterminer modifiers with *rod* have become so entrenched that they have acquired the status of a lexicalized unit: they are mentioned in dictionaries as a set phrase and are defined via the adjectival component without any reference to the TN in the explanation. We list such phrases below with equivalents in other languages:
– *takogo roda* 'such' lit. 'of such kind' (Evgen'eva 1999; Lopatin 2013; Ushakov 1939; Ozhegov and Shvedova 2010); see Polish *tego rodzaju*, Czech *toho druhu/takového typu* and Crotian *takve vrste*, Belarusian *takoha rodu/takoha kštaltu*[20]

---

20 *Takoha kštaltu, taki* 'such' is preferred in Belarusian. Similarly, *takogo rodu* in Ukrainian is considered a calque from Russian, a structure overused in legal administration but to be avoided in everyday use of the language (it is recommended to use *takyj* 'this, such' instead).

- *vsjakogo/raznogo roda* 'all sorts, different$_{PL}$' lit. 'of every/different kind' (Lopatin 2010 and Ozhegov and Shvedova 2010), see Ukrainian *usjakoho/riznoho rodu*, Belarusian *roznaha kštaltu*, Polish *wszelkiego rodzaju*, Bulgarian *vsjakakǎv rod/različen rod*, Croatian *svake/razne vrste* and Czech *všeho druhu*
- *drugogo/inogo roda* 'different' lit. 'of a different kind' (Lopatin 2013); see Polish *innego rodzaju*, Belrusian *inšaha rodu*, Bulgarian *drug rod* and Croatian *druge vrste*
- *svoego roda* 'sui generis, to a certain extent, kind of, from a certain point of view' lit. 'of its own kind' (Evgen'eva 1999; Lopatin 2013; Ushakov 1939; Ozhegov and Shvedova 2010; Kuznetsov 1998); see Ukrainian *svoho rodu*, Belarusian *svajho rodu*,[21] Polish *swego rodzaju*, Czech *svého druhu*,[22] Bulgarian *svoevo roda*[23] and Croatian *svoje vrste*[24]

Some languages allow two types of modifier structures: genitival, as demonstrated above, and adpositional. The latter are parallel in their function to the genitival modifiers with the same determiners, and in the case of Russian are also mentioned in dictionaries as fixed phrases:
- Russian *v svoëm rode* 'from a certain point of view, sui generis' lit. 'in its own kind', see also Ukrainian *u svojemu rodi*
- Russian *v nekotorom rode* 'to some degree, somewhat, partially' lit. 'in some way', see also Croatian *u nekoj vrsti/do neke vrste*
- Russian *v ètom/takom rode* 'approximately, approximately such, approximately so' lit. 'in this/such kind', Croatian *u ovoj vrsti/u takvoj vrsti*

With the exception of Croatian, these structures seem to be rare in South Slavic languages (e.g. Serbian *na neku vrstu*). Syntactically, adpositional phrases function as adverbials in Russian and can therefore modify verbs or adjectives (27), unlike the parallel genitival modifiers.

---

21 Attested in literature, possibly under the Russian influence. Normative dictionaries recommend *svoeasablivy, pa-svojmu, taki* instead.
22 Attested only in written language.
23 bookish, archaic
24 *Svoje roda* is recognised by Croatian native speakers as old-fashioned and possibly offensive (with the possibility of using it as an insult). Note that this different meaning ('particular, not like other people') is also attributed to Russian *v svoem rode* alongside its hedging meaning. In older usages, *rod* can be found in this construction, which suggests that the scope of taxonomic uses of Croatian *rod* has narrowed.

(27) Rus. *otvet   ètot*
         answer-NOM.M.SG   this-NOM.M.SG
      v svoem rode   *daže*   ***interesnej***
      in its.own-PRP.M.SG kind-PRP.M.SG   even   interesting-COMP
      samogo   voprosa.
      itself-ADJ.GEN.M.SG question-GEN.M.SG
      'This answer is **kind of** even **more interesting** than the question itself.' (RNC)

What is interesting is that some rare adpositional phrases are attested in functions similar to negative quantifiers, e.g. Russian *ni v koem rode* 'in no way' lit. 'in no kind', as in (28).[25] Parallel uses can be found in Ukranian and Belarusian data, see (29)–(30). However, both examples were interpreted by our informants as unnatural and a calque of the corresponding Russian phrase (indeed, Belarusian/Ukrainian-Russian mixed speech is common in the region due to a very close language contact). Croatian *ni u kakvom rodu* (lit. 'in no kind') 'by no means, in no case' is recognised by native speakers as outdated.

(28) Rus. *A   napominanie   o   proigryše*
          and   reminder-NOM.N.SG   about   loss-PRP.M.SG
      ni v koem rode   *ne   pomogaet.*
      not in which-PRP.M.SG kind-PRP.M.SG   not   help-PRS.3SG
      'A reminder of the loss does not help **in any way**.'(https://www.wattpad.com/924379598-артур-луи-и-адель-глава-4, accessed 5 February 2021)

(29) Bel. *Tamu   hèta* ***ni ŭ jakim rodze***
          that's.why it   not in which-PRP.M.SG kind-PRP.M.SG
      ja   ne   mahu   nazvac'   il'hotaj
      I-NOM   not   can-PRS.1SG   call-INF   benefit-INS.F.SG
      'That's why I can't call it **in any way** a benefit.' (https://euroradio.fm/ministerskiya-zarobki-vyrasli-da-2-milyonau-750-tysyach, accessed 5 February 2021)

---

25 In present-day Russian, the archaic pronominal form *koj* 'which' (instead of *kakoj* 'which') is found in only a few set phrases.

(30) Ukr. *Fil'm*   «*1917*» **ni v jakomu rodi**   *ne*
film-NOM.M.SG   not in which-PRP.M.SG kind-PRP.M.SG not
proslavljaje   *vijnu*
glorify-PRS.3SG   war-ACC.F.SG
'The film *1917* **in no way** glorifies the war' (https://posmotrim.com.ua/uk/, accessed 5 February 2021)

3.2 Nominal qualifiers: Lexical approximation, mitigation, etc.

In Polish and Russian the nominal qualifier function is fulfilled by the TN *rodzaj/rod*. It should be emphasized that such a function is not recent. For instance, in Polish, uses of *rodzaj* in the context of expressing approximation were widely exploited in dictionary definitions, in correlation with postdetermination, as early as the sixteenth century, e.g. *Vitulus item marinus, Nieyáki rodzay morskich ryb alias Phoce* '*Vitulus item marinus*, some kind of sea fish' (Mączyński 1564). The inclination towards contexts expressing imprecision is so strong in the case of Polish *rodzaj*, as in (31), that it started to enter constructions with the vagueness marker *coś* 'something' in the left-hand slot even before forming standard bi(multi-)nominal constructions (comp. *coś w stylu* Y in Kisiel, this volume, chapter 14). Russian etymological dictionaries do not include the approximation meaning but the data suggest that it is not new, see (32). In Kuznetsov (1998) one of the meanings of *rod* is defined as 'something or somebody similar to something or somebody, a likeness of something or somebody', see the previously mentioned example (12). The same meaning 'something (someone) like someone or something, a resemblance of someone or something' is mentioned in Belarusian TSBM (ER).

(31) Pol. *Ich*   *dorobek*   *eseistyczny*   *to*   *zaledwie*
their   output-NOM.M.SG essayistic-NOM.M.SG   it   merely
dodatek   *do*   *największych*   *arcydzieł*
addition-NOM.M.SG   to   greatest-GEN.PL   masterpiece-GEN.PL
a   *niekiedy –*   *jak*   *w*   *przypadku*   *Prousta –*
and   sometimes   like   in   case-LOC.M.SG   Proust-GEN.M.SG
rodzaj   **uwertury**   *czy*   *nawet* *literackiej*
kind-NOM.M.SG   overture-GEN.F.SG   or   even   literary-GEN.F.SG
wprawki
exercise-GEN.F.SG
'Their essayistic output is merely an addition to their greatest masterpieces or sometimes – as in the case of Proust – it is **a kind of overture** or even a literary exercise.' (NCP)

(32) Rus. *Sledovatel'no,   oni   byli   nekotoryj*
         Consequently,   they-NOM.PL be-PST.PL   some-NOM.M.SG
     rod   *našix*   *tak nazyvaemyx*   *intermedij.*
     kind-NOM.M.SG   our-GEN.PL   so.called-GEN.PL   interlude-GEN.PL
     'Consequently, they were **some kind of** our so-called interludes.' (RNC, 1750)

The qualifier function can be fulfilled by various TNs in different Slavic languages: *tip* in Serbian, *vid* in Bulgarian, *vrsta* (although rarely) in Croatian, and *riznovyd* and *gatunok* in Ukrainian, see, for instance, (33).

(33) Ukr. *Bo   pujactvo —   takož   riznovyd*
         Because   drunkenness-NOM.N.SG   also   variety-NOM.M.SG
     podoroži!
     travel-GEN.F.SG
     'Because drinking is also **a form of travel**!' (RNC Parallel, 2001)

Besides lexical approximation, qualifiers can mark the unexpected use of metaphors, as in (34), or mitigate potentially offensive statements or requests (35). In some languages, like Bulgarian, a TN has to be supported by an indefinite pronoun to fulfil this function, such as *njakakăv* 'some' in (36).

(34) Pol. *hm,   może   ludzie   nie   reagują   bo*
         yhm   maybe   people-NOM   not   react-PRS.3PL   because
     boją się   że   jak   oni   będą   w   potrzebie
     afraid-PRS.3PL   that   when   they   be-FUT.3PL   in   need-LOC
     to   też   nikt   nie   zareaguje?   może   to
     then   also   no.one-NOM   not   react-FUT.3SG   maybe   it-NOM
     rodzaj   *„psychicznej"*   *zemsty?*
     kind-NOM.SG   psychological-GEN.F.SG   revenge-GEN.F.SG
     'Maybe people don't react because they're afraid that when they're in need, then nobody will react either. Maybe it's **a kind of "psychological" revenge**?' (NCP)

(35) Pol. (...) *sam   uważam   WOŚP   za   **rodzaj***
              myself   consider-PRS.1SG   WOŚP   for   kind-NOM.SG
     wielkiej   mistyfikacji.
     huge-GEN.F.SG   hoax-GEN.F.SG
     'I personally see WOŚP as **a kind of big hoax**.' (http://tech4.nowoscimediaokpi.pl/, accessed 5 February 2021)

(36) Bul. *Smjatam tova za* **njakakǎv vid mistifikacija.**
think-PRS.1SG this for some-M.SG kind-M.SG mystification-F.SG
'I consider it **a kind of mystification**.'

Note that the hedging structures (genitival and adpositional modifiers with the reflexive pronoun 'one's own') discussed in the previous section have similar functions, as do some of the grammaticalized prepositional and participle uses described below.

3.3 Extranominal uses

Grammaticalization of structures with TNs involves the fossilization of the noun in one of its forms, either by itself, e.g. the erstwhile genitive forms Russian *tipa*, Polish and Ukrainian *typu*, Belarusian and Ukrainian *kštaltu*,[26] and Croatian *vrste*,[27] the instrumental forms Ukrainian *kštaltom* (obsolete) and Belarusian *kštaltam* (obsolete),[28] or in combination with a preposition, e.g. Russian *vrode* (<*v rode* lit. 'in the kind of'), *po tipu* (lit. 'by the type'), Polish *w rodzaju* (lit. 'in the kind of'), *z rodzaju* (lit. 'from the kind of'), *w typie* (lit. 'in the type', *na kształt* (lit. 'on the form of'), Ukrainian *na kštalt*,[29] and Belarusian *nakštalt*. A certain pattern is not necessarily linked to a specific TN root and languages differ as to which particular pattern is used with which TN. For instance, the pattern *v* 'in' + TN$_{LOC/PRP.M.SG}$ (as in French *dans le genre de* and German *in der Art von*) is apparent in Russian *vrode* and Polish *w rodzaju*, but it has not produced new units in the case of Ukrainian *rid* or Belarusian *rod*. In Polish, both *rodzaj* and *typ* have fol-

---

[26] Belarusian and Ukrainian *kštaltu* seem to be fairly recent; consider a 2015 forum post arguing that *kštaltu* does not exist in the Belarusian literary standard, and *nakštalt* should be used instead: "What is this fashion for the new preposition 'kštaltu'? It is what, a hybrid of Polish *kształt* and Moscow's *tipa* bred in the incubators of informal-colloquial jargon?" (translated, https://by-mova.livejournal.com/1265215.html, accessed 5 February 2021).
[27] *Vrste* can be found in spoken Croatian, but it is not common: the adverbs *kao* 'like' and *poput* 'like' are preferred.
[28] Hrinčenko (v. 2, 1958: 336) documents the instrumental form *kštaltom* 'in a similar manner' in nineteenth-century Ukrainian: *Vikopajemo pečeru kštaltom zimovnika* 'We dig a cave like a wintering ground'. Belarusian *kštaltam* is also mentioned as an obsolete preposition equivalent to *nakštalt* in Šuba (1993 ER).
[29] It is likely that a contamination of *ščos' na kštalt* 'something like' and *ščos' typu* 'something like' gave rise to *ščos' na typu*, which is currently spreading in spoken Ukrainian, mainly among younger users, e.g. *To ščos' na typu štatyvu* 'It is something like a tripod' (http://foto.ua/gallery/photos/236073.html, accessed 5 February 2021).

lowed this pattern (*w rodzaju* and *w typie*), but Russian *tip* has not. Bulgarian, in which the nominal case system has been nearly lost, features strings *ot tipa na* (lit. 'from the type of'), *ot vida na* (lit. 'from the kind of'), *ot sorta na* (lit. 'from the sort of') and *ot roda na* (lit. 'of/from the kind of'), in which *-a* is a definite article used with nouns in the position of a grammatical object.

Most of the grammaticalized items function as prepositions, but some of them further develop into particles or conjunctions. Note that as prepositions, they require a genitive complement (except for the analytical Bulgarian), a grammatical feature inherited from TNs. As particles and conjunctions, they lose case governance, and their scope broadens such that is no longer limited to an NP but can include either a part of or an entire proposition. Among the most conspicuous functions are markers of (approximative) similarity (37)–(38) or exemplification (39)–(41) or hedging (42); in the latter case they are functionally similar to nominal qualifiers or hedging modifiers described previously. They are frequently found in combination with (potential) locutions, often in quotation marks, which raises the question whether at least some of them may have acquired a quotative status, since they are used in the same contexts as traditional quotatives or markers of reported speech. Consider for example, a Bulgarian translation of Russian standard deverbal particle markers of reported speech *deskat'* and *mol* with *edin vid* in (43)–(44).

(37) Ukr. *V Ukrajini buduvatymut' rezervnu*
in Ukraine-PRP.F.SG build-FUT.3.SG reserve-ADJ.ACC.F.SG
armiju **na kštalt** švejcars'koji
army-ACC.F.SG NA KŠTALT Swiss-ADJ.GEN.F.SG
'Ukraine will build a reserve army **similar to/like** the Swiss one.' (https://www.youtube.com/watch?v=0IDMC6rUB8E, accessed 5 February 2021)

(38) Bel. *Prèzydèntam mae byc' čalavek*
president-INS.M.SG have-PRS.3SG be-INF person-NOM.M.SG
kštaltu *Daškeviča.*
KŠTALTU Dashkevich-GEN.M.SG
'A man **like** Dashkevich should be president' (https://www.svaboda.org/a/30112946.html, accessed 5 February 2021)

(39) Pol. (...) *nigdy nie używa określeń* **w rodzaju**
never not use-PRS.3SG expression-GEN.PL W RODZAJU
"dyktatura, junta, reżim" (...)
dictatorship-NOM junta-NOM regime-NOM
'He never uses **such** words **as** dictatorship, junta, regime' (NCP)

(40) Rus. *Logika končennogo knigomana,*
Logic-NOM.F.SG finished-GEN.M.SG book.lover-GEN.M.SG
vrode *menja*
VRODE I-GEN
'It is the logic of a complete book maniac, **such as** me' (RNC)

(41) Bul. *bjaxa zahvărlili srednovekovnite si tehniki*
discard-PPRF.3PL medieval-PL own technique-PL
ot sorta na *„Smărt črez razčlenjavane" i*
of sort-M.SG.DEF of death through dismemberment-N.SG and
se bjaha nasočili kăm kăde-kăde po-humannite
direct-REFL.PPRF.3PL to more.humane
„Obrabotvane" i „Transformacija"
processing-N.SG and transformation-F.SG
'[A]bandoned their medieval techniques **such as** "Death by Dissection" and turned to the more humane "Processing" and "Transformation".' (BulNC)

(42) Bul. *Varenka Nelidova beše ne samo*
Varenka-F.SG Nelidova-F.SG be-IPFV.3SG not only
snažna i s pravilni čerti, no
well.built-F.SG and with correct-PL feature-PL but
v neja imperatorăt **edin vid** *čerpeše*
in she emperor-M.SG.DEF EDIN VID draw-IPFV.3SG
uverenost v tova, kolko se e razvilo i
confidence-F.SG in that how.much develop-REFL.PRF.3SG.N and
otišlo s gigantski krački napred vsičko naokolo.
go-PRF.3SG.N with giant-PL step-PL forward everything around
'Not only did Varenka Nelidova have a well-built figure and a fine-featured face, but the emperor **kind of** drew confidence from her in how everything had developed and moved forward with giant steps.' (RNC parallel).

(43) Rus. *Ja kak-to pis'meco ej podkatil, v*
I-NOM once letter-ACC.N.SG she-DAT roll.up-PST.M.SG in
takom, znaeš', vozvyšennom duxe.
such-PRP.M.SG know-PRS.2SG sublime-PRP.M.SG spirit-PRP.M.SG
Vljublen, **deskat',** *bezumno i s trepetom*
in.love-ADJ.M.SG QUOT madly and with awe-INS.M.SG
ožidaju vašego otveta.
wait.for-PRS.1SG your-GEN.M.SG answer-GEN.M.SG

Bul. **Edin vid,** vljuben　　　　săm　　　　bezumno i　s
　　　EDIN VID　in.love-ADJ.M.SG　be-PRS.1SG madly　and with
trepet　　očakvam　　otgovora　　　　vi.
awe-M.SG wait-PRS.1SG answer-M.SG.DEF your
'I once made a pass at her with a letter, in such, you know, a sublime style.
I am in love, **I was like**, I am madly and anxiously waiting for your answer.'
(RNC Parallel)

(44) Rus. Podnjala　　ruku –　　　　**mol**,　ne　takaja
　　　　raise-PST.F.SG hand-ACC.F.SG QUOT not such-NOM.F.SG
ja　　persona,　　čtoby　nazyvat'　svoe
I-NOM worthy-NOM.F.SG to　call-INF one's-REFL.ACC.N.SG
imja –　　　i,　izobraziv　　　polupoklon
name-ACC.N.SG and having.portrayed-TRSGR half.bow-ACC.M.SG
v　storonu　　šefa,　　　skazala (. . .).
in side-ACC.F.SG boss-GEN.M.SG say-PST.F.SG
Bul. Vdigna　　　dlan –　　**edin vid**, ne　săm　　čak
　　　raise-AOR.3SG hand- F.SG EDIN VID not be-PRS.1SG REINF
takava　　persona,　če　　da　se predstavjam
such-F.SG worthy-F.SG that SUBJ introduce-REFL.PRS.1SG
poimenno, i　s　　počitelno　sveždane　na
by.name　and with respectful-N.SG droop-N.SG of
glava　　v　posoka　　kăm　　šefa,　　　kaza (. . .).
head-F.SG in direction-F.SG towards boss-M.SG.DEF say-AOR.3SG
'She raised her hand – **like**, I'm not such an important person to introduce
myself by name – and, with a respectful nod of the head towards her boss,
said (. . .).' (RNC Parallel)

Two distinctive functions seem to be specific to Russian particle *vrode*: firstly, that of a quasi-assertive (or a sensory evidential) whereby "the speaker refrains from a confident judgment, despite having direct information on the actual state of affairs" (Bylygina & Shmelev 1997), as in (45), and secondly, as a part of the implied concessive-adversative construction '*vrode X but Y*', which can be described as "prise en compte d'une incompatibilité" [taking account of some incompatibility] (Sakhno 2010), as in (46). Such uses have not been observed in Polish or Czech, nor in South Slavic languages like Serbian, Bulgarian or Croatian. They are discussed in more detail in Kisiel and Kolyaseva (this volume, chapter 13).

(45) Rus. U Èsli, **vrode kak,** černyj pojas po
at Esley VRODE KAK black-NOM.M.SG belt-NOM.M.SG by
karatè, takže on očen' dolgo zanimalsja kapoèjra
karate also he-NOM very long do-PST.M.SG capoeira
i ajkido.
and aikido
'Esley, **as far as I remember / as far as I have heard,** has a black belt in karate, and he also did capoeira and aikido for a very long time.' (RNC) [the speaker has some direct evidence that Esley has a black belt].

(46) Rus. **Vrode by** krugom neprijatnosti. No sem'ja
VRODE BY around trouble-NOM.PL but family-NOM.F.SG
slonov i v samom dele byla sčastliva,
elephant-GEN.PL REINF actually be-PST.F.SG happy-F.SG
potomu čto vse oni očen' ljubili drug druga.
because all-PL they-NOM very love-PST.PL one.another
'[*Vrode by*] they were surrounded by troubles. But the elephant family was indeed happy, because they all loved each other very much.' [= Even though they were in trouble, the family was happy]. (RNC)

3.4 Functions aquired by tip/typ and its derivatives

As a point of special interest highlighted in this volume, we draw attention to the functions acquired by *tip/typ*. Although these nouns were borrowed by the Slavic languages relatively recently compared to other TNs, they have developed grammaticalized/pragmaticalized items, such as *tipa/typu*. In some languages, like Russian or Ukrainian, they are rather extensive, but in others they seem to be predominantly used as markers of lexical or semantic approximation and exemplification, functions that are also typical of other TNs as discussed above. The approximative and exemplifying uses are observed in Russian, Polish, Czech, Serbian, Ukrainian, Bulgarian and spoken Croatian. In the case of Croatian we observe a borrowing from Italian (*tip*) in the region of Rijeka/Istria; however, the borrowing has not yet been fully accepted as part of the lexicon and is currently only used in spoken discourse. Quotatives, on the other hand, are not as universal. In Czech, for instance, quotative uses of *typu* are very limited and are only attested with impersonal subjects in contexts like (47). This is different from the standard Czech quotative particle *prý/prej*, Russian particles *mol, deskat'* or English *be like* which require a defined reported speaker to whom certain words are attributed by the current speaker (see for example the conceptualization of quotatives as "double voiced utterances" in Spronck [2012], following Vološinov [1973] and Jakobson [1957]). In fact, we observed such quotative uses of *tipa/typu* only in the East Slavic languages, Russian and Ukrainian.

(47) Cze. to   bylo   hnedka   **typu**   že   že
          it   be- PST.PTCP.N.SG immediately   type-GEN.M.SG   that that
          pracuju   ž*   že   sem   měl   **málo peněz**
          work-PRS.1SG   t*   that am   have- PST.PTCP.M.SG little money-GEN.PL
          'they immediately said, like, you know, that I work and I had little money'
          (ORAL_06H089N)

Although *typu* can be also found in Belarusian data, even in academic contexts (e.g. the definition of the preposition *pa* in Šuba (1993): *U vyrazax* **typu** *raz pa razu, kroplja pa kropli i pad. abaznačae "adno ŭsled za druhim"* – 'In expressions **like** *time and time again, drop by drop*, etc. denotes "one after another"'), it is viewed as a calque from Russian, in contrast to the synonymous *nakštalt*. The alien nature of the item is emphasised and mocked in the form *cipa*, which may be used for ironic or sarcastic purposes. While *typu* is a semantic calque, *cipa* is a mere phonetic adaption of the Russian *tipa* (in Belarussian, *c* corresponds to the Russian palatalised [t'], as in *tipa*). Since, in general, the use of Russian words in Belarusian discourse is perceived as stylistically low, and in any case something negative, the evidently "Russian" *cipa* makes the statement sound somewhat unserious or derisive.[30]

Below we delineate the main functions developed by Slavic nouns *tip/typ* and their grammaticalized derivatives and illustrate them with examples from various languages.

Lexical or semantic approximation

(48) Rus. *Nu   t... to est'   zaxodiš'/   nu   tut   takoe*
          well   th... that is   enter-PRS.2SG well here such-NOM.N.SG
          tipa dekorativnogo   krylečka (...)'
          TIPA   decorative-GEN.M.SG   porch-GEN.M.SG
          'Well th... that is you come in / well there is here such...**sort of a decorative porch** (...)' (RNC)

---

[30] We thank Uladzimir Koshchanka for sharing this observation.

(49) Cze. *neni   to   **typ**   **Pavarottiho**   *je   to*
         he.is.not it   type-NOM.M.SG Pavarotti-GEN.M.SG   he.is   it
     *spíš   **typ**   **Carrerase***
     rather type-NOM.M.SG   Carreras-GEN.M.SG
     'he is not **like Pavarotti**, he's rather **like Carreras**' (ORAL_10P006N)

Mitigation (metadiscursive/illocutionary)

(50) Rus. *- Èto   čto/   ja   dolžna   delat'?*
          this-ACC.N.SG what   I-NOM   must-F.SG do-INF
     *- Nu / net / nu. . . nu   ja   dumal /   **tipa** /*
     well   no   well   well   I-NOM   think-PST.M.SG   TIPA
     pomožeš'.
     help-FUT.2SG
     '- What / is it me who has to do that?
     – well / no / well. . . well I thought / **like** / you would help.' (RNC)

Exemplification

(51) Pol. *samochody   **typu kombi**   lub   **van***
          car-NOM.PL   TYPU kombi-NOM.SG   or   van-NOM.SG
     'cars **such as kombi** or **van**' (NCP)

(52) Cze. ***starý   dědky**   **typu**   já   nevim*
          old-NOM.PL   grandpa-NOM.PL   type-GEN.SG   I   not.know-PRS.1SG
     Nazareti**   a   **Pink Floydi**   a   **Rolling Stones
     Nazareth-NOM.PL   and   Pink.Floyd-NOM.PL   and   Rolling.Stones-NOM.PL
     'grandpas **such as** – I don't know – **Nazareth and Pink Floyd and Rolling Stones**' (ORAL_10H007N)

(53) Rus. *a   prezident   isključitel'no   zanimaetsja*
          and   president-NOM.M.SG   exclusivey   engage.in-PRS.3SG
     *vojažami   po   različnym   gosudarstvam /   **tipa**   **Angoly***
     travel-INS.PL in   various-DAT.PL state-DAT.PL   TIPA   Angola-GEN.F.SG
     *i   **Bangladeš**/   i   ustanovlenija   s*
     and   Bangladesh-GEN.F.SG   and   establishing-GEN.N.SG   with
     nimi   dobrososedskix   otnošenij.
     they-INS   neighborly-GEN.PL   relation-GEN.PL

'... and the president deals exclusively with trips to various states / **such as Angola and Bangladesh** / and establishing good neighbourly relations with them.' (RNC)

(54) Hrv. *U skoroj bi budućnosti moglo*
in soon-LOC.F.SG COND future-LOC.F.SG could-N.SG
biti pokušaja, u tzv. kućnim
be-INF attempt-NOM.M.SG in so.called home-ADJ.LOC.PL
laboratorijima, proizvodnje kemijskih
laboratory-LOC.PL production-GEN.F.SG chemical-GEN.PL
droga **tipa ecstasyja** *i* **amfetamina.**
grug-GEN.PL TIPA ecstasy-NOM.M.SG and amphetamine-NOM.M.SG
'In the near future there could be attempts, in the so-called home laboratories, to produce chemical drugs **such as** ecstasy and amphetamines.' (Riznica corpus)

(55) Bul. *Az obiknah moite obrečeni, nemi*
I get.used-AOR.1SG my-PL.DEF doomed-PL wordless-PL
prijateli, privărzah se i kăm
friend-PL become.attached-AOR.1SG and to
prijatelkite im **ot tipa na**
female.friend-PL.DEF they-DAT from type-M.SG.DEF of
prelestnata **Balabanica** *ot Momčilovo, i na ošte*
lovely-F.SG.DEF Balabanitsa-F.SG from Momchilovo and of even
po-prelestnata **Hadžidie**, *vnučkata*
more.beautiful-F.SG.DEF Hadjidie granddaughter-F.SG.DEF
na djado Rašid.
of grandfather-M.SG Rashid-M.SG
'I got used to my doomed, wordless friends and became attached to their owners **such as** the lovely **Balabanica** from Momchilovo, and to the even more lovely **Hadjidie**, the granddaughter of grandfather Rashid.' (RBCorpus).

Quotative / marker of reported speech

(56) Rus. *Nu ja- ja takaja... ja uže*
well I-NOM I-NOM such-NOM.F.SG I-NOM already
išču— nu netu ix voobšče
search-PRS.1SG REINF there.is.no they-GEN at.all

> nigde/ ja takaja dumaju/ tipa/ nu/ ja
> nowhere I-NOM such-NOM.F.SG think-PRS.1SG TIPA well I-NOM
> takaja vylezaju/ vižu ètu
> such-NOM.F.SG get.out-PRS.1SG see-PRS.1SG this-ACC.F.SG
> tëtku/ takaja/ **tipa**/ "Izvinite/ a gde
> woman-ACC.F.SG such-NOM.F.SG TIPA excuse.me PART where
> tut očki?"
> here glasses-PL
> 'Well, I'm like... I'm already looking — well, I don't have them anywhere at all / I'm thinking / like / well / I'm getting out [of the solarium] / I see this woman / I'm like / **I'm like** / "Sorry / where are the glasses here?"' (RNC)

(57) Ukr. *Ja kažu druhu šo **typu** vona*
I-NOM say-PRS.1SG friend-DAT.M.SG that TYPU she-NOM
ne xoče myrytys', i šo možno
not want-PRS.3SG make.up-INF and that may-IMPRS
zabyty na nai
say.the.hell-INF on she-ACC
'I tell my friend [*typu*] that she doesn't want to make peace, and that I could tell her to go to hell' (https://vk.com/wall-93124539_31954, accessed 5 February 2021)

(58) Pol. *No, ja mówię, rozmowa schodziła też na*
well I say-PRS.1SG conversation-NOM.SG go-PST.3SG also on
jakieś pewnie uboczne tematy,
some-ACC.PL surely side-ADJ.ACC.PL subject-ACC.PL
pewnie i ten, o którym pan
surely also this-ACC.M.SG about which-LOC.M.SG you-POLITE
*mówi, **typu**, że pan Adam*
say-PRS.3SG TYPU that mister-NOM Adam-NOM
Michnik coś żartował z panią
Michnik-NOM something-NOM joke-PST.3SG.M with miss-INS.F.SG
minister Jakubowską
minister-INS.F.SG Jakubowska-INS.F
'Well, I say, the conversation also touched on some side subjects, possibly also the one you mention, **like**, that Adam Michnik joked about something with minister Jakubowska.' (NCP)

In contrast to Romance languages, no clear instances of *tipa/typu* as a numerical approximator or a structuring device have been observed. Even though there are some isolated instances of Russian *tipa* in combination with numerals, in contexts like (59) and (60) the idea of 'inexactitude' cannot be entirely attributed to *tipa*, as it is already conveyed by *v rajone* 'around' or *čto-to* 'something'.

(59) Rus. *Sovsem nedavno... Odinnadcatogo čisla?* **Tipa**
 quite recently eleventh-GEN.M.SG date-GEN.M.SG tipa
 v rajone odinnadcatogo čisla /
 in vicinity-PRP.M.SG eleventh-GEN.M.SG date-GEN.M.SG
 po-moemu. Možet devjatogo...
 to.my.mind maybe nineth- GEN.M.SG
 'Very recently ... on the eleventh? **Like** around the eleventh / I think. Maybe on the ninth ...' [the speaker cannot remember the date] (RNC)

(60) Rus. *No u nix est' i platnye uslugi —*
 but at they-GEN there.is and paid-NOM.PL service-NOM.PL
 «virtual'naja škola», ***čto-to***
 virtual-NOM.F.SG school-NOM.F.SG something-NOM.N.SG
 tipa 100 rublej *v mesjac za*
 TIPA hundred-GEN rouble-GEN.PL in month-ACC.M.SG for
 predmet, no my ne pol'zuemsja.
 discipline-ACC.M.SG but we-NOM not use-PRS.1PL
 'But they also have paid services — "the virtual school", **something like 100 roubles** a month per subject, but we do not use it.' (RNC)

Although *tipa/typu* do not seem to be used to signal narrative progress or to mark the beginning of an argument, they can be used as an elaboration/explanation marker (see elaborative and inferential discourse markers in Fraser [2009: 296]). Consider examples (61) and (62), in which the speaker requests their interlocutor to elaborate on the question they posed using *typu*. Note that this is more than requesting an example. In (62) for instance, it is also a sign of annoyance of how general A's question is, in a frame, 'I am acting as if I did not know what you mean so that you have to explain yourself'. The discourse can be interpreted as follows: A suggests that being interested in such men (as previously mentioned) is shameful, so B asks for a definition of "such men" because B is annoyed with the inference that it is bad to be interested in them. On the other hand, had B reacted with "*W rodzaju?*", (s)he would want nothing more than an example of such men mentioned by A. In Russian and Ukrainian, *tipa/typu* has developed further and can be interpreted in certain contexts as an explanatory marker meaning 'that is' (as with It. *tipo*, Voghera 2013) or signalling the speaker's inference regarding the reasons or goals of somebody's actions or statements (Kolyaseva 2018, Kolyaseva

2021a), as in (63) in which *tipa* introduces the speaker's interpretation of why the extra sum is paid. Alternatively, it can introduce explanation for the speaker's own actions, e.g. in (64), in which the speaker's lack of expertise in humanities is explained by his identification as a techie.

(61) Ukr. A: *A ty ljubiš muzyky?* B: ***Typu?***
and you-NOM like-PRS.2SG music-ACC.F.SG TYPU
'A: Do you like music? B: **Like what**?'

(62) Pol. A: *Interesujesz się takimi facetami?* B: ***Typu?***
interest-REFL.PRS.2SG such-INS.PL man-INS.PL TYPU
'A: You fancy such men? B: **Like**? [=What do you mean?]'

(63) Rus. *A u nas vyxodit/ koroče/ stipendija*
and at we-GEN come.out-PRS.3PL in.short stipend-NOM.F.SG
*i pljus trista rublej **tipa** na*
and plus three.hundred-NOM rouble-GEN.PL TIPA for
prožitočnyj minimum/ na-naverno.
subsistence-ADJ.ACC.M.SG minimum-ACC.M.SG maybe
'And we receive / in short / a stipend plus three hundred roubles, **like** for a living wage / I guess.'

One final specific use developed in some of the Slavic languages is that of a 'falsity' marker equivalent to air quotations, as in (64), discussed as 'quasi'-use in Kolyaseva (2018, see also 2021a). In addition to Russian *tipa*, this function is fulfilled by Ukrainian *typu* and similar contexts can be found on the Belarusian web, as in (65), in which *typu* can be interpreted as marking that, in the speaker's view, the special forces' care for citizens is nothing but simulated. However, our Belarusian informants identified it as a feature of trasianka, the Belarusian-Russian mixed speech. It is possible that the uses observed in Ukrainian data are also a result of Russian influence.

(64) Rus. *ŠČas poem i tože pridkmaju kakoj-nibud'*
now eat-FUT.1SG and also invent-FUT.1SG some-ACC.M.SG
***tipa** smešnoj slučaj kotoryj **tipa** so*
TIPA funny-ACC.M.SG case-ACC.M.SG which-ACC.M.SG TIPA with
mnoj nedavno proizošel.
I-INS recently happen-PST.M.SG
'I'm gonna eat right now and then I will also come up with a [*tipa*] funny story that has recently [*tipa*] happened to me.' [= the story is not funny, and it did not happen] (from Kolyaseva 2018: 90)

(65) Bel.* *Dlja   musaroŭ   padobnaha   kštaltu*
         for   cop-GEN.M.SG   similar-GEN.M.SG   form-GEN.M.SG
   specaperacyi   hèta   ne   tol'ki   praca.   Hèta
   special.operation-NOM.F.PL it.is not only   work-NOM.F.SG   it.is
   mahčymasc'   atrymac'   asalodu
   opportunity-NOM.F.SG   get-INF   bliss-ACC.F.SG
   ad   uladarannja   nad   ljudz'mi.   Hètae
   from   domination-GEN.N.SG   over   people-INS.PL   this-NOM.N.SG
   ix   žadanne   prajaŭljaecca   ŭ   kožnaj
   their   desire-NOM.N.SG   manifest-PRS.3SG   in   every-LOC.F.SG
   *drobjazi.   Navat   kali   jany   robjac'   **typu***
   trifle-LOC.F.SG   even   if   they-NOM   do-PRS.3PL   typu
   "dabro"   zatrymanym.
   good-ACC.N.SG   detainee-DAT.PL
   'For these kind of cops, special operations are not just a job. It is an opportunity to enjoy domination over people. This desire of theirs is manifested in every small detail. Even if they [typu] do "good" to the detained.'
   (https://vk.com/@mikola_dziadok-sobr-i-gubazk-antrapalagchnyya-nazrann, accessed 5 February 2021)

References

Bańkowski, Andrzej. 2000. *Etymologiczny słownik języka polskiego* [Etymological dictionary of Polish]. Warsaw: Wydawnictwo naukowe PWN.
BER 1971– = *Bălgarski etimologičen rečnik* [Bulgarian etymological dictionary]. Sofia: Izdatelstvo na Bălgarskata akademija na naukite, Akademično izdatelstvo „Prof. Marin Drinov". https://ibl.bas.bg/ber/ (accessed 5 February 2021).
Besedje 2011 = Ahačič, Kozma, Andreja Legan Ravnikar, Majda Merše, Jožica Narat & France Novak. 2011. *Besedje slovenskega knjižnega jezika 16 stoletja* [Words of the Slovene literary language of the 16th century]. Ljubljana: Založba ZRC, ZRC SAZU. https://www.fran.si/iskanje?FilteredDictionaryIds=140&View=1&Query=* (accessed 5 February 2021).
Bezlaj, France. 1977–2007. *Etimološki slovar slovenskega jezika*. Knj. 1–5. [Etymological dictionary of the Slovenian language. Books 1–5]. Ljubljana: Mladinska knjiga, Založba ZRC.
Boryś, Wiesław. 2005. *Słownik etymologiczny języka polskiego* [Etymological dictionary of Polish]. Kraków: Wydawnictwo literackie.
Brückner, Aleksander. 1895. *Kazania średniowieczne* [Medieval sermons]. Kraków: Akademia Umiejętności.
Brückner, Aleksander. 1927. *Słownik etymologiczny języka polskiego* [Etymological dictionary of the Polish language]. Kraków: Krakowska Spółka Wydawnicza. https://polona.pl/item/slownik-etymologiczny-jezyka-polskiego (accessed 5 February 2021).

Bulygina, Tatyana V. & Alexei D. Shmelev. 1997. *Jazykovaja konceptualizacija mira (na materiale russkoj grammatiki)* [Language conceptualization of the world (based on Russian grammar)]. Moscow: Jazyki russkoj kul'tury.

Čerkasova, Evdokija T. 1967. *Perexod polnoznačnyx slov v predlogi*. [The transition of contentful words into prepositions]. Moscow: Nauka.

Černyx, Pavel JA. 1999. *Istoriko-ètimologičeskij slovar' sovremennogo russkogo jazyka*. V 2 t. [Historical and etymological dictionary of modern Russian language. In 2 vol.]. Moscow: Russkij jazyk.

Cyganenko, Galina. P. 1989. *Ètimologičeskij slovar' russkogo jazyka* [Etymological dictionary of the Russian language]. Kiev: Rad. šk.

Davidse, Kristin, Lieselotte Brems, Peter Willemse, Emeline Doyen, Jessica Kiermeer & Elfi Thoelen. 2013. A comparative study of the grammaticalized uses of English 'sort (of)' and French 'genre (de)' in teenage forum data. In Emanuele Miola (ed.), *Standard and non-standard languages on the Internet. Languages Go Web*. Studi e Ricerche, 41–66. Alessandria: Edizionidell' Orso. https://kuleuven.limo.libis.be/discovery/search?query=any,contains,lirias1820602&tab=LIRIAS&search_scope=lirias_profile&vid=32KUL_KUL:Lirias&foolmefull=1

DRMJ = *Digitalen rečnik na makedonskiot jazik* [Digital dictionary of the Macedonian language]. http://www.makedonski.info/ (accessed 5 February 2021).

DWDS = *Digitales Wörterbuch der deutschen Sprache*. https://www.dwds.de (accessed 5 February 2021).

ESBM 1978– = *Etymalahičny sloŭnik bielaruskaj movy* [Etymological dictionary of the Belarusian language]. Minsk: Navuka i technika, Belaruskaja navuka.

ESSČ = *Elektronický slovník staré češtiny* [Electronic dictionary of Old Czech]. Prague, Institute of the Czech Language, Academy of Sciences of the Czech Republic, http://vokabular.ujc.cas.cz (version 1.1.14).

ESUM 1982–2012 = *Etymolohičnyj slovnyk ukrajins'koji movy*. В 7 т. [Etymological dictionary of the Ukrainian language. In 7 vols.]. Kiev: Naukova dumka.

Fraser, Bruce. 2009. An account of discourse markers. *International Review of Pragmatics* 1(2). 293–320.

Hrinchenko, Borys D. 1907–1909. *Slovar' ukrajins'koji movy* [Dictionary of the Ukrainian language]. http://hrinchenko.com (accessed 5 February 2021).

HSBM 1982–2017 = *Histaryčny sloŭnik belaruskaj movy* [Historical dictionary of the Belarusian language, in 37 vol.]. Minsk: Belaryskaja navuka.

IJuM 1906 = Istoriko-juridičeskie materialy, izvlečennye iz" aktovyx"ъ knig" gubernij Vitebskoj i Mogilevskoj [Historical and legal materials extracted from the act books of Vitebsk and Mogilev provinces]. Issue 32. Vitebsk: Tipo-Litografija Br. Podzemskixъ. https://dlib.rsl.ru/viewer/01003871079#?page=376 (accessed 5 February 2021).

ISSČ = *Internetový slovník současné češtiny* [Online dictionary of modern Czech]. https://www.nechybujte.cz/slovnik-soucasne-cestiny (accessed 5 February 2021).

Jacobson, Roman. 1957 [1973]. Shifters, verbal categories and the Russian verb. In Roman Jacobson, *Selected writings II, Word and language*, 130–147. The Hague: Mouton.

Jungmann, Josef. 1834–1839. *Slovník česko-německý* [Czech-German dictionary]. Prague: W knjžecj arcibiskupské knihtiskárne.

Kastelec, Matija & Gregor Vorenc 1680–1710 = Stabej, Jože. 1997. *Slovensko-latinski slovar po: Matija Kastelec – Gregor, Dictionarium Latino-Carniolicum* (1680–1710). [Slovenian-Latin dictionary by: Matija Kastelec – Gregor Vorenc, Dictionarium Latino-Carniolicum

(1680–1710)]. Ljubljana: Založba ZRC, ZRC SAZU. https://fran.si/138/katelec-vorenc-slovensko-latinski-slovar/datoteke/Vorenc_Predgovor.pdf. (accessed 5 February 2021).

Kolyaseva, Alena. 2018. The 'new' Russian quotative *tipa*: Pragmatic scope and functions. *Journal of Pragmatics* 128. 82–97.

Kolyaseva, Alena. 2021a. The divergent paths of pragmaticalization: the case of the Russian particles *tipa* and *vrode*. *Journal of Pragmatics*. https://doi.org/10.1016/j.pragma.2021.08.003 (accessed 5 February 2021).

Kolyaseva, Alena. 2021b. The nominal uses of the Russian *rod* ('genus', 'genre', 'kind') and *tip* ('type'): the starting point of desemanticization. *Slovo a Slovesnost* 82. 3–44.

Kolyaseva, Alena. 2022. The Russian prepositional TIPA and VRODE in online student discourse: evidence of attraction? *Linguistics* 60 (5). 1451–1485.

Králik, Ľubor. 2015. *Stručný etymologický slovník slovenčiny* [Brief etymological dictionary of Slovak]. Bratislava: Veda, vydavateľstvo SAV.

Kuznetsov, Sergei A. 1998. *Bol'šoj tolkovyj slovar' russkogo jazyka* [The Big explanatory dictionary of Russian language]. Saint-Petersburg: Norint.

Lapteva, Olga A. 1983. Tipa ili vrode ? [Tipa or vrode?]. *Voprosy JAzykoznanija* [Topics in the Study of Language] 1983 (1). 39–51.

Lazareva, Viktoria. 2016. K èvoljucii taksonomičeskix terminov: russkoe *tipa* i ego funkcional'nye raznovidnosti [On the evolution of taxonomic terms: Russian *tipa* and its functional varieties]. *Europa Orientalis* 35. 543–565.

Lopatin, Vladimir V. 2013. *Tolkovyj slovar' sovremennogo russkogo jazyka* [Explanatory dictionary of modern Russian language]. Moscow: Eksmo.

Machek, Václav. 1968. *Etymologický slovník jazyka českého* [Etymological dictionary of the Czech language]. Prague: Československá Akademie Věd.

MAS 1999 = *Slovar' russkogo jazyka v 4-x tomax (Malyj akademičeskij slovar')* [Dictionary of the Russian language in 4 volumes (Minor academic dictionary)], Evgen'eva (ed.). Moscow: Rus. jaz., Poligrafresursy.

Mączyński, Jan. 1564. *Lexicon Latino-Polonicum ex optimis Latinae linguae scriptoribus concinnatum*. Królewiec: Typographus Ioannes Daubmannus. https://www.wbc.poznan.pl/dlibra/publication/14839/edition/23849/content (accessed 5 February 2021).

Nikolskij, Boris M. 1999. O vos'mi častjax slova: problema istočnikov [On the eight parts of speech: the problem of sources]. In Natal'ja N. Zapolskaja (ed.), *Èvoljucija grammatičeskoj mysli slavjan XIV–XVIII vv.* [The evolution of grammatical thought of the Slavs in 14–18th centuries], 9–33. Moscow: Institut slavjanovedenija RAN.

Ohienko, Ivan (Metropolitan Ilarion). 1979–1994. *Etymolohično-semantyčnyj slovnyk ukrajins'koji movy* [Etymological and semantic dictionary of the Ukrainian language]. Winnipeg: Volyn.

Ozhegov, Sergey I. & Natalia YU. Shvedova. 2010: *Tolkovyj slovar' russkogo jazyka* [Explanatory dictionary of Russian language]. Moscow: Atberg.

Pfeifer, Wolfgang et al. 1993. *Etymologisches Wörterbuch des Deutschen*, digitalisierte und von Wolfgang Pfeifer überarbeitete Version im Digitalen Wörterbuch der deutschen Sprache, https://www.dwds.de/wb/etymwb/search?q=. (accessed 5 February 2021).

Polikarpov-Orlov, Fedor P. 1704. *Leksikon trejazyčnyj, sireč' rečenij slavjanskix, èllino-grečeskix i latinskix sokrovišč iz različnyx drevnix i novyx knig sobrannoe i po slavjanskomu alfavitu v čin raspoloženoe* [Trilingual lexicon, i.e. of Slavic, Hellenic-Greek and Latin treasures collected from various ancient and new books and arranged according to the Slavic alphabet]. Moscow: Tipografija carskaja.

Preobraženskij, Aleksandr G. 1910–1949. *Ètimologičeskij slovar' russkogo jazyka* [Etymological dictionary of the Russian language, in 3 vol.]. Moscow & Leningrad: Tipografija G. Lissnera i D. Sovko, Izd-vo Akademii nauk.
RBE 2001– = *Rečnik na bălgarskija ezik* [Dictionary of the Bulgarian language]. Sofia: Prof. Marin Drinov. https://ibl.bas.bg/rbe/ (accessed 5 February 2021).
Rejzek, Jiří. 2009. *Český etymologický slovník* [Czech etymological dictionary]. Praha: LEDA.
RSHKJ 1967–1976 = Mihailo Stevanović (ed.), *Rečnik srpskoxrvatskoga književnog jezika* [Dictionary of Serbo-Croatian literary language]. Novi Sad: Matica Srpska.
RSJ 2007 = Vujanić, Milica et. al. (eds.), *Rečnik srpskoga jezika* [Dictionary of Serbian language]. Novi Sad: Matica Srpska.
Rudnyc'kyj, Jaroslav B. 1962–1982. *Etymolohičnyj slovnyk ukrajins'koji movy*: u 2-x t. [Etymological dictionary of the Ukrainian Language: in 2 vols.]. Winnipeg & Ottawa: Ukrainain Mohylo-Mazepian Academy of Sciences. http://litopys.org.ua/djvu/rudnycky_slovnyk.htm (accessed 5 February 2021).
Sakhno, Serguei. 2010. *Les avatars du sens et de la fonction dans le phénomène de la grammaticalisation: Description systématique du lexème russe vrode 'dans le genre de' comparé à d'autres lexèmes russes grammaticalisés à fonctionnement proche*. Monographie inédite présentée en vue de l'obtention d'une habilitation à diriger des recherches. Nanterre, Université Paris Ouest.
Shaposhnikov, Alexander. K. 2010. *Ètimologičeskij slovar' sovremennogo russkogo jazyka*. [Etymological dictionary of the modern Russian language]. Moscow: Flinta, Nauka.
Skok, Petar. 1971–1973. *Etimologijski rječnik hrvatskoga ili srpskoga jezika* [Etymological dictionary of the Croatian or Serbian language]. Zagreb: Jugoslavenska akademija znanosti i umjetnosti.
Słownik staropolski [The dictionary of Old Polish]. https://pjs.ijp.pan.pl/sstp.html (accessed 5 February 2021).
Słownik warszawski: Słownik języka polskiego [Dictionary of Polish]. 1900–1927. J. Karłowicz, A. A. Kryński, W. Niedźwiedzki (eds.). Warszawa: drukarna Gazety Handlowej, drukarnia Współczesna.
Snoj, Marko. 2016. *Slovenski etimološki slovar*, [Slovenian etymological dictionary], 3rd ed. Ljubljana: Založba ZRC, ZRC SAZU.
Spronck, Stef. 2012. Minds divided, speaker attitudes in quotatives. In Isabelle Buchstaller & Ingrid Van Alphen (eds.), *Quotatives: Cross-linguistic and cross-disciplinary perspectives*, 71–116. Amsterdam: Benjamins.
Sreznevsky, Izmail I. 1893–1912. *Materialy dlja slovarja drevne-russkago jazyka po pis'mennym" pamjatnikam"* [Materials for the dictionary of the Old Russian language based on manuscripts]. Saint Petersburg: Imperatorskaja akademija nauk.
SRJ 11–17 vv. 1975– = *Slovar' russkogo jazyka XI–XVII vv.* [Dictionary of the Russian language of 11–17 c.] Moscow & St. Petersburg: Nauka, Nestor-Istoria. http://etymolog.ruslang.ru/index.php?act=xi-xvii (accessed 5 February 2021).
SRJ 18 v. 1984– = *Slovar' russkogo jazyka XVIII v.* [Dictionary of the Russian language of the 18th century]. Leningrad/St. Petersburg: Nauka.
SSJ 1959–1968 = *Slovník slovenského jazyka*. Š. Peciar (Ed.). [Dictionary of the Slovak language]. Bratislava: Vydavateľstvo SAV. https://www.juls.savba.sk/ssj_peciar.html (accessed 5 February 2021).

SSJČ 1960–1971 = *Slovník spisovného jazyka českého* [Dictionary of the standard Czech language]. http://www.ujc.cas.cz/elektronicke-slovniky-a-zdroje/Slovnik_spisovneho_jazyka_ceskeho.html (accessed 5 February 2021).

SSKJ 2014 = *Slovar slovenskega knjižnega jezika* [Dictionary of the Slovene Literary Language]. Ljubljana: Cankarjeva založba. https://fran.si/130/sskj-slovar-slovenskega-knjiznega-jezika (accessed 5 February 2021).

SSUM 14–15 st. 1977–1978 = *Slovnyk staroukrajins'koji movy XIV–XV st., u 2 t.* [Dictionary of the Old Ukrainian language of the XIV–XV centuries, in 2 vols.]. Kiev: Naukova dumka.

ŠRHJ = Matea Birtić, Goranka Blagus Bartolec, Lana Hudeček, Ljiljana Jojić, Barbara Kovačević, Kristian Lewis, Ivana Matas Ivanković, Milica Mihaljević, Irena Miloš, Ermina Ramadanović, Domagoj Vidović. *Školski rječnik hrvatskoga jezika* [School dictionary of the Croatian language]. https://rjecnik.hr (accessed 5 February 2021).

Šuba, Pavel. 1993. *Tlumačal'ny sloŭnik belaruskix prynazoŭnikaŭ* [Explanatory dictionary of Belarusian prepositions]. Minsk: Narodnaja asveta. http://slounik.org/prynaz/ (accessed 10 August 2021).

SUM 1970–1980 = *Slovnyk ukrajins'koji movy. Akademičnyj tlumačnyj slovnyk* [Dictionary of the Ukrainian language. Academic explanatory dictionary]. http://sum.in.ua (accessed 5 February 2021).

The dictionary of 17th and 1st half of 18th century Polish – the card index. https://www.rcin.org.pl/dlibra/publication/20029?language=en#structure (accessed 5 February 2021).

Thomson, Francis J. 1988/1989. The Bulgarian contribution to the reception of Byzantine culture in Kievan Rus': The myths and the enigma. *Harvard Ukrainian Studies* (12/13). 214–261.

TLFi = *Trésor de la Langue Française informatisé*. http://atilf.atilf.fr/tlf.htm. (accessed 5 February 2021).

Troc, Michał Abraham. 1779. *Nowy dykcyonarz to iest mownik polsko-niemiecko-francuski* [A new dictionary, i.e. Polish-German-French phrasebook]. Leipzig: Johann Friedrich Gleditsch.

TSBM = *Tlumačal'ny sloŭnik belaruskaj movy* [Explanatory dictionary of the Belarusian language] (rv-blr.com) https://verbum.by/rvblr (accessed 5 February 2021).

Ushakov, Dmitry N. 1939: *Tolkovyj slovar' russkogo jazyka v 4 t.* [The explanatory dictionary of the Russian language in 4 volumes]. Moscow: Gos. izd-vo inostr. i nac. slov.

Vasmer, Max. 1986–1987 [1950–1958]. *Ètimologičeskij slovar' russkogo jazyka*: v 4 t. [Etymological dictionary of the Russian language: in 4 vol.] (translated by O.N. Trubačev). Moscow: Progress.

Voghera, Miriam. 2013. A case study on the relationship between grammatical change and synchronic variation: the emergence of tipo[–N] in Italian. In Anna Giacalone Ramat, Caterina Mauri & Piera Molinelli (eds.), *Synchrony and Diachrony. A dynamic interface*, 283–312. Amsterdam: Benjamins.

Vološinov, Valentin N. 1973. *Marxism and the philosophy of language*. Translated by Ladislav Matejka & I. R. Titunik. New York & London: Seminar Press.

WSJP = *Wielki słownik języka polskiego* [The great dictionary of the Polish language]. https://wsjp.pl/index.php?pwh=0 (accessed 5 February 2021).

Xaburgaev, Georgij A. 1986. *Staroslavjanskij jazyk* [Old Church Slavonic]. Moscow: Prosveščenie.

Zubatý, Josef. 1918. *Naše řeč*, ročník 2 (1918), číslo 5. 131–140.

Corpora

BulNC = *Bulgarian National Corpus*. https://dcl.bas.bg/bulnc/ (accessed 5 February 2021).
Cvrček, V., Vondřička, P.: SyD. 2011. Korpusový průzkum variant. Charles University in Prague. http://syd.korpus.cz (accessed 5 February 2021).
Korba = Elektroniczny korpus tekstów polskich z XVII i XVIII w. (do 1772 r.) [On-line corpus of Polish 17th and 18th century tekst (until 1772)]. https://korba.edu.pl/query_corpus/ (accessed 5 February 2021).
NCP = *Narodowy Korpus Języka Polskiego* [National Corpus of Polish]. http://nkjp.pl/ (accessed 5 February 2021).
ORAL = *Czech National Corpus* – ORAL v.1. Institute of the Czech National Corpus, Prague. http://www.korpus.cz (accessed 5 February 2021).
RBCorpus = *Korpus parallel'nyx russkix i bolgarskix tekstov* [Corpus of parallel Russian and Bulgarian texts]. http://rbcorpus.com/opisanie_rus.php (accessed 5 February 2021).
Riznica = *The Croatian Language Corpus*. Institute of Croatian Language and Linguistics. http://riznica.ihjj.hr (accessed 5 February 2021).
RNC = *Russian National Corpus*. https://ruscorpora.ru/new/en/index.html (accessed 5 February 2021).
SYN7 = *Czech National Corpus* – SYN v.7. Institute of the Czech National Corpus, Prague. http://www.korpus.cz (accessed 5 February 2021).

Anna Kisiel & Alena Kolyaseva

13 Towards a comprehensive typology of type noun constructions in Slavic languages, with a special focus on Polish and Russian

Abstract: This chapter proposes a typology of lexical and grammaticalized uses of the two major TNs in Polish and Russian: *typ/tip* 'type' and *rodzaj/rod* 'kind'. The classification is built on similarities and differences between the meanings, usages and collostructional requirements of the two items within each language, as well as between the counterparts in both languages. The final proposal aims at showing that two languages from one language group can be alike in terms of constructions with TNs in their nominal uses and differ greatly in their non-representational meanings. The analysis is based on examples extracted from the Polish and Russian national corpora, confronted with analogous contexts in Ukrainian and Bulgarian. The classification intends to be generic and specific at the same time: by presenting a range of constructions with TNs and the results of their grammaticalization, the article attempts to offer a typology of possible TN uses and their developments in present-day Slavic languages.

1 Introduction

The broad range of functions discussed in various typologies of constructions formed by taxonomic nouns (TNs) in Romance and Germanic languages includes a number of disparate uses, such as quotative marker, approximator (Mihatsch 2016), quantifier (Mihatsch 2016; Davidse et al. 2013), nominal qualifier (Davidse et al. 2013), attributive modifier (De Smedt, Brems, and Davidse 2007), complex determiner (Denison 2005) and discourse markers that convey a speaker's attitude or support speaker-hearer interaction (Aijmer 2002: 175–209).

Although Slavic TNs have not enjoyed the same level of scholarly attention as their English, French, Italian, Spanish and Portuguese counterparts, most of such functions can also be observed in Slavic languages, in some more than in others. Perhaps, the most evident and well-discussed example is Russian *tipa* 'like, sort

---

Anna Kisiel, KU Leuven, e-mail: anna.kisiel@kuleuven.be
Alena Kolyaseva, KU Leuven, e-mail: alena.kolyaseva@kuleuven.be

of' (< tip-a$_{GEN.SG}$, lit. 'of the type'), whose ongoing grammaticalization and active expansion in oral discourse was first signalled in Lapteva (1983). In particular, its new function as a quotative or a marker of reported speech has been commented upon in multiple crosslinguistic overviews (Foolen 2008; Buchstaller 2014; Wiemer 2011) and specifically discussed in Daiber (2010), Spronck (2016) and Kolyaseva (2018). Additionally, Russian *vrode* 'like, kind of' (< v rod-e$_{PRP.SG}$, lit. 'in the kind of') has been the subject of two (post)doctoral theses (Semenova 2000; Sakhno 2010). In contrast, Polish has been rather neglected. Apart from Kisiel (this volume, chapter 14) and two articles on derivative predicates (Bartmiński 2001; Maryn-Stachurska 2011) no research has been done in the field of TNs and their constructions.

To our knowledge, the first comparative examination involving Slavic items was undertaken in Janebová and Martinková (2017) on Czech translations of English TNs. The fact that Slavic languages have entered crosslinguistic discussion to such a small extent is disappointing as they feature TN-derived items that are not registered in other languages, such as 'quasi'-uses of *tipa* in Russian (Kolyaseva 2018) or the use of Russian *vrode* in (implied) adversative constructions, the function labelled in Sakhno (2010: 113) as "prise en compte d'une incompatibilité" [taking an incompatibility into account]. This paper is an attempt to offer a comprehensive typology of possible uses of TNs in present-day Slavic languages, with a focus on Polish and Russian, by presenting a range of TN constructions and the results of their grammaticalization. We believe that such a description is an important contribution to the ongoing discussion of the crosslinguistic phenomenon, since most Slavic languages are typologically different from those that have been widely discussed in this regard. When it comes to the nominal phrase, Slavic languages are highly synthetic (except for the Eastern South subgroup), as opposed to the analytical English and modern Romance languages. They have preserved a strong case system and have not developed articles (except for Bulgarian and Macedonian). The fact that these languages express syntactic relationships by other means makes Slavic TN constructions particularly interesting to consider.

The material in this chapter is organized following a reanalysed typology of lexical and grammaticalized uses of TNs in Russian (Kolyaseva and Davidse [2016] 2018), with an aim to integrate other available accounts of the grammaticalized items into a holistic picture. The classification proposed in this article intends to be generic and specific at the same time, providing a fine-grained description of the primary TNs: Polish *typ* and Russian *tip* 'type', Polish *rodzaj* and Russian *rod* 'kind'. It is formed on the basis of similarities and differences between the meanings and usages of Polish *typ* and *rodzaj* and Russian *tip* and *rod*, as well as between the counterparts in each language. The final proposal aims to demonstrate how two languages from one language group can be alike in terms of nominal uses of TN constructions and yet differ greatly in their non-representational meanings. The analysis is based on examples extracted from the Polish and Russian national corpora, and in some cases corroborated with analogous contexts in Ukrainian and Bulgarian.[1]

By providing a comprehensive overview embracing the major possible uses of the primary TNs, the presented typology aims to illuminate the range of possibilities for TN development in Slavic to date. However, some uses can stay inactive in certain Slavic languages as, for example, particle uses do in Polish (Section 4.3). Some meanings or functions that are shared by most (if not all) Slavic languages might be performed by different TNs. For example, the items based on the root *rod-* are present in all Slavic languages but only in some, like in Russian and Polish, do they develop the general taxonomic meaning 'kind'. In others, they are used only in the 'family' meaning or as terms (e.g. referring to grammatical gender, voice, or genus), while the general taxonomic meaning is conveyed by other linguistic items (see Janebová and Martinkova, this volume, chapter 15, on Czech *druh*). Due to the limitations of this study, we do not report on developments specific to other Slavic languages that are not examined in this paper.

2 Non-taxonomic meanings: typ_{0A}/tip_{0A}, typ_{0B}, $rodzaj_{0A}/rod_{0A}$, $ród_{0B}/rod_{0B}$

Apart from the taxonomic meanings that are at the centre of our interest here, *typ/tip* and *rodzaj/rod* also have several other meanings. For the sake of clarity, they need to be identified at this early stage of classification and will subsequently not be considered in the chapter.

The semantic specificity of non-taxonomic *typ/tip* and *rodzaj/rod* correlates with certain grammatical features and collocational preferences. For example, typ_{0A}/tip_{0A}[2] 'a guy, a fellow' referring to a man (especially one who is odd, dangerous or of undesirable qualities) takes adjectives consistent with a negative picture of the person it evokes, such as Polish *dziwny, groźny, masywny typ* 'weird, grim, bulky

---

[1] We are grateful to our informers, native speakers of Ukrainian and Bulgarian, Roman Tymoshuk, Yurij Ganoshenko and Steliana Aleksandrova for their critical read and comments on an earlier version of this paper.

[2] The subscript numbers and letters should be interpreted as follows: the numbers mark separate meanings, starting with 0 for the uses that are not further considered in this paper (non-taxonomic and terminological) and 1 for taxonomic uses that are analysed in more detail; the letters mark semantic variation within a group of meanings (in the case of non-taxonomic meanings) or syntacto-collocational variation within one meaning (in the case of taxonomic meanings).

type', Russian *podozritel'nyj, zlovrednyj, grubyj tip* 'suspicious, malicious, rude type'. Though combinations with adjectives with more positive semantics can be observed both in Russian and in Polish (as in (1)), such contexts concern rather the person's oddity than the speaker's approval of their behaviour. This specific meaning manifests in Slavic languages grammatically, reflecting the distinction between animate and inanimate nouns. In line with a widely accepted understanding of a semantically driven distribution of case endings among masculine nouns (cf. Orzechowska 1998), most Polish animate nouns receive the *-a* ending in the genitive (*nauczyciela* 'teacher$_{GEN}$', *kota* 'cat$_{GEN}$'), while abstract and collective nouns take a less frequent *-u* (see *strachu* 'fear$_{GEN}$' and *lasu* 'forest$_{GEN}$' respectively), as in example (2). Russian does not distinguish between typ$_{OA}$ and typ$_I$ in the genitive (both take the *-a* ending), but the difference concerns the accusative: animate nouns in 1st declension take the accusative form that coincides with the genitive (*konja* 'horse$_{ACC=GEN}$', *stroitelja* 'builder$_{ACC=GEN}$'), while inanimate nouns of the same declension type take the accusative form that coincides with the nominative (*stol* 'table$_{ACC=NOM}$', *nož* 'knife$_{ACC=NOM}$'), as in example (3). Such case syncretism as a manifestation of the grammatical category of animacy is characteristic of all Slavic languages that have retained the case system. Also note that unlike the taxonomic meanings, *typ$_{OA}$/tip$_{OA}$* are semantically complete and do not require a genitival complement (vs. *typ jabłek* 'type of apples' in (2) or *tip razvitija* 'type of development' in (3)).

(1) Rus. *Èto on zvonil ej nasčet Niki...*
it he-NOM call-PST.M.SG she-DAT about Nika-GEN.F.SG
Kakoj **interesnyj** **tip...**
what-NOM.M.SG interesting-NOM.M.SG type-NOM.M.SG
'It was him who gave her a call about Nika . . . What an **interesting type**'.

(2) Pol. *Jonagold? Nie lubię tego* **typu**
jonagold-NOM not like-PRS.1SG this-GEN.M.SG type-GEN.M.SG
[jabłek].
apple-GEN.PL
vs.
Nie lubię tego **typa.**[3]
not like-PRS.1SG this-GEN.M.SG type-GEN.M.SG
'Jonagold? I don't like this **type** [of apple].' – 'I don't like this **guy**.'

---

[3] Constructed examples are based on the sentences from *The National Corpus of Polish* and *Russian National Corpus*, unless otherwise stated; they have been modified (mainly shortened) to emphasize the point under discussion.

(3) Rus. *Začem, — govorit, — Egorov, ty privël*
why say-PRS.1SG Egorov-NOM.M.SG you-NOM bring-PST.M.SG
s soboj ètogo **tipa?**
with self-INS this-ACC.M.SG type-ACC.M.SG
vs.
. . . opredelit' **tip** *razvitija strany*
define-INF type-ACC.M.SG development-GEN.N.SG country-GEN.F.SG
'Yegorov, he says, why have you brought this **guy** with you?!' – '. . . to define the **type of** country's **development**'

Specific collocational preferences are also characteristic of another Polish *typ*_{OB} 'choice', which only allows possessive pronouns (see (4)) or, less often, a noun (especially a proper noun) in the genitive (see (5)) referring to a possessor. Interestingly, even though such a use of *typ* does not allow for a noun in the genitive pointing to the group from which the choice is being made, the derivative verb *typować kogoś na coś/do czegoś* 'to bet, to choose' (lit. choose_{INF} someone_{ACC} for something_{ACC}/to do something_{GEN}) opens a slot for exactly such a noun.

(4) Pol. *Jakie są wasze ulubione*
how-NOM.PL be-PRS.3PL your-NOM.PL favourite-NOM.PL
piosenki traktujące o tym uczuciu?
song-NOM.PL treat-P.ACT-NOM.PL about this-LOC.N.SG feeling-LOC.N.SG
Moje typy *na dzisiaj:* Bob Marley- Waiting In Vain
my-NOM.PL type-NOM.PL for today-ACC.M.SG Bob Marley- Waiting In Vain
(no, ba), Julian Marley- Rock With Me (. . .)
well Julian Marley- Rock With Me
'What are your favourite songs about this feeling? **My choice** for today is: Bob Marley. . .'

(5) Pol. *Jeżeli chodzi o* **typy** *pana*
if be.about-PRS.3SG type-ACC.PL mister-GEN.M.SG
Tomasza, to przedstawiają się następująco:
Tomasz-GEN.M.SG then present-PRS.3PL self following-ADV
piłkarze – 1. Radosław Sobolewski,
footballer-NOM.PL 1. Radosław Sobolewski-NOM.SG
2. *Mauro Cantoro (. . .)*
2. Mauro Cantoro (. . .)-NOM.SG
'As for the **choices** of Mr. Tomasz, they are as follows: footballers 1. Radosław Sobolewski, 2. Mauro Cantoro (. . .)'

Finally, the meanings of Polish *rodzaj*$_{OA}$, Russian *rod*$_{OA}$, Czech *rod*$_{OA}$, Ukrainian *rid*$_{OA}$ etc. referring to grammatical gender, voice, literary genre or biological genus (all with very limited collocational options) are excluded from further analysis regardless of their clear taxonomic meaning, as terminology is not in the scope of this paper. Interestingly, in Polish, there is interplay between this terminological meaning and infrequent uses of *rodzaj* as a synonym of 'sex' (6) or even 'a family' (7) – a meaning that has been mainly preserved in infrequent and obsolete *ród* 'a kin, a family', as in grammaticalized *ród kobiecy* 'female race' (lit. kin$_{NOM.M}$ female$_{NOM.M}$), *ród męski* 'male race' (lit. kin$_{NOM}$ male$_{NOM.M}$), and *ród człowieczy* 'human race' (lit. kin$_{NOM}$ human$_{NOM.M}$).[4] By contrast, with Russian *rod* the 'kin' meaning has not been lost, though it is most commonly used in contexts referring to realia of the past and not so frequently in those referring to the present day. In dictionaries, *rod*$_{OB}$ is presented as a separate, homonymous lexeme, and furthermore, it differs from *rod*$_1$ 'kind' (as well as from the terminological meanings) paradigmatically. *Rod*$_{OB}$ allows forms of the locative and partitive cases ending in -*u*,[5] which are characteristic of only a small number of Russian nouns. These forms stand in contrast to the -*e* ending of the genitive and prepositional case forms used in the same contexts for other nouns: consider *v moëm rodu* 'in my family$_{LOC}$, in my kin$_{LOC}$' vs. *v ètom rode dejatel'nosti* 'in this type$_{PRP}$ of occupation' and *15 let ot rodu* '15 years-old' (lit. '15 years from birth$_{PRT}$') vs. *nezavisimo ot roda dejatel'nosti* 'irrespective of the type$_{GEN}$ of occupation'.[6] As such, Russian *rod* does not normally refer to females or males, but it can be employed stylistically in this meaning, as in (8), similar to Polish (6). This use is analogical to the stabilized collocation *čelovečeskij rod* 'humankind' that invokes the original 'kinship' meaning; see also the creative use of *rod* in (9).

---

4 Similar uses to (7) are registered in *The Dictionary of 16th century Polish* but are nowadays only present in spoken language and seem to be stylistically marked.
5 Remnants of the *-ŭ stem declension type that merged in Old East Slavic with the *-ŏ stem declension type. As *-u in the partitive and the locative are not productive, their lack in taxonomic *rod* and their presence in *rod*$_{OB}$ indicates that the former appeared later (see Kolyaseva and Kisiel, this volume, chapter 12, for the timeline).
6 To avoid terminological confusion, we gloss prepositional case as PRP, reserving PREP for 'preposition'.

(6) Pol. *To   był   bardzo   trendowy   człowiek*
         it   be-PST.3SG   very   trendy-NOM.M.SG   person-NOM.M.SG
    rodzaju   żeńskiego.
    kind-GEN.M.SG female-GEN.M.SG
    'That was a very trendy person of **female gender**.'

(7) Pol. *Jednej   nieuczciwości   opisanej   w*
         one-ACC.F.SG   dishonesty-ACC.SG   describe-PASS.PTCP.F   in
    pani   liście   nie warto   chyba   rozciągać
    your-POLITE-LOC.F.SG   letter-LOC.F.SG   not worth   perhaps   extend-INF
    *na   cały   **rodzaj   kobiecy**?*
    on   whole-ACC.M.SG kind-ACC.M.SG   female-ACC.M.SG
    'One example of dishonesty that you describe in your letter should perhaps not be extended on the whole **female kind**?'

(8) Rus. *Ves'   **ženskij   rod**   zadoxnulsja:*
         entire-NOM.M.SG female-NOM.M.SG   kind-NOM.M.SG   choke-PST.M.SG
    vybiraj   ljubuju!
    chose-IMP.SG any-ACC.F.SG
    'The whole **female kind** held its breath: choose any!'

(9) Rus. *Maks   sdvinul   s   mërtvoj   točki*
         Max-NOM.M.SG   move-PST.M.SG   from   dead-GEN.F.SG   point-GEN.F.SG
    *ves'   svoj   **obez'janij   rod***
    entire-ACC.M.SG   one's.own-ACC.M.SG   monkey-ADJ.ACC.M.SG   kind-ACC.M.SG
    'Max has moved his whole **monkey race** from the dead point'

After excluding these non-taxonomic meanings from further consideration, we proceed to a typology of the uses of TNs in the following sections. We first describe constructions in which TNs retain their nominal grammatical features. As we show, there are nominal constructions that are free and fully compositional, but there are also structures that are either semi-fixed or lexicalized, in which the original lexical meaning of the TN has been bleached or altered. We then proceed to discuss grammaticalized items that have lost nominal properties and have been reanalysed as functional linguistic items serving grammatical or communicative, pragmatic, functions.

3 Nominal constructions

Nominal constructions are those constructions in which the TNs *typ/tip* and *rodzaj/rod* have not lost their nominal properties and have (to varying degrees) retained their taxonomic meaning. We distinguish between two types of nominal constructions: head and modifier uses. These are distinguished by the syntactic role of the TN in relation to the superordinate word – as its grammatical head (i.e. [head: TN + [complement: N_{GEN}]]) or its modifier ([head: N + [modifier: Adj_{GEN} + TN_{GEN}]] or [head: N/Adj/V + [modifier: w/v + $Adj_{LOC/PRP}$ + $TN_{LOC/PRP}$]][7]). Among head uses, the qualifier use is of particular interest. Unlike English qualifier constructions which are no longer considered binominal (Denison 2002; Keizer 2007), from the syntactic point of view Slavic TNs are regarded as the head of qualifier constructions. This is evident from the direction of case governance, even though semantically the TNs' meaning has shifted towards a rather secondary role. The modifier uses are subdivided into genitival modifier constructions and constructions with an adpositional phrase containing one of the TNs. Interestingly, the adpositional phrases with TNs are limited in terms of their collocability, and the most frequent of them are considered as semi-fixed modifiers, raising the question as to whether they have lexicalized. Overall, nominal constructions are the most similar among the analysed languages, and we expect most Slavic languages to follow the pattern presented here.

3.1 Head uses: typ_{1A}/tip_{1A} and $rodzaj_1/rod_1$ versus typ_{1B}/tip_{1B}; typ_{1C}

The starting point of the classification presented in this paper are head uses of *typ/tip* and *rodzaj/rod* with a general taxonomic meaning. In such uses they open a right-hand slot for a genitive complement (singular or plural). In the left-hand slot they allow for both qualifying (10)–(11) and classifying modifiers (12)–(13) as well as numerals (14)–(15). Note that by head use, we mean that a TN is a head of a complement N_{GEN} referring to a superordinate notion, e.g. *typ instalacji* 'type of installation', *tip gosudarstva* 'type of state'. The NP TN+N_{GEN} can, of course, form part of a larger NP. For instance, in (14)–(15) it complements the numeral *dwa/dva* 'two'.

---

[7] As discussed in the corresponding section, this construction is strictly adnominal in Polish.

(10) Pol. *W budynku   przy   Młynarskiej   jest*
     in building-LOC.M.SG next.to Młynarska-LOC.F.SG be-PRS.3SG
     *jeszcze stary   **typ**   instalacji*
     still   old-NOM.M.SG type-NOM.M.SG installation-GEN.F.SG
     gazowej.
     gas-ADJ.GEN.F.SG
     'In the building at Młynarska St. there is still the **old type of gas installation**.'

(11) Pol. *Powstał   tam   jakoby   **nowy***
     come.into.exsitence-PST.M.3SG there supposedly new-NOM.M.SG
     ***rodzaj**   kukurydzy   czy może   koniczyny?*
     kind-NOM.M.SG corn-GEN.F.SG or   maybe clover-GEN.F.SG
     'They apparently created **a new kind of corn** or perhaps clover?'

(12) Pol. *Trudno   o   bardziej **klasyczny**   **typ***
     hard-ADV about more   classic-ACC.M.SG type-ACC.M.SG
     ***przestępstwa**   o   charakterze   terrorystycznym.*
     crime-GEN.N.SG about character-LOC.M.SG terrorist-ADJ-LOC.M.SG
     'It is hard to think of a more **classic type of crime** of a terrorist nature.'

(13) Rus. *Èto samyj   dešëvyj   i   samyj*
     it   the.most-NOM.M.SG cheap-NOM.M.SG and the.most-NOM.M.SG
     ***nizmennyj**   rod   original'nosti.*
     low-NOM.M.SG kind-NOM.M.SG originality-GEN.F.SG
     'This is the cheapest and **lowest kind of originality**'.

(14) Rus. *Nesmotrja na istoričeskuju   molodost'   svetskogo*
     despite   hictoric-ACC.F.SG youth-ACC.F.SG secular-GEN.N.SG
     gosudarstva,   možno   vydelit'   kak minimum dva
     state-GEN.N.SG possible-PRED distinguish-INF as.minimum   two-ACC.M
     ego   tipa.   Pervyj   tip -
     it-GEN.N.SG type-GEN.M.SG first-NOM.M.SG type-NOM.M.SG
     *vnekonfessional'noe   gosudarstvo,   **vtoroj -***
     non-confessional-NOM.N.SG state-NOM.N.SG second-NOM.M.SG
     ateističeskoe   gosudarstvo.
     atheistic-NOM.N.SG state-NOM.N.SG
     'Despite the secular state being historically young, at least **two types** can be distinguished. **The first type** is a non-confessional state, **the second** is an atheistic state'.

(15) Pol. *Co   nasuwało   słuszne   podejrzenie,*
         what   draw-PST.N.3SG right-ADJ.ACC.N.SG suspicion-ACC.N.SG
     *że   Andersen   znał   **dwa   rodzaje***
     that Andersen-NOM.M know-PST.M.3SG two-ACC   kind-ACC.PL
     podróży.   Pierwszy   rodzaj   *zmuszał   go*
     travel-GEN.F.SG first-NOM.M.SG kind-NOM.M.SG force-PST.M.3SG   he-ACC
     do   szerokiego   otwierania   oczu.
     to   wide-GEN.N.SG open-GRD-GEN.N.SG   eye-GEN.PL
     'What is open to conjecture is that Andersen knew **two kinds of travel. The first kind** made him open his eyes wide.'

Interestingly, *typ/tip* and *rodzaj/rod* do not show clear differences here. However, their different origins can sometimes motivate the prioritization of one above the other in certain contexts. *Typ/tip* is a borrowing and shares its Greek (via Latin) origin with its equivalents in other languages, whereas *rod-* (in *rodzaj/rod*) is an inherited root present in the whole Slavic world.[8] Even though in present-day Polish and Russian, the taxonomic uses of *typ/tip* and *rodzaj/rod* are semantically very similar, they take a different angle when presenting the same thing – *typ/tip* points to a group of objects sharing a certain feature (or features) and therefore being different from other groups, while *rodzaj/rod* emphasizes family resemblance, the fact that all objects in the group are in some way similar. For this reason, *rodzaj/rod* can be used when the resemblance is questioned (as in Polish *dziwny rodzaj posiłku* 'a strange$_{\text{NOM.M.SG}}$ kind$_{\text{NOM.M.SG}}$ of meal $_{\text{GEN.M}}$', *niecodzienny rodzaj zabawy* 'unusual$_{\text{NOM.M.SG}}$ kind$_{\text{NOM.M.SG}}$ of fun$_{\text{GEN.M}}$', Russian *strannyj rod op'janenija* 'strange$_{\text{NOM.M.SG}}$ kind$_{\text{NOM.M.SG}}$ of drunkenness$_{\text{GEN.N.SG}}$') or when talking about a subgroup that while preserving all the features of the main group adds a new feature (Polish *motywujący rodzaj strachu* 'motivating$_{\text{NOM.M.SG}}$ kind $_{\text{NOM.M.SG}}$ of fear$_{\text{GEN.M}}$' is as much fear as other kinds of fear but has a new, motivational, function). However, full semantic adjectives do not typically premodify *rodzaj/rod*, which prefers adjectives with pronominal semantics or no modifiers at all. By contrast, *typ/tip*, invoking classification, naturally combines with adjectives which specify the type.

The comparison of nominal head constructions in Russian in Kolyaseva (2021b) revealed that they are not as typical for *rod* as they are for *tip*. While *tip* has the collocational potential to be combined with any N2, *rod* is often found in fixed collocations such as *rod vojsk* ('type of army$_{\text{GEN}}$'), *rod dejatel'nosti* ('occupation', lit. 'kind of activity$_{\text{GEN}}$'), etc. Due to the semantic persistence of its base

---

8 As pointed out by the reviewer of this paper, it has cognates also in non-Slavic languages, cf. *rod-* < PSl. **rod-* < PIE. **H̯erdh-* (the same root is in: Gr. *orthós*, San. *várdhati* etc.).

meaning invoking origin, *rod* is associated with the meaning 'nature or character of something'. However, in certain contexts this distinction between the two nouns is obscured, e.g. *tip* could be substituted for *rod* in (16).

(16) Rus. *Rassmotrim* **tri** **roda** **tekstov:**
Consider-IMP.1PL three-ACC kind-GEN.M.SG text-GEN.PL
primer v naučnom izloženii,
example-NOM.M.SG in scientific-PRP.N.SG narration-PRP.N.SG
pritču v religioznom tekste i
parable-ACC.F.SG in religious-PRP.M.SG text-PRP.M.SG and
basnju.
fable-ACC.F.SG
'Consider **three kinds of texts**: an illustration in a scientific text, a parable in a religious text, and a fable.'

For *typ/tip*, we also register another meaning (*typ/tip*$_{1B}$), 'a character (mainly literary) embodying characteristic features of some group of people' (Evgen'eva 1999), e.g. *tip krest'janina* 'the peasant type' (lit. 'type peasant$_{GEN.SG}$') or *gamletovskij tip* 'Hamlet type', or *don-kixotovskij tip ljudej* 'Don Quixote type of people', as in (17–18). With this meaning, Polish *typ* takes a postmodifier pointing to the type of art the character performs in, to his/her function in the story or its creator. In some cases, such uses of Polish *typ* can be transformed into binominal constructions (*allenowski typ bohatera* 'Allen-like type of character'), which are standard in Russian and Ukrainian (18). However, in most cases such transformation in Polish results in a change of meaning (for example *typ kobiecy* 'a female character' vs *kobiecy typ postaci* 'feminine type of character'; *typ komiczny* 'a comic character' vs *komiczny typ postaci* 'comical type of character'). The postposition of the modifier suggests its classifying nature, as postposition in Polish is reserved for classifying adjectives.

(17) Pol. *Jego postać to tak zwany* **typ**
his character-NOM.M.SG it so.called-NOM.M.SG type-NOM.M.SG
allenowski, *zdziwaczały, neurotyczny*
Allen-ADJ.NOM.M.SG eccentric-NOM.M.SG neurotic-NOM.M.SG
introwertyk z ironicznym poczuciem humoru.
introvert-NOM.M.SG with ironic-INS.N.SG sense-INS.N.SG humor-GEN.M.SG
'His character is a so-called **Woody Allen type**, an eccentric, neurotic introvert having an ironic sense of humour.'
(https://www.dawne.teatralia.com.pl/ideal-realnym-swiecie-ruby/, accessed 23 April, 2020)

(18) Rus. *No imponiroval emu imenno ètot,*
     but attract-PST.M.SG he-DAT precisely this-NOM.M.SG
     don-kixotovskij tip ljudej.
     Don.Quixote-ADJ.NOM.M.SG type-NOM.M.SG people-GEN.PL
     'But he liked precisely this, **Don Quixote type of people**.'

At the same time, *typ*$_{1B}$ can bring a parallel characteristic to non-fictional objects, pointing to race (Polish *typ nordycki* 'Nordic race', Russian *vostočnyj tip lica* 'oriental type of face', *sredizemnomorskij tip* 'Mediterranean type') or origin (Polish *typ południowy* 'Southern type'), social characteristics (Russian *krest'janskij tip* 'peasant type'), and temperament (Polish *typ choleryczny* 'choleric type', Russian *melanxoličeskij tip* 'melancholic type'). Many such uses in Polish seem to be stabilizing as labels, as they obtain a classifying sense due to the postposition of the adjective.

Even though the classifying adjectival modifier is more naturally postposed in Polish, it can also be placed before *typ*. In neither of the cases can *typ*$_{1B}$ take a N$_{GEN}$ complement referring to humans. There is, in fact, only one expression with these adjectives that follows the pattern given at the beginning of this section: *nordycki/południowy typ urody* 'Nordic/southern type of beauty' (similar to *mieszany typ skóry* 'combination skin' lit. 'mixed type of skin'). Also, in this usage Polish *typ* can never appear in the plural. Regardless of these grammatical and collocational differences, *typ*$_{1B}$ should be considered a specialized usage of *typ*$_1$ rather than a new linguistic entity. The difference between *typ*$_{1B}$ and *typ*$_{1A}$ results from the difference in character of the accompanying modifier rather than from changes to *typ* itself.

Finally, *typ*$_{1C}$ appears in the construction *typ*$_{1C}$ + N$_{GEN}$ in contexts such as Polish *typ ofiary* 'of a victim mentality' (lit. type$_{NOM.M.SG}$ victim$_{GEN.F}$) and can be considered another special case of the characterization of a human object. Similarly to *typ*$_{1B}$, *typ*$_{1C}$ cannot take plural forms. The order of the elements of the construction is fixed and the only modifier that can be added to it is a qualifying adjective. This brings us to the essence of *typ*$_{1C}$: it is the special nature of N$_{GEN}$ that leads to the characterization of the object in such a construction. The N$_{GEN}$ here should not be identified with the N$_{GEN}$ in structures like (10)–(15), where it rather has a function of a hypernym and where the adjectival element differentiates the object in question from other objects that could be included in the class defined by that hypernym. For example, in (10), what can be found in the building at Młynarska street is a gas installation and what distinguishes it from other gas installations is that it is old (see also (19)). If, on the other hand, we say that someone is *typ ofiary/naukowca/społecznika* etc. 'has a victim/scientist/social worker etc. mentality', we do not include this person in the class of victims (*ofiara*), scientists (*naukowiec*) or social workers (*społecznik*) but rather point to a certain resemblance between this person's behaviour and the (stereo)typical behaviour of objects included in the class. In other words, we say that this person has certain (probably even definitional) features of a member of a certain group without really being a member of the group, as in (20).

(19) Pol. *Terroryzm to typ przestępstwa.*
terrorism-NOM.SG it type-NOM.M.SG crime-GEN.N.SG
vs
Są różne typy przestępstw,
be-PRS.3PL various-NOM.PL type-NOM.PL crime-GEN.N.PL
terroryzm to jeden z nich.
terrorism-NOM.M.SG it one-NOM.M.SG from they-GEN
'Terrorism is a type of crime. – There are various types of crimes, terrorism is one of them.'

(20) Pol. *Janusz to typ ofiary.*
Janusz-NOM.M it type-NOM.M.SG victim-GEN.F.SG
vs
**Są różne typy ofiar,*
be-PRS.3PL various-NOM.PL type-NOM.PL victim-GEN.PL
Janusz to jeden z nich.
Janusz-NOM.M.SG it one-NOM.M.SG from they-GEN
'Janusz has a victim mentality. – *There are various types of victims, Janusz is one of them.'

3.2 Head use as nominal qualifier: rodzaj$_1$/rod$_1$

Rodzaj/rod in its head use can function as a qualifier, which seems to stem from its prototypical meaning that emphasizes origin. As mentioned in the previous section, due to this meaning, *rodzaj$_1$/rod$_1$* can be used to question the degree of a family resemblance, and thus indicate that the speaker is not completely confident in defining certain phenomena or objects the way they do. For instance, in (21), the speaker does not mean to say that there is a typology of constitutions, with the law in question representing one of the types. By contrast, it is evident that in the speaker's opinion the document in question does not completely qualify as a constitution, but they could not come up with a better definition (perhaps, for the lack of a more appropriate notion), and *constitution* is used because it is what this decree resembles the most.

(21) Rus. *Ešče ran'še, 19 marta 1918*
yet earlier 19th-GEN.M.SG March-GEN.M.SG 1918th-GEN.M.SG
goda byl prinjat (...) **rod**
year-GEN.M.SG be-PST.M.SG pass-PTCP.M.SG kind-NOM.M.SG
konstitucii *pod skromnym (...) nazvaniem*
constitution-GEN.F.SG under modest-INS.N.SG title-INS.N.SG
« Osnovnoj zakon ob organizacii
main-NOM.M.SG law-NOM.M.SG about organization-PRP.F.SG
Sovetskoj vlasti v g. El'ce i
Soviet-GEN.F.SG authority-GEN.F.SG in Yelets-PRP.M.SG and
Eleckom uezde ».
Yelets-ADJ.PRP.M.SG county-PRP.M.SG
'Even earlier, on March 19, 1918, **a kind of constitution** under the modest (...) title 'The Main Law on the Organization of Soviet Authority in the Town of Yelets and the Yelets County' was adopted'.

Polish *rodzaj* in this function is often correlated with vagueness modifiers *pewien* 'a', *jakiś* 'a, some', see (22), which reinforce the reading 'I am not quite sure if this thing (you know what I am talking about) can be called this'. As expected, taxonomic typ_1/tip_1 which implies inherent classification is not used in such hedging contexts. We can imagine a dialogue such as that in (23), but we would expect speaker B to provide a differentiating characteristic (e.g. . . . *który nie jest już używany* '. . . that is no longer in use') to specify the type. However, if the speaker (B) wished to use a vague rather than a classifying description, B should use $rodzaj_1/rod_1$ instead.

(22) Pol. *Przyjaźń to w końcu też* **jakiś**
friendship-NOM.F.SG it in.the.end also some-ADJ.NOM.M.SG
rodzaj miłości, *ale pozbawionej*
kind-NOM.M.SG love-GEN.F.SG but deprive-PASS.PTCP.GEN.F.SG
podtekstów seksualnych.
innuendo-GEN.PL sexual-GEN.PL
'In the end, friendship is also a **kind of love** but without sexual innuendo.'

(23) Pol. A: *Co to jest?*
what it be-PRS.3SG
B: *To* **taki** *typ instalacji*
it such-NOM.M.SG type-NOM.M.SG installation-GEN.F.SG
gazowej.
gas-ADJ-GEN.F.SG
'A: What is this? B: It is **a certain type of gas installation**.'

3.3 Genitival modifier with an adjective: typu/tipa versus rodzaju/roda

The base taxonomic constructions with typ_1/tip and $rodzaj_1/rod_1$ can be transformed into constructions in which the hypernym acts as a head and the taxonomic noun is used in the genitive as a modifier, for example, Polish *instalacja gazowa starego typu* 'gas installation of an old type' for (10) or Russian *originalnost' samogo nizmennogo roda* 'originality of the cheapest kind' for (13). Note that it is a composite adnominal modifier, consisting of the genitival form of a TN which is in its turn modified by an agreeing adjective: $N + [Adj_{GEN.M} + TN_{GEN}]$. These uses are very similar in Polish and Russian, except for one disparity related to structural characteristics of the languages. In Polish, classifying adjectives can also take the position after *typu*, e.g. *poezja klasycznego typu – poezja typu klasycznego* 'a classical type of poetry'. Russian does not distinguish syntactically between classifying and qualitative adjectives, and adjectival postmodification does not occur: *èkonomika sovetskogo tipa* 'Soviet type of economy' is possible but not **èkonomika tipa sovetskogo* (Kolyaseva and Davidse 2018). However, as the inflectional nature of the language allows for a relatively free word order, the entire modifier string $Adj_{GEN.m} + TN_{GEN}$ can be moved to the premodifier position ($[Adj_{GEN.m} + TN_{GEN}] + N$) depending on the informational structure of the sentence. Regardless of its position, the word order within the modifier itself does not change.

In general, genitival uses of *rodzaju/roda* and *typu/tipa* in such modifier structures are by far more common in the singular than the plural forms *typów/tipov*, *rodzajów/rodov*. A quantitative account for Russian structures is offered in Kolyaseva (2021b). For Polish TNs, a brief glance at the corpus data suggests a similar distribution. At the same time, we observe that *typu/tipa* typically combines with classifying adjectives, whereas *rodzaju/roda* prefers pronominal markers (adjectival determiners), as in (24)–(25) (see also a similar account for Czech *druh* in Janebová and Martinková, this volume, chapter 15). Such preferences are in line with the meanings of *typ/tip* and *rodzaj/rod*: *typu/tipa* serves further subcategorization, while *rodzaju/roda* either defines the level of membership in the group (Polish *jakiegoś rodzaju* 'of a kind', lit. 'some$_{GEN.M.SG}$ kind$_{GEN.M.SG}$') or comments on the status of a certain object as a member of the group (Polish *dziwnego rodzaju* 'of a strange kind' lit. 'strange$_{GEN.M.SG}$ kind$_{GEN.M.SG}$', Russian *osobogo roda* 'of a special kind' lit. 'special$_{GEN.M.SG}$ kind$_{GEN.M.SG}$').

(24) Rus. ***Takogo roda*** *tradicii projavljajut*
such-GEN.M.SG kind-GEN.M.SG tradition-NOM.PL manifest-PRS.3PL
sebja i v ostal'nyx oblastjax duxovnoj i
self-ACC and in rest-ADJ.PRP.PL field-PRP.PL spiritual-GEN.F.SG and
material'noj kul'tury.
material-GEN.F.SG culture-GEN.F.SG
'**Such traditions** also manifest themselves in other areas of spiritual and material culture.'

(25) Pol. *Czyli kaszel, podwyższona*
in.other.words cough-NOM.M.SG higher-NOM.F.SG
temperatura, katar i inne
temperature-NOM.F.SG running.nose-NOM.M.SG and other-NOM.PL
tego rodzaju *„przyjemności".*
this-GEN.M.SG kind-GEN.M.SG pleasure-NOM.PL
'In other words, cough, fever, running nose and other **"pleasures" of this kind**.'

Interestingly, in Russian *tip* and *rod* in the modifier structures are characterized by different distributional patterns in terms of their syntactic position. As shown in Kolyaseva (2021b), modifiers with *tip* are generally postposed ($N + [Adj_{GEN.M} + TN_{GEN}]$), as is standard for Russian nominal modifiers. However, premodification ($[Adj_{GEN.M}+TN_{GEN}] + N$), as in (24), is characteristic of the most frequent constructions with *rod*, namely those serving the purposes of textual anaphoric reference, hedging and the indication of variety and quantification. Given that premodification is typical for Russian simple adjectival modifiers, such distribution has been pointed out in Kolyaseva (2021b) as indirect evidence of routinization of those modifier strings with *rod* and their automation as a single processing item.

It is worth mentioning that modifier structures such as Polish *wszelkiego rodzaju/typu*$_{GEN.SG}$ 'of all possible kinds' and *różnego rodzaju/typu*$_{GEN.SG}$ 'of different kinds', and Russian *vsex rodov*$_{GEN.PL}$ 'of all kinds', *raznogo roda*$_{GEN.SG}$ 'of different kinds', *raznogo tipa*$_{GEN.SG}$ 'of different types', and *vsjačeskogo roda*$_{GEN.SG}$ 'of all possible kinds' can acquire a function comparable to the quantifier uses in English and Romance languages (English *all kinds of arguments*, Spanish *todo tipo de juramento*). Sometimes it is unclear in the context whether these uses refer to differing sorts or rather to a multitude, 'all sorts of', as in (26)–(27). Note that singular structures are possible (and even preferred) despite plural semantics, as in (27).

(26) Rus. *oficial'nye*   *i*   *delovye*   **dokumenty**
        official-NOM.PL and business-ADJ.NOM.PL document-NOM.PL
        vsex   ***tipov***   *i*   *vsevozmožnye*   ***nadpisi***
        all-GEN.PL type-GEN.PL and all.kinds.of-ADJ.NOM.PL inscription-NOM.PL
        '**all types of** official and business documents (**all sorts of documents**?) and all kinds of inscriptions'

(27) Rus. *pytalas'*   *podsunut'*   ***raznogo***   ***roda***
        try-PST.F.SG slip-INF different-GEN.M.SG kind-GEN.M.SG
        proizvedenija,   *ničego*   *ne*   *nravitsja.*
        work.of.art-ACC.PL nothing-NOM.N.SG not like-REFL.PRS.3SG
        'I tried to slip in **various kinds (all sorts of?) books**, [the child] doesn't like anything.'

One such expression, namely *swego rodzaju/svoego roda* as in (28)–(30), counterparts of which are used in most Slavic languages, has lexicalized as a vagueness marker or hedge.[9] An indirect supporting argument in favour of the lexicalization of the construction in both languages consists in its syntactic position as a premodifier: while the neutral position for the nominal genitival modifier is postmodification, *swego rodzaju/svoego roda* always precedes the noun that it hedges. Also note that *rodzaj/rod* in this construction is always used in the singular.

(28) Rus. *Èto*   ***svoego***   ***roda***   ***objazatel'noe***
        it one's.own-GEN.M.SG kind-GEN.M.SG obligatory-NOM.N.SG
        bljudo   *dlja*   *ljubogo*   *gurmana*
        dish-NOM.N.SG for any-GEN.M.SG gourmet-GEN.M.SG
        'This is a **kind of must-have dish** for any gourmet.'

(29) Pol. *Zbudowanie*   *nowoczesnego*   *systemu*
        build-GRND.NOM.N.SG modern-GEN.M.SG system-GEN.M.SG
        finansów   *publicznych*   *będzie*   *więc*   *napotykać*
        finances-GEN.PL public-GEN.PL be-FUT.3SG so meet-INF
        barierę   *finansową,*   *co*   *jest*
        barier-ACC.F.SG financial-ACC.F.SG what-NOM be-PRS.3SG

---

[9] In these languages where *rod*-based units do not develop the general taxonomic meaning, such construction requires a semantically parallel element, e.g. Czech *svého druhu* (Janebová and Martinková 2017).

swego	*rodzaju*	*paradoksem.*
one's.own-GEN.M.SG	kind-GEN.M.SG	paradox-INS.M.SG

'Therefore building a modern system of public finances will face a financial barrier, which is **a kind of paradox**.'

(30) Ukr. *Ci   zaxody   stajut'   svoho*
     this-NOM.PL action- NOM.PL become-PRS.3PL one's.own-GEN.SG.M
     rodu   « kul'tovymy   podijamy ».
     kind-GEN.SG iconic-INS.PL event-INS.PL
     'These events have become **kind of "iconic events"**.'

3.4 Adpositional phrases

There is a structural possibility in Slavic languages for TNs to form adpositional phrases. An examination of structures in Polish and Russian reveals that while the genitival modifier structures discussed above are uniform in both languages, adpositional constructions are realised rather differently.

A construction that stands in parallel to the genitival modifier is an adpositional phrase that is formed by *w* ('in') + Adj$_{LOC.SG}$ + TN$_{LOC.SG}$ in Polish and *v* ('in') + Adj$_{PRP.SG}$ + TN$_{PRP.SG}$ in Russian, essentially the same construction. In Polish, this construction is realised only by *typ*. Both parallel structures with *typ* are similar in the sense that they modify a noun (Polish *blondynka w typie*$_{LOC.SG}$ *nordyckim*$_{LOC.SG}$ = *blondynka typu*$_{GEN.SG}$ *nordyckiego*$_{GEN.SG}$ 'a Nordic type of blonde girl'). However, *typ*'s collocability with adjectives in adpositional phrases is limited to classifying (often human-related) adjectives. Prepositional phrases with Polish *rodzaj*, on the other hand, are not used as adpositions but instead have become a source for the new adjectival expression *jedyny w swoim rodzaju* 'one of a kind' (lit. 'singular in its.own$_{LOC.SG}$ kind$_{LOC.SG}$') and the hedge *coś w tym rodzaju* 'something like this' (*lit.* 'something in this$_{LOC.SG}$ kind$_{LOC.SG}$').

By contrast, in Russian such an adpositional structure is possible for *rod* but not for *tip*. Furthermore, while the genitival modifier can only modify a noun, the adpositional phrase *v* + Adj + *rod-(e)*$_{PRP.SG}$ is not necessarily adnominal, as in (31) and (34), but it can also fill adverbial slots and modify adjectives and verbs, as in (32) and (33). In other words, the adpositional structures are functionally parallel to genitival modifier constructions but have different grammatical properties. The adnominal genitival modifier is a bound syntaxeme, while the adpositional phrase in Russian is a free syntaxeme.[10] Examples include Russian *v nekotorom*PRP.SG *rode*PRP.SG 'in a way' vs. *N + nekotorogo*GEN.SG *roda*GEN.SG 'of some kind', *v svoëm*PRP.SG *rode*PRP.SG 'in a way' vs. *N + svoego*GEN.SG *roda* GEN.SG, *v takom*PRP.SG *rode*PRP.SG 'such, in such a way' vs. *N + takogo*GEN.SG *roda*GEN.SG 'of such kind', and *v ètom*PRP.SG *rode*PRP.SG 'in this kind/way' vs. *N + ètogo*GEN.SG *roda*GEN.SG 'of this kind'. Interestingly, such expressions are realised in Polish only by the genitival modifier *rodzaju* (as in *tego rodzaju* 'of this kind', *pewnego rodzaju* 'of some kind', etc.).

(31) Rus. *Bojus'   tol'ko, čto **molitva**   v*
       be.afraid-PST.1SG only that prayer-NOM.F.SG in
       ***takom   rode**   u   tebja   ne   poslednjaja.*
       such-PRP.M.SG kind-PRP.M.SG at you-GEN.SG not last-NOM.F.SG
       'I am just afraid that **such a prayer** will not be your last one'.

(32) Rus. *Kažetsja,   ètot   idiot   i   dal'še*
       seem-PRS.3SG this-NOM.M.SG idiot-NOM.M.SG and further
       *sobiralsja   **vydurivat'** v   **takom   rode.***
       going.to-PST.M.SG fool-INF   in such-PRP.M.SG kind-PRP.M.SG
       'It seemed that this idiot was going to continue **to fool around like that.**'

(33) Rus. *Disput   **prodolžalsja**   v   **takom že***
       dispute-NOM.M.SG continue-PST.M.SG in same-PRP.M.SG
       strannom   rode.
       strange-PRP.M.SG kind-PRP.M.SG
       'The dispute **went on in the same strange way.**'

(34) Rus. *Teper' **čto-to**   v   **ètom   rode,***
       now   something-ACC.N   in this-PRP.M.SG kind-PRP.M.SG
       po-moemu,   pereživaet   Pet'ka.
       in.my.opinion live.through-PRS.3SG Petka-NOM.M.SG
       'Now, Petka is experiencing **something like that**, in my opinion.'

The range of adjectives acceptable in the Russian adpositional structure is even more limited than in the corresponding genitival construction with *rod*. As expected, full lexical adjectives are extremely rare (consider (33), although even in this example the adjective is accompanied by a pronoun). The range of

---

[10] See Zolotova (1973) on free and bound syntaxemes.

typical adjectives is narrow, and confined to pronominal adjectives forming the following combinations: (i) *v ètom rode* (*lit.* 'in this kind', *v takom rode* (*lit.* 'in such kind') with the function of approximative anaphoric reference (31)–(34), and (ii) *v nekotorom rode* ('in some way'), *v kakom-to rode* ('in some way'), *v svoem rode* 'of a kind' which are used for hedging purposes (signalling that the proposed definition is valid only 'from a certain point of view', as in (35)–(36)).[11] These are semi-fixed structures which despite forming a lexically bound linguistic item are still compositional, since the adjectives can alternate, even though the choice is extremely limited. A question could be raised as to whether at least some of them (especially *v svoëm rode*[12]) have lexicalized, i.e. are used as fixed constructions no longer directly associated in the minds of the speakers with the TN *rod*.

(35) Rus. *vydajuščajasja žadnost'* — *èto tože* **v**
outsatnding-NOM.F.SG greed-NOM.F.SG it also in
svoëm rode dostiženie.
one's.own-PRP.M.SG kind-PRP.M.SG achievement-NOM.N.SG
'outstanding greed is also an achievement **in its own way**.' (=*svoego roda* 'kind of').

(36) Rus. *Ispol'zovanie telefonnoj svjazi v*
use-NOM.N.SG telephone-ADJ.GEN.F.SG connection-GEN.F.SG in
propasti — **v nekotorom rode** *iskusstvo.*
abyss-PRP.F.SG in some-PRP.M.SG kind-PRP.M.SG art-NOM.M.SG
'Using telephone communication in an abyss is **in some way** an art.'

There is a clear tendency for the adpositional constructions to either lexicalize or become a base for the grammaticalization of multiword expressions in Slavic languages. One such collocation was mentioned earlier, Polish *jedyny w swoim rodzaju* 'one of a kind, *lit.* 'the only in its kind', which is used to refer to something or somebody that is unique and has equivalents in other Slavic languages, for example, Russian *edinstvennyj v svoëm rode* (37), Ukrainian *jedynyj u svojemu rodi*, Czech *jediný svého druhu*, and Bulgarian *edinstven po roda si*.

---

[11] For a quantitative account, see Kolyaseva (2021b).
[12] The fixed adpositional structure *v svoem rode* is semantically parallel to the lexicalized genitival structure *svoego roda*.

(37) Rus. ètogo   sočinenija,   v   **svoem**
           this-GEN.M.SG   work-GEN.N.SG   in   one's.own-PRP.M.SG
     rode   **edinstvennogo,**   bolee   ni   na   čto
     kind-PRP.M.SG   singular-GEN.M.SG   more   not   on   something-ACC.N
     ne   poxožego
     not   similar-GEN.M.SG
     'this work, **one of a kind**, not similar to anything else'

As a result of the fact that Russian *rod* enters adpositional structures and can function as an adjunct, while Polish *w rodzaju* requires nominal fillers in both left-hand and right-hand slots and must be regarded as a secondary preposition (see Section 4.1), some expressions are classified differently in the two languages. For example, the vagueness marker Polish *coś w tym rodzaju* 'something like this' (*lit.* something in this$_{\text{LOC.SG}}$ kind$_{\text{LOC.SG}}$) will be recognized as potentially grammaticalizing usage of a preposition *w rodzaju*, whereas parallelly built Russian *čto-to v takom/ètom rode* 'something like this' (*lit.* 'something in this kind') will be characterized as a combination of *čto-to* 'something' modified by the adpositional construction *v* + Adj$_{\text{PRP.SG}}$ + TN$_{\text{PRP.SG}}$. In addition, general extenders,[13] as in (38) and (39), regardless of their structure with obligatory nominal elements in the left-hand slot (*coś* 'something' in Polish and *i vsë* 'and everything' in Russian), will be considered different in nature: prepositional in Polish and modifying in Russian.

(38) Pol. *Przy*   *KKP*   *ma*   *być*   *tworzona*
           next.to   KKP   have-PRS.3SG   be-INF   establish-PASS.PTCP.NOM.F.SG
     Rada   *Prasowa*   *czy* *coś*   *w*
     commitee-NOM.F.SG   press-ADJ.NOM.F.SG   or   something-NOM.N   in
     tym   **rodzaju.**
     this-LOC.M.SG   kind-LOC.M.SG
     'In KKP they plan to establish the Press Committee or **something like that**.'

(39) Rus. *A*   *s*   *odnim*   *mal'čikom-*   *sirotoj*   « *s*
           and   with   one-INS.M.SG   boy-INS.M.SG   orphan-INS.SG   from
     toj   *storony* »   *vzjalas'*   *rabotat'*   *tol'ko*
     that-GEN.F.SG   side-GEN.F.SG   take-PST.F.SG   work-INF   only
     nikomu   *ne*   *izvestnaja*   *anglijskaja*   *učitel'nica,*
     nobody-DAT   not   known-NOM.F.SG   English-NOM.F.SG   teacher-NOM.F.SG

---

[13] Otherwise known as terminal tags, see Dines (1980) and Romaine and Lange (1991).

	i	načala,		kak	umela		opisyvat'		ego	učebu
	and	start-PST.F.SG		as	can-PST.F.SG		describe-INF		his	study-ACC.F.SG
	v	škole			volšebnikov.		**I**		**vse**	**v**
	in	school-PRP.F.SG			wizard-GEN.PL		and		everything-NOM	in
	takom			**rode.**						
	such-PRP.M.SG			kind-PRP.M.SG						

'And only an unknown English teacher embarked on working with an orphan-boy "from the other side" and began, as best as she could, to describe his studies at the school of wizards. **And that kind of thing.**'

4 Grammaticalized uses

Besides the nominal uses discussed above, the development of TNs in Slavic languages has reached a stage representing a classic case of grammaticalization, whereby content words come to be used as functional items (Hopper and Traugott 1993). More precisely, a certain form of a word (e.g. the genitive form, Polish *typu*/Russian *tipa*) or a compositional structure (e.g. a prepositional phrase, Polish *w typie*/Russian *po tipu*) stabilizes in a new function, losing or modifying the lexical meaning of the base-word. This implies decategorization, i.e. losing the TN's nominal properties and moving into the class of *non-compositional* prepositions or particles. The process seems to have gone further in Russian than in Polish which has not developed many particle uses.

Characteristics of the grammaticalization process that manifest here are phonetic attrition, hypercorrection and univerbation, among others. The first two concern the Russian particle *tipa*, which developed from and is homophonous with the genitive of the noun *tip*. In informal communication such as internet fora, another spelling of *tipa* – *tipo* – is not unusual; see (40). Since both variants can be employed in the same contexts, it is possible to consider *tipo* as an incorrect spelling of *tipa*, given that in standard Russian, phonemes /a/ and /o/ neutralize in an unstressed position. This can be taken as evidence that *tipa* is no longer associated with its original nominal form, since the ending -*o* is not within the repository of case endings of the noun *tip*. Rather, the fact that Russian adverbials typically end with -*o* suggests that the speakers associate the item with the grammatical semantics of this category. However, *typo* also appears in Ukrainian where it is considered an incorrect and highly colloquial form of Ukrainian *typu*. The very fact of its existence, given the lack of neutralization in Ukrainian, suggests that variants ending in -*o* do not necessarily result from hypercorrection but may represent another stage of the grammaticalization chain *tipa > tipo*. Furthermore, in colloquial speech and writing, the Russian particle *tipa/tipo* can be phonetically reduced to *tip*, as in (41), which is especially characteristic of internet communication. In general, variation (*tipa, tipo, tip*) predominantly concerns those cases that are considered particle uses in this paper, but occasional instances when *tipo* governs a genitive complement and is thus classified as a preposition are also attested.

(40) Rus. U nego nos na maske i
at he-GEN nose-NOM.M.SG on mask-PRP.F.SG and
kryl'ja. **Tipo** *žuravl'*.
wing-NOM.PL TIPO crane-NOM.M.SG
'He has a nose and wings on his mask. Like, he is a crane.'

(41) Rus. nu **tip** soznatel'noe otnošenie k
well TIP conscious-NOM.N.SG attitude-NOM.N.SG to
učebe, *nè?*
study-DAT.F.SG not
'Well, **like**, it's a conscious attitude towards learning, no?'
(vk.com, accessed 23 April 2020).

Univerbation (in Lehman's [2019] terms) concerns Russian preposition and particle *vrode* which derives from a prepositional phrase *v + rod-(e)*_{PRP.SG} 'in the kind of' that has become welded into one word and thus non-compositional. In a parallel development, *po tipu* 'like, similar to, for example', which is derived from a prepositional phrase with *tip* (*po tip-u*_{DAT.SG} 'according to the type, by the type of'), continues to be spelt with two words but is nonetheless considered in Kolyaseva and Davidse (2018) to be a grammaticalized complex preposition and particle, analogical in its functions to *tipa*. While the prepositional phrase *v rode* does not occur in present-day Russian, the grammaticalized uses of *po tipu* represent a case of divergence, as the combination of the preposition *po* and the noun *tip* does not cease to exist. The criteria for distinction between the nominal structure *po tipu* and the homonymous grammaticalized prepositional item are offered, among others, in Artemenko (2018). Interestingly, Lazareva (2016: 550) reports an instance of case contamination (*po tipa*) which she interprets to be based on the shared grammaticalized meaning of *po tipu* and *tipa*. This example from the Oral Corpus seems to remain isolated to date.

The main two classes formed by grammaticalized TN constructions are prepositions and particles.[14] Prepositions are defined as a functional part of speech which formalizes the subordination of one lexical word to another in a phrase or a sentence, and thus expresses their relation to each other (Russkaja Grammatika 1980, § 1655). The meaning of a preposition is determined by the type of relation they communicate. We distinguish a central meaning of the prepositions Polish *typu*, Russian *tipa*, Polish *w typie*, Russian *po tipu*, Russian *vrode* and Polish *z rodzaju*[15] – the relation of (approximative) similarity. In Russian, there is another meaning the prepositional items can acquire, that of exemplification, but in Polish the counterpart exemplificatory items behave as particles. For this reason, we first discuss the prepositions expressing the relation of similarity (Section 4.1), and then move on to cases in which defining part-of-speech characteristics of these items is either problematic or different in the analysed languages (Section 4.2).

The relational grammatical meaning of a preposition is that it connects two representational items and is essentially an important marker of syntactic relation between these two items. By contrast, particles do not form syntactic relations between words and can be removed without damaging the syntactic structure of a sentence. They can serve multiple functions but their meaning as a word class can be defined as either the relation of the proposition to reality or the attitude of the speaker to the message that is being communicated (Russkaja Grammatika 1980, § 1689; Grochowski, Kisiel and Żabowska 2014). They thus belong to the communicative level of speech (Beziaeva 2002), not the propositional level. The polyfunctionality of Russian TN-derived particles is addressed in Section 4.3.

4.1 Prepositions – Similarity marker: typu$_1$/tipa$_1$, w typie$_1$/po tipu$_1$, vrode$_1$, z rodzaju$_1$

Prepositional Polish *typu*/Russian *tipa*, Polish *w typie*/Russian *po tipu*, Polish *w rodzaju*/Russian *vrode* and Polish *z rodzaju*[16] are structurally closer to the base

---

[14] The diffused grammatical nature of the Russian units has been commented upon in various studies, starting from Lapteva (1983). For instance, Lazareva (2016) notes that *tipa* in its diverse meanings is functionally similar to the preposition, adverb and conjunction. Also see the account of *tipa* as a complementizer in Benigni (this volume, chapter 16).

[15] As prepositions, these units are no longer compositional and as such are not glossed further in the paper.

[16] The structure *iz* 'from'+ TN_{GEN} is productive in Russian, but surprisingly not for *tip* and *rod* (e.g. *iz serii* lit. 'from the series', *iz razrjada* lit. 'from the category', *iz sorta* lit. 'from the sort').

tip₁/typ₁ and *rod₁/rodzaj₁* than homographic particles. The main sign of such cognation is the inherited complement N_SG.GEN in prepositional uses, in other words, persistence (Hopper 1991).

Even though these prepositions share two structural matrices, the genitive form and the prepositional phrase, they are not semantically identical. The one that stands out most is Polish *typu*. In (42), the objects marked by the nouns in the genitive (Gomułka, Kliszko) are presented as prototypical elements of the class to which the objects determined by the left-hand noun (*półinteligenci* 'dumbheads') are similar. This type of relation, interestingly, brings Polish *typu* close to exemplification markers. The main difference between *X typu Y* as a similarity operator and *X typu Y* as an exemplification marker is that in case of the latter the object designated by the noun in the Y position is a member (representative) of the class in the X position. The former does not prejudice the membership of X and Y in the same class. It simply says that we can know about X something that we know about the class represented by Y. Obviously, it is highly likely that X and Y are in fact members of one class.

(42) Pol. **Półinteligenci   typu   Gomułki   czy**
         half-intelligent-NOM.PL TYPU Gomułka-GEN.M.SG or
     Kliszki   *nie   mogą   pojąć,   że   w*
     Kliszko-GEN.M.SG not can-PRS.3PL understand-INF that in
     perspektywie   historycznej   humanistyka
     perspective-LOC.F.SG historical-LOC.F.SG the.humanities-NOM.F.SG
     jest   bazą   technologicznej   nadbudowy.
     be-PRS.3SG base-INS.F.SG technological-GEN.F.SG superstructure-GEN.F.SG
     '**Dumbheads like Gomułka or Kliszko** cannot comprehend that from a historical perspective the Humanities are the basis for technological superstructure.'

Polish *w typie* is more frequently employed as a similarity marker (43) than an exemplification marker. Its functions match those of Russian *tipa* and *po tipu*. Similar to music groups and The Wilde Geese in (43), the room and the garage in (44) are both presented as separate entities. It is not that the garage is a type of room, the reading we would get with a nominal construction. Rather, the room in (44) is *similar to* a garage (just as groups which are popular in the speaker's country are *similar* to The Wilde Geese in (43)), i.e. it has certain properties typical of a garage (e.g. small, probably relatively dark, etc.), yet this circumstance does not make it a garage. In other words, there is no equivalency between the referents of the two nouns that these prepositions connect. Likewise, in (45), the street in question is characterized as similar to the Arbat, a 1 km long street in

Moscow, based on certain properties such as the length and width of the street. The structure *po tipu* invokes the lost 'prototype' meaning that can still be found in the texts of the early 19th century. However, in modern texts, the preposition *po tipu* is used synonymously with *tipa*, and the street in (45) is not necessarily modelled on Moscow's Arbat. In the similarity meaning, Russian *tipa* and *po tipu* are synonymous to another grammaticalized preposition, *napodobie* (< *na* 'on' + *podobie*$_{ACC}$ 'semblance, similarity').

(43) Pol. W   naszym   kraju   najpopularniejsze
         in   our-LOC.M.SG country-LOC.M.SG   most.popular-NOM.PL
         są   więc **grupy**   **w typie** **The Wilde Geese**.
         be-PRS.3PL   so   group-NOM.PL   W TYPIE
   'In our country, **groups like The Wilde Geese** are therefore the most popular.'

(44) Rus. On   razmestilsja   v   **pomeščenii**   **tipa**
         he-NOM   settle.down-PST.M.SG   in premise-PRP.N.SG   TIPA
         garaža,   soveršenno   neprimetnyj   pristroj
         garage-GEN.M.SG completely   inconspicuous-NOM.M.SG   annex-NOM.M.SG
         k   mnogoètažke.
         to high-rise.building-DAT.F.SG
   'He moved into **a garage-like room**, a completely inconspicuous extension to a high-rise building.'

(45) Rus. Širokaja,   protjažennaja   **ulica**   **po tipu**
         wide-NOM.F.SG   extended-NOM.F.SG   street-NOM.F.SG   PO TIPU
         moskovskogo   **Arbata**   s   množestvom
         Moscow-ADJ.GEN.M.SG   Arbat-GEN.M.SG   with   multitude-INS.N.SG
         magazinčikov,   kafe,   teatrov.
         shop-GEN.PL   café-GEN.PL   theatre-GEN.PL
   'A long, wide **street similar to the Moscow's Arbat** with many shops, cafes, and theatres.'

Polish *w rodzaju* has an identical structure and similar meaning to *w typie*; however, it is only rarely used with a similarity meaning. Typically, it functions as a marker of exemplification (see Section 4.2) and its participation in similarity contexts is limited to the hedge *coś w rodzaju* N$_{GEN}$ 'something like', as in (46). Polish *X z rodzaju Y* is similar to *X w typie Y* in that it requires a Y denoting an object whose dominating features would determine the range of the class to which the object designated by X belongs. However, *z rodzaju* is rather used to name the feature than an object typically having such a feature. As a consequence, it has a strong preference for a noun phrase complement (as in *klasyczna garsonka z rodzaju tych w dobrym gatunku* 'classical two-piece of the good quality kind') or a sentence (as in *pomysły z rodzaju tych, które zmieniają bieg dziejów* 'ideas of the kind that change the course of history'). *Z rodzaju* is therefore used when a multi-word description of a class is required.

(46) Pol. *Następnego   dnia   urządzili   sobie*
           next-GEN.M.SG   day-GEN.M.SG   organize-PST.3PL self-DAT
    coś   w rodzaju   uroczystej   wieczerzy.
    something-ACC W RODZAJU   solemn-GEN.F.SG dinner-GEN.F.SG
    'The following day they organized **something like a solemn dinner**.'

In Russian, prepositional *tipa* and *vrode* seem to perform the same functions, for instance in (44) *tipa* can be replaced by *vrode* without alteration of the meaning.[17] An interesting example is (47), in which *vrode* becomes close in function to an adverbial or a conjunction, but the genitive form of the noun does not allow us to classify this form as something other than a preposition, given that in Russian a combination of a preposition with a dependent form is easily separated from the main word, can acquire independence and is capable of relatively independent functioning in the sentence (Russkaja Grammatika 1980, §1655). Such uses are not accepted for Polish TN similarity markers.

(47) Rus. *Stena   polučalas'   židen'koj,   **vrode***
           wall-NOM.F.SG   come.out-PST.F.SG runny-INS.F.SG   VRODE
    pletnja (...)
    wattle-GEN.M.SG
    'The wall turned out thin, **like a wattle fence**.'

Characteristically, in both languages, TN-derived prepositions can also participate in vagueness constructions with indefinite pronouns Polish *coś*/Russian *čto-to* 'something' and, more rarely, Polish *ktoś* / Russian *kto-to* 'someone', for example, Polish *potrzebować **kogoś w rodzaju** Balcerowicza* 'to need **someone like** Balcerowicz', Russian *ustraivajut **čto-to vrode** srednevekovogo disputa* 'arrange **something like** a medieval dispute', Polish *specjalne regimenty: **coś w typie** jednostek karnych* 'special regiments: **something like** a penitentiary unit', and Russian *diagnoz: **čto-to tipa** mikroinfarkta* 'diagnosis: **something**

---

17 A quantitative account modelling selection between prepositional *tipa* and *vrode* is offered in Kolyaseva (2022).

like microinfarction'. Due to the approximative element of the meaning, such constructions can be viewed as hedging devices, whereby the speaker signals that they are not fully committed to the proposition (see also approximation use in Sakhno [2017]). Interestingly, Polish *typu* and *z rodzaju* do not form such expressions. In both cases, it is the filler of the right-hand slot that clashes with the concept of vagueness: both a typical representative and a key feature of a class are seen as specifying the scope of the class.

4.2 Exemplification marker – Between a preposition and a particle: typu$_2$/tipa$_2$, w typie$_2$/po tipu$_2$, z rodzaju/vrode$_2$, z rodzaju$_2$

The previous discussion on two Polish prepositions in the similarity function has proven that the line between similarity and exemplification has to be drawn carefully: on the one hand Polish *typu*, due to employing an idea of a representative, approaches the exemplification meaning, while on the other hand, the exemplification marker *w rodzaju* can, under certain circumstances, operate in similarity contexts.

Overall, the distinction between similarity and exemplification markers in Polish is rather clear-cut. They differ both semantically and formally, the similarity marker being a preposition, whereas the exemplification one does not govern the case of the right-hand noun and has to be qualified differently. To start with, similarity markers allow for singular and plural nouns in the left-hand slot and require the genitive in the right-hand context. Conversely, exemplification markers permit only plural nouns in the left-hand slot and open a right-hand position for a noun (or series of nouns) in the nominative (48) and also (predominantly!) for quoted words (49). Regardless of the functional ambiguity of such a marker, no differentiation is drawn here between exemplifying uses and quotatives. The reason is that in both cases the structure is the same: a noun (in the plural) in the left-hand slot, a pause after the particle and an enumeration or quotation in the right-hand slot. Such a difference in prosody clearly differentiates them from similarity markers. Moreover, following demonstration theory (Clark and Gerrig 1990; Fox Tree and Tomlinson 2008) quotations can be perceived as examples of what was said or could be said, which would support an interpretation of the TN-derived item as an exemplification marker.

(48) Pol. *Dlatego warto też sięgać i po inne*
therefore worth also reach-INF and for other-ACC.PL
metody typu hipnoza, regresing, *(...).*
method-ACC.PL TYPU hypnosis-NOM.F.SG regressing-NOM.M.SG
'Therefore it is also worth trying other **methods such as hypnosis, regressing**, (...).'

(49) Pol. *Wynika to prawdopodobnie z*
result-PRS.3SG it probably from
przekazanych mu przez rodziców
convey-PASS.PTCP.GEN.PL he-DAT by parent-ACC.PL
komunikatów typu: "Złe dzieci nie
message-GEN.PL TYPU bad-NOM.PL children-NOM.PL not
mają prawa do istnienia".
have-PRS.3PL right-GEN.N.SG to exist-GRD.GEN.SG
'It may result from the **statements** conveyed by his parents **such as "Bad children have no right to exist."**'

Interestingly, Polish *w rodzaju, z rodzaju* and *w typie* only permit quotations (see *cudaczne zwroty w rodzaju "brylantowa melodya"* 'bizarre expressions such as "diamond melody"', *patriarchalizm z rodzaju "gdzie są moje skarpetki!"* 'patriarchy such as "where are my socks!"' and *sposób relacji w typie "właściwie nic się nie stało"* 'reporting style such us "nothing actually happened"' respectively). *W rodzaju* is here visibly more frequent than the other two, which is understandable since it is the only item in this group that does not have a homograph in the class of similarity markers.

Sporadically, some exemplification markers, especially *w rodzaju*, can be used without a visible nominal context, as in (50). This predominantly occurs in spoken language and is limited to uses with quotations in the right-hand position.

(50) Pol. *Większość w rozmowie prywatnej*
majority-NOM.F in conversation-LOC.F.SG private-LOC.F.SG
*jednoznacznie odpowiada **w rodzaju** "za tę*
unequivocally answer-PRS.3SG W RODZAJU for this-ACC.F.SG
cenę wiadomo, że to replika".
price-ACC.F.SG know-IMPERS that it replica-NOM.F.SG
'In a private conversation most people unequivocally answer **like**, "For this price it is clear that it is a replica."' (www.kobieta.gazeta.pl, accessed Jan 2020)

In Russian the exemplification marker remains a preposition. Unlike in Polish, the right-hand slot is filled by a noun in the genitive (or an item which substitutes for it), sometimes without a preceding pause, making such constructions with an exemplification marker formally indistinguishable from those with a similarity marker (note that there may be a pause before the similarity marker too, for example in (47), which would be ungrammatical in Polish). The distinction between the two functions is thus semantic; however, since they are closely related (as with English *like* which also combines both functions), in some contexts it is not clear whether the items in question convey similarity or exemplification. In general, Russian *X tipa /po tipu/vrode Y* expresses the relation of similarity when X is being compared to Y but X and Y are perceived as more or less separate entities, i.e. X is presented as similar to Y but their referents do not coincide or subsume each other (X is not Y and Y is not X), as in (44) or (47). The same structure expresses the relation of exemplification if Y is presented as an example of X, i.e. X subsumes Y. The reference of X is thus not that concrete; it is presented as a class with many possible elements, one of which is Y. Y is given as a typical representative of the class, as in (51) in which the Soviet emulations of Gaudi are clearly not being compared to the Palace of Rituals in Tbilisi – the latter is rather mentioned as a shining example of such imitations. Note that just as is the case for similarity markers, prepositional *tipa* and *vrode* are interchangeable in the function of exemplification and can even be used in the same sentence for paraphrasing purposes.

(51) Rus. *Odnovremenno stroilis' i funkcional'nye*
simultaneously build-PASS.PST.3PL and functional-NOM.PL
žilye **kompleksy** *tipa moskovskogo*
residential-NOM.PL complex-NOM.PL TIPA Moscow-ADJ.GEN.N.SG
Čertanova, *i fantastičeskie* **podražanija**
Chertanovo-GEN.N.SG and fantastic-NOM.PL imitation-NOM.PL
Gaudi **vrode Dvorca** *toržestvennyx*
Gaudi-DAT.M.SG VRODE palace-GEN.M.SG ceremonial-GEN.PL
obrjadov v Tbilisi.
ritual-GEN.PL in Tbilisi-PRP.M.SG
'At the same time, functional residential complexes **such as** Moscow's Chertanovo and fantastic imitations of Gaudi **such as** the Palace of Rituals in Tbilisi were built.'

Similarly to their Polish equivalents, Russian *tipa* and *vrode* can introduce a list of examples, but even then they require the genitive form of the dependent form, as in (52), discussed in Kolyaseva and Davidse (2018: 208). A bright-turquoise jacket or a bright red one are given as just some examples of the bright colours that the speaker has in her wardrobe.

(52) Rus. *To est'   v   moem   garderobe   est'*
that.is   in   my-PRP.M.SG   wardrobe-PRP.M.SG   there.is-PRS.3SG
i   beloe /   i   černoe (. . .)   i   daže   jarkie
and white-NOM.N.SG and   black-NOM.N.SG   and   even   bright-NOM.PL
kakie-to   letnie /   jarkie   dostatočno
some-NOM.PL   summer-ADJ.NOM.PL   bright-NOM.PL   enough
cveta   *tam /   m . . .* ***tipa   birjuzovogo***
colour-NOM.M.PL   there   m . . .   TIPA   turquoise-GEN.M.SG
kakogo-nibud' / ***jarko-birjuzovogo   pidžaka***
some-GEN.M.SG bright.turquoise-GEN.M.SG   jacket-GEN.M.SG
ili ***jarko-krasnogo.***
or   bright.red-GEN.M.SG
'That is, in my wardrobe there are the white / and the black (. . .) or even some bright summer / bright enough colours / mmm . . . such as some **turquoise / a bright turquoise jacket or a bright red one**.'

Two non-standard cases must be mentioned in relation to Russian *tipa* and *vrode*. First of all, there are examples in which the second noun (Y) takes the nominative form, as in (53) and (54), which brings into question their status as prepositions. However, note that while with Polish TN-derived exemplification markers a noun realising the position of Y must take the nominative form, cases with a nominative are only marginal in Russian. Furthermore, apart from the lack of the genitive, such Russian constructions are indistinguishable from the standard prepositional structures with *tipa* or *vrode* – consider (54), in which there is no reason to believe that *tipa* is being employed differently than in (52) in which it is followed by a genitive. As *vrode* and *tipa* are evidently part of a syntactic structure expressing relation between X and Y, Kolyaseva and Davidse (2018) analysed them as elliptical. In other words, the obligatory genitive is present implicitly but is not realised in the phrase (i.e. *slovami tipa [slova] "strukturalizm"* 'words like [the word$_{GEN}$] "structuralism"'; *žurnalami tipa [žurnala] "Stil"* 'journals like [the journal$_{GEN}$] "Style"'). This is different from exemplification markers in Polish, which no longer require the genitive form.

(53) Rus. *Ne   nužno   zabivat'   golovu   škol'nikov*
         not   necessary-PRED   fill.up-INF   head-ACC.F.SG   schoolkid-GEN.PL
slovami   vrode   "strukturalizm"...
word-INS.N.PL   VRODE   structuralism-NOM.M.SG
'No need to bother schoolchildren with **words like "structuralism"**.'

(54) Rus. *A   byvaet,   čto   prixodjat   so*
         and   happen-PRS.3SG   that   come-PRS.3PL   with
*specializirovannymi   **žurnalami   tipa   « Stil' »,***
specialized-INS.M.PL   journal-INS.M.PL   TIPA   style-NOM.M.SG
« Inter'er ».
Interior-NOM.M.SG
'And sometimes they come with specialized **magazines such as "Style", "Interior"**.'

The second non-standard case concerns contexts in which *tipa* and *vrode* are complemented by quotations, as in (55). Here again, the lack of a noun in the genitive form might cast doubt upon the status of these items as a preposition. However, this circumstance alone cannot be taken as evidence that *tipa* and *vrode* in such contexts are no longer prepositions. Russian prepositions can be complemented by a nominal form or by a structure that substitutes for it, in this case a quotation; consider example (56). Moreover, such structures are not confined in Russian to the markers of exemplification, as in Polish. In many cases they can be rather defined as expressing the relation of approximate similarity; consider a synonymous similarity marker *napodobie* 'similar to' in the same context in (57).

(55) Rus. *Prosto   obidno   za   naše   pokolenie,*
         just   shame-PRED   for   our-ACC.N.SG   generation-ACC.N.SG
kogda   slyšiš'   o   sovetskix   fil'max
when   hear-PRS.2.SG   about   Soviet-PRP.PL   film-PRP.PL
*otzyvy   **vrode:** "Da   ja   vašče   ne   v"exal,*
review-ACC.PL   VRODE   EMPH   I-NOM   at.all   not   drive.in-PST.M.SG
če   režisseru   nado   bylo",   èto   "A,
what-ACC.N   director-DAT.M.SG   need   be-PST.N.SG   it   ah
gde   oni   ves'   fil'm   prosto
where   they-NOM   entire-ACC.M.SG   film-ACC.M.SG   simply
xodjat   tuda-sjuda?"
walk-PRS.3PL   back.and.forth

'It is just a shame for our generation when you hear **comments** about Soviet films **like: "I didn't get it at all, what the producer wanted", "Ah, it's where they just walk back and forth during the whole movie?"'**

(56) Rus. *odni*   *opirajutsja*   *na:*   *"bog*   *be*
          some-NOM.PL   rely.on-PRS.3PL   on   god-NOM.M.SG   be-AOR.3SG
slovo",   *drugie:*   *"slovo*   *be*
word-NOM.N.SG   other-NOM.PL   word-NOM.N.SG   be-PST.3.SG
u   *boga".*
at   god-GEN.M.SG
'(. . .) some **rely on: "God was the word"**, others: "God had the word".'

(57) Rus. *Žena*   *ž*   *ego, Efrosin'ja,*   *ne*
          wife-NOM.F.SG   CONTRAST   his   Euphrosyne-NOM.F.SG   not
tol'ko   *ne*   *spala,*   *no*   *prebyvala*   *v*   *jarosti*   *i,*
only   not   sleep-PST.F.SG   but   reside-PST.F.SG   in   rage-PRP.F.SG   and
uvidev   *v*   *rastvorennom*   *okne*
see-TRNSGR   in   opened-PRP.N.SG   window-PRP.N.SG
znakomuju   *figuru, (. . .),*   *zakričala*   *čto-to*
familiar-ACC.F.SG   figure-ACC.F.SG   shout-PST.F.SG   something-ACC.N
napodobie: *"Pogibeli*   *na tebja*   *netu!»*   *ili*
similar.to-PREP   perdition-GEN.F.SG   on   you-ACC.SG   there.is.no   or
« Dušegub   *okajannyj! »*   *On*   *točno*   *ne*
murderer-NOM.M.SG   curst-NOM.M.SG   he-NOM   exactly   not
pomnil,   *čto*   *ona*   *kriknula,*
remember-PST.M.SG   what-ACC.N   she-NOM   shout-PST.F.SG
potomu čto   *vmeste*   *s*   *poslednimi*   *slovami*   *v*
because   together   with   last-INS.PL   word-INS.PL   into
nego   *poletela*   *glubokaja*   *tarelka. . .*
he-ACC   fly-PST.F.SG   deep-NOM.F.SG   plate-NOM.F.SG

'His wife, Euphrosyne, not only did not sleep, but was outraged, and having noticed the familiar silhouette through an open window, (. . .), screamed **something like "Bastard!" or "You swine!"** He didn't remember exactly what she had shouted, because along with the final words a deep dish had flown at him . . .'

In all these cases, the TN-derived units remain part of the syntactic structure, modifying the left-hand slot noun. Given the structural possibility of a preposition being followed by quoted text instead of a nominal form (as in 56), these cases are classified as prepositional. Nonetheless, it is clear that such contexts are favourable towards transition to the particle status and most likely allowed for the development of quotative particles.

4.3 Particles: tipa, po tipu, vrode

The grammaticalization into particles has taken a more extensive form in Russian than in Polish. With respect to particle uses, Polish has been developing multiple exemplification markers and hedges in the last few decades, some of them based on taxonomic nouns, others on nouns that do not have a base taxonomic meaning and yet whose derivative structures follow the pattern by which TN-derived items have developed (see Kisiel, this volume, chapter 14). Russian, on the other hand, expands and diversifies the uses of existing units such as *tipa*, *po tipu* and *vrode*. The pragmatic functions described below concern mainly Russian particles, since in Polish such uses have not been developed. Ukrainian *typu* demonstrates similar functions to Russian *tipa*.

Since the Russian particles *tipa, po tipu* and *vrode* are polyfunctional (Sakhno 2010; Kolyaseva 2021a), restrictions of space do not allow us to describe the functional nuances in much detail, but we aim to spot the most common uses and pinpoint those that, as far as we are aware, are not attested for TNs in other languages. For instance, *tipa* (*po tipu*) and *vrode* have been associated with a qualifying (or approximator) and a quotative function (Sakhno 2010; Kolyaseva 2018), as well as a filler use, which are rather standard for the grammaticalization of TNs in other languages and will not be discussed here in detail.

Bulygina and Shmelev (1997: 302) list *vrode* among quasi-assertives whereby "the speaker refrains from a confident judgment, despite the fact that they have direct information on the actual state of affairs", as they are not convinced of its reliability. As the authors state, this information is obtained as a result of sensory perception or recall, or is received from other people.[18] Indeed, *vrode* is often used as an uncertainty marker that allows the speaker to hedge their responsibility for the accuracy of the information. For instance, the speaker in (58) is not sure whether the fledglings under her balcony are sparrows. However, and importantly, she has some evidence which suggests that the proposition is likely to be true, e.g. the fledglings look or sound like sparrows.

---

18 The development of a similarity marker into a sensory evidential is not unusual; see for example Bužarovska (2006) on the Macedonian *kako da*. For an account of the particle as a 'portmanteau' word between modality and evidentiality, see Kosta (2013).

(58) Rus. *pod   našim   balkonom   nedavno   vyvelis'*
         under   our-INS.M.SG balcony-INS.M.SG recently hatch-PST.PL
         *kakie-to   ptency,   **vrode   by**[19]**,   vorob'i...***
         some-NOM.PL   fledgling-NOM.PL VRODE   SBJV   sparrow-NOM.PL
         'Some fledglings, sparrows **it seems**, have recently hatched under our balcony...'
         (https://www.nashideti.site/2019/03/27/krasnohvostye-podbalkonniki/, accessed 23 April 2020)

Tipa cannot be used in this function: in the same context it is likely to be interpreted as an approximator ('something like sparrows'). Yet, *tipa* is also engaged in marking epistemic modality. As a quotative, *tipa* allows speakers to distance themselves from the reported statement, thus conveying an agnostic, neutral stance.[20] Needless to say, the quotation can be either actual or hypothetical as is the case in (59). As shown in Kolyaseva (2018), the agnostic stance is not far from doubt and disagreement, and *tipa* has also developed as a falsity marker (equivalent to air quotation) signalling that the information conveyed in the statement is not true. The context of use is associated with pretence, a deliberate attempt by someone to make something appear true while the speaker knows or is convinced that it is not true and points it out by using the particle *tipa*. Consider example (60) in which a mother is stealthily observing a scene of conflict between children (her son and a neighbour's child), pretending she is not watching. It is *tipa* that introduces the 'falsity' nuance in the context and signals to the reader that her attention is not at all absorbed by her phone. If *tipa* is left out of the sentence, the proposition is presented as true: the mother is engrossed in her reading and does not pay attention to the children's interaction. This specific meaning can be also observed in Ukrainian *typu*, for example in (61).

---

19 *Vrode* is often used together with *by* and *kak*, forming complex particles *vrode by*, *vrode kak*. *Tipa* does not combine with *by*.
20 In the quotative use, unlike in the previously discussed prepositional uses introducing a quotation, *tipa* can be substituted by other Russian quotatives *mol* or *deskat'*.

(59) Rus. *Net   takogo   otkrytogo   pis'ma /*
          there.is.no such-GEN.M.SG open-GEN.M.SG   letter-GEN.M.SG
*čto / **tipa**/ Sergej   Šnurov /   zatknites'*
that TIPA Sergey-NOM.M.SG Shnurov-NOM.M.SG shut.up-IMP.PL
i   bol'še ne   pojte.
and   more   not sing-IMP.PL
'There is no such an open letter / that / **like** / Sergey Shnurov / shut up and do not sing again.'

(60) Rus. *On   by   s   udovol'stviem   vmazal*
          he-NOM   COND   with   pleasure-INS.N.SG smack-COND.M.SG
Matveju   za   to,   čto   tot   ne
Matthew-DAT.M.SG for that-ACC.N.SG that that-NOM.M.SG   not
gotov   otdavat'   igrušku,   no   ja   xot'
ready-M.SG give.away-INF toy-ACC.F.SG but I-NOM though
*i   molču   i   voobšče **tipa** uperlas'*
and keep.silent-PRS.1SG and at.all   TIPA   fix.one's.eyes-PST.F.SG
v   svoj   telefon,   no   vsë-taki
in   one's-ACC.M.SG   telephone-ACC.M.SG but still
sliškom   blizko.
too   close-ADV
'He would have liked to biff Matthew for not being ready to give him the toy, but even though I am keeping quiet, and am **"busy"** with my phone, I am still too close.'
(https://www.nashideti.site/2019/03/20/dvor-detstvo/, accessed 23 April 2020)

(61) Ukr. *Slon –   toj   pidnjavsja,   Sjeryj*
          elephant-NOM.M.SG   this-NOM.M.SG   rise-PST.M.SG Gray-NOM.M.SG
*pidnjavsja,   Vit'ka –   **typu**, ne   znaje   šče*
rise-PST.M.SG Vitka-NOM.M.SG TYPU   not know-PRS.3SG yet
'Slon got up, Seryj got up, Vitka – **as if** he doesn't know yet' (Dereš L.).

What is remarkable about this 'quasi' use is that from the strict categorization sense of the noun *tip* with its inherited 'typical representative' meaning (model, prototype) *tipa* developed into a sense which includes peripheral members in ad hoc categories by indicating their 'fuzzy boundaries' (approximator uses) and eventually on to marking that something is out of these boundaries and is not a member of the category. Both approximator and quasi-uses coexist as two distinct functions of *tipa*. Sakhno (2010: 120–121) reports a similar 'quasi' use for *vrode*, but it does not seem to be typical of it. For instance, substitution for *tipa* by *vrode* in (60) is likely to shift the interpretation to the perspective of the child, who, based on what he can observe, believes that the woman is not watching.

However, a meaning somewhat related to the field of 'misleading appearance' can be traced in *vrode* as part of the (implied) concessive-adversative construction, a use labelled as "prise en compte d'une incompatibilité" [taking some incompatibility into account] in Sakhno (2010: 113). Such constructions imply two propositions – one with *vrode* (P1) and another one (P2) that is in certain contradiction to P1 and is introduced by an adversative conjunction, such as *a* or *no* 'but'.[21] These constructions often involve the pragmatic effect of failed expectations: *vrode* precedes a proposition (predication) that makes the speaker expect a certain development of the situation – which, to their surprise, does not occur. In (62), the speaker is fairly certain that the person they are talking about is sensible, hence they would have expected him to have refrained from an imprudent act. But in reality, the person has done something which in the judgment of the speaker is not compatible with being a smart person. The collision of the expectation and reality does not refute the original assumption (the person is considered smart in (62) or the view unobstructed in (63)). Note, that the second proposition might not be realised but is implied, as in (62). As discussed in Savchenko (2016: 49), without *vrode* the second contradictory part is no longer expected. However, the structure is also characterised by a specific intonational pattern that distinguishes it from other uses of *vrode* and makes the listener expect or infer from the context the second contradictory part.

(62) Rus. *Čelovek   vzroslyj,   **vrode   umnyj,***
         person-NOM.M.SG adult-NOM.M.SG   VRODE   smart-NOM.M.SG
         dolžen   byl   ponimat',   vo   čto
         must-M.SG   be-PST.M.SG understand-INF into   what-ACC.N
         vvjazyvaetsja...
         get.involved-PRS.3SG
         'He is an adult, **[vrode] a smart one**, he should have understood what he was getting into...' [implied P2: but he did get involved anyway]

---

21 Sakhno (2017) notes that *vrode* in such structures functions as a connector.

(63) Rus. *I* **vrode vsë** *bylo vidno, i*
and VRODE everything-NOM.N.SG be-PST.N.SG seen-PRED and
vsë ravno neponjatno...
all.the.same incomprehensible-PRED
'And **although I could see clearly**, **but** all the same I could not understand it...'

Tipa, on the other hand, is often used in clarification contexts and has developed an explanatory function, as in (64).[22] Regarding this specific use, one might raise the question as to whether the item can be regarded as an explanatory conjunction rather than as a particle, since it explains and clarifies the content of the preceding sentence or its element, in the meaning 'that is, that is to say/this means/because/with the purpose of' (Kolyaseva 2018).

(64) Rus. *Nam dali listočki dlja rozygryša*
we-DAT give-PST.PL sheet-ACC.PL for draw-GEN.M.SG
prizov – èto tože očen' amerikanskaja praktika,
prize-GEN.PL it also very American-NOM.F.SG practice-NOM.F.SG
indoor prizes – **tipa** *na ljubom meroprijatii*
TIPA on any-INS.M.SG event-PRP.M.SG
razygryvajutsja kakie-to podarki- prizy...
raffle-PRS.3PL some-NOM.M.SPL present-NOM.M.PL prize-NOM.M.PL
'We were given some pieces of paper for the raffle of prizes – this is also a very American practice, the indoor prizes – **like** [*tipa*] gifts or prizes are raffled out at any event...'

Overall, Russian *tipa* (like Ukrainian *typu*) is so pervasive in informal discourse that it is sometimes regarded as a verbal tic (which is common for pragmatic markers). It is problematic to define it semantically in some contexts, because it does not add to the propositional content of the sentence, as in (65) in which the speaker does have in mind calling a hairdressing salon, nothing else. Such uses can be considered fillers. However, one might also consider characterising them as discourse markers, fulfilling an interpersonal or social function. This use also encompasses the sequence *tipa togo* ('something like that', < tipa + that$_{\text{GEN.N.SG}}$), as in (66), in which the string *tipa togo* loses its representational or even similative meaning, becoming semantically empty: it does not refer to anything similar to what the deictic pronoun *to* 'that' could stand for. As this pronoun loses any possible reference, the

---

[22] The same function can be observed in Ukrainian contexts.

string can only be regarded as a verbal tic. There is evidence to suggest that *vrode* is also reaching this stage as a "figure of modesty" whereby certain speakers avoid black-and-white judgments (Bulygina and Shmelev 1997: 302), though perhaps 'overuse' of *vrode* happens to a lesser extent than that of *tipa* which has come to be used as a hesitation marker.

(65) Rus. *ty*   *takaja*   *zvoniš'*   **tipa** *v*
           you-NOM such-NOM.F.SG   call-PRS.2.SG   TIPA   to
    parikmaxerskuju.
    hair.salon-ACC.F.SG
    '...and you call, **sort of**, a hair salon'

(66) Rus. *Mne*   *ešče*   *xotelos',*   *èto,*   **tipa** *togo*,
           I-DAT   more   want-PST.N.SG   HESITATION MARKER   TIPA   TOGO
    zakazat'...
    order-INF
    'I also wanted, err, **sort of**, to order...'

5 Conclusions

TNs in Polish and Russian show a high level of agreement in their most basic, nominal uses. Apart from the difference in word order stemming from Polish differentiation between qualifying and classifying adjectives and subsequent variation of structures with genitive or preposition (or both), Polish *typ*, *rodzaj* and Russian *tip*, *rod* are semantically and syntactically alike (see Table 1).

Despite these similarities, it would be much too far-reaching to regard these two languages as identical in relation to how TNs behave. First, they show different structural preferences. While Polish favours genitival structures (*swego rodzaju*, *pewnego typu* 'of a kind' etc.), Russian offers adpositional structures in parallel to the genitival ones. In Russian, adpositional phrases are more limited in terms of their lexical content, but, on the other hand, they are also less limited in terms of what they can modify (a genitival modifier is strictly adnominal, while adpositional structures are more independent and can take adverbial slots). Second, different expressions with TNs are lexicalizing in both languages. What follows a combinatory pattern in one language might be considered fixed collocation in the other (for example, Russian *rod vojsk* 'type of army'). Third, in the course of the grammaticalization process, Polish and Russian drift apart. For example, Polish similarity and exemplification markers can be differentiated on collosyntactic

Table 1: The collocational potential of *typ/tip* and *rodzaj/rod* in their taxonomic and derivative meanings with regard to left (L) and right (R) slots as well as the mid-position (M) slot in the case of prepositional phrases. For particle uses, X marks the possibility of use of a certain TN-derived item. Pronom marks adjectives with pronominal semantics such as *this*. Other adjectives are marked as following: QUAL – qualifying, such as *interesting*; CLASS – classifying, such as *classic*; ART – art-related, such as *comic*; and HUM – human-related, such as *Nordic*.

		Nominal uses								Prepositional uses						Particle uses	
		Adj				Pronom	Num	N	N_GEN	V	Adv	N	N_VAG	N_GEN	tych-Phrase	N_NOM, N_NOM...	QUOT	parenthesis
		QUAL	CLASS	ART	HUM													
Polish	typ	L	L	R	R/L	L	L	R										
	typu	L	R/L	R	L		(Adj) R L				L			R		R		X
	w typie	R	R	R			L	L	R		L L		R			R		
	rodzaj	L	L			L	L	R										
	rodzaju	L	L			L	(Adj) L L											
	w rodzaju					M					L		R				R	
	z rodzaju								R		L			R			R	
Russian	tip	L	L	L	L	L	L	R		L								
	tipa	L	L	L	L	L	L				L L		R			R		X
	po tipu		L	L		M		R		L	L L		R			R		X
	rod	L	L	L	L	L	L	R		L								
	roda	L	L	L	L	L	L	L										
	v rode					M	L/R			L/R	L/R							
	vrode										L L		R	R		R		X

grounds (genitive versus nominative/quotation), whereas in Russian this distinction is purely functional. The fact that in both languages similarity operators and exemplification markers interfuse paradoxically brings Polish and Russian closer. However, the development of particle uses sets the two languages on two quite different paths. Russian *tipa* and *vrode* progress the expansion of modality in spoken language, whereas Polish chooses to build on prepositional structures, developing multiple new hedges, such as *coś w tym rodzaju* 'or something like this'. It is therefore clear that the two languages have been going their separate ways for some time. A diachronic data analysis is needed to trace when this detachment started and how.

References

Aijmer, Karin. 2002. *English discourse particles: Evidence from a corpus*. Amsterdam: John Benjamins.

Artemenko, Maria V. 2018. Otymennyj reljativ "po tipu": semantiko-sintagmatičeskie svojstva [Nominal relator "po tipu": semantic and syntagmatic features]. *Filologičeskie nauki. Voprosy teorii i praktiki* [Philological sciences. Questions of theory and practice] 6 (84). 312–316.

Bartmiński, Jerzy. 2001. Operatory "typowy" i "prawdziwy" w strukturze semantycznej tekstu [The operators 'typical' and 'real' in the semantic structure of a text]. *Prace Filologiczne* 46. 41–47.

Beziaeva, Maria G. 2002. *Semantika kommunikativnogo urovnja zvučaščego jazyka: Voleiz"javlenie i vyraženie želanija govorjaščego v russkom dialoge* [Semantics of the communicative level of the sounding language: The expression of the speaker's volition and wish in Russian dialogue]. Moscow: Izd-vo Moskovskogo universiteta.

Buchstaller, Isabelle. 2014. *Quotatives: New trends and sociolinguistic implications*. Oxford: Wiley Blackwell.

Bulygina, Tatyana V. & Alexei D. Shmelev. 1997. *Jazykovaja konceptualizacija mira (na materiale russkoj grammatiki)* [Language conceptualization of the world (based on Russian grammar)]. Moscow: JAzyki russkoj kul'tury.

Bužarovska, Eleni. 2006. Pathways of semantic change: From similarity marker to sensory evidential. *Slavia Meridionalis* 6. 185–208.

Clark, Herbert H. & Richard J. Gerrig. 1990. Quotations as demonstrations. *Language* 66. 764–805.

Daiber, Thomas. 2010. Quotativmarker im Russischen (типо/типа). *Zeitschrift für Slawistik* 55 (1). 69–89.

Davidse, Kristin, Lieselotte Brems, Peter Willemse, Emeline Doyen, Jessica Kiermeer & Elfi Thoelen. 2013. A comparative study of the grammaticalized uses of English 'sort (of)' and French 'genre (de)' in teenage forum data. In Emanuele Miola (ed.), *Standard and non-standard languages on the Internet. Languages Go Web. Studi e Ricerche*, 41–66. Alessandria: Edizionidell' Orso.

De Smedt, Liesbeth, Lieselotte Brems, & Kristin Davidse. 2007. NP-internal functions and extended uses of the "type" nouns *kind*, *sort*, and *type*: Towards a comprehensive, corpus-based description. In Roberta Facchinetti (ed.), *Corpus Linguistics 25 Years on*, 227–257. Amsterdam: Rodopi.

Denison, David. 2002. History of the *Sort of* construction family. Paper presented at ICCG2: Second International Conference on Construction Grammar, Helsinki. https://www.humanities.manchester.ac.uk/medialibrary/llc/files/david-denison/Helsinki_ICCG2.pdf (accessed 23 April 2020).

Denison, David. 2005. The Grammaticalisations of *sort of*, *kind of* and *type of* in English. Paper presented at New Reflections on Grammaticalization 3, University of Santiago de Compostela.

Dines, Elizabeth. 1980. Variation in discourse – 'and stuff like that'. *Language in Society* 9. 13–31.

Evgen'eva, Anastasija P. (ed.). (1999): *Slovar' russkogo jazyka v 4 tomax* [The Dictionary of Russian language in 4 volumes] / Russian Academy of Sciences, Institute of Linguistic Studies. 4 ed., RP. Moscow: Russ. yaz., Poligrafresursy.

Foolen, Ad. 2008. New quotative markers in spoken discourse. In Bernt Ahrenholz, Ursula Bredel, Wolfgang Klein, Martina Rost-Roth & Romuald Skiba (eds.), *Empirische Forschung und Theoriebildung. Beiträge aus Soziolinguistik, Gesprochene-Sprache- und Zweitspracherwerbsforschung. Festschrift für Norbert Dittmar zum 65. Geburtstag*, 117–128. Frankfurt: Peter Lang.

Fox Tree, Jean E. & John M. Tomlinson Jr. 2008. The rise of *like* in spontaneous quotations. *Discourse Processes* 45 (1). 85–102.

Grochowski, Maciej, Anna Kisiel & Magdalena Żabowska. 2014. *Słownik gniazdowy partykuł polskich* [Nest dictionary of Polish particles]. Kraków: PAU.

Hopper, Paul J. 1991. On some principles of grammaticization. In Elizabeth Closs Traugott & Bernd Heine (eds.), *Approaches to grammaticalization*, Vol. I. 17–36. Amsterdam: John Benjamins.

Hopper, Paul J. & Elizabeth C. Traugott. 1993. *Grammaticalization*. Cambridge: Cambridge University Press.

Janebová, Markéta & Michaela Martinková. 2017. NP-Internal *kind of* and *sort of*: Evidence from an English-Czech Parallel Translation Corpus. In Markéta Janebová, Michaela Martinková, & Ekaterina Lapshinova-Koltunski (eds.), *Contrasting English and other languages through corpora*, 164–217. Newcastle upon Thyne: Cambridge Scholars Publishing.

Keizer, Evelien. 2007. *The English noun phrase. The nature of linguistic categorization*. Cambridge: Cambridge University Press.

Kolyaseva, Alena & Kristin Davidse. 2016. A typology of lexical and grammaticalized uses of Russian *tip*. *Leuven Working Papers in Linguistics*. 171–210.

Kolyaseva, Alena & Kristin Davidse. 2018. A typology of lexical and grammaticalized uses of Russian *tip, tipa, po tipu*. *Russian Linguistics* 42 (2). 191–220.

Kolyaseva, Alena. 2018. The 'new' Russian quotative *tipa*: Pragmatic scope and functions. *Journal of Pragmatics* 128. 82–97.

Kolyaseva, Alena. 2021a. The divergent paths of pragmaticalization: the case of the Russian particles *tipa* and *vrode*. *Journal of Pragmatics*. https://doi.org/10.1016/j.pragma.2021.08.003 (accessed 30 October 2021).

Kolyaseva, Alena. 2021b. The nominal uses of the Russian *rod* ('genus', 'genre', 'kind') and *tip* ('type'): The starting point of desemanticization. *Slovo a Slovesnost 82* (1). 3–44.

Kolyaseva, Alena. 2022. The Russian prepositional TIPA and VRODE in online student discourse: evidence of attraction? *Linguistics* 60 (5). 1451–1485.

Kosta, Peter. 2013. How can I lie if I am telling the truth? The unbearable lightness of being of strong and weak modals, modal adverbs and modal particles in discourse between epistemic modality and evidentiality. In Nadine Thielemann & Peter Kosta (eds.), *Approaches to Slavic interaction*, 167–184. Amsterdam: John Benjamins.

Lapteva, Olga A. 1983. *Tipa* ili *vrode* ? [Tipa or vrode?]. *Voprosy JAzykoznanija* [Topics in the Study of Language] 1983 (1). 39–51.

Lazareva, Viktoria. 2016. K èvoljucii taksonomičeskich terminov: russkoje *tipa* i ego funkcional'nye raznovidnosti [On the evolution of taxonomic terms: Russian *tipa* and its functional varieties]. *Europa Orientalis* 35. 543–565.

Lehmann, Christian. 2019. Univerbation. *CLIPP*, https://christianlehmann.eu/publ/lehmann_univerbation.pdf (accessed 23 April 2020).

Maryn-Stachurska, Dagmara. 2011. O cechach składniowych i semantycznych jednostek "typowy" i "typowo" [On syntactic and semantic features of 'typical' and 'typically']. *Prace Filologiczne* LX. 197–206.

Mihatsch, Wiltrud. 2016. Type-noun binominals in four Romance languages. *Language Sciences* 53. 136–159.

Orzechowska, A. 1998. Rzeczownik [A noun]. In Renata Grzegorczykowa, Roman Laskowski & Henryk Wróbel (eds.), *Gramatyka współczesnego języka polskiego*, t. 2: Morfologia [Grammar of modern Polish. Morphology], 270–331. Warszawa: PWN.

Romaine, Suzanne & Deborah Lange. 1991. The use of *like* as a marker of reported speech and thought: A case of grammaticalization in progress. *American Speech* 66. 227–279.

Russkaja Grammatika [The Russian Grammar]. 1980. Vol. l. *Fonetika. Fonologija. Udarenie. Intonacija. Slovoobrazovanie. Morfologija* [Phonetics. Phonology. Stress. Intonation. Word formation. Morphology]. The USSR Academy of Sciences. The Institute for the Russian Language. Moscow: Nauka.

Sakhno, Serguei. 2010. *Les avatars du sens et de la fonction dans le phénomène de la grammaticalisation : Description systématique du lexème russe* vrode *'dans le genre de' comparé à d'autres lexèmes russes grammaticalisés à fonctionnement proche.* Monographie inédite présentée en vue de l'obtention d'une habilitation à diriger des recherches. Nanterre, Université Paris Ouest.

Sakhno, Serguei. 2017. Polyfonctionnalité et transcatégorialité des morphèmes russes *vrode, tipa*: fonctionnement et aspects typologiques. In Thierry Ponchon, Hava Bat-Zeev Shyldkrot & Annie Bertin (eds.), *Mots de liaison et d'intégration: Prépositions, conjonctions et connecteurs*, 197–214. Amsterdam: John Benjamins.

Savchenko, Darya S. 2016. Vrode ničego xorošego, a xorošo! Protivitel'nye oboroty s časticami v ustnoj reči [It's like there's nothing good, but there is! Adversative constructions with particles in colloquial speech]. *Kommunikativnye Issledovanija* [Communication Studies] 3(9). 48–54.

Semenova, Oksana V. 2000. *Morfologičeskij status i sintaksičeskie funkcii slova* vrode. [The morphological status and syntactic functions of the word *vrode*]. Dissertation for the degree of candidate of philological sciences, Moscow, Moscow State Pedagogical University.

Spronck, Stef. 2016. Evidential fictive interaction (in Ungarinyin and Russian). In Esther Pascual & Sergeiy Sandler (eds.), *The conversation frame: Forms and functions of fictive interaction*, 255–275. Amsterdam: John Benjamins.

Wiemer, Björn. 2011. Hearsay in European languages: Toward an integrative account of grammatical and lexical marking. In Gabriele Diewald & Elena Smirnova (eds.), *Linguistic realization of evidentiality in European languages*, 59–129. Berlin: De Gruyter Mouton.

Zolotova, Galina A. 1973. *Očerk funkcional'nogo sintaksisa russkogo jazyka* [Essay on the functional syntax of the Russian language]. Moscow: Nauka.

Anna Kisiel
14 Polish *w stylu* and the rise of hedges

Abstract: The main aim of this chapter is to confirm the hypothesis that the development path of nouns that are not considered taxonomic resembles the path of grammaticalization of parallel constructions with TNs. This means that the pattern established for the development of constructions with TNs has a wider range than originally assumed as other nouns not typically labelled as TNs may share it. The author verifies this hypothesis by a collostructional and semantic study of (i) the lexical uses immediately preceding the first grammaticalized uses and (ii) the grammaticalized uses of *w stylu* (lit. 'in style$_{\text{LOC.SG}}$') in modern Polish. The grammaticalization paths of *w stylu* are identified based on a qualitative and quantitative corpus study in the span of 20th and 21st century.

The data indicates that the two main uses of grammaticalized *w stylu* – the prepositional and particle uses – differ syntactically, mainly with regard to the type of the required right-hand filler. It also shows that the fact that both meanings of *w stylu* are similarity-based allows for it to be used in a hedging function if it co-occurs with vagueness markers (like *coś* 'something', *rzeczy* 'things') or demonstratives in anaphoric use or undergoes a position switch (to a final-tag).

1 Introduction

Constructions with taxonomic nouns (henceforth TNs) have received ample attention in Germanic, Romance and, even if only recently, Slavic languages (see respective chapters in this volume). The research concentrates primarily on the three main TNs, namely *sort*, *kind*, *type* (hence another term *SKT-nouns*; Denison 2002), while other TNs such as *class*, *form*, *manner*, *kin*, *variety*, *brand*, *species*, *category* (Brems 2011) are less often brought into focus. At the same time, it is hypothesized that other nouns not recognized as TNs can nonetheless develop similar functions.

The two main hypotheses in this chapter concern the evolution of Polish *w stylu*. The first one suggests that the development path of *w stylu* resembles the path of grammaticalization of parallel constructions with TNs as presented

---

Acknowledgements: This work was supported by KU Leuven Internal Funds (research project 3H190236).

Anna Kisiel, KU Leuven, e-mail: anna.kisiel@kuleuven.be

https://doi.org/10.1515/9783110701104-014

in Figure 1 even though the base noun *styl* 'style, manner' has not been widely accepted as a TN (Danon-Boileau and Morel 1997; Denison 2002; Mihatsch 2016). This means that the pattern identified for the development of TN constructions has a wider range than originally assumed as other nouns not typically labelled as TNs may share it. The second hypothesis aims at differentiating the dynamics in the pattern followed by constructions with TNs vis-à-vis other nouns. What seems to be typical for the development of constructions with non-taxonomic nouns is that they tend to develop particle functions either before or simultaneously with prepositional ones and that particle functions are more common than prepositional functions. Such a development can be observed not only for *w stylu*, but also for *w guście* (<*gust* 'taste'), *na kształt* (<*kształt* 'shape'), *na wzór* (<*wzór* 'pattern'), *spod znaku* (<*znak* 'sign'), *z nurtu* (<*nurt* 'stream'), and *z serii* (<*seria* 'series'), etc. For example, in written language, the distribution of *w stylu* between nominal, prepositional and particle uses shows a strong preference for nominal uses (based on an analysis of 100 random occurrences in the National Corpus of Polish, the proportion is 56:14:28, respectively). However, in spoken language almost all uses (95% of occurrences in Spokes) represent particle uses, predominantly quotatives. Once again, this supports a long-entrenched thesis that spoken language is the locus of the most radical linguistic change (Halliday 1978).

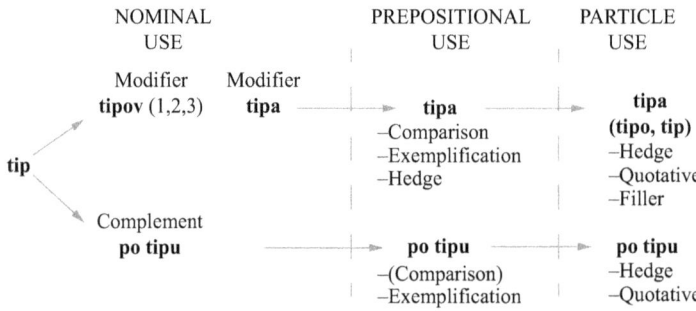

Figure 1: Hypothesized grammaticalization paths for constructions Russian *tip* (Kolyaseva and Davidse 2018).

It is worth noting that contrary to TNs the base non-taxonomic nouns discussed here either do not form a genitival modifier at all (comp. parallel (1a) with (2a) and (1b) with blocked (2b)) or such a modifier is extremely rare and does not seem fully correct (compare parallel to (1a–2a) *ciekawy kształt budynku* 'an interesting shape of a building' with parallel to (1b–2b) ?*budynek ciekawego kształtu* 'a building of an interesting shape' and a better alternative with the preposition *o*: *budynek o ciekawym kształcie* 'a building with an interesting shape').

(1) a. *ciekawy   typ   budownictwa*
       interesting-NOM.SG type-NOM.SG   architecture-GEN.SG
       'an interesting type of architecture'

    b. *budownictwo   ciekawego   typu*
       architecture-NOM.SG interesting-GEN.SG type-GEN.SG
       'architecture of an interesting type'

(2) a. *ciekawy   styl   budownictwa*
       interesting-NOM.SG style-NOM.SG   architecture-GEN.SG
       'an interesting style of architecture'

    b. **budownictwo   ciekawego   stylu*
       architecture-NOM.SG interesting-GEN.SG style-GEN.SG
       'architecture of an interesting style'

Therefore, in the case of the development of constructions with non-taxonomic nouns, we will be looking only at preposition-driven units (the lower row in Figure 1).

There are several possible explanations for the aforementioned acceleration towards particle uses alongside prepositional uses. The hypothesis of language contact-driven development has to be rejected for the reasons discussed in Kolyaseva (2018) for Russian. Firstly, particle uses of *w stylu* appear in the mid-twentieth century, at least two decades before the development of English quotatives such as *be like* and slightly before the first similar registered occurrences of Russian *tipa*. Secondly, at the time of the rise of the particle *w stylu*, Poland was isolated from other countries with the exception of Russia where so-called new quotatives (Blyth, Recktenwald and Wang 1990; Kolyaseva 2018) developed no sooner than in Polish.[1] Most likely, particle uses of *w stylu* and similar sequences are a result of language-internal development. It is naturally intriguing why such an innovation appeared around the same time in many European languages (Buchstaller and Van Alphen 2012). However, the issue will not be further debated in this chapter.

In order to present the development of *w stylu*, I will start by discussing its meaning from a synchronic perspective. Section 2 presents syntactic, prosodic and semantic differences between the preposition *w stylu* and the homophone particle. The former is compared with the compositional adverbial phrase *w stylu* and

---

[1] Poland also had some contact with other countries of the Eastern Bloc. However, access to those countries was rather limited.

the similarity marker *jak* 'how, like'; the latter is compared with other exemplification markers developed from TN and non-TN constructions. Section 3 delivers the analysis of diachronic material supporting the proposed difference between a preposition and a particle. Sections 4 and 5 concentrate on hedges (both in prepositional and particle uses) as the newest development of constructions with taxonomic and quasi-taxonomic nouns. Hedging is here treated as a special function of constructions with *w stylu* enabled by its primary meanings rather than as a completely new meaning. In Section 4, I discuss possible syntactic and contextual triggers of the hedging function as well as the influence of hedging on discourse flow.

2 *W stylu* in present-day Polish I: Prepositions versus particles

This section offers an overview of the grammaticalized uses of Pol. x *w stylu* y, their distribution and connectivity as compared to items similar in meaning. I argue that *w stylu* has evolved into similarity (3) and exemplification (4) markers. In its similarity function, it can be recognised as a preposition, whereas in its exemplification function as a particle. Both uses can be distinguished by syntactic factors: while the similarity marker preserves the case requirement of the base noun (compare the grammaticalized (3) with the nominal *styl tej książki* 'the style$_{NOM.SG}$ of this$_{GEN.SG}$ book$_{GEN.SG}$'), the exemplification marker adjoins a noun in the nominative. This innovation (i.e. a change of case requirement) is coupled with a change in prosody (a pause between the particle *w stylu* and y).

(3) książki   *w stylu*   "Dziennika   Bridget   Jones"
     book-NOM.PL   W STYLU   diary-GEN.M.SG Bridget-GEN.F.SG Jones-GEN.F.SG
     'Bridget Jones' Diary-style books'

(4) książki   *w stylu*   "Dziennik   Bridget   Jones"
     book-NOM.PL   W STYLU   diary-NOM.M.SG Bridget-GEN.F.SG Jones-GEN.F.SG
     'books like (for example) Bridget Jones' Diary'

In its similarity function, x *w stylu* y, permits in the y-position not only nouns in the genitive but also nominal phrases with deictic expressions (in the genitive), as in Table 1, and adjectival phrases with a participle, as in (5). This is similar to prepositional constructions with *typ* 'type' and *rodzaj* 'kind, genre' (see Kisiel 2018; Kisiel and Kolyaseva, this volume, chapter 13).

(5) książki   w stylu   pisanych   po   pracy
    book-NOM.PL W STYLU   written-GEN.PL after work-GEN.F.SG
    'written-after-work-style books'

Table 1: The range of uses of *w stylu*.

	nominal uses	prepositional uses	particle uses
styl	*ciekawy/fascynujący styl budownictwa* 'an interesing/fascinating style of architecture'	similarity: *budynki w stylu wieżowca* 'tower block-style buildings'	exemplification: *budynki w stylu: wieżowiec, drapacz chmur itd.* 'buildings like a tower-block, skyscraper etc.'
	chiński styl budownictwa 'the Chinese style of architecture' *styl Gaudiego* 'the style of Gaudi'	*budynki w stylu tych wybudowanych po wojnie* 'built-after-the-war-style buildings	*budynki w stylu "narysowałem kwadrat i pokolorowałem"* 'buildings like "I drew a square and coloured it"'
	budownictwo w stylu chińskim 'architecture in a Chinese style'	hedge: *coś w stylu wieżowca* 'something like a tower-block'	hedge: *coś/rzeczy w stylu wieżowiec* 'something/things like a tower-block'
	budownictwo w stylu Gaudiego 'architecture in the style of Gaudi'	*coś w tym stylu* 'something like this	*coś/rzeczy w stylu "narysowałem kwadrat i pokolorowałem"* 'something/things like "I drew a square and coloured it"'

Similarity is the base concept for the noun *styl* 'style', which can be defined as 'how something is done'. This has some important implications, the main one being that nominal (adverbial) uses of *w stylu*, as in (6), can be confused with prepositional uses (3) and (5) (see also Table 1). In the literature on Polish prepositions, the grammaticalization path from an adverb to a preposition is seen as very typical (Wątor 1976; Gawełko 2012). This interplay between an adverb and a preposition is particularly visible in the case of so-called secondary prepositions (*przyimki wtórne*, cf. Lesz-Duk 2011; Milewska 2003; Janowska 2015; Nowak 2008), which are reported to be indistinguishable from adverbs. Authors have hitherto pointed out the lack of criteria separating prepositional and adverbial uses (Nowak 2008) or claimed that the difference between these uses boils down to the two types of contexts in which they appear: with a noun (*jest obok domu* 'is next to the house') and with a contextual ellipsis of a noun (*jest obok* 'is close') (Karolak in Polański 1999). In this chapter, the difference between the nominal-adverbial and grammaticalized-prepositional uses is based on a difference between the right-slot fillers: x *w stylu* y in its nominal uses opens a y-slot for a descriptive element (mainly adjectives, as in (7)), whereas in prepositional uses both x and y positions are filled with nominal elements from the same class (cf. *budynki w stylu mozaiki Gaudiego 'Gaudi's mosaics'-style buildings'). The descriptive element (y) in nominal uses of *w stylu* can also point to a maker (see (6) and (8)) and therefore bring a more general description of x by evoking works (characteristic) of a certain person. In both (7) and (8), we tend to reconstruct the information on the right (y) as relating to how buildings made by the Chinese or Gaudi look, yet all that is communicated about the architecture is that 'it is done as the Chinese/Gaudi would do it'. Incidentally, it is likely that in (8), quite a few Polish speakers will not actually think about the buildings designed by Gaudi, but rather about his mosaics, stained glass and ironwork, something that the preposition *w stylu* forbids. It is also worth mentioning that these uses based on the recognition of someone's authorship have evolved into a specialized phraseme *coś (nie) jest w czyimś stylu* 'something is (not) one's style' as in (9).

(6) książki   w   stylu   Douglasa   Adamsa
    book-NOM.PL in   style-LOC.M.SG Douglas-GEN.M.SG Bridget-GEN.M.SG
    'books in the style of Douglas Adams'

(7) budownictwo   w   stylu   chińskim
    architecture-NOM.N.SG w   style-LOC.M.SG Chinese-LOC.M.SG
    'architecture in a Chinese style'

(8) budownictwo   w   stylu   Gaudiego
    architecture-NOM.N.SG w   style-LOC.M.SG Gaudi-GEN.M.SG
    'architecture in the style of Gaudi'

(9) To   nie w stylu   mojej   matki,   żeby
    it-NOM.N.SG not W STYLU   my-GEN.F.SG   mother-GEN.F.SG   in.order.to
    kłamać.
    lie-INF
    'Lying is not my mum's style.'

The difference between nominal and prepositional uses involves a change in function (from descriptive to relational). The preposition *w stylu*, which has undergone such a change, marks similarity between two given objects (or groups of objects). It is semantically close to the similarity marker *jak* 'like, how', which has been defined by Chojak (2009) on the basis of the notion of knowledge: *płakała jak Bridget Jones* 'she cried like Bridget Jones' is understood as 'she cried in such a way that we can know about her crying something that we know about Bridget

Jones' crying'. *Jak* and the preposition *w stylu* can be considered synonymic markers with complimentary distribution: *jak* is used with predicates (verbs, adjectives and adverbs), whereas *w stylu* prefers binominal constructions. This syntactic requirement is more specific than has previously been acknowledged for the homophone nominal uses.[2] It is paired with a change in meaning of the preposition *w stylu* in comparison with the nominal *w stylu*. If we compare (3) *książki w stylu "Dziennika Bridget Jones"* 'Bridget Jones' Diary-style books' and (6) *książki w stylu Douglasa Adamsa* 'books in the style of Douglas Adams', the semantic difference becomes clear. In nominal uses like in (6), *w stylu* characterizes a certain group of objects (books) by referencing a creator of this type of object (a writer, Douglas Adams). *Styl* retains its base meaning here and the whole prepositional phrase is used to describe the left-side noun rather than to establish a relation between the two objects. Contrarily, in (3), it is precisely the relation between the two objects that is of most relevance. Nominal uses of x *w stylu* y with a nominal x can be read as 'x is made in the same way that y made similar objects', whereas prepositional uses should be read as x *w stylu* y 'you can know about x something you know about y'.

The exemplification function is also based on the concept of similarity: x *w stylu* y 'x is such that you can know something about it when you know something about a certain class represented by y'. As will be shown in Section 3, it is impossible to tell which of the preposition or the particle developed first. It would seem logical for the preposition to precede the particle as it is semantically less complex (propositional versus (meta)textual) and more closely tied to nominal uses (for example with regard to syntactic requirements). That would be in line with most models of the unidirectional grammaticalization of *like* (eg. Romaine and Lange 1991). Yet, the preposition *w stylu* has never been significantly frequent and it seems justified to suggest an interrelationship between the two. This argument is supported by the fact that both the preposition and the particle can be used as hedges.

The particle x *w stylu* y is mainly used in bi(multi-)nominal constructions but the y-position can also be filled by a quotation, as in (10). Quotative uses are by far the most popular in spoken language, yet apart from this pragmatic specification, there is no difference between uses like (4) and (10). The function of the

---

[2] Nominal uses with predicates in left-hand context are also possible, even though they might be rare, as in *Będzie pan pracował w stylu Zbigniewa Bońka latając po Europie, by podglądać potencjalnych kadrowiczów czy też jak Jerzy Engel bazując na zapisach magnetowidowych?* 'Will you work in the style of Zbigniew Boniek and fly all around Europe to observe potential players for the national team or more like Jerzy Engel, simply watching videos?'

particle *w stylu* in quotative contexts is to present a quotation as an example of what someone said or could say.

(10) słowa   w stylu   "najdroższa,   jedyna"
     word-NOM.PL   W STYLU   dearest-NOM.F.SG the.one-NOM.F.SG
     'words like "dearest, beloved"'

In the spoken language the particle x *w stylu* y can be used without any accompanying noun in the x-position, as in (11). This confirms its non-prepositional status. Contrary to the homophone preposition, the particle *w stylu* is removable (in quotative contexts). However, if *w stylu* introduces something that did not occur nor was intended to occur but is more a summary of what a quoted speaker had in mind, "a recollection which is often more accurate in general meaning than in precise wording" (Romaine and Lange 1991: 230), as in (11), then the reduction of the particle is blocked. The presence of a marker like *w stylu* is in such uses required precisely in order to dismiss a verbatim reading.[3]

(11) PiS   wprawdzie   nie   pochwala   tej
     PiS   admittedly not   approve-PRS.3SG   this-GEN.F.SG
     metody,   ale   mówi   w stylu: cel
     method-GEN.F.SG   but   say-PRS.3SG   W STYLU   goal-NOM.M.SG
     uświęca   środki
     sanctify-PRS.3SG   measure-ACC.PL
     'Admittedly, PiS does not approve of this method but says something like, "The ends justify the means."' (NCP)

It is important to differentiate particle uses in (11) from very infrequent nominal uses with left-sided verbal context. In such nominal uses a speaker describes the way something is done as similar to the way another person does it (or rather *did it* as such a person serves here as a point of reference for the action in question). Particle *w stylu*, even though semantically also rooted in the notion of similarity, does not simply deliver a comparison between two objects. It rather states that we can know something about what is being spoken about (be it an object or an action) when we recognize a certain class represented by an object (or an action) to which y refers. For example, in the nominal (12a) the way Lovecraft writes is compared (described as similar) to Poe's style of writing, whereas in (12b), which

---

[3] This is of course to the extent that a quotation in the spoken language can ever be verbatim (see Tannen 1989; Clark and Gerrig 1990).

exemplifies the particle use, we can know what a certain person writes about the papists when we recognize the type of attitude represented by the quotation. Similarly, in (13a) the behaviour of Posadzki is compared to the behaviour of a communist comrade, whereas in (13b) we can only understand the type of behaviour represented by an enthusiast in question when we correctly recognize the attitude hidden behind the quoted proverb.

(12) a. *Czy Lovecraft   pisze   w stylu*
    Q   Lovecraft-NOM.M.SG write-PRS.3SG in style-LOC.M.SG
    Edgara Allan Poe?
    Edgar.Allan.Poe-GEN.M.SG
    'Does Lovecraft write in the style of Edgar Allan Poe?' (NCP)
  b. *O   takich   samych   okrucieństwach   papistów*
     about   this-LOC.PL   same-LOC.PL   atrocity-LOC.PL papist-GEN.PL
     pisze   w stylu   „olaboga,   ale go   męczą,
     write-PRS.3SG   W STYLU   holy.moly   but he-ACC   torment-PRS.3PL
     biedny   on,   biedny...".
     poor-NOM.M.SG   he-NOM   poor-NOM.M.SG
     'About similar atrocities of the papists he writes something like, "Holy moly! How they torment him! Poor, poor him."' (NCP)

(13) a. *UPR zwróciła Posadzkiemu   uwagę,   że*
     UPR   Posadzki-DAT.M.SG   point.out-PST.F.3SG that
     zachowuje się   w stylu   towarzysza
     behave-PRS.3SG in style-LOC.M.SG   comrade-GEN.M.SG
     partyjnego   przekonywującego   naród (...)
     party-ADJ.GEN.M.SG   convincing-GEN.M.SG   nation-ACC.M.SG
     'UPR pointed out to Posadzki that he behaved like (=in the style of) a comrade persuading the nation.' (NCP)
  b. *A   pasjonat,   który   przez*
     and enthusiast-NOM.M.SG   which-NOM.M.SG   through
     niechęć   do   historii   filozofii
     aversion-ACC.F.SG   towards   history-GEN.F.SG philosophy-GEN.F.SG
     nie   ma   zamiaru   ich   sobie
     not   have-PRS.3SG   intention-GEN.M.SG they-ACC   himself
     przyswoić   zachowuje się   w stylu   „na złość
     internalize-INF   behave-PRS.3SG   W STYLU   for anger-ACC.F.SG

babci	odmrożę	sobie	uszy".
grandmother-GEN.F.SG	frostbite-FUT.1SG	myself	ear-ACC.PL

'And an enthusiast who does not intend to internalize them due to his aversion to the history of philosophy behaves like "I'll cut off my nose to spite my face".' (NCP)

The difference between the exemplification function of x *w stylu* y and other exemplification markers, including the ones based on TNs (x *w rodzaju* y, x *typu* y, see Kisiel and Kolyaseva, this volume, chapter 13) is that the object(s) referred to by the x-complement of x *w stylu* y are in fact like objects from a set determined by the y-complement, making this construction much more closely aligned to the similarity marker. *W stylu* does not settle the question as to whether or not a x-object belongs to a set so characterized. Consider the difference between *szli ze sloganami w stylu "Maryja rządzi", "z Maryją na wieki"* 'they walked with slogans like "Mary rules", "Mary forever"' and ... *sloganami typu...* '... with such slogans as ...'. In the first case, the y-complement defines the slogans in question as produced by Catholic ultras; however, we do not know exactly what slogans were presented during the march. In the second case, a speaker gives an example of such a slogan and even though it might be that not all the slogans during the march were the same to the letter, they involved Mary and expressed a certain appreciation for her. In other words, *w stylu* establishes a similarity between some elements of a certain class and the presented object(s).

3 *W stylu* in the history of Polish

The noun *styl* entered the Polish language system in the second half of the seventeenth century with the meaning 'way of expressing thoughts', as observed in the definition in Linde (1807) 'for the Romans a tool to write, later transferred to naming various ways of speaking and writing'. This meaning became very quickly extended. *Słownik wileński* (1861) registers uses of *styl* with reference not exclusively to speaking and writing but to human activity at large, with the following definitions: 'a way to write, compose'; *fig.* 'a way of composing and producing, which is characteristic for an artist'; *fig.* 'a method of construction, a kind' (*dom drewniany w stylu rodzinnym* 'a wooden house in a family style'); and 'regulated time division and layout'. A few decades later, *Słownik warszawski* (1900–1927) adds a new general and figurative meaning 'a manner, a kind, a sort; a scale'. Yet none of the dictionaries until the second half of the twentieth century (until *Słownik* Doroszewskiego) note *w stylu*, not even in examples of nominal uses. *Inny słownik języka polskiego* (2000) registers *coś w tym stylu* 'something like this', an informal nominal phrase or an exclamation with a similar function. Finally, the most recent dictionary, *Wielki słownik języka polskiego* (2015-), registers *w stylu* as a preposition with two meanings: pointing to an object to which another object has become similar, and introducing exemplary elements of a certain set.

This semantic development is supported by the data extracted from the National Corpus of Polish (see Table 2). Nominal uses dominate until the mid-twentieth century when the new quotative and hedging uses appear. Interestingly, the prepositional uses that appear only slightly earlier are from the outset less frequent than particle uses. The variation of hedging structures grows with time, including hedges based on the binominal structure of the preposition: *coś w stylu* x_{GEN}. This coincides with the first occurrences of *typu* 'like' in its function as an exemplifier. It would be tempting to suggest that this innovation for *typu* stimulated the constructions with non-taxonomic nouns to develop similar meanings. However, quotative *w rodzaju* was popular as early as the 1930s. As mentioned earlier, it can be hypothesized that the twentieth century, particularly the second half, brought popularization of the particle uses of TN constructions and that some other nouns which in the meantime had developed quasi-taxonomy uses followed this pattern before managing to fully develop prepositional uses. However, this is a hypothesis that needs to be verified by analyzing the historical data for all nominal constructions that developed the functions in question.

Table 2: The sequence of appearance of new uses of *w stylu* since the nineteenth century.

Period	Occurrences	New uses
1800–1900	11	– nominal uses only
1901–1910	6	
1911–1920	0	
1921–1930	21	– extension of adverbial contexts – 1923 *bajkopisarstwo w stylu la Fontaine's* 'science-fiction writing in the style of La Fontaine'
1931–1940	21	
1941–1950	5	– 1946 prepositional: *dowcip w stylu zagadek ormiańskich* 'Armenian riddle-style joke'
1951–1960	24	– quotative uses: *pytanie w stylu "czego się napiję, kawy czy herbaty?"* 'a question like, "What would you like to drink, tea or coffee?"' – hedges: *coś w stylu procesów* 'something like trials'; . . . *albo coś w tym stylu* 'or something like this'; . . ., *coś w tym stylu* 'something like this'

Table 2 (continued)

Period	Occurrences	New uses
1961–1970	35	
1971–1980	53	
1981–1990	73	
1991–2000	4767	– hedges: *coś w stylu „. . ."* 'something like, ". . ."'; *ktoś w stylu Marlowe'a* 'someone like Marlowe'; *coś w stylu, że . . .* 'something like that . . .'; *. . . czy coś w tym stylu* 'or something like this' – exemplification: *babskie gazety w stylu Claudia czy Oliwia* 'girls' magazines like Claudia or Oliwia'
2001–2010	30996	
2011–2019	9	

4 *W stylu* in present-day Polish II: Hedges and exemplification markers

Recent decades have witnessed growth in the range and use of hedges cross-linguistically (Namsaraev 1997; Gries and David 2007; Fetzer 2010; Adamczyk 2015; Doboszyńska-Markiewicz 2015) and quotatives (Blyth, Recktenwald, and Wang 1990; Macaulay 2001; Bakht-Rofheart 2002, Cukor-Avila 2002; Tagliamonte and D'Arcy 2004; Buchstaller 2006; Fox Tree and Tomlinson 2008; Tagliamonte, D'Arcy, and Rodríguez Louro 2016). It has been reported that the increase in the use of these devices is often paired with the widening variety of contexts they can participate in (see, for example, Fox Tree and Tomlinson 2008 for quotative *like*). The acceleration of language change in the last half a century "is not a coincidence. Scholars have documented extreme changes in all areas of science, technology, and human interaction in this period. (. . .) We suggest that these unmatched developments – stemming from social, cultural, and political changes – lead to a concomitant linguistic renaissance" (Tagliamonte, D'Arcy, and Rodríguez Louro 2016: 838–839). The development of TN constructions and similar is a part of this global change.

TNs and similar constructions show a clear tendency to perform the function of hedges. *W stylu*, based on the concept of similarity, seems particularly well designed to play the role of a hedge (Buchstaller and Van Alphen 2012). Participation of *w stylu* in the hedging function started in the mid-twentieth century with one important innovation shared by both the preposition and particle uses: co-occurrence with the referential vagueness marker *coś* 'something'. Interestingly, a similarity marker *coś w stylu* y has always been more common than x *w stylu* y and *coś w stylu* y in the exemplification function is even more frequent. As Table 3 shows, the similarity marker *coś w stylu* y is less frequent in written language than the exemplification marker *coś w stylu* y (even assuming that all contexts like (14)–(15) should be accounted for as examples of *coś w stylu* y$_{\text{GEN.SG}}$ hosting indeclinable nouns).

(14) Lepsze by było jakby każdy kraj
 better would-3SG be-PST.N.3SG as every-NOM.M country-NOM.M.SG
 miał takie same prawo a
 have-PST.M.3SG such-ACC.N.SG same- ACC.N.SG law- ACC.N.SG and
 jeden przewodniczył na jakiś okres
 one- NOM.M.SG preside-PST.M.3SG for some-ACC.M.SG period-ACC.M.SG
 coś w stylu UE.
 something-NOM.N W STYLU UE
 'It'd be better if every country had the same regulations and one of them would preside for a period of time; something like the EU.' (NCP)

(15) To mi wygląda na coś w stylu portfolio.
 it I-DAT look.like-PRS.3SG something-ACC.N W STYLU portfolio
 'It looks to me like something like a portfolio.' (NCP)

The relation between *coś* 'something' and the preposition and the particle *w stylu* is not a simple one. In many cases *coś w stylu* is visibly compositional, i.e. in contexts where *coś* 'something' is required by a superordinate verb in the clause, like in *dostać coś w stylu nagrody* 'to get something like a prize' or *powiedzieć coś w stylu "spadaj, durniu"* 'to say something like, "get lost, you fool"'. The separation of *coś* and *w stylu* is sometimes emphasized by added *takiego* [*taki*$_{\text{GEN}}$] 'such', especially in informal language, as in (16)–(17). *Coś* is also not the only possible companion for *w stylu*. In recent years, *w stylu* can also co-occur with *rzeczy* 'things', as in (18); see Dines 1980.[4] Sporadically, *coś* 'something' can be replaced by *ktoś* 'someone' if a noun filling the y-position of the preposition *w stylu* refers to a person (#10 in Table 3). This is not at all necessary since *coś* 'something' works well with reference to human objects (see (17)); such hypercorrectness is yet one more argument for the compositionality of *coś w stylu*.

---

[4] Even though 0-filler in left-sided context is becoming more and more popular in spoken language, nominal context is still dominant for both the preposition and the particle *w stylu*.

(16) *Istnieje   coś   takiego   w stylu   ombre   tylko*
    exist-PRS.3SG something-NOM.N this-GEN.N.SG W STYLU ombre only
    żeby   przyciemnić   włosy   zamiast   rozjaśniania?
    to   darken-INF   hair-ACC.PL instead   bleaching-GRND.GEN
    'Is there something like ombre but to darken hair instead of bleaching it?'
    (Internet, www.wykop.pl accessed Jan 2020)

(17) *wiem   że   jest   teraz   coś   takiego*
    know-PRS.1SG that   be-PRS.3SG   now   something-NOM.N this-GEN.N.SG
    w stylu   „rzecznik   pasażerów"
    W STYLU   spokesman-NOM.M.SG   passenger-GEN.PL
    'I know there is now something like "a passenger spokesman"'
    (Internet, info.wyborcza.biz accessed Jan 2020)

(18) *Jednak jeśli już   naprawdę   język   Cię*
    yet   if   already   really   tongue-NOM.M.SG   you-ACC
    świerzbi,   nie   mów   rzeczy   w stylu: „Jesteś
    itch-PRS.3SG not   say-IMPER   thing-ACC.PL W STYLU   be-PRS.2SG
    marnym   kierowcą,   jak   każda
    poor-INS.M.SG   driver-INS.M.SG   like   every-NOM.F.SG
    baba".
    woman-OFFENS-NOM.F.SG
    'If you really have to say something, don't ever say things like, "You are a poor driver, like every woman"' (NCP)

One might argue that the presence of the pronoun *tym* [*ten*$_{LOC}$] 'this, the' in phrases such as #2–5 and #8–9 in Table 3, some of which are very frequent in both written and spoken language, points to nominal character of *w stylu*. However, *ten*$_{LOC}$ does not function as a determiner of *styl* 'a style' but rather has an anaphoric function and refers to a previously given nominal phrase. For example, the sentence in #2 in Table 3. below can be transformed into the phrase *coś w stylu drugich narodzin* 'something like a second birth'. In other words, *tym*, by referring to something previously mentioned, replaces the function of y. The possibility of replacing the y-noun by a demonstrative pronoun has been observed for many secondary prepositions (Przybylska 1988; Milewska 2003; Nowak 2008). It has also been noticed that demonstratives are a common source of quotatives in many of the world's languages (Buchstaller and Van Alphen 2012).

14 Polish *w stylu* and the rise of hedges — 559

Table 3: The development of the range of hedging constructions with *w stylu*, based on NCP (full version) and Spokes.

		NCP		Spokes
#	Phrase	First occurrence	Total number	
1	*coś w stylu* N$_{GEN.SG}$ 'something like N'	1954 *Cóż by to była za gratka, gdyby się udało (. . .) zmontować jakiś proces przeciwko komunistom (. . .).* ***Coś w stylu procesów*** *organizowanych przez przyjaciół pani Luce w jej własnym kraju.* 'What a treat it would be if we could put the communists on trial. **Something like the processes** organized by Miss Luce's friends in her own country.'	1155	0
2	*. . . . coś w tym stylu* '. . . something like that'	1955 *(. . .) czy też coś się zmieni i nasza pamięć wystartuje od zera. Drugie narodziny,* ***coś w tym stylu****.* 'or something will change and our memory will restart. A second birth, **something like that**.'	326	19
3	*albo coś w tym stylu* 'or something like that'	1957 *Wtedy krzycz: „ratunku! bandyci!" –* ***albo coś w tym stylu****.* 'Then yell "Help! Bandits!" **or something like that**.'	541	5
4	*coś w tym stylu* 'something like this'	1987 *Tak, w tym miejscu M-ski niechybnie powiedziałby jakiś morał (. . .) coś w rodzaju: „Kto się prawdy nie boi, niczego się nie boi", bez wątpienia powiedziałby* ***coś w tym stylu****, ale (. . .)* 'Yes, in this moment M-ski would certainly moralize, something like "One who is not afraid of the truth, is not afraid of anything", certainly he'd say **something like this** but. . .'	163	4
5	*czy coś w tym stylu* 'or something like this'	1991 *Nie będę przytaczał, aby znowu nie być przez kogoś oskarżony (. . .) o naruszenie czyichś praw autorskich* ***czy coś w tym stylu****.* 'I will not quote it so that I'm not again accused of violating someone's authorship **or something like that**.'	1283	8
6	*coś w stylu „. . ."*/N$_{NOM.SG}$, N$_{NOM.SG}$ 'something like ". . ."'	1995 *Przecież w tych gazetach seks przedstawiany jest jako dobry sposób na rozładowanie stresu!* ***Coś w stylu****: „Masz zły humor? – Jedź z dziewczyną za miasto, tylko nie obiecuj, że ją kochasz".* 'But in those newspapers, sex is presented as a good way to relax! **Something like** "Are you in a bad mood? Take a girl out of the city, just don't tell her you love her"'	1216	21
7	*coś w stylu, że* 'something like that p'	1997 *Nawet Wrońska powiedziała* ***coś w stylu, że*** *Danka po śmierci Romka bardzo się zmieniła.* 'Even Wrońska said **something like that** Danka has changed a lot after Romek's death.'	76	3

Table 3 (continued)

#	Phrase	NCP First occurrence	Spokes Total number	
8	*lub coś w tym stylu* 'or something like this'	1998 (...) *kiedy mężczyźni wypowiadają się o kobietach jakby były istotami drugiej kategorii **lub coś w tym stylu**.* 'when men say things about women as if they were second category beings **or something like this**.'	401	0
9	*bądź coś w tym stylu* 'or something like this'	1999 *Jednak mój ostatni post skierowany właśnie do Amarota zasługuje chyba na odpowiedź (choćby zauważenie, że jestem głupi **bądź coś w tym stylu**)* 'But my last post to Amarot deserves, I think, an answer (even if it's just pointing out that I'm stupid **or something like that**).'	8	0
10	*ktoś w stylu* $N_{GEN.SG}$ 'someone like N'	1999 *Dla szczegółów poczytaj Chandlera (ale to NIE ma być **ktoś w stylu** Marlowe'a) albo lepiej Dashiella Hammetta.* 'For details read Chandler (but it should not be **anyone like** Marlow) or even better, Dashiell Hammett.'	4	0

It is worth noting that the whole series with *coś* (*coś w tym stylu/guście/rodzaju* 'something like this') and particularly terminal tags (Dines 1980; Romaine and Lange 1991), i.e. markers taking the final position (*czy coś/albo coś* 'or something', *czy coś w tym stylu/czy coś w tym guście/czy coś w tym rodzaju/albo/lub/ bądź coś w tym stylu/guście/rodzaju* 'or something like this'[5]) have the special function of dismissing precision. In using them the speaker informs the interlocutor that s/he is not willing to be more specific. This dismissal ('I do not think it is important to be more specific about it') does not have to be negative. It can also be a sign of trust in shared knowledge ('you know what I am talking about'). The importance of this series in discourse is confirmed by its extended uses, for example, as a response weakening what the interlocutor has said, as in (19); see the vast range of variants in Table 3.

(19) A: *Więc to groźba?* B: *Coś w tym*
so it threat-NOM.F.SG something-NOM.N w this-LOC.M.SG
stylu.
style-LOC.M.SG
'A: Is it a threat? B: Something like that.'

---

5 These should be considered as variants. "Syntactic variants, it can be argued, are only weakly equivalent, probably no transformation being free of change in meaning." (Dines 1980:15)

Another argument supporting the compositionality of *coś w stylu* refers only to the particle *w stylu* and was mentioned earlier: the x-position of x *w stylu* y can be left empty as long as the grammatical structure of a sentence does not require the presence of an object, such as a verb that does not demand a complement. In (20) the speaker, by using *w stylu*, introduces an example of what she means by organizing outsourcing in HR. Here, the left-side slot is only seemingly empty as x can be extracted from the preceding context. There are also contexts where the addition of *coś* 'something' (or any other noun for that matter) is blocked. Those uses, such as in (21), are typical for spoken language and will be discussed below in more detail.

(20) *a   oni   jeszcze   tam   na   tej   stronie*
     and   they-NOM   still   there   on   this-LOC.F.SG   website-LOC.F.SG
     ich   czytam   oni   mają   też   takie
     their   read-PRS.1SG they-NOM   have-PRS.3SG   also   this-ACC.PL
     *robią   chyba   **haerowy**   też   **autsorsing***
     do-PRS.3SG   maybe   HR-ADJ.ACC.M   also   outsourcing-ACC.M.SG
     *czasem   nie?   wiesz   **w stylu**   lancze*
     sometimes   no   know-PRS.2SG   W STYLU   lunch-NOM.PL
     chyba   czy   coś
     perhaps   or   something-NOM
     'and they still / there on their website / I read / they have also these / I think / **HR** / also / **outsources** sometimes, doesn't it? You know, **like** lunches maybe, or something' (Spokes)

(21) *wiesz   jakoś   tak   ona   autentycznie   w*
     know-PRS.2SG   somehow   so   she-NOM   really   in
     głowie   ma   już   zakodowane   jak
     head-LOC.F.SG   have-PRS.3SG   already   code-PASS   how
     *mówi   o   godzinie   y   **w stylu**   szósta*
     say-PRS.3SG   about   hour-LOC.F.SG   eee   W STYLU   sixth-NOM.F.SG
     to   mówi   o   szóstej   w   nocy
     then   say-PRS.3SG   about   sixth-LOC.F.SG   in   night-LOC.F.SG
     czaisz
     understand-PRS.2SG
     'you know / somehow she really has it already coded in her head when she talks about hours // **like** / six / then she says / at six in the night / see?' (NCP)

So far, all hedging uses discussed in this paper have been triggered by the addition of *coś* 'something'. The question is whether either the preposition and the particle *w stylu* can be used as hedges alone. As mentioned previously, the meaning of both types of *w stylu*, which is based on the concept of similarity, facilitates hedging. The buildings (*budynki*) in *budynki w stylu Palau Güell Gaudiego* 'Gaudi Palau Güell style buildings' are given only a rough description based on what they resemble. If our understanding of hedging is based on the concept of fuzziness (as in the original work of Lakoff (1972)), then identifying similarity with hedging would be too far-reaching. The same can be said about the exemplification marker. Identifying an object by showing its similarity to a class defined by an illustrative member is certainly not the most straightforward method, but even within this usage, *w stylu* does not comment on the degree to which the object fits a certain category as a typical hedge does. This common misconception about exemplification markers has been previously highlighted by some researchers. For example, Dines (1980) discussing final tags such as *and stuff like that* emphasizes that they "operate on 'parts' to relate them to 'wholes' (. . .) The presence of a clause-terminal tag indicates that an underlying general notion has been realised by a specific example." (Dines 1980: 22). It therefore appears clear that it is *coś* 'something' that carries the hedging meaning in the constructions discussed. The only possible use of *w stylu* without *coś* 'something' in a hedging function involves contexts like (21) in which *w stylu* delays giving an example, which could be regarded as epistemic hedging if hedging were associated with tentativeness.[6] In the sentence presented, the delay results from the speaker's need to consider which example would best communicate what he/she is trying to say. As pointed out by Dines (1980), exemplification markers signalize implicitness rather than inexplicitness. Due to the syntactic independence of *w stylu* from the rest of the sentence (21), its function here is similar to that of a filler.

Finally, a few words must be said about the particle *w stylu* allowing for a quotative complement. Contrary to *like*, its very close equivalent in English, *w stylu* indicates that there is a distinction between the reported words and the original (cf. Romaine and Lange 1991; Fox Tree and Tomlinson 2008). This is supported not only by contexts like (22) where this lack of exact correspondence is marked in an explicit way, but also by adding, for example, a marker reporting on a speaker's choice regarding what should be said (like *raczej* 'rather' in (23)).

---

6 Epistemic perspective has been reported for some of the uses of TN-constructions, as in: "Rather than viewing *like* as a marker of vagueness, it can be more appropriately construed as a marker of intersubjectivity. By presupposing similar background knowledge and experience, *like* is used as a basis for saying less while simultaneously conveying that there is more for the addressee to add in order to flesh out unstated meanings" (Levey 2003:30).

One might argue that this points to a hedging function of the quotative *w stylu* (on the potential of units evolved from the core meaning of similarity to function as hedges see e.g. Hasund, Opsahl, and Svennevig 2012). I argue that it is not the case. A quotation appears here as an example of what was/can be said and as such does not have to be an exact copy of the words uttered. Even though there are certain differences between exemplificative x *w stylu* y with a N_{NOM} and with a quotation in the y-position, such as the possibility to remove *w stylu* in the latter case but not in the former, I opt for a joint analysis of these uses as two instances of one particle's occurrence. In both types of contexts, the meaning of *w stylu* remains the same (as presented in Section 1) and the y can be explained through demonstration theory (Clark and Gerrig 1990; Fox Tree and Tomlinson 2008). Both N_{NOM} and a quotation represent only certain aspects of how something is to give a general idea to an interlocutor as to what is being discussed.

(22) na scenę   wyszedł   Paweł   Kukiz   i
     on stage-ACC.F.SG come-PST.M.3SG   Paweł-NOM.M   Kukiz-NOM.M   and
     powiedział   coś   **w stylu**   (**nie pamiętam**
     say-PST.M.3SG   something-ACC   W STYLU   not   remember-PRS.1SG
     dokładnie):   „Polska   śle   wielkie   pieniądze
     exactly   Poland-NOM.F   send-PRS.3SG   big-ACC.PL   money-ACC.PL
     do   dalekiej   Azji,   by   pomóc   umierającym   dzieciom,
     to   far-GEN.F.SG Asia-GEN.F   to   help-INF dying-DAT.PL   child-DAT.PL
     tymczasem   dzień   dnia   w   Polsce
     while   day-NOM.M.SG   day-GEN.M.SG   in   Poland-LOC.F
     cierpią   i   głodują   dzieci   i   nikt
     suffer-PRS.3PL   and   starve-PRS.3PL child-NOM.PL and   no.one-NOM.M
     tego   nie   zauważa"
     this-GEN.M.SG   not   notice-PRS.3SG
     'Paweł Kukiz went on the stage and said something like (**I don't remember exactly**): "Poland sends huge amounts to distant Asia to help dying kids, while every day Polish kids suffer and starve, and no one notices."' (NCP)

(23) stwierdzenie (...)   całkowicie   inne,   **raczej w stylu**
     statement-NOM.N.SG   completely   different-NOM.N.SG rather W STYLU
     „Jeśli   nauczyciel X   jest   pedofilem,   to
     if   teacher-NOM.M.SG   be-PRS.3SG   paedophile-INS.M.SG   then
     nauczyciel Y   również   nim   jest?"
     teacher-NOM.M.SG   also   he-INS   be-PRS.3SG
     'It is a completely different statement, **more like**, "If teacher X is a paedophile, then is teacher Y one, too?"' (NCP)

For this very reason, it is also possible for *w stylu* + QUOT to report on thoughts (24) or hypothetical and not real words (25), which differentiates it from verbs introducing reported speech, like *powiedzieć* 'to say' (Bogusławski 2005). Moreover, *w stylu* can also report on specific prosody or intonation, such as when it introduces a song in (26), or other non-verbal expressions like laughter (known as token mimicry, see Rimmer 1988; Levey 2003) as in (27). It can even accompany gestures, as in *Ona na to w stylu* [groźna mina, warkot] 'And she goes like [makes an angry face and snarls]'. Contrary to *like*, it can also introduce reported speech in combination with *że* 'that', as in (28). In recent years, these uses have developed into the new function of the explanation marker (similar to *to znaczy że* 'in other words'; lit. 'it means that'), such as in (29) where a speaker explains what s/he means by a certain device "dying". These new (and not yet stabilized) uses were rendered possible precisely because the particle *w stylu* does not introduce an exact quotation but rather an impression of what has been said.

(24) *Ale kiedy ochłonąłem, dorwały mnie dziwne*
but when calm.down-PST.M.1SG grab-PST.3PL I-ACC weird-NOM.PL
myśli, w stylu „coś było nie tak
thought-NOM.PL W STYLU something-NOM.N be-PST.N.3SG not so
hm... czy ja czegoś nie udawałem?".
hmm... Q I-NOM something-GEN.N not pretend-PST.M.1SG
'But when I calmed down, weird thoughts came to me like, "Wasn't there anything wrong hmm... or was I not pretending something?"' (NCP)

(25) *Nie sądzę... ale zaraz oczywiście posypie się*
not think-PRS.1SG but soon obviously bepowder-FUT.3SG
lawina lawina tekstów w stylu „jeśli
avalanche-NOM.F.SG avalanche-NOM.F.SG text-GEN.PL W STYLU if
ma super charakter to...", czy
have-PRS.3SG super-ACC.M.SG character-ACC.M.SG then or
też „niektórym się tacy faceci podobają..."
also some-DAT.PL such-NOM.PL guy-NOM.PL fancy-PRS.3PL
– BULLSHIT!
'I don't think so... but thick and fast we will get a bunch of texts like, "If he has a good character then..." or "Some [women] like those kind of men..." – BULLSHIT' (NCP)

(26) *heh ja   znam   coś   w stylu . . .*
          I-NOM   know-PRS.1SG something-ACC   W STYLU
      „pszczółka   maja   sobie   lata   aaaahaaaa (. . .)"
      bee-DIM.NOM.F.SG Maya-NOM   oneself   fly-PRS.3SG
      "Huh I know something like, "Maya the bee is flying around aaaaahaaaa'"
      (NCP)

(27) *Ale   to   było   takie,   że   tylko się można*
      but   it-NOM.N   be-PST.N.3SG such-NOM.N   that   only   can
      było   z   śmiać,   w stylu: tego   ha, ha, ha,
      be-PST.N.3SG from laugh-INF W STYLU   this-GEN.N.SG
      ale   fajna   sprawa.
      but   cool-NOM.F.SG thing-NOM.F.SG
      'But it was like you could only laugh at it, like, "Ha, ha, ha, how cool!"' (NCP)

(28) *Poza tym   wasze   uwagi   w stylu,   że   jest*
      besides   your-NOM.PL   remark-NOM.PL   W STYLU   that be-PRS.3SG
      okropnie   brzydka,   niezgrabna   itp.   to   już   lekka
      awfully   ugly-F.SG   clumsy-F.SG   etc.   it   already slight-NOM.F.SG
      przesada.
      exaggeration-NOM.F.SG
      'Besides, your remarks like **that** she is horribly ugly, clumsy etc. are a bit of an exaggeration.' (NCP)

(29) *Ale   gaśnie   w stylu   że   ekranik   przestaje*
      but   die-PRS.3SG   W STYLU   that   screen-NOM.M.SG   stop-PRS.3SG
      świecić
      give.light-INF
      'But it dies, I mean, the screen stops giving light.' (NCP)

5 Conclusions

In this chapter, I have shown how syntactic development is correlated with semantic-pragmatic change. All the meanings and functions of *w stylu* are based on the concept of similarity. This means that in all cases it allows for a selective depiction of certain aspects of what is given in the right slot. However, this base concept is represented differently depending on *w stylu*'s function: characterizing (nominal uses), relational (prepositional uses), (meta)textual (particle uses), as illustrated in Figure 2. The function of *w stylu* also correlates with syntactic features: in nominal uses y-filler is mainly adjectival, whereas prepositional uses require both the positions of x and y are occupied by nominal elements that belong to the same class. Particle uses, on the other hand, appear together with syntactic loosening (i.e. no case requirements, strong pauses, possible 0-filler in the x-position). This path, though similar to that taken by taxonomic nouns (Figure 1), has in the case of nouns like *styl* 'a style' been shortened so that the prepositional and particle uses appear around the same time.

nominal:		preposition:	hedge:
styl y.GEN 'how y is made' *styl* x.GEN 'how x makes things'	y *w stylu* x.GEN 'y made in the same way that x made similar objects'	y *w stylu* x.GEN 'you can know about y something you know about x' **particle:** [y] *w stylu* x.NOM-series/QUOT 'y is such that you know it when you know the class represented by x'	+*coś*; zero-y; *tym*; QUOT 'what you know about x is not exactly or not all you can know about y'

Figure 2: The meanings of *w stylu*.

The similarity-based meanings allow both the preposition and the particle to be used in a hedging function. However, this function is enabled by additional co-occurring elements: vagueness markers like *coś* 'something' and *rzeczy* 'things', demonstratives in anaphoric use (*ten* 'this'), and a position switch (to a final tag). Very recently, spoken language has begun to permit new filler-like uses of particle *w stylu*. At the same time, a new 'explanatory' use has appeared, which means that the future path of the particle *w stylu* is as yet undetermined.

References

Dictionaries and corpora

Linde, Bogumił. 1807–1814. *Słownik języka polskiego*. Warszawa: Drukarnia Księży Pijarów.
Słownik warszawski: Karłowicz, Jan, Adam Antoni Kryński & Władysław Niedźwiedzki (eds.). 1900–1927. *Słownik języka polskiego*. Warszawa: PWN.
Słownik wileński. 1861. Wilno: Maurycy Orgelbrand.
Słownik Doroszewskiego: Doroszewski, Witold (ed.). 1958–1969. *Słownik języka polskiego*:. Warszawa: PWN
Bańko, Mirosław (ed.). 2000. *Inny słownik języka polskiego*. Warszawa: PWN.

Wielki słownik języka polskiego https://www.wsjp.pl/ (accessed 5 May 2019)
Narodowy Korpus Języka Polskiego http://nkjp.pl/ (accessed 5 May 2019)
Spokes http://spokes.clarin-pl.eu/ (accessed 5 May 2019)

Other references

Adamczyk, Magdalena. 2015. Do hedges always hedge? On non-canonical multifunctionality of *jakby* in Polish. *Pragmatics* 25 (3). 321–344.

Bakht-Rofheart, Maryam. 2002. *Avoidance of a new standard: Quotative use among Long Island teenagers*. Paper presented at NWAVE 31, Stanford University, California.

Blyth, Carl, Sigrid Recktenwald & Jenny Wang. 1990. I'm like, 'Say what?!'. A new quotative in American oral narrative. *American Speech* 65. 215–227.

Bogusławski, Andrzej. 2005. Do teorii czasownika powiedzieć [Addendum to the theory of the verb powiedzieć 'to say']. *Polonica* 24–25. 139–155.

Brems, Lieselotte. 2011. *Layering of size and type noun constructions in English*. Berlin, Boston: De Gruyter Mouton.

Buchstaller, Isabelle. 2006. Social stereotypes, personality traits and regional perception displaced: Attitudes towards the 'new' quotatives in the U.K. *Journal of Sociolinguistics* 10 (3). 362–381.

Buchstaller, Isabelle & Ingrid Van Alphen. 2012. Introductory remarks on new and old quotatives. In Isabelle Buchstaller & Ingrid Van Alphen (eds.), *Quotatives: Cross-linguistic and cross-disciplinary perspectives*, xii–xxx. Amsterdam: Benjamins.

Chojak, Jolanta. 2009. *Zrozumieć jak. Studium składniowo-semantyczne* [Towards understanding of jak 'how; when' as'. A syntactic-semantic study]. Warszawa: Wydział Polonistyki UW.

Clark, Herbert H. & Richard J. Gerrig. 1990. Quotations as demonstrations. *Language* 66. 764–805.

Cukor-Avila, Patricia. 2002. She say, she go, she be like: Verbs of quotation over time in African American Vernacular English. *American Speech* 77. 3–31.

Danon-Boileau, Laurent & Mary-Annick Morel. 1997. Question, point de vue, genre, style. . .: les noms prépositionnels en français contemporain. *Faits de langues* 9. 193–200.

Denison, David. 2002. *History of the sort of construction family*. Paper presented at ICCG2, Helsinki.

Dines, Elizabeth. 1980. Variation in discourse-and stuff like that. *Language in Society* 9. 13–31.

Doboszyńska-Markiewicz, Katarzyna. 2015. O „jakby nieostrości" i jej „swego rodzaju" operatorach (linguistic hedges) – uwagi wstępne [On jakby nieostrości 'a sort of hedging' and its operator swego rodzaju 'of a sort'. Preliminary remarks]. *Linguistica Copernicana* 12. 137–155.

Fetzer, Anita. 2010. Hedges in context: Form and function of *sort of* and *kind of*. In Gunther Kaltenböck, Wiltrud Mihatsch & Stefan Schneider (eds.), *New approaches to hedging*, 49–71. Bingley: Emerald.

Fox Tree, Jean E. & John M. Tomlinson Jr. 2008. The rise of *like* in spontaneous quotations. *Discourse Processes* 45 (1). 85–102.

Gawełko, Marek. 2012. Przyimki polskie a tendencja analityczna języków indoeuropejskich [Polish prepositions and the analytic tendention in Indo European languages]. *Studia z Filologii Polskiej i Słowiańskiej* 47. 9–38.

Gries, Stefan T. & Caroline V. David. 2007. This is kind of/sort of interesting: Variation in hedging in English. In Päivi Pahta, Irma Taavitsainen, Terttu Nevelainen & Jukka Tyrkkö (eds.), *Studies in variation, contacts and change in English*, vol. 2: *Towards multimedia in corpus studies*. Helsinki: University of Helsinki. http://www.helsinki.fi/varieng/journal/volumes/02/gries_david/ (accessed 5 May 2019).

Halliday, M.A.K. 1978. *Language as social semiotic. The social interpretation of language and meaning*. London: Arnold.

Hasund, Kristine, Toril Opsahl & Jan Svennevig. 2012. By three means: The pragmatic functions of three Norwegian quotatives. In Isabelle Buchstaller & Ingrid Van Alphen (eds.), *Quotatives: Cross-linguistic and cross-disciplinary perspectives*, xii–xxx. Amsterdam: Benjamins.

Janowska, Aleksandra. 2015. *Kształtowanie się klasy polskich przyimków wtórnych* [The forming of Polish secondary prepositions]. Katowice: Wydawnictwo Naukowe UŚ.

Kisiel, Anna. 2018. *Polish type noun constructions: x to typ y-a, x w typie y-a*. Paper presented at Pragmatic functions of type nouns: a crosslinguistic perspective, 20.06.2018 Tübingen.

Kolyaseva, Alena. 2018. The 'new' Russian quotative *tipa*: Pragmatic scope and functions, *Journal of Pragmatics* 128. 82–97.

Kolyaseva, Alena & Kristin Davidse. 2018. A typology of lexical and grammaticalized uses of Russian *tip, tipa, po tipu*. *Russian Linguistics* 42 (2). 191–220.

Lakoff, George 1972. Hedges: A study in meaning criteria and the logic of fuzzy concepts. In Paul M. Peranteau, Judith N. Levi & Gloria C. Phares (eds.), *Papers from the 8th Regional Meeting of the Chicago Linguistic Society (Chicago Linguistic Society 8)*, 183–228. Chicago, Ill.: Chicago Linguistic Society.

Lesz-Duk, Maria. 2011. *Przyimki wtórne w języku polskim: Stan współczesny i ewolucja* [Secondary prepositions in Polish: A present-day situation and their evolution]. Częstochowa: Wydawnictwo Akademii im. Jana Długosza.

Levey, Stephen. 2003. He's like 'Do it now!' and I'm like 'No!'. *English Today* 19 (1). 24–32.

Macaulay, Ronald. 2001. You're like 'why not?' The quotative expressions if Glasgow adolescent. *Journal of Sociolinguistics* 5. 3–21.

Mihatsch, Wiltrud. 2016. Type-noun binominals in four Romance languages. *Language Sciences* 53. 136–159.

Milewska, Beata. 2003. *Przyimki wtórne we współczesnej polszczyźnie* [Secondary prepositions in modern Polish]. Gdańsk: Wydawnictwo UG.

Namsaraev, Vasili. 1997. Hedging in Russian academic writing in sociological texts. In Raija Markkanen & Hartmut Schröder (eds.), *Hedging and Discourse. Approaches to the Analysis of a Pragmatic Phenomenon in Academic Texts*, 64–80. Berlin-NY: De Gruyter.

Nowak, Tomasz. 2008. *Przyimki lokatywno-inkluzyjne we współczesnym języku polskim. W głębi, w obrębie, w środku, we wnętrzu* [Locative-inclusive prepositions in modern Polish. W głębi 'in the depths of', w obrębie 'within', w środku 'inside', we wnętrzu 'inside, in the bowels of']. Katowice: Wydawnictwo Uniwersytetu Śląskiego.

Polański, Kazimierz (ed.). 1999. *Encyklopedia językoznawstwa ogólnego* Encyclopedia of general linguistics]. Wrocław: Zakład Narodowy im. Ossolińskich.

Przybylska, Renata. 1988. Wydzielanie przyimków wtórnych we frazach temporalnych [Separating secondary prepositions in temporal phrases]. *Język Polski* 4–5. 243–248.

Rimmer, Sharon E. 1988. Sociolinguistic Variability in Oral Narrative. Diss. Aston U.

Romaine, Suzanne & Lange, Deborah. 1991. The use of *like* as a marker of reported speech and thought: A case of grammaticalization in progress. *American Speech* 66. 227–279.

Tagliamonte, Sali & Alex D'Arcy. 2004. He's like, she's like: The quotative system in Canadian youth. *Journal of Sociolinguistics* 8. 493–514.

Sali Tagliamonte, Alexandra D'Arcy & Celeste Rodríguez Louro. 2016. Outliers, impact and rationalization in linguistic change. *Language* 92 (4). 824–849.

Tannen, Deborah. 1986. Introducing constructed dialogue in Greek and American conversational and literary narrative. In Florian Coulmans (ed.), *Direct and Indirect Speech*, 311–322. Berlin: Mouton.

Wątor, Ignacy. 1976. *Rozwój funkcji wyrazów i wyrażeń polskich od przysłówkowej do przyimkowej* [The evolution of words and phrases from adverbial to prepositional]. Rzeszów: Wydawnictwo WSP.

Markéta Janebová, Michaela Martinková & Volker Gast
15 Czech type nouns: Evidence from corpora

Abstract: In Czech, a West Slavic language, there are two major type nouns: *druh* 'kind/sort' (a group of individuals sharing the same characteristics, or a collection of characteristic features), and *typ* 'type' (a model, example, or an individual with characteristic features; a group of individuals or things with the same features). While the type meaning of *druh* developed from the animate reading ('member of a group; companion'), *typ* is a nineteenth-century borrowing, arguably via German, which originally goes back to Latin and Greek. In this exploratory corpus-driven study, we investigate the discourse functions of these nouns by analysing their distributional patterns in informal spoken Czech as represented by the ORAL v.1 corpus and in original Czech fiction translated into English. By means of statistical analyses, we determine which contextual properties condition a preference for one or the other. The data suggests that in Czech, *druh*, unlike *typ*, mostly retains its "subtype" meaning, even though there is evidence of its gaining approximative functions (quantifying and hedging). These changes are quite complex: the categorial shift is marked by changes in case assignment, agreement, and positional variation. *Typ*, on the other hand, has acquired exemplifying, similative, and quotative functions.

1 Introduction and aims

In many languages, type nouns, i.e. nouns originally denoting a type or subclass, have acquired "pragmatic, interpersonal, and speaker-based functions" (Traugott 1995: 32).[1] In English, *sort*, *kind*, and *type*, or "SKT-nouns" as Denison

---

1 See e.g. Aijmer (2002), Denison (2005), Davidse et al. (2008), and Janebová and Martinková (2017) for English, Voghera (2013) and Mihatsch (2016) for Romance languages, Kolyaseva and Davidse (2018) for Russian, and Kisiel (2018) for Polish.

Acknowledgements: The first author gratefully acknowledges the support granted by the Faculty of Arts, Palacký University Olomouc (grant no. FPVC2016/11). We would also like to thank Emma Walters and the anonymous reviewers for their valuable comments and suggestions.

Markéta Janebová, Palacký University Olomouc, e-mail: marketa.janebova@upol.cz
Michaela Martinková, Palacký University Olomouc, e-mail: michaela.martinkova@upol.cz
Volker Gast, Friedrich Schiller University Jena, e-mail: volker.gast@uni-jena.de

https://doi.org/10.1515/9783110701104-015

(2005) calls them, have been studied extensively from both the synchronic and diachronic perspectives. There are clear syntactic, semantic, and pragmatic differences between the English type nouns in their head use in the NP1-*of*-NP2 pattern and outside the NP1-*of*-NP2 pattern; however, the difference between the head use and the non-head use (or taxonomic and non-taxonomic, respectively) of the type nouns within the NP1-*of*-NP2 pattern is more difficult to grasp, especially in monolingual corpora.[2]

For this reason, in a previous study (Janebová and Martinková 2017) we investigated NP-internal uses of two English type nouns, *kind* and *sort*, i.e. the NP1-*of*-NP2 structures where NP1 contains *kind* or *sort*,[3] adopting a different methodology than previous monolingual studies. Following Johansson, we systematically exploited "the bilingual intuition of translators" (2007: 52): we turned to the parallel translation corpus InterCorp (Čermák and Rosen 2012) to investigate the status of the two type nouns (in American English) through their translation equivalents in a typologically different language, namely the inflectional and articleless Czech. Because Czech type nouns have not undergone the same kind of grammaticalization as the English ones, we expected a wide range of corresponding Czech translations which would explicate the functions of the NP-internal uses of English type nouns, and thus might cast new light on their status in the NP1-*of*-NP2 structure. Attention was also paid to the determiners and modifiers which appear in each construction and the discourse functions of the constructions.[4]

Our previous research (Janebová and Martinková 2017) not only showed how the pragmatic and discourse functions of the English type nouns in the NP1-*of*-NP2 structure are made "visible" through translation, but also suggested that the corresponding translations are dependent on the element preceding *sort/kind*. As for the translation equivalents of the English type nouns, in ca. 17% of

---

[2] The term "head use" of a type noun covers hyponymy statements such as *a robin is a sort of bird* (Aijmer 2002: 176); Denison (2005) and Traugott (2008) call it a "binominal construction". Type nouns can also appear as "non-heads" in constructions such as *When thanks is not forthcoming, we feel a kind of emptiness* (Denison 2005). Unlike the binominal construction, this one has a hedging function (Traugott 2008).
[3] The low frequencies of *type* in our subcorpus did not make it possible to carry out the same statistical analysis as with the other two, and *type* was excluded from the research.
[4] A subcorpus of American post-1980 fiction (3,424,121 tokens, sentence-aligned with the published Czech translations) was created. In other words, the corpus we created is a unidirectional translation corpus in which the originals are English and Czech is represented only in translations.

all the cases, a Czech type noun was used in the translation: *druh* 'kind/sort' was the most frequent equivalent (57%), followed by *typ* 'type' (31%). Other taxonomic nouns as translation equivalents (e.g. *značka* 'brand' or *forma* 'form') were much less frequent.[5] The remaining Czech translation equivalents of the English type nouns – where no Czech taxonomic noun was used – fall into two main groups: textual markers (or markers which refer to the common ground between the speaker and the hearer) and epistemic (imprecision) markers or hedges (see Aijmer 1984). The hedging and textual functions of the English type nouns are typically expressed by a Czech pronoun or a phoric adjective (e.g. *the kind/sort* is translated as *podobný* 'similar', *that kind* as *takový* 'such') or an approximator (e.g. *trochu* 'a bit' or *jaksi* 'somehow').

As for the element preceding *sort/kind*, the following predictors turned out to be statistically significant: premodification of the type noun (in NP1), i.e. the kind of determiner or modifier preceding the type noun; and premodification of the noun in NP2. For example, *some* in the premodification field of a type noun dispreferred a Czech type noun equivalent. Additionally, there were significant differences between the two English type nouns in this respect,[6] and we concluded that *sort* appears to be more hedge-like than *kind*: *some sort of* is significantly more frequent than *a sort of*, which was not the case with *kind* (the fact that the indefinite article is less common with *sort of* than with *kind of* could be related to a more prominent loss of the referential function in the sense of Keizer (2007: 159)).

In our (2017) study, Czech was the target language, and the question arose as to whether the correlations that were observed might be a translation effect. Corpus data suggests that to a certain extent this might be the case: our analysis of a comparable monolingual corpus of fiction written in Czech (created on the basis of InterCorp 8 data; 9,738,866 tokens of Czech translations from English and 9,690,113 tokens of non-translated [original] Czech) revealed that, for example, the string *ten typ* 'that kind/sort/type' is almost three times more frequent in translations from English (9.96 pmw) than in original Czech texts (3.92 pmw). To eliminate this possible effect of 'translationese' and to understand the functions of the two main Czech type nouns *druh* and *typ*, research on non-translated original Czech data was needed.

---

[5] There was not a single occurrence of *rod* 'genus', the cognates of which have acquired general taxonomic meanings in Russian and Polish.
[6] *Sort* was attracted by two categories in the premodification field in NP1, not strongly, but significantly, as the regression model showed: adjectives and *some*.

Given the fact that there is a lack of detail regarding the distribution of Czech type nouns in linguistic literature, as well as in major Czech grammars and dictionaries, we decided to carry out an exploratory corpus-based study both of original Czech fiction translated into English and of spoken Czech. The questions our present study seeks to answer are as follows:
1. Is there any difference between the distribution of the type nouns *druh* and *typ* in Czech?
2. If so, which aspects of the linguistic context condition the choice between the type nouns in Czech?
3. Are there any parallels to the grammaticalization path suggested for the Russian type noun *tip* in Kolyaseva and Davidse (2018)?

The study is structured as follows: in the first section, we introduce type nouns in Czech as they are described in dictionaries of Standard Czech and in etymological dictionaries, and present previous research on type nouns in Russian. In Section 2, we discuss our methodology, and in Section 3, we analyse the uses of type nouns attested in the corpora of original Czech fiction and of spoken Czech. In Section 4, we offer statistical analyses of the distribution of *druh* and *typ*, and in Section 5 present our conclusions.

1.1 Type nouns in the history of Czech

The grammaticalization of type nouns (TNs) in Germanic and Romance languages and, recently, also in Russian, an East Slavic language, has been well researched (see Kolyaseva and Davidse (2018) for an overview of the studies): these type nouns include the cognates of 'type', 'kind', 'genus', 'genre', 'species', 'sort', 'form', 'category', and 'class'. However, for Czech, a West Slavic language, similar studies are lacking. In this section, we will focus on the etymology of the nouns *druh* and *typ*, but we will also briefly discuss the etymology of *rod*, as it has cognates in other Slavic languages in which extensions of its taxonomic meaning have been observed.

Machek (2010: 130) notes that the taxonomic meaning of *druh* is an extension of its sense 'a member of a group; a companion' (cf. *družina* 'group, suite' and *druhý* 'the second'). The taxonomic meaning arose from fixed phrases such as *toho druh* [that.GEN companion.NOM.SG] or *těch druh* [those.GEN companion.NOM.SG], as in (1):

(1) ten   nůž   je   **mého**   **druh**
    that   knife is   my.**GEN.SG**   companion/kind.**NOM.SG**
    'that knife is like / such as mine [that knife is a companion of my knife]'[7]

When phrases such as these ceased to be semantically transparent,[8] *toho druh* changed to *toho druhu* [that.GEN companion.GEN.SG 'of that kind'], which gave rise to a new meaning of *druh*, namely 'sort' (Machek 2010: 130).

The history of the noun *typ* is much less clear (it is not included in Machek (2010) at all). According to Rejzek (2001), *typ* is a nineteenth-century borrowing which is understood to have come into Czech via German, having originated from Latin and Greek (Rejzek 2001: 687), although there is no direct evidence of this (Rejzek, p.c.). The German type noun *der Typus* is a late sixteenth-century borrowing from Latin, but it acquired a new form – *der Typ* – together with a new meaning at the beginning of the twentieth century, namely 'a special type, a prototype'. Under the influence of French, *Typ* (originally *Type*), started to be used in the meaning of 'a strange man' in the first half of the twentieth century, and in present-day German it also means 'a (young) male' (all of these meanings are established in Czech as well).[9]

Figure 1 shows the frequencies of *druh(u)* and *typ(u)* from the late nineteenth century to 2009. *Typ*, originally very rare, became more and more common during the course of the first half of the twentieth century. The second half of the twentieth century shows shifting frequencies between the two type nouns. In texts from the twenty-first century, *typ* clearly prevails.

---

[7] All translations are our own, with the exception of examples from the parallel translation corpus InterCorp (IC).
[8] The 'companion' meaning of *druh* is attested in the 14th century. According to Machek (2010), the fixed phrases giving rise to the taxonomic meaning were common in Middle Czech (i.e. ca. 1500–1775); however, Zubatý (1918) provides evidence of such taxonomic uses of *druh* from ca. 1450. We did not find any such occurrences in the Middle Czech textbank (*Středněčeská textová bank*a; accessible via the web application *Vokabulář webový* at http://vokabular.ujc.cas.cz), or in Middle Czech texts as represented in the diachronic corpus Diakorp (Kučera et al. 2015). Because of the limited space of this study, this issue has to be left for further research.
[9] *Das Wortauskunftssystem zur deutschen Sprache in Geschichte und Gegenwart* (DWDS), s.v. "Typ", https://www.dwds.de/wb/Typ.

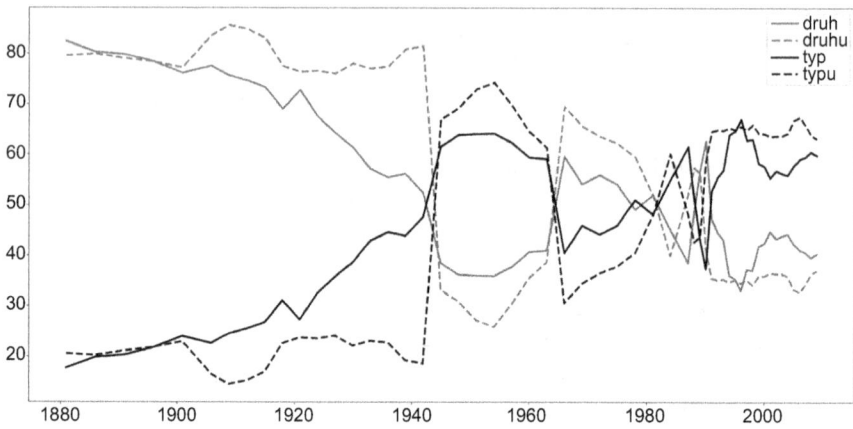

Figure 1: Diachronic distribution of *druh* and *typ* in the nominative/accusative case (*druh*/*typ*) and in the genitive/dative/locative case (*druhu*/*typu*).[10]

The etymology of *rod* can be traced back to the proto-Slavic word for 'lineage' or 'descent' (cf. also *rodina* 'family'), according to Machek (2010: 514). In Jungmann's Czech-German dictionary from 1837, it is also mentioned in the terminological sense of 'genus' in contrast to *druh* 'species'. In addition, *rod* is used in the grammatical sense as 'gender' and '(verbal) voice'. As for the subtype meanings associated with *druh* and *typ*, the Dictionary of Standard Czech [*SSČ*] does not list any for *rod*.[11]

One might argue that the reason for the lack of research on Czech type nouns is obvious: in Czech, type nouns have not been grammaticalized to the same extent as, for example, Russian or English. In monolingual dictionaries of Czech,

---

[10] Figure 1 was generated on the basis of the data provided by SyD (Cvrček and Vondřička 2011), a corpus tool which allows researchers to compare the distribution of variants in Czech. For diachronic searches, it uses the Diakon corpus, which includes Czech data from the 14th century on. However, since it does not facilitate a search for lemmas, the data presented here are the proportions of both type nouns in their nominative/accusative and genitive/dative/locative singular forms only.

[11] On the basis of our previous (2017) study, as well as preliminary corpus findings, we decided to exclude *rod* from our further analysis. First, as already mentioned, there was not a single case of *rod* as a translation equivalent of the English type nouns *type*, *kind*, and *sort* in our (2017) study; second, we did not notice any categorial shifts in *rod*. The vast majority of cases are covered by the terminological use (e.g. *rod Paleocastor* 'the Paleocastor genus') and the lineage use (e.g. *z rodu Hamrů* 'from the Hamr family'). The only exception is the prepositional phrase *z rodu* 'of descent.GEN.SG', where we noticed an extension of meaning. Here *z rodu* can mean "belonging to the category", e.g.

no extensions of meanings of *druh* or *typ* are recorded.¹² Furthermore, with one exception,¹³ in all the examples given in such dictionaries, the Czech type noun is the head of the noun phrase. This seems to suggest that there is nothing to study. And yet, as we will see shortly, a closer look shows a less uniform picture.

1.2 Type nouns in Russian

Before we proceed to our study of the distribution of type nouns in present-day Czech, let us begin with an overview of the Russian type noun *tip* 'type'. According to Kolyaseva and Davidse (2018), *tip* can participate in the following constructions: 1. nominal constructions, where *tip* is the head of the noun phrase complemented by the superordinate noun (TN+N2), as in (2a), or the genitival modifier of the superordinate noun (N1+TN), as in (2b); 2. prepositional constructions (3), and 3. particle constructions, exemplified in (4) and (5). In the first – binominal – construction, *tip* retains its lexical meaning in both positions. In the second construction, as Kolyaseva and Davidse (2018) argue, it functions as a "simple preposition" *tipa* or a "complex preposition" *po tipu*; here *tip* has lost its nominal property and expresses a semantic relationship between two noun phrases, namely exemplification, comparison, or hedging. In the third construc-

(i) *Mám   v   hlavě   uloženo   mnoho   vzpomínek   na   koncerty,   ale   jedna*
    I-have in   head   stored   many   memories   of   concerts,   but   one
    je   z   rodu   těch   opravdu   svátečních.
    is   of   descent.GEN.SG those   truly   festive
    'In my head there are many memories of concerts, but one is of a truly festive kind.'
    (SYN15_ lnpa1312:9:2)

This extended use of *z rodu* is, however, very rare in written language (only 30 tokens in the SYN15 corpus of synchronic written Czech out of 121 million tokens) and even more rare in spoken Czech (one token in the ORAL v1 corpus of spontaneous Czech out of six million tokens). This made it impossible to carry out the same analysis with *rod* as with *druh* and *typ*.

12 For example, the meanings of *druh* listed in the *SSČ* are as follows:

I. masc. animate
   1. companion, friend [archaic]
   2. a person's life partner (not married)

II. masc. inanimate
   1. a group of individuals belonging to some class, sharing the same characteristics; cf. *species*
   2. a collection of characteristic features, character, type

13 The example, *kniha svého druhu* 'book of its kind', is discussed below in Section 3.2.

tion, *tipa* and *po tipu* are used as hedging or quotative markers (or even as a filler in the case of *tipa*) and "are not part of any dependency relations" (Kolyaseva and Davidse 2018: 214).

(2) a. [...] *vybor*   **tipa**   *reaktora* [...]
       choice.NOM.M.SG type.GEN.M.SG reactor.GEN.M.SG
       'the choice of the type of reactor'
       (Quoted in Kolyaseva and Davidse 2018: 197)

   b. [...] *ėkonomika*   *sovetskogo*   **tipa** [...]
      economy.NOM.F.SG Soviet.GEN.M.SG type.GEN.M.SG
      'economy of the Soviet type'
      (Quoted in Kolyaseva and Davidse 2018: 199)

(3) [...] *zvezda*   **tipa** *Solnca*   *našego*
    star.NOM.F.SG tipa   Sun.GEN.M.SG our.GEN.M.SG
    'a star like the Sun of ours'
    (Quoted in Kolyaseva and Davidse 2018: 206)

(4) *Ėto normal'naja kniha—**Tipa** detskoj   medicinskoj*
                             child.ADJ.GEN.F.SG medical.GEN.F.SG
    Ėnciklopedii.
    encyclopedia.GEN.F.SG
    'It is a good book. A sort of children's medical encyclopedia.'
    (Quoted in Kolyaseva and Davidse 2018: 206; translation our own)

(5) *Tam rebjata byli / ja im govorju / **tipa** / podoždite menja* [...]
    'There were guys there / I say to them / like / wait for me.'
    (Quoted in Kolyaseva and Davidse 2018: 216)

In the following sections, we will investigate whether the Czech type nouns *druh* and *typ* show any parallels to the grammaticalization path suggested for the Russian type noun *tip* in Kolyaseva and Davidse (2018).

2 Data and method

To investigate the uses of type nouns *druh* and *typ* in original Czech, we again used corpora created by the Institute of the Czech National Corpus at Charles University in Prague. For written language, InterCorp (Čermák and Rosen 2012) was used as a basis for the creation of a subcorpus of original post-1950[14] Czech fiction (2,946,414 tokens), aligned with English translations. For the analysis of spoken Czech, we resorted to ORAL v.1 (Kopřivová et al. 2017), a corpus of 6,361,707 tokens, the majority of which (5,598,175 tokens) are informal spontaneous dialogues between friends and relatives recorded in their natural environments over a span of ten years (2002–2011). The rest (763,532 tokens) comprises more formal encounters such as job interviews, conversations at the office or in shops, and recordings of lectures.

Both corpora are lemmatized, which enabled us to perform case-insensitive lemma queries for both *druh* and *typ*. Table 1 summarizes the absolute frequencies (AF) of *druh* and *typ* before filtering in both the InterCorp subcorpus of Czech fiction (cz-fic) and in ORAL, during which unintelligible tokens of *typ*, as well as animate readings of *druh* ('friend, companion'), were removed, and the absolute as well as relative frequencies (RF) of each of the type nouns after filtering.

Table 1: Absolute (AF) and relative (RF) frequencies of *druh* and *typ* in InterCorp (cz-fic) and in ORAL (n=841).

	druh				*typ*			
	before filtering		after filtering		before filtering		after filtering	
	AF		AF	RF (pmw)	AF		AF	RF (pmw)
InterCorp (cz-fic)	205		136	46.2	117		114	38.7
ORAL	286		236	37.1	373		355	55.8

As for the English translation equivalents of the two Czech type nouns in fiction, the situation is different than in our previous research. In our (2017) study, a Czech type noun was used to translate ca. 17% of the two English type nouns *kind* and *sort* (the number included all Czech taxonomic nouns, not only *druh* and *typ*), i.e. only 17% of the cases of *kind* and *sort* were interpreted taxonomically. If we look at original Czech fiction translated into English, the Czech type nouns *druh* and *typ* are translated by an English SKT-noun in 55% of all cases, and if we include other English taxonomic nouns such as *variety* or *model*, the number is

---

[14] This corpus is, unfortunately, not comparable to the corpus used for our (2017) analysis in terms of size or time-span, for the reason that Czech is a small language (ca. 10.7 million L1-users, according to the data from http://www.ethnologue.com/language/) and there will always be more translations into Czech than from Czech.

even higher, ca. 60%. The second most frequent translation equivalent of *druh* is *species* (the first one being the SKT-nouns mentioned above). This indicates that unlike in English, the taxonomic meaning of the Czech type nouns *druh* and *typ* still prevails, but it is worth noting that there is zero correspondence in 15% and 18% of the translations of *druh* and *typ* respectively. Zero correspondence typically appears when the Czech type noun is not part of a taxonomic binominal construction, i.e. when there is no superordinate noun in the Czech original, but, for example, a proper name or a quotative phrase. The fact that such non-taxonomic usage of Czech type nouns often does not have an English translation equivalent suggests that Czech type nouns might have developed meanings which English type nouns have not. We also observed differences between the Czech type nouns: *typ* has a wider range of translation equivalents than *druh* (18 vs. nine respectively), which might indicate that *typ* has developed meanings which it does not share with *druh*.

Before we proceed to more quantitative analyses in Section 4, we present a qualitative analysis by exemplifying the main uses of the type nouns *druh* and *typ* attested in the two corpora (for reference purposes, we also resort to written data in the SYN v.7 corpus (Křen et al. 2017)).

3 Type nouns in corpora of written and spoken Czech

It has been mentioned that Czech monolingual dictionaries only acknowledge the nominal taxonomic use for *druh* and *typ*, and that in almost all of their printed examples the type noun is the head. However, the corpus data presented in Table 2 shows that the Czech type nouns are attested in both types of binominal constructions defined in Kolyaseva and Davidse (2018): the TN+N2 pattern in (6), and the N1+TN pattern in (7). In addition, in the TN+N2 structure the type noun can have a taxonomic function, as in (6) and (7), or a non-taxonomic function (8), and, as example (9) demonstrates, there does not need to be a nominal complement at all.

(6) *Je* **moc** **druhů** *tajných* *věd.*
 is many kind.GEN.PL secret.GEN.PL teaching.GEN.PL
 'The science of the occult comes in various forms.'
 (IC_Fuks-MysiNatalieMoosha)

(7) **Další součinnosti tohoto druhu** se nebudeme
    further cooperation.DAT.SG this.GEN.SG kind.GEN.SG REFL we.will.not
    vyhýbat.
    avoid
    'We won't rule out further cooperation of this kind, either.'
    (IC_Lustig-ModlitbaProKHor)

(8) vona neni **typ Mirky**
    she is.not type.NOM.SG Mirka.GEN.SG
    'she is not like Mirka'
    (ORAL_07A2116N)

(9) **víkendového rodiče typu** jednou za štrnáct dní na
    weekend parent type.GEN.SG once in fourteen days for
    víkend
    weekend
    'a once-in-two-weeks-for-the-weekend kind of parent'
    (ORAL_06H089N)

As Table 2 shows, while non-taxonomic *druh* comprises 5% of all uses in fiction and only 2% in spoken Czech, the non-taxonomic use of *typ* represents ca. 20% of all cases in fiction as well as in spoken Czech.

Table 2: An overview of the uses of *druh* and *typ* in original Czech fiction and in spoken Czech.

	druh		typ	
	Czech fiction (n = 136)	Spoken Czech (n = 236)	Czech fiction (n = 114)	Spoken Czech (n = 355)
Taxonomic head use	75%	93%	69%	74%
Taxonomic non-head use	20%	5%	12%	6%
Non-taxonomic use	5%	2%	19%	20%

In most uses, there are distributional differences between *druh* and *typ*. In the following subsections, we discuss the uses of both type nouns separately. However, in our discussion we follow formal criteria (i.e. whether a construction is binominal or not, and whether the type noun is the head or not) rather than semantic criteria (i.e. whether the type noun is taxonomic or not). This leads us to adopt the term "binominal" as a purely descriptive label for constructions containing a type noun and another noun; in other words, we do not adopt the prepositional use that appears in Kolyaseva and Davidse (2018): in this way, we will be able to grasp the motivation of the extension from the prototypical binominal taxonomic use to other uses. We start with the head use, i.e. cases in which the type noun is the head of the noun phrase: what we consider criterial is the fact that it is not limited to any particular case form (in other words, it can appear in all seven cases), it can be premodified and/or determined, and it can also be postmodified, typically by a relative clause.

3.1 Binominal head use

The prototypical use of a type noun is the one classified as "nominal" in Kolyaseva and Davidse (2018): TN+N2.GEN, where TN is the type noun with a taxonomic meaning, and N2 is a noun in the genitive referring to the superordinate. Both *typ* and *druh* can be used here; however, *typ* is preferred in the sense of 'model' (10), while *druh* is preferred in the sense of 'species' (11) or 'variety'.

(10) **v nejmodernějším typu bavoráku**
in the.most.modern.LOC.SG type.LOC.SG BMW.GEN.SG
'in the most modern type of BMW'
(ORAL_06A099N)

(11) ale ta strupatost to je prej **ňákej druh**
but that potato scab it is allegedly some kind.NOM.SG
plísně
fungus.GEN.SG
'but this potato scab, it is allegedly some kind of fungus'
(ORAL_ 02A004N)

In English, a binominal construction with an indefinite article or an indefinite pronoun is a bridging context for the non-taxonomic (hedging) use of type nouns *kind* and *sort*. The indefiniteness marker in the NP1-*of*-NP2 pattern "may trigger the inference that because the class membership is not uniquely identifiable, it is not exact" (Traugott 2008: 228–229). Traugott (2008: 229) mentions the degree modifier use of *sort of* in the NP1-*of*-NP2 pattern, which conveys "the speaker's assessment that the entity referred to is not an adequate or prototypical exemplar of NP2 [. . .], or that NP2 is not an exactly appropriate expression". For example, *a sort of a frog* can mean a "frog-like thing" (Traugott 2008: 227). However, this was not attested in our Czech corpora, as indefinite pronouns were only used in prototypical taxonomic sentences in our data. Indefinite pronouns are "typically used where the referent is unknown to the speaker (though it need not be unknown)" (Haspelmath 1997: 132), and in our Czech data, the lack of knowledge of the referent does not concern the class membership: the speaker is familiar with the superordinate category, but may lack specific knowledge of the subtype (see, for example, [11]).[15]

Nevertheless, there were cases in which *typ* could not be classified as taxonomic; unlike in English, this was not because of an indefiniteness marker but because the noun following *typ* was not a superordinate noun. *Typ* is lexicalized here (it cannot be replaced with *druh*), meaning "an individual or a thing with characteristic features"; in our data, it is an individual (+Human). This use of *typ* evokes similarity to certain properties of the people involved, creating an ad hoc category, i.e. it does not hedge an existing one (as in example [12]). Typically, the noun is a proper name with a unique referent, and the whole NP appears in the predicative position.

(12) neni   to   **typ**   ***Pavarottiho***   je   to   spíš
     he.is.not   it   type.NOM.SG   Pavarotti.GEN.SG   he.is   it   rather
     typ   ***Carrerase***
     type.NOM.SG   Carreras.GEN.SG
     'he is not like Pavarotti, he's rather like Carreras'
     (ORAL_10P006N)

This usage anticipates Kolyaseva and Davidse's (2018: 204) "prepositional type 2.1", in which "its [of *tipu*] semantic role has been reduced to expressing a relation". However, unlike in Russian, *typ* still retains some of its nominal features – in (13) it is determined by the demonstrative pronoun *ten* and the similative demonstrative *takový* 'such'. On the other hand, it is never premodified by adjectives; the demonstratives here "function to coordinate the interlocutors' joint focus of attention, which is one of the most basic functions of human communication" (Diessel 2006: 463) and, relying on the "common ground", they help create an ad hoc category (see Umbach and Gust (2014), according to whom the kinds "need not be given in advance and are instead ad-hoc generated by the use of the similarity demonstrative").[16]

---

15 Another piece of evidence is the fact that *druh* does not co-occur with referential vagueness markers such as *něco* 'something' or *někdo* 'somebody' (no occurrences of *něco/někdo druhu* were attested in SYN2015 or ORAL v.1). *Typ* is extremely rare with referential vagueness markers (only 4 tokens of *něco typu* 'something like' were found in SYN2015 and none in ORAL).
16 In the spoken Czech data, *takový* is almost five times more frequent than in fiction (4,442.68 pmw), and the most frequent use is the one referred to as "recognitional", i.e. non-phoric. By

Like in the Russian use marked as prepositional – and unlike in the taxonomic use given above – the NP appears not only in the genitive, but also in the nominative:

(13) *takový rozervanec* **takový ten typ** *Karel*
such savage such that type.NOM.SG Karel.NOM.SG
Hynek Mácha
Hynek.NOM.SG Mácha.NOM.SG
'such a romantic savage, such as [the Czech poet] Karel Hynek Mácha'
(ORAL_09A166N)

To sum up, we have identified two different binominal constructions with *typ* as head – one in which *typ* fulfils a taxonomic function (N2 is a superordinate noun in the genitive) and one in which *typ* is used as a similative creating ad hoc subcategories. Unlike in the first type, N2 in the latter construction can be in the genitive as well as in the nominative.

3.1.1 Nominal head use with no overt N2

There are also cases of the lexicalized *druh* and *typ* in which there is no overt N2. *Druh* is only interchangeable with *typ* when the meaning is still taxonomic, i.e. the superordinate noun is present or recoverable from the context, or when there is a quantifier; see for example (14) and (15):

(14) *Maxim Gavrilič si nacpal plná ústa* **několika druhy** [*sýra*]
Maxim Gavrilič REFL stuffed full mouth several kind.INSTR.PL
současně
at.once
'Arashidov [sic] stuffed his mouth with several varieties [of cheese] at once'
(IC_Skvorecky-Mirakl)

---

using *takový*, the speaker aims to "signal [to] the hearer that the speaker is referring to specific, but presumably shared, knowledge. It invites the hearer to signal the need for further clarification regarding the intended referent" (Himmelmann 1996: 240). Although we gloss *takový* as 'such' in this paper, it is worth pointing out that the English similative *such* does not have the recognitional use, and the demonstrative *this* is used in this function instead (see Auwera and Coussé 2016). Therefore, where appropriate, we translate the recognitional *takový* as *this*; see, for example, (16) and (17).

(15) [*toto triko*] *bylo barevné* [...] *ano* [pause] *a dělaly se*
    this T-shirt was coloured   yes   and were.made REFL
    dva typy
    two type.NOM.PL
    '[this T-shirt] was coloured [...] yes, and there were two kinds'
    (ORAL_09A66N)

However, in the lexicalized (+Human) meaning, only *typ* can be used. Apart from more or less well-established classes, as in (16), *typ* (but not *druh*) can also express ad hoc categorization; here *typ* is typically premodified, as in (17), or postmodified by a relative clause, as in (18).

(16) *sme voba* **takový** *ty* **severský**
    we.are both such.NOM.PL that.NOM.PL Scandinavian.NOM.PL
    typy *no*
    type.NOM.PL yeah
    'we are both these Scandinavian types, you know'
    (ORAL_06A148N)

(17) *já sem* **takovej přesolovací typ**
    I am such.NOM.SG oversalting.NOM.SG type.NOM.SG
    'I am this oversalting type'
    (ORAL_05H057N)

(18) *Zuzka asi opravdu nebude* **ten** **typ**
    Susie probably really will.not.be that.NOM.SG type.NOM.SG
    co by měla *jako zástupy nápadníků*
    what.REL would have.PAST.PTCP.F.SG like crowds of.suitors
    'Susie probably won't be the type to have crowds of suitors'
    (ORAL_08A003N)

The relative pronoun and the verb in the relative clause do not necessarily agree in gender and number with the type noun which the clause postmodifies; in (18) the past participle *měla* has the feminine form, while there is no binominal construction with a feminine noun in the formal antecedent (the relative pronoun *co* is not gender-sensitive). In other words, even if the construction is not overtly binominal, the fact that the superordinate noun (*žena* 'woman') is retrievable from the context may influence the agreement. For this reason, we include such cases in our data.

3.2 Binominal non-head use

Within the nominal use, the type noun can also function as a genitival modifier of the superordinate head noun and is in obligatory postposition: N1+TN.GEN. Both *druh* and *typ* have been attested in this use, but there are clear differences in their distribution. In the non-head use, *druh* as a genitival modifier appears only with quantifiers (19), possessives, or demonstratives, or when premodified by the adjectives *stejný* 'same', *jiný* 'different', *další* 'further', and *různý* 'various' (20).[17] In example (21), a shift from the taxonomic to the quantifying meaning of *všeho druhu* [all.GEN.SG kind.GEN.SG] can be observed (the universal quantifier *všechen* 'all' would be incompatible with the singular type noun *druh* in its meaning of totality, and therefore has to be interpreted as 'various').[18] In all of these examples, *typ* could be used as well, but it was not attested in our corpora. When we compared the frequency of *všeho druhu* 'of every kind' and *všeho typu* 'of every type' in the synchronic corpus of written Czech SYN v.7,[19] the difference was striking: 24,746 (4.98 pmw) versus 180 tokens (0.04 pmw) respectively. In the quantifying use, *druh* is thus clearly more entrenched than *typ*.

(19) **zboží   jednoho   druhu**
    goods.NOM.SG one.GEN.SG kind.GEN.SG
    'goods of one kind'
    (ORAL_05A130N)

---

17 These are a subset of the adjectives listed by Davidse et al. (2008: 143–146), who maintain that the range of adjectives in the premodification of the taxonomic type noun is limited to qualitative attributes such as *new, wrong*, and *special*, and postdeterminer adjectives (*same, (an)other, certain, particular*). For the purpose of our analysis, we call the whole group "postdeterminer adjectives". These adjectives help single out "subclasses for particular attention" or set off "subtypes against other subtypes" (2008: 146).
18 See the reference to English *all sorts/kinds of* in Davidse et al. (2008: 158); *all* and the type noun are said to form "a fixed expression" with a quantifier sense "many/much", which is said to have arisen through lexicalization and a "pragmatic-semantic shift"; if "all possible subtypes are involved, then a natural implication is that there are many instances" (Davidse et al. 2008: 160). Brems and Davidse (2010: 188) regard the fact that the English type noun can appear in the singular as "overtly reflecting the reanalysis that had taken place".
19 A subcorpus of original Czech data (4,968,169,874 tokens) was created for this purpose.

(20) přijelo   sem   obrovské množství **nových**   **aut**
     came   here huge   amount   new   car.GEN.PL
     nejrůznějších   **druhů**
     various.GEN.PL.SUP   kind.GEN.PL
     'there had been a tremendous influx of all sorts of new cars'
     (IC_Topol-Chladnou_zemi)

(21) tam   je   **spousta** těch   **supermarketů**   všeho   **druhu**
     there   is   lots   those   supermarket.GEN.PL   all.GEN.SG kind.GEN.SG
     'there are a lot of supermarkets of all kinds'
     (ORAL_07A68N)

Rather surprisingly, in spoken language, there were no examples of *svého druhu* (or *svýho druhu*, i.e. the substandard form) such as *kniha svého druhu* 'book of its kind' (the only example of *druh* in the non-head use found in *SSČ*), and there was only one example of *svého druhu* in our subcorpus of original Czech fiction. In order to obtain more data, we decided to analyse the occurrence of *svého druhu* in the synchronic corpus of written Czech SYN v.7 again. Its relative frequency is 8.7 pmw; however, it turns out that *svého druhu*, in addition to the taxonomic meaning exemplified in (22), can have other uses as well.

(22) **jediná**   **škola**   **svého**   **druhu**
     only.ADJ.NOM.SG   school.NOM.SG   its.own.POSS.REFL.GEN.SG   kind.GEN.SG
     v   republice
     in   republic
     'the only school of its kind in the country'
     (SYN7_ mf101021:322:11:3)

In a random sample of 200 examples of *svého druhu* in SYN v.7, 23 tokens are in premodification, functioning as a hedge;[20] as in (23) and (24). Note that only *svého druhu* can appear in premodification; any other modifier or determiner would be ungrammatical in this position, as would be *typ*: **tohoto druhu škola* [this.DEM.GEN.SG kind.GEN.SG school.NOM.SG], **svého typu škola* [its.own.POSS. REFL.GEN.SG type.GEN.SG school.NOM.SG].

---

20 This use is very similar to what Traugott (2008: 229) describes as the degree modifier use of *sort of* in the NP1-*of*-NP2 pattern, discussed in Section 3.1.

(23) ty   koncerty beru   jako   poklidnou   víkendovou   záležitost,
     the   concerts I.take as   relaxed   weekend   affair
     jako **svýho**   **druhu**   **čundr**
     as   its.own.POSS.REFL.GEN.SG   kind.GEN.SG   camping.ACC.SG
     'I treat the gigs as a relaxed weekend affair, like some sort of camping trip'
     (SYN7_ rockpop: 383:83:3)

(24) rebelové   ve   velmi   chudých   zemích   fungují   jako
     rebels   in   very   poor   countries function   as
     svého   **druhu**   **soukromé**
     its.own.POSS.REFL.GEN.SG   kind.GEN.SG   private.NOM.PL
     firmy
     company.NOM.PL
     'rebels in very poor countries behave like private companies of sorts'
     (SYN7_zahor_ohniskanap:1:148:116)

In other words, *druh* (but not *typ*) can serve as a hedge when it is determined by the reflexive pronoun *svůj*, and the categorial shift is quite prominent because the phrase *svého druhu* appears in the premodification of the head noun. Here the change of the default postposition of the modifier *druh* has a pragmatic effect: cf. (22), where the type noun *druh* is in the postposition and retains its lexical meaning. In some of the examples the phrase *svého druhu* no longer modifies a noun (as in (25)); it thus becomes very similar to the hedge *svým způsobem* 'in a way', which can modify verbs as well as nouns and adjectives.

(25) tento   typ   pojistek   může   být   i   **svého**
     this   type   insurance   can   be   also   its.own.POSS.REFL.GEN.SG
     druhu   „**praktický**"
     kind.GEN.SG   practical.ADJ.NOM
     'this type of insurance can also be sort of "practical"'
     (SYN7_ln120426:59:17)

Whereas the non-head use of *druh* (exemplified in (21)) is very rare in spoken language, *typ* as a non-head (i.e. the genitive form *typu*) appears both in fiction and spoken language. If the type noun is premodified by a classifying adjective, only *typ* is used, and the meaning is taxonomic (as in (26)–(28) below):

(26) *Ale Pluto se podobá* **planetám** *zemského*
but Pluto REFL resembles planet.DAT.PL earth.ADJ.GEN.SG
typu
type.GEN.SG
'But Pluto resembles earth-like planets'
(IC_Fuks-MysiNatalieMoosha)

(27) *neni vyloženě na dálnici že to je jenom* **silnice**
not exactly on motorway that it is just road.NOM.SG
dálničního *typu*
motorway.ADJ.GEN.SG type.GEN.SG
'it is not exactly on the motorway; it is just a motorway-type road'
(ORAL_07A158N)

(28) *sejra* [...] *je to je to* [pause] **hermelínovýho** *typu*
cheese [...] is it is it Camembert.ADJ.GEN.SG type.GEN.SG
plísňovej
mouldy.NOM.SG
'the cheese is a kind of Camembert, mouldy cheese'
(ORAL_10A43N)

This use is analogous to an identifying apposition where instead of a classifying premodifier, there is a classifying nominal complement of *typ*; see (29).[21]

(29) *stát se pilotem* **stihačky** *typu*
to.become REFL pilot.INSTR.SG aircraft.GEN.SG type.GEN.SG
MIG *z povolání.*
MIG.NOM.SG by profession
'[...] to become a MiG pilot.'
(IC_Skvorecky-PribehIng_2)

The identifying apposition, we believe, is a bridging context to what Kolyaseva and Davidse call the prepositional use of the type noun: "its semantic role has been reduced to expressing a relation" (2018: 204). The structure exemplified in (30) is ambiguous between appositive identification (the construction set used

---

[21] All examples of the appositive identification, e.g. (29), have zero English correspondence, mainly because in English, unlike in Czech, the second appositive may appear in the premodification field.

was in fact Merkur), exemplification (several brands of construction sets could have been used, including Merkur), and similarity (the construction set used resembles Merkur because it also consists of reusable metal strips and plates).

(30) deset dvacet **stavebnic** **typu** **Merkur**
ten twenty construction sets type.GEN.SG Merkur.NOM.SG
'ten or twenty Merkur construction sets / ten or twenty construction sets like Merkur'
(ORAL_ 02A025N)

Typ (or more precisely, its genitive form *typu*) is not referential here and cannot be premodified or predetermined by demonstratives. It can take a whole range of complements (see below in Section 3.3); if there is an NP, it never includes a superordinate noun. The construction can be regarded as binominal in the sense that *typu* expresses a relationship between a more general noun and a more specific one.[22] The relation may be that of exemplification, as in (31)–(34), where the second appositive exemplifies the reference of the more general noun – or similarity (where an ad hoc kind is created; see (35)).

(31) [...] *chtějí mít z Prahy* **moderní** **velkoměsto**
they.want to.have from Prague modern.ACC.SG metropolis.ACC.SG
typu **Paříže** [...]
type.GEN.SG Paris.GEN.SG
'those mastodons in the town hall] want to turn Prague into a modern city along the lines of Paris [...]'
(IC_Urban-Lord_Mord)

(32) **starý dědky** **typu** *já nevim* **Nazareti**
old grandpas type.GEN.SG I do.not.know Nazareth.NOM.PL
a **Pink Floydi** *a* **Rolling Stones**
and Pink Floyd.NOM.PL and Rolling Stones.NOM.PL
'grandpas such as – I don't know – Nazareth and Pink Floyd and Rolling Stones'
(ORAL_10H007N)

---

22 We hesitate to call this use of *typ* prepositional because – among others – the complement is very constrained: if it is a proper name, it does not allow modification such as **lidi typu ten blbec Karel* [people type.GEN.SG that idiot.NOM.SG Charles.NOM.SG] (Petr Biskup, p.c.).

(33) **osobnostem**   **typu**   **Halíka**   bych   určitě   dal
personality.DAT.PL   type.GEN.SG   Halík.GEN.SG   I.would   definitely   give
přednost
preference
'I'd definitely prefer personalities such as [the Czech Catholic priest] Halík'
(ORAL_03A005N)

(34) *vybíral*   *cíle*   *jako*   **typu**   *dvoumetrový*   *rozložitý*
he.picked   targets   like   type.GEN.SG   two.metre.NOM.SG   huge.NOM.SG
skinhead   který   začal   močit   doprostřed   chodníku
skinhead.NOM.SG   who   started   to.urinate   in.the.middle.of   pavement
'he picked targets such as a huge two-metre-tall skinhead who started urinating in the middle of the street'
(ORAL_05A060N)

(35) [...] *je*   *to*   *bývalá* [...]   **žena**   **typu**   **Mileny**
is   it   former   woman.NOM.SG   type.GEN.SG   Milena.GEN.SG
Pelentové
Pelentová.GEN.SG
'she used to be [...] a Milena Pelentová type of woman [i.e. a woman obsessed with men]' [transl. MJ&MM]
(IC_skvorecky-hrichy_pater)

The appositive identification in (29) differs from exemplification and similarity in that it only allows an NP complement in the nominative, while exemplification and similarity uses allow both the nominative and the genitive (as in (32) and (33)). Only *typ* in its exemplification and similarity uses can be replaced with *jako* 'like, such as' (although *jako* would only take a nominative complement in these cases), which is not possible in the appositive identification.

3.3 Non-binominal non-head use

While the previous section dealt with nominal complements of *typ* (*druh* does not appear in this usage), a whole range of other complements was attested in the corpora. The complement can be an adverb phrase, as in (36), or a whole sentence, as in (37).

(36) **víkendového rodiče typu** *jednou za štrnáct dní na*
weekend parent type.GEN.SG once in fourteen days for
víkend
weekend
'a once-in-two-weeks-for-the-weekend kind of parent'
(ORAL_06H089N)

(37) *uplně nejvíc miluju* **tu léčbu typu** *nejprve*
absolutely most I.love that treatment type.GEN.SG first
se to musí zhoršit aby se to začalo zlepšovat
REFL it must worsen so REFL that began improve
'most of all I love the it-must-first-get-worse-so-it-can-get-better kind of treatment'
(ORAL_09A188N)

This is again similar to Russian, where, as Kolyaseva and Davidse (2018: 209) observed, "the complements may be proper names, abbreviations or words and phrases that are put in quotation marks or that are used as quotations". The quotative interpretation is at hand when the noun preceding *typ* denotes a speech event, and what follows is a representative example of many other possible wordings of the same content:[23]

(38) **takový rady typu** *jako víš co* **uvolněte**
such advice type.GEN.SG like you.know what relax
se *a* **nebojte se** *mluvit no*
REFL and do.not.be.afraid REFL to.speak yeah
'such advice like, you know, "Relax and don't be afraid to speak," right'
(ORAL_09A025N)

In some examples of the quotative use, there is no nominal element at all – neither head nor complement – and *typ* is used predicatively to introduce both direct and indirect speech, as in (39) and (40) respectively:

---

[23] In this respect, *typ* is similar to the English *be like*, which is said to make "no claim to verbatim reconstruction of dialogue" (D'Arcy 2017: 16).

(39) **toto je typu** jako **teď tady máš tatínka a ten**
this is type.GEN.SG like now here you.have daddy and he
tě bude bavit
you will entertain
'this is like, "Here's your daddy now and he will entertain you"'
(ORAL_06H089N)

(40) **to bylo** hnedka **typu** že že pracuju ž* že
it was immediately type.GEN.SG that that I.work t* that
sem měl málo peněz
am had little money
'they immediately said, like, you know, that I work and I had little money'
(ORAL_06H089N)

In contrast to Russian, the quotative use of *typ* is very limited; it was only attested with impersonal subjects, unlike the Czech quotative particle *prý/prej*,[24] exemplified in (41), and unlike the English quotative *be like*.[25]

(41) a **my prej** ale my jedeme už teď a strašně
and we QUOT but we go already now and terribly
jsme spěchali [...] a **voni prej** teďka něco
we.were rushed and they QUOT now something
jede jo?
goes yeah
'and we said, "But we are going now," and we were in a terrible rush [...] and they said, "Oh, is there a train now?"'
(ORAL_02A022N)

---

24 On the polyfunctional particle *prý* (substandard form *prej*), see Martinková and Janebová (2017). The anonymous reviewer raised the question of whether there are contexts in which *typ* would be used rather than *prý/prej*. The quotative particle *prý/prej* introduces direct speech (i.e. it can be used with [understood] personal subjects, unlike *typ*), but it could also be used in a predicative construction with the demonstrative impersonal subject *to* in (40), i.e. *to bylo hnedka prý/prej že . . .*; on the other hand, it would be ungrammatical with the deictic pronoun *toto* in (39).
25 As D'Arcy (2017: 19) notes: "What is striking about early examples of *be* is that, though never robust in terms of overall frequency, this verb typically occurred with non-referential *it* [. . .]." However, "[i]n current use, *it* occurs at (near) categorical rates with *be like*."

4 Data analysis

In Section 3 we discussed the major uses of type nouns attested in present-day spoken Czech and original Czech fiction. As the data shows, in contrast to the definitions and examples given in dictionaries of Standard Czech, *druh* and *typ* are not limited to the binominal taxonomic construction and have other uses. In the next step, we carried out quantitative analyses in order to determine which properties of the linguistic context influence the distribution of type nouns in Czech, thus complementing the results of our qualitative analysis. In what follows we describe the annotation of the data (Section 4.1), followed by a presentation of the results of a logistic regression analysis which allows us to identify associations between specific variables and the use of *druh* and *typ* as response variables (Section 4.2), and random forest and conditional inference tree analyses, which give us an idea of the relative importance of the variables (Section 4.3). Readers less familiar with statistics may wish to proceed directly to Section 4.4 and the Conclusions, where the implications of our results are summarized.

4.1 Annotation of the data and descriptive statistics

Each observation was coded for the variables shown in Table 3. These variables were used as predictors for the use of either *druh* or *typ* (the response variable). The first three variables capture the structural properties of the relevant noun phrases: 1. the determiner of the type noun, 2. the head status of the type noun, and 3. the complement. Moreover, we coded the data for two semantic properties: 4. the animacy of the referent of the type noun (±Human), and 5. the type of premodifying adjective used (distinguishing between what we call postdeterminer adjectives in the sense of Davidse et al. (2008: 143) and other adjectives). The final variable is modality (written or spoken).

Table 3: Predictors for the selection of the type nouns *druh* and *typ*.

1. DETERMINER (DET): determiner of the type noun	
0	no determiner
DEF	definite determiners, i.e. demonstratives and possessive pronouns
SIM	similative demonstrative
INDEF	indefinite
QUANT	quantifier
INTER	interrogative

Table 3 (continued)

2. HEAD STATUS (HEAD)	
YES	type noun is the head
NO	type noun is not the head
3. COMPLEMENT OF THE TYPE NOUN (X2)	
0	no complement
SN	superordinate noun
ID	identification
EX	exemplification[26]
COMP	comparative clause[27]
QUOT	quotative phrase
POSTMOD	other postmodifiers (e.g. relative clause)
4. PREMODIFIER (PREMOD)	
0	no premodifier
PD_ADJ	postdeterminer adjective
ADJ	all other adjectives
5. HUMAN REFERENT (HUM)	
YES	referent is human
NO	referent is non-human
6. MODALITY (MOD)	
SPOK	spoken
WRIT	written

The distribution of all the categories combining with *druh* and *typ* in both modalities is shown in the form of barplots in Figure 2.

4.2 Bayesian logistic regression analysis

We used logistic regression in order to understand the relationships between the predictor variables summarized in Table 3 and the response variable TYPE NOUN

---

[26] Since the relation of similarity discussed in Section 3.2 is hard to differentiate from the exemplification relation, both are coded as EX in our data.
[27] We use the term in the sense of Quirk et al. (1985: 1127): "In a comparative construction, a proposition expressed in the matrix clause is compared with a proposition expressed in the subordinate clause with respect to some STANDARD OF COMPARISON."

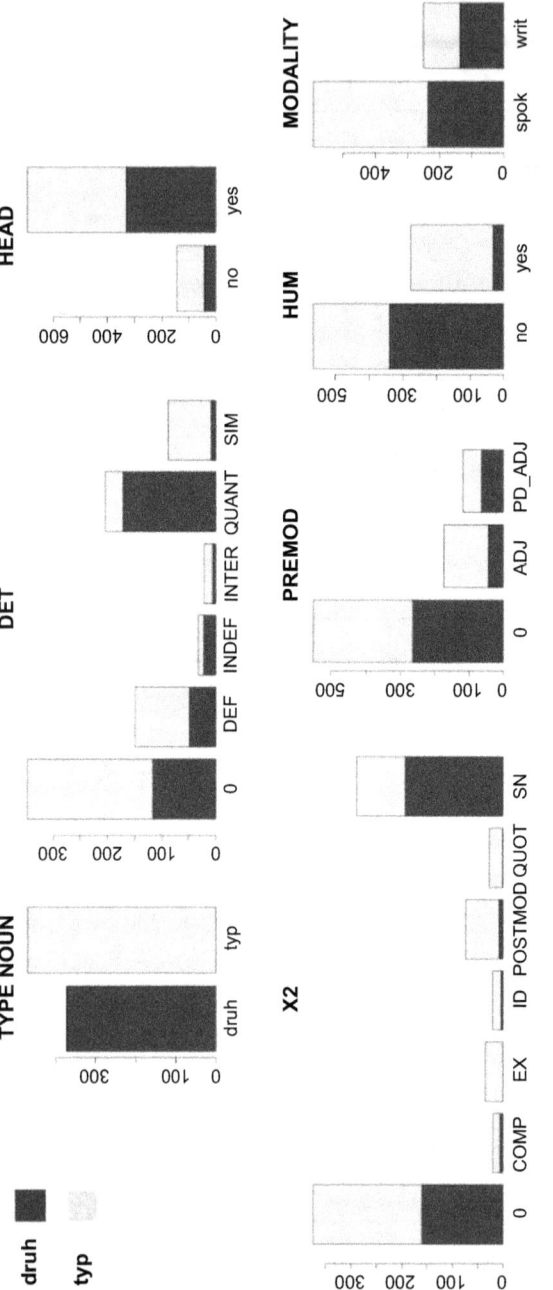

Figure 2: The absolute frequencies of *druh* and *typ* relative to the other variables.

(*typ* vs. *druh*). Given that the data contained instances of complete separation, we used Bayesian regression as implemented in the package 'brms' for R (Bürkner 2017, 2018). The model statistics cannot be displayed here for reasons of space and are provided in the Appendix. The Bayesian R^2-value is 0.48.

Significant two-way interactions ($p < 0.05$) were found between the following pairs of variables:
- HUM(AN REFERENT) and MOD(ALITY)
- PREMOD(IFIER) and HEAD

In the following sections we discuss the results by predictor variable, visualizing them in terms of the coefficients with 95% credible intervals. Regression coefficients indicate the relationship between predictor variables and the response variable (TYPE NOUN). For categorical predictors (like the ones used in the present study) they have to be interpreted relative to the reference level, which will be indicated in each case. A value higher than 0 shows a (relative) preference for *typ*, a value lower than 0 indicates (relative) association with *druh*. For interacting variables we also show conditional effects, i.e. the probability of finding a specific observation under the condition that the other variables are at a specific level. While regression coefficients can be used to compare predictors with each other in terms of their association with specific levels of the response variable, conditional effects indicate probabilities of finding *typ* and *druh*, for each level of the predictor variable, under specific conditions. The condition used in each case is that the other predictor variables are at their reference levels.[28] The reference levels are:
- DET: 0
- PREMOD: 0
- X2: 0
- HEAD: no
- HUM: no
- MOD: spoken

4.2.1 Determiners

The coefficients for the levels of the variable DETERMINER are shown in Figure 3. The reference level is 'no determiner'. Remember that positive values indicate

---

[28] The conditional probability plots were created with the function conditional_effects() of the package 'brms' for R.

(relative) association with *typ*, negative values show association with *druh*. The levels INDEF and QUANT are clearly associated with *druh*, while INTER shows a significant association with *typ*.

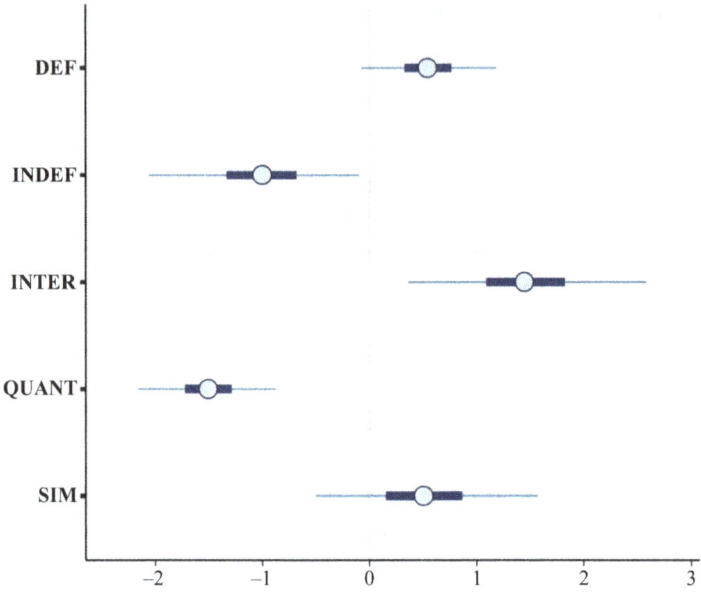

Figure 3: Effects of the variable DETERMINER.

For convenience, examples (19) and (11) are repeated here as (42) and (43) respectively, to exemplify the typical uses of quantifiers and indefinites with *druh*.

(42) **zboží   jednoho   druhu**
     goods.NOM.SG   one.GEN.SG   kind.GEN.SG
     'goods of one kind'
     (ORAL_05A130N)

(43) ale   ta   strupatost   to   je   prej   **ňákej   druh**
     but   that   potato scab   that   is   allegedly   some   kind.NOM.SG
     plísně
     fungus.GEN.SG
     'but this potato scab that is allegedly some kind of fungus'
     (ORAL_ 02A004N)

Even though there is no significant interaction between the variables DETERMINER and MODALITY, the coefficients for two types of determiners, definite and similative ones, vary substantially between spoken and written texts. The interaction is in fact almost significant, with p = 0.052. We therefore show the conditional effects for a model including the interaction between DET and MOD in Figure 4. The plot shows that in the spoken modality, definite determiners tend to favour *typ*, while in the written modality, they favour *druh*. The similative demonstrative *takový* does not show any specific preference in spoken language, but it leans heavily towards *typ* in written language.

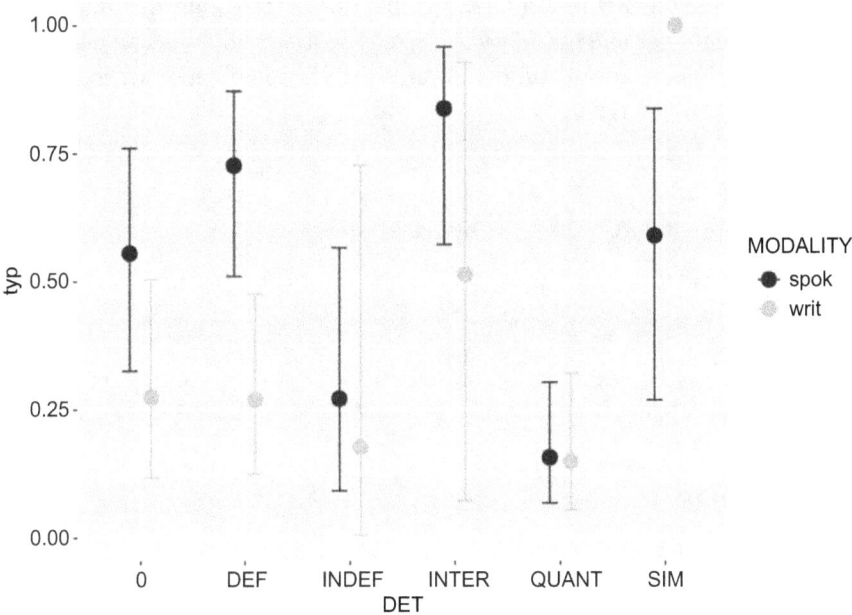

Figure 4: Conditional effects for the levels of DETERMINER interacting with MODALITY.

The association of the similative demonstrative pronoun with *typ* is illustrated with example (44):

(44) **takovej** klasickej stydlavej **typ** ruskýho mafióza
  such classical bashful type.NOM.SG Russian.GEN.SG mobster.GEN.SG
  'that classical bashful Russian mobster type'
  (IC_ Pekarkova-Dej_mi_ty_pr)

4.2.2 Head status and premodifier

The variables HEAD STATUS and PREMODIFIER interact and are therefore treated together in this subsection. The reference levels are 'no' for HEAD and '0' for PREMODIFIER. These levels are therefore not represented in the plots. The top two lines in Figure 5 show the coefficients for ADJ and PD_ADJ if the type noun is not head: ADJ tends towards *typ*, PD_ADJ tends towards *druh* in this context (in comparison with the context of an absent modifier). The two rows at the bottom show the interaction with HEAD: if the type noun is head, the distribution is shifted in the direction of *druh* for ADJ, and it is shifted in the direction of *typ* for PD_ADJ. The line in the middle shows that there is no significant association between HEAD = yes and *typ* or *druh* if there is no premodifier (in comparison to HEAD = no). The balance is shifted towards *druh* in combination with ADJ, and it is shifted towards *typ* in combination with PD_ADJ (see the bottom two lines in Figure 5).

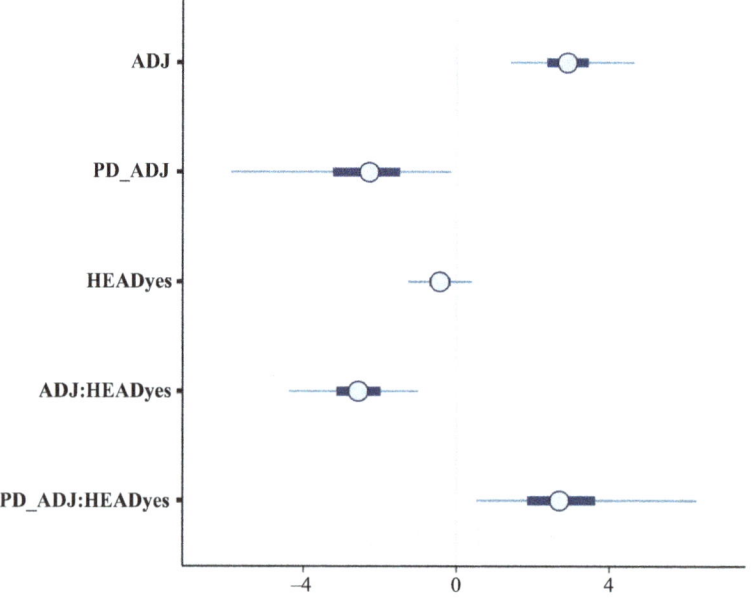

Figure 5: Effects of the interacting variables HEAD and PREMODIFIER.

The interaction between the two variables is illustrated with the conditional effects (estimated probabilities) in Figure 6, which visualizes the probability of finding *typ* for the combinations of the two variables PREMODIFIER and HEAD, given that all other variables are at their reference levels. This figure shows that the interaction effects are primarily due to the behaviour of non-head uses of type nouns. The probability of finding ADJ or PD_ADJ with *typ* as head is approximately 50%, i.e. there is no preference for either type noun. However, in the non-head use, *typ* is significantly more likely than *druh* with ADJ as a premodifier, while with PD_ADJ as a premodifier, *druh* is significantly more likely than *typ*.

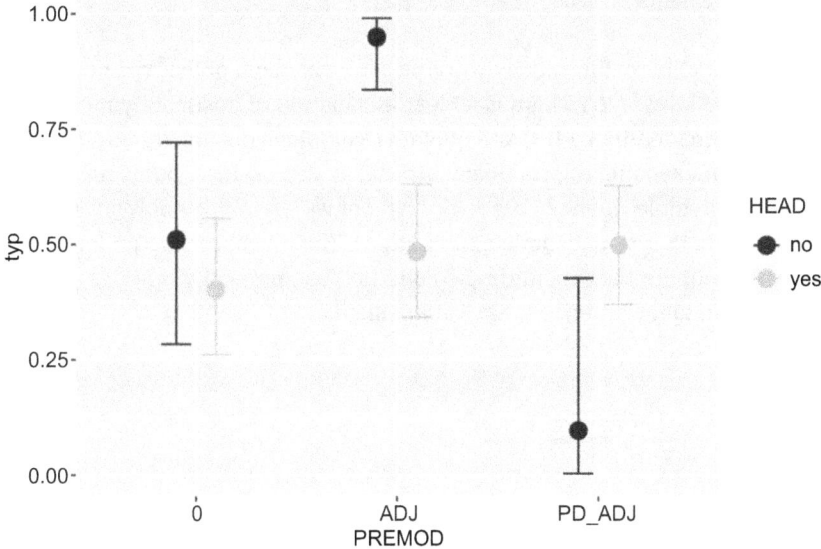

Figure 6: Conditional effects of the interacting variables HEAD and PREMODIFIER.

The distributional preferences shown in Figure 6 are exemplified below: in (20), repeated here as (45), a non-head *druh* is modified by a postdeterminer adjective, and in (28), repeated here as (46), a non-head *typ* is modified by a classifying (non-postdeterminer) adjective.

(45) přijelo sem obrovské množství **nových aut**
came here huge amount new car.GEN.PL
nejrůznějších druhů
various.GEN.PL.SUP kind.GEN.PL
'there had been a tremendous influx of all sorts of new cars'
(IC_Topol-Chladnou_zemi)

(46) **sejra** [...] je to je to [pause] **hermelínovýho** **typu**
cheese [...] is it is it Camembert.ADJ.GEN.SG type.GEN.SG
plísňovej
mouldy.NOM.SG
'the cheese is a kind of Camembert, mould cheese'
(ORAL_10A43N)

4.2.3 Complements

Figure 7 shows the coefficients for the type of complement of the type noun (X2). The reference level is '0'. There is a clear association of postmodifying clauses (POSTMOD) and identifying (ID) and quotative complements (QUOT) with *typ*. The coefficient for exemplifying complements (EX) is also positive, but is not shown because its credible intervals are very large, since EX is invariably realized as *typ* in our data (a case of complete separation). The plot shows no preference of either type noun for the superordinate noun (SN) or comparative clauses (COMP), in comparison to the absence of any complement.

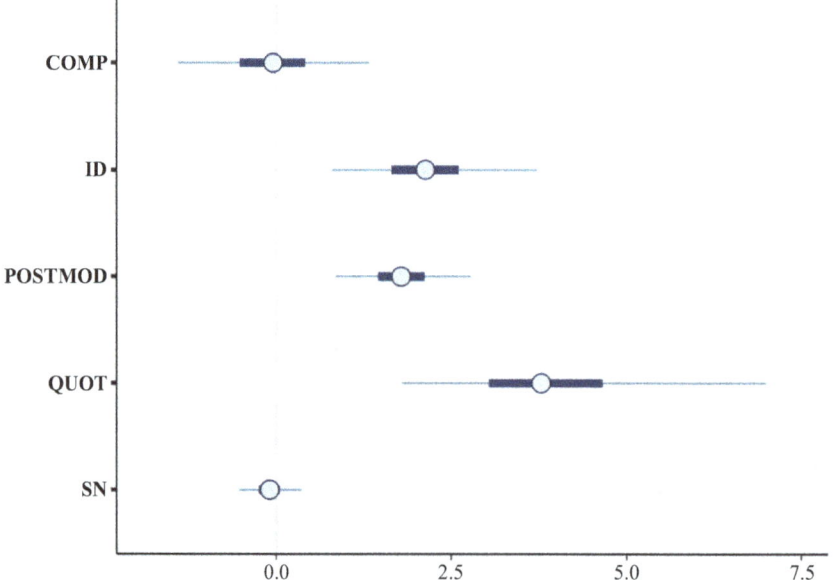

Figure 7: Effects of the variable X2 (complement).

For convenience, examples (10) and (11) are repeated here as (47) and (48) to exemplify that that is no preference of either type noun for the superordinate noun; example (37), repeated here as (49), exemplifies the preference for *typ* with quotative complements.

(47) v   nejmodernějším   typu   bavoráku
      in   the.most.modern.LOC.SG   type.LOC.SG   BMW.GEN.SG
      'in the most modern type of BMW'
      (ORAL_06A099N)

(48) ale   ta   strupatost   to   je   prej   **ňákej   druh**
      but   that potato scab   it   is   allegedly some   kind.NOM.SG
      plísně
      fungus.GEN.SG
      'but this potato scab, it is allegedly some kind of fungus'
      (ORAL_ 02A004N)

(49) *uplně   nejvíc   miluju*   **tu**   *léčbu*   **typu**   *nejprve*
      absolutely   most   I.love   that   treatment   type.GEN.SG   first
      se   to   musí   zhoršit   aby   se   to   začalo   zlepšovat
      REFL   it   must   worsen   so   REFL   that   began   improve
      'most of all I love the it-must-first-get-worse-so-it-can-get-better kind of treatment'
      (ORAL_09A188N)

4.2.4 Human referent and modality

HUMAN REFERENT is the only purely semantic variable in our data. As it interacts with modality, these variables are discussed together in this subsection. The reference levels are 'no' for HUM and 'spoken' for MODALITY. The top row in Figure 8 shows that *typ* is strongly associated with type nouns in noun phrases referring to human referents if MODALITY is spoken, in comparison to non-human referents. *Druh* shows an affinity to the written modality with non-human referents (the reference level), in comparison with *typ*. The line at the bottom, representing the interaction between HUM and MOD, shows that if the referent is human and MODALITY is written, the distribution is shifted towards *druh*.

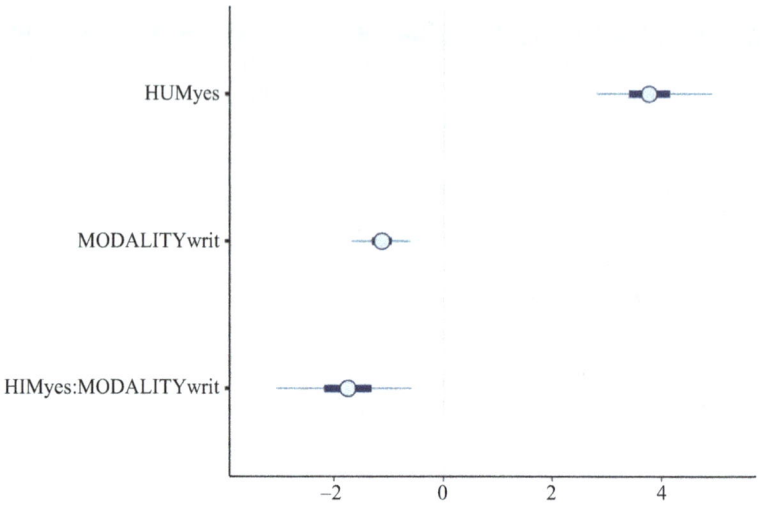

Figure 8: Effects for the interacting variables HUMAN REFERENT and MODALITY.

Figure 9 shows the conditional effects for the choice of *typ*, for HUMAN REFERENT (HUM) and MODALITY, i.e. the probabilities of using *typ* given that all other variables are at their reference levels. The likelihood of *typ* being used in the spoken modality is higher than in the written modality, and this preference is even stronger with human referents than with non-human referents.

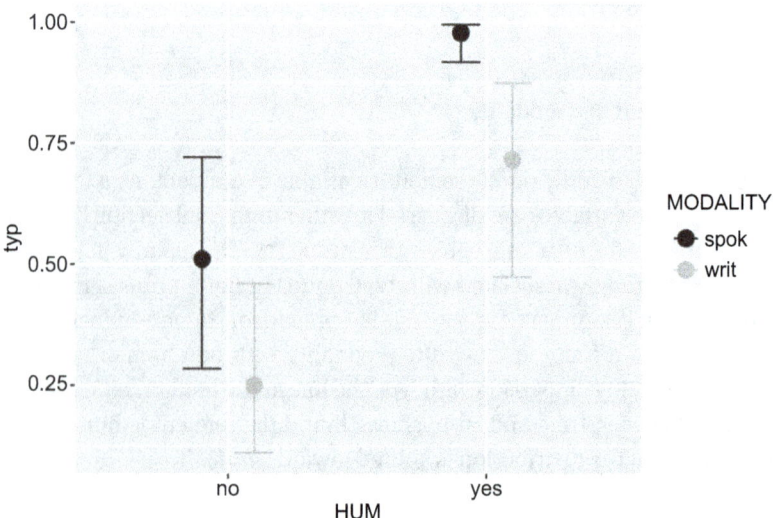

Figure 9: Conditional effects for the interacting variables HUMAN REFERENT and MODALITY.

The association of human referents with *typ* in both modalities can be illustrated with example (12), repeated below for convenience as (50). The association of non-human referents with *druh* in the corpus of fiction is illustrated with example (20), repeated below for convenience as (51). Examples of *druh* with a human referent, as in (52), were only attested in the written modality and are very rare overall.

(50) neni   to   **typ**   **Pavarottiho**   je   to   spíš
     he.is.not   it   type.NOM.SG   Pavarotti.GEN.SG   he.is rather it   rather
     typ   **Carrerase**
     type.NOM.SG   Carreras.GEN.SG
     'he is not like Pavarotti, he's rather like Carreras'
     (ORAL_10P006N)

(51) přijelo sem   obrovské   množství   **nových**   **aut**
     came   here   huge   amount   new   car.GEN.PL
     nejrůznějších   **druhů**
     various.GEN.PL.SUP   kind.GEN.PL
     'there had been a tremendous influx of all sorts of new cars'
     (IC_Topol-Chladnou_zemi)

(52) V   takovymhle   pajzlu   neni   **člověk**   **mýho**   **druhu**
     in   this   dive   is.not   man.NOM.SG   my.GEN.SG   kind.GEN.SG
     nikdy   sám [...]
     never   alone
     'People like me are never alone in a dive like this [...]'
     (IC_skvorecky-hrichy_pater)

4.3 Conditional inference tree algorithm

The regression analysis has shown associations between the various predictor variables and the response variable (use of *druh* vs. *typ*). In order to determine the relative importance of the variables, we used conditional inference trees and random forests.[29] The results of the random forest analysis are shown in Figure 10.

---

[29] We used conditional inference trees with the package 'ctree' for R (Hothorn et al. 2006).

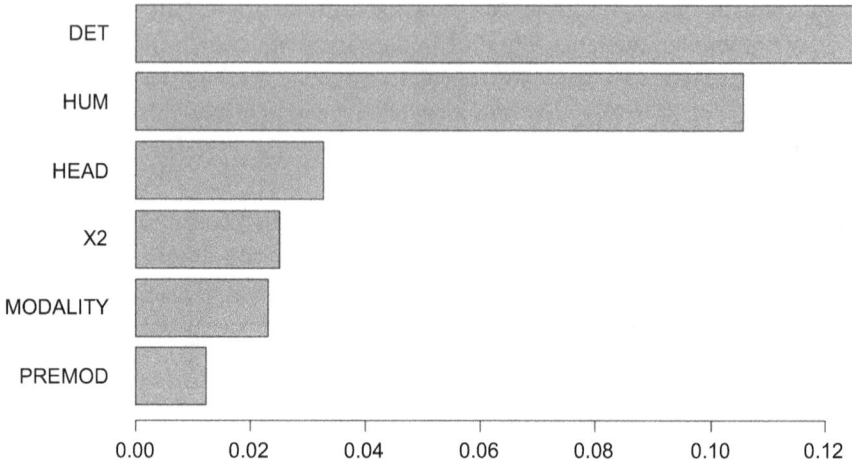

Figure 10: Importance of variables according to a random forest analysis.

Figure 10 shows that DET(ERMINER) and HUM(AN REFERENT) are the most important variables differentiating between *druh* and *typ*. In the following two sections we will inspect conditional inference trees – separately for the spoken and written modalities – to gain a better understanding of the interplay between the various predictor variables and the response variable TYPE NOUN.

4.3.1 Distribution of the type nouns *druh* and *typ* in spoken Czech

Figure 11 shows the conditional inference tree for the distribution of the type nouns *druh* and *typ* in spoken Czech. The first important split is between indefinite pronouns and quantifiers (INDEF/QUANT) on the one hand, and the other determiners (0/DEF/INTER/SIM) on the other. The next split is between human and non-human referents (HUM).

As Figure 11 shows, the only condition under which *druh* prevails in spoken Czech is with DET=INDEF or DET=QUANT, and HUM=no (Node 3). In other words, if there is an indefinite pronoun or a quantifier, and if the type noun does not refer to a human being, there is a strong preference for *druh* (see for example (21), repeated here for convenience as (53)). The only condition under which the distribution of *druh* and *typ* is comparable is DET ∈ {0, DEF, INTER, SIM}, HUM=no, and HEAD=yes (Node 7). This means that the distribution of the two type nouns is similar if the determiner is neither indefinite nor a quantifier (i.e. zero, inter-

15 Czech type nouns: Evidence from corpora — 607

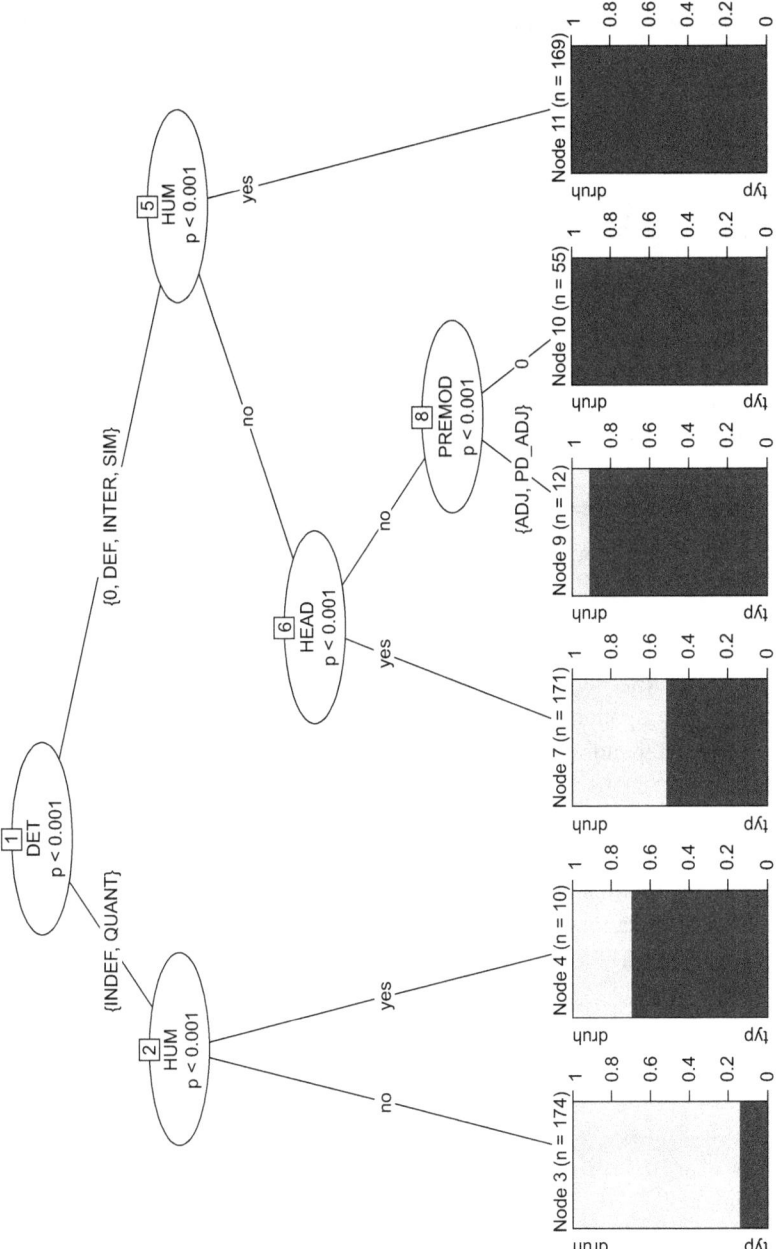

Figure 11: The conditional inference tree for the distribution of the type nouns *druh* and *typ* in spoken Czech.

rogative, similative, demonstrative, or possessive), if the type noun does not refer to a human being, and if the type noun is the head (see *typ* in example (10), repeated below as (54), and *druh* in example (55)). In all other cases, we can see a clear preference for *typ*, as in (17), repeated below as (56), where there is neither a quantifier nor an indefinite pronoun (DET ∈ {0, DEF, INTER, SIM}), and there is a human referent (HUM=yes). Sentence (37), repeated below as (57), exemplifies a non-head use of *typ* with no human referent (DET ∈ {0, DEF, INTER, SIM}, HUM=no, HEAD=no).

(53) tam je **spousta** **těch** **supermarketů**   **všeho**   **druhu**
     there is lots   those   supermarket.GEN.PL all.GEN.SG kind.GEN.SG
     'there are a lot of supermarkets of all kinds'
     (ORAL_07A68N)

(54) v **nejmodernějším**   **typu**   **bavoráku**
     in the.most.modern.LOC.SG type.LOC.SG BMW.GEN.SG
     'in the most modern type of BMW'
     (ORAL_06A099N)

(55) asi   záleží   na **druhu**   **půstu**
     perhaps it.depends on kind.LOC.SG fast.GEN.SG
     'perhaps it depends on the kind of fast'
     (ORAL_03A022N)

(56) já sem **takovej**   **přesolovací**   **typ**
     I   am   such.NOM.SG oversalting.NOM.SG type.NOM.SG
     'I am this oversalting type'
     (ORAL_05H057N)

(57) uplně   nejvíc miluju   **tu**   **léčbu**   **typu**   **nejprve**
     absolutely most   I.love that treatment type.GEN.SG first
     se   **to** **musí** **zhoršit** **aby** **se**   **to** **začalo** **zlepšovat**
     REFL it   must   worsen   so   REFL that began   improve
     'most of all I love the it-must-first-get-worse-so-it-can-get-better kind of treatment'
     (ORAL_09A188N)

4.3.2 Distribution of the type nouns *druh* and *typ* in original Czech fiction

The conditional inference tree for the distribution of the two type nouns in written Czech is shown in Figure 12.

The first split in the tree in Figure 12 is between human and non-human referents. The next split occurs between the type of complementation. There is only one condition under which there is a clear preponderance of *druh* in Czech fiction, i.e. with HUM=no and X2 ∈ {0, COMP, POSTMOD} (Node 8); in other words, if the type noun does not refer to a human being and there is a comparative clause or another postmodifying clause or no complement, *druh* is used; see for example (20), repeated below as (58). On the contrary, if the type noun does not refer to a human being, but the complement is exemplifying (EX), identifying (ID), or quotative (QUOT), *typ* is preferred (Node 9); see for example (31), repeated below as (59), and (60). The other condition in which *typ* is clearly preferred involves reference to a human being, no superordinate noun in the complement (X2=0, EX, POSTMOD, QUOT), and head status (HEAD=yes) (Node 5), as in (61).

(58)   *přijelo sem obrovské množství **nových aut***
       came   here huge   amount   new   car.GEN.PL
     nejrůznějších   druhů
     various.GEN.PL.SUP kind.GEN.PL
     'there had been a tremendous influx of all sorts of new cars'
     (IC_Topol-Chladnou_zemi)

(59)   [...] *chtějí mít   z   Prahy **moderní**   **velkoměsto***
     they.want to.have from Prague modern.ACC.SG metropolis.ACC.SG
     typu*   *Paříže [...]
     type.GEN.SG Paris.GEN.SG
     'those mastodons in the town hall] want to turn Prague into a modern city along the lines of Paris [...]'
     (IC_Urban-Lord_Mord)

(60)   [...] *ten děd   mě naučil hlavně **slogany typu**:*
         the old.man me taught mainly slogans type.GEN.SG
     seber   rýč*,** [...] ***víc   hnoje, chceš   cigáro?
     pick-up rake   more manure you.want cigarette
     'Mostly all the old fogy taught me was phrases like: get the rake, [...] more manure, want a smoke?'
     (IC_Topol-Sestra)

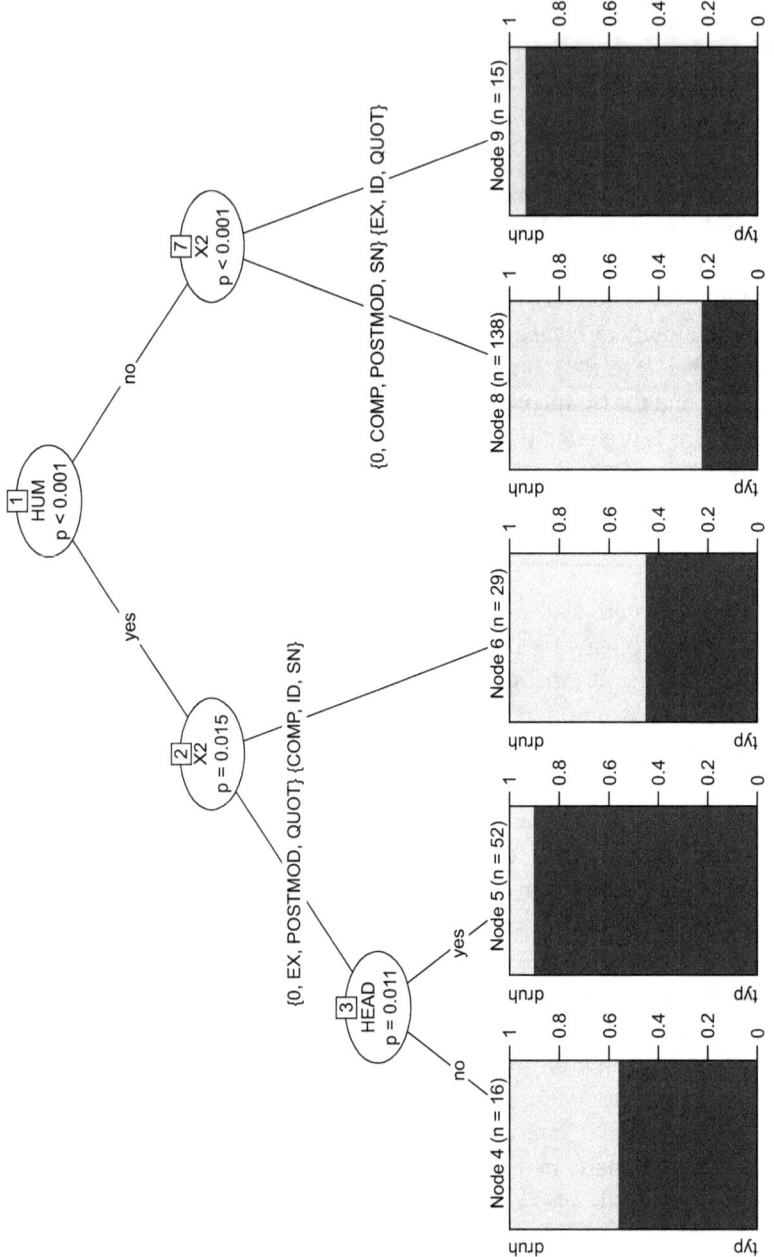

Figure 12: The conditional inference tree for the distribution of the Czech type nouns in original Czech fiction.

(61) [...] **takovej černovlasej, olivovej italskej typ**
such black-haired olive.ADJ Italian type.NOM.SG
'he was olive-skinned, an Italian type'
(IC_skvorecky-hrichy_pater)

4.4 The role of variables: Interpretation of the data

As the data shows, the type of referent is an important predictor for the distribution of *typ* vs. *druh*: in original Czech fiction, it is the most influential factor (it creates the first split in the conditional inference tree in Figure 12), and in spoken Czech the second most influential factor (it creates the second split in spoken Czech in Figure 11). In both modalities, there is a clear association of human referents with *typ*.

The type of determiner used is the most influential factor for spoken Czech (it creates the top split in the conditional inference tree in Figure 11). If there is an indefinite pronoun or a quantifier, and if the type noun does not refer to a human being, there is a strong preference for *druh*. The fact that *druh* – but not *typ* – strongly correlates with quantifiers and indefinite pronouns indicates that it is associated with the subtype meaning. *Typ*, on the other hand, collocates with definite determiners (demonstratives and possessives) in spoken language and the similative demonstrative *takový*,[30] i.e. *typ* creates ad hoc kinds based on properties retrievable from the context or based on "common ground".

As for 'type of modifier' as a predictor, the fact that *druh* is associated with postdeterminer adjectives, which single out subclasses, while *typ* is associated with the other – non-postdeterminer – ones indicates the different paths of lexicalization and grammaticalization of the two type nouns. The taxonomic meaning of *druh* is lexicalized into the quantitative meaning ("various"), which is not the case with *typ*.

The head status of the type noun has also been shown to be an important predictor. In spoken Czech, the distribution of the two type nouns is similar only if the noun phrase with the type noun does not refer to a human being, and if the type noun is the head of the phrase (and if the determiner is neither indefinite or

---

30 The regression model only shows a strong correlation of the similative demonstrative with *typ* in the written modality; see Figure 4. The imbalance in the distribution that can be observed in Figure 2 is partly due to the covarying variables HUM and HEAD. While we would need more data to get a more precise understanding of the exact relationships between these variables, the correlation between SIM and *typ* is compatible with our intuitions, and is confirmed by inspection of the data.

a quantifier). It is in the non-head use that the type nouns have been observed to be prone to an extension of meaning. For *druh*, this extension of meaning consists in the lexicalization into the quantitative meaning; *typ*, on the other hand, has acquired new functions which are associated with the last predictor, the type of complement.

The type of complement used also has a bearing on the distribution of the type nouns. We have seen that there is no preference of either type noun for the superordinate noun, or, to put it differently, in the prototypical binominal construction, *druh* and *typ* are comparable. Outside the binominal construction, only *typ* is to be found: if there is no superordinate noun, and the complement is exemplifying or quotative, *typ* is selected.

5 Conclusions

Our analysis reveals significant distributional differences between the Czech type nouns (TNs) *druh* and *typ*. There are two types of binominal constructions in Czech: TN+N2, where the type noun is the head and N2 is in the genitive (binominal head use), and N1+TN, where the type noun functions as a genitival modifier (binominal non-head use), and it is in obligatory postposition. Both can be taxonomic as well as non-taxonomic.

Reference to subtypes can be expressed in both the ways mentioned above. However, the distribution of *druh* and *typ* with the subtype meaning is only comparable in the prototypical taxonomic usage, namely in the head construction TN+N2.GEN, if N2 is a superordinate noun which does not refer to a human being.

In the taxonomic non-head construction N1+TN.GEN, both *druh* and *typ* have been attested, but there are statistically significant differences in the determination and premodification of the type nouns. *Druh* is strongly associated with quantifiers and – in the non-head use – with postdeterminer adjectives such as *stejný* 'same', *jiný* 'different', and *další* 'further', which help single out "subclasses for particular attention" or set off "subtypes against other subtypes" (Davidse et al. 2008: 146). It is also associated with indefinite pronouns. This, together with the fact that *druh* does not take nominal complements other than superordinate nouns, shows that *druh* still retains its subtype meanings (indeed 98% of the occurrences of *druh* in spoken Czech and 95% of those in fiction are taxonomic; see Table 2). *Druh* refers to well-established and countable kinds, or, in the case of indefinite pronouns, it has a referent which may be known or unknown to the speaker (in the sense of Haspelmath (1997)), but there is no referential vagueness: the speaker is familiar with the superordinate category, but may lack specific knowledge of the subtype. In other words, *nějaký druh* 'some kind' does not hedge an existing category.

The non-head use is prone to the weakening of the taxonomic meaning. We have observed a shift from the taxonomic to the quantifying meaning of the non-head *druh* in *všeho druhu* [all.GEN.SG kind.GEN.SG]. We also observed an extension of the taxonomic meaning of *druh* marked by a categorial shift; when determined by the reflexive pronoun *svůj*, the non-head *druh* can function as a hedge. The categorial shift is quite prominent because as a hedge, the phrase *svého druhu* [its.own.POSS.REFL.GEN.SG kind.GEN.SG] appears in the premodification of the head noun, while in its taxonomic meaning it can only appear in postposition. This use, however, was only attested in the reference corpus of written Czech SYN v.7, not in our corpora of original Czech fiction and spoken Czech.

Having described the distribution of *druh*, let us now turn to *typ*. Unlike *druh*, which correlates strongly with quantifiers and indefinite pronouns, *typ* collocates with definite determiners (in spoken language) and the similative demonstrative *takový* (significantly so in fiction). In other words, *typ* creates ad hoc kinds based on properties retrievable from the context or based on "common ground". As Table 2 shows, the non-taxonomic use of *typ* represents 20% of all its occurrences in our corpora. Unlike in Russian, where the extension of meaning is motivated by the non-head use of the type noun (Kolyaseva and Davidse 2018), we observed an extension in the head structure TN+N2 as well: our data show that *typ*, and not *druh*, appears in the lexicalized usage ("individual with characteristic features"). In such a case, the N2 (if present) has a unique referent, typically a proper name, in both the genitive and nominative (while only the genitive can be used taxonomically). In this way, *typ* is used as a similative creating ad hoc categories.

In non-head uses expressing a relationship, *typ* (i.e. its genitive form *typu*), and not *druh*, was attested. In the extended meaning, *typ* has an exemplifying function or expresses similarity, and the N2 can be used in both the nominative and genitive. In some cases, the complement does not even contain a noun, and *typ*, like its Russian counterpart, is followed by "phrases that are put in quotation marks or that are used as quotations" (Kolyaseva and Davidse 2018). We also regard tokens in which a noun complemented by the genitival form of *typ* is used to refer to a speech event as quotative. In none of these can *typ* be considered a fully-fledged quotative particle as observed in Russian (Kolyaseva and Davidse 2018); at most, it occurs in the predicative position. Unlike the Czech quotative particle *prý/prej*, it does not allow personal subjects, but only the impersonal pronouns such as *to* 'it'.

In other words, as the spoken data in particular suggests, *druh* (unlike *typ*) mostly retains its "subtype" meaning, even though there is evidence of its gaining approximative functions (quantifying and hedging) in fiction. These changes are quite complex: the categorial shift is marked by changes in case assignment, agreement, and positional variation (from obligatory postposition to premodification). *Typ*, on the other hand, has acquired exemplifying, similative and quotative functions, but was not attested in the hedging function in our corpora (instead of qualifying an existing category, it creates its own).

The task that awaits us is twofold: in the next step, historical corpus data should be investigated against the backdrop of evidence from other languages (Slavic languages as well as German, as a contact language of Czech) so that possible grammaticalization paths of the two type nouns *druh* and *typ* can be established.

Appendix

Formula

brm(typ ~ DET + PREMOD * HEAD + X2 * DET + HUM * MOD, family = 'bernoulli', control = list (max_treedepth = 20))

Table 4: Reference level of the response variable: *druh*.

	Estimate	Est.Error	l-95% CI	u-95% CI	Rhat	Bulk_ESS	Tail_ESS
Intercept	0.03	0.47	−0.92	0.95	1	1782	2489
DET_DEF	0.54	0.32	−0.07	1.18	1	2013	2508
DET_INDEF	−1.02	0.5	−2.06	−0.09	1	3462	3015
DET_INTER	1.46	0.56	0.36	2.58	1	2809	2620
DET_QUANT	−1.51	0.33	−2.16	−0.88	1	1872	2334
DET_SIM	0.51	0.52	−0.5	1.57	1	2774	2647
MOD_writ	−1.14	0.27	−1.69	−0.62	1	2734	2985
PREMOD_ADJ	2.93	0.84	1.39	4.64	1	1699	2168
PREMOD_PD_ADJ	−2.47	1.46	−5.89	−0.14	1	1464	1007
HEAD_yes	−0.43	0.42	−1.26	0.42	1	2397	2542
X2_COMP	−0.05	0.69	−1.4	1.32	1	3355	3053
X2_EX	63.59	64.61	5.29	243.49	1	1027	609
X2_ID	2.15	0.74	0.78	3.72	1	2418	2406
X2_POSTMOD	1.79	0.49	0.84	2.77	1	2711	2815
X2_QUOT	3.94	1.33	1.79	7	1	2734	1970
X2_SN	−0.09	0.23	−0.53	0.37	1	2945	2984
HUM_yes	3.79	0.55	2.8	4.92	1	1850	2185

Table 4 (continued)

	Estimate	Est.Error	l-95% CI	u-95% CI	Rhat	Bulk_ESS	Tail_ESS
PREMOD_ADJ:HEADyes	−2.6	0.87	−4.39	−1	1	1787	2512
PREMOD_PD_ADJ:HEADyes	2.86	1.46	0.51	6.29	1	1529	962
MOD_writ:HUMyes	−1.76	0.64	−3.08	−0.58	1	1794	2137

References

Aijmer, Karin. 1984. *Sort of* and *kind of* in English conversation. *Studia Linguistica* 38. 118–128.
Aijmer, Karin. 2002. *English discourse particles: Evidence from a corpus*. Amsterdam: John Benjamins.
van der Auwera, Johan & Evie Coussé. 2016. *Such* and *sådan* – the same but different. *Nordic Journal of English Studies* 15 (3). 15–32.
Brems, Lieselotte & Kristin Davidse. 2010. The grammaticalization of nominal type noun constructions with *kind/sort of*: chronology and paths of change. *English Studies* 91 (2). 180–202.
Bürkner, Paul-Christian. 2017. brms: An R package for Bayesian multilevel models using Stan. *Journal of Statistical Software* 80 (1). 1–28.
Bürkner, Paul-Christian. 2018. Advanced Bayesian multilevel modeling with the R package brms. *The R Journal* 10 (1). 395–411. doi:10.32614/RJ-2018-017.
Čermák, František & Alexandr Rosen. 2012: The case of InterCorp, a multilingual parallel corpus. *International Journal of Corpus Linguistics* 17 (3). 411–427.
Cvrček, Václav & Pavel Vondřička. 2011. SyD – korpusový průzkum variant [SyD – corpus study of variants]. Charles University in Prague. http://syd.korpus.cz.
D'Arcy, Alexandra. 2017. *Discourse-pragmatic variation in context. Eight hundred years of LIKE*. Amsterdam: John Benjamins.
Davidse, Kristin, Lieselotte Brems & Lieselotte De Smet. 2008. Type noun uses in the English NP: A case of right to left layering. *International Journal of Corpus Linguistics* 13 (2). 139–167.
Denison, David. 2005. The grammaticalisations of *sort of*, *kind of* and *type of* in English. Paper presented at *New Reflections on Grammaticalization* 3, Santiago de Compostela, 17–20 July. http://www.humanities.manchester.ac.uk/medialibrary/llc/files/david-denison/Santiago_NRG3_paper.pdf (accessed 1 December, 2016).
Diessel, Holger. 2006. Demonstratives, joint attention, and the emergence of grammar. *Cognitive Linguistics* 17. 463–489.
Elektronický slovník staré češtiny [Electronic dictionary of Old Czech]. 2006–. Institute of the Czech Language, Academy of Sciences of the Czech Republic, Prague. http://vokabular.ujc.cas.cz (version 1.1.14, accessed 12 June, 2020).
Haspelmath, Martin. 1997. *Indefinite pronouns*. Oxford: Oxford University Press.

Himmelmann, Nikolaus. 1996. Demonstratives in narrative discourse: A taxonomy of universal uses. In Barbara A. Fox (ed.), *Studies in anaphora*. 205–254. Amsterdam: Benjamins.

Hothorn Torsten, Kurt Hornik & Achim Zeileis. 2006. Unbiased recursive partitioning: A conditional inference framework. *Journal of Computational and Graphical Statistics* 15 (3). 651–674.

Janebová, Markéta & Michaela Martinková. 2017. NP-internal *kind of* and *sort of*: Evidence from a parallel translation corpus. In Markéta Janebová, Ekaterina Lapshinova-Koltunski & Michaela Martinková (eds.), *Contrasting English and other languages through corpora*, 164–217. Newcastle upon Tyne: Cambridge Scholars.

Johansson, Stig. 2007. Seeing through multilingual corpora. In Roberta Facchinetti (ed.), *Corpus linguistics 25 years on*, 51–72. Amsterdam: Rodopi.

Jungmann, Josef. 1837. *Slovník česko-německý, Díl III., P–R* [Czech-German dictionary, Vol. III, P–R]. 1st ed. Praha.

Keizer, Evelien. 2007. *The English noun phrase. The nature of linguistic categorization*. Cambridge: Cambridge University Press.

Kisiel, Anna. 2018. Polish type noun constructions: x to typ y-a, x w typie y-a. Paper presented at the workshop *Pragmatic functions of type nouns: A crosslinguistic perspective*, University of Tübingen, 19 June 2018.

Kolyaseva, Alena & Kristin Davidse. 2018. A typology of lexical and grammaticalized uses of Russian *tip, tipa, po tipu. Russian Linguistics* 42. 191–220. https://doi.org/10.1007/s11185-018-9193-9.

Kopřivová, Marie, David Lukeš, Zuzana Komrsková, Petra Poukarová, Martina Waclawičová, Lucie Benešová & Michal Křen. 2017. ORAL: korpus neformální mluvené češtiny [ORAL: corpus of informal spoken Czech], version 1 from 2. 6. 2017. Institute of the Czech National Corpus, Prague. http://www.korpus.cz.

Křen, Michal, Václav Cvrček, Tomáš Čapka, Anna Čermáková, Milena Hnátková, Lucie Chlumská, Tomáš Jelínek, Dominika Kováříková, Vladimír Petkevič, Pavel Procházka, Hana Skoumalová, Michal Škrabal, Petr Truneček, Pavel Vondřička & Adrian J. Zasina. 2017. Corpus SYN, version 7 from 29. 11. 2018. Institute of the Czech National Corpus, Prague. http://www.korpus.cz.

Kučera, Karel, Anna Řehořková & Martin Stluka. 2015. DIAKORP: Diachronní korpus [DIAKORP: Diachronic corpus]. Version 6 from 18. 12. 2015. Prague, Institute of the Czech National Corpus. http://www.korpus.cz.

Machek, Václav. 2010. *Etymologický slovník jazyka českého* [Etymological dictionary of Czech]. 5th ed. Prague: Nakladatelství Lidové noviny.

Martinková, Michaela & Markéta Janebová. 2017. What English translation equivalents can reveal about the Czech "modal" particle *prý*: A cross-register study. In Karin Aijmer & Diana Lewis (eds.), *Contrastive analysis of discourse-pragmatic aspects of linguistic genres*, 63–90. Cham: Springer.

Mihatsch, Wiltrud. 2016. Type-noun binominals in four Romance languages. *Language Sciences* 53. 136–159.

Quirk, Randolph, Sidney Greenbaum, Geoffrey Leech & Jan Svartvik. 1985. *A comprehensive grammar of the English language*. London: Longman.

Rejzek, Jiří. 2001. *Český etymologický slovník* [Czech etymological dictionary]. Prague: LEDA.

Slovník spisovné češtiny pro školu a veřejnost (SSČ) [Dictionary of Standard Czech for schools and the public]. 2009. Prague: Academia.

Středněčeská textová banka [Middle Czech text bank]. Prague, Institute of the Czech Language, Academy of Sciences of the Czech Republic.Version 1.1.4. http://vokabular.ujc.cas.cz/banka.aspx?idz=SDTB.

Traugott, Elizabeth Closs. 1995. Subjectification in grammaticalization. In Dieter Stein & Susan Wright (eds.), *Subjectivity and subjectivisation: linguistic perspectives*, 31–54. Cambridge: Cambridge University Press.

Traugott, Elizabeth Closs. 2008. Grammaticalization, constructions and the incremental development of language: suggestions from the development of degree modifiers in English. In Regine Eckardt, Gerhard Jaeger & Tonjes Veenstra (eds.), *Language evolution: cognitive and cultural factors*, 219–240. Berlin: Mouton de Gruyter.

Umbach, Carla & Helmar Gust. 2014. Similarity demonstratives. *Lingua* 149. 74–93.

Voghera, Miriam. 2013. A case study on the relationship between grammatical change and synchronic variation: The emergence of tipo[-N] in Italian. In Anna Giacalone Ramat, Caterina Mauri & Piera Molinelli (eds.), *Synchrony and Diachrony. A Dynamic Interface*, 283–312. Amsterdam: John Benjamins.

Zubatý, Josef. 1918. Jeden [One]. *Naše řeč* 2 (5). 131–140.

Corpora

Czech National Corpus – Diakorp. Institute of the Czech National Corpus, Prague. http://www.korpus.cz.

Czech National Corpus – InterCorp. Institute of the Czech National Corpus, Prague. http://www.korpus.cz.

Czech National Corpus – ORAL v.1. Institute of the Czech National Corpus, Prague. http://www.korpus.cz.

Czech National Corpus – SYN2015. Institute of the Czech National Corpus, Prague. http://www.korpus.cz.

Czech National Corpus – SYN v.7. Institute of the Czech National Corpus, Prague. http://www.korpus.cz.

Part 4: **Comparative analyses**

Valentina Benigni
16 The complementizer function of *type*-nouns in ad hoc concept construction: Evidence from Italian and Russian

Abstract: The purpose of this study is to explore the semantic and pragmatic aspects of the complementizer function of *type*-nouns (cognates of *type*) in Italian and Russian and their role in the construction of *ad hoc* concepts. Italian *tipo* and Russian *tipa* have undergone a series of diachronic changes associated with semantic bleaching of their original taxonomic meaning and loss of morphosyntactic properties, followed by the development of non-nominal uses and functional meanings. Specifically, this paper presents and discusses a discourse instantiation of the abstract syntactic pattern [X (*of*) *type* (*of*) Y] shared both by Italian and Russian, whose semantic and pragmatic content can be summarized as follows: X and Y are chunks of discourse with varying degrees of syntactic complexity, involving single word forms, phrases, clauses, or fully-fledged sentences; X introduces a concept or a statement that requires further specification to become meaningful; Y provides additional information with respect to X; the *type*-noun behaves as a polyvalent complementizer, establishing an underspecified logical-semantic relation between X and Y and enhancing cohesion at the inter-clausal level. A theme that runs throughout the paper is the mechanism by which the pattern under study triggers the formation of ad hoc concepts, viewed from a Relevance-theoretic perspective. The principle of Relevance appears to provide an adequate explanation of why the speakers interpret, construct, and exploit the *type*-complementizer in discourse the way they do.

1 Research aims and methodology

The purpose of this study is to explore the semantic and pragmatic aspects of the complementizer function of *type*-words (cognates of *type*) in Italian and Russian, specifically, their role in the construction of *ad hoc* concepts. I assume a broad defi-

---

Acknowledgements: I would like to thank Anna Alexandrova, Sapienza University of Rome, for her useful comments on the Russian data.

Valentina Benigni, Roma Tre University, e-mail: valentina.benigni@uniroma3.it

nition of a complementizer as a marker capable of taking a full clause as an argument. Needless to say, Romance and Slavic languages exhibit multiple differences at the morphosyntactic level. However, they also show some interesting similarities. Italian *tipo* and Russian *tipa* exhibit a series of diachronic changes usually associated with grammaticalization, namely, semantic bleaching and loss of their taxonomic lexical meaning as well as the loss of morphosyntactic properties characteristic of nouns, followed by the development of non-nominal syntactic patterns and respective functional ('grammatical') meanings. The more recently developed non-nominal uses, which in turn are highly diversified, do not replace the older nominal ones. Instead, all these patterns co-exist in synchrony. In this paper, I present a detailed analysis of a discourse pattern based on a non-nominal use of *type*-words which is shared by Italian and Russian and involves a set of similar formal and semantic-pragmatic characteristics. While the structural properties of the pattern in question can be represented in a very general manner by the schema [X (*of the*) *type* (*of*) Y], the level of semantic and pragmatic content can be summarized as follows:

- X and Y are chunks of discourse with varying degrees of syntactic complexity, involving single word forms, phrases, clauses, or fully-fledged sentences;
- X introduces a concept or a statement that requires further specification to become meaningful;
- Y provides additional information with respect to X;
- the *type*-noun behaves as a polyvalent complementizer, denoting that Y relates to X.

The polyvalent complementizer thus establishes a semantically underspecified relation between the two entities, represented by X and Y, henceforth also respectively referred to as the pre-*type* and post-*type* positions.

The X and Y components are loosely connected both at the semantic and morphosyntactic levels. Hence, the *type*-word enhances textual cohesion at the inter-clausal level. Consider the following examples:

(1) Rus. *Segodnja utrom* [...]   [*odelas'*]$_X$ ***tipa***
    today   in.the.morning dress-REFL.PST.F.SG   TIPA
    [*leto   na   dvore*]$_Y$
    summer- NOM.N.SG on court-PRP.M.SG
    'This morning I [...] dressed **like** it's summer outside' (https://forum.cofe.ru/, accessed 1 March 2020)[1]

---

[1] In the glosses the *type*-word is not translated but is cited in uppercase letters. The interlinear word-by-word glossing is followed by a freer paraphrase.

16 The complementizer function of *type*-nouns in ad hoc concept construction — 623

(2) It. [*L'*   *amore*   *di*   *Chicory*   *per*   *gli*   *altri*   *è*]$_X$ ***del***   ***tipo*,**
the   love   of   Chicory   for   the   others   is   of.the   type
[*io*   *ti*   *do*   *e*   *tu*   *mi*   *dai*]$_Y$ *non*   *è*   *proprio*
I   you-DAT.SG   give   and   you   me-DAT.SG   give   not   is   exactly
l'   *amore*   *incondizionato*   *di*   *cui*   *tanto*   *si*   *parla.*
the   love   unconditional   of   which   a.lot   REFL   talk-PRS.3SG
'Chicory's love for others is **of the** *quid pro quo* **type**. . . it is not exactly the unconditional love that we talk about so much.' (AIM, florencefiorionline.com)

In (1), Russian *tipa* (lit. 'of the type') introduces an existential clause (*leto na dvore* 'it is summer now', lit. 'summer [is] in the courtyard'), which functions as a manner argument of the verb *odet'sja* 'dress'. The whole construction metonymically represents the concept GO OUT LIGHTLY DRESSED. I consider it as a case of metonymy understood in a broad sense, where a season stands for a particular item of clothing worn in that period of the year. The association underlying this type of metonymy is 'extrinsic', i.e. non-inherent and unconventional (Croft and Cruse 2004: 217; see also Radden and Kövecses 1999: 22). In (2), the Italian genitive-like prepositional phrase *del tipo* 'of the type' introduces two coordinate declarative sentences (*io ti do e tu mi dai* 'I give you and you give me'). The latter present a generic assertion which is an equivalent of the Latin idiomatic expression *quid pro quo*. Its function is to categorize Chicory's love for others as a form of SELF-INTERESTED LOVE. This interpretation is reinforced by the subsequent sentence, in which it is explicitly stated that Chicory's love is not truly unconditional.

Both in terms of structure and function, the complementizer use of *type*-nouns is closely related to both their taxonomic uses and their similative-approximative uses. The Italian data on this topic were previously discussed in Mihatsch (2007) and Voghera (2013, 2014), while the respective Russian situation was accounted for in Lapteva (1983), Daiber (2010), Sergeeva (2010), Benigni (2014), Kolyaseva and Davidse (2018), and Kolyaseva (2018), among others. However, the pattern discussed in the present paper constitutes a distinct case, inasmuch as Y does not introduce either a subtype or a prototypical exemplar. While the subtype is a feature of the taxonomic use, the prototypical exemplar of the class individuated by X pertains to the similative-approximative uses. In the pattern under study, the *type*-item rather provides an informative content, which, in a more or less direct manner, contributes to the specification of the meaning of X. In other words, in the complementizer use, X and Y are not linked by the IS-A relation, i.e., a taxonomic relation, which associates an entity to its hypernym. For instance, compare (3a) and (3b):

(3) It. a. *pantaloni   stretti   **tipo**   jeans*
       trousers-M.PL   tight-M.PL   type   jeans
       'tight trousers **like** jeans' (AIM, ondaosservatorio.it)
    b. *pantaloni   **tipo**   "acqua   alta"   a   Venezia*
       trousers-M.PL type   water-F.SG high-F.SG in Venice
       '(short) trousers **like** "high water in Venice"' (AIM, linus.blog.
       deejay.it)

In the taxonomic construction (3a), jeans are presented as a type of tight trousers. In turn, in the complementizer construction (3b), a specific subtype of trousers is indirectly referred to by means of metonymic extension. The phenomenon of high water in Venice recalls the habit of rolling up one's trouser legs in order to keep them from getting wet. This conceptual association leads to the construction of the ad hoc concept RIDICULOUSLY SHORT TROUSERS. In (3b), just as in (1) above, the *type*-item allows for the replacement of an explicit similative-conditional or similative-temporal relation (respectively, expressed by an *as if*-clause or by a *like when*-clause) with a more generic metonymic relation.

Moreover, the complementizer use of the *type*-word overlaps with its quotative and pseudo-quotative use. In quotative contexts, the *type*-word is a device adopted for the incorporation of direct speech. The quotation thus illustrates the content of a *verbum dicendi* or of a noun referring to a communicative act, hosted in the pre-*type* position. In turn, in pseudo-quotative contexts, characterized by the absence of verbs or nouns of communication in X, the propositional content Y, which is a verbalization in the form of reported speech of the concept expressed in X, is introduced by the *type*-complementizer, as in the example below. The pseudo-quotative *type*-word can be paraphrased as meaning 'as if to say; as if to mean':

(4) Rus. [*kot   vstaet   obratno i   tykaet*
         cat-NOM.M.SG   stand-PRS.3SG   back   and   bump-PRS.3SG
         mordočkoj   v   dver']$_x$ **tipa**   [*otkryvaj   davaj*]$_Y$!
         muzzle-INS.F.SG in   door-ACC.F.SG TIPA   open-IMP.2SG   HORT
         'the cat gets back and bumps his nose against the door – **like**, "Come on, open it!' (ARM, mau.ru)

In (4), the cat's desire to open the door is packaged as a fictitious quotation, containing the exhortative sentence *otkryvaj davaj* 'come on, open (it)'. Furthermore, in the preceding piece of discourse, it is claimed by the speaker that the feline shows communicative behaviour, since in a past life he might have been a human. Hence, unsurprisingly, his behaviour is verbalized through a pseudo-quotation.

The concept THE CAT'S BEHAVIOUR IS LIKE THAT OF A HUMAN BEING, emerging from the co-text, is thus reinforced by the construction.

These partially overlapping uses of *type*-words in both languages lead me to investigate more closely the discursive functions associated with this hyper-clausal pattern.

As far as the methodology is concerned, the study adopts a usage-based constructional approach of functional-cognitive orientation. Since in both languages the constructions are characteristic of colloquial registers and hence more likely to appear in conversational contexts, I have made use of web corpora, which typically contain a large amount of informal conversations, characterized by an extensive use of "loose" cohesive mechanisms. Russian data were mainly extracted from the web corpus Araneum Russicum Maius (ARM) and the Russian National Corpus (RNC). Italian data were taken from Araneum Italicum Maius (AIM) and Perugia Corpus (PC). In addition, some examples were taken from InterCorp, a large multilingual parallel corpus, which includes translations of (predominantly) fictional texts, as well as directly from the Web. Both the corpora of the Araneum Family and Intercorp can be accessed through the KonText platform (Benko 2014). These corpora contain collections of spoken discourse and CMC (Computer-Mediated Communication, i.e. forum posts, comments, and chats). All examples have been left in their original form, including misspellings and typos.

Data are discussed within the framework of Construction Grammar, which allows capturing the overall meaning and function of the hyper-clausal pattern under scrutiny. Its primary function consists in connecting two chunks of discourse, thus enhancing cohesion and coherence at the inter-clausal level. Moreover, the *type*-construction is frequently used by speakers as a means of encoding complex non-lexicalized concepts which are not stored in the mental lexicon and are hence constructed ad hoc in response to specific communicative needs. This parameter is examined from the perspective of the Relevance Theory (Wilson and Carston 2007), which states that communication is a collaborative process between speakers and hearers. Speakers, in fact, use words flexibly – by widening or narrowing their meanings via processes of metonymic and metaphorical extension – and construct ad hoc concepts by activating related semantic frames. For their part, hearers make inferences based both on the discourse and on their own encyclopedic knowledge, selecting from the speakers' discourse those pieces of information, which are "relevant" to the context.

The paper is structured as follows. In Section 2, I analyze the formal properties of the pattern under study in the following order: the *type*-form (Section 2.1), the pre-*type* position (Section 2.2), and the post-*type* position (Section 2.3). In particular, in Section 2.3.1, I discuss the explicative and labelling functions associated with a subtype of the complementizer *type*-construction, whose distinctive formal parameter is Y realized as a NP.

The focus of Section 3 is on how the complementizer *type*-noun enhances cohesion at the inter-clausal level. The most salient feature of this complementizer, which follows from the whole discussion of the data, is that it allows for an implicit and/or underspecified logical-semantic relation between X and Y.

In Section 4, the use of the complementizer *type*-construction in habitual and potential contexts is accounted for.

Finally, a theme that runs throughout the paper is the mechanism by which the pattern under study triggers the formation of ad hoc concepts, viewed from a Relevance-theoretic perspective. The principle of Relevance appears to provide an adequate explanation of why the speakers interpret, construct, and exploit the *type*-complementizer in discourse the way they do.

2 Structural properties of the construction

In this section the three components of the *type*-complementizer construction are presented: the *type*-word, the chunk of discourse that precedes it (also referred to as X or the pre-*type* position) and the chunk of discourse that follows it (also referred to as Y or the post-*type* position). This is the standard situation, and I have chosen to follow it for ease of exposition. However, this classification is not meant to be rigid, and, as is shown further, various deviations from this prototypical structure can be found.

One of the parameters of variation is concerned with the lexical units and multiword expressions pertaining to the domain of communication found in the pre-*type* position. For instance, phrasal units involving elements belonging to different semantic classes can occur in this position, e.g., the vague noun *banal'nosti* 'platitudes', preceded by the generic verb of communication *govorit'* 'say' in (5):

(5) Rus. [*Možno govorit' banal'nosti*]$_X$ **tipa** ["*s nami*
 possible-PRED say-INF platitude-ACC.PL TIPA ["with we-INS
 ostalis' ego knigi"]$_Y$
 remain-PST.PL his book-NOM.F.PL
 'One can say platitudes **of the kind** "his books remained with us."' (ARM, terra-america.ru)

The same items can be classified, from a functional standpoint, as shell nouns, i.e. abstract nouns enclosing complex concepts and used as cohesive devices (Schmid 2000). Different classes of shell nouns can be employed to evoke specific frames for different kinds of world knowledge. Thus, for instance, Rus. *scena* /It. *scena* 'scene; situation' pertain to the class of *visual stimuli*.

Moreover, aside from the *type*-word itself, which is an item with clear word-hood status, the morphosyntactic boundaries of the X and Y components can be fuzzy, inasmuch as both can be represented by single words (mainly nouns or verbs), but also by (non-predicative) phrases, incomplete clauses, sentences or higher-level discourse units, involving more than one fully-fledged sentence.

2.1 The type-word

The complementizer use of the Russian and Italian *type*-nouns (Rus. *tipa* and It. *tipo*) directly developed from their original taxonomic meaning in constructions such as (3a), discussed above. The taxonomic construction can be thus represented by the following schema:

[N_1 (*of the*) *type* (*of*) N_2],

where N_2 is a subtype of the class or category identified by N_1. As is well known, there is a general crosslinguistic tendency for taxonomic nouns to undergo grammaticalization and pragmaticalization. This process involves, firstly, the loss of semantic content and, secondly, the development of functional as well as pragmatic meanings and discourse functions. Similar grammaticalization processes take place in different languages and have been already thoroughly discussed in the literature (cf. Mihatsch 2007, 2016; Voghera 2013). In the first step, taxonomic nouns tend to turn into approximation markers, which means that N_2 is employed in order to narrow the reference of N_1, as in (6) and (7):

(6) Rus. *Ja   xotela   podat'   priznaki   žizni   i*
        I   want-PST.F.SG give-INF   sign-ACC.PL   life-GEN.F.SG   and
        [*izdat'   kakoj-to   zvuk*]$_X$ ***tipa*** [*kašlja*]$_Y$
        produce-INF   some-ACC.M.SG   sound-ACC.M.SG   TIPA   cough-GEN.M.SG
        'I wanted to give signs of life and make some sound, **such as** a cough or the like.' (ARM, kusakin.squarespace.com)

(7) It. c'era   anche   [un   odore]$_X$ **tipo** [di cane   bagnato]$_Y$²
       there.was also   a-M.SG   smell-M.SG TIPO   of dog-M.SG wet-M.SG
    'there was also a smell **like** wet dog' (AIM, saurosandroni.com)

In (6) above, the speaker compares the sound produced by the subject with a cough (*kašel*), whereas in (7) s/he facilitates the identification of the specific type of bad smell by referring to *cane bagnato* 'wet dog'. When the approximation function emerges, N_1 and N_2 are linked not so much by a broadly understood relation of hypernymy/hyponymy, as by a particular case of generic/specific relation. In the latter case, N_1 tends to be a vague or general noun (for instance Rus. *zvuk* 'sound' in (6) or It. *odore* 'smell' in (7)), whereas N_2 has more specific semantics. As was noted by Voghera (2013), in Italian the appositional (or 'non-nominal') construction [N_1 *tipo* N_2] (8c) derives from the double genitive construction [N_1 *del tipo di* N_2] (8a), in which both *tipo* and N_2 are governed by the preposition *di* 'of' (in the coalesced form with the definite article and in the simple form, respectively). In present-day language, both constructions co-exist. However, the appositional construction is preferred by speakers in colloquial contexts. Moreover, an appositional construction [N_1 *del tipo* N_2], which only has the ellipsis of the second preposition *di*, is also possible (8b):

(8) It. a. [un   odore   [del   tipo   [~~odore~~
           a-M.SG   smell-M.SG of-DEF.M.SG   TIPO   smell-M.SG
           [di   cane   bagnato]]]]
           of   dog-M.SG   wet-M.SG
       b. [un   odore   [[del   tipo] [cane   bagnato]]]
           a-M.SG smell-M.SG of-DEF.M.SG   TIPO   dog-M.SG   wet-M.SG
       c. [[un   odore]   [tipo]   [(di)³ cane   bagnato]]
           a-M.SG smell-M.SG TIPO   dog-M.SG wet-M.SG

In (8b–c) above, a metonymic extension is obtained. The head noun *odore* 'smell' of the post-*type* constituent has been omitted (cf. footnote 3), so that the name of the animal directly stands for the smell referred to. Voghera (2013: 296) observes that in this subtype of construction, *tipo* introduces an adjec-

---

2 In this construction N_2 is omitted, leaving a "gap" before its complement, as shown in (8a). Thus, the *type*-noun grammaticalizes from a taxonomic noun, introducing a NP, into a similative-exemplificative marker, which separates the complement from the head noun.
3 As discussed in the footnote above, in the process of grammaticalization of the *type*-noun into a similative-exemplificative marker, the *quasi*-appositional construction [N_1 *tipo di* N_2] (with retention of the second preposition *di*) can also be observed (cf. (7)).

tive-like element, performing an attributive function. For the same reason, the use of the (second) preposition becomes redundant. This mechanism is extensively adopted in the complementizer construction which is under discussion in this paper. Thus, it may be assumed that the complementizer use has derived directly from the taxonomic use. It represents an independent line of development that has evolved simultaneously alongside the expansion of the hedging and quotative functions.

With the rise of the hedging function, the *type*-noun becomes a shield, reducing the degree of liability concerning the truth value of the constituent in its scope. By this stage of development along the grammaticalization cline, the *type*-noun has lost its original taxonomic meaning, inasmuch as it is no longer used to map a hyponym to its hypernym. It rather renders the meaning of the following lexical item approximate. In Russian, *tipa* (a lexicalized and fossilized genitive singular form of the noun *tip* 'type') loses the nominal valency associated with a genitive-marked NP and becomes compatible with NPs inflected for cases other than genitive (9) and other types of phrases, comprising VPs (10):

(9) Rus. *Est'   takaja   zabava   byt'   **tipa***
         there.is such-NOM.F.SG amusement-NOM.F.SG be-INF TIPA
         oppozicionerom
         dissident-INS.M.SG
         'Some people find amusement in being kind of dissident'
         (ARM, slavyansk2.ru)

(10) Rus. *Pravda,   slyšala,   čto   oni   čto-to*
          However hear-PST.F.SG that they-NOM something-NOM.N.SG
          ***tipa**   porugalis'*
          TIPA   have.a.row-PST.PL
          'however, I've heard that they **sort of** had a row.' (ARM, hurricaneofjoy.livejournal.com)

Hence, as far as the non-nominal uses are concerned, Russian *tipa* has developed the same functions of the appositional Italian *tipo*.

Once their usage has spread significantly, It. *tipo* and Rus. *tipa* tend to act as fillers or hesitation devices. However, these uses are beyond the scope of this paper. In fact, the development of the complementizer construction occurs at the beginning of the grammaticalization process when the *type*-noun is still characterized by the function of relating X to Y. However, it differs from the mere taxonomic use inasmuch as it has developed the ability of connecting heterogeneous lexical and phrasal items, including chunks of discourse.

2.2 The pre-type position

The lexical ingredients that constitute the pre-*type* content are the focus of the present section.

2.2.1 Low referential NPs

The most frequent content to appear in the pre-*type* position is a NP with weak referentiality, which can be an indefinite pronoun, a vague noun or a shell noun.

It is widely accepted that vague nouns are deictic words (cf. It. *cosa* 'thing', *roba* 'stuff', Rus. *vešč'* 'thing', *štuka* 'stuff, thing'), whose meaning cannot be understood without co-textual and contextual information (Halliday and Hasan 1976). At the discourse level, they express either exophoric or endophoric reference and function as nominal placeholders when the speaker is not able to produce the intended reference immediately (for a discussion of Italian vague nouns *cosa* 'thing' and *roba* 'stuff', see Benigni 2016). Consider, for instance, the following Italian example in which the pre-*type* position contains the statement that the subject would enjoy doing 'a great deal of other things' (*un sacco di altre cose*). The content of the vague items, followed by the *type*-word, is illustrated in the post-*type* position by two coordinate infinitive VPs (*imparare a dipingere la stoffa* 'to learn how to dye a fabric' and *realizzare i quadri con la sabbia* 'to make sand paintings'):

(11) It. a volte   penso   che   sono   giovane   e
         sometimes think-PRS.1SG that   be-PRS.1SG   young-SG   and
    [mi   piacerebbe   fare   un   sacco   di   altre   cose]$_X$.
    I-DAT like-COND.3SG do-INF a-M.SG great.deal of   other   thing
    Tipo [*imparare   a   dipingere   la   stoffa   o   realizzare*
    TIPO   learn-INF   to   dye-INF   the   fabric   or   make-INF
    i   quadri   con   la   sabbia]$_Y$
    the painting-M.PL with   the   sand
    'Sometimes I think I am young and I'd enjoy doing a great deal of other things, **such as** learning how to dye a fabric or making sand paintings'
    (AIM, verdespirito.blog.kataweb.it)

Moreover, vague nouns with derogatory connotations (which in fact tend to undergo semantic bleaching and hence gradually lose their offensive content in present-day language) are highly frequent in this function both in Italian and Russian where they conventionally convey the speaker's negative attitude towards the content of the utterance. For instance, in (12), *vsjakaja fignja social'naja* 'all the social bullshit' alludes to a traditional *cliché*, according to which a female is supposed be weaker than a male:

(12) Rus. *Vot   togda   i   [nadobitsja   vsjakaja*
             here.is   then   EMPH   need-REFL.PRS.3SG.   various-NOM.F.SG
      *fignja   social'naja]*ₓ,   **tipa**   ['ženščina   dolžna*
      bullshit-NOM.F.SG   social-NOM.F.SG   TIPA   woman-NOM.F.SG   must-F.SG
      *byt'   slaboj']*ᵧ
      be-INF   weak-INS.F.SG
      'Then all the social bullshit is needed, **such as** "A woman must be weak"' (ARM, lita.ru)

Furthermore, as in the above example, reference to commonplace thoughts and, at the same time, distancing from the latter, is often stressed by the use of quotation marks in written discourse.[4]

Another relevant class of semantically vague nouns is presented by what has been labelled as shell nouns,[5] involving abstract general nouns such as It. *storia* 'story', *faccenda* 'affair', *situazione* 'situation' or Rus. *dejatel'nost'* 'activity', *problema* 'problem', *situacija* 'situation', etc. These lexical items behave as conceptual containers (or shells) for context-dependent propositional content. They are usually associated with specific lexical-syntactic patterns (cf. It. *il fatto che...* 'the fact that...' or Rus. *delo v tom...* 'the point is...'), including the complementizer *type*-construction. In the latter case, the shell noun has a cataphoric function creating anticipation of the shell content. The indefinite nature of the shell noun is often supported by the occurrence of the indefinite article in Italian, or of an indefinite adjective with a similar function in Russian. Con-

---

4 As far as the Italian *tipo* is concerned, Voghera (2013: 297) claims that most of the segments of discourse introduced by *tipo* are "'reported speech or thought' *lato sensu*: that is, they are commonplaces, maxims, formulaic expressions, or pieces of common knowledge". Thus, according to the scholar, the prevalent discourse function associated with this use is not straightforward quotation but rather expressive labelling and characterization of specific items or situations.
5 Although Schmid (2000) includes vague nouns into the class of shell nouns, for the purposes of the present study a distinction is made between the two concepts. Vague nouns may identify a referent only on the basis of contextual information, whereas shell nouns are able to do so with the general properties of a referent independently of the latter (cf. *una cosa senza senso* 'something meaningless', lit. 'a thing without sense', vs. *una storia senza senso* 'a nonsensical/meaningless story').

sider (13) below, in which two occurrences of the *type*-word, a nominal and a non-nominal one, present two asyndetically linked phrases of different syntactic statuses, meaning 'dance and drink coffee together'. They are conceptualized as possible concrete instantiations of the indefinite NP *kakaja-to dejatel'nost'* 'some (certain, unspecified or unknown) activity'. Thus, the flow of information goes from generic to specific:

(13) Rus. *Poigrat' v nastol'nye igry/ [poučastvovat'*
 play-INF in table-ADJ.ACC.PL game-ACC.PL participate-INF
 *v kakoj-to dejatel'nosti]$_X$ **tipa** [tancev]$_Y$ **tipa***
 in some-PRP.F.SG activity-PRP.F.SG TIPA dance-GEN.PL TIPA
 [popit' kofe vmeste]$_Y$
 drink-INF coffee-ACC.M together
 'To play table games/ take part in some activity, **such as** dancing and (such as) drinking coffee together.' (RNC, spoken language)

However, it should be kept in mind that the Russian indefinite adjectives, particularly *kakoj-nibud'*, along with the indefinite semantics, often carry a pejorative pragmatic meaning.[6] As shown in (13) above, the *type*-word behaves as a polyvalent complementizer, which when duplicated can take nominal and verbal complements (the nominal *tanec* 'dance' in the genitive plural and the infinitive phrase *popit' kofe vmeste* 'to drink coffee together'). In this case, both have eventive semantics, as they denote human activities. Along with the shell noun in the pre-*type* position, the possibility of embedding and combining different syntactic units leads to the enhancement of cohesion at the inter-clausal level.

Schmid (2000: 4) defines shell nouns as "conceptual shells for complex, proposition-like pieces of information" and classifies them into six semantic groups, each of which can be found in the pre-*type* position, namely, factual, linguistic, mental, modal, eventive, and circumstantial.

In both languages under study, the most frequent class (both in terms of tokens and types) is presented by 'linguistic' shell nouns (e.g., It. *espressione* 'expression', *parole* 'words', Rus. *vopros* 'question', *zapros* 'inquiry, request', *ssylka* 'reference'), which allow the speaker "to portray linguistic activities and their contents and products" (Schmid 2000: 131). Furthermore, shell nouns express the speaker's

---

[6] The pejorative meaning could be derived from either (1) the basic indefinite meaning, 'it is not asserted that X exists' → 'X is insignificant/worthless', or, alternatively, (2) the secondary meaning 'approximate quantity of X' → 'little quantity of X' (Ward 1977: 452).

16 The complementizer function of *type*-nouns in ad hoc concept construction — 633

attitude towards the reported utterance. For instance, in (14) below, the Italian noun *solfe* 'the same old songs' negatively characterizes the content of the catchphrase *la cultura salverà il mondo* 'culture will save the world'. In this context, the *type*-word links the shell noun to the shell content. This use is associated with the pseudo-quotative function, often involving speech verbs such as *dire* 'say' in the pre-*type* position:

(14) It. Persino   i   punti   di   catene commerciali   come   la
          even   the   point-PL of   chain stores   such.as   the
          Feltrinelli   chiudono i battenti.   Non   sta   a   me   [dire]ₓ:
          Feltrinelli   are closing down   not   is   to   me   say-INF
          'vive la France'   e   [solfe]ₓ   **tipo**   che   [la   cultura
          'vive la France'   and   the.same.old.songs TIPO   that   the   culture
          salverà   il   mondo]ᵧ
          will.save   the   world
          'Even chain stores such as Feltrinelli are closing down. I don't mean to say "Vive la France" and (repeat) the same old songs **like** "Culture will save the world" (AIM, lecittadelledonne.it)

Similarly, in the Russian pseudo-quotative example below, the verbal content of the VP *vyskazat' svoe "fi"* 'voice one's contempt' (lit. 'speak out one's "meh"'), is verbalized in the post-*type* position by a first-person utterance used in a generalized way:

(15) Rus. I   každaja   b'juti-guru   nepremenno
         and   each-NOM.F.SG   beauty-guru-NOM.F.SG   necessarily
         dolžna   [vyskazat'   svoe   "fi"   v adres
         must-ADJ.F.SG   speak.out-INF   her.own-REFL.ACC.N.SG "meh"   towards
         Botoksa   i   drugix   ukolov   v
         Botox-GEN.M.SG   and   other-GEN.PL   injection-GEN.PL   in
         lico]ₓ,   **tipa**   ["ja   vsja   takaja
         face-ACC.N.SG TIPA I-NOM   all-NOM.F.SG   such-NOM.F.SG
         rasprekrasnaja   ot prirody i   kolot'sja   ne   sobirajus'"]ᵧ
         lovely-NOM.F.SG   by nature and   inject-REFL.INF   not   be.going.to-PRS.1SG
         'And it is imperative that each beauty-guru has to voice her opposition to Botox and other cosmetic injectables **like,** "I'm so lovely by nature and I'm not going to make use of injections".' (https://omorfia.ru/users/85187/blog/20002, accessed 1 March 2020)

Another common class is that of mental shell nouns (It. *scoperta* 'discovery', *idea* 'idea', Rus. *mysli* 'thoughts', *reakcija* 'reaction, attitude'). As Schmid (2000) notes, linguistic and mental shell nouns share some common traits: linguistic shell nouns report utterances, whereas mental shell nouns introduce ideas. Schmid also claims that "since speakers only have direct access to their own idea, their reports on the thoughts of other people also depend on the language" (Schmid 2000: 184); according to this perspective, the *type*-noun introduces the shell content, which verbalizes thoughts at the ideational level:

(16) Rus. *Očen' želatel'no čtoby èto byla ne prosto*
very desirable-PRED that this be-COND.F.SG not just
*[golaja ideja]$_X$ (**tipa** ["davajte kak-nibud'*
naked-NOM.F.SG idea-NOM.F.SG TIPA let's-IMP.2PL somehow
skinem Putina i zaživëm vol'no")]$_Y$ a
remove-IMP.1PL Putin-ACC.M.SG and live-IMP.1PL freely but
čto-to bolee konkretnoe
something-NOM.N.SG more specific-NOM.N.SG
'It is very desirable that it wouldn't be just a mere idea (**like,** "Let's topple Putin somehow and live freely"), but something more specific.' (ARM, rusimperia.info)

Circumstantial shell nouns are well represented by the noun 'situation' (*situazione* in It. and *situacija* in Rus.): the lemma occurs 44 times in the ARM and 35 in AIM in cataphoric function, followed by the *type*-word introducing the shell content, as in (17) and (18):

(17) It. *Condivido i malumori che nascono in*
share-PRS.1SG the ill.feeling-PL that arise-PRS.3PL in
*[situazioni]$_X$ **tipo** ["ho scattato 70 foto e non*
situation-PL TIPO "have-PRS.1SG taken 70 photos and not
me ne piace nemmeno una!"]$_Y$
me CL like-PRS.3SG not.even one-F.SG
'I share the ill-feeling that arises in situations **like,** "I took 70 photos and I don't like any of them!"' (AIM, animaegusto.it)

(18) Rus. *Odnim slovom, rabota njanej*
one- INS.N.SG word-INS.N.SG job-NOM.F.SG nanny-INS.F.SG
tebe podojdet esli ty ljubiš' detej,
you-DAT.SG suit-FUT.3SG if you-NOM love-PRS.2SG children-ACC.PL

> u   tebja   krepkie   nervy   i   spokojnyj
> at   you-GEN.SG   strong-NOM.PL   nerve-NOM.PL   and   calm-NOM.M.SG
> xarakter [. . .].   Tebe   pridetsja   stalkivat'sja
> character-NOM.M.SG   you-DAT.SG   have.to-REFL.FUT.3SG   deal-INF
> [s situacijami]ₓ   **tipa**   ["nečajanno   razbil
> with situation-INS.PL   TIPA   inadvertently   smash-PST.M.SG
> okno   ili   ljubimuju   maminu
> window-ACC.N.SG   or   favourite-ACC.F.SG   mother's-ADJ.ACC.F.SG
> vazu"]ᵧ
> vase-ACC.F.SG

'In a word, the nanny job suits you if you love children, you have strong nerves and a calm character. [. . .] You will have to deal with situations **like** "[The child] inadvertently smashed a window or Mother's favourite vase"' (ARM, blondinka.by)

Nouns introducing a sensorial stimulus (e.g. It. *scena* 'scene', *rumore* 'noise', *odore* 'smell'; Rus. *šum* 'noise') seem to behave analogously to shell nouns, especially in Italian. In the following example, the pre-*type* element introduces a noun (*scene* 'scenes') referring to a visual stimulus, whose content is specified in the post-*type* position by a NP (*due gemelli Columbiani* 'two Colombian twins') modified by two relative clauses (the second one embedded within the first one):

(19) It. *ogni tanto   mentre   torni   a   casa   [ti*
          sometimes   while   go-PRS.2SG   to   home   you-DAT.SG
          *capitano   scene]ₓ **tipo**   [due   gemelli   Columbiani   che*
          happen-PRS.3PL   scenes TIPO   two   twin-PL   Colombian   who
          improvvisano   un   live   di   rumba,   flamenco,   cumbia   e
          improvise   a   live   of   rumba   flamenco   cumbia   and
          ritmi   Afro-Americani   davanti a   dozzine   di   passeggeri
          rhythm-PL   African-American-PL   in.front.of dozens   of   passengers
          che   aspettano   il   treno]ᵧ.
          who   wait   the   train
          'From time to time, on your way home, you happen to see (certain) scenes **such as** two Colombian twins improvising a live performance of rumba, flamenco, cumbia and African-American rhythms in front of dozens of passengers waiting for a train.' (AIM, alain.it)

In Russian the reference to a sensorial stimulus is more frequently realized by Stimulus Subject Perception verbs (Levin 1993) (e.g. *vygljadet'* 'to look, appear, seem', *paxnut'* 'smell'), which evoke the sensorial domain: in (20) the *type*-noun introduces an imperative clause, typical for chain letters, which exemplifies the way the situation looks (note also the use of the "visual" discourse markers *na pervyj vzgljad* 'at first glance; seemingly'):

(20) Rus. *I   xotja,   [na   pervyj   vzgljad*
          and   although   on   first-ACC.M.SG   sight-ACC.M.SG
*èto   vygljadit]ₓ   **tipa**   ["Perešlite   èto*
this-NOM.N.SG   look-PRS.3SG   TIPA   forward-IMP.PL   this-ACC.N.SG
pis'mo   sta   čelovekam   i   budet
letter-ACC.N.SG   hundred-DAT   person-DAT.PL   and   be-FUT.3SG
vam   sčast'e"]ᵧ   na samom dele   èto
you-DAT.PL   happiness-NOM.N.SG   in.reality   this-NOM.N.SG
ne   tak.
not   like.this
'Although at first sight it looks **like** "Please forward this letter to one hundred people, and you will be happy", but that's not really true.' (https://egoland.ru/sistema-dostizheniya-celej-duxovnyj-vybor-zavershenie/, accessed 1 March 2020)

The pre-*type* position may be occupied by an indefinite pronominal element. In the following example, the pre-*type* position is filled by the indefinite pronoun *koe-čto* 'something; one thing', referring to something known to the speaker/writer ("realis indefinite" in Haspelmath [1997]'s terms). Specifically, this indefinite pronoun has the ability to evoke a set of contextually related items and displays a presentational function, whereas the *type*-word introduces a declarative sentence which specifies the content of the pronoun:

(21) Rus. *Snačala   ja   byl   vo xmelju,   no   potom*
          at.first   I-NOM   be-PST.M.SG   in hops-PRP.M.SG   but   later
*[stal   **koe-čto**   primečat]ₓ.   **Tipa**,   [u*
start-PST.M.SG   something-ACC.N.SG   notice-INF   TIPA   at
vas   tut   sidit   broker,   ves'
you-GEN.PL   here   sit-PRS.3SG   broker-NOM.M.SG   entire-NOM.M.SG
razodetyj   i   čitaet   "Financial Times"
dressed.up-NOM.M.SG   and   read-PRS.M.SG
utrom   v   voskresen'e,   kogda   birža
in.the.morning   in   Sunday-ACC.N.SG   when   stock.market-NOM.F.SG

zakryta]ᵧ.   Ne   sovsem   real'no [. . .]
closed-NOM.F.SG   not   entirely realistic-PRED
'I was a bit groggy before, then [I started noticing **things**]. **Like**, [you've got a stockbroker over here, all dressed up reading the Financial Times on a Sunday morning when the market's closed] ᵧ. Unlikely [. . .]' (InterCorp, subtitles)⁷

2.2.2 Verbs requiring a manner adverb

In the pre-*type* position there may be verbs expressing the manner of behaviour (such as the hypernym verb 'to behave, to act [in some way]': It. *comportarsi*, Rus. *vesti sebja*, or specific behavioural verbs, both transitive and intransitive, referring to the manner of walking, dressing or looking at something, and so on): this kind of verb requires a manner argument to become meaningful and informative. In the following example the subject acts in the way expressed by the post-*type* declarative sentence:

(22) Rus. [vedet   sebja]ₓ   **tipa** \   ["kruče   menja
            behave-PRS.3SG self-ACC   TIPA   cool-COMP   I-GEN
      tol'ko gory\"]ᵧ
      only   mountain-NOM.PL
      'behaves **like** \ "No one is cooler than me\"' (https://retwork.com/reviews/detail/?id=58542, accessed 1 March 2020)

The *type*-noun introduces metaphorical content (lit. 'only the mountains are tougher than me'), which fills the slot of a manner argument: the meaning of the whole complementizer-*type* construction may be paraphrased as HE IS OVERCONFIDENT. The Russian adjective *krutoj* has probably developed the extended meaning 'tough' from the original meaning 'abrupt; steep; hard' via metonymic extension.

In (23) the verb *guardare* 'to look/to have a look (at sb/sth)' denotes the subject's attitude towards the topic and is specified by a manner complement:

---

[7] The example is taken from the multilingual subcorpus of movie subtitles of the parallel corpus InterCorp.

(23) It. *Thomas e Christine, dopo il tiramisù* [...] *hanno*
Thomas and Christine after the tiramisu have
continuato a bere. Vino Rosso [...] *io* [*li guardavo*]ₓ
kept.on to drink wine red I them was.looking.at
tipo [*incontri ravvicinati del terzo tipo*]ᵧ
TIPO Close encounters of the Third Kind
'After tiramisu Thomas and Christine [...] kept on drinking. Red wine [...] I was looking at them **as if** (it were) "Close Encounters of the Third Kind"'
(AIM, danein.blog.kataweb.it)

The *type*-word introduces the reference to the movie "Close Encounters of the Third Kind", which ironically conveys the subject's astonishment towards the restaurant customers Thomas and Christine: thus, the meaning of the whole construction is I'M LOOKING AT THEM WITH WONDER.

Sometimes an adverb of manner (including a deictic one: e.g. 'in this way', It. *così*; Rus. *takim obrazom*) is already present in the pre-*type* position. Here, it performs a cataphoric function, in which case its meaning is specified by the content in the post-*type* position:

(24) Rus. *Ja koroče, na neë* [*tak posmotrel*]ₓ **tipa**
I-NOM in.short at she-ACC this.way look-PST.M.SG TIPA
[*"davaj poznakomimsja*⁸*"*]ᵧ, *i* [*rezko tak*
let's get.acquainted-IMP.1PL and immediately this.way
golovu otvernul]ₓ, **tipa** [*« ne xočeš'* - *ne*
head-ACC.F.SG turn.away-PST.M.SG TIPA not want-PRS.2SG not
nado! »]ᵧ
necessary-PRED
'In short, I looked at her this way, **like** "Shall we talk?" and immediately (this way) turned my head away, **like** "If you don't want to – your loss!"'
(http://risovach.ru/kartinka/4080084, accessed 1 March 2020)

In (24) the exhortative sentence *davaj poznakomimsja* 'let's get acquainted' in the post-*type* position is coreferential with the deictic adverb *tak* 'in this way' in the pre-*type* position: together they contribute to express the way the subject (*ja* 'I') is looking at the woman (*na neë* 'to her'), revealing the desire to know her. In the coordinated complementizer-*type* construction the content of the post-*type*

---

8 *Davaj poznakomimsja* (lit. 'Let's get to know each other') is a standard conversation starter used to introduce oneself to a person in informal situations (the next question would be "What's your name?", etc.).

sentence *ne xočeš' – ne nado...* 'if you don't want to – your loss!') is coreferential with the verbal phrase *rezko tak golovu otvernul* lit. 'immediately this way turned my head away' and communicates the speaker's awkward attitude towards the woman. The overall meaning of this double complementizer *type*-construction may be paraphrased as A WAY OF GETTING ACQUAINTED WITH A WOMAN WITHOUT SEEMING TOO BOLD.

The possibility of using complementizer *type*-constructions in Russian to illustrate the manner (and, implicitly, the reason) of behaviour has already been observed by Sergeeva (2010: 251), who gives the following example:

(25) Rus. *Da   ničego   / nu   / prosto imeetsja v vidu   / čto*
          EMPH   nothing / well / just   assume-PRS.3SG   / that
          / možet byt' mimo prošël   i   ne   zametil
          / may.be   by   pass-PST.M.SG and not   notice-PST.M.SG
          *daže ego   / **tipa** tebe   on   voobšče   po figu*
          even he-ACC / TIPA   you-DAT.SG he-NOM   absolutely   don't.care
          'Yes, nothing / well / just / I mean / that simply / you maybe passed by and didn't even notice him / **as if** you don't care about him' (RNC, spoken language)

In this example the post-*type* declarative sentence reports through free indirect discourse the explanation provided by the subject to justify his behaviour. *Tebe* 'you.$_{DAT}$' may be coreferent with *ego* 'he.$_{ACC}$', or refer to a generic recipient: in this case, *tipa* retains part of its original "(proto-)typical" meaning, as it refers to the "most likely" explanation that could be offered for such behaviour ("I pass by, because I don't care about you").

2.2.3 Fully-fledged sentences

Finally, the pre-*type* position can be occupied by a fully-fledged sentence (even a complex one), containing a general statement, thus the *type*-word acts in effect like a general-purpose connector linking the predicative content of X and Y.

In the following example, X is a biclausal construction consisting of a matrix clause (*è noto che* 'it's well known that'), followed by a subject complement clause (*l'italico soffre stress post-traumatico da cellulare scarico* 'the Italian suffers from the dead-phone post-traumatic stress disorder'), whereas Y is a biclausal construction consisting of two coordinated clauses linked by a cause-effect relation (*l'iPhone smette di scrivere e tu smetti di vivere* 'the iPhone stops typing and you stop living'). Y somewhat reformulates and specifies the content of X: the use of the second person singular involves displacement from here-and-now, thus the post-traumatic stress disorder is regarded as the Italian's generalized hyperbolic reaction to the battery going flat:

(26) It. È   noto   che   [*l'italico   soffre   stress post-traumatico*
          is   known   that   the.Italian   suffers   stress post-traumatic
          da   cellulare   scarico]ₓ **tipo** **che**   [*l'iPhone   smette   di*
          from   phone   dead   TIPO   that   the.iPhone   stops   of
          scrivere   e   tu   smetti   di   vivere]ᵧ
          type-INF   and   you   stop   of   live-INF
'It is well known that the Italian suffers from the 'dead-phone post-traumatic stress disorder' **such that** the iPhone stops typing and you stop living' (AIM, hano.it)

Analogously, in (27) X contains a declarative clause, which metaphorically illustrates the subject's attitude towards the topic (*Šajmiev prosto umyvaet ruki* 'Šajmiev simply washes his hands [of this]'), whereas Y contains a simple clause (*on ne pri delax* 'he has nothing to do [with it]'), which acts as a sort of explanation for X:

(27) Rus. *Takim obrazom,* [*Šajmiev   prosto   umyvaet*
           thus   Šajmiev-NOM.M.SG   simply   wash-PRS.3SG
           ruki]ₓ,   **tipa**   [*on   ne pri delax*]ᵧ
           hand-ACC.PL   TIPA   he-NOM   not.in.business
'Thus, Šajmiev simply washes his hands (of this), **like** he has nothing to do (with it)' (ARM, journalufa.com)

Although on the semantic level Y is connected to X by a cause-effect relation, on the syntactic level it is not clear whether Y is subordinate to X, or, in other words, whether *tipa* 'type' should be considered as a subordinating causal conjunction (equivalent to 'because'), a similative-conditional connective (equivalent to 'like; as if'), or an inter-clausal explicative connective (equivalent to 'in fact').

2.3 The post-type position

The post-*type* position can be realized by different types of constituents: a rough subdivision can be made between a) nominal elements; b) subordinate clauses (complement, infinitive), which are syntactically dependent on X and c) fully-fledged syntactically independent sentences.

16 The complementizer function of *type*-nouns in ad hoc concept construction — 641

The most salient features of both syntactically dependent and independent elements are the loose semantic and syntactic relations that link Y to X.

2.3.1 Explicative and labelling NPs

In the post-*type* position, a simple NP (possibly modified by a relative clause, a prepositional or a participial phrase that give more detail about it) can occur: for the purposes of this work I only deal with those cases where this NP exhibits a frame-metonymic connection to the pre-*type* element, leaving aside cases of hypernym-hyponym relation, already widely discussed.

Two structurally similar (but functionally different) patterns can be found; the first one has an explicative function:

(28) It. *Insomma, avrei dovuto filmare* [*una storia*]$_X$ **tipo** [*la
     in.short should.have film-INF   a   story   TIPO the
     giovane operaia   messa incinta dal   figlio del   padrone
     young   worker-F knocked up   by.the son   of.the boss
     che viene salvata dall'   operaio*]$_Y$.
     who is   saved   by.the   worker-M
     'In short, I should have filmed a story **like** the young (female) worker, knocked up by her boss' son, who is saved by the (male) worker' (PC)

The NP in the post-*type* position (*la giovane operaia* 'the young [female] worker'), modified by a participial phrase (*messa incinta dal figlio del padrone* 'knocked up by her boss' son') and a relative clause (*che viene salvata dall'operaio* 'who is saved by the [male] worker'), evokes a culture-specific frame (the man who abuses his power towards the woman), which summarizes the plot of the 'story' (*una storia*) mentioned in the pre-*type* position. Thus, the NP fulfills an explicative function based on the interlocutors' shared knowledge.

Example (29) is functionally very similar:

(29) Rus. *Važno   otmetit', čto   pomimo* [*trěšovyx   i
          important-PRED note-INF that besides trashy-GEN.PL   and
          poleznyx   istorij*]$_X$ **tipa** [*"èlektrogeneratora,
          useful-GEN.PL   story-GEN.PL   TIPA   electric.generator-GEN.M.SG
          rabotajuščego   na moče"*]$_Y$,   *vstrečaetsja   eščë
          powered-GEN.M.SG   on urine-PRP.F.SG   occur- PRS.3SG   further

mnogo interesnogo.
a.lot   interesting-GEN.N.SG
'It is important to note that in addition to **such** trashy and useful stories **as** "Urine-powered generator", there are many other interesting things.'
(ARM, hopesandfears.com)

The post-*type* NP, headed by a noun (*èlektrogeneratora* 'electric generator.M.GEN. SG') and modified by a participial phrase (*rabotajuščego na moče* 'powered.M.GEN. SG by urine'), recalls the content of 'trashy and useful stories' known by the interlocutors: unlike the Italian *tipo*, which is used in an appositional way, Russian *tipa* assigns the genitive case to the NP it governs, showing the stronger syntactic dependency of Y on X in this language. Nevertheless, in both languages, the *type*-noun acts on a semantic level as a general-purpose connector, which establishes a generic semantic connection between X and Y. This kind of semantic connection is not straightforward; the *type*-noun simply signals that X and Y may be understood as part of the same semantic frame, since the associative mechanism is predominantly based on the speakers' cultural, background or encyclopedic knowledge about the world.

The second pattern present in both languages has a labelling function: in this case the *type*-word introduces a NP, which functions as a label for the pre-*type* element; the label is often put between quotation marks in written communication. In the following example the label *fame chimica* 'chemical hunger' provides a sort of definition for the behaviour described by the complex declarative sentence in the pre-*type* position (constituted by a conditional clause [*quando sono agitata* 'when I'm nervous'] followed by the main clause [*inghiottirei qualsiasi cosa* 'I would swallow anything']):

(30) It. [*io quando sono agitata inghiottirei   qualsiasi cosa*]$_X$,
        I   when   am   nervous would.swallow any   thing
tipo [*"fame chimica"*]$_Y$
TIPO   chemical hunger
'when I'm nervous, I would swallow anything, **like** "chemical hunger"'
(AIM, notedicioccolato.blogspot.it)

The explicative and the labelling patterns are structurally quite similar but display different discourse-structuring functions. The explicative pattern has an analytical function, since it uses Y to explain in more detail the generic meaning of X, whereas the labelling pattern has a synthetic function, since it uses Y to give a label to the vague predicative content of X.

2.3.2 Infinitive clauses

The post-*type* position can be occupied by an infinitive clause licensed by the presence in the pre-*type* position of a low referential NP (see Section 2.2.1). In this case the *type*-noun can be paraphrased by a similative-exemplificative marker such as Italian *come per esempio* and Russian *kak naprimer* lit. 'such as for example'. This syntactic pattern seems to be more frequent in Italian, probably due to the prevalence of general and vague nouns in the pre-*type* position (31) and to the fact that infinitive forms show fewer syntactic constraints, i.e. they may undergo nominalization and occur with prepositions; however, this pattern is occasionally attested also in Russian (32):

(31) It. *Una fatica non trascurabile, avrei voluto vedere voi*
a effort not insignificant would have see-INF you-PL
*protagonisti di [scene]ₓ **tipo:** [sbagliare l' ultima nota*
protagonists of scenes TIPO get.wrong-INF the last note
e dover ricominciare tutto dall' inizio!]ᵧ
and must-INF start.again-INF all from.the beginning
'(It is) quite a significant effort. I would have liked to have seen you as protagonists of scenes **like** "Getting the last note wrong and having to start all over again!"' (AIM, catetering.it)

(32) Rus. *Očevidno, čto "dlja sebja" [ideja*
obvious-PRED that for oneself-GEN idea-NOM.F.SG
*vygljadit]ₓ **tipa** ["poslušat' doklad X, lično*
look-PRS.3SG TIPA listen-INF lecture-ACC.M.SG X in.person
poobščat'sja s Y, i nažrat'sja na afterpati"]ᵧ
hang.out-INF with Y and get.pissed-INF at afterparty-PRP
'Obviously, "for oneself" the idea looks **like** "Listening to the lecture by X, having a little chat with Y, and getting pissed at the afterparty"'(https://habr.com/ru/post/332126,/ accessed 1 March 2020)

In (31) the infinitive clause illustrates the content of the noun scene 'scenes', vaguely referring to a visual stimulus, while in (32) it illustrates the content of the mental shell noun *ideja* 'idea', followed by the Stimulus Subject Perception Verb (Levin 1993) *vygljadit* 'looks like'.

2.3.3 Completive clauses

Sometimes the *type*-word may precede the declarative complementizer 'that', giving rise to a compound form (It. *tipo che*; Rus. *tipa čto* 'TYPE that'). In Italian (see also [14] and [26]) the construction with the compound complementizer replaces the one with the standard complementizer *che* 'that' in cases where the syntactic slot for the completive clause is already occupied (33)–(34):

(33) It. [...] *accade che lui ti baci. E da lì in poi*
happens   that he you-ACC.SG kisses And from then on
[*tutto   è   possibile*]$_X$... **Tipo che** [*questa persona*
everything is possible   TIPO CHE this   person
inizi   ad entrarti nei   pensieri]$_Y$
begins to   seep-INF into.the.PL thoughts
'[...] it happens that he kisses you. And from then on everything is possible... **such that** this person begins to seep into your thoughts' (AIM, veneredimilo.it)

(34) It. *Naturalmente* [*si scoprono   cose   molto interessanti*]$_X$,
of.course   are discovered things very   interesting,
tipo che [*una delle due   società   mercenarie* [...] *nel 1994*
TIPO CHE   one of.the two   companies mercenary   in 1994
aveva firmato (grazie alla mediazione del   Pentagono) un
had signed   thanks to.the mediation of.the Pentagon   a
contratto con la   Croazia per addestrare l'   esercito croato]$_Y$
contract with the Croatia to   train-INF the   army   Croatian
'Of course, very interesting things are discovered, **like that** one of the two mercenary companies [...] had (thanks to the Pentagon) signed a contract with Croatia in 1994 to train the Croatian army' (AIM, mirumir.altervista.org)

Both in (33) and (34) the standard complementizer could have introduced the completive only if the slot for the subject had not already been occupied, but the presence of the subject (*tutto* 'everything' in [33] and *cose molto interessanti* 'very interesting things' in [34]) prevents its use (cf. [33] → **tutto è possibile che...*; [34] → **si scoprono cose molto interessanti che...*). The use of the compound complementizer *tipo che* gives the possibility of introducing an additional subject-completive, coreferent with the subject in pre-*type* position. In Russian, the construction with *tipa čto* is less frequent and is often connected to a speech-act noun or to a verb of communication in the pre-*type* position, as in (35)–(36):

(35) Rus. *nado   kakie to   [bumažki]ₓ   sobirat'*   **tipa čto**
          necessary-PRED some-PL   paper-ACC.PL gather-INF   TIPA ČTO
          [u   rebënka   net   tuberkulëza]ᵧ [...].
          at   child-GEN.M.SG there.is.no   tuberculosis-GEN.M.SG
          'it is necessary to gather some papers – **like that** the child does not have tuberculosis [...]' (ARM, svadba-kursk.ru)

(36) Rus. *[...] ja   govorju   o   tex,   kto   tol'ko*
          I   talk-PRS.1SG   about   that-PRP.PL who-NOM   just
          učitsja   xodit'   – vot   takie   DOLŽNY   [učit'
          learn-PRS.3SG walk-INF   – DEICT   such-NOM.PL must-PL   teach-INF
          *osnovy]ₓ –   **tipa čto**   [xodjat   na   nogax,   a*
          basics-ACC.PL   TIPA ČTO   walk-PRS.3PL   on   foot-PRP.PL and
          lazjat   na   rukax]ᵧ
          climb-PRS.3PL on   hand-PRP.PL
          '[...] I am talking about those who are just learning to walk – they MUST learn the basics – **such as** walking on their feet and climbing on their hands' (ARM, cotoha.info)

In (35) in the pre-*type* position the object argument is realized by a noun referring to a communicative act (*bumažki* 'papers'), followed by the compound *type*-complementizer *tipa čto*, which introduces an object-completive clause, exemplifying the content of the object: the meaning of the whole construction can be reformulated as gathering documents which provide information on the child's health. In (36) the object-completive introduced by the compound *type*-complementizer *tipa čto* is coreferent with the noun *osnovy* 'the basics' in the pre-*type* position: the fact that feet are made to walk and hands are made to climb can be considered a metaphor for basic knowledge (in the co-text there is another expression [*učitsja xodit'* 'learning to walk'] that points to the same conceptual metaphor LEARNING THE ROPES IS LIKE LEARNING TO WALK).

2.3.4 Independent clauses

The analyzed data show that all the main types of independent clauses are allowed in the post-*type* position (declaratives, interrogatives, including rhetorical questions, imperatives, exclamatives, etc.). In the Italian example (37), the post-*type* position is occupied by a rhetorical question, which functions as a pseudo-quotation expressing the subject's surprise; on a syntactic level the rhetorical question realizes the slot for the manner argument of the verb, while on a semantic level it allows the speaker to represent the subject's emotional state, which can be paraphrased as SHE LOOKS AT HERSELF WITH SURPRISE:

(37) It. Era   bellissima [...] [si guardava]ₓ   **tipo:** ["*oddio*
         was   pretty-F   was.looking.at.herself TIPO   oh.my.God
     ma   chi   sono"]ᵧ *però*   *era   contenta*
      but who   am   however was   happy-F
     'She was so pretty [...] she looked at herself **like**, "Oh my God, is it really me?" but she was happy' (AIM, ilblogdellapresy.blog.deejay.it)

As for Russian, example (22) shows that in the post-*type* position a declarative sentence can be found (*kruče menja tol'ko gory* 'no-one is cooler than me'): the use of both the first-person pronoun and quotation marks suggests that the statement should be read as a pseudo-quotation, which metaphorically expresses the way the subject behaves. On a syntactic level the declarative sentence in Y fills the manner slot of the verb *vedet sebja* '[he] behaves' in X.

3 Cohesive mechanisms

In this section, the role of the *type*-word in contexts of loose cohesion will be discussed in more detail. In (37) a partial co-reference between the pre-*type* and post-*type* elliptic subject arguments can be observed: the third-person subject of the first sentence and the first-person subject of the second sentence point to the same referent. Some inferential operations are performed by the hearer in order to work out the intended meaning; these operations rely on the context, and on encyclopedic and shared knowledge: firstly, the verb *guardarsi* 'to look at oneself', as discussed in Section 2.2.2, requires a manner adverb to become meaningful. Secondly, the question in the post-*type* position is used as a rhetorical expression of surprise. Finally, the *type*-word triggers a pseudo-quotative interpretation of the sentence (note also the use of quotation marks).

However, the construction can also be used in cases in which X and Y exhibit neither syntactic coreference nor semantic coherence (or 'intrinsic metonymic associations', according to Croft and Cruse 2004: 217). In the following example from the Russian writer Pelevin, X and Y are not linked by the classic hypernym-hyponym relation ('plebeian orgasm' is not a kind of jacket), but rather by an associative mechanism: the semantic frame activated by the co-text ('an outfit worn by particularly prudent businessmen') establishes an extrinsic metonymic relation between the ad hoc concept of 'plebeian orgasm' and the outfit of the prudent businessman and deduce the intended meaning (AN OUTFIT WHICH COULD BRING COMMON PEOPLE TO ORGASM). In this case the *type*-word has a labelling function:

(38) Rus. *Na nem byl [pidžak]*ₓ ***tipa***
on he-PRP be-PST.M.SG jacket-NOM.M.SG TIPA
*["orgazm plebeja"]*ᵧ *[. . .] – narjad, kotoryj*
orgasm-NOM.M.SG plebeian-GEN.M.SG outfit-NOM.M.SG which-ACC.M.SG
nadevajut osobo rasčetlivye biznesmeny
put.on-PRS.3PL particularly prudent-NOM.PL businessmen-NOM.PL
'He was wearing a jacket **of the** "commoner's orgasm" **type** [. . .] an outfit worn by particularly prudent businessmen' (RNC, V. Pelevin)

In (39) X is occupied by a NP which introduces a causal clause, while Y is realized by a NP modified by a participle and a relative clause: Y specifies the content of X, in fact the meaning of the vague noun *cosa* 'something' is made explicit by *un aereo perso da un artista* 'an aeroplane lost by an artist'; analogously, the meaning of the general predicate (*non andava bene* 'was not going well') is made more specific (*scombinava tutto il programma* 'messed up the whole programme):

(39) It. *[Momenti di demoralizzazione perché una cosa non*
moments of demoralization because a thing not
*andava bene]*ₓ ***tipo*** *[un aereo perso di un*
go-IPRF.3SG well TIPO an aeroplane lost of an-M
*artista che ci scombinava tutto il programma]*ᵧ
artist which we-DAT.PL messed.up all the programme
'Moments of demoralization because something was not going well, **like** an aeroplane lost by an artist which messed up the whole programme' (PC)

4 The complementizer *type*-construction in habitual and potential contexts

Although it has not been explicitly mentioned, the complementizer *type*-construction is frequently associated with habitual or generic ((5), (12), (17), (19), (22), (26), (37)) and irrealis moods (in particular with potential (11), (15), (16), (18), (30),

(33) or counterfactual (28) contexts):[9] such uses, analogous to the exemplificative uses, relate to the etymologically primary meaning of the *type*-noun which identifies a "model", an "ideal" or a "typical exemplar" (cf. Mihatsch 2007: 227). In other words, if in the exemplifying use the *type*-noun introduces a "typical" instantiation of a previously mentioned concept, here it refers to a habitual or generic "behavioural pattern" which is "typical" for the situation given in X. In the co-text, this use is frequently associated with iterative verbal forms (cf. It. Imperfect tense and Rus. Imperfective aspect), predicative verbs (such as It. *è umano che...* 'it is normal that' in (40)) and adverbs of frequency (It. *ogni tanto* 'from time to time', Rus. *često* 'often', see (41)):

(40) It. è   umano il   fatto che   quando al   potere
     is   human the fact   that when   in.the power
     si alternano   due   gruppi [...] [si   finisca   per fare
     alternate-REFL two   groups   IMPRS end.up.SBJV.3SG   to make
     accordi   sottobanco]ₓ [...] **tipo** [io sistemo   tuo   figlio a
     agreements backroom-ADV   TIPO   I   arrange   your   son   to
     dirigere   il   ministero   e   tu   fai   prendere
     run-INF   the ministry   and you.SG make-PRS.2SG   get-INF
     l' appalto   milionario   al   mio]ᵧ [...]
     the contract millionaire to.the   mine
     'It is normal that when two parties alternate in power [...] we end up making backroom deals [...] **such as** "I'll arrange for your son to run the ministry and you help mine get the million-dollar contract" [...]' (AIM, cobraf.com)

(41) Rus. [Istorii   často   načinajutsja   tak]ₓ –   **tipa**
         story-NOM.PL   often   begin-PRS.3PL like.this TIPA
         [čelovek   priexal   iz   Saxalina   na
         man-NOM.M.SG   come-PST.M.SG   from   Sakhalin-GEN.M.SG for
         dva   dnja   v   komandirovku   v   Rigu]ᵧ
         two-ACC   day-GEN.M.SG   on   business.trip-ACC.F.SG to Riga-ACC.F.SG
         'Stories often begin like this – **like**, "A man came from Sakhalin to Riga for two days on a business trip"' (ARM, audioveda.ru)

---

9 Givón (1995: 116) observes an interesting semantic similarity between habitual and irrealis clauses: "From a communicative perspective, habitual marked clauses tend to be strongly asserted, i.e. pragmatically like realis. Semantically, however, they resemble irrealis in some fundamental ways. To begin with, unlike realis, which typically signals that an event has occurred (or state persisted) at some specific time, a habitual-marked assertion does not refer to any particular event that occurred at any specific time".

In other cases the use of the *type*-noun has the ability to envisage possible scenarios: in the co-text this use is frequently associated with *if*-clauses, temporal clauses (It. *quando*..., Rus. *kogda*... 'when....'), and counterfactual situations (cf. the use of past conditional in (28) with modal verbs: *avrei dovuto filmare* 'I should have filmed').

As previously mentioned, the use of the *type*-noun in habitual/generic, potential and counterfactual contexts overlaps with other uses: first of all with the exemplificative one (where It. *tipo*/Rus. *tipa* introduces a "prototypical", "ideal" instance of a category or concept), but also with the labelling and quotative uses (where It. *tipo*/Rus. *tipa* assigns a "possible" label to the referent and signals a "supposed" quote). In the following example, the post-*type* sentence (*neizvestno, kak vse složitsja* 'it is not known how everything will turn out') can be considered both a pseudo-quotation of the sentence uttered in that context and a label for situations of uncertainty:

(42) Rus. [...] *volnenie   i   trevoga   po povodu*
            excitement-NOM.N.SG and anxiety-NOM.F.SG about
     predstojaščego   sobytija   narastajut   po mere
     upcoming-GEN.N.SG   event-GEN.N.SG   grow-PRS.3PL   according.to
     približenija   ètogo   sobytija.   Osobenno
     approaching-GEN.M.SG this-GEN.N.SG   event-GEN.N.SG Especially
     èto   kasaetsja   [otvetstvennyx žiznennyx
     this-NOM.M.SG   concern-PRS.3SG important-GEN.PL life-ADJ.GEN.PL
     *peremen   i   situacij]ₓ   **tipa** ["neizvestno,   kak*
     change-GEN.PL   and   situation-GEN.PL TIPA not.known-PRED how
     vse   složitsja"]ᵧ
     everything-NOM.N.SG turn.out-FUT.3SG
     'Excitement and anxiety about the upcoming event grow as the event approaches. This is especially true for big life changes and situations **like** "It is not known how everything will turn out"' (ARM, lib.znate.ru)

Kolyaseva (2018) highlights a subuse of the quotative function of the *type*-noun in Russian, where *tipa* "gradually loses the function of reporting someone's speech, and becomes a means of conveying the idea that, according to the speaker, the information is simply not true. It then becomes synonymous to *quasi-*, *pseudo-* and is often used to convey sarcasm" (Kolyaseva 2018: 89). This use could be defined as "simulative", in that it constitutes a means by which the speaker tells the listener that the lexical item Y under the scope of the *type*-word acquires the additional meaning 'not really Y, but something that looks like Y'.[10] For the sake of illustration, consider the following example:

(43) Rus. ščas poem i tože pridumaju kakoj-nibud' **tipa**
       now eat-FUT.1SG and also invent-FUT.1SG some-ACC.M.SG TIPA
       smešnoj slučaj, kotoryj **tipa** so mnoj
       funny-ACC.M.SG case-ACC.M.SG which-NOM.M.SG TIPA with I-INS
       nedavno proizošel
       recently happen-PST.M.SG
    'I'm gonna eat right now and then I will also come up with a **TIPA** funny story that has recently **TIPA** happened to me.' (Kolyaseva 2018: 90)

As Kolyaseva points out, the "funny" story is 'not at all funny' and it has not really happened to the speaker: the "simulative" reading is also triggered by the presence in the co-text of the "ideational" verb *pridumat'*, lit. 'invent' in addition to the future time reference and the use of *kakoj-nibud'* 'some', the irrealis indefinite (Haspelmath 1997). Moreover, the comment *tipa ser'eznyj* is frequently used on Russian social media under photos or videos to suggest that the subject has adopted a 'deliberately serious' expression. Thus, the Russian "simulative" function of the *type*-word also falls within the domain of irrealis. However, the two languages differ with respect to this feature, because in Russian it refers to a fictional context, whereas in Italian it rather evokes a potential situation. Example (43) could be translated into Italian by replacing *tipa* with *tipo*:

---

10 Sakhno (2017) observes that also *vrode* 'like' (< *v* 'in' + *rode* 'kind.M.LOC.SG'), another Russian polysemous similative-approximative marker derived from the grammaticalization of a taxonomic noun, can be used to convey "illusion" and "simulation": used in this way, *vrode* means 'apparently', 'as if', 'it looks/it's like', 'supposedly' ("Dans les emplois de ce type, *vrode* signifie 'apparemment', 'comme si', 'on dirait', 'soi-disant'" Sakhno 2017: 203). Sakhno illustrates this use through an example taken from Šukšin:

*Vit'ka prjamo tut že, za stolom celoval Ritu, a Rita slabo bila rukoj Vit'ku po pleču, **vrode ottalkivala**, a sama l'nula tugoj grud'ju i drugoj rukoj obnimala za šeju.* (V. Šukšin)

Fr.: 'Vitka embrassait Rita sans quitter la table, Rita donnait des faibles coups de poing sur l'épaule de Vitka, **comme si elle le repoussait, mais en réalité**, elle serrait son opulente poitrine contre la sienne et enlaçait son cou de l'autre bras.'

Eng.'Vitka kissed Rita right there, at the table, and Rita weakly punched Vitka on the shoulder, **as if she were pushing him away, but in reality** she was rubbing her opulent chest against him and hugging his neck with the other arm'

Sakhno's translation into French makes the simulative meaning of *vrode* more explicit through the insertion of a modal adverbial *en réalité* 'in reality'.

(44) It. ora   mangio   e   mi invento   anche   **tipo**
         now   eat-PRS.1SG and   come.up.with-REFL.PRS.1SG also   TIPO
    una storia divertente, che   **tipo** mi   è successa   tempo fa
    a   story   funny   that TIPO   to.me happen-PST.F.SG time ago
    'I'm gonna eat right now and then I will also come up with **TIPO** a funny story that **TIPO** has recently happened to me.'

In this case, however, the use of the *type*-word emphasizes that the elements that fall within its scope ('a funny story' that 'has recently happened to me') should be considered as potential, since they constitute "possible types" of stories that can be invented and are likely to have happened. The difference between Russian *tipa* and Italian *tipo* illustrated in (43) and (44) suggests that the two forms developed through different paths of grammaticalization and pragmaticalization: the "simulative" use of *tipa* constitutes a semantic extension of the similative-approximative function (X looks like Y > X pretends to be Y), whereas the potential use of *tipo* is more tightly connected with the similative-exemplificative function (Y represents a typical exemplar of X > Y represents a possible exemplar of X).

5 Conclusion

Both in Italian and Russian the *type*-noun has developed several "non-nominal" uses, which are organized around core functions such as exemplification and instantiation (explicative function), synthesis and generalization (labelling function), categorization by analogy and approximation, and indirect quotation of others' speech. The boundaries between different functions are fuzzy because these uses are often overlapping and interwoven, as shown, for instance, in (42).

This aspect has already been discussed in other works; however, as far as I know, the role of the *type*-noun as a generic complementizer in contexts where the pre-*type* and post-*type* discourse segments are characterized by loose conceptual connections had not previously been fully investigated.

Very frequently the *type*-complementizer is used in a specific lexical and morphosyntactic pattern to connect a cataphoric shell noun (in particular a linguistic, mental or circumstantial shell noun, as well as a noun referring to a sensorial stimulus) to its shell content. Moreover, both It. *tipo* and Rus. *tipa*, appear in contexts where X and Y are linked together by unconventional or marked metonymic relations, that is, relations of contiguity located outside the world of reality on the conceptual level[11] (cf. (3b): the phenomenon of high water in Venice > the habit of rolling up trouser legs in order to keep them from getting wet > ridiculously short trousers). In such contexts, the *type*-noun interplays with background and contextual knowledge, as well as with the surrounding text (the co-text) in guiding selective information processing.

As a general-purpose complementizer, the *type*-word comes into play when other syntactic cohesive means are not available or simply omitted: for instance, the *type*-complementizer can be used in substitution of more explicit means, such as the similative-conditional and similative-temporal connectives 'as if' and 'like when'. In fact, as has already been observed, the *type*-construction is frequently associated with the habitual/generic and irrealis moods, where it is used to introduce potential scenarios which can be realized in terms of both possible situations (in Italian) and fictional contexts (in Russian).

In other words, the use of the *type*-complementizer enhances cohesion in the ongoing construction of meaning, and at the same time allows the speaker/writer to avoid making the semantic relations that exist between X and Y explicit.

References

Benko, Vladimír. 2014. Aranea: Yet another family of (comparable) web corpora. In Petr Sojka, Aleš Horák, Ivan Kopeček & Karel Pala (eds.), *Text, Speech and Dialogue. 17th International Conference, Brno, Czech Republic, September 8–12, 2014*, 247–256. Cham: Springer International Publishing Switzerland.

Benigni, Valentina. 2014. Strategie di approssimazione lessicale in russo e in italiano. In Olga Inkova, Marina di Filippo & François Esvan (eds.), *L'archittetura del testo. Studi contrastivi slavo-romanzi*, 203–224. Alessandria: Edizione dell'Orso.

Benigni, Valentina. 2016. *Roba da matti!* La resa dei nomi vaghi nella traduzione dall'italiano al russo. In Olga Inkova & Andrea Trovesi (eds.), *Langues slaves en contraste / Slavjanskie jazyki in comparatione / Lingue slave a confronto*, 307–342. Bergamo: Bergamo University Press – Sestante Edizioni.

Croft, William & D. Alan Cruse. 2004. *Cognitive Linguistics*. Cambridge: Cambridge University Press.

Daiber, Thomas. 2010. Quotativmarker im Russischen (tipo/tipa). *Zeitschrift für Slawistik* 55 (1). 69–89.

---

[11] As Radden and Kövecses observe, the notion of "contiguity" "is at the core of most definitions of metonymy" (Radden and Kövecses 1999: 19–20). They account for "metonymic contiguity" within Lakoff's theory of Idealized Cognitive Models (ICMs), which includes not only all the associations commonly related to a conceptual entity (that is, people's encyclopedic knowledge of a particular domain) but also the cultural models in which they occur: this network of conceptual relationships gives rise to new associations which may be exploited in metonymic shifts.

Givón, Talmy. 1995. *Functionalism and grammar*. Amsterdam & Philadelphia: John Benjamins.
Halliday, Michael A. K. & Ruqaiya Hasan. 1976. *Cohesion in English*. London: Longman.
Haspelmath, Martin. 1997. *Indefinite pronouns*. Oxford: Clarendon Press.
Kolyaseva, Alena & Kristin Davidse. 2018. A typology of lexical and grammaticalized uses of Russian *tip, tipa, po tipu*. *Russian Linguistics* 42 (2). 191–220.
Kolyaseva, Alena. 2018. The 'new' Russian quotative *tipa*: Pragmatic scope and functions. *Journal of Pragmatics* 128. 82–97.
Lapteva, Olga Alekseevna. 1983. *Tipa* ili *vrode* [*Tipa* or *vrode*]. *Voprosy jazykoznanija* [Topics in linguistics] 1. 39–51.
Levin, Beth. 1993. *English verb classes and alternations: A preliminary investigation*. Chicago & London: The University of Chicago Press.
Mihatsch, Wiltrud. 2007. The construction of vagueness: "Sort of" expressions in Romance languages. In Günter Radden, Klaus-Michael Köpke, Thomas Berg & Peter Siemund (eds.), *Aspects of meaning construction*, 225–245. Amsterdam & Philadelphia: John Benjamins.
Mihatsch, Wiltrud. 2016. *Type*-noun binominals in four Romance languages. *Language Sciences* 53. 136–159.
Radden, Günter & Zoltán Kövecses. 1999. Towards a theory of metonymy. In Klaus-Uwe Panther & Günter Radden (eds.), *Metonymy in language and thought*, 17–59. Amsterdam & Philadelphia: John Benjamins.
Sakhno, Sergueï. 2017. Polyfonctionnalité et transcatégorialité des morphèmes russes *vrode, tipa*: fonctionnement et aspects typologiques. In Thierry Ponchon, Hava Bat-Zeev Shyldkrot & Annie Bertin (eds.), *Mots de liaison et d'intégration: Prépositions, conjonctions et connecteurs*, 197–214. Amsterdam & Philadelphia: John Benjamins.
Schmid, Hans-Jörg. 2000. *English abstract nouns as conceptual shells: From corpus to cognition*. Berlin & New York: Mouton de Gruyter.
Sergeeva, Ekaterina Nikolaevna. 2010. *Tipa* kak evidencialnyj marker v russkoj razgovornoj reči [*Tipa* as evidential marker in Russian colloquial speech]. In Nikolaj Nikolaevič Kazanskij (ed.), *Acta Linguistica Petropolitana. Trudy Instituta lingvističeskix issledovanij*, VI(3), 149–153. Sankt-Peterburg: Nauka.
Voghera, Miriam. 2013. A case study on the relationship between grammatical change and synchronic variation. The emergence of *tipo*[-N] in Italian. In Anna Giacalone Ramat, Caterina Mauri & Piera Molinelli (eds.), *Synchrony and diachrony. A dynamic interface*, 283–312. Amsterdam & Philadelphia: John Benjamins.
Voghera, Miriam. 2014. Da nome tassonomico a segnale discorsivo: una mappa delle costruzioni di tipo in italiano contemporaneo. *Studi di grammatica italiana* 33. 197–221.
Ward, Denis. 1977. On indefinite pronouns in Russian. *The Slavonic and East European Review* 55 (4). 444–469.
Wilson, Deirdre & Robyn Carston, 2007. A unitary approach to lexical pragmatics: Relevance, inference and ad hoc concepts. In Noel Burton-Roberts (ed.), *Pragmatics*, 230–259. London: Palgrave.

Hélène Vassiliadou, Elena Vladimirska, Marie Lammert,
Céline Benninger, Francine Gerhard-Krait, Jelena
Gridina & Daina Turla

17 Clear vs. approximate categorization in French and Latvian

Abstract: This paper aims to put into perspective various issues surrounding categorization and approximation, two frequently opposed yet essentially indissociable operations, by comparing the taxonomic expressions in two languages belonging to different language groups (French and Latvian). We mean to verify in particular whether the expressions exhibit the same kind of semantic multifunctionality in the studied languages or, on the contrary, if we observe specific constraints in each language (lexical and grammatical variations, syntactic marking, etc.). One way to illustrate these issues is to focus on the analysis of the nouns preceding and following the type nouns in the binominal structures (X = N1 *type noun* Y = N2). It is also important to reinvestigate the terminological imbroglio that closely affects *approximation*, *imprecision*, *vagueness* and *categorization*. Thus, with reference to psychological literature, we will show that the principle of categorization itself functions by means of relating elements, in a similar way to *approximation*. We also challenge formal and semantic correlations attached to often juxtaposed interpretative types (clear, approximate, non-prototypical categorization or vagueness). However, we must temper this challenge for Latvian: with its morphological syntax, it marks lexicogrammatical differences in a more clear-cut way than French.

Acknowledgements: Project PHC *Osmose: De la Taxinomie à l'approximation dans les langues naturelles* funded by the Ministry of Europe, Foreign Affairs and the Ministry of Higher Education, Research & Innovation (MESRI). We are grateful towards all our anonymous reviewers for their comments and suggestions, to the editors and Emma Walters for their proofreading and precious insights as far as the final version of this text is concerned.

Hélène Vassiliadou, University of Strasbourg, e-mail: vassili@unistra.fr
Elena Vladimirska, University of Latvia, e-mail: jelena.vladimirska@lu.lv
Marie Lammert, University of Strasbourg, e-mail: mlammert@unistra.fr
Céline Benninger, University of Strasbourg, e-mail: benninge@unistra.fr
Francine Gerhard-Krait, University of Strasbourg, e-mail: gerhard@unistra.fr
Jelena Gridina, University of Latvia, e-mail: jelena.gridina@lu.lv
Daina Turla, University of Latvia, e-mail: daina.turla-pastare@lu.lv

https://doi.org/10.1515/9783110701104-017

1 Introduction

In recent decades, research on clear and approximate categorization and their manifestations in languages has generated numerous studies on syntax, semantics, pragmatics, psycholinguistics, philosophy, logic, etc. This is of particular interest, given that these two operations have formally similar realizations even in languages belonging to different groups. The existence of a large number of type nouns such as *sorte, type, espèce* in French, *вроде* in Russian, *είδος [idos], τύπος [tipos]* in Greek, *jakby* in Polish, *sort, kind* in English, etc. testifies to the productivity of these realizations.[1] If many of these nouns serve to both categorize in a clear or in an approximate manner, the fundamental question one can raise is that of identifying the processes of interpretation concerned, since there is not always a consensus on it.

In the present paper, our starting point is to avoid opposing approximation and categorization by arguing for the inherent semantic indeterminacy of most type nouns. The indeterminacy in question encompasses the definition of *hedges* (Lakoff 1973) which may render a categorical reading clearer or less clear. The indeterminacy of type nouns consists of a set of meanings that can cover taxonomy, as well as several types of approximation and vagueness (Gerhard–Krait and Vassiliadou 2017b) which will be discussed in Section 2.3.

In what follows, we will show that approximate uses of type nouns emerge in context. This perspective mostly complies with cognitive and linguistic processes of categorization: when we cannot categorize in a clear manner, we use such type nouns in order to locate an instance compared to other representations that are more stable (Feldermeier and Kutas 2001). Thus, the principle of categorization itself proceeds by means of relating different instances to a category.

It is then important to underline that we can adequately describe taxonomic and approximate interpretations by semantic means without appealing to pragmatic factors. It is assumed in the current literature that the taxonomic value corresponds to the semantics of type nouns, whereas approximate interpretations are systematically associated with pragmatic values (see for example Mihatsch 2007a, 2009). This kind of reasoning leads to a series of a very narrow functional, semantic and pragmatic coincidences: approximation is correlated with vagueness, vagueness or fuzziness are often correlated with pragmatics, the boundaries of vagueness and indeterminacy are "difficult to fix" and fuzzy in turn (Bazzanella 2011); finally, new type noun usages are also directly analyzed

---

1 See *i.a.* Flaux and Van de Velde (2000); Rosier (2002); Denison (2005); Aijmer, Foolen and Simon-Vandenbergen (2006); Keizer (2007); Mihatsch (2007b, 2016); Brems (2011); Davidse et al. (2013); Benigni (2014); Gerhard-Krait and Vassiliadou (2014, 2017a); Adamczyk (2015); Voghera (2017); Kolyaseva and Davidse (2018).

with a pragmatic meaning. For instance, *genre*, *style* and *type* in French, when they enter into a construction perceived as an exemplification are assimilated *ipso facto* to approximation (Chauveau-Thoumelin 2016). Additionally, as Inkova (forth.) pointed out, many studies consider approximation and exemplification as two sides of the same coin. In examples (1)-(3), it seems however difficult to interpret the type noun as approximative:

(1) *Dans ce cas, on peut envisager une séparation par un meuble de rangement, **type** commode ou buffet.* (*amenagement-salon.com*)
'In this case, one can consider separation by a storage unit, **such as** a chest of drawers or a dresser.'

(2) *Il possède principalement des armes **style** fusil laser mais il est aussi armé de sabre laser, juste au cas ou il devrait se battre au corps à corps.* (*forumactif.org*)
'He mainly owns **rifle-style weapons**, but he is also armed with a lightsaber, just in case he has to fight hand-to-hand.'

(3) *Dans une casserole (**genre** cocotte), mettre à chauffer à feu vif l'huile d'olive (ou margarine)* (*L'Est Républicain*, in Chauveau-Thoumelin 2016: 11)[2]
'In a pot (**specifically** a casserole dish), heat the olive oil (or margarine) to a high temperature'

In these particular cases, it seems difficult to talk about approximation, insofar as the noun given in Y (*commode, dresser, rifle, pot*) is a sub-type of X (in structures such as X = N1 *type noun* Y = N2), despite the fact that we can see a case of 'loosening' (Carston 1996), since there are many features contained in Y that are not contained in X. This hyponymy is intrinsically associated with these lexical units and glossing with 'approximately' does not accurately express the meaning

---

[2] This example is particularly interesting because, in French, in the absence of a stable category label which designates all the different types of pots and pans (besides "*ustensile de cuisine*" 'kitchen utensil' whose extension is broad), "*casserole*" is used both as a hypernym and as the co-hyponym of its hyponyms (it designates a particular type of pot or pan that has distinctive features). A quick look at some specialized sites confirms that in French lexicon, "*cocotte*" is mostly seen as a sub-type of "*casserole*". For instance, on https://www.knivesandtools.fr/fr/ct/quelle-casserole-choisir.htm, we can read the following: "*Quelle casserole choisir? Lorsque l'on y regarde de plus près, on remarque qu'il existe un nombre incroyable de types de casseroles.*" [Which pan to choose? When you look more closely, there are an incredible number of different types of pots and pans available.] Then a list of these types (with their specific features) is given, and we can find "*cocotte*" among them. There is no single-word hypernym in English for 'pots and pans', so the translation of *casserole* as 'pot' is not an exact equivalent.

of the type noun usage. The function of the type noun is to explain or to highlight a vertical categorization by picking out one or more of a larger set of alternatives. Following Lo Baido (2018), we consider that exemplification implies categorization because "though differentiated, exemplifying constructions are all characterized by the same function, that is, to signal that the expressions in their scope are examples and that they have to be processed as triggers of a higher-level category." (Lo Baido 2018: 69).[3]

Even in (4) where *genre* is combined with the 'postiche-name'[4] *chose* 'thing', approximative reading is not triggered. "The kind of thing I never say" sketches a category, certainly difficult to name, but sufficiently unifying to be able to include not only formulations of the "*ce nous*/'that we'" type, but also those of what it implies (see Benninger and Vassiliadou 2020):

(4) « *Ma femme, a-t-il enchaîné brusquement, elle était du Portugal comme vous. De Faro. Vous connaissez, hein. – Non. Nous sommes du nord. Faro, c'est dans le sud. – Ah.* » *Il avait l'air déçu.* « *C'est un beau pays, paraît-il, ai-je rattrapé, contrarié.* » *Ce nous, qui m'était venu sans prévenir, me restait en travers de la gorge.* **Le genre de chose** *que je ne dis jamais.* (Garat A. –M., *On ne peut pas continuer comme ça*, 2006)
'« My wife, he said/continued abruptly, was from Portugal like you. From Faro. You know, eh. – No. We're from the north. Faro is in the south. – Ah ». He looked disappointed. « It's a beautiful country, it seems, I corrected myself, upset ». That *we*, which came out unexpectedly, stuck in my throat. **The kind of thing** I never say.'

We illustrate the above general statements by:
– presenting some recent psychological insights on the similarities between taxonomic, approximative and ad hoc categorization (Section 2.1),
– formulating our criticism of existing descriptions, which associate taxonomic vs approximative categorization too strictly with specific syntactic constructions (Section 2.2),
– showing that, in many cases, the solution to the problem raised lies in a more profound analysis of the semantic properties of the nouns that appear in the post-positioned group (X=N1 *taxonomic or metalinguistic marker*[5]/*type noun* Y=N2) (Sections 2.3 and 3).

---
3 See also Landolsi (2018).
4 'Postiche noun' (see Kleiber 1987a) can be seen translated approximatively by 'fake noun'.
5 Following Flaux and Van de Velde (2000), we consider type nouns as metalinguistic markers.

Finally, we put these issues into perspective by comparing the use of type nouns in French and Latvian, a language whose type nouns had not previously been studied (Section 4). In our investigation we consider only literal readings, excluding metaphorical interpretations. Noticeably, for the purpose of demonstration, we use both natural and constructed examples, the former from monolingual and parallel corpora and the latter created on the basis of natural utterances. And we have to keep in mind that translations in English are tricky and do not always convey the lexical specificities of French or Latvian.

2 Categorization and approximation: An antagonistic approach?

The existence of multiple readings of so-called metalinguistic, taxonomic or (sub) categorizer nouns is a well-known phenomenon widely commented upon and analyzed. However, we contend that the problem of noun interpretation has not yet been solved. In the given scientific context, a single or multiple reading is not necessarily agreed upon. Moreover, it is hard to assemble formal argumentation that would help to dissociate them. In most of the existing literature, interpretation is taken for granted and intuition plays a major role.

The amount and nature of interpretations or semantic effects must also be clarified as there are different ways to categorize. We can either categorize in a strict manner or by approximation. If all categorization proceeds *via* approximation, then where is the line to be drawn between the two operations? Does a categorization through approximation cease to be a categorization after all? Are ad hoc categories (see also Section 3) necessarily approximate? The term *approximation* itself is also difficult to pin down as there is no accepted sense to guide one in its application (Bat-Zeev Shyldkrot, Adler, and Asnes 2016).[6] And if there are different ways to approximate, then once again, what guides the interpretation?

Things become complicated when pragmatic approximation is defined through pragmatic vagueness which is in turn defined in the same way as semantic vagueness, that is the imprecise or unclear use of language and the impossibility for a speaker or hearer to say with certainty if an element X belongs or not to the category Y. Nevertheless, we should not forget that vagueness has also a

---

[6] See the distinctions made by Voghera and Collu (2017) about informational, relational and discourse vagueness; see also the discussion in Roubaud and Temple (1988), Mihatsch (2009), Gerhard-Krait and Vassiliadou (2017a).

semantic dimension (for example, vagueness applied on concepts, vague predicates, etc.). In semantics, it is admitted that "a word is vague when there are 'borderline cases', i.e. objects for which it is impossible to say whether the word applies or not; we are then in the realm of neither true nor false" (Fuchs 1986: 235).[7] In other words, "a predicate 'F' is vague just in case for any objects a and b, if a and b are very close in respects relevant to the possession of F, then 'Fa' and 'Fb' are very close in respect of truth." (Smith 2007: 157). In semantics the problem thus arises when the truth value of a membership is difficult to assign. Vagueness can then be defined as "closeness" and vague predicates are intrinsically tolerant predicates.[8] Type nouns exploit these very aspects of vagueness.

The pragmatic version of approximation also plays on the undecidable character of an inclusion or a categorical belonging, but it reflects a speaker's attitude: "there is no perfect choice, but several lexical units more or less distant from the target" (Mihatsch 2009: 103).[9] Approximation is then a tool available to the speaker to signal a particular use of the language, contextually marked by an intention to signify uncertainty (Channell 1994: 20) or any other form of precautionary usage (modality, ignorance, avoidance strategy, connivance, etc.).

As soon as we move outside a purely taxonomic framework, there is a great temptation to invoke approximation. As a result, the approximation model becomes too powerful to account for all cases in which speakers express the need for enriching or lessening the linguistic material following the type noun or in which only "some of the lexical properties contained in the concept are communicated and sorting out which properties are relevant and which are not is a matter for pragmatic inference" (Andersen 2000: 22). To sum up, when something is not a precise description of what the speaker had in mind, we tend to speak of approximation.

---

[7] « Un terme est vague lorsqu'il existe des 'cas frontières', c'est-à-dire des objets pour lesquels il est impossible de dire si le terme s'applique ou non ; on est alors dans le domaine du ni vrai ni faux » (Fuchs 1986: 235). See also Kleiber (1987b: 159) for whom vagueness is defined "with respect to generality, i.e. with respect to the fact that a sign as a type is meant to be used for different referential occurrences" (Le vague est défini « par rapport à la généralité, c'est-à-dire par rapport au fait qu'un signe en tant que type est destiné à être utilisé pour des occurrences référentielles différentes »).

[8] Let's point out here that *vagueness*, in philosophical terms, "is neither a semantic nor an epistemological notion but rather a psychological notion, for its correct explication is in terms of a certain kind of partial belief". (Schiffer 2003: 205).

[9] « Il n'y a pas de choix parfait, mais plusieurs unités lexicales plus ou moins éloignées de la cible » (Mihatsch 2009: 103).

2.1 Some psychological insights

The principles of categorization are at the centre of human thought in a general manner and, in particular, at the center of all the models of lexical and semantic access, seeing that meaning construction and representation of our knowledge are related to the processes of memory, attention, etc. (Feldermeier and Kutas 2001). We know however that linguistic categories do not correspond exactly to conceptual categories (Genome and Lombrozo 2012) and that there is no bi-univocal relationship between the possible difficulty of saying something and that of identifying and categorizing a referential object. Prasada (2010: 37) highlights this fact by explaining that "the mechanisms that allow us to think and talk of particular entities as instances of kinds are formally distinct from the mental mechanisms exploited by exemplar theories to represent and store information about particular entities as such." It is therefore naïve to think that the environment of our human existence is replete with "readily identifiable organisms and objects" (Ungerer and Schmid 1996: 60). The question of categorization related to semantic treatment is very complex, being dependent upon neural networks, whose constituents are modulated by a myriad of features, characteristics and semantic representations (Sachs et al. 2008).

If our ability to categorize functions well enough, it is because we live in a highly structured and coherent world, as argued in the theory of the Uniformity of Nature (Witkin and Tenenbaum 1983). According to this theory, humans, with the little knowledge they have about the world, can convert observable facts (even about an unknown object) into highly informative categorizations. The general tendency would then be to categorize based on generic representations and not on a specimen, an instance (Prasada 2000). However, as Pelletier (2010) points out, the question still remains open: do the features associated with categories exist in the real world or in the speakers' mind? Two explanatory trends are generally advanced in psycholinguistics: the first postulates that a member of a category can be seen as such by a well-defined rule of the type: *X is or X is not in the category* (cluster/group model). It is based on the necessary and sufficient conditions in order to classify a member in a category (Smith and Medin 1981; see also the Aristotelian model). The second postulates that belonging to a category is a matter of the graduated distance of the member from a typical member of the category (Rosch Theory of the prototype). However, experimental studies tend to show that humans favor the presence of an essential or defining feature when making classifications rather than typicality (Medin and Ortony

1988).[10] Moreover, when people represent a concept, they do not always have in mind fixed rules that guide them to find what belongs to a category and what does not (see also Hampton 2010: 81).

Consequently, when categories are named and excluding scientific taxonomies, is there a lexically organized way of perceiving the category and projecting it? Is an ad hoc category[11] really different from a lexically and semantically established one?[12] In (5), "these high school courses that took place after lunch or the sitcoms" belongs to the ad hoc category "these kinds of things that remind us our childhood." Following Barsalou (2010), we can say that an ad hoc category shares the same structure in terms of typicity as a well-established category, the comparison of similarity imposing a graduated structure to the category, regardless of the type of the category concerned. Indeed, as we can see it in example (5), when we interpret utterances, we count on our "inferential capabilities" that "enable us to construct ad hoc concepts out of lexically encoded concepts" (Carston 1996: 62):

(5) *Cela doit être* **le genre de choses qui nous rappellent l'enfance**, *comme ces cours au collège qui se déroulaient après manger ou les séries...* (FrTenTen12)
'This might be **the kind of thing** that reminds us of our childhood, like these high school courses that took place after lunch or the sitcoms...'

Most researchers adopt a middle path towards the combination of a core concept requiring strict definition and a peripheral identification process (Pinker and Prince 1991). According to this approach, both processes, categorization and approximation, are initiated by the same language act or the same speaker's communicative intention: fill the absence of denomination, inherently ambiguous terms, the content of the concept is vague or indeterminate (language as a source; Hampton 2010), difficulty of identifying a reality (the speaker as a source or a hard-to-define reality, the general complexity of the world or of the language), speaker's hesitations (knowledge of the world or of the language itself; "hesitation between two cognitively close categories", Mihatsch 2006: 236; 2007a and

---

10 As one of our anonymous reviewers pointed out, "things are probably more complex than that. Thus, if the feature [fly] is probably an essential feature to structure the bird category (a prototypical bird flies), other features intervene to distinguish entities that fly and are not birds: *plane* (non-animated), *flying saucer* (non-animated + shape)." See the extensive literature on the *Necessary and Sufficient Conditions model*, in particular the synthesis proposed by Kleiber (1990).
11 See Barsalou (1991, 1995, 2013), Mauri and Sansò (2018).
12 Mauri (2017).

b), extensive categories as in Lakoff's famous 'balan' example which includes "women, fire, and dangerous things [. . .] also birds that are not dangerous, as well as exceptional animals such as platypus, bandicoot, and echidna" (Lakoff 1987: 5), speakers' strong tendency for modality or mitigation (Sweetser 1989) that makes a category-statement look like an approximation.

It is also important to distinguish between the meaning that speakers explicitly attribute to items and the intuition involved in assigning characteristics to members of a category. For example, something that walks like a duck and quacks (like a duck) may not be a duck. To put it another way, an item may be devoid of any characteristics that would make it a member of the category and still be part of it (Carey 2009). Thus, when resembling or triggering associations with something else, we do not necessarily approximate. Likewise, type nouns suggest that alternative modes of expression may be equally appropriate even when non-identical resemblance between X and Y is involved.

Moreover, cognitive studies show that categorization does not depend on existing denominations. In other words, categories can exist despite the absence of established denominations. Knowledge in the field of neuroscience (as a result of different types of tasks, such as word generation, semantic priming, classification or comparison; Kahlaoui et al. 2010) also tends to confirm that conceptual knowledge is organized according to semantic characteristics and that sensory features are important for our ability to distinguish natural objects, while functional features affect the distinction of artefacts. It has also been observed that natural objects trigger stronger activation in areas of visual association, whereas artefacts activate areas where actions are represented (Chao and Martin 2000). Finally, Sachs et al. (2008) have shown that there are no differences in activation when making taxonomic categorizations and when making thematic categorizations close to what we find under the approximation label as mentioned above.

To sum up, taxonomic, approximative and ad hoc categorization all involve the same basic mechanism of categorization, which is to relate elements to a category. The element may be included as a core or as a peripheral element in the category, or it may not be included in the category at all, but it bears similarities to elements of the category.

2.2 Interpretative types and formal correlations

In this section, following De Smedt, Brems, and Davidse (2007), we would like to address some critiques of existing descriptions where taxonomic vs. approximative categorization may have been associated too readily with specific constructions.[13] There are indeed difficulties in defining the relevance of the proposed structural associations and their operational character, when interpretative types are coordinated to formal correlations:

- either by applying a number of tests to a precise structure (the nature of the article in *un/une espèce/genre de*, or its definite character, concordance of gender and number inside and outside the noun phrase, dislocations/transformations, semi-suffix uses, head uses, etc.)
- or by showing that a given interpretation is associated with a specific structure more often than with others as in the distinction between binominal and qualifying constructions in English type noun structures which is generally associated with respectively straight taxonomizing (example 6) and qualification (example 7) in one way or another of the category used:[14]

(6) *There are three main **types of** rock: igneous, sedimentary and metamorphic.*

(7) *We had **a sort of** holiday, I guess.*

Loose use or rough description in (7) involves the relaxing of linguistically encoded meaning: the speaker means that what they had may not be what one could ideally call a holiday (for multiple reasons that can be inferred based on our shared knowledge of a 'prototypical' holiday; the extension of 'holiday' may be difficult to grasp). Still, what they had is what approaches the most the concept of *holiday* (for instance, they were not at work). We do not question here that the speaker's intention is to "downtone" of what might seem a "high-flown label" (De Smedt, Brems, and Davidse 2007). We question once more (as in Section 2 above) the notion of approximation itself and the rapid exclusion of categorization meaning for type nouns, even in highly grammaticalized cases.

Type nouns are linguistic units that have "an unspecified meaning boundary [...] so that its interpretation is elastic in the sense that it can be stretched or shrunk according to the strategic needs of communication" (Zhang and Parvaresh 2019: 4). As De Smedt, Brems, and Davidse (2007: 229) pointed out "there is no formally motivated classification" of type-noun uses. If we consider Aijmer's (2002) description of *sort of*, despite her fine-grained analysis, we observe that the particles' sub-uses

---

[13] We cannot proceed here to a deep detailed syntactic analysis; let it suffice to point out the difficulties encountered in the practice of systematic pairing between a construction and a semantic specification. See Rouget (1997), Aijmer (2002), Denison (2002), Rosier (2002), Keizer (2007), Brems and Davidse (2010).
[14] We thank the editors for this suggestion.

(interpersonal, affective, hedging, detensifying, etc.) are contextually dependent and account for pragmatic/discourse effects without direct connection with syntax: "the structural relation between the type noun in head position and postmodifier *of* + second noun" does not change (De Smedt, Brems, and Davidse 2007: 232).[15]

Likewise, Prince, Bosk, and Frader (1982), from the outset, attribute an inherent approximate value to markers as *genre*, *style*, *kind* and *sort*. From a semantic point of view, their meaning is not intrinsically akin to "approximately" and they do not convey to the expression they modify a fuzzy or vague value:

(8) *I saw **a kind of** insect.*

Utterance (8), metaphorical usage put aside, can for example indicate that "I saw an insect that I do not know/which has never been listed/that I cannot name but I clearly identify the occurrence as an insect" (see Section 2.3 for details).

As far as French is concerned, Rosier (2002: 83) immediately associates for instance *une sorte de* to approximation. Similarly, dictionary definitions using *une sorte de* ('sort of/kind of') are analyzed or regarded as *definition by approximation* such as in:

(9) *Blouson = sorte de veste serrée à la taille, fabriquée le plus souvent en tissu imperméable et résistant, en cuir, etc.* (TLFi)
'Jacket = a kind of straight fitted short coat (. . .)'[16]

However, there is no approximation, since a 'blouson' belongs to the category 'veste' even if it may not reach a very similar point of the body as coats do. Or to put it differently, the definition in (9) embodies the idea that 'blouson' and 'veste' share the salient property of being 'short' and that provides the means for creating an equivalent class.

Categorical status as well as distribution criteria are invoked to explain the multiple readings of *genre*, one of the French markers that is mostly seen as an approximator. Thus, some researchers[17] attach formal correlates to an interpre-

---

15 Not all researchers necessarily agree with these statements. We do not deny that syntax may be one clue among others. We merely point out that it is not sufficient.

16 *Jacket* is defined as a 'short coat' in https://dictionary.cambridge.org. We encounter the same phenomenon as the one in example (3). 'Veste' in French stands both for a hypernym and a co-hyponym.

17 Yaguello (1998), Rosier (2005), Vigneron-Bosbach (2016), Vladimirska (2016), Haillet (2018). It is surprising that the main value of *genre*, that of a categorizer, is not part of the classification proposed by Haillet (2018: 238) who distinguishes three lexical entities: $genre_1$ which "serves to

tative type by showing that a given interpretation is associated in a privileged way with a construction: "*genre*-preposition" or "*genre* as qualifying particle" (Davidse and Doyen 2009: 140) is considered approximative[18] (11), whilst structures such as *ce/le/un genre de* (10) are seen as categorizing ones:

(10) *J'aime **ce genre de** voitures/j'aime les voitures **de ce genre**.*
'I like **this kind/sort of** car'/'I like cars **of this kind/sort**'

(11) *Il y a pas mal de sportifs de haut niveau qui ont l'interdiction de faire tout un tas de sports en dehors de leur boulot (**genre du** ski de piste), je trouve étrange que Kubica ait pu faire du rallye, moi aussi.* (racingstub.com)
'There are quite a number of top athletes who are prohibited from doing a whole lot of sports besides their work (**such as/like** downhill skiing), I also find it strange that Kubica was able to go rally driving.'

Yet, in (11), *ski de piste* ('downhill skiing') is a kind of sport that top athletes are not allowed to practise.[19] There is no conceptual discrepancy between what is said and what is meant (Danon-Boileau and Morel 1997).

The alleged meanings of specific constructions are intimately related to the complexity and multiplicity of pragmatic values embodied under the global approximation label. This can ultimately result in sidestepping semantics and losing sight of the main semantic properties of both type nouns and nouns entering especially the binominal constructions, as we will show hereafter. What falls within the realm of pragmatics is why the speaker's intention is to inject vagueness into his speech. In binominal constructions, some nouns allow vagueness because they can leave the door open to multiple interpretations (out of context) and some nouns do not permit approximation. Another side of the problem concerns the ability to identify an instance which can belong to different categories. In any case, type nouns themselves are *a priori* undetermined in language use (as are *hedges*), but this does not mean that the sentences they appear in become

---

represent the speaker as contesting what an explicit segment X says", *genre₂* which serves to exemplify and *genre₃* which signals approximation.

18 Davidse and Doyen (2009: 140) state that all uses of *genre* as a 'qualifying particle' "qualify the description of whatever element it has in its scope as approximate". Exemplifying meaning is often seen as a stage between categorization and approximation or as a use that easily triggers approximation. Of course, not all scholars equate exemplification with approximation (see Kolyaseva and Davidse 2018 for instance or Haillet 2018 who makes a distinction between them).

19 Even if we could reason in terms of exemplification, that does not change the fact that there is no approximation in this example as stated in our Introduction (cf. also Lo Baido 2018; Gerhard-Krait, Lammert, and Vassiliadou 2019; Vassiliadou and Fotiadou 2022).

vague too. A question of interest here concerns the nouns (well-established kinds vs. not well-established kinds for instance) that can give rise to approximation.

2.3 Four possibilities/four types of readings

To illustrate the aforementioned issues, we proceed with some French examples that can help us identify four different interpretations. We exemplify hereby four possible readings triggered by the combination of nominal constructions placed on the left and right context of type nouns. We favour simple constructions as in *X est une sorte/un genre de Y* ('X is a type/sort of Y'), though it is obvious that differences may arise and that some of the readings may be preferred to others when the sentence structure is a predicative one, or when the context contains details that orient the interpretation. X (= N1) corresponds most of the time to a token of the category Y (= N2). As mentioned, we perceive no semantic difference between *X est un type de Y* ('X is a type/kind of Y') and the genitive structure *Y de type X* ('X is of the type/kind of Y').[20] Even if it is syntactic parsing or the mechanism itself (subordination vs. superordination) that differs, the global reading remains the same: X can be seen as subtypes or instances of the category mentioned depending on the nature of the noun.

2.3.1 First reading: Clear categorization

The first reading involves clear, frank and straightforward belonging (inclusion) to a category that leads to a taxonomic reading:

(12) *Le pingouin est **une sorte de/une espèce** d'oiseau.*
    'A penguin is a **kind of/a type of** bird.'

(13) *Le psychiatre est **une sorte de** médecin.*
    'A psychiatrist is **a kind of** doctor.'

The only possible way to interpret the utterances (12) and (13) is to consider X as being necessarily a Y. We can paraphrase typical categorization by:
- X is a Y/It is a Y
- X belongs to the class of Y
- X is a type of/a variety of Y

---

[20] We put aside colloquial uses and registers.

In a general way, the context can direct the interpretation. In (12) and (13), the generic sentence associated with a Be-Hierarchy between a hyponym and a hypernym leaves no room for doubt (Murphy and Wisniewski 1989). However, the same interpretation can easily emerge into a non-binominal construction, as in (14), which is a predicative context. Thus, some pre-established music subtypes are mentioned in the interaction:

(14) MB: *et autrement qu- s-* **quelle sorte de musique** *alors est-ce que vous aimez euh?*
MG475 : *j'aime bien euh le symphonies de Beethov*
MB: *(...) enfin ça c'est* **de la grande musique** *quoi euh (...) mais autrement vous aimez* **le jazz** *ou* (Cocoon)
'MB: and otherwise wh- **what kind of music** do you like, hm?'
MG475: I like uh Beethoven symphonies
MB: (...) yes well that's what we call **great music** uh (...) but besides this, do you like **jazz** or'

That is also the case in utterances (15) and (16):

(15) *Je sens* **une sorte d'***odeur. / Ça te fait penser à quoi* **cette sorte d'***odeur? / J'entends* **une espèce de** *bruit.*
'I smell **a kind of** odour.' / 'What does that **kind of** smell remind you of?' / 'I hear **a kind of** noise.'[21]

(16) *C'est* **une forme/sorte de** *mouvement.*
'It is **a form/sort of** movement.'

However, if (15) and (16) can imply a subcategorization, they do so because of the semantic nature of nouns such as *odeur* 'odour' (Kleiber 2012; Vassiliadou and Lammert 2016; Gerhard-Krait and Vassiliadou 2017b) and *mouvement* 'movement' (Kleiber 2011) that do not have preestablished sub-categories. Therefore,

---

21 We have the same phenomenon in English with N-*like* expressions which are a way of categorizing the utterance into the category of N:

To get a better understanding of how to deal with *noise-like* signals, let's examine the best approach for measuring them (...) (http://www.mwrf.com/test-amp-measurement/techniques-making-measurements-noise-signals-spectrum-analyzer)

We show that these mirror *movement-like* deficits are associated with axonal guidance defects of two identified groups (...) (http://www.ncbi.nlm.nih.gov/pmc/articles/PMC3931503/).

they can only signal that there is a token of a smell or a movement. If anyone asks, "What kind of smell is this?", we can answer: *a kitchen smell, a smell of roses*, etc. *A sort of* or *a kind of smell* will always be a smell. If there is an identification problem, it will always concern the subcategory level, i.e., the type noun targets the subcategory of odour. Thus, it will not be an ordinary case of X into a Y categorization, 'sort of' having no effect on 'odour' itself. Some nouns such as *noise* (in 15) have hyponyms in French, so it is not a problem to identify which category they belong to; however, the denomination[22] or the identification of their tokens are at stake.

2.3.2 Second reading: Non-prototypical categorization

The second case is when an X is inside a category, while derogating from the model of reference. There is therefore a doubtful inclusion into a category, in the sense that X is not a good exemplar of it: X is a Y but does not look like a prototypical Y. In other words, X presents an important difference from the prototype, as in (17):

(17) *L'aîné portait au bras un grand panier carré où, sur un lit de branches de pin, s'étalaient quelques fleurs fanées ; il tenait à la main* **une sorte de bouquet, je devrais dire : de balai**, *dont il mâchurait puis crachait les pétales ; les fleurs étaient si sales, si flétries que je n'ai pu les reconnaître.*
– *il n'est pas bien joli,* **ton bouquet**, *mon pauvre garçon, lui ai-je dit ; qui est-ce qui va bien pouvoir t'acheter ça?*
Alors d'un coup de main il a rassemblé dans son panier une poignée d'œillets point trop fanés :
– *tenez, m'sieur ; ça c'est du frais.* (A. Gide, *Journal*, 1939)
'The eldest carried a large square basket, where, on a bed of pine branches, were spread some faded flowers; he held in his hand **a kind of bouquet**, or I should say **a kind of a broom**, whose petals he had chewed and then spat out; the flowers were so dirty, so withered that I could not recognize them.
– This is not a very pretty bouquet, is it, my poor boy, I said to him; who might buy that from you?
Then in a quick hand gesture, he gathered in his basket a handful of carnations that were not at all faded:
– here you go, sir; these ones are fresh.'

---

22 Denomination refers, in French, to the naming process as well as the relationship between the word and its referent.

The boy holds a bunch of flowers that does not look like a bunch of flowers because of their withered aspect. Despite this, it is still a bunch of flowers. The account developed above suggests in line with Prasada (2000, 2010) that the difficulty in analysing these kinds of examples lies in the establishment of connections between kinds of things and their properties.

2.3.3 Third reading: Approximate categorization

The third case is one of non-belonging or non-inclusion. X looks like a Y but stays outside of the category because of at least one excluding feature:
- X is a kind of/resembles a Y, but it is not a Y
- X looks like a Y, but it is not a Y
- X is almost a Y

In (18) even if a lynx looks like a big cat, it is not a cat, in (19) a psychologist is not a psychiatrist (not a doctor), and in (20) research on literature is not a police investigation even if the person has this impression based on similarities between the two types of investigation:

(18) *Le lynx est **une sorte de/espèce de** chat.*[23]
'The lynx is **a kind of/a species** of cat.'

(19) *Le psychologue est **une sorte de** psychiatre.*
'A psychologist is **a kind/sort of** psychiatrist.'

(20) (en parlant d'une recherche littéraire) *FJ944 : pour moi ça a été une euh une enquête **une genre une sorte d'**enquête euh d'enquête policière* (Cocoon)
'(the discussion is about research on literature) FJ944: for me it was an uh an investigation **a kind a sort of** police investigation.'

Insertion of *type*, which is almost exclusively taxonomic in French, is not possible in this third case, which means it can be used as a diagnostic to ascertain the correct interpretation:
- *X est un type de Y ('*X is a type of Y').

---

[23] In biological taxonomies, 'cat' refers to the family *Felidae* and further down the taxonomy and in everyday language the subspecies "domestic cat". *The lynx is a (domestic) cat* is not completely incorrect in English, due to the dual meaning of 'cat' as a genus and a species name, whereas *Le lynx est un chat* is a falsifiable proposition in French.

Applying a second diagnostic tool, if we remove the marker (*Le lynx est un chat*, 'The lynx is a (domestic) cat'), we fall into metaphorical usage by categorizing an element into a class that is the wrong one.

2.3.4 Fourth reading: Vagueness

Finally, the last case concerns purely vague examples such as the ones in (21)-(22), which bear no truth value. We consider this as a fourth possible interpretation known in the literature as a *vague* or *undecidable interpretation* (Kleiber 1987b; Lupu 2003; Mihatsch 2010):

(21) *J'ai vu **une sorte de** lévrier.*
'I saw **a kind of** a greyhound dog.'

(22) ***Une sorte de** lévrier a mordu un enfant.*
'**A kind of** a greyhound dog bit a child.'

With no other form of specification, (21) and (22) potentially correspond to all three types of situations. We cannot choose one or the other because there is nothing in the context that allows us to be sure whether the (token of) X belongs to the category of Y, or not (in a clear or doubtful manner). Thus, "*lévrier*" ('greyhound') is either:
- a subcategory (subtype/breed) of greyhound (Afghan greyhound, whippet, etc.),
- an atypical greyhound, but still a greyhound (because of numerous reasons), or
- not a greyhound at all (but another subspecies of dog).

If we remove the marker, the only interpretation is that of strict/clear categorization.

3 Some interesting categories in French

As we have already observed, in French, a specific set of markers is used for four distinct readings. However, most of the time, the differences observed are not connected to the markers themselves, but rather to the nouns (N2) that are used in Y position. We can illustrate this in a succinct way with the help of some arte-fact and abstract nouns as well as nouns designating ad hoc categories. These linguistic items present interesting semantic properties and raise particular issues as far as categorization is concerned, demonstrating that it is necessary to take into account the very semantics of nouns used with type noun constructions.

Artefacts are known for representing complex categories because they do not necessarily have a prototypical form; besides, they do not always share a predominant feature, except for function. What is important, therefore, is their function, as opposed to natural objects whose form is of prime importance. There is of course an intimate relationship between form and function and there are some forms that are more recognizable than others. The boundary between 'being Y' and 'not being Y' is much less clear with artefacts than it is with other categories. *Function* is indeed one of the salient aspects in regard to identification and it can take primacy over shape and Gestalt features (i.e. no formal scheme is necessarily associated with the category):

(23) *Il marchait avec **une sorte de canne**, un bâton sculpté avec goût qu'il avait trouvé on ne sait où (. . .).*
'He walked with **a kind of cane**, a stick designed/sculpted with taste that he had found somewhere'.

(24) *Il s'est fabriqué **une sorte de couvre-chef** avec un mouchoir.*
'He made himself **a kind of a hat** from a handkerchief he had'.

The point of these examples is to show that explaining things in terms of approximation is more delicate with these nouns. Considering a tastefully designed/sculpted *stick* that someone is using to walk with, as in (23), we might say that it is a *cane* and we might even say that the function (and the shape) of a simple stick can transform it into a cane. The difference between *mouchoir* 'handkerchief' and *couvre-chef*[24] 'hat' is that the handkerchief is used in (24) as a hat, while out of context and seen all by itself, one would not say that a handkerchief was a hat but. . . a handkerchief. In other words, we are somehow projecting representations onto the categories.[25]

---

24 'Couvre-chef' and 'mouchoir' are etymologically related in French (see De Antoine Court de Gébelin 1778: 218).
25 In English: While they often seem to be interchangeable words, *walking sticks* and *walking canes* are actually two very different types of product with different uses. Many people get them mixed up, but if you read on, you will be one of the elite few who know the difference between walking sticks and canes. The main difference, of course, is function (. . .) (https://justwalkers.com/mobility-blog/walking-canes-vs-walking-sticks).

A different way to show how vague predicates function is to examine abstract nouns. Vague predicates are usually intensive abstract nouns and have need of a support[26] i.e. the support gives them a qualitative feature. Intensive nouns refer to entities (i) that have neither temporal nor spatial extension (Flaux and Van de Velde 2000; e.g. a little courage does not last for less time than a lot of courage) and (ii) for which the distinction between quality and quantity is abolished: the qualifiers attached to them imply inevitably a degree of intensity (cf. *a great, deep, angelic, black, violent love*). As such, intensity is a characteristic dimension of some abstract names. Among them, emotion and property names are particularly interesting. These vague predicates are considered as intensive and syncategorematic nouns. That means they do not exist without a support (Kleiber 2014). The gradeability of corresponding adjectives (most abstract nouns are the nominal form of adjectives) colours these nouns with intensity effects:

(25) *Il a fait preuve d'**une forme de** courage. / **L'espèce, la sorte de** courage dont il fait preuve. / **Le type d'**amour qu'on lui porte. / **Ce genre d'**amour…*
'He manifested **a form of** courage.' / '**The kind, the sort of** courage that he shows.' / '**The kind/type of** love we feel towards him.' / '**This kind of** love.'[27]

So, *amour* 'love', *courage* 'courage', etc., are already vague predicates, that is categories for which we do not know exactly where the semantic boundaries lie. On the one hand, it is hard to decide whether they are instances of the category or not; on the other hand, their semantic profile is arduous to establish, and adding vagueness to vague would be problematic. Instead, we can start from the premise that these are some kinds of organizing words. It is the love that is exemplified by the person that feels love. Thus, "a kind of filial love" can be paraphrased as "love that is of the filial type", a type of love that we can feel for someone who is not necessarily our child, as in (25). But, if this is not love, what is it? It may be a kind of love that resembles friendship, for instance, nevertheless we are still in

---

26 That means that vague predicates require the presence of an element on which they must apply, called *support*. These nouns (called *relational* or *syncategorematic*) convey a relationship expressed by a genitive construction (Partee 1997; Kleiber 2014).
27 In English: By preoccupying ourselves with *romantic love*, we risk neglecting other *types of love* that are more stable or readily available and that may, especially in the longer term, prove more healing and fulfilling. The seven types of love discussed below are loosely based on classical readings (…) (cf. familial love, friendship love, etc.) (https://www.psychologytoday.com/us/blog/hide-and-seek/201606/these-are-the-7-types-love).

the category of *love*. We can also predicate *a kind of love* for an occurrence of love or a form of love that we do not understand or that does not correspond to our conceptualization of love precisely because we know that the forms of love are multiple and diverse.

A similar way of accessing categorization can be observed with nouns that have a very general meaning like *action* 'action' and *événement* 'event' that denote somehow immediate experiences which can correspond to semantic primes (Goddard and Wierzbicka 2014). What these nouns denote can be immediately identified as such, even if their lexical definition or their meaning is hard to express:

(26) *Le consentement explicite vous oblige à faire **une sorte d'action** afin de démontrer que vous exprimez votre consentement* (www.statmt.org/Reverso Context)
'Expressed consent requires you to do **some sort of action** to demonstrate that you are expressing your consent'[28]

Sort of action is an action, and it is peculiar to interpret it as an approximation. In (26), it is a type of action that expresses consent. And as there is no denomination (no name) for this kind of action, "sort of" helps to create a subcategory, that of "consent action". Further specifications can be brought up by context. *Kind/Sort of action* leads in this context to an ad hoc subtype. As soon as a noun, in the first position (X, N1), does not correspond to a taxonomic hierarchy, all of its tokens are named ad hoc. Are ad hoc categorizations approximations? We do not think so. With ad hoc categories (i.e. not lexical, pre-established categories), taxonomic expressions either target tokens (occurrences) directly or create subtypes (*via* complex expressions such as *things we take for camping*, *things we save from a fire*, *household things*) in the same way general nouns do:

(27) *Si c'est du massif, je te conseille d'utiliser un bois qui bouge pas trop **genre** le chêne, le hêtre, le pin des bois avec des fibres rigides, si tu vois ce que je veux dire.* (Chauveau-Thoumelin, 2016: 7)
'If it is solid wood, I suggest you use **a variety/kind of** wood which does not move that much, **like** oak, beech, pine with rigid fibres, if you know what I mean.'

---

28 In English, 'a psych evaluation' is a kind of action:
– I suggest you bring him in for a psych evaluation.
– Without something more substantial, I can't justify *that kind of action* (*Opus subtitles* 2016).

In (27), the classification of "wood" is made on the basis of the characteristic "which does not move that much" and an ad hoc class is formed. We choose a particular characteristic within the class of "wood" and we get a new class with subcategories like "wood that doesn't move as much", such as 'oak', etc.

With abstract nouns, an inherent classification problem becomes visible as soon as linguistic categories are (lexically) missing or when we are dealing with "mere classes/types/equivalence classes" that are not strictly speaking "kinds" (Prasada and Dillingham 2006). To sum up, approximate categorization (third reading) is hardly conceivable with the linguistic items described in this section. Thus, clear categorization is the privileged one.

4 Evidence from Latvian

Before discussing the four readings in Latvian, it is important to mention a few particularities of Latvian concerning taxonomic markers and their use.

The majority of Latvian taxons (*valsts* 'kingdom', *tips* 'type', *klase* 'class', *kārta* 'order', *dzimta* 'family', *ģints* 'genus', *suga* 'species') have never extended beyond the scientific domain. Many of the following examples are modifier uses (attributive or semi-suffix uses) according to Brems and Davidse (2010). *Klase* 'class', *kārta* 'order' and *dzimta* 'family' do appear in our corpora but they are relatively rare in contexts other than specialized or technical ones:

(28) *No trifeļu ģints Latvijā atrastas trīs dažādas **trifeļu sugas**.* (http://nosketch.korpuss.lv/)
'In Latvia three different **species** of truffles [lit. truffle GEN-PL species NOM.PL] from the truffle **genus** [lit. truffle GEN-PL **genus** GEN-SG] have been found.' (Reading 1: clear categorization)

Unlike French, these taxonomic markers cannot appear together with artefacts and abstract nouns, except the pure taxonomic cases:

(29) *Īsta draudzība – tas ir **pirmais draudzības tips**, kas ir balstīts uz savstarpēju uzticību, mīlestību un sapratni.* (https://zvaigznutulks.lv/)
'Real friendship – this is the first **type** of friendship [lit. first friendship GEN-SG **type** NOM-SG] that is based on mutual trust, love and understanding.' (Reading 1: clear categorization)

Abstract nouns (examples 30 and 32) as well as artefacts (31), are generally preceded by non-taxonomic markers, whose semantics originates in comparison or exemplification, like *tāds kā* and *it kā* (*such as, as, like*, etc.):[29]

(30) *Dažādi nodarbojāmies, tomēr manī vēl joprojām bija **tāds kā nemiers**.*
(http://nosketch.korpuss.lv/)
'We did different things, but I still had [something] **like** anxiety [lit. [something] **like** an anxiety NOM.SG].'

(31) *Viņš improvizēja. Viņš sēdēja uz pakāpiena kādu ārdurvju priekšā, viņš bija zemē izklājis **tādu kā galdautu**, uz tā bija novietots viņa vijoles futrālis, kurā bija iesviestas pāris monētas.* (http://nosketch.korpuss.lv/)
'He improvised. He was sitting on the steps in front of the door; he had laid on the floor [something] **like** a tablecloth [lit. [something] **like** a tablecloth ACC.SG], on which he had placed his purple case, containing a few coins.'

(32) *Tad es jūtos . . . neērti . . . Man ir **it kā kauns**, ka pievēršu sev pārāk lielu uzmanību.* (http://nosketch.korpuss.lv/)
'Then I feel . . . uncomfortable . . . I feel **a kind of** shame [lit. I have **kind of** shame NOM.SG] that I pay too much attention to myself.'

From the list of taxonomic markers, we have retained two items, *suga* ('species') and *tips* ('type'), whose uses go beyond strictly scientific domains, and which are remarkable both for their frequency in the corpora and for their semantic and morphosyntactic specificities.[30]

4.1 Clear categorization

Suga and *tips* ensure above all the first reading (see Section 2.3.1), that is to say, they build a clear and unambiguous categorial membership. It is also important to specify that, in Latvian, the defining determinant is always placed before its

---

29 As one of our reviewers noticed, "in many languages, comparison markers compete with taxonomic nouns to express approximative categorization".
30 Whilst *tips* 'type' (from the Latin *typus*) is known in several Indo-European languages, *suga* 'species' is a borrowing from the Livonian language (Karulis 2001: 954), a member of the Uralic family with no direct links to Latvian (which is a Baltic language).

incident, so in example (33), the defining determinant *drauga* 'friend' (in the genitive) appears before *suns* 'dog':

(33) *mana drauga suns*
 'My friend's dog'
 [lit. my friend-GEN-SG dog NOM.SG]

Therefore, the syntactic structure proper to French and English, as in the example seen above, *J'ai vu une sorte de lévrier* 'I saw a kind of greyhound' (only as far as the fourth reading 'vagueness' is concerned) will trigger in Latvian a pure taxonomic reading with the following order: specific item in the genitive + taxonomic marker + generic items[31] (as in 34 below):

(34) *Es redzēju **kurtu sugas suni**.*
 'I saw a greyhound (dog).'
 [lit. greyhound GEN-PL **breed** GEN-SG dog ACC.SG]

We consider this word order as an additional constraint prohibiting here any other type of reading except taxonomic one. Unlike English and French, where the taxonomic marker precedes the specific item, the taxonomic marker in Latvian is always following the specific item. In addition, the presence of both specific and generic items is mandatory. This order is very rigorous and does not imply doubting or vagueness as to the specification/identification of X. Indeed, the markers which in Latvian imply an approximate reading precede the specific item, but these markers do not come from taxonomy (except *tipa* which will be discussed later in this section).[32] Thus, for example, the marker *tāds kā* (*like*) X which implies an undecidable reading. However, it is important to notice that undecidable reading is constrained when the noun falls under pre-established taxonomy, as it is the case with 'greyhound'. Therefore, the utterance in (35) is perceived in Latvian as artificial, whereas (36) and (37) are attested in our corpus, as illustrated in the complete examples given in (38) and (39):

(35) *Es redzēju **tādu kā kurtu**.*
 'I saw [something] **like** a greyhound.'
 [lit. [something] **like** a greyhound ACC.SG]

---

[31] As we have seen above, the specific term is generally a hyponym and the generic term corresponds to a hypernym.
[32] See a similar discussion for Russian syntax in Kolyaseva and Davidse (2018).

(36) *Es redzēju **tādu kā cilvēku.***
'I saw [something] **like** a man.'

(37) ***tādu kā gaiteni***
'**like** a corridor'

(38) *Tad tumsa pilnīgi izgaisa, un es redzēju **tādu kā cilvēku**. Viņš bija tērpies viss baltā.* (http://livars.blogspot.com/)
'Then the darkness was completely illuminated, and I saw [something] **like** a man. [lit. [something] **like** a man ACC.SG]. He was dressed in white.'

(39) *Es redzēju **tādu kā gaiteni** – tas bija tumšs, sienas bija kā no tumšiem akmeņiem, tas bija ļoti, ļoti garš.* (http://kokteilis.la.lv/)
'I saw [something] like a corridor – it was dark, the walls were **like** dark stones, it was very, very long.'
[lit. [something] **like** a corridor ACC.SG]

The marker *suga* most often participates in the construction of ad hoc categories and is used when taxonomy is not strictly defined. Thus, in the examples below, the Y category is not a pre-existing one, but constructed in and by the discourse. In (40), the category of lovers is built first and then the token (*he*, the man) X is excluded from it. In (41), the man X is identified as being a member, as belonging to the category Y: *izlutināto vīriešu suga* [lit. spoiled men-GEN-PL type-GEN-SG], 'a spoiled **type** of guy':

(40) *Mēs dzeram lētu skrūvi – šņabi ar toniku, vai džinu ar toniku, man bija vienalga. Es garšu nejutu. Esmu izstāstījusi sarunu ar Āri, bet māsa smējās un paskaidroja: – **Viņš nav no mīlnieku sugas**, viņš ir sportists, kurš jēgu redz tikai darbā.* (http://nosketch.korpuss.lv/)
'We drank cheap drinks – vodka tonic, or gin tonic, I couldn't care less. I didn't taste it. I told her about my conversation with Aris, but my sister laughed and said: "He's not from that **species** of lovers [lit. he is not from lovers-GEN-PL **species**-GEN-SG], he's an athlete who only deems work sensible."'

(41) *Ilgi skatījās brūnajā dzērienā. Garas, tumšas, biezas uz augšu uzliektas skropstas kā bērnam. **Izlutināto vīriešu suga**. Aizkustinoša nevarība un maigums*

piemita šai pozai. Vai arī es esmu līdzīga tām sievietēm, kas, sastapušas šāda tipa vīriešus, pārtop žēlsirdīgajās māsās, apmātās būtnēs. (http://nosketch.korpuss.lv/)
'Long, dark, thick, curved eyelashes like those of a child. A spoiled **type** of guy.
[lit. spoiled men-GEN-PL **species**-GEN-SG]. A moving incapacity and softness emanating from this pose. Am I one of those women who, upon meeting this **type** of man, turn into nurses, possessed beings?'

The learned character of *suga* gives a stability and an almost scientific rigour to the ad hoc category, and it is therefore never used as a hedge.

Tips had a different history, most probably because being a loan from Russian типа (t'ipa). It entered standard Latvian by giving rise to two derivative forms: *tipa*, an invariable form derived from the genitive of *tips* 'type', and *ķipa*, with palatalized [k].[33] The latter is peculiar to the informal register of oral Latvian: it is classified as slang by online dictionary *tezaurs.lv*.[34]

Latvian *tips* allows all four readings, depending on the syntactic organization of the utterance and the semantic properties of the noun. Thus, the first reading is ensured by the following morphosyntactic organization of the utterance: X Noun-GEN-PL *tipa*-GEN Y, with the first noun in the genitive plural. This order is more common and is used in cases of scientific taxonomy; it communicates clear categorization (as with *suga*):

(42)   *Pekiniešu **tipa suņuks***
       'A Pekingese (**type of**) puppy'
       [lit. pekingese-GEN-PL **type**-GEN.SG puppy- NOM.SG]

In what follows, we will analyse the examples with *tips* allowing different readings: from non-prototypical categorization to approximate and vagueness reading. We are going to review a certain number of syntactic, semantic and morphological parameters (such as singular or plural of the specific item, semantics of the scope of the marker, position of the specific item relative to the generic item, etc.), whose combination can trigger a particular kind of reading.

---

33 Upeniece (2009: 29).
34 https://tezaurs.lv/%C4%B7ipa:3.

4.2 From clear categorization to vagueness: Problem of singular/plural opposition of the specific item

The change of the number of the first item from the plural to the singular immediately questions the clear categorization. X Noun-GEN-SG *tipa*-GEN Y with the first item in the genitive singular can have varied readings: non-prototypical categorization, approximate categorization and, finally, vagueness:

(43) *Pekinieša **tipa suņuks***
 'A Pekingese-**type** puppy'
 [lit. pekingese -GEN-SG **type**-GEN.SG puppy-NOM.SG]

As the example (43) shows, the change in the number of the noun leaves the reading open: it can just as well be a dog breed of Pekingese as a dog resembling a Pekingese but not belonging to the breed. It should be noted that in the case of pre-established taxonomies such as *dog breeds*, Latvian prefers the *suga* marker which permits only a reading of clear categorization, to the marker *tips*, and the preceding item in the genitive plural to the genitive singular (44):

(44) *Pekiniešu **sugas** suns*
 'A Pekingese (**breed**) puppy'
 [lit. pekingese-GEN-PL **breed**-GEN.SG dog-NOM.SG]

In cases such as the one illustrated in (43), we have a series of parameters allowing the uncertain reading: the marker *tips*, the singular of the noun preceding the marker, as well as the semantics of the second item which does not refer to a representative member of the class (see *suņuks* = a small dog, a puppy, so not representative of a breed or species of dog). The following examples illustrate the same phenomena:

(45) *Apes novada Dārzciemā (pie dolomītu karjera) pieklīdis **pekinieša tipa suņuks** ar zaļu blusu siksniņu. Nogādāts dzīvnieku mājā Astes un Ūsas Alūksnē.* (http://nosketch.korpuss.lv/)
 'In the district of Ape Darzciems (near the dolomite quarry), a Pekingese-**type** puppy [lit. pekingese-GEN-SG **tipa**-GEN.SG. puppy-NOM.SG.]. has been found with a green flea strap. He is currently at the shelter *Astes un Usas* in Aluksne.'

(46) Suņukam ir 5 mēneši, spriežot pēc izskata, tāds **vilka tipa puikiņš sanāk**. Mūsu uzdevums – sameklēt Cīkariņam labas mājas. Nav suņuks ne pārāk diža auguma, ne dikti daiļa un cēla izskata. Viens feins suņuks, kuram vajag mājas un kārtīgus saimniekus. (http://nosketch.korpuss.lv/)
'The puppy is 5 months old, judging from its appearance, **a sort of** a little wolf [lit. that wolf-GEN-SG **tipa**-GEN.SG puppy-NOM.SG]. Our goal is to find it a good home. It's not so big, nor gracious nor beautiful. A nice puppy in need of a home and a decent owner.'

In (45) and (46), the whole context leads us to a vague reading: there is no certainty as to either the age or the breed of the puppy, which is only identified by its appearance. Thereby, we cannot say with certainty that changing the number of the noun disambiguates the reading. The singular, erasing the differentiation between the occurrences of the class, appears regularly where diversity (individuation) is not at stake.

(47) Viesu ērtībai teritorijā būs organizētas ēdināšanas zonas ar bufetēm un **restorāna tipa apkalpošanu**, VIP zonas ar lieliskiem bāriem un **restorāna tipa apkalpošanu**. (http://nosketch.korpuss.lv/)
'For the convenience of the guests, there will be catering areas organized with buffets and restaurant-**type** service, VIP areas with excellent bars and restaurant-**type** service.'
[lit. restaurant-GEN-SG **type**-GEN.SG service-ACC.SG] (Reading 1: clear categorization)

In the example (47) above, since restaurant-type service is the type of service found in a restaurant, we have here the first reading.

(48) Tātad, saskaņā ar mūsu abu rakstisko vienošanos, būvēsim māju, kurā būs viena 25 m2 liela dzīvojamā istaba (vienlaikus guļamistaba, virtuve, ēdamistaba un viesistaba – to laikam sauc par **studijas tipa mājokli**).
'Thus, in accordance with our two written agreements, we will build a one-room house of 25 m^2 (a bedroom, a kitchen, a dining room and a living room – this is **what would be called** a 'studio' type of dwelling).'
[lit. studio-GEN-SG **type**-GEN.SG dwelling-ACC.SG] (Reading 1: clear categorization)

In the example (48), the noun 'studio' refers to a pre-established category (a studio flat is a type of dwelling: X is a type of Y) and invokes a taxonomic reading.

With ad hoc categories too, there is a trend towards the plural use as in (49). Nevertheless, there are also cases where the plural is impossible, for example with categories built from a proper name, as in (50):

(49) *Mūziklu **tipa** franču pilsētiņa.*
 'A **musicals-type** French town.'
 [lit. musicals-GEN-PL **type**-GEN.SG. French town-NOM.SG.]

(50) *Es balsošu par Godmaņa **tipa** cilvēku.*
 'I will vote for a Godmanis **type of** person.'
 [lit. Godmaņa-GEN-SG **type**-GEN.SG person- ACC.SG.]

We want to highlight that among linguists there is no unanimous agreement on the conditions requiring the use of the singular or the plural. In general, the choice seems to be dependent on the semantic features of the noun:[35] the singular relates to a generalized feature, *ielas kurpes* 'street shoes' [lit. GEN-SG shoes-NOM-PL], *mājas zvirbulis* 'house sparrow' [lit. house GEN-SG. sparrow NOM-SG], *skolotāja profesija* 'teaching profession' [lit. teacher GEN-SG profession NOM-SG], *ziemas apģērbs* 'winter clothes' [lit. winter GEN-SG clothes NOM.PL], etc. The plural mostly refers to scientific terminology like the classification of plants, diseases, insect biotopes, etc. However, it is recognized that linguistic tradition (norms and prescriptive grammar) plays a preponderant role in the choice of singular or plural forms. The trends noted above during the analysis of our corpus thus call for a more in-depth study.

4.3 Approximate categorization

The utterances triggering an approximate reading can have two variants of morphosyntactic organization. The first one (with the first item in genitive singular) coincides with the one that we discussed above, and which suggests a clear categorization. The third reading (non-inclusion in the category) relates then to the semantics of the name constituting the scope of the marker.

---

[35] Valsts Valodas Komisija (VVK). Morfoloģiskais aspekts. http://www.vvk.lv/index.php?sadala=221&id=711.

(51) *Tīna par pašas godam nopelnītu un rūpīgi krātu naudiņu iegādājusies sev automašīnu Rover 75. Mašīna ir otrā lielā dziedātājas dāvana sev, kas pirkta par pašas pelnītu naudu – pirmā bija ausu monitori. **"Tas ir Jaguāra tipa auto** – abi ir līdzīgi un nereti tiek jaukti. Sen jau biju noskatījusi šo mašīnu, jo arī mans tētis tādu iegādājās.* (http://nosketch.korpuss.lv/)
'Tina bought herself a car, the Rover 75, with her carefully saved money, the car which is the second greatest gift that the singer has offered herself, the first being the ear monitor. "It's a Jaguar-**type** car – the two are similar and are often mixed. I've been looking for this car for a long time because my father bought it too.'
[lit. It is Jaguar-GEN-SG **type**-GEN.SG car NOM.SG]

Being a well-known brand of car (pre-established category) *Tas ir Jaguāra tipa auto/It's a Jaguar-type car* (51) implies that the car in question looks like a Jaguar but is not a Jaguar. We are dealing here with a non-inclusion of X to the category Y.

The second variant allowing an approximate reading is specific to the familiar register of Latvian and concerns the discursive semantics of *tips*. This implies the change of morphological, syntactic and semantic parameters. Thus, *tipa* (or oral palatalized variant *ķipa*) does not require genitive case: Noun-NOM-SG/PL *tipa* (invariable form) Noun NOM.SG/PL. It is a case of non-taxonomic reading par excellence. Its scope is very wide: NP, VP, etc., as well as an entire sentence and *tipa* is always anterior to its scope. Its function can be compared to those of *genre* in oral French or *like* in English:

(52) *No kabatas izvilka vīrieša iedoto naudaszīmi un atlocīja – tas bija **no kāda spēļu žurnāla izgriezts tipa desmitnieks**.* (http://nosketch.korpuss.lv/)
'She took out the banknote that the man had given her and unfolded it – it was **like** a tenner [ten-dollar bill], cut from some game magazine.'
[lit. from some game magazine cut out **type** tenner NOM.SG]

In (52), the 'tenner' that was supposed to be a banknote is in fact just a piece of paper, but the only way to describe it is using the category of banknote. We thus have an approximate categorization (reading 3): X (the piece of paper) does not belong to the category of banknotes but looks like it.

It is interesting to compare example (53) to (54) below. In (53), the invariable form of the marker *tipa* leads to approximate categorization, whereas in (54), the construction with the first item in the genitive preceding the taxonomic marker allows a clear categorization:

(53) *Cittautieši tiek diskriminēti un [. . .] valdība gribot celt šiem,* **tipa, geto priekšpilsētas** *ar pastāvīgi pagarināmām uzturēšanās atļaujām.*
'Non-Latvians are discriminated against and the government [. . .] wants to build for them **like** ghetto suburbs, with constantly renewed residence permits.'
[lit. **like** ghetto suburbs NOM.PL][36]

(54) *Sociālo spriedzi rada nabadzīgu imigrantu pieplūdums urbānajos centros. Izolētas, turīgas kopienas ārpus pilsētām kontrastē ar* **geto tipa pilsētu centriem**. (http://nosketch.korpuss.lv/)
'Social tensions are caused by the influx of poor immigrants into urban centres. Isolated and wealthy communities outside of the cities contrast with ghetto-**type** downtowns.'
[lit. ghetto GEN.SG.**type**-GEN.SG of city GEN.PL centre INSTR.PL]

In the examples (55)–(56), *X ķipa Y* means that *X looks like Y but it is not a real, true Y*:[37]

(55) *un tad vietējā "influencere" ieliek instagramā bildi, kur ir aizdedzinātas vairākas sveces MEŽĀ.* **ķipa sveču konkursiņš** *un tā. es saprotu, ka bildei, bet nu kur prāts?* (twitter.com)
'and then a local "influencer" posts a photo on Instagram where several candles are lit IN A FOREST. **Supposedly** a candle contest and all that. I understand that it's for a photo, but where is the brain?'
[lit. **like** a candle GEN.PL contest NOM.SG]

(56) *Vakar sakatījos filmu par rembo. Tur darbība kā vienmēr, ir sliktie un labie,* **ķipa labie**, *un viņi kādu glābj.* (twitter.com)
'The action is as always, there are the bad ones and the good ones, the **supposed** good ones, and they are saving someone.'
[lit. good ones NOM.PL **like** good ones NOM.PL]

The staging of the picture in (55) wants to look like a candle contest but is really a fake; the "good ones" in (56) are fake good guys but they are presented as if they

---

[36] The noun *ghetto*, as a loan word, remains invariable in Latvian.
[37] This use of *tipa* is very close to the use of Russian *tipa* that Kolyaseva and Kisiel (Ch. 12, this volume) call a 'falsity marker.'

were truly good. So, here, *tipa* specifies X as having the appearance of Y, while the real X is different, or even the opposite of what Y represents.

4.4 From non-prototypical categorization to vagueness

The reading suggesting non-prototypical categorization is the least frequent in our corpora. This reading is more appropriate for contexts comprising non-taxonomic markers. The examples which allow the second reading are also open to an approximate one (the third reading), and it is only the broader context that can remove the ambiguity:

(57) *Krūtī iedūrās adata – **tā bija, tipa, valsts simbolbroša**.* (http://nosketch.korpuss.lv/)
'The chest was pierced by a needle – it was **like** a national symbol-brooch.'
[lit. it was **type** brooch-national symbol NOM.SG]

In (57), the needle (a priori any needle, unspecified) is identified (recognized) as a part of a national traditional symbol-brooch: *simbolbroša/symbol-brooch* is a compound word in Latvian and designates a whole category of Latvian traditional symbols which one hangs on the chest. We can therefore admit that the jewel in question looked like this type of brooch-symbol, but we cannot be sure if it was indeed the traditional brooch but not immediately identifiable, or another brooch of the same style. The interpretation therefore remains undecidable.

That said, *tipa/ķipa* is conducive to building an undecidable reading. So, when we say:

(58) *Viņš ir **ķipa ārsts**.*
'He is **like** a doctor.'
[lit. **like** a doctor NOM.SG]

three readings are acceptable: non prototypical categorization ('X is not a typical representative of Y but is still Y'), approximate categorization ('X is not really Y') and vagueness interpretations. In (59), three interpretations are possible: flying saucer as a subtype of the vessel (clear categorization), an atypical member of the category (non-prototypical categorization) or a vessel resembling to a flying saucer, but not being one (approximate categorization):

(59) Un no tā sarkanuma tāds kuģis kā no miglas izpeld, tāds gaisa **kuģis, tipa lidojošais šķīvītis**, un balss, tāda pērkonīga, pa visu debesi saka [. . .]. (http://nosketch.korpuss.lv/)
 'And from this redness, a ship comes out of the fog, **like** an airship, kind of a flying saucer and a voice, so soft, all over the sky says [. . .].'
 [lit.: airship NOM.SG, **like** a flying saucer NOM.SG.]

5 Discussion

In this article, we put in perspective the complexity of distinguishing semantic and pragmatic approaches as far as the words *approximation* and *vagueness* are concerned. It is nevertheless difficult to ensure that interpretations are well-grounded, and that one interpretation prevails over the others. However, this way of proceeding allowed us not to oppose approximation and categorization, but to consider them as two interpretative options instantly available to language users. Moreover, as the type-noun markers are vague terms when out of context, we suggest that one of the keys to the solution of the problem lies in a more profound analysis of the lexical properties of nouns used with those markers and the parameters that allow for their semantic specification (see Section 3). We also pointed out that when clear categorization is not easily achievable, speakers tend to use terms such as *espèce/suga* in order to locate a token (instance) in reference to more stable representations. Semantic and pragmatic dimensions are finally difficult to distinguish. In fact, what seems to prevail is that when speakers use type nouns, there is always an intent; thus, what is important to make clear is the identification of the speaker's intention.

We also verified whether the same semantic multifunctionality of the studied expressions is present in the studied languages or if, on the contrary, it implies specific constraints in the languages under examination. Thus, we observed in Latvian the same tendencies as to the complementarity of the approximation and categorization operations, but more rigidity than French as to the distinction of these operations: with the exception of *tipa*, taxonomic markers do not go beyond the categorial reading.[38] Lexical and grammatical variations, syntactic categories such as word-order, and declensions play a major role as far as Latvian is concerned. A more systematic study of the use of *suga*, *ķipa* and *tipa* remains

---

38 As suggested by one of our anonymous reviewers, "in French, only *genre* 'genus' and *espèce* 'species' allow categorization outside of scientific taxonomy; other taxonomic nouns (*classe* 'class', *famille* 'family', *règne* 'kingdom', etc.) do not allow it."

to be done. The parameters we exposed, namely the noun involved (comparison or taxonomic markers), the cases (nominative or genitive), and the grammatical number (singular or plural), should also be studied separately in relation to the interpretation of the utterances. Finally, we pointed out that type nouns are categorization markers above all and that categorization processes can follow various paths and take on different faces. The inherent indeterminacy of type nouns must be factored into any analysis of their usage.

For the present paper, we insisted on markers derived from taxonomic expressions. We have observed that most of them remain taxonomic par excellence, and do not combine with abstract nouns and artefacts. The grammatical number of the noun to the left of the marker (X) partially determines whether or not the utterance is open to an approximate categorization; however, an approximate reading still depends on the semantic features of the noun in Y position and does not occur when it modifies a term of scientific or pre-established taxonomy. More research must be done by examining in a systematic and quantitative way the pairing between type noun markers and nouns appearing in the second (Y) position of the structure (X *marker* Y) in order to reveal the possible affinities, recurrences and preferences of certain markers to combine with specific noun types.

References

Adamczyk, Magdalena. 2015. Do hedges always hedge? On non-canonical multifunctionality of *jakby* in polish. *Pragmatics* 25(3), 321–344. https://doi.org/10.1075/prag.25.3.01ada (accessed 20 December 2021).

Aijmer, Karin. 2002. *English discourse particles. Evidence from a corpus*. Amsterdam & Philadelphia: John Benjamins.

Aijmer, Karin, Ad Foolen & Anne-Marie Simon-Vandenbergen. 2006. Pragmatic markers in translation: a methodological proposal. In Kerstin Fischer (ed.), *Approaches to discourse particles*, 101–114, Amsterdam: Elsevier.

Andersen, Gisle. 2000. The role of the pragmatic marker *like* in utterance interpretation. In Gisle Andersen & Thorstein Fretheim (eds.), *Pragmatic markers and propositional attitude*, 17–38, Amsterdam: John Benjamins.

Barsalou, Lawrence W. 1995 [1991]. Deriving categories to achieve goals. In Gordon H. Bower (ed.), *The psychology of learning and motivation: Advances in research and theory*, 1–64, San Diego, CA: Academic Press.

Barsalou, Lawrence W. 1995. Storage side effects: Studying processing to understand learning. In Ashwin Ram & David Leake (eds.), *Goal-driven learning*, 407–419. Cambridge, MA: MIT Press/Bradford Books.

Barsalou, Lawrence W. 2010. Grounded cognition: Past, present and future. *TopiCS* 2(10). 716–724. https://doi.org/10.1111/j.1756-8765.2010.01115.x (accessed 20 December 2021).

Barsalou, Lawrence W. 2013. *Ad hoc* categories. *Memory & Cognition* 1. 211–227. https://doi.org/10.3758/BF03196968 (accessed 20 December 2021).

Bat-Zeev Shyldkrot, Hava, Silvia Adler & Maria Asnes (eds.). 2016. *Nouveaux regards sur l'approximation et la précision*. Paris: Honoré Champion.

Bazzanella, Carla. 2011. Indeterminacy in dialogue. *Language and dialogue* 1(1). 21–43. https://doi.org/10.1075/ld.1.1.04baz (accessed 20 December 2021).

Benigni, Valentina. 2014. Strategie di approssimazione lessicale in russo e in italiano. In Olga Inkova, Marina di Filippo & François Esvan (eds.), *L'archittetura del testo. Studi contrastivi slavo-romanzi*, 203–224. Alessandria: Edizioni dell'Orso.

Benninger, Céline & Hélène Vassiliadou. 2020. Quand *chose* et *genre* se croisent : Catégorisation et noms atypiques. In Machteld Meulleman, Silvia Palma & Anne Theissen (eds.), *Mélanges en l'honneur d'Emilia Hilgert*, 105–124. Reims: EPURE.

Brems, Lieselotte. 2011. *Layering of size and type noun constructions in English*. Berlin & Boston: De Gruyter Mouton.

Brems, Liselotte and Kristin Davidse. 2010. The Grammaticalisation of nominal type noun constructions with *kind/sort of*: Chronology and paths of change. *English Studies* 91(2). 180–202. https://doi.org/10.1080/00138380903355023 (accessed 20 December 2021).

Carey, Susan. 2009. *The origin of concepts*. Oxford: Oxford University Press.

Carston, Robyn. 1996. Enrichment and loosening: complementary processes in deriving the proposition expressed. *UCL Working Papers in Linguistics* 8. 61–88. https://www.phon.ucl.ac.uk/publications/WPL/96papers/carston.pdf (accessed 20 December 2021).

Channell, Joanna. 1994. *Vague Language*. Oxford: Oxford University Press.

Chao, Linda L. & Alex Martin. 2000. Representation of manipulable man-made objects in the dorsal stream. *Neuroimage* 12(4). 478–484. https://doi.org/10.1006/nimg.2000.0635 (accessed 20 December 2021).

Chauveau-Thoumelin, Pierre. 2016. De l'exemplification à la catégorisation approximative : étude de la construction [[X]SN genre [Y]SN], SHS Web of Conferences 27, paper presented at the Congrès Mondial de Linguistique Française – CMLF 2016, 1–16. https://doi.org/10.1051/shsconf/20162712005n (accessed 20 December 2021).

Danon-Boileau, Laurent & Marie-Annick Morel. 1997. *Question, point de vue, genre, style. . .* : les noms prépositionnels en français contemporain, *Faits de langues* 9. 193–200. https://www.persee.fr/docAsPDF/flang_1244-5460_1997_num_5_9_1155.pdf (accessed 20 December 2021).

Davidse, Kristin & Emeline Doyen. 2009. Using teenage versus adult forum data for the study of language change: Is the grammaticalization of French *genre* as advanced as that of English *sort* and *kind*? In Stef Slembrouck, Miriam Taverniers & Micke Van Herreweghe (eds.), *From will to well. Studies in linguistics offered to Anne-Marie Simon-Vandenbergen*. 135–146. Gent: Academia Press.

Davidse, Kristin, Lieselotte Brems, Peter Willemse, Emeline Doyen, Jessica Kiermeer & Elfi Thoelen. 2013. A comparative study of the grammaticalized uses of English 'sort (of)' and French 'genre (de)' in teenage forum data. In Emanuele Miola (ed.), *Standard and non-standard languages on the internet. Languages Go Web*, 41–66. Alessandria: Edizioni dell'Orso.

Denison, David. 2002. History of the *sort of* construction family. Paper presented at the Second International Conference on Construction Grammar. University of Helsinki, 6–8 September 2002.

Denison, David. 2005. The grammaticalisations of *sort of*, *kind of* and *type of* in English. Paper presented at New Reflections on Grammaticalization 3, University of Santiago de Compostela, 17–20 July 2005.

De Smedt, Liesbeth, Lieselotte Brems & Kristin Davidse. 2007. NP-internal functions and extended uses of the 'type' nouns *kind*, *sort*, and *type*: towards a comprehensive, corpus-based description. In Roberta Fachinetti et al. (eds.), *Corpus linguistics 25 years on*, 225–255. Amsterdam: Rodopi.

Flaux, Nelly & Danièle Van de Velde. 2000. *Les noms en français: esquisse de classement*. Paris: Ophrys.

Feldermeier, Kara D. & Marta Kutas. 2001. Meaning and modality: influences of context, semantic memory organization and perceptual predictability on picture processing. *Journal of Experimental Psychology* 27. 202–224. https://doi.org/10.1037/0278-7393.27.1.202 (accessed 20 December 2021).

Fuchs, Catherine. 1986. Le vague et l'ambigu : deux frères ennemis. *Quaderni di Semantica* 2. 235–245.

Genome, James & Tania Lombrozo. 2012. Concept possession, experimental semantics, and hybrid theories of reference. *Philosophical Psychology* 25. 1–26. https://doi.org/10.1080/09515089.2011.627538 (accessed 20 December 2021).

Gerhard-Krait, Francine & Hélène Vassiliadou. 2014. Lectures taxinomique et/ou floue appliquées aux noms : quelques réflexions. . . *Travaux de linguistique* 69. 57–75. https://doi.org/10.3917/tl.069.0057 (accessed 20 December 2021).

Gerhard-Krait, Francine & Hélène Vassiliadou. 2017a. Lectures taxinomique, approximative et floue : quelques pistes supplémentaires, Présentation. *Syntaxe et Sémantique* 18. 11–18. https://doi.org/10.3917/ss.018.0011 (accessed 20 December 2021).

Gerhard-Krait, Francine & Hélène Vassiliadou. 2017b. Clapotis, murmures et autres manifestations sonores: les méandres de l'approximation catégorielle. *Syntaxe et Sémantique* 18. 19–43. https://doi.org/10.3917/ss.018.0019 (accessed 20 December 2021).

Gerhard-Krait, Francine, Marie Lammert & Hélène Vassiliadou. 2019. Exemplification et sous-catégorisation: identité de mécanismes et altérité des moyens. Paper presented at the 4th *International Symposium*, *Language for International Communication* LINCS 2019, Université de Lettonie, Riga, 11–12 April 2019.

Goddard, Cliff & Anna Wierbzbicka. 2014. *Words & meanings: Lexical semantics across domains. Languages & cultures*. Oxford: Oxford University Press.

Haillet, Pierre Patrick. 2018. Entité lexicale: *genre*. In Claude Anscombre, Maria Luisa Donaire & Pierre Patrick Haillet (eds.), *Opérateurs discursifs du français 2, Éléments de description sémantique et pragmatique*, 237–248. Berne: Peter Lang.

Hampton, James. 2010. Stability in concepts and evaluating the truth of generic statements. In Francis Jeffrey Pelletier (ed.), *Kinds, things, and sStuff. Mass terms and generics*, 80–99. Oxford: Oxford University Press.

Inkova, Olga. Forth. Approximation et structures sémantiques apparentées. *Langages*.

Kahlaoui, Karima, Bernadette Ska, Clotilde Degroot & Yves Joanette. 2010. Neurobiological bases of the semantic processing of words. In Jackie Guendouzi, Filip Loncke & Mandy J. Williams (eds.), *The handbook of psycholinguistic and cognitive processes*, chapter 5, 99–118. New York and London: Taylor & Francis Group.

Karulis, Konstantins. 2001. *Latviešu etimoloģijas vārdnīca*. Riga: Avots.

Keizer, Evelien. 2007. *The English noun phrase. The nature of linguistic categorization*. Cambridge : Cambridge University Press.

Kleiber, Georges. 1987a. Mais à quoi sert donc le mot *chose* ? Une situation paradoxale. *Langue française* 73. 109–128. https://www.jstor.org/stable/41558288 (accessed 20 December 2021).

Kleiber, Georges. 1987b. Quelques réflexions sur le vague dans les langues naturelles. In Sylvie Mellet (ed.), *Hommage à Guy Serbat*, 157–172. Paris: Société pour l'Information Grammaticale.

Kleiber, Georges. 1990. *La sémantique du prototype. Catégories et sens lexical*. Paris: PUF.

Kleiber, Georges. 2011. Dans le « sens » du mouvement : éléments de sémantique conceptuelle du nom MOUVEMENT. In Sarah Dessì Schmid, Ulrich Detges, Paul Gévaudan, Wiltrud Mihatsch and Richard Waltereit (eds.), *Rahmen des Sprechens. Beiträge zu Valenztheorie, Varietätenlinguistik, Kreolistik, Kognitiver und Historischer Semantik. Peter Koch zum 60. Geburtstag*, 271–283. Tübingen: Gunter Narr.

Kleiber, Georges. 2012. De la dénomination à la désignation. Le paradoxe ontologico-dénominatif des odeurs. *Langue française* 174. 45–58. https://doi.org/10.3917/lf.174.0045 (accessed 20 December 2021).

Kleiber, Georges. 2014. Détermination et noms de propriétés : la réponse en termes de 'variétés'. In Emilia Hilgert, Silvia Palma, Pierre Frath & René Daval (eds.), *Des théories du sens et de la référence*, 123–138. Reims: EPURE.

Kolyaseva, Alena and Kristin Davidse. 2018. A typology of lexical and grammaticalized uses of Russian *tip, tipa, po tipu*. *Russian Linguistics* 42(2). 191–220. https://doi.org/10.1007/s11185-018-9193-9 (accessed 20 December 2021).

Lakoff, George. 1973. Hedges: A study in meaning criteria and the logic of fuzzy concepts. *Journal of Philosophical Logic* 2(4). 458–508. https://asset-pdf.scinapse.io/prod/2082550766/2082550766.pdf (accessed 20 December 2021).

Lakoff, George. 1987. *Women, fire and dangerous things: What categories reveal about the mind*, Chicago: University of Chicago Press.

Landolsi, Houda. 2018. *L'exemplification et ses marqueurs*. Uppsala: Acta Universitatis Upsaliensis, *Studia Romanica Upsaliensia*, 86. https://doi.org/10.4000/praxematique.5303 (accessed 20 December 2021).

Lo Baido, Maria C. 2018. Categorization *via* exemplification: Evidence from Italian. *Folia Linguistica Historica* 39. 69–95. https://doi.org/10.1515/flih-2018-0007 (accessed 20 December 2021).

Lupu, Mihaela. 2003. Concepts vagues et catégorisation. *Cahiers de Linguistique Française* 25. 291–304. https://clf.unige.ch/files/8814/4102/7666/16-Lupu_nclf25.pdf (accessed 20 December 2021).

Mauri, Caterina. 2017. Building and interpreting *ad hoc* categories: a linguistic analysis. In Joanna Blochowiak, Cristina Grisot, Stéphanie Durrleman-Tame & Christopher Laenzlinger (eds.), *Formal models in the study of language*, 297–326. Berlin: Springer.

Mauri, Caterina & Andrea Sanso (eds.). 2018. *Linguistic strategies for the construction of* ad hoc *categories: synchronic and diachronic perspectives*, Special Issue *Folia Linguistica Historica* 39. https://doi.org/10.1515/flih-2018-0001 (accessed 20 December 2021).

Medin, Douglas & Andrew Ortony. 1988. Psychological essentialism. In Stella Vosniadou and Andrew Ortoni (eds.), *Similarity and analogical reasoning*, New York: CUP.

Mihatsch, Wiltrud. 2007a. Taxonomic and meronomic superordinates with nominal coding. In Andrea Schalley & Dietmar Zaefferer (eds.), *Ontolinguistics. How ontological status shaped the linguistic coding of concepts*, 359–377. Berlin: Mouton de Gruyter.

Mihatsch, Wiltrud. 2007b. The Construction of vagueness: *Sort of* expressions in Romance languages. In Günter Radden, Klaus-Michael Koepcke, Thomas Berg & Peter Siemund (eds.), *Aspects of meaning constructing meaning: From concepts to utterances*, 225–245. Amsterdam/Philadelphia: John Benjamins.
Mihatsch, Wiltrud. 2009. L'approximation entre sens et signification : un tour d'horizon. In Dominique Verbeken (ed.), *Entre sens et signification – Constitution du sens : points de vue sur l'articulation sémantique-pragmatique*, 100–116. Paris: L'Harmattan.
Mihatsch, Wiltrud. 2010. Les approximateurs quantitatifs entre scalarité et non-scalarité. *Langue française* 165. 125–153. https://doi.org/10.3917/lf.165.0125 (accessed 20 December 2021).
Mihatsch, Wiltrud. 2016. Type-noun binominals in four romance languages. *Language Sciences* 53. 136–159. https://doi.org/10.1016/j.langsci.2015.05.009 (accessed 20 December 2021).
Murphy, Gregory L. & Edward J. Wisniewski. 1989. Categorizing objects in isolation and in scenes: What a superordinate is good for? *Journal of Experimental Psychology. Learning, Memory, and Cognition* 15(4). 572–586. https://doi.org/10.1037/0278-7393.15.4.572 (accessed 20 December 2021).
Partee, Barbara. 1997. Uniformity vs. versatility: The genitive, a case study, appendix to Theo Janssen, Compositionality. In Johan van Benthem & Alice ter Meulen (eds.), *The Handbook of Logic and Language*, 464–470. Amsterdam: Elsevier.
Pelletier, Francis Jeffrey. 2010. *Generics*: A philosophical introduction. In Francis Jeffrey Pelletier (ed.), *Kinds, things, and stuff. Mass terms and generics*, 3–15. Oxford: Oxford University Press.
Pinker, Steven & Alan Prince. 1991. *The nature of human concepts: insight from an unusual source*, Unpublished manuscript.
Prasada, Sandeep. 2000. Acquiring generic knowledge, *Trends in Cognitive Sciences* 4. 66–72. https://doi.org/10.1016/S1364-6613(99)01429-1 (accessed 20 December 2021).
Prasada, Sandeep. 2010. Conceptual representation and some forms of genericity. In Francis Jeffrey Pelletier (ed.), *Kinds, things, and stuff. Mass terms and generics*, 36–59. Oxford: Oxford University Press.
Prasada, Sandeep & Elaine Dillingham. 2006. Principled and statistical connections in common sense conception. *Cognition* 99. 73–112. https://doi.org/10.1016/j.cognition.2005.01.003 (accessed 20 December 2021).
Prince, Ellen, Charles Bosk & Joel Frader. 1982. On hedging in physician-physician discourse. In Robert J. Di Pietro (ed.), *Linguistics and the Professions*, 83–97. Norwood: Ablex.
Rosier, Laurence. 2002. *Genre* : le nuancier de sa grammaticalisation. *Travaux de linguistique* 44. 79–88. https://doi.org/10.3917/tl.044.0079 (accessed 20 December).
Rosier, Laurence. 2005. La polysémie des mots *genre, style, type*. In Olivier Soutet (ed.), *La polysémie*, 231–243. Paris: Presses Paris Sorbonne.
Roubaud, Marie-Noëlle & Liz Temple. 1988. L'approximation lexicale. *Reflets* 27. 12–13.
Rouget, Christine. 1997. *Espèce de, genre de, sorte de* : Approximatifs ou sous-catégorisateurs ? In Paulo de Carvalho & Olivier Soutet (eds.), *Psychomécanique du langage*, 289–298. Paris: Champion.
Sachs, Olga, Susanne Weis, Timo Krings, Walter Huber & Tilo Kircher. 2008. Categorical and thematic knowledge representation in the brain: Neural correlates of taxonomic and thematic conceptual relations, *Neuropsychologia* 46. 409–418. https://doi.org/10.1016/j.neuropsychologia.2007.08.015 (accessed 20 December 2021).

Schiffer, Stephen. 2003. *The things we mean*. Oxford: Oxford University Press.
Smith, Edwars & Douglas Medin. 1981. *Categories and concepts*, Cambridge: M.A.: Harvard University Press.
Smith, Nicholas. 2007. Vagueness as closeness. *Australasian Journal of Philosophy* 83(2). 157–183. https://doi.org/10.1080/00048400500110826 (accessed 20 December 2021).
Sweetser, Eve. 1989. *From etymology to pragmatics: The mind-as-body metaphor in semantic structure and semantic change*. Cambridge: Cambridge University Press.
Ungerer, Friedrich & Hans-Jörg Schmid. 1996. Levels of categorization. In Friedrich Ungerer & Hans-Jörg Schmid (eds.), *An introduction to cognitive linguistics*, chapter 2, London: Longman.
Upeniece, Aiga. 2009. Vides ietekme jauniešu valodas izvēlē: saziņa bibliotēkā. [Environmental impact in choosing a youth language: communication in the library]. *Latvian language practice: observations and suggestions. A collection of popular scientific articles*. Atb. red. L. Lauze. Nr. 4, 21–30, Rīga: LU Akadēmiskais apgāds. https://www.valodaskonsultacijas.lv/uploads/suggested_sources/4/pdf/Valodas_prakse_4.pdf#page=4 (accessed 20 December 2021).
Vassiliadou, Hélène & Marie Lammert. 2016. Odour names and hedonic dimension: evidence from Greek and French. In Melissa Barkat-Defradas & Elisabeth Motte (eds.), *Words for odours: Language skills and cultural insights*, 229–253. Cambridge: Cambridge Scholars.
Vassiliadou, Hélène & Fotiadou, Georgia. 2022. Catégorisation claire et approximative en grec et en français. In Rea Delveroudi, Sophie Vassilaki & Evanggelia Vlachou (eds.), *Approches linguistiques comparatives Grec-Français*, 123–140. Athènes: Presses Universitaires d'Athènes.
Vigneron-Bosbach, Jeanne. 2016. *Analyse constrastive des marqueurs* genre *en français,* like *en anglais et* so *en allemand dans des corpus d'oral et d'écrit présentant un faible degré de planification*. Graz : Université de Poitiers et Université Karl-Franz de Graz, dissertation.
Vladimirska, Elena. 2016. Entre le dire et le monde : le cas du marqueur discursif *genre*. In Hava Bat-Zeev Shyldkrot, Silvia Adler & Asnes Maria (eds.), *Nouveaux regards sur l'approximation et la précision*, 195–209. Paris: Honoré Champion.
Voghera, Miriam. 2017. Quando vaghezza e focus entrano in contatto: Il caso di *un attimo, anzi un attimino*. In Roberta D'Alessandro, Gabriele Iannàccaro, Diana Passino & Anna M. Thornton (eds.), *Di tutti i colori. Studi linguistici per Maria Grossmann*, 385–397. Leiden: University.
Voghera, Miriam & Laura Collu. 2017. Intentional vagueness: a corpus-based analysis of Italian and German. In Maria Napoli & Miriam Ravetto (eds.), *Exploring intensification: Synchronic, diachronic and cross-linguistic perspectives*, 371–389. (Studies in Language Companion Series 189). Amsterdam: John Benjamins Publishers.
Witkin, Andrew & Jay Tenenbaum. 1983. What is perceptual organization for? *IJKAI* 2. 1023–1026.
Yaguello, Marina. 1998. *Genre*, une particule d'un genre nouveau. *Petits faits de langue*, 18–24. Paris: Le Seuil.
Zhang, Grace Qiao & Vahid Parvaresh. 2019. *Elastic language in persuasion and comforting: A cross-cultural perspective*. Cham: Palgrave Mac Millan.

Corpora/dictionaries

Cambridge Dictionary. https://dictionary.cambridge.org/fr/ (accessed 22 May 2018).
Collection de Corpus Oraux Numériques, Cocoon (https://cocoon.huma-num.fr) (accessed 12 February 2019).
De Antoine Court de Gébelin. 1778. *Monde primitif: Dictionnaire étymologique de la langue françoise*, Paris: BNF.
Frantext. Base textuelle du XIIe au XXIe siècle, Nancy, ATILF (http://www.frantext.fr/) (accessed 15 March 2018).
FrTenTen French Web Corpus 2014 (https://app.sketchengine.eu) (accessed 12 February 2019).
lvTenTen Latvian Corpus form the Web, (https://app.sketchengine.eu) (accessed 13 April 2018).
Reverso Context (context.reverso.net) (accessed 12 February 2019).
Tezaurs Latvian (https://tezaurs.lv) (accessed 12 February 2019).
Trésor de la langue française informatisé (Tlfi) (http://atilf.atilf.fr) (accessed 12 February 2019).
Valsts Valodas Komisija (VVK). Morfoloģiskais aspekts. 2002 (http://www.vvk.lv/index.php?sadala=221&id=711) (accessed 13 April 2018).

Kate Beeching
18 Sociopragmatic variation, *sort of* and *genre* in English and French

Abstract: Type-nouns come to be exploited pragmatically for a range of functions, some of which coincide across different languages or national varieties of a language. *Sort of* and *genre*, for example, can both be used to express approximation, uncertainty, and as a focaliser. There are, however, areas where they are dissimilar: the use of *sort of* as a metacommenter is uncommon for *genre* while on the other hand *genre* can be used as a quotative in the way that *like* is in English. In Canadian French *comme* is more often used both as a quotative and an approximator. The recent rise in frequency of *genre* in European French, but more particularly in Canadian French, and access to the *Corpus de Français Parlé au Québec* allow us to examine language change in synchrony and to test theories of semantic and syntactic change, weighing up the role of psycholinguistic, sociolinguistic and language-internal factors.

1 Introduction: Aims and rationale

Pragmatic uses of expressions derived from type-noun constructions have been widely attested in different languages (see, for example, Mihatsch 2007, 2010). The motivations and syntactic pathways for pragmatic-semantic changes such as these have been the object of considerable debate in the literature. Since Sweetser's (1990) seminal work on etymology, we have better understood the cognitive basis and metaphorical exploitations which provide the link between pragmatic ambiguity, semantic change and lexical polysemy. Traugott (1982) and Traugott and Dasher's (2002) work in which they developed their IITSC (Invited Inferencing Theory of Semantic Change) made some predictions regarding the unidirection-

---

Acknowledgements: Many thanks to the organisers and participants at the "Pragmatic functions of type-nouns: a crosslinguistic phenomenon" workshop organised by Wiltrud Mihatsch and Inga Hennecke in Tübingen (18–20 June 2018) firstly for inviting me and secondly for their comments on my presentation. I would also like to thank Gaétane Dostie, Bernd Heine, Elizabeth Traugott and two anonymous reviewers for their very helpful and encouraging remarks on drafts of this paper which have enriched it considerably. Remaining faults remain of course entirely my own responsibility

Kate Beeching, University of the West of England, Bristol, e-mail: Kate.beeching41@gmail.com

ality of changes, from propositional to textual to expressive, truth-conditional to procedural, subjective to intersubjective, more lexical to less lexical. There have been ongoing debates as to whether the development of pragmatic markers (henceforth PMs[1]) should be considered as cases of grammaticalization, pragmaticalization, lexicalization, idiomaticization or cooptation. My own work (Beeching 2005, 2007a) has stressed the importance of PISC (Politeness-Induced Semantic Change) and factors to do with the nature of spoken interaction as motivations specifically for the development of PMs. Brinton (2017), meanwhile, has tested some of the predictions made by Traugott and Dasher (2002) and highlighted some pathways of syntactic change, from lexical item and from clausal construction to pragmatic marker. Brinton is scrupulous in limiting any conclusions about pathways of change to the evidence revealed through painstaking analysis of occurrences traced diachronically. Thus, as she finds little evidence to support the development of *hwaet* (the ancestor of modern-day *what*) from propositional to textual to interpersonal in the manner familiar from Traugott, she concludes that the pragmatic senses arise naturally via context-induced inferences from the interrogative sense. Brinton pushes the grammaticalization versus pragmaticalization debate to one side by suggesting that it all depends what you include in grammar. She is equally rather sceptical about Heine's (2013) notion of cooptation, which involves, in relation to pragmatic markers, a sudden rather than gradual change. She suggests (2017: 37) that: "cooptation would not seem to explain why any particular form might be suited (and hence coopted) to serve a certain pragmatic function."

Heine (2018: 28) responds that in early theories of grammaticalization, "cognitive-communicative explanations were proposed to understand some of the motivations underlying grammaticalization" and similar cognitive-communicative motivations underlie cooptation – which Heine (2018: 45) likens to pragmaticalization.

Heine et al. (2017) give a fuller description of types of cooptation and Heine (2018) provides a very detailed rationale for the fact that PMs (which he calls

---

1 The nomenclature used to describe expressions such as *well, you know, I mean, sort of* and *like* is still far from settled. I have chosen to call *sort of* and *genre* pragmatic markers following Aijmer and Simon-Vandenbergen (2006: 2) who draw the distinction between discourse markers and pragmatic markers as follows:

> Discourse marker is the term which we use when we want to describe how a particular marker signals coherence relations. Pragmatic markers as we see them are not only associated with discourse and textual functions but are also signals in the communication situation guiding the addressee's interpretation. The term as we are using it can also be defined negatively: if a word or a construction in an utterance does not contribute to the propositional, truth-functional content, then we consider it a pragmatic marker.

DMs) do not arise in the first instance as a result of grammaticalization. They are first coopted sentence elements which are used as discourse elements in the same way that parenthetical remarks like *frankly*, or *sadly*, can be used to comment on discourse rather than as part of sentence grammar. He argued in Heine (2013) that DMs are grammaticalized theticals. They are conventionalized in the sense that they are recurrently used fixed markers.

The current chapter argues that investigating synchronic data on *genre* using the sociolinguistic lens of apparent time (see following paragraph), coupled with notions to do with discourse practice, can provide motivations for, and evidence of, relatively sudden changes – cooptation – and that cooptation allows for rapid propagation of lexical items which adopt a new function or functions, which conventionalize(s), becoming PMs. The linguistic form can, however, subsequently be used in regrammaticalized constructions.

Sociolinguistic approaches to variation have generally focussed on phonology in the Labovian variationist mould. Sociolinguists differentiate between *real time* where samples are taken at different historical periods and *apparent time* where data from different generations recorded at the same point in time can indicate change. So, for example, it is currently very likely in British English that *like* is used to a much greater extent by 18–24 year-olds than by 50+ year-olds and this might indicate a linguistic change in progress. A fairly consistent finding has been that there is a peak in apparent time change in progress in adolescence, a factor captured in Labov's (2001) logistic incrementation model. It seems that, when a change begins, it reaches a peak in adolescence as young speakers carry the change further than the previous generation. Labov (2001: 455) suggests that the peak in apparent time is a general requirement of synchronic change.

The difficulties of applying classic Labovian methodologies to discourse-pragmatic features are discussed in Beeching (2016a: 41–45) and will not be rehearsed in full here. Suffice it to say that, due to the structural promiscuity of DMs, it is more difficult to establish a Labovian "envelope" whereby all presences (AND absences) of the feature under investigation are accounted for. It is also problematic to do so because variants of the variable need to "mean" the same, or be at least equivalent ways of doing the same thing (and PMs rarely mean exactly the same). One way to get round some of these problems is to look at distributional frequencies in a corpus, in the kind of "variant-centred" analysis favoured by Dinkin (2016). Looking at *like*, Dinkin (2016: 240) claims that "there has been a change in discursive practice toward greater ambiguity in degree of literality in vernacular conversation, and that as a result of this *sociolinguistic* change (in Coupland's sense), a variant that indexes vague literality gains ground at the expense of its various competitors as a set of *linguistic* changes."

Dinkin proposes that this change in discursive practice is further-reaching than D'Arcy's (2012) notion that quotative *be + like* has developed because of a stronger tendency for speakers to cite the direct speech (or thought) of others[2] (i.e. a different sort of change in discursive practice).

In another paper in the same special issue of *Language Variation* Tamminga, MacKenzie, and Embick (2016) highlight the role of the individual in what they call DVIQ (dynamics of variation in individuals). They differentiate three types of conditioning (2016: 303):

a. Sociolinguistic factors, the effect of which we term *s-conditioning*
b. Internal linguistic factors, *i-conditioning*
c. Physiological and psycholinguistic factors, *p-conditioning*

The current chapter aims to contribute to these debates by tracing some rather synchronic developments in French *genre* which also conform to the notion of a change in discursive practice towards vague literality. These developments will be compared with what appears to have happened historically in the case of *sort of*.[3] Both *genre* and *sort of* are derived from type-nouns and both are used for a range of pragmatic purposes, linked to approximation. They have, however, followed different paths and it is interesting to speculate on what is universal (typically *p-conditioning*), what is a regular pathway of change and what we can only put down to each word has its own history (typically *i-conditioning*). Large spoken corpora, accompanied by demographic metadata, may provide the dated evidence we need to see how a new development, like the rise of PM *genre*, comes about, typically as a form of *s-conditioning*.

The focus of this chapter is, then, the pragmaticalized uses of *sort of* and *genre* (hedging, approximating and metacommenting) in English and French, such as we see illustrated in examples (1)–(5):

---

[2] This is a hypothesis shared by Cheshire and Secova (2018: 230) who suggest that the reporting of inner thought using direct quotation appears to be increasing, possibly as a form of pragmatic borrowing from English *like*, but also as a "discourse style, perhaps disseminated via global communication flows." The evidence presented for all the functions of *genre* in both Cheshire and Secova (2018: 217) and in the current paper suggest that the quotative is, indeed, part of a larger move towards vague literality, since the youngest speakers use *genre* more frequently for other pragmatic marking purposes than for quotative uses.

[3] A detailed examination of the extent to which both *genre* and *sort of* might be said to be competing with the similatives *comme* and *like* in the semantico-pragmatic space around "vague literality" highlighted by Dinkin (2016) will have to be postponed to a different article.

(1) I'm **sort of** lacking in experience.

(2) Now we're at university you know **sort of** moving on...

(3) I know that sounds really bad but (laughs) I just **sort of** I'd rather **sort of** get myself up together first and then like then if I want to help people do it after that like. (examples from UWE Role-play Corpus 2010–2014, described in Beeching 2016a)

(4) *A: il dit des mots **genre** en français soutenu.* (Secova 2018: 163)
'he says words **sort of** in formal French'.

(5) *Kelly elle est devenue **genre** conseillère d'orientation on sait pas trop là.* (Corpus de Français Parlé au Québec, cited in Beeching 2018: 137)
'Kelly she became **sort of** a careers advisor not quite sure'.

In examples (1)–(5) *sort of* and *genre* precede a lexeme, noun or verb phrase which they modify or which the speaker is struggling to find. They could be regarded as pause-fillers, giving the speaker processing time, time to retrieve the item they need. They suggest approximation, not exactly this but something of this sort. They can be considered to be distancing the speaker from the noun phrase they come up with, suggesting that they are unhappy with its adequacy to express their meaning. To that extent they are multifunctional, simultaneously hedging, approximating and metacommenting.

PM *genre* is a more recent development in French than *sort of* in English. Where young people in English use *like*, young people in France use *genre*. (And young French Canadians also use *comme*).

The structure of the chapter is as follows. Section 2 gives some general background about the development of the PM *sort of* from the type-noun construction *a sort of*, leading to some research questions about the French PM *genre*. Section 3 reviews the literature on *genre* in European French. Section 4 presents the method and corpus consulted as part of the current study of *genre*, charts the synchronic developments in the use of *genre* (and, to a lesser extent, *comme*) in the Quebec corpus, and discusses the new evidence in relation to previous findings about *genre*. The conclusions in Section 5 answer the research questions proposed at the end of Section 2, weighing up the factors which come into play in the spread of type-noun derived PMs like *genre* and *sort of* in the manner of Tamminga, MacKenzie, and Embick (2016).

2 Conceptual framework. From type-noun to pragmatic marker: *A sort of* to *sort of*

Both *sort of* and *genre* derive from binominal type-noun constructions *a sort of cake*, *un genre de pâtisserie* ('a sort of cake').

The historical evolution which leads from type-nouns to hedges and other pragmatic functions is a fascinating one and one which we can profitably explore cross-linguistically. In my chapter on *sort of* in Beeching (2016a), the previous literature on type-noun constructions led me to identify six type-noun constructions:

Head/binominal: A *type of* cheese
Postdeterminer: These *kinds of* people
Nominal qualifier: a *kind of* large Pin-cushion
Quantifier usage: All *sorts of* people. Some *sort of* a business
Descriptive modifier-attributive: a loose *sort of* woman
Descriptive modifier-semi-suffix use: a good knockabout *kind of* a wife

Denison (2002, 2011) proposed that the postdeterminer and qualifier constructions developed from the head construction and that the postdeterminer developed first, paving the way for the qualifying construction. Taking a diachronic corpus approach, Brems and Davidse (2010) identified two further constructions, the quantifier and descriptive modifier, and suggest that these pre-dated and helped facilitate the postdeterminer and qualifying constructions.

What is of interest in the descriptive modifier usage is that the type noun is preceded by lexical material – often rather distinctive and foregrounded adjectival material. The attributive and semi-suffix usage are distinguished purely on the basis of the length of the modifying material which precedes the type-noun. I suggested (Beeching 2016a: 180), on the basis of close analysis of examples drawn from the Old Bailey Corpus (1675–1913) that the pragmaticalization of *sort of* may have originated, and is at the very least reflected in, the type of question forms widely used by counsel. These elicit further nominal qualifying adjectival material, indicated in examples (6)–(11).

(6)   What sort of a night? (Rather darkish, a very foggy night)

(7)   What sort of a handkerchief was it? (A silk handkerchief)

(8)   What sort of a shilling? (A Victorian shilling of 1859)

(9) What sort of a watch? (A silver watch)

(10) What sort of trunk? (It was made of wood, but covered with leather, it was a lead colour).

(11) What sort of a light did it appear? (It seemed to come along the floor; it was a light of a greater body than a candle).

These are not taxonomic – counsel is not talking of a taxonomy of nights, handkerchiefs, shillings and watches – but request rather further description generally involving adjectival modification. Once *sort of* becomes pragmatically ambiguous with respect to its categorical reference versus its general descriptive qualities it can be recruited for approximative and hedging uses. Note the re-analysis from: [a sort] of [cake] to: a [sort of] cake.

The earliest examples of bald nominal qualification i.e. with no adjectival modification in the Old Bailey Corpus[4] are in 1782 and 1783, reproduced in (12) and (13) below.

(12) Fuller made a *sort of* snatch back.

(13) There was a *sort of* scolding.

Given that French adjectives generally follow the noun, and that the descriptive modifier will not naturally precede *genre* in the way it does with *sort of* in English, one is led to wonder how the shift occurs in French and to the following research questions:
- Is there any evidence that *genre* takes a similar course of development historically as that followed by *sort of*?
- What role do syntactic and sociolinguistic factors (as opposed to cognitive factors) play in the evolution of pragmatic functions?

---

[4] An anonymous reviewer wonders whether it is possible to make hypotheses about the evolution of the construction [a sort of] in English from such a particular corpus. As I explain in Beeching (2016a:46–49), the Old Bailey Corpus is as close a record of spoken forms as we can get before the advent of the tape recorder. There are 10,578 occurrences of *sort of* in the Corpus which constitutes a robust body of evidence and the evolution from categorising to more pragmatic uses in the seventeenth century is very clear. It is nonetheless the case that the Old Bailey Proceedings are (transcriptions of) interactions in the law courts and are thus arguably not representative of all speech. The Proceedings could, however, be said to be just as, if not more, representative of everyday speech than some of the more literary sources commonly used for historical linguistics.

3 Literature review. Functions of *genre* in contemporary European French

Yaguello (1998) provides an excellent list of examples drawn from her teenage children in the 1990s (reproduced here as examples (14)–(25)):

(14) *Elle est genre méchante avec les cas, cette prof.*
 'She's sort of nasty to people with learning difficulties, that teacher'.

(15) *Il saute genre 1m 30 sans peine*
 'He can jump like / ?sort of 1m 30 easily'.

(16) *Elle telephone genre dix fois par jour*
 'She phones like /?sort of 10 times a day'.

(17) *Elle fait des contrôles genre toutes les semaines.*
 'She does tests like / ?sort of every week'.

(18) *Elle me dit « Trois heures de cours dont une de dessin ? Ça fait deux ça » genre le dessin ça ne compte pour rien.*
 'She says to me "Three hours of lessons one of which is art ? That only makes two" like /*sort of art doesn't count for anything'.

(19) *Elle me demande tout le temps de l'aider, genre elle a rien compris au cours.*
 'She asks me to help all the time like / *sort of she hasn't understood the lesson at all'.

(20) *Elle fait une tête, genre tout le monde devrait être à ses pieds.*
 'She pulls a face like / *sort of everyone should jump to it and do what she wants'.

(21) *Tu sais à quelle heure elle nous remplace son cours genre pour pas nous déranger ? à huit heures samedi !*
 'you know what time she's replacing the lesson like /?sort of not to put us out ? eight o'clock on a Saturday!'

(22) *Le chinois, c'est vraiment une belle langue, genre à l'épicerie, hier, la vendeuse, quand elle parlait, c'était comme si elle chantait.*

'Chinese is really a beautiful language, like (=for example) (*sort of) (I mean) at the grocer's yesterday the salesgirl, when she was talking, it was as if she was singing'.

(23) *Il a vraiment rien dans la tête, celui-là, genre il ouvre son cartable et ya toujours quelque chose qui lui manque.*
'He's really brainless, that guy, like/sort of/I mean (=for example, one reason I say that is) he opens his school bag and there's always something missing'.

(24) *Ce jean, il me va mieux, genre il me serre déjà moins.*
'These jeans are better for me, like/?sort of/I mean (= for example, the reason I say that is) they're not so tight'.

(25) *Un jour elle nous fait l'imparfait et genre la semaine d'après on passe au passé simple.*
'One day she's doing the imperfect with us and like /sort of (=for example) the following week we go on to the past historic.'

The broad range of pragmatic functions served by *genre* is amply illustrated by these examples. It functions as an approximative with adjectives, numerals and expressions of time ((14)–(17)). Examples (18)–(20) verge on quotative uses *as if she was saying*, *art doesn't count*, *she hasn't understood*, *everyone should jump to it*.

In (21) *genre* introduces the notion *as if this wouldn't be putting us out* but can be interpreted more ironically or sarcastically in the context as *on the pretext that this won't put us out*. In (22)–(24) *genre* introduces a justification or explanation. Finally, in (25), with "*et genre*" there is an implicit criticism of the teacher for jumping so quickly from one topic to the next. Discourse connective *genre* triggers the instruction to link the previous utterance with the following one in various ways. It signals *Here comes an example of what I have just said* and/or *Here comes a justification for what I have just said*. The sense is either ambiguous or disambiguated by the context.

Yaguello's examples make a strong case for participant observation (by a linguist) in collecting telling illustrations of new uses of linguistic forms. She does not specifically provide exemplification of the quotative use which we find in 21st. century corpora – and my guess is she would have done had she heard examples of it – this suggests that this usage at the very least is incoming. Davidse et al.'s (2013) study of *genre* in the online forum *Adojeunz*[5] investigated in 2008 and 2009 provides evidence to confirm this – on the one hand, they found 50 examples of quotative uses of *genre* which constituted 10% of the total use of *genre*. On the other, a 23 year-old discussant from Liège did not recognise some of the adolescent uses of *genre* as part of his own idiolect. Of the different quotative forms used in the Multicultural Paris French (MPF) corpus, Cheshire and Secova (2018: 212) identify 2 examples of *dire genre*, 2 of *faire genre* and 20 of standalone *genre*, amounting to 2.8% of all the quotative forms.

Isambert (2016: 85) highlights the very recent evolution of new uses of *genre* in European French, citing the opprobrium of the Académie Française in the following terms example (26):

(26) *Il m'a répondu genre j'en sais rien*, phrase d'où toute syntaxe a disparu, pourrait se dire *Il m'a répondu à peu près, approximativement, en gros qu'il n'en savait rien*.
'*He was like I don't know*, a phrase from which all syntax has disappeared, and could be glossed *He replied along the lines of, approximately, in general, that he did not know*'.

Isambert remarks that, in addition to the wry smile occasioned by the purist remark about the dearth of all syntax in the citation (and the insertion of *ne* in the "corrected" gloss provided by academician), one is arrested by the fact that, though the *Académie* has recognised the approximative use of the marker, its quotative use (introducing the direct speech *j'en sais rien*) is not recognised.

Isambert points out that *genre* in French derives from the word meaning *genus*, as in *genre humain* ('humankind'). It is only in the 15th century that the sub-type meaning *sort of* or *type of* emerges. He goes on to trace the development of the more recent uses of *genre* from examples with a noun phrase of the type + (*du*) *genre* + Proper Noun. He cites the Balzac example in (27):

(27) *Une porcelaine de la plus charmante fragilité*, **genre** *Saxe, et qui coûtait plus qu'un service d'argenterie*. (*Splendeurs et misères des courtisanes*, 1847, base FRANTEXT*)*.
'A china of the most charming fragility, Saxe-**style**, and which cost more than a canteen of silver'.

---

[5] As this is an online forum we do not know whether contributors are European or Canadian French speakers. The site, however, appears to be Canadian.

The only surprising thing about this is the omission of *"du"* (*"du genre Saxe"*) – this omission of the preposition is, however, important according to Isambert, as it means that *genre* now acts as a preposition.

At this stage examples are all common noun + *genre* + Proper noun, where the proper noun is conceived as an exemplary representative of the category denoted by the first term. Common names come later, as in example (28):

(28) *Ce sont des groups africains avec des des mo- des instruments typiquement africains* **genre** *calebasses euh* **genre** *kora (corpus CFPP,* 1951[6])
'These are African groups with the the mo- typically African instruments **such as** calebashes er **such as** koras.'

This use expands syntactically to include not only nominal groups but prepositional groups:

(29) *A : et alors les les jeunes à la dérive vous réagissez comment y en a beaucoup hein – B : Ouais y en a beaucoup ouais – C :* **genre** *avec des chiens et tout oui (corpus CFPP,* 1981)

(30) 'A : and so the the young people who're drifting how do you react there are lots of them aren't there – B : Yeah there are lots yeah – C : **like** with dogs and everything yeh'

Isambert argues that the semantic schema A *genre* B is maintained whereby B denotes a sub-category of A. However, B becomes less of a representative entity and more of an approximative entity (and this is reflected in the way that the English translations in the present paper move from *such as* to *like*). Isambert stresses the fact that only speakers born at the earliest in the 1970s use constructions in which one of the elements is not a noun.

The next stage is one in which A is not an entity which has sub-categories as such:

(31) *on est partis se poser sur un truc* **genre** *un petit stade (forum internet)*
'we went off to sit down on a thingy **sort of** a small stadium'.

The first element here is so vague it cannot be considered to be something which a small stadium can be a category of. This is an important stage as it allows the binary A *genre* B to dissolve in examples such as (32):

---

[6] Date of birth of the speaker.

(32) *Mais c'est bizarre, il y a pas des, il y a pas **genre** un parti écolo ou euh ?(corpus PFC, 1973)*
'But it's weird, isn't there, isn't there **like** a green party or er?'

The element which follows *genre* is no longer necessarily a NP but can be prepositional or verbal. It often precedes numerals in an apparently approximative function and, most recently, has a quotative function, introducing direct speech or putative (in)direct speech, as in (33):

(33) *fais pas **genre** tu connais les joueurs, ça sert à rien.(Corpus CLAPI, 1990)*
'don't come **like** you know the players, that won't do any good'.

Finally, *genre* breaks free from any kind of NP construction and can be used almost anywhere as a hedge (34):

(34) *Typés européens, pour des européens, c'est un peu, **genre**, normal. (forum internet).*
'European type-casts, for Europeans, is a bit **kind of/sort of/like** normal'.

And as a pause-filler (35):[7]

(35) *Après **genre** même (..) même ça dépend tu vois **genre** on peut dire qu'on part à à beaucoup tu vois **genre** euh beaucoup **genre** deux voitures (. .) et moi j'emmène mes petits cousins **genre** ma cousine et mes petits cousins* (MPF, Anna6b, Marie, 2389)
'Afterwards **like** even (. . .) even it depends you see **like** you can say that we travel in in lots you see er lots **like** two cars (. . .) and I take my little cousins **like** my (female) cousin and little cousins'.

---

[7] An anonymous reviewer notes that this is a complex example and that *genre* has different functions. It is certainly the case that the functions of PMs in general and *genre* in particular are often difficult to pin down and particular examples can be multifunctional and open to different interpretations. For example, all of the occurrences of *genre* in (35) can be categorised as pause-fillers used to buy time while the speaker formulates what is to come next. In *beaucoup **genre** deux voitures*, *genre* could be considered to mark a repair (not lots, but two) or exemplification (lots, for example 2). A similar remark could be made about *mes petits cousins **genre** ma cousine et mes petits cousins*. The speaker may be correcting (his/her female cousin is not one of the small cousins) or illustrating (or both).

Isambert also notes a discourse connective *genre* and a focalising or narrative break use of *et genre*. He is particularly keen to stress the difficulties of tracing a linear path through these different developments and suggests that previous diachronic studies may have been presented a more systematic picture because only certain functions have survived. What is blindingly clear is the difference in the evolutionary development of *sort of* and *genre* and this may (or may not) explain some of the differences in their functional equivalence.

Both *sort of* and *genre* derive from binominal type-noun expressions but *sort of* (and, for that matter, *kind of*) generally has scope over a following lexical item (verb or noun). *Genre* on the other hand is more similar to *like* in having far more variable scope, expressing approximation when associated with numbers/quantification, and modulation or metacommenter when associated with noun phrases. What is more, *genre* can be a discourse connective with different functions ranging from *as if* to *for example*. *Sort of* and *genre* have reached different stages of pragmaticalization. Isambert argues that the changes are less systematic than long-term diachronic studies seem to suggest. The pragmaticalized and canonical senses of both *sort of* and *genre* co-exist in polysemy.

In previous works where I've compared *sort of* and *genre* in English and French (Beeching, 2016b and 2018), I've taken a variational pragmatics approach and departed from tradition by adopting an onomasiological, rather than a semasiological analysis. As we have seen in the translated examples above, *genre* is more naturally translated by the similative *like* than by the type-noun-derived *sort of*. This is a question which is worth pursuing in the quest to tease out the factors which impact language change, whether these involve s- , i- or p-conditioning.

Back in 2004, Fleischmann and Yaguello highlighted the similarities between *genre* in French and *like* in English and their functional evolution (Figure 1, p. 141)

Propositional	**Textual**	**Expressive**
Expression of COMPARISON (Similarity/Approximation/ PARADIGMATIC EXAMPLE)	FOCUS	INTERPRETIVE QUOTATIVE HEDGE

At some point in their history both *like* and *genre* express "*quelque chose de ce genre*" ('something of this type') whereby an item is considered in relation to a norm or paradigm. Interestingly from a sociolinguistic point of view, Fleischmann and Yaguello remark (2004: 130) that

> *genre* is infrequent, though attested, in Canadian French; the Ottawa-Hull Corpus (. . .) suggests that francophone Canadians prefer *comme* (. . .), which may be a loan translation of *like*.

Hennecke (2017: 363) confirms this for Manitoban French where she says: "In Manitoban French, where the pragmatic functions [...] are taken by *comme*, the lexical unit *genre* occurs rarely, even in its use as a noun."

It seems then that, though *genre* was developing pragmatic functions in European French from at least the 1980s, this was not the case for Canadian French, where *comme* was used for similar purposes, apparently calqued on English *like*.

The current study breaks new ground by drawing for its data on a corpus of Quebec French – the *Corpus de Français Parlé au Québec* – in which pragmatic uses of both *genre* and *comme* (not to mention the collocates *comme genre* and *genre comme*) are very much in evidence. As scholars had found little evidence for the use of *genre* as a pragmatic marker in earlier collections of Canadian data, we appear to have the opportunity here to see language change as it is happening before our very eyes, in synchrony. This also gives us the opportunity to trace implicational hierarchies in the development of successive meanings, through the uses made of the form for different functions by younger and younger age-groups.

4 Synchronic developments: *genre* (and *comme*) in the Quebec Corpus

4.1 Methods

Having discovered, serendipitously, that there were fairly numerous occurrences of *genre* in the relatively recently established *Corpus de Français Parlé au Québec*, recorded in the 2000s, I took a classic corpus linguistic and semantico-pragmatic approach to the analysis of their distributional frequency and functions.

The *Corpus de Français Parlé au Québec* (Corpus of French Spoken in Quebec, see Dostie 2016 for further details) is a corpus of everyday spoken French of some 688,542 words, recorded and transcribed in the 2000s. Conversations are in groups of three or four with a student observer doing the recordings. Speakers are grouped according to age-groups of 5 years, starting at age 15 and ending at 85+ (so 15–20; 20–25; 25–30 and so on). Although there are few speakers in each age-group (around seven to eight), the fine-grained nature of this age differentiation allows us to trace apparent-time developments across the age groups, particularly since the online software is set up to do this.

Quantitative and qualitative analyses of all occurrences of *genre* were conducted in order to gauge the extent to which the form has grammaticalized, how any new functions are spreading, and whether there is an implicational hierarchy in the order in which one function succeeds another.

Functions of *genre* were divided into canonical, hedge/filler, approximative with numerals, discourse connective, quotative, postposed and *genre que* uses. These functions are illustrated in examples (36)–(42).

(36) Canonical
*il avait un pogo c'est **un genre de** poteau.*
'he had a pogo it's **a sort of** stick'.

(37) Hedge/filler
*c'est **genre** mon but dans la vie là*
'it's **like** my aim in life'.

(38) Approximative with numerals
*c'était **genre** euh soixante-dix*
'it was **like** er 70'.

(39) Discourse connective
*je pédale je pédale pis là ça fait un bon cinq minutes là que je pédale (.) <p> •<all>° (.) pis là je me retourne (.) pis là il y a un dude qui est (dit en riant) (.) à deux mètres de moi debout **genre** il a de l'eau à peu près à mi-cuisse (dit en riant)*
'I'm pedalling and pedalling it's a good five minutes I've been pedalling for and then I turn round and then there's a dude who is (laughter) two metres from me standing **sort of** he's got water about mid-thigh (laughter)'.

(40) Postposed
J : *négociation de l'entente notre entente elle finit {le:;le euh} trente et un mars (en posant son index sur la table comme pour insister sur ses propos) (0:06:25.6)*
S : *OUH[1 :*
JN : *[1 tu parles de convention collective **genre**/*
J : *tu parles de [nom de l'entreprise non transcrit pour préserver l'anonymat]*
'J : negotiation of the agreement our agreement it finishes {the:; the er} thirty first of March (putting his index finger on the table as if to insist on what he's saying)
S : OOH
JN : you're talking about a collective agreement **like**/
J : you're talking about [name of business not transcribed to maintain anonymity]'.

(41) Quotative
vraiment pas sympathique t'sais j- je rentre dans l'appart {elle est;et;elle} la coloc est dans le divan **genre** •bon ben je me lèverai pas pour te dire salut/°
'really not nice y'know I- I come back to the flat {she is ; and ; she} the flatmate is on the sofa **like** •OK well I'm not getting up to say hello'.

(42) genre que
mais t'sais euh: tu t'assis **genre genre que** ton bedon il sort
'but y'know er : you sit **so so** (=in such a way/such that) your tummy it sticks out'.

The difficulties of distinguishing between the different functions of PMs is well-known, particularly given their multifunctionality. For example, the discourse connective *genre* in example (39) can also be classified as postposed (but mid-utterance) and *genre que* in (42) can very logically be classified as discourse connective. It was interesting and important, however, to distinguish between these syntactic positions and on the basis of examples such as the above it was possible to allocate most occurrences to a positional or functional type.

4.2 Results

Figure 1 shows the raw number of tokens of *genre* and *comme* found in the Quebec Corpus for each of the age-groups, 15–20, 20–25 and so forth.

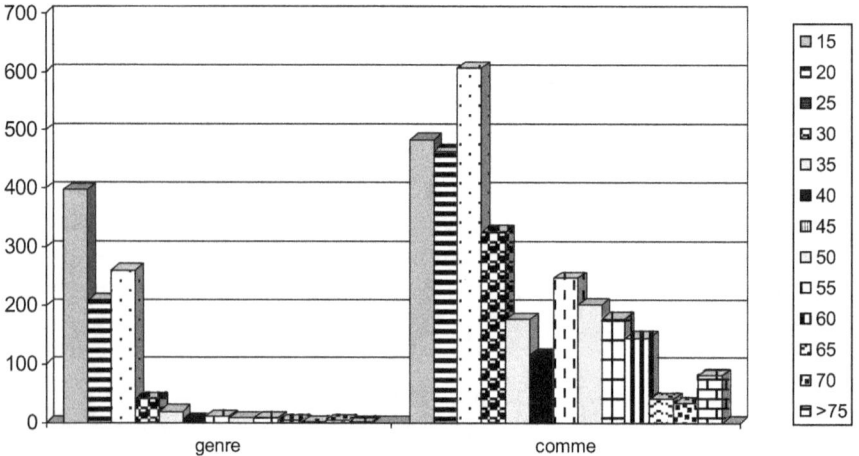

Figure 1: Number of tokens of *genre* and *comme* as a function of age in the Quebec Corpus.

The form *comme* is overall a great deal more frequent than *genre* – this is unsurprising given the wide range of grammatical uses that can be made of *comme* (in addition to its pragmatic marking functions). It is most frequent, however, in the younger speakers from age 15 to age 30 after which its usage drops dramatically with very low rates in the 65+ age-groups. The highest rates of use are in the 25–30 year-olds.

Genre, by contrast, has extremely low rates of use in anyone over 30 – but high rates of use in the 15–30 year-olds, with the very highest rates in the 15–20 year-old group. As we can see more clearly in Figure 2, the frequency of occurrence of *genre* rises extremely dramatically in the under-30s.

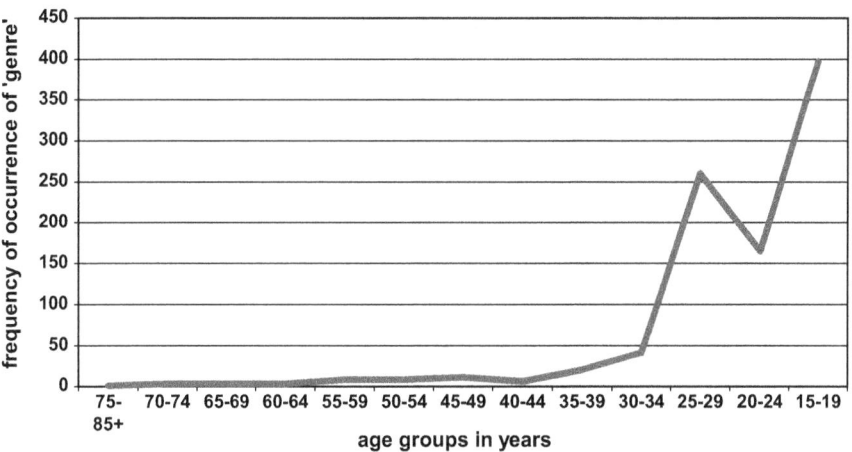

Figure 2: Numbers of occurrences of *genre* according to age-group.

This looks very much like the classic peak in apparent time which Labov (2001) identifies as being a characteristic of synchronic change. *Comme* reached its peak 10 years previously and is a change carried by the 25 year-olds. The youngest generation of speakers in the Corpus appear to be using both *comme* and *genre* in a development which echoes Dinkin's (2016) finding about the rise in variants which index "vague literality." However, although it is a reasonable assumption that a rise in frequency reflects a rise in pragmatic functions (as semantically bleached elements are more easily implementable in different contexts), a qualitative analysis of the forms must be made to verify this, and this is what was done.

Table 1 displays the raw token rates and percentages of *genre* subtypes per age-group.

Table 1: Tokens and percentages of *genre* by function and age-group.

age-group	tokens	CAN N	CAN %	HED N	HED %	APP N	APP %	DIS CON N	DIS CON %	PP N	PP %	QUOT N	QUOT %	GQUE N	GQUE %
75–85+	1	1	100	0	0	0	0	0	0%	0	0%	0	0%	0	0%
70–74	3	3	100%	0	0%	0	0%	0	0%	0	0%	0	0%	0	0%
65–69	3	3	100%	0	0%	0	0%	0	0%	0	0%	0	0%	0	0%
60–64	3	3	100%	0	0%	0	0%	0	0%	0	0%	0	0%	0	0%
55–59	8	7	88%	0	0%	1	12%	0	0%	0	0%	0	0%	0	0%
50–54	8	8	100%	0	0%	0	0%	0	0%	0	0%	0	0%	0	0%
45–49	11	7	64%	1	9%	0	0%	1	9%	2	18%	0	0%	0	0%
40–44	6	4	67%	2	33%	0	0%	0	0%	0	0%	0	0%	0	0%
35–39	20	7	35%	8	40%	2	10%	0	0%	2	10%	1	5%	0	0%
30–34	41	15	37%	12	29%	3	7%	1	2%	8	20%	1	2%	1	2%
25–29	260	25	10%	146	56%	18	7%	9	3%	49	19%	8	3%	5	2%
20–24	165	10	6%	81	49%	19	12%	4	2%	39	24%	8	5%	4	2%
15–19	397	16	4%	273	69%	32	8%	5	1%	50	13%	14	4%	7	2%

Legend: CAN=canonical (binominal); HED=hedge; APP=approximative (before numerals); DISCON=discourse connective; PP=postposed; QUOT=quotative; GQUE=*genre que*

Speakers aged 50 and over use *genre* exclusively in its canonical taxonomic function in formulations such as *quel genre d'accident* ('what sort of accident'). We see sporadic occurrences of hedging, discourse connective and postposed uses in the 45–49 and 40–44 year-olds but the numbers are very small. The frequency begins to pick up in the 35–39 year-olds and 30–34 year-olds where all functions are in evidence. It is, however, with the 20–29 year-olds that frequencies soar, all uses are in evidence, the percentage of canonical uses diminishes while hedging uses rise. The number of tokens more than double in the 15–19 year-olds – unfortunately, we do not have word counts for this corpus so we cannot normalize the data. What we can say is that all of the functions are in evidence in the youngest speakers, and that the balance of uses shifts dramatically from canonical to hedging – this is even more exaggeratedly the case if we include the postposed examples (PPs) as hedges (which they are from a functional point of view, albeit their positional difference at the end of the utterance). In the 15–19 year-olds, only 4% are canonical uses, while 69% are hedging/filling uses. It is unsurprising that frequencies rise given the increased flexibility of *genre* once it is coopted for discourse purposes. Figure 3 makes it easier to gauge the extent to which there is an implicational hierarchy in the order in which the different functions of *genre* can develop.

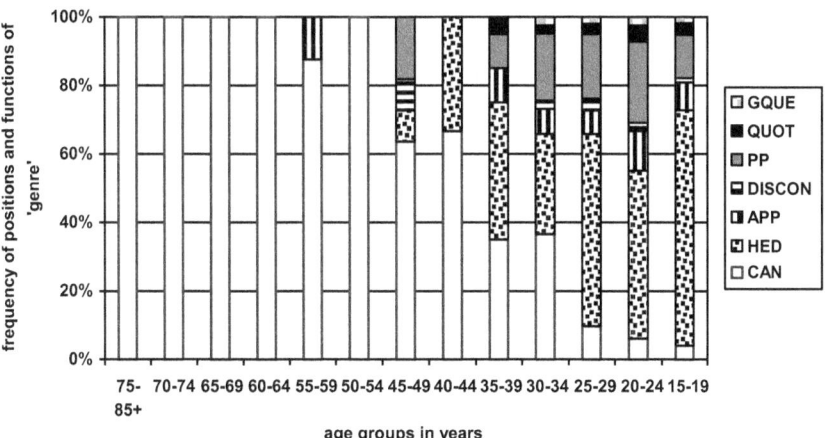

Figure 3: Percentage frequency of positions and functions of *genre* in different age groups. Legend: CAN=canonical (binominal); HED=hedge; APP=approximative (before numerals); DISCON=discourse connective; PP=postposed; QUOT=quotative; GQUE=*genre que*

The synchronic data displayed in Figure 3 give some indication of the order in which different functions of *genre* start to emerge. That is, if we believe the younger speakers start to adopt new functions of *genre* which are incoming. There may of course be particular effects due to discourse preferences in the young or old or due to imbalances in the corpus (more speakers in the 25–29 age-group for example). Ongoing research will be welcome to test hypotheses suggested here. Overall, the evidence is that hedging is by far the most ubiquitous pragmatic use of *genre*, and the one which emerges most strongly first of all. The 45–49 group has some fairly anomalous results with a number of discourse connectives and postposed uses as well as hedging uses. It seems that postposed *genre* does not of necessity antedate hedging functions (in other positions in the utterance) but that, indeed, as *genre* begins to have scope-over-discourse rather than scope-over-NP, it can begin to be postposed. The rather high proportion of PPs in the 45–49 group (18%) might suggest that postposition marks the transition from truncated noun phrase ([*du*] *genre* X) to pragmatic marker – but we have only 2 tokens (see Table 1) – insufficiently robust data to argue the case – particularly as hedging examples elsewhere in the utterance are proportionately higher in the succeeding age-groups.

We can also note that the quotative does not appear till after the discourse connective and postposed examples.

Genre que is the last to appear with 17 tokens in the Quebec French. This latter usage flies in the face of previous assertions concerning the irreversibility in the process of change for PMs, that is, that they are syntactically (and semantically) non-obligatory. The emergence of the connective *genre que* which is obligatory from a syntactic view-point suggests a process of reobligatorification or regrammaticalization.[8] We have to be a little cautious in making such an assertion, as numbers are small and when we look at some of the other examples of *genre que* in the Corpus, their status as subordinating conjunctions is drawn into some doubt: it is possible that they are examples of postposed *genre* + *que*.

(43) *mais ça dépend lesquelles là à midi là il y en a une t'sais moi je reprenais mes points de: l'autre jour **genre que** j'étais en congé pis c'était comme •ah mais on peut pas faire ça°*
'but it depends which ones like at mid-day like there is one y'know I was picking up the points I made: the other day **like the fact that** I was on holiday so it was like ah but you can't do that'.

---

8 We see a similar process in the development of quotative *be like* as *like* in this construction is syntactically obligatory. Indeed in the quotative example (40), both *genre* and *like* are syntactically obligatory – it may therefore be the case that *genre que* arises out of the obligatorification engendered by the quotative.

The loose connecting force of *que* and its possible extension and omission in spoken vernacular French is highlighted by Gadet (2003: 47), where she cites examples such as "*il est venu que j'étais malade* ('he came that I was ill' [= as/when/because I was ill])."

In example (43), by this type of interpretation, *genre* provides Dinkin's vague literality while *que* provides the link between the two clauses. The plurality of *mes points* and the singular *I was on holiday* suggests that this is an example, so *genre* introduces an example of the points she made, such as being on holiday.

There is tentative evidence of further development of *genre que* in the CFPQ as we can see in examples such as (44) and (45).

(44) *j'osais pas l'écrire dans la fiche* **genre que** *j'aime pas full les mets épicés parce que c'est ça t'sais tu vas là POUR ÇA t'sais*
'I didn't dare write it on the form **sort of that** I don't really like spicy foods because that's it y'know you go there FOR THAT y'know'

In (44) *genre* could be interpreted as a postposed approximator and the complementizer *que* fulfils the projection about what she was writing or it can be interpreted as 'for example that. . .' It is not interpretable as purposive or resultative. Example (45) is very similar, the complementizer *que* follows *écris* ('write') and *genre* serves as an approximator.

(45) *mais t'écris* **genre que** *t'es full sportive que tu fais tous les sports du monde pis là: il y a pas de fille qui fait ça fait que là ils vont te mettre avec un gars*
'but you write **sort of that** you are really sporty that you do all the sports in the world but then: there aren't any girls who do that so they're going to put you with a boy'.

4.3 Discussion

Cheshire and Secova (2018) found that, in Parisian French, discourse marker and discourse particle[9] uses of *genre*, at 58% and 18% respectively, were by far

---
9 Cheshire and Secova (2018: 219) explain that they "adopt D'Arcy's (2005) distinction between a discourse marker, which occurs at the periphery of the clause with scope over the entire clause, and a discourse particle, which has narrow scope over an element within the clause." I have taken a less syntactic and more functional approach overall with "hedges" roughly equivalent to "discourse particles" and "discourse connectives" equivalent to "discourse markers." Cheshire and Secova's "quotatives" would presumably be described as discourse markers as they occur at

the most ubiquitous of the uses in the younger speakers (born 1992–1999). In the Quebec data, too, the hedging uses are the most common at 69%.

Cheshire and Secova do not comment on postposed uses of *genre* in the Parisian data and neither did Yaguello (1998). The increase in frequency of postposed *quoi* in European French has been highlighted in Beeching (2007b and 2007c). Postposed *quoi* does not exist in Canadian French and it is tempting to posit a "division of labour" (Mosegaard-Hansen 2005) whereby the end-slot in European French is occupied by *quoi* and therefore does not require to be, or cannot be, occupied by *genre*.[10] The significance of postposition is highlighted by Heine (2013: 1231, citing Brinton (2008: 127)) in a discussion of the evolution of *I mean*. One of the key stages in the development of discourse-marking *I mean* is that it "can begin to be postposed to the phrasal element." Degand (2014), too, suggests that there is a move, in the development of DM *alors,* from mid to postposed to preposed positions. There is no evidence whatsoever that this progression has occurred for *genre* in Parisian/European French – but the move from binominal to prepositional, mid- to postposed positions does occur for Quebec French. The evidence from the CFPQ corpus provides further support for Cheshire and Secova's (2018: 215) contention (for Parisian French) that "the emergence of the quotative function occurs when speakers begin to use the lexical item *genre* in an increasing number of syntactic categories and pragmatic functions." Cheshire and Secova are, however, at pains to emphasize that they do not believe the quotative emerges from the discourse marker. They remark (2018: 215):

> Instead, quotative *genre* emerges once the lexical item *genre* becomes syntactically multi-functional, a property that is typical of new similarity quotative expressions in other languages. Young speakers in Paris harness *genre* in all its syntactic roles, both old and new, as a quotative expression.

The interconnection between taxonomic expressions, (deliberate) vagueness and exemplification can be seen in similar forms such as *sort of*, *kind of* and *type (of) thing* in English. It is less commonly found in a conjunctival expression, though we do find *tipo che* in Italian and in Russian *tipa čto* (see Benigni, Ch. 16, this volume), the first of which expresses consequence as well as introducing exemplification though there is hesitation about the resultative nature of the

---

the periphery of the clause – but the quotatives can include the nominal *du genre* as well as the prepositional *genre*.

10 The current coexistence, too, of *comme* and *genre* as quotatives in Canadian French appears to counter any arguments in favour of a division of labour – though it may be that one or other wins out in the end, with *comme* coming in to Canadian French through bilingual contact with English (cf. *like*) and *genre* emerging either independently or through contact with European French.

second. The well-established (possibly archaic) *de sorte que* ('so that') in French (which covers both purposive and resultative meanings) is long-lived evidence of the way that a taxonomic noun, *sorte*, can form a conjunctival connector. Fleischman and Yaguello (2004: 130) had noted that "resourceful French speakers enhance the connective capacity of *genre* with *que*, thereby enabling it to function as a kind of generic subordinator and thus increasing its syntactic scope." Cheshire and Secova (2018: 219) discuss one example of *genre que* in their MPF data, reproduced here as (46):

(46)   ma petite soeur qui a treize ans elle adore parler de ça **genre que** c'est comme si c'était sa sa grande soeur en fait (Mehda)
'my little sister who is thirteen years old she loves talking about that **sort of like** it's as if it was her older sister in fact'

Cheshire and Secova point out that this is the only example of *genre que* in their data and it is immediately followed by *c'est comme si* ('it's as if'), suggesting that the speaker is correcting herself. They argue that *genre* here has the meaning of comparison.

Benigni refers to the complementizer function of *tipo che* as existing in ad hoc concept constructions – and *genre que*, too, currently appears to be pressed to a number of contextually bound functions which may in future coalesce more firmly around exemplification, and purposive or resultative functions, similar to *de sorte que*. For the moment, the collocation exists in Quebec French (but not, at least in any numbers, in European French) and may or may not conventionalize in a particular form-function construction.

5 Conclusions

As we have seen, *un genre* in French has a similar nominal meaning to 'genre' in English. It derives from the word meaning *genus* and, in the 15th. Century, the sub-type meaning *sort of* or *type of* emerges. But it is out of this, via a contraction of *du genre* to *genre*, giving it a prepositional status, that the new pragmaticalized meanings evolve, first apparently attached to nouns, adjectives and numerals but then as a discourse connective roughly translatable as 'as if' (Yaguello 1998; Isambert 2016; Cheshire and Secova 2018). Syntactic factors appear to play an important role in the differential evolution of *sort of* and *genre:* heavy adjectival qualification (semi-suffix usage) BEFORE the noun in English which is not possible in French led to the different status of *sort of*. *Sort of* appears before verbs and adjectives as well as nouns, but they tend to be full lexical items and the scope of *sort of* is generally limited to those items rather than to the full utterance. *Sort of* tends not to appear as a discourse connective, and does not function as a quotative.

D'Arcy (2012) argues that it is only after occurring as a conjunction – *he went away like he was unhappy with the situation* – that *like* starts to appear in the quotative *be like* construction. Cheshire and Secova (2018) argue that it is after *genre* frees itself from its nominal status and becomes syntactically more mobile that the quotative arises. The Quebec data presented here confirms some of the previous findings for Parisian French but distinguishes itself from the Parisian data in some ways (having postposed *genre* – and with quotative *genre* coexisting with quotative *comme*) and adds some further intriguing possibilities to our debates. *Genre* has a) outpragmaticalized *sort of* – but this is very recent – and b) even more recently has undergone re-obligatorification in expressions like *faire genre* and *genre que*.

Going back to previous theories which have attempted to find regularities in the development of PMs, *sort of* and *genre* do not entirely conform to the unidirectional path from propositional to textual to interpersonal. There appears to be a universal tendency, at least across Indo-European languages, for taxonomic nouns to be recruited for interpersonal purposes, expressing approximation, a tendency towards a hedging usage in contemporary discourse which I have referred to as Politeness Induced Semantic Change and which Dinkin (2016) terms "vague literality." There is a cognitive, metaphorical, pathway which leads from a relationship between superordinate and co-hyponyms to exemplification. (*A robin is a sort of bird* entails *An example of a bird is a robin*). Exemplification slides into approximation via peripheral membership of a prototype – this is an example of a bird, but may not have ALL the criteria required to be a bird, in other words it is vaguely a bird. The approximation sense then breaks free from the taxonomic sense and can be used in a wider range of contexts. To use Heine et al.'s (2017) term, the very rapid rise in frequency of *genre* which we see in the Quebec data presented here suggests that type-nouns like this can be coopted very readily and conventionalize very quickly in their new metacommenting function. They are grammaticalized theticals. In Tamminga, MacKenzie, and Embick (2016) terminology, this exemplifies p-conditioning of a cognitive sort. The functional differences between *sort of* in English and *genre* in French appear to be related to i-conditioning (internal language-specific factors). The approximative function of *sort of* derives from the weighty pre-modifying descriptive material which leads it to move from taxonomy to peripheral membership or approximation, with the item-to-be-hedged following *sort of*. By contrast, the syntax of French leads from *du genre Saxe* to *genre Saxe* and this one-word, rather than two-word, expression, has greater syntactic freedom: *genre* can appear in a postposed position as well as in syntactically obligatory forms such as the quotative *être/faire genre* and (potentially) *genre que*. We cannot say why *genre* has only relatively recently developed PM functions by comparison with the very longstanding PM functions of *sort of*. However, we have evidence to support a particular type of s-conditioning in its evolution, the incrementation pattern posited by Labov in 2001 which is very clearly demonstrated in Figures 1 and 2. Hennecke (2017: 363) presumes that: "the newly emerged functions of *comme* in Canadian French, which arose in the course of the twentieth century, are due to long-term language contact with English and underlie the process of pragmaticalization."

Contact-induced change and shifts in discourse processes can be described as macro-sociolinguistic conditioning of an almost conscious sort. We cannot point to contact-induced change as a motivation for the development of *genre* in Quebec French unless Quebec French speakers have contact with European French speakers – which, as far as I know, is not the case. It is possible that, like the development of *coudon* (see Dostie 2009), pragmatic uses of *genre* crossed the Atlantic and continued to develop in Quebec but not elsewhere. An investigation of a historical corpus of Quebec French may be able to answer this question. But the apparent time data in Table 1 and Figures 2 and 3 which reveal that it is only in the younger generation of speakers that PM uses are prevalent undermines this hypothesis. What we can assert on the basis of the current data is the rapid expansion of *genre* once it has hedging and approximating functions. Changes in discursive practice, effects of language contact and peak in apparent time (all s-conditioning) come into play alongside semantic bleaching/pragmatic enrichment, a form of p-conditioning, as general conditions for synchronic change, and ones which appear to operate cross-linguistically. Evidence from the data on *genre* tentatively challenges the notion that, once an item has pragmaticalized, the change is irreversible. The existence of *genre que* (also exemplified in Italian *tipo che*) suggests that, after discourse grammaticalization/pragmaticalization, there can be a process of reobligatorification, in a new cycle of grammaticalization.

References

Aijmer, Karin & Anne-Marie Simon-Vandenbergen. 2006. Introduction. In Karin Aijmer & Anne-Marie Simon-Vandenbergen (eds.) *Pragmatic markers in contrast*, 1–10. (Studies in Pragmatics 2). Oxford: Elsevier.

Beeching, Kate. 2005. Politeness-induced semantic change: The case of *quand même*. *Language Variation and Change* 17 (2). 1–27.

Beeching, Kate. 2007a. A politeness-theoretic approach to pragmatico-semantic change. *Journal of Historical Pragmatics* 8 (1). 69–108.

Beeching, Kate. 2007b. Social identity, salience and language change: The case of post-rhematic *quoi*. In Wendy Ayres-Bennett & Mari Jones (eds.), *The French language and questions of identity*, 140–149. London: Legenda.

Beeching, Kate. 2007c. La co-variation des marqueurs discursifs *bon, c'est-à-dire, enfin, hein, quand même, quoi* post-rhématique et *si vous voulez* : Une question d'identité?. *Langue Française* 154 (2). 78–93.

Beeching, Kate. 2016a. *Pragmatic markers in British English. Meaning in social interaction*. Cambridge: Cambridge University Press.

Beeching, Kate. 2016b. Insights from contrastive linguistics: Translating *sort of* into French. In Maryvonne Boisseau, Catherine Chauvin, Catherine Delesse & Yvon Keromnes (eds.), *Linguistique et traductologie: Les enjeux d'une relation complexe,* 85–98. Arras: Artois Presses Université.

Beeching, Kate. 2018. Metacommenting in English and French. A variational pragmatics approach. In Kate Beeching, Chiara Ghezzi & Piera Molinelli (eds.), *Positioning the self and other(s). Linguistic perspectives*, 127–152. Amsterdam: John Benjamins.

Brems, Lisselotte & Kristin Davidse. 2010. The reanalysis and grammaticalization of nominal type noun constructions with *kind of/sort of*: Chronology and paths of change. *English Studies* 91. 180–202.

Brinton, Laurel. 2017. *The evolution of pragmatic markers in English. Pathways of change*. Cambridge: Cambridge University Press.

Cheshire, Jenny & Maria Secova. 2018. The origins of new quotative expressions. *Journal of French Language Studies* 28 (2). 209–234.

D'Arcy, Alexandra. 2012. The diachrony of quotation. Evidence from New Zealand English. *Language Variation and Change* 24 (3). 343–369.

Davidse, Kristin, Lieselotte Brems, Peter Willemse, Emeline Doyen, Jessica Kiermeet & Elfi Thoelen. 2013. A comparative study of the grammaticalized uses of English "sort of" and French "genre (de)" in teenage forum data. In Emanuele Piola (ed.) *Languages go web. Standard and non-standard languages on the internet*, 41–66. Alessandria: Edizione dell'Orso.

Degand, Liesbeth. 2014. 'So very fast then'. Discourse markers at left and right periphery. In Kate Beeching & Ulrich Detges (eds.), *Discourse functions at the left and right periphery*, 151–178. Leiden: Brill.

Denison, David. 2002. History of the *sort of* construction family. Paper presented at the Second International Conference on Construction Grammar, University of Helsinki, 7 September. Outline draft version available from: http://www.humanities.manchester.ac.uk/medialibrary/llc/files/david-denison/Helsinki_ICCG2.pdf (accessed 02 February 2022).

Denison, David. 2011. The construction of SKT. Plenary paper presented at Second Vigo-Newcastle-Santiago-Leuven International Workshop on the Structure of the Noun Phrase in English (NP2), Newcastle upon Tyne. Powerpoint presentation available from: https://www.escholar.manchester.ac.uk/api/datastream?publicationPid=uk-ac-man-scw:172513&datastreamId=SUPPLEMENTARY-1.PDF (accessed 02 February 2022).

Dinkin, Aaron. 2016. Variant-centered variation and the *like* conspiracy. *Language Variation* 16 (2). 221–246.

Dostie, Gaétane. 2009. Discourse markers and regional variation in French: A lexico-semantic approach. In Kate Beeching, Nigel Armstrong & Françoise Gadet (eds.), *Sociolinguistic variation in contemporary French*, 201–214. Amsterdam: Benjamins.

Dostie, Gaétane. 2016. Le corpus de français parlé au Québec (CFPQ) et la langue des conversations familières : exemple de mise à profit des données à partir d'un examen lexico-sémantique de la séquence *je sais* pas. *Corpus* 15. https://journals.openedition.org/corpus/2945 (accessed 12 March 2019).

Fleischmann, Suzanne & Marina Yaguello. 2004. Discourse markers across languages? Evidence from English and French. In Carol Lynn Moder & Aida Martinovic-Zik (eds.) *Discourse across Languages and Cultures,*129–147. Amsterdam: John Benjamins.

Gadet, Françoise. 2003. *La variation sociale en français*. Paris: Ophrys.

Heine, Bernd. 2013. On discourse markers. Grammaticalization, pragmaticalization, or something else?. *Linguistics* 51 (6). 1205–1247.

Heine, Bernd. 2018. Are there two different ways of approaching grammaticalization? In Sylvie Hancil, Tyne Breban & José Vicente Lozano (eds.) *New trends in grammaticalization and language change,* 23–54. Amsterdam: John Benjamins.

Heine, Bernd, Gunther Kaltenböck, Tania Kuteva & Haipping Long. 2017. Cooptation as a discourse strategy. *Linguistics* 55(4). 813–855.

Hennecke, Inga. 2017. The impact of pragmatic markers and hedging on sentence comprehension: a case study of *comme* and *genre*. *Journal of French Language Studies* 27. 355–380.

Isambert, Paul. 2016. Genre: une mode récente mais qui vient de loin. *Journal of French Language Studies* 26 (1). 85–96.

Labov, William. 2001. *Principles of linguistic change. Vol 2: Social Factors.* Oxford: Blackwell.

Mihatsch, Wiltrud. 2007. The construction of vagueness: *sort of* expressions in Romance languages. In Günter Radden, Klaus-Michael Köpke, Thomas Berg & Peter Siemund (eds.), *Aspects of meaning construction,* 225–245. Amsterdam: Benjamins.

Mihatsch, Wiltrud. 2010. The diachrony of rounders and adaptors: Approximation and unidirectional change. In Gunther Kaltenböck, Wiltrud Mihatsch & Stefan Schneider (eds.), *New approaches to hedging.* Studies in Pragmatics 8, 93–122. Bingley: Emerald.

Mosegaard-Hansen, Maj-Britt. 2005. A comparative study of the semantics and pragmatics of *enfin* and *finalement*, in synchrony and diachrony. *Journal of French Language Studies* 15. 153–171.

Secova, Maria. 2018. Direct speech, subjectivity and speaker positioning in London English and Paris French. In Kate Beeching, Chiara Ghezzi & Piera Molinelli (eds.), *Positioning the self and other(s). Linguistic Perspectives*, 155–175. Amsterdam/Philadelphia: John Benjamins.

Sweetser, Eve. 1990. *From etymology to pragmatics. Metaphorical and cultural aspects of semantic structure.* Cambridge: Cambridge University Press.

Tagliamonte, Sali and Alexandra D'Arcy. 2009. Peaks beyond phonology: Adolescence, incrementation and language change. *Language* 85 (1). 58–108.

Tamminga, Meredith, Laurel MacKenzie & David Embick. 2016. The dynamics of variation in individuals. *Language Variation* 16 (2). 300–336.

Traugott, Elizabeth Closs. 1982. From propositional to textual and expressive meanings: Some semantic-pragmatic aspects of grammaticalization. In Winfred P. Lehmann & Yakov Malkiel (eds.), *Perspectives on historical linguistics,* 245–271. Amsterdam: John Benjamins.

Traugott, Elizabeth Closs & Richard B. Dasher. 2002. *Regularity in semantic change.* Cambridge: Cambridge University Press.

Yaguello, Marina. 1998. *Petits faits de langue.* Paris: Seuil.

Language index

Baltic languages 676
Belarusian 40, 459–489, 494
– Old 467
– *see also* Old Ruthenian
Belarusian-Russian mixed speech 481, 494
– *see also* trasianka
Bulgarian 24, 44, 458, 460–465, 470, 475, 480, 483, 485, 487–489, 495, 502–503, 520

Catalan 22, 36–37, 245–248, 250–254, 260, 271, 275, 292, 299–300
Celtic 253
Croatian 40, 458, 461, 464, 467–468, 480–488
Czech 2, 6–7, 17, 21, 24, 36, 45, 220, 238, 571–619
– Middle 466, 471, 575
– Old 466–467, 468
– Present-day 459, 577, 594

Dutch 9, 30, 41, 55–93, 344
– Middle 86
– Present-day 55, 59–60, 82, 86, 89, 91–92

English 1–53, 55–93, 95–139, 141–179, 181–209, 695–721
– American V, 24, 41, 141–146, 155, 159, 164–165, 177–178, 183–184, 188, 191, 200, 207, 572
– Australian 146
– British V, 24, 41, 141–146, 167, 200, 697
– Canadian 143–147, 151–154, 158, 161, 165, 175–175
– Hong Kong 41, 143–145, 147, 151–154, 158, 161, 165, 175–175
– Middle 18, 22, 38, 55, 57, 59, 63–69, 73–75, 78, 86, 134, 263
– Modern 55, 59, 65–66, 69, 71, 74–76, 86
– New Zealand 41, 143–145, 147, 151–154, 158, 161, 165, 175–175
– Old 5, 7, 12, 29–30, 55, 57, 59–63, 65–67, 69–70, 74–75, 78, 86, 95, 121, 134–136
– Philippine 41, 143–145, 147, 151–154, 158, 161, 165, 175–175
– Present-day 15–16, 55, 59–60, 65–66, 73, 78, 80, 82, 90–91, 134–135, 150
– Singapore 143–145, 147, 151–154, 158, 161, 165, 175–175

Franco-Provençal 245, 247, 254, 260, 277
French 1–53, 245–309, 311–349, 655–693, 695–721
– Canadian 294, 695–721
– creoles 273
– Middle 253
– Old 6, 22, 69, 251, 264

Galician 37, 245–246, 248, 260, 267, 271, 275, 290, 299–300
German 1–53, 211–243
– High 6–9, 29, 216, 267
– Low 6, 8
– Middle 6, 8–9, 467
– Modern 216
– Old 7–8
– Present-day 575
Germanic languages 30, 36, 55–56, 92, 247, 270
Greek
– Ancient 5, 11, 457–458, 470
– Classical 5–10, 250–252

Hungarian 250–254

Italian 245–309, 351–391, 621–653
– ancient 354, 361–362

Ladin 37, 246, 295, 299
Latin 4–12, 21–22, 36, 104, 108, 117, 247–254, 262, 354, 363, 458–461, 465–472, 510, 570, 575, 623, 666
– medieval 250, 363, 386
Latvian 2, 32, 45–46, 458, 655–693
Livonian 676

Macedonian 458, 460–464, 502
Middle Czech 466, 471, 575

Norwegian 1–53, 92, 263, 265, 285
Norse
– Old 56
– West Old 7–10, 29–31

Occitan 245–248, 251, 253–254, 260, 277, 294
Old East Slavic 465, 506
Old Church Slavonic 465, 469
Old Ruthenian 467, 472
– see also Old Belarusian
– see also Old Ukrainian

Polish 1–53, 457–569
– Old 8, 10, 467, 472
– Present-day 510, 548, 556
Portuguese 1–53, 245–309, 393–413

Romance languages 245–310
Rhaeto-Romance 245–246, 248
Río de la Plata Spanish 415–453
Romanian 3, 36–37, 245–301
Rumantsch 37
– Sursilvan 246, 250–253, 261, 264, 275–276, 294–295, 301
– Rumantsch Grischun 246, 275, 294, 300
Russian 1–53, 56–60, 76, 91, 95–98, 136, 203, 363, 457–498, 501–543, 621–653
– Old 465, 469
– Present-day 481, 510, 524

Sardinian 37, 245–252, 261, 269, 276, 296, 299–301
– Campidanese 245–251, 276, 301
– Logudorese 245–251, 276, 301
Scandinavian languages 5, 12, 31, 92
– North 8, 21, 33, 36
Serbian 24, 460–467, 480, 483, 487–488
Spanish 1–53, 245–309, 415–455
– Argentinian 290
– see also Río de la Plata Spanish
– Old 264
– Peninsular 291, 452
Slavic languages
– East 457–460, 465–466, 489, 574
– South 457, 459, 467, 480, 487
– Eastern South 458–459, 465, 502
– Western South 7, 10, 458–459
– West 457, 459
Slovak 7, 458–471
Slovenian 458–471
synthetic 55–65, 317, 451, 502, 642
Swedish 3–46, 92, 227, 285, 352

trasianka 494
– see also Belarusian-Russian mixed speech
Turkish 250–251

Ukrainian 41, 44, 458–500, 501–539
– Old 467
– see also Old Ruthenian
– Soviet 470
Ukrainian-Russian mixed speech 481
Uralic language family 676

Subject index

adjective
- attributive 20, 73, 96–97, 107
- classifying 17, 107, 117, 148–149, 264, 418, 510, 515, 587
- descriptive 64, 149–151
- determiner-like 8, 27, 256
- modifying 5–18, 25, 62, 124, 148, 153, 264, 265–268, 333, 339–340, 478, 503–504, 518, 519–520, 540, 550, 586, 601, 611–612
- *see also* modifier
- phoric 15, 65, 572
- pronominal 28, 520, 573
- relational 420, 424, 427, 428
- qualifying 30, 429, 512, 515
- quantifying 62, 65, 66, 69

adjectival use 71, 368, 388
adverb (type noun functioning as) 34–36, 372, 377, 388–389, 524, 549
adverbial function 32, 162, 367, 375
adverbial use 25, 34, 162, 190, 257, 264, 272, 375, 549
agreement 14, 16, 18, 27
- gender 28–29, 283, 327–328
- number 28, 96, 146–147, 368
- case 58, 614
ambiguous 18, 161, 226, 266, 328, 334, 365–366, 375, 394, 421–422, 425, 472, 590, 662, 701, 704
ambiguity 16, 171, 223, 262, 265–267, 399, 422, 528, 685, 695, 697
analogy 69, 300, 365, 367, 371, 373, 386, 651
analytical 55, 57, 59, 65–66, 70, 74–75, 78, 91–92, 485, 502
apposition 5, 12, 20, 29, 30–31, 61–66, 75, 78–79, 83, 98–99, 107, 108, 116, 117, 126–136, 221, 323, 418, 419, 420, 421, 425, 428, 446–447, 589, 628, 629, 642
approximator 1, 3, 22–29, 36, 162–163, 166, 245, 270–285, 295, 311–312, 320, 338, 398, 407, 410, 445, 450, 492, 501, 534–536, 573, 665, 695, 708
- *see also* qualifier, qualification

approximative V, 15, 23, 24, 26, 28, 38, 39, 141, 159, 170, 246, 258, 272–278, 279, 282–284, 300, 330, 342, 377, 398, 403, 406, 410, 411, 421, 425, 428, 444, 448, 450, 477, 485, 488, 520, 524, 528, 571, 613, 623, 650, 651, 657, 658, 663, 666, 676, 701, 703, 704, 705, 706, 709, 712, 713, 718
- function 28, 159, 276, 411, 651, 706, 718
- use 15, 23, 26, 38–39, 246, 258, 272–278, 300, 623, 704
approximation 15, 22–23, 26, 28, 35, 160, 170–171, 176, 185, 188–189, 191, 195, 197, 202, 204, 206, 256, 266, 270–274, 284, 287, 330–331, 348, 351, 375, 386–388, 396–397, 399, 401, 411, 421, 426, 428, 440, 444–445, 447, 450–451, 457, 482–483, 488–489, 528, 627–628, 651, 655–674, 686, 695, 698–699, 707, 718
- *see also* imprecision, uncertainty
argument
- manner 623, 637, 645
- object 645
- subject 646

bleaching 74, 85, 621–622, 631, 719
borrowing 6, 11, 40, 45, 220, 299, 461, 467–468, 488, 510, 571, 575, 676, 698
booster 163–164, 168, 177, 447, 448
- *see also* intensifier
bridging context 18, 34, 366, 473, 583, 589

calque 3, 5–8, 10–11, 21, 31, 36–37, 250, 260, 292, 294–296, 299, 457–458, 465, 467, 479, 481, 489, 708
case
- accusative 135, 504, 576
- dative 31, 135, 576
- genitive 29–31, 32–33, 36, 38, 42, 56–59, 60–70, 86, 91–92, 134–136, 240, 478, 480, 504–505, 508–509, 515–519, 531, 539–541, 546, 582–584, 586, 591, 612–613, 623, 628–629, 667, 677, 679, 680–683

726 — Subject index

- partitive 221–223
- instrumental 496
- locative 518, 580, 588
- nominative 71, 105, 110–112, 118–120, 126, 132, 135, 337, 504, 528, 531, 541, 548, 576–577, 584, 591, 613,
- prepositional 135, 506

case assignment 571, 614

categorization
- approximate 656–693
- clear 667, 671, 675–683
- doubtful 23, 271, 669
- non-prototypical 656, 669, 679–680, 685
- subcategorization 3, 26, 33, 515, 668–686

category
- ad hoc 43, 195, 238, 312, 345, 583, 662, 679
- new 197
    subcategory 12, 144, 147, 189, 328, 335, 395–396, 420, 669, 671, 574

change
- semantic 6–7, 10, 94, 361, 541, 692, 695, 718–721

Cognitive Grammar 57, 60

coalescence 14, 33
- see also univerbation

coherence 406, 409, 411, 462, 625, 647, 697

cohesion 343, 406, 407, 621–623, 625–626, 632, 646, 65

cohyponym 23, 271, 286, 657, 665, 718
- see also hyponym, hypernym

collocation 21–22, 42, 44, 146, 155, 168, 172, 462, 474, 506, 510, 520

collocational
- preferences 503, 505
- patterns 44, 142–143, 371

common ground 157, 175, 410, 573, 583, 611, 613
- see also shared knowledge

comparison
- similative 33, 35, 36, 77, 82, 286, 293, 369, 374, 375, 420, 425, 463, 475, 584, 599, 613, 623, 707

complement
- appositional 78, 83, 117, 134
- postcomplement 61, 66, 78–79, 83, 99, 104–121, 129, 133–137

- precomplement 78, 110–111, 124–126, 141–145
- superordinate 134

compromiser 162, 163, 166, 447, 448, 451

concept construction 621–653, 717

conjunction
- adversative 537
- causal 640
- explanatory 538

connective
- discourse 703, 707, 709–714, 717–718
- explicative 640

connector 287, 295, 439, 537, 639, 642, 717

construction
- adjectival 364–366, 372
- adverbial 257
- binominal 4, 14, 18, 20, 29, 38, 59, 78, 95–96, 123, 162, 255–256, 276, 369, 511, 551, 572, 580, 582, 584–585, 612, 666, 668
- complementizer 624, 626, 629
- concessive-adversative 487, 537
- trinominal 33–35, 284–285, 734

Construction Grammar 45, 142, 625

conditional inference tree 594, 605–612

conventionalization 168, 290, 300

countercultures 41, 292, 298–299

decategorialization 41, 56, 96, 135, 385, 387

decategorization 522

degree modification 76, 477

determiner
- complex 3, 5, 18, 20–22, 56, 62–63, 67–74, 81, 87–88, 91, 96–97, 116, 124, 155, 256, 262, 502
- see also postdeterminer
- interrogative 18, 80, 86, 526, 342
- phoric 80–81, 155, 258

diachronic change 90, 622

diminisher 447, 448, 451

discourse marker 38, 42–43, 77, 81, 141–142, 146, 160, 166, 169–177, 181–182, 189–191, 201, 204, 207, 375–378, 388–389, 393–394, 397–398, 405–410, 493, 501, 538, 636, 697, 715–716
- see also pragmatic marker

discourse particle 77, 81–82, 89, 91, 715
– see also pragmatic marker
discourse-pragmatic 182–183, 189–190, 195, 204, 206, 697
doubt 432, 437, 535
downtoning 80, 160, 162–164, 168, 171, 664

enunciative 397, 398, 400–402, 406, 410
etymology 8–9, 217, 251, 253, 574, 576, 695
epistemic 35, 145, 400, 402, 432, 435, 437, 535, 562, 573
– marker of certainty 432, 435
– marker of doubt 432, 437
evidential 35, 487, 534
exemplificative 563, 628, 642, 648–651
exemplifying 45, 82, 89, 239, 378, 488, 528–534, 571, 580, 602, 609, 612–614, 645
experiment 211, 214–215, 228–229, 236, 238, 240, 661
explanation marker 35, 44, 564

face 153, 163, 174, 403, 431
false start 172, 201, 394
falsity marker 494, 535–537, 684
– see also simulative, 'quasi' use
filler 82, 89, 99, 130, 153, 190, 404–408, 410, 436, 439, 521, 528, 534, 538, 545, 549, 562, 566, 578, 629, 699, 706, 709
– see also hesitation marker
focus marker 1, 35–36, 245, 436
fossilization 2, 18, 26, 33, 279, 281, 484
function
– discourse VI, 45, 171, 183, 189–190, 201, 207, 396, 403, 571–572, 627, 631
– grammatical 1–2, 78–80, 84–86, 96–97, 133
– pragmatic VI, 1–3, 24, 32, 43, 39, 42–43, 142–143, 162, 174, 177, 182–183, 185, 285, 351, 379, 507, 534, 695–696
Functional Discourse Grammar 60
fuzzy 65, 142, 169, 227, 330, 345, 371, 393, 402, 536, 627, 651, 657, 665

grammaticalization VI, 4, 14, 18, 23, 41, 44, 56–57, 70, 73, 78, 90–91, 96, 142, 177, 264, 271, 279–284, 293, 299, 361–362, 380, 385, 386, 415–416, 418, 421, 425–426, 428, 431, 438–452, 484–488, 501–502, 520, 522–524, 534, 539, 545–546, 549, 551, 572, 574, 578, 611, 614, 622, 627–629, 650–651, 696–697, 714, 719
grammaticalized 2, 9, 11–12, 15, 22, 27–28, 44, 55, 68, 264, 270, 280, 295, 415–417, 422, 425, 438, 444, 450, 457, 463, 472, 474–478, 485–489, 501–502, 506–507, 545, 548, 576, 664, 697, 708, 718
general extender 20, 153, 257, 261, 373, 379, 380, 387, 521
– see also list extender, terminal tag
generalization 24, 87, 101, 110, 367, 657
given 19, 191, 194, 559, 583
– see also old

head
– head-complement 60, 62, 65, 70, 75–76, 78, 101–102, 112, 121, 128, 132
– head-modifier 20, 69, 78–79, 101, 134
– reversal 26–30, 62, 91
– shift 15, 121
head status 5, 11, 14, 18–19, 26, 37, 75–76, 78, 96, 120, 123, 128, 152, 257, 264, 270, 277, 279, 318, 594–595, 600, 609, 611
hedge 174, 185, 188, 227, 307, 321, 330, 377, 440, 517, 526, 546–547, 556, 562, 566, 573, 583, 588, 613, 679, 706–709, 712
– see also mitigation, vagueness marker
hesitation 38, 77, 171, 172–173, 175–177, 182, 189, 201, 399, 400, 404, 405, 407, 408, 409, 410, 629, 662, 716
hesitation marker 190, 539
– see also filler
hyponym 271, 396, 406, 411, 420, 572, 628–629, 641, 646, 657, 668–669, 677
– see also cohyponym, subordinate
hypernym 512, 515, 623, 628–629, 637, 641, 647, 657, 668, 677

illocutionary 285, 287, 397, 402–403, 406, 410, 432, 437, 440, 490
imprecision 22, 25, 46, 145, 185, 188, 189, 195, 196, 202, 271, 287, 394, 398, 410, 482, 573, 655
– see also approximation

inference 73, 80, 159, 186, 227, 393, 493, 582, 625, 660, 695–696
inferable 186, 191–192, 207, 331
intensification 156, 163
intensifier 142, 146, 155–157, 161, 163, 164, 447, 448
– see also booster, downtoning
interpersonal 76, 89, 157, 171, 172, 175, 177, 401, 403, 409, 431, 538, 572, 665, 696, 718
– see also intersubjective
intersubjectification 297, 431
intersubjective 157, 163, 377, 400, 401, 431, 696
– see also interpersonal
intersubjectivity 401, 562
irrealis 375, 377, 434, 647–648, 650, 652
Invited Inferencing Theory of Semantic Change 695

language contact 40–41, 135, 295, 299–300, 472, 481, 547, 719
lexicalization 96, 135, 326, 418, 421, 425, 517, 586, 611–612, 696
lexicalized 22, 154, 386, 396, 424, 479, 507–508, 517, 520, 583–585, 611, 613, 625, 629
lexicography 472
list extender 261
– see also general extender, terminal tag

metacomment 153, 162, 167, 169–171, 175–177, 299, 695, 698–699, 707, 719
metalinguistic 22, 24, 76, 82, 89, 171, 266, 287, 371, 658–659
mitigation 2, 24, 35, 39, 43–44, 50, 188–191, 202, 206, 287, 291, 307–308, 391, 402, 415–457, 482, 490, 663
– see also hedge
mitigator 1, 153, 163, 174, 185, 188, 245, 285, 416, 444, 448, 450, 451
modifier
– adverbial 25, 141
– attributive 1, 15, 17, 149–151, 184, 189, 245, 265, 371, 477, 501
– descriptive 25–26, 67, 73–74, 79–80, 91, 127, 137, 477, 700–701

– postmodifier 56–60, 66, 72–91, 98, 103–105, 112–127, 133–134, 146, 189, 192, 511, 595
– premodifier 20, 56, 62, 66–91, 98, 107, 116–134, 265–270, 477, 515–517, 595, 600–601

new
– discourse-new 187, 193–193, 197, 207
– hearer-new 187, 197
noun
– shell 343, 627, 630–634, 643, 651
– taxonomic 1–55, 211–240, 245–309, 311–313, 352, 393–395, 406, 415–455, 457–501, 515, 534, 546–548, 555, 566, 573, 579, 627–628, 650, 717
– vague 373, 379, 626, 630, 647
NP-external 25, 27, 42, 181–209, 279
NP-internal 42, 108, 113, 134, 181–184, 189, 191, 194–197, 206–207, 306, 572

old, see also given
– hearer-old 187, 193, 197, 207

particle 34, 40, 77, 81, 82, 89, 91, 450, 463, 485, 487, 503, 522, 524, 528, 534–541, 545–554, 555, 557, 561–566, 577, 613, 664, 666, 715
pejorative 76, 84, 395, 632
politeness 89, 163, 166, 403, 431, 451
Politeness-Induced Semantic Change (PISC) 696, 718
polysemy 6, 253, 259, 395, 410, 418, 696, 707
pragmatic marker 25, 31–44, 142, 171, 175–176, 245, 270–271, 284–300, 538, 696, 700, 708, 714
– see also discourse marker, discourse particle
pragmaticalized 1–2, 11, 32–33, 36, 40, 45–46, 285, 288–290, 445, 463, 481, 698, 707, 717, 719
pragmaticalization 4, 36–37, 41, 96, 285–292, 297–300, 394, 627, 651, 696, 700, 707, 719–721
prenominal 5, 15, 18, 20, 30–31

preposition
- comparative 35, 288
- complex 81, 90, 369, 523, 577
- similative 32–35, 89, 287
- similative-exemplificative 628, 643, 651
pronoun
- demonstrative 171, 558, 583, 599
- indefinite 373, 483, 582, 606, 608, 611, 630, 636
- personal 374, 613
- reflexive 227, 484, 588, 613
postdeterminer 1, 8, 18–29, 142, 151–158, 177, 245, 256–260, 270, 278–285, 300, 339, 458, 478–479, 586, 594–595, 602, 611–612, 700
- see also determiner
postnominal 17–18, 20, 22, 192, 257

qualification 43, 311–349, 379, 664, 701, 717
qualifier 1, 5, 22, 27, 39, 42, 75–77, 89–90, 141, 153, 160–179, 181–190, 206, 246, 256, 270, 272, 281–283, 445, 457, 477, 482–483, 501, 508, 513, 700
- see also approximation, approximator
quasi-assertive 487, 534
'quasi' use 494, 502, 536
   - see also falsity marker, sumulative
quantification 20, 23, 26–28, 35, 72–73, 111, 133, 263, 337, 346, 406, 428, 430, 447–448, 450–451, 478, 516, 707
quantifier 1, 5, 14, 18–30, 38–39, 62, 68–69, 73, 132, 138, 153–155, 176, 183, 255–256, 269–270, 283, 300, 367, 396, 447–450, 501, 516, 584, 586, 594, 606, 608–612, 700
quotative
- function 36, 45, 166, 173, 294, 397, 406, 476, 546, 571, 614, 629, 633, 649, 706
- marker 1, 35, 77, 81–82, 89–101, 173–174, 245, 501, 578
- use 39, 295, 473–474, 535, 592–593, 624, 703–704
- para-quotative 474
- pseudo-quotative 624, 633, 647

reanalysis 25, 78, 134, 264–266, 283, 361, 369, 586
reduction 33, 38, 361, 386, 552

reference
- dual 13, 71, 109–112, 114, 118, 131–132
- generic 71–72, 74, 109–114, 118–119
referentiality
- non-referential 71, 110–111, 114,118, 131–132, 193
- weak 630
reformulation 295, 400, 405, 407, 408, 422, 425, 431
Relevance Theory 625
repair 706
- see also self-repair

scope 16, 25, 38, 42, 43, 71, 76, 81, 106, 107, 108, 124, 130, 160, 169, 171, 181, 182, 189, 190, 195, 207, 265–267, 288, 291, 361, 373, 374, 375, 379, 406, 408, 415, 416, 428–438, 440, 441, 448–450, 485, 629, 649, 651, 658, 666, 679, 682, 683, 707, 714, 715, 717, 718
self-repair 190, 201
- see also repair
semantic change 6–7, 10, 94, 361, 541, 692, 695,718–721
semantic theory 211, 214, 235, 239
semantic-pragmatic 43, 75, 142, 395, 406, 408, 411, 435, 443, 565, 622
semantico-pragmatic 698, 708
semi-suffix 1, 15, 97, 123, 148, 151–153, 175, 184, 265, 270, 371, 477, 700, 717
shared knowledge 187, 373, 401, 410, 560, 641, 646, 664
- see also common ground
similarity
- demonstrative 237–238
- marker 524–528, 530, 532, 534, 548, 550, 554, 557
- function 528, 548,
- use 374, 472, 524–528, 534, 548–549, 550–551, 557, 590–591, 707
simulative 649–651
- see also falsity marker, 'quasi' use
sociolinguistic 2, 24, 37, 39, 43, 46, 246, 387, 394, 417, 695–719
subjectification 14, 297, 431
subjective 15, 22, 109, 157, 163, 164, 167, 264, 265, 361, 384, 385, 431, 477, 696

subjectivity marker 385
subordinate 31, 128, 445, 447, 455, 607, 652
– *see also* hyponym
superordinate 7–8, 19, 23, 32–33, 56,
    63–66, 75, 78, 83, 96–103, 105, 107,
    113–114, 116, 120, 130–1136, 148,
    153–154, 171, 280, 285–286, 293,
    386, 420, 508, 557, 577, 580–590, 595,
    602–603, 609, 612, 691, 718
– *see also* hyperonym, hypernym

taxonomic
– meaning 5–10, 44–45, 217, 247–253,
    278, 351–366, 386–387, 416–420, 427,
    458–472, 503–508, 517, 534, 574–575,
    580, 582, 587, 611, 613, 621, 637, 639
– relation 44, 635
terminal tag 521, 560, 562
– *see also* general extender
time
– apparent 697, 708, 711, 719
– real 697
truth
– commitment 402, 437, 443
– conditions 23, 317
– value 227, 437, 629, 660, 671
– *see also* falsity marker, doubt
truth-conditional 25, 696
truth-functional 38, 285, 287, 696

uncertainty 159, 196, 400, 534, 649,
    660, 696
univerbation 27, 522, 523
use
– lexical: 30, 37–38, 132, 135, 279–280, 295,
    428, 485, 545
– grammatical 445, 712

vagueness marker 296, 482, 517, 521, 545,
    557, 566, 583
– *see also* hedge
variation
– constructional 133
– positional 572, 614
– semantic 503
– sociopragmatic 695–719
– structural 59–79, 539
– synchronic 99

www.ingramcontent.com/pod-product-compliance
Lightning Source LLC
Chambersburg PA
CBHW051551230426
43668CB00013B/1812